MEDITATIONS ON THE TAROT

Meditations
on the
TAROT

A Journey into Christian Hermeticism

Anonymous

TRANSLATED BY ROBERT POWELL

JEREMY P. TARCHER / PUTNAM
a member of Penguin Putnam Inc.
New York

Most Tarcher/Penguin books are available at special quantity discounts
for bulk purchase for sales promotions, premiums, fund-raising,
and educational needs. Special books or book excerpts also can
be created to fit specific needs. For details, write
Penguin Group (USA) Inc. Special Markets,
375 Hudson Street, New York, NY 10014.

Jeremy P. Tarcher/Penguin
a member of
Penguin Group (USA) Inc.
375 Hudson Street
New York, NY 10014
www.penguin.com
Originally published in French in 1980 by Aubier Montaigne.
Originally published in English in 1985 by Amity House.
First Jeremy P. Tarcher Edition 2002

Library of Congress Cataloging-in-Publication Data

Meditations on the tarot : a journey into Christian hermeticism /
Anonymous ; translated by Robert Powell.
p.   cm.
Originally published: 1985.
Includes bibliographical references.
ISBN 1-58542-161-8
1. Tarot.   2. Hermeticism.   I. Powell, Robert, date.
BF1879.T2 M48   2002   2001059016
133.3'2424—dc21

Printed in the United States of America
9   10

CONTENTS

Foreword

These meditations on the Major Arcana of the Tarot are Letters addressed to the Unknown Friend. The addressee in this instance is anyone who will read all of them and who thereby acquires definite knowledge, through the experience of meditative reading, about Christian Hermeticism. He will know also that the author of these Letters has said more about himself in these Letters than he would have been able to in any other way. No matter what other source he might have, he will know the author better through the Letters themselves.

These Letters were written in French because in France — since the eighteenth century until the present time — there exists a literature on the Tarot, a phenomenon which is found nowhere else. On the other hand, there existed in France — and it still persists — a continuous *tradition* of Hermeticism, in which is united a spirit of free research with one of respect for the tradition. The purpose of these Letters therefore will be to "incarnate" into this tradition, i.e. to become an organic part of it, and in this way to contribute support to it.

As these Letters are intended only to serve, to sustain, and to support the Hermetic tradition — from its first appearance in the epoch of Hermes Trismegistus, lost in the remoteness of antiquity and become legendary — they are a definite manifestation of this millennium-old current of thought, effort, and revelation. Their aim is not only to revive the tradition but also, and above all, to immerse the reader (or rather the Unknown Friend) in this current — be it temporarily or for ever. For this reason the numerous citations of ancient and modern authors which you will find in these Letters are not due to literary considerations, nor to a display of erudition. They are *evocations* of the masters of the tradition, in order that they may be present with their impulses of aspiration and their light of thought in the current of meditative thought which these Letters on the twenty-two Major Arcana of the Tarot represent. For these are in essence twenty-two spiritual exercises, by means of which you, dear Unknown Friend, will immerse yourself in the current of the living tradition, and thus enter into the community of spirits who have served it and who are still serving it.

And the citations in question only serve the aim of a "relief setting" for this community. For the links in the chain of the tradition are not thoughts and efforts alone; they are above all *living beings* who were thinking these thoughts and willing these efforts. The essence of the tradition is not a doctrine, but rather a community of spirits from age to age.

There remains nothing more to say in this introduction to the Letter-Meditations on the Tarot, because all other questions concerning them will find a response in the Letters themselves.

Your friend greets you, dear Unknown Friend,
from beyond the grave.

MEDITATIONS ON THE TAROT

Meditation on the
First Major Arcanum of the Tarot

THE MAGICIAN
LE BATELEUR

Spiritus ubi vult spirat: et vocem
ejus audis, sed nescis unde veniat,
aut quo vadat: sic est omnis,
qui natus est ex spiritu.
(John iii, 8)

The wind blows where it wills, and
you hear the sound of it, but you do
not know whence it comes or whither
it goes; so it is with every one
who is born of the Spirit.
(John iii, 8)

Into this happy night
In secret, seen of none,
Nor saw I aught,
Without other light or guide,
Save that which in my heart did burn.
(St. John of the Cross)*

LETTER I

THE MAGICIAN

Dear Unknown Friend,

The words of the Master cited above have served me the key for opening the door to comprehension of the first Major Arcanum of the Tarot, "The Magician", which is, in turn, the key to all the other Major Arcana. This is why I have put them as an epigraph to this Letter. And then I have cited a verse from the "Songs of the Soul" of St. John of the Cross, because it has the virtue of awakening the deeper layers of the soul, which one has to appeal to when the concern is the first Arcanum of the Tarot and, consequently, all the Major Arcana of the Tarot. For

*Canciones del Alma, The Dark Night of the Soul, verse iii; trsl. G. C. Graham, London, 1922, p. 29.

3

the Major Arcana of the Tarot are authentic *symbols*, i.e. they are "magic, mental, psychic and moral operations" awakening new notions, ideas, sentiments and aspirations, which means to say that they require an activity more profound than that of study and intellectual explanation. It is therefore in a state of deep contemplation — and always ever deeper — that they should be approached. And it is the deep and intimate layers of the soul which become active and bear fruit when one meditates on the Arcana of the Tarot. Therefore this "night", of which St. John of the Cross speaks, is necessary, where one withdraws oneself "in secret" and into which one has to immerse oneself each time that one meditates on the Arcana of the Tarot. It is a work to be accomplished in solitude, and is all the more suitable for recluses.

The Major Arcana of the Tarot are neither allegories nor secrets, because allegories are, in fact, only figurative representations of abstract notions, and secrets are only facts, procedures, practices, or whatever doctrines that one keeps to oneself for a personal motive, since they are able to be understood and put into practice by others to whom one does not *want* to reveal them. The Major Arcana of the Tarot are authentic symbols. They conceal and reveal their sense at one and the same time according to the depth of meditation. That which they reveal are not *secrets*, i.e. things hidden by human will, but are *arcana*, which is something quite different. An arcanum is that which it is necessary to "know" in order to be fruitful in a given domain of spiritual life. It is that which must be actively present in our consciousness — or even in our subconscious — in order to render us capable of making discoveries, engendering new ideas, conceiving of new artistic subjects. In a word, it makes us *fertile* in our creative pursuits, in whatever domain of spiritual life. An arcanum is a "ferment" or an "enzyme" whose presence stimulates the spiritual and the psychic life of man. And it is symbols which are the bearers of these "ferments" or "enzymes" and which communicate them — if the mentality and morality of the recipient is ready, i.e. if he is "poor in spirit" and does not, suffer from the most serious spiritual malady: self-complacency.

Just as the *arcanum* is superior to the *secret*, so is the *mystery* superior to the arcanum. The mystery is more than a stimulating "ferment". It is a spiritual *event* comparable to physical birth or death. It is a change of the entire spiritual and psychic motivation, or a complete change of the plane of consciousness. The seven sacraments of the Church are the prismatic colours of the white light of one sole Mystery or Sacrament, known as that of the Second Birth, which the Master pointed out to Nicodemus in the nocturnal initiation conversation which He had with him. It is this which Christian Hermeticism understands by the *Great Initiation*.

It goes without saying that nobody initiates anyone else, if we understand by "initiation" the Mystery of the Second Birth or the Great Sacrament. This Initiation is operative from above and has the value and the duration of eternity. The Initiator is above, and here below one meets only the fellow pupils; and they recognise each other by the fact that they "love one another" (cf. John xiii, 34-35).

There are no longer any more "masters" because there is only one sole *Master*, who is the Initiator above. To be sure, there are always masters who teach their doctrines and also initiates who communicate some of the secrets which they possess to others who thus become in their turn the "initiates"— but all this has nothing to do with the Mystery of the Great Initiation.

For this reason Christian Hermeticism, in so far as it is a human concern, initiates no one. Amongst Christian Hermeticists nobody assumes for himself the title and the function of "initiator" or "master". For all are fellow pupils and each is master of each in some respect — just as each is a pupil of each in some other respect. We cannot do better than to follow the example of St. Anthony the Great, who

> subjected himself in all sincerity to the pious men whom he visited and made it his endeavour to learn for his own benefit just how each was superior to him in zeal and ascetic practice. He observed the graciousness of one, the earnestness at prayer in another; studied the even temper of one and the kindheartedness of another; fixed his attention on the vigils kept by one and on the studies pursued by another; admired one for his patient endurance, another for his fasting and sleeping on the ground; watched closely this man's meekness and the forebearance shown by another; and in one and all alike he marked especially devotion to Christ and the love they had for one another. Having thus taken his fill, he would return to his own place of asceticism. Then he assimilated in himself what he had obtained from each and devoted all his energies to realizing in himself the virtues of all. (St. Athanasius, *The Life of Saint Anthony*, ch. 4; trsl. R. T. Meyer, Westminster, 1950, p.21)

It is the same conduct which must be applied by the Christian Hermeticist in that which concerns knowledge and science — natural, historical, philological, philosophical, theological, symbolical and traditional. It amounts to learning the *art of learning*.

Now, it is the Arcana which stimulate us and at the same time guide us in the art of learning. In this sense, the Major Arcana of the Tarot are a complete, entire, invaluable school of meditation, study, and spiritual effort — a masterly school in the *art of learning*.

Dear Unknown Friend, Christian Hermeticism therefore has no pretension to rival either religion or official science. He who is searching here for the "true religion", the "true philosophy", or the "true science" is looking in the wrong direction. Christian Hermeticists are not masters, but servants. They do not have the pretension (that is, in any case, somewhat puerile) of elevating themselves above the holy faith of the faithful, or above the fruits of the admirable efforts of workers in science, or above the creations of artistic genius. Hermeticists are not guarding the secret of future discoveries in the sciences. They do not know, for example, just as everyone at present is ignorant of it, the effective remedy against cancer. Moreover they would be monsters if they were to guard the secret of the remedy against this bane of humanity without communicating it. No, they do not know it, and they will be the first to recognise the superiority of the future benefactor of the human race, that savant who will discover this remedy.

Likewise they recognise without reserve the superiority of a Francis of Assisi — and of many others — who was a man of the so-called "exoteric" faith. They know also that each sincere believer is potentially a Francis of Assisi. Men and women of faith, of science and of art are their superiors in many essential points. Hermeticists know it well and do not flatter themselves to be better, to believe better, to know better or to be more competent. They do not secretly guard a religion, which to them is appropriate, to replace the existing religions, or a science to replace the current sciences, or arts to replace the fine arts of today or yesterday. That which they possess does not comprise any tangible advantage or objective superiority with regard to religion, science and art; what they possess is only the *communal soul of religion, science and art*. What is this mission of conserving the communal soul of religion, science and art? I am going to reply with a concrete example, as follows:

You know without doubt, dear Unknown Friend, that many — and several of them are writers — in France, Germany, England, and elsewhere, promulgate the doctrine of the so-called "two churches": the church of Peter and the church of John, or of "two epochs" — the epoch of Peter and the epoch of John. You know also that this doctrine teaches the end — more or less at hand — of the church of Peter, or above all of the papacy which is its visible symbol, and that the spirit of John, the disciple loved by the Master, he who leaned on his breast and heard the beating of his heart, will replace it. In this way it teaches that the "exoteric" church of Peter will make way for the "esoteric" church of John, which will be that of perfect freedom.

Now, John, who submitted himself voluntarily to Peter as leader or prince of the apostles, did not become his successor after his death, although he outlived Peter by many years. The beloved disciple who listened to the beating of the Master's heart was, is, and always will be the representative and guardian of this heart — and as such he was not, is not, and never will be the *leader* or *head* of the Church. Because just as the heart is not called upon to replace the head, so is John not called upon to succeed Peter. The heart certainly guards the life of the body and the soul, but it is the head which makes decisions, directs, and chooses the means for the accomplishment of the tasks of the entire organism — head, heart and limbs. The mission of John is to keep the life and soul of the Church *alive* until the Second Coming of the Lord. This is why John has never claimed and never will claim the office of directing the body of the Church. He *vivifies* this body, but he does not direct its actions.

Now Hermeticism, the living Hermetic tradition, guards the communal soul of all true culture. I must add: *Hermeticists listen to* — and now and then hear —

the beating of the heart of the spiritual life of humanity. They cannot do otherwise than live as guardians of the life and communal soul of religion, science and art. They do not have any privilege in any of these domains; saints, true scientists, and artists of genius are their superiors. But they live for the mystery of the communal heart which beats within all religions, all philosophies, all arts and all sciences — past, present and future. And inspired by the example of John, the beloved disciple, they do not pretend, and never will pretend, to play a directing role in religion, science, art, in social or political life; but they are constantly attentive so as not to miss any occasion to *serve* religion, philosophy, science, art, the social and political life of humanity, and to this to infuse the breath of life of their communal soul — analogous to the administration of the sacrament of Holy Communion. Hermeticism is — and is only — a stimulant, a "ferment" or an "enzyme" in the organism of the spiritual life of humanity. In this sense it is itself an *arcanum* — that is to say the antecedent of the Mystery of the Second Birth or the Great Initiation.

This is the spirit of Hermeticism. And it is in this spirit that we now return to the first Major Arcanum of the Tarot. Of what does this first Card consist?

A young man, wearing a large hat in the form of a lemniscate, standing behind a small table on which are arranged: a yellow-painted vase; three small yellow discs; another four red discs, in two piles, each divided down the middle by a line; a red beaker with two dice; a knife withdrawn from its sheath; and lastly a yellow bag for carrying these various objects. The young man — who is the Magician — holds a rod in his right hand (from the standpoint of the observer) and a ball or yellow object in his left hand. He holds these two objects with perfect ease, without clasping them or showing any other sign of tension, encumbrance, haste or effort. What he does with his hands is with perfect spontaneity — it is easy play and not work. He himself does not follow the movement of his hands; his gaze is elsewhere.

Such is this Card. . .That the series of symbols, that is to say of the revealers of the Arcana, which is the game of Tarot, is opened by an image representing a player of tricks — a magician (or juggler) who plays — is truly astonishing! How may this be explained?

The first Arcanum — the principle underlying all the other twenty-one Major Arcana of the Tarot — is *that of the rapport of personal effort and of spiritual reality*. It occupies the first place in the series because if one does not understand it (i.e. take hold of it in cognitive and actual practice), one would not know what to do with all the other Arcana. For it is the Magician who is called to reveal the practical *method* relating to all the Arcana. He is the "Arcanum of the Arcana", in the sense that he reveals that which it is necessary to know and to will in order to enter the school of spiritual exercises whose totality comprises the game of Tarot, in order to be able to derive some benefit therefrom. In fact, the first and fundamental principle of esotericism (i.e. of the way of experience of the reality of the spirit) can be rendered by the formula:

> *Learn at first concentration without effort; transform work into*
> *play; make every yoke that you have accepted easy and every*
> *burden that you carry light!*

This counsel, or command, or even warning, however you wish to take it, is most serious; this is attested by its original source, namely the words of the Master Himself: "My yoke is easy, and my burden is light" (Matthew xi, 30).

Let us examine in succession the three parts of this formula, in order to penetrate the Arcanum of "active relaxation" or "effort without effort". Firstly — *learn at first concentration without effort* — what is this in a practical and theoretical sense?

Concentration, as the faculty of fixing maximum attention on a minimum amount of space (Schiller said that he who wants to complete something of worth and of skill, "*der sammle still und unerschlafft, im kleinsten Punkt die grösste Kraft*", i.e. that "quietly and unceasingly he directs the greatest force upon the smallest point"), is the practical key to all success in every domain. Modern pedagogy and psychotherapy, the schools of prayer and spiritual exercises — Franciscan, Carmelite, Dominican and Jesuit — occult schools of every type and, lastly, ancient Hindu yoga, all approaches are in agreement about this. Patanjali, in his classic work on yoga, formulates in his first sentence the practical and theoretical essence of yoga — the "first arcanum" or the key of yoga — as follows:

> *Yoga citta vritti nirodha* (Yoga is the suppression of the oscilla-
> tions of the mental substance, *Yoga Sutras* 1.2)

— or, in other terms, *the art of concentration*. For the "oscillations" (*vritti*) of the "mental substance" (*citta*) take place automatically. This automatism in the movements of thought and imagination is the opposite of concentration. Now, concentration is only possible in a condition of *calm* and *silence*, at the expense of the automatism of thought and imagination.

The "to be silent" therefore preceeds the "to know", the "to will" and the "to dare". This is why the Pythagorean school prescribed five years silence to beginners or "hearers". One dared to speak there only when one "knew" and "was able to", after having mastered the art of being silent — that is to say, the art of concentration. The prerogative "to speak" belonged to those who no longer spoke automatically, driven by the game of the intellect and imagination, but who *were able to* suppress it owing to the practice of interior and exterior silence, and who *knew* what they were saying — again thanks to the same practice. The *silentium* practised by Trappist monks and prescribed for the time of "retreat", generally to all those there who are taking part, is only the application of the same true law: "Yoga is the suppression of the oscillations of the mental substance" or "concentration is the willed silence of the automatism of the intellect and imagination".

There are nevertheless two sorts of concentration to be distinguished, which are essentially different. The one is *disinterested concentration* and the other is *interested concentration* . The first is due to the will free of *enslaving* passions, obsessions and attachments, whereas the other is the result of a *dominating* passion, obsession, or attachment. A monk absorbed in prayer and an enraged bull are, the one and the other, concentrated. But the one is in the peace of contemplation whilst the other is carried away by rage. Strong passions therefore realise themselves as a high degree of concentration. Thus, gluttons, misers, arrogant people and maniacs occasionally achieve a remarkable concentration. But, truth to tell, it is not a matter of *concentration* but rather *obsession* in connection with such people.

True concentration is a free act in light and in peace. It presupposes a disinterested and detached will. For it is the condition of the will which is the determining and decisive factor in concentration. This is why yoga, for example, demands the practice of *yama* and *niyama* (*yama* — the five rules of moral conduct; *niyama* — the five rules of mortification) before the preparation of the body (through respiration and posture) for concentration and the practice of the three degrees of concentration itself (*dharana, dyana, samadhi* — concentration, meditation and contemplation).

Both St. John of the Cross and St. Teresa of Avila do not tire of repeating that the concentration necessary for spiritual prayer is the fruit of moral purification of the will. It is therefore useless to strive to concentrate oneself if the will is infatuated with something else. The "oscillations of the mental substance" will never be able to be reduced to silence if the will itself does not infuse them with its silence. It is the *silenced will* which effects the silence of thought and imagination in concentration. This is why the great ascetics are also the great masters of concentration. All this is obvious and stands to reason. However, what occupies us here is not just concentration in general but particularly and especially *concentration without effort*. What is this?

Look at a tightrope walker. He is evidently completely concentrated, because if he were not, he would fall to the ground. His life is at stake, and it is only perfect concentration which can save him. Yet do you believe that his thought and his imagination are occupied with what he is doing? Do you think that he reflects and that he imagines, that he calculates and that he makes plans with regard to each step that he makes on the rope?

If he were to do that, he would fall immediately. He has to eliminate all activity of the intellect and of the imagination in order to avoid a fall. He must have suppressed the "oscillations of the mental substance" in order to be able to exercise his skill. It is the intelligence of his rhythmic system — the respiratory and circulatory system — which replaces that of his brain during his acrobatic exercises. In the last analysis, it is a matter of a miracle — from the point of view of the intellect and the imagination — analogous to that of St. Dionysius, apostle of the Gauls and first bishop of Paris, whom tradition identifies with St. Dionysius the Areopagite, disciple of St. Paul. In particular, he was

beheaded with the sword before the statue of Mercury, contess-
ing his faith in the Holy Trinity. And at once the body of
Dionysius stood erect, and took his head in its hands; and with
an Angel guiding it and a great light going before, it walked
for two miles, from the place called Montmartre to the place
where, by its own choice and by the providence of God, it now
reposes. (Jacobus de Voragine, *Legenda aurea*; trsl. G. Ryan and
H. Ripperger, *The Golden Legend*, New York, 1948, pp. 620-
621).

Now, the tightrope walker, he too has the head — that is to say, the intellect and
imagination — severed for the time of the exercise of his skill, and he also walks
from one point to another, carrying his head in his hands, under the guidance
of another intelligence than that of his head, which acts through the body's
rhythmic system. For the tightrope walker, the juggler, and the magician, their
skill and ability are, fundamentally, analagous to the miracle of St. Dionysius;
because with them as with St. Dionysius, it is a matter of transposing the centre
of directing consciousness from the head to the chest — from the cerebral system
to the rhythmic system.

Concentration without effort is the transposition of the directing centre of the
brain to the rhythmic system — from the domain of the mind and imagination
to that of morality and the will. The great hat in the form of a lemniscate which
the Magician wears, like his attitude of perfect ease, indicates this transposition.
For the lemniscate (the horizontal eight: ∞) is not only the symbol of infinity,
but also that of *rhythm*, of the respiration and circulation — it is the symbol of
eternal rhythm or the *eternity of rhythm*. The Magician therefore represents the
state of concentration without effort, i.e. the state of consciousness where the centre
directing the will has "descended" (in reality it is elevated) from the brain to the
rhythmic system, where the "oscillations of the mental substance" are reduced
to silence and to rest, no longer hindering concentration.

Concentration *without effort* — that is to say where there is nothing to suppress
and where contemplation becomes as natural as breathing and the beating of the
heart — is the state of consciousness (i.e. thought, imagination, feeling and will)
of perfect calm, accompanied by the complete relaxation of the nerves and the
muscles of the body. It is the profound silence of desires, of preoccupations, of
the imagination, of the memory and of discursive thought. One may say that the
entire being becomes like the surface of calm water, reflecting the immense
presence of the starry sky and its indescribable harmony. And the waters are deep,
they are so deep! And the silence grows, ever increasing...what silence! Its growth
takes place through regular waves which pass, one after the other, through your
being: one wave of silence followed by another wave of more profound silence,
then again a wave of still more profound silence...Have you ever *drunk silence*?
If in the affirmative, you know what concentration without effort is.

To begin with there are moments, subsequently minutes, then "quarters of an hour" for which complete silence or "concentration without effort" lasts. With time, the silence or concentration without effort becomes a fundamental element *always present* in the life of the soul. It is like the perpetual service at the church of Sacré-Coeur de Montmartre which takes place, whilst in Paris one works, one trades, one amuses oneself, one sleeps, one dies... It is in like manner that a "perpetual service" of silence is established in the soul, which continues all the same when one is active, when one works, or when one converses. This "zone of silence" being once established, you can draw from it both for rest and for work. Then you will have not only concentration without effort, but also *activity without effort*. It is precisely this that comes to expression in the second part of our formula:

transform work into play

The changing of work, which is duty, into play, is effected as a consequence of the presence of the "zone of perpetual silence", where one draws from a sort of secret and intimate respiration, whose sweetness and freshness accomplishes the anointing of work and transforms it into play. For the "zone of silence" does not only signify that the soul is, fundamentally, at rest, but also, and rather, that there is contact with the heavenly or spiritual world, *which works together with the soul*. He who finds silence in the solitude of concentration without effort, *is never alone*. He never bears alone the weights that he has to carry; the forces of heaven, the forces from on high, are there taking part from now on.

In this way the truth stated by the third part of the formula:

make every yoke that you have accepted easy and every burden
that you carry light,

itself becomes experience. For silence is the sign of real contact with the spiritual world and this contact, in turn, always engenders the influx of forces. This is the *foundation* of all mysticism, all gnosis, all magic and all practical esotericism in general.

All practical esotericism is founded on the following rule: it is necessary to be *one* in oneself (concentration without effort) and *one* with the spiritual world (to have a zone of silence in the soul) in order for a revelatory or actual spiritual experience to be able to take place. In other words, if one wants to practise some form of authentic esotericism — be it mysticism, gnosis, or magic — it is necessary to be the *Magician*, i.e. concentrated without effort, operating with ease as if one were playing, and acting with perfect calm. This, then, is the *practical teaching* of the first Arcanum of the Tarot. It is the first counsel, commandment or warning concerning all spiritual practice; it is the aleph of the "alphabet" of practical rules of esotericism. And just as all numbers are only aspects (multiples) of unity, so are all other practical rules communicated by the other Arcana of the Tarot only aspects and modalities of this basic rule.

Such is the practical teaching of the Magician. What is its theoretical teaching?

It corresponds in every point to the practical teaching, its theoretical operation being only the mental aspect of the practice. Just as the latter proceeds from concentration without effort, i.e. puts *unity* into practice, so does the attendant theory consist in the basic *unity* of the natural world, the human world and the divine world. The tenet of the basic oneness of the world plays the same fundamental role for all theory as that of concentration for all practice. As concentration is the basis of every practical achievement, the tenet of the basic unity of the world is the same with regard to all knowledge — without it no knowledge is conceivable.

The tenet of the essential unity of all that exists precedes every act of knowledge, and every act of knowledge presupposes the tenet of the unity of the world. The ideal — or ultimate aim — of all philosophy and all science is TRUTH. But "truth" has no other meaning than that of the reduction of the plurality of phenomena to an essential unity — of facts to laws, of laws to principles, of principles to essence or being. All search for truth — mystical, gnostic, philosophical and scientific — *postulates* its existence, i.e. the fundamental unity of the multiplicity of phenomena in the world. Without this unity nothing would be knowable. How could one proceed from the known to the unknown — and this is indeed the method of progress in knowledge — if the unknown had nothing to do with the known? If the unknown had no relationship with the known and was absolutely and essentially a stranger to it? When we say that the world is knowable, i.e. that knowledge as such exists, we state through this fact itself the tenet of the essential unity of the world or its knowability. We declare that the world is not a mosaic, where a plurality of worlds which are essentially strangers to one another are fitted together, but that it is an *organism* — all of whose parts are governed by the same principle, revealing it and allowing reduction to it. The relationship of everything and of all beings is the *conditio sine qua non* of their knowability.

The open recognition of the relationship of all things and beings has engendered an exactly corresponding method of knowledge. It is the method generally known under the title THE METHOD OF ANALOGY; its role and its import in so-called "occult" science has been illumined in an admirable way by Papus in his *Traité élémentaire de science occulte* (Paris, 1888 pp. 28ff). Analogy is not a tenet or postulate — the essential unity of the world is this — but is the first and principal method (the *aleph* of the alphabet of methods) whose use facilitates the advance of knowledge. It is the first conclusion drawn from the tenet of universal unity. Since at the root of the diversity of phenomena their unity is found, in such a way that they are at one and the same time different and one, they are neither identical nor heterogeneous but are *analagous* in so far as they manifest their essential kinship.

The traditional formula setting forth the method of analogy is well known. It is the second verse of the *Emerald Table* (*Tabula Smaragdina*) of Hermes Trismegistus:

Quod superius est sicut quod inferius, et quod inferius est sicut quod est superius, ad perpetranda miracula rei unius. That which is above is like to that which is below and that which is below is like to that which is above, to accomplish the miracles of (the) one thing. (*Tabula Smaragdina*, 2; trsl. R. Steele and D. W. Singer, *Proceedings of the Royal Society of Medicine* xxi, 1928, p. 42; see the appendix to Letter I concerning the problem of the authenticity of the *Tabula Smaragdina*).

This is the classic formula of analogy for all that exists in *space*, *above* and *below*; the formula of analogy applied in *time* would be:

Quod fuit est sicut quod erit, et quod erit est sicut quod fuit, ad perpetranda miracula aeternitatis. That which was is as that which will be, and that which will be is as that which was, to accomplish the miracles of eternity.

The formula of analogy applied in space is the basis of *typological* symbolism, that is, of symbols expressing correspondences between *prototypes* above and their manifestations below; the formula of analogy applied in time is the basis of *mythological* symbolism, that is, of symbols expressing correspondences between *archetypes* in the past and their manifestations in the present. Thus the Magician is a typological symbol; he reveals to us the *prototype* of the MAN OF SPIRIT. Whilst the Biblical accounts of Adam and Eve, Cain and Abel, and if you wish, also, the *schisme d'Irschou* of Saint-Yves d'Alveydre (cf. *Mission des Juifs*, vol. ii, Paris, 1956, pp. 191ff.) are, on the other hand, *myths* ; they reveal the *archetypes* which manifest themselves endlessly in history and in each individual biography—they are mythological symbols pertaining to the domain of time. These two categories of symbolism, based on analogy, constitute through their mutual relationship a cross:

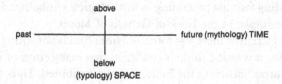

Here is something written on myth (i.e. on the symbolism of time, or history, according to our definition) by Hans Leisegang, the author of a classic book on gnosis:

Every myth expresses, in a form narrated for a particular case, an eternal idea, which will be intuitively recognised by he who re-experiences the content of the myth. (Hans Leisegang, *Die Gnosis*, Leipzig, 1924, p. 51)

And this is what Marc Haven says concerning typological symbols in the chapter on symbolism in his posthumous book *Le Tarot*:

> Our sensations, symbolising external movement, do not resemble them (i.e. the phenomena) any more than the undulations of sand in the desert resemble the wind which raises it up into sand dunes, or any more than the ebb and flow of the sea resembles the combined movements of the sun and moon. They are symbols of it...The opinion of *Kant*, *Hamilton* and *Spencer*, which reduces inner movements to simple symbols of a hidden reality is truer and more rational (than naive realism — author's note). Science ought to resign itself to being only a symbolism conscious of itself...But the symbolic has quite another significance: the "science of sciences" as it was called by the ancients (cf. Decourcelle, *Traité des symboles* , Paris, 1806), the universal and divine language, which proclaims and proves the hierarchy of forms from the archetypal world down to the material world and the relationships which unite them; it is, in a word, the living and tangible proof of the kinship of beings. (Marc Haven *Le Tarot*, Lyons, 1937, pp. 19-20, 24)

Above, therefore, two definitions — of symbols of time or of myths, and of that of space or of the correspondence of worlds "from the archetypal world down to the material world"— are formulated, the one by a German savant (Hans Leisegang) at Leipzig in 1924 and the other by a French Hermeticist (Marc Haven) at Lyons in 1906, which express exactly the ideas of the two types of symbolism (mythological and typological) which we are setting forward here. The *Emerald Table* only alludes to typological symbolism or space — analogy between that which is "above" and that which is "below". This is why it is necessary to add to it, by extension, the corresponding formula pertaining to mythological symbolism or time, which we find, for example, in the book of Genesis of Moses.

The distinction of these two forms of symbolism is not entirely devoid of practical import; it is owing to their confusion that many errors of interpretation of ancient sources, including the Bible, must be attributed. Thus, for example, certain authors take the Biblical account of Cain and Abel as a typological symbol. They want to see in it symbols of "centrifugal and centripetal forces" etc. However, the story of Cain and Abel is a *myth*, i.e. it expresses, in a form narrated for a particular case, an "eternal" idea. Consequently, it refers to *time*, to history, and not to space and its structure. It shows us how brothers can become mortal enemies through the very fact that they worship the same God in the same way. The source of religious wars is revealed here; and it is not the difference in dogma nor that of cult or ritual which is the cause, but uniquely the *pretention to equality* or, if one prefers, the *negation of hierarchy*. Here also is the world's first revolution — the archetype (Goethe's *Urphänomen*) of all revolutions which have taken place and which will take place in the future of humanity. For the cause of all wars and revolutions — in a word, of all violence — is always the same: the negation of hierarchy. This cause is found already, germinally, at such a lofty level as that of the communal act of worship of the same God by two brothers — this is the staggering revelation of the story of Cain and Abel. And as murders, wars and revolutions continue, the story of Cain and Abel remains ever valid and relevant. Being always valid and relevant throughout the passage of centuries, this is a myth and, moreover, a myth of the first order.

It is the same with the accounts of the Fall of Adam and Eve, the Deluge and Noah's ark, the tower of Babel, etc. These are *myths*, i.e. in the first place *historical* symbols referring to time, and not symbols expressing the unity of the worlds in physical, metaphysical and moral space. The Fall of Adam and Eve does not reveal a corresponding fall in the divine world, within the womb of the Holy Trinity. Neither does it express directly the metaphysical structure of the archetypal world. It is a particular event in the terrestial history of mankind whose importance will cease only with the end of human history; in a word it is a true *myth*.

On the other hand it would be erroneous to interpret, for example, the vision of Ezekiel, the *Merkabah*, as a myth. The vision of the celestial chariot is a symbolic revelation of the archetypal world. It is a typological symbol; it is that which, furthermore, the author of the *Zohar* so well understood, which is why he took the vision of Ezekiel as the central symbol of cosmic knowledge — according to the rule of analogy that that which is above is as that which is below. For the *Zohar* knows this rule well. Not only does it make implicit use of it, but also it gives it an explicit expression. It is thus that we read in the *Zohar*:

> For as it is above so it is below: as all the supernal "days" are filled with blessing by the (heavenly) Man, so are the days here below filled with blessing through the agency of Man (i.e. the righteous). ("Waera", *Zohar* 25a; trsl. Sperling-Simon-Levertoff, London-Bournemouth, 1949, vol. iii, p. 84)

India also has her version of the Hermetic maxim. Thus the *Vishvasara Tantra* states the formula:

> What is here is there. What is not here is nowhere.*

The use of analogy is not limited, however, to the "accursed sciences" — magic, astrology and alchemy — and to speculative mysticism. It is, truth to tell, universal.

Vishvasara Tantra; trsl. Arthur Avalon, *The Serpent Power*, London, 1919, p. 72.

For neither philosophy, nor theology, nor science itself can do without it. Here is the role that analogy plays in the logic which is the basis of philosophy and the sciences:

(1) The procedure of *classification* of objects on the basis of their resemblance is the first step on the way of research by the inductive method. It presupposes the *analogy* of objects to be classified.

(2) Analogy (argument by analogy) can constitute the basis of *hypotheses*. Thus the famous "nebular hypothesis" of Laplace was due to the analogy that he observed in the direction of the circular movement of the planets around the sun, the movement of satellites around the planets, and the rotation of the planets about their axes. He concluded therefore, from the analogy manifesting itself in these movements, their common *origin*.

(3) As J. Maynard Keynes says in his *A Treatise on Probability*: "Scientific method, indeed, is mainly devoted to discovering means of so heightening the known analogy that we may dispense as far as possible with the methods of pure induction." (J. Maynard Keynes, *A Treatise on Probability*, London, 1921, p. 241)

Now "pure induction" is founded on simple enumeration and is essentially only conclusion based on the experience of given statistics. Thus one could say: "As John is a man and is dead, and as Peter is a man and is dead, and as Michael is a man and is dead, therefore man is mortal." The force of this argument depends on number or on the *quantity* of facts known through experience. The method of analogy, on the other hand, adds the *qualitative* element, i.e. that which is of *intrinsic* importance, to the quantitative. Here is an example of an argument by analogy: "Andrew is formed from matter, energy and consciousness. As matter does not disappear with his death, but only changes its form, and as energy does not disappear but only modifies the mode of its activity, Andrew's consciousness, also, cannot simply disappear, but must merely change its form and mode (or plane) of activity. Therefore Andrew is immortal." This latter argument is founded on the formula of Hermes Trismegistus: that which is below (matter) (energy) is as that which is above (consciousness). Now, if there exists a law of conservation of matter and energy (although matter transforms itself into energy and vice versa), there must necessarily exist also a law of conservation of consciousness, or immortality.

The ideal of science, according to Keynes, is to find the means to elaborate the scope of *known* analogy so far as to be able to do without the hypothetical method of pure induction, i.e. to transform the scientific method into *pure analogy*, based on pure experience, without the hypothetical elements immanent in pure induction. It is by virtue of the method of analogy that science makes discoveries (in passing from the known to the unknown), formulates fruitful hypotheses, and pursues a methodical, directing aim. Analogy is its beginning and its end, its alpha and its omega.

In that which concerns speculative philosophy or metaphysics, the same role is reserved there for analogy. All conclusions of a metaphysical nature are based only on the analogy of man, Nature and the intelligible or metaphysical world. Thus the two principal authorities of the most methodical and most disciplined philosophy—mediaeval Scholastic philosophy—St. Thomas Aquinas and St. Bonaventura (of whom one represents Aristotelianism and the other Platonism in Christian philosophy) not only make use of analogy but also assign it a very important theoretical role in their doctrines themselves. St. Thomas advances the doctrine of *analogia entis*, the analogy of being, which is the principal key to his philosophy. St. Bonaventura, in his doctrine of *signatura rerum*, interprets the entire visible world as the symbol of the invisible world. For him, the visible world is only another Holy Scripture, another revelation alongside that which is contained in the Holy Scripture properly said:

> *Et sic patet quod totus mundus est sicut unum speculum plenum luminibus praesentantibus divinam sapientiam, et sicut carbo effundens lucem.* And it thus appears that the entire world is like a single mirror full of lights presenting the divine wisdom, or as charcoal emitting light. (Bonaventura, *Collationes in Hexaemeron* ii, 27)

Now, St. Thomas and St. Bonaventura have been proclaimed (by Sixtus V in 1588, and again in 1879 by Leo XIII) *"duae olivae et duo candelabra in domo Dei lucentia"* ("two olive trees and two chandeliers shining in the house of God"). You see therefore, dear Unknown Friend, that we are able, you and I, to declare openly our faith in analogy and proclaim aloud the formula of the *Emerald Table*, consecrated by tradition, without appearing thereby to be infidels to philosophy, science, and the official doctrines of the Church. We are able to use it in good conscience as philosophers, as scientists and as Catholics. There is nothing to be said against it according to these three points of view.

But the sanction accorded to analogy does not stop here: the Master Himself has endorsed it by the use which He made of it. As well as the parables, the *a fortiori* argument which He made use of in His sayings demonstrates it. The parables, which are *ad hoc* symbols, would be devoid of sense and purpose, if they were not statements of analogous truths made in the language of analogy and making appeal to the sense of analogy. With respect to the argument *a fortiori*, its entire strength lies in analogy which is its foundation. Here is an example of an *a fortiori* argument employed by the Master:

> What man of you, if his son asks him for bread, will give him

a stone? Or if he asks for a fish, will give him a serpent? If you
then, who are evil, know how to give good gifts to your children,
how much more will your Father who is in heaven give good
things to those who ask him. (Matthew vii, 9-11)

Here we have the analogy of terrestrial kinship (human) to celestial kinship
(divine), on which is founded the force of the *a fortiori* argument, where "how
much more" is the result of imperfect manifestation in relation to the ideal prototype. The analogy of father and Father is the essence here.

At this point, a feeling of unease could arise in the conscientious reader: "There
are many arguments and authorities cited *in support of* the method of analogy,
but what is there here as an argument *against* this method, as regarding its weaknesses and dangers?"

Well, it must be acknowledged quite plainly and frankly that the method of
analogy presents many negative sides and many dangers, errors and serious illusions. This is because it is entirely founded on *experience*; and all superficial, incomplete or false experience is bound to give rise to superficial, incomplete and
false conclusions, by analogy, in a direction parallel with the experience from which
they are the outcome. Thus in making use of insufficiently powerful telescopes
"canals" were seen on Mars—straight, continuous lines—where it was inferred by
analogy that these "canals" must be artificial and that consequently the planet
was inhabited by civilised beings. Now, the subsequent perfecting of telescopes
and exact observation has demonstrated that the "canals" are not at all continuous,
but that they display breaks, and are not rectilinear as they first appeared. The
argument by analogy therefore loses its value in this case, owing to the error of
experience on which it was based.

With respect to the occult sciences, Gerard van Rijnberk has published (cf. *Le
Tarot*, Lyons, 1947, p. 203) a table of astrological "correspondences" of the Tarot
according to different authors. There, for example, the seventh card —"The Chariot"
—corresponds to the sign Gemini (according to Etteila), to Sagittarius (according
to Fomalhaut), to Gemini (according to Shoral), to Sagittarius (according to an
anonymous author), to the planet Mars (according to Basilide), to the planet Venus
(according to Volguine), to the Sun (according to Ely Star), to the sign of Libra
(according to Snijders), to the planet Venus (according to Muchery), to the sign
of Cancer (according to Crowley), and to the sign of Gemini (according to
Kurtzahn). Here the relativity of the correspondences obtained by means of the
method of analogy is readily apparent.

But, on the other hand, the concordance of correspondences between the metals
and the planets, obtained by the same method, is maintained by ancient, mediaeval and modern authors. Greek astrologers of the fourth century B.C., continuing the Babylonian tradition, where gold corresponds to the Sun and to the god
Enlil, and silver to the Moon and to the god Anu, accepted the following correspondences: Gold—Sun, Silver—Moon, Lead—Saturn, Tin—Jupiter, Iron—

Mars, Copper—Venus, and Mercury—Mercury (cf. E. J. Holmyard, *Alchemy*, London, 1957, pp. 18-19).* The same correspondences were accepted by astrologers and alchemists of the Middle Ages, and again today by all authors in the occult sciences and in Hermeticism (including Rudolf Steiner and other anthroposophical authors), which correspondences you will find in the book by Papus, *Traité élémentaire de science occulte* (Paris, 1888 p. 145). On the subject of the universality of these analogous correspondences between the planets and metals, I may add that the forty-four years of my studies and experiences in this domain have not led me to modify anything in the table of given correspondences and that, on the contrary, they have supplied numerous proofs—direct and indirect—which have confirmed their truth.

It must be concluded, therefore, that the *method of analogy* on the one hand is in no way infallible but on the other hand it is qualified to lead to the discovery of essential truths. Its effectiveness and value depend on the fullness and exactitude of the experience upon which it is based.

Let us return now to the Arcanum "The Magician". As concentration without effort finds expression in the whole picture of the Card—as well as in all its details—and thus constitutes the practical Arcanum here, one also finds expressed in it the method of analogy, which constitutes the theoretical Arcanum. For, seen from the level of the intellect, the practice of the method of analogy corresponds completely to the practice of concentration without effort. Also, it appears there not as "work" but rather as "play".

The practice of analogy on the intellectual plane of consciousness does not, in fact, demand any effort; either one perceives ("sees") analogous correspondences or one does not perceive or "see" them. Just as the magician or juggler has had to train and work for a long time before attaining the ability of concentration without effort, similarly he who makes use of the method of analogy on the intellectual plane must have worked much—i.e. to have acquired long experience and to have accumulated the teachings which it requires—before attaining the faculty of immediate perception of analogous correspondences, before becoming a "magician" or "juggler" who makes use of the analogy of beings and of things without effort as in a game. This faculty constitutes an essential part of the realisation of the task that the Master charged his disciples with: "Truly, I say to you,

*Trans. note: E. J. Holmyard's research concerning the planetary metals, cited here by the author, stands in need of some modification. The list of correspondences between the planets and the metals given by Holmyard is the standard one found in Arabic alchemical texts. It is also referred to by the Christian astrologer Theophilus of Edessa, who lived in Baghdad in the eighth century A.D. (cf. Arthur Ludwich, *Anecdota astrologica*, Leipzig, 1877, p. 121). This list is almost identical to the earliest known list of the planetary metals, that of the second century A.D. Greek astrologer Vettius Valens (cf. *Anthologiarum* i, 1; ed. W. Kroll, Berlin, 1908), with the exception that Valens gives electrum (an alloy of gold and silver) as the metal corresponding to Mercury, instead of quicksilver. It is possible that the Arabic alchemical tradition took over the correspondences between the planets and metals from the Greek astrological tradition, and later substituted quicksilver for electrum. (It is not surprising that quicksilver is not mentioned by Vettius Valens, as its distillation became established only later—at some time around the fourth century A.D.).

whoever does not receive the kingdom of God like a child shall not enter it" (Mark x, 15).

The little child does not "work"—he plays. But how serious he is, i.e. concentrated, when he plays! His attention is *still* complete and undivided, whereas with he who approaches the kingdom of God it becomes *again* entire and undivided. And this is the Arcanum of intellectual geniality: the vision of the unity of beings and things through the immediate perception of their correspondences—through consciousness concentrated without effort. The Master did not want us to become puerile; what he wanted is that we attain the geniality of intelligence and heart which is analogous—not identical—to the attitude of the child, who carries only easy burdens and renders all his yokes light.

The Magician represents the man who has attained harmony and equilibrium between the spontaneity of the unconscious (in the sense given to it by C. G. Jung) and the deliberate action of the conscious (in the sense of "I" or ego consciousness). His state of consciousness is the *synthesis* of the conscious and the unconscious—of creative spontaneity and deliberately executed activity. It is the state of consciousness that the psychological school of C. G. Jung calls "individuation", or "synthesis of the conscious and unconscious elements in the personality", or "synthesis of the self" (C. G. Jung and C. Kerényi, *Introduction to a Science of Mythology*; trsl. R. F. C. Hull, London, 1951, p. 115). This synthesis renders possible concentration without effort and intellectual vision without effort, which are the practical and theoretical aspects of all fruitfulness in both practical and intellectual realms.

Friedrich Schiller seems to have had consciousness of this Arcanum when he advanced his doctrine of the synthesis between intellectual consciousness, imposing heavy burdens of duties and of rules, and the instinctive nature of man, in the *Spieltrieb* (the urge to play). The "true" and the "desired" must, according to him, find their synthesis in the "beautiful", for it is only in the beautiful that the *Spieltrieb* renders the burden of the "true" or the "just" light and raises at the same time the darkness of instinctive forces to the level of light and consciousness (cf. Friedrich Schiller, *Letters on the Aesthetic Education of Man*; trsl. E. M. Wilkinson and L. A. Willoughby, Oxford, 1967, pp. 331-332, note). In other words, he who sees the beauty of that which he recognises as true cannot fail to love it— and in loving it the element of constraint in the duty prescribed by the true will disappear: duty becomes a delight. It is thus that "work" is transformed into "play" and concentration without effort becomes possible.

But the *first* Arcanum, the Arcanum of practical and theoretical fruitfulness, whilst proclaiming the effectiveness of *serious play* (which is the complete Tarot) contains at the same time a serious warning: there is Play and play, there is the Magician and the magician; this is why anyone who confuses lack of concentration with concentration without effort, and streams of simple mental associations with the vision without effort of correspondences by analogy, will necessarily become a *charlatan*.

The Arcanum of "The Magician" is twofold. It has two aspects: he invites us on the path which leads to *geniality*; and he warns us of the danger of the path which leads to charlatanism. I must add that often—too often, alas!—the teachers of occultism follow the two paths at the same time and that which they teach contains elements of genius mixed with elements of charlatanism. May the first Arcanum of the Tarot be always present before us as a kind of "guardian of the threshold"; may he invite us to cross the threshold of work and effort in order to enter into activity without effort, and knowledge without effort, but may he at the same time warn us that the more we go beyond the threshold, the more work, effort and experience on this side of the threshold will be indispensable for the attainment of real truth. May the Magician say to us, and may he repeat it each day:

> To perceive and to know, to try and to be able to, are all different things. There are mirages above, as there are mirages below; you only *know* that which is verified by the agreement of all forms of experience in its totality—experience of the senses, moral experience, psychic experience, the collective experience of other seekers for the truth, and finally the experience of those whose knowing merits the title of wisdom and whose striving has been crowned by the title of saint. Academia and the Church stipulate methodical and moral conditions for one who desires to progress. Carry them out strictly, before and after each flight into the region beyond the domain of work and effort. If you do this, you will be a sage and a mage. If you do not do this— you will be only a charlatan!

Appendix to Letter I:

Historical Note Concerning the Emerald Table

Here is the Latin text of the *Emerald Table*, known since the time of Albertus Magnus, as given by Julius Ruska, *Tabula Smaragdina* (Heidelberg, 1926), p. 2:

> *"Versio Tabulae Smaragdinae Hermetis"* —*Qualis ea vulgo Latino Idiomate, e Phoenicio expressa circumfertur*— *Verba secretorum Hermetis Trismegisti.*
> 1. *Verum, sine mendacio, certum et verissimum.*
> 2. *Quod est inferius, est sicut (id) quod est superius, et quod*

> *est superius, est sicut (id) quod est inferius, ad perpe-*
> *tranda[1] miracula rei unius.*
>
> 3. *Et sicut omnes res fuerunt ab uno, meditatione[2] unius: sic*
>   *omnes res natae fuerunt ab hac una re, adaptatione.[3]*
> 4. *Pater ejus est Sol, mater ejus Luna; portavid illud ventus in*
>   *ventre suo; nutrix ejus terra est.*
> 5. *Pater omnis thelesmi totius mundi est hic.*
> 6. *Vis (virtus) ejus integra est, si versa fuerit in terram.*
> 7. *Separabis terram ab igne, subtile a spisso, suaviter, cum*
>   *magno ingenio.*
> 8. *Ascendit a terra in coelum, iterumque descendit in terram,*
>   *et recepit vim superiorum et inferiorum. Sic habebis gloriam*
>   *totius mundi. Ideo fugiat (fugiet) a te omnis obscuritas.*
> 9. *Hic (haec) est totius fortitudinis fortitudo fortis: quia vincet*
>   *omnem rem subtilem, omnemque solidam[4] penetrabit.*
> 10. *Sic mundus creatus est.*
> 11. *Hinc adaptationes erunt mirabiles, quarum modus est hic.*
> 12. *Itaque vocatus sum Hermes Trismegistus, habens tres partes*
>   *Philosophiae totius mundi.*
> 13. *Completum est quod dixi de operatione Solis.*

The following English translation from the Latin text *Tabula Smaragdina* is based on that by Robert Steele and Dorothy Singer, *Proceedings of the Royal Society of Medicine* xxi (1928), p. 42, who also discuss the manuscript tradition of the text, its content, and the sources of the text (ibid., pp. 41-57).

1. True it is, without falsehood, certain and most true.
2. That which is above is like to that which is below, and that which is below is like to that which is above, to accomplish the miracles of (the) one thing.
3. And as all things were by contemplation (meditation) of (the) One, so all things arose from this one thing by a single act of adaptation.
4. The father thereof is the sun, the mother the moon; the wind carried it in its womb; the earth is the nurse thereof.
5. It is the father of all works of wonder (*thelema*) throughout the whole world.
6. The power thereof is perfect, if it be cast on to earth.

---

1. According to K. C. Schmieder, *Geschichte der Alchemie* (Halle, 1832), p. 30, one meets also the variants *"penetranda"* and *"praeparanda"*.
2. According to an Arabic manuscript, discovered subsequently, this should read *"mediatione"*.
3. Another (inexact) variant is *"adoptione"*.
4. Another variant is *"et omne solidum"*.

7. It will separate the element of earth from that of fire, the subtle from the gross, gently and with great sagacity.
8. It doth ascend from earth to heaven; again it doth descend to earth, and uniteth in itself the force from things superior and things inferior. Thus thou wilt possess the glory of the brightness of the whole world, and all obscurity will fly far from thee.
9. This thing is the strongest of all powers, the force of all forces, for it overcometh every subtle thing and doth penetrate every solid substance.
10. Thus was this world created.
11. Hence there will be marvellous adaptations achieved, of which the manner is this.
12. For this reason I am called Hermes Trismegistus, because I hold three parts of the wisdom of the world.
13. That which I had to say about the operation of *sol* is completed.

As the above (Latin) text has been known in the Occident only since Albertus Magnus (1193/1206-1280) and as no other text or manuscript for an earlier date could be found over the centuries, historians at the beginning of this century were of the opinion that Albertus Magnus was the author of the *Emerald Table*. It was considered apocryphal not only from the point of view of its authenticity as a work of Hermes Trismegistus, but also from the point of view of its intrinsic authenticity as a work worthy of inclusion in the *Corpus Hermeticum* (= the collection of apocryphal texts from the first centuries of our era attributed to authors writing under the name — or pseudonym — of Hermes Trismegistus). Now, the text of the *Emerald Table* is not contained in what is considered to be the most complete edition of the *Corpus Hermeticum* — that of Walter Scott, *Hermetica* (4 volumes; Oxford, 1924). The same remark applies also to *Corpus Hermeticum* edited and translated by Nock and Festugière (4 volumes; Paris, 1960). Scott wrote the following:

> ...the masses of rubbish which fall under the...head...of writings concerning astrology, magic, alchemy and kindred forms of pseudo-science...the contents of which are also ascribed to Hermes Trismegistus. (Walter Scott, *Hermetica*, Oxford, 1924, vol. i; p. 1)

The criterion which Scott makes use of to establish if a writing attributed to Hermes Trismegistus is to be included in the *Corpus Hermeticum* or to be rejected is whether it is concerned with religious and philosophical problems or not. In other words, the writings dealing with problems of religion and philosophy belong to the *Corpus Hermeticum*, whereas the others are not worthy of inclusion, e.g. those writings concerned with *Nature* (in a "pseudo-scientific" manner) are to be rejected. However, Hermes himself says:

> I bear in mind that many of my writings have been addressed
> to him (Ammon), as again *many of my treatises on
> Nature*...have been addressed to Tat... (*Asclepius*, Prologue;
> trsl. W. Scott, *Hermetica*, vol. i, p. 287.)

How can it be permitted to reject all the writings on Nature and to consider the sole category ("addressed to Ammon") as authentic, when one has knowledge of the fact that the author of a writing (*Asclepius*), recognised as authentic in the *Corpus Hermeticum*, has proclaimed in an explicit manner that he is the author of another category of writings, namely those concerned with Nature? With respect to the *Emerald Table*, the affinity of its ideas with those expressed in *Asclepius* are all too apparent. Thus, for example, Hermes says:

> (Air) enters into earth and water; and fire rises into air. That
> only which tends upward is life-giving; and that which tends
> downward is subservient to it. Moreover, all that descends from
> on high is generative; and that which issues from below is
> nutritive. Earth, which alone stands fast in its own place, receives
> all that is generative into itself, and renders back all that it has
> received. (*Asclepius*; trsl. W. Scott, *Hermetica*, vol. i, p. 289)

Why should these ideas be considered as more "religious and philosophical" than those of the *Emerald Table*, which also speaks of movements above and below and of *generation* by father sun and mother moon, and similarly of the *nourishing* function of the earth? Perhaps because at the time of Walter Scott's researches no other text of the *Emerald Table* had been found prior to the thirteenth century?

Now, in 1926 the *Heidelberger Akten der Von-Portheim-Stiftung* published a work by Julius Ruska: *Tabula Smaragdina. Ein Beitrag zur Geschichte der hermetischen Literatur*. This book contains a description of G. Bergsträsser's manuscript in Arabic. This manuscript comprises 97 folios, of which 25 relate the history of Joseph, 40 contain an alchemical treatise, which includes as a summary the text of the *Emerald Table* (in Arabic, like the entire manuscript), followed by 32 folios devoted to other subjects, notably particulars concerning the calendar of the prophet Daniel. The alchemical treatise was written by a priest named Sagijus of Nabulus—its contents originating from the master Balinas the Wise (which is the Arabic name for Apollonius of Tyana), who himself had discovered it in an underground chamber. Here is a rendering in English of the German translation of the Arabic text of the *Emerald Table* that is given in Bergsträsser's manuscript (cf. Ruska, pp. 113-114):

Here is that which the priest Sagijus of Nabulus has dictated concerning the entrance of Balinas into the hidden chamber (the following words of wisdom were found at the end of the book by Balinas the Wise): After my entrance into the chamber, where the talisman was set up, I came up to an old man sitting on a golden throne, who was holding an emerald table in one hand. And behold, the following—in Syriac, the primordial language —was written thereon:

1. Here (is) a true explanation, concerning which there can be no doubt.
2. It attests: The above (comes) from the below, and the below from the above—the work of the miracle of the One.
3. And things have been (formed) from this primal substance through a single act. How wonderful is this work! It is the main (principle) of the world and is its maintainer.
4. Its father is the sun and its mother the moon; the wind has borne it in its body, and the earth has nourished it.
5. (It is) the father of talismen and the protector of miracles,
6. whose powers are perfect, and whose lights are confirmed(?),
7. a fire that becomes earth. Separate the earth from the fire, so you will attain the subtle as more inherent than the gross, with care and sagacity.
8. It rises from earth to heaven, so as to draw the lights of the heights to itself, and descends (again) to the earth; thus within it are the forces of the above and the below; because the light of lights (is) within it, thus does the darkness flee before it.
9. (It is) the force of forces, which overcomes every subtle thing and penetrates into everything gross.
10. The structure of the small world (microcosm) is in accordance with the structure of the great world (macrocosm).
11. And accordingly proceed the knowledgeable.
12. And to this aspired Hermes, who was threefold graced with wisdom.
13. And this is his last book, which he concealed in the chamber.

But Julius Ruska is not the only one to have discovered an Arabic text of the *Emerald Table*. The author of *Alchemy*, E. J. Holmyard (Pelican, London, 1957), points out that he found a shortened text of the *Emerald Table* in Arabic. This text is part of the *Second Book of the Element of the Foundation* by Jabir or Geber (722-815). Prior to this discovery, made in 1923, only the mediaeval Latin text was known of. Subsequently, another variant in Arabic was discovered by Ruska in a book entitled *The Secret of Creation* attributed to Apollonius. Jabir (or Geber) himself, in giving the text of the *Emerald Table* states that he is quoting Apollonius. Now, Kraus has shown that *The Secret of Creation* was written, at least in its final edition, during the Caliphate of al-Ma'mun (813-833), and it includes parallels with a book written at this same time by Job of Edessa. The latter was a scholar whose translations from Syriac into Arabic merited the praise of even such a severe critic as Hunain ibn Ishaq. Therefore, even if Job did not write *The Secret of Creation*, he probably drew from the same, more ancient sources as the author of the said treatise. Kraus has shown that one of these sources was the writings of Nemesius, bishop of Emesa (Homs) in Syria during the second half of the fourth century A.D. Nemesius wrote in Greek, but his book *On the Nature of Man* does not contain the text of the *Emerald Table*. To summarise, it can be concluded that the most ancient rendering of the *Emerald Table* that is known, namely that in Arabic, was probably translated from Syriac, but this can equally well have been based on an original Greek text. Whether this original dates back to the time of Apollonius is an insoluble problem (cf. Ruska, op. cit., pp. 78-79, pp. 96-97).

The present state of historical studies on the *Emerald Table* is therefore as follows: it was known in Arabic as a translation from Syriac at the beginning of the ninth century; two variants in Arabic are extant; there is no reason to reject the Arabic tradition that it was translated from Syriac, or for that matter the tradition that it originated with Apollonius.

One could add that if there is no reason to doubt that it originated with Apollonius, there is no more reason to reject the tradition that Apollonius in his turn found it in the manner described by the priest Sagijus of Nabulus. Be that as it may, it is immediately apparent that the *Emerald Table* is of a considerably more ancient origin than was believed up to 1923, and consequently there is room to reconsider the opinion that it is not worthy of inclusion in the *Corpus Hermeticum*.

For our part, we have every reason—subjective as well as objective—sufficient for us *in foro interno* (i.e. in good conscience) to be sure that the *Emerald Table* is without doubt the only absolutely authentic fragment in the whole *Corpus Hemeticum*. And this, moreover, in the sense that its author is neither the "third Hermes" nor the "second", but actually the first, that is to say the founder of the Hermetic tradition as such—in which tradition the principal links (according to Ficino, writing in 1471) are: Hermes Trismegistus—Orpheus—Pythagoras—Philolaus (*Divi Platonis nostri praeceptor*)—Plato—the Neopythagoreans (Apollonius)—the Neoplatonists (Plotinus).

Meditation on the
Second Major Arcanum of the Tarot

THE HIGH PRIESTESS
LA PAPESSE

Wisdom has built her house,
she has set up her seven pillars.
(Proverbs ix, 1)

LETTER II

THE HIGH
PRIESTESS

Dear Unknown Friend,

As set forth in the preceding Letter, the Magician is the arcanum of intellectual geniality and cordiality, the arcanum of true spontaneity. Concentration without effort and the perception of correspondences in accordance with the law of analogy are the principal implications of this arcanum of spiritual fecundity. It is the arcanum of the *pure act* of intelligence. But the pure act is like fire or wind: it appears and disappears, and when exhausted it gives way to another act.

> The wind blows where it wills, and you hear the sound of it,
> but you do not know whence it comes or whither it goes; so it
> is with everyone who is born of the Spirit. (John iii, 8)

The pure act in itself cannot be grasped; it is only its *reflection* which renders it perceptible, comparable and understandable or, in other words, it is by virtue of the reflection that we become conscious of it. The reflection of the pure act produces an inner representation, which becomes retained by the memory; memory becomes the source of communication by means of the spoken word; and the communicated word becomes fixed by means of writing, by producing the "book".

The second Arcanum, the High Priestess, is that of the reflection of the pure act of the first Arcanum up to the point where it becomes "book". It shows us how Fire and Wind become Science and Book. Or, in other words, how "Wisdom builds her house".

As we have pointed out, one becomes conscious of the pure act of intelligence only by means of its reflection. We require an inner mirror in order to be conscious of the pure act or to know "whence it comes or whither it goes". The breath of the Spirit—or the pure act of intelligence—is certainly an event, but it does not suffice, itself alone, for us to become conscious of it. Con-*sciousness* (*con-science*) is the result of two principles—the active, activating principle and the passive, reflecting principle. In order to *know* from where the breath of the Spirit comes and where it goes, Water is required to reflect it. This is why the conversation of the Master with Nicodemus, to which we have referred, enunciates the absolute condition for the *conscious* experience of the Divine Spirit—or the Kingdom of God:

> Truly, truly, I say to you, unless one is born of Water and the
> Spirit, he cannot enter the Kingdom of God. (John iii, 5)

"Truly, truly"—the Master refers here twice to "truth" in this mantric (i.e. magical) formula of the reality of con-sciousness. By these words he states that full consciousness of the truth is the result of "inbreathed" truth and reflected truth. Reintegrated consciousness, which is the Kingdom of God, presupposes two renovations, of a significance comparable to birth, in the two constituent elements of consciousness —active Spirit and reflecting Water. Spirit must become divine Breath in place of arbitrary, personal activity, and Water must become a perfect mirror of the divine Breath instead of being agitated by disturbances of the imagination, passions and personal desires. Reintegrated consciousness must be born of Water and Spirit, after Water has once again become Virginal and Spirit has once again become divine Breath or the Holy Spirit. Reintegrated consciousness therefore becomes born within the human soul in a way *analogous* to the birth or historical incarnation of the WORD:

> *Et incarnatus est de Spiritu Sancto ex Maria Virgine.* (by the
> power of the Holy Spirit the Word became incarnate from the
> Virgin Mary)

The re-birth from Water and Spirit which the Master indicates to Nicodemus is the re-establishment of the state of consciousness prior to the Fall, where the Spirit was divine Breath and where this Breath was reflected by virginal Nature. This is *Christian yoga*. Its aim is not "radical deliverance" (*mukti*), i.e. the state of consciousness without breath and without reflection, but rather "baptism from Water and the Spirit", which is the complete and perfect response to divine action. These two kinds of baptism bring about the reintegration of the two constituent elements of consciousness as such—the active element and the passive element. There is no consciousness without these two elements, and the suppression of this duality by means of a practical method such as that inspired by the ideal of unity (*advaita*—non-duality) must necessarily lead to the extinction not of being but rather of consciousness. Then this would not be a *new birth* of consciousness, but instead would be its *return* to the pre-natal embryonic cosmic state.

On the other hand, this is what Plotinus says concerning the duality underlying all forms and every level of consciousness, namely the active principle and its mirror:

> . . .when the mirror is there, the mirror-image is produced, but when it is not there or is not in the right state, the object of which the image would have been is (all the same) actually there. In the same way as regards the soul, when that kind of thing in us which mirrors the images of thought and intellect is undisturbed, we see them and know them in a way parallel to sense-perception, along with the prior knowledge that it is intellect and thought that are active. But when this is broken because the harmony of the body is upset, thought and intellect operate without an image, and then intellectual activity takes place without a mind-picture. (Plotinus, *Ennead* I. iv. 10; trsl. A. H. Armstrong, London, 1966, pp. 199 and 201)

This is the Platonic conception of consciousness, the thorough study of which can serve by way of introduction to the nocturnal conversation of the Master with Nicodemus on the reintegration of consciousness or the aim of Christian yoga.

Christian yoga does not aspire directly to unity, but rather to the *unity of two*. This is very important for understanding the standpoint which one takes towards the infinitely serious problem of unity and duality. For this problem can open the door to truly divine mysteries and can also close them to us. . .for ever, perhaps, who knows? Everything depends on its comprehension. We can decide in favour of monism and say to ourselves that there can be only one sole essence, one sole being. Or we can decide—in view of considerable historical and personal experience —in favour of dualism and say to ourselves that there are two principles in the world: good and evil, spirit and matter, and that, entirely incomprehensible though this duality is at root, it must be admitted as an incontestable fact. We can, moreover, decide in favour of a third point of view, namely that of *love* as the cosmic principle which presupposes duality and postulates its *non-substantial but essential* unity.

These three points of view are found at the basis of the Vedanta (*advaita*) and Spinozism (monism), Manichaeism and certain gnostic schools (dualism), and the Judaeo-Christian current (love).

In order to give more clarity and precision to this problem, as well as to attain greater depth — we shall take for our point of departure what Louis Claude de Saint-Martin says concerning the number *two* in his book *Des Nombres* ("On Numbers").

> Now, in order to show how they (numbers) are related to their base of activity, let us begin by observing the working of *unity* and of the number *two*. When we contemplate an important truth, such as the universal power of the Creator, his majesty, his love, his profound light, or suchlike attributes, we bear ourselves wholly towards this supreme model of all things; all our faculties are suspended in order to fill us with him, and we really only make ourselves one with him. This is the active image of unity, and the number *one* in our languages is the expression of this unity or invisible union which, existing intimately between all attributes of this unity, must equally exist between it and all its produced creations. But if, after having borne all our faculties of contemplation towards this universal source, we return our gaze to ourselves and fill ourselves with our own contemplation, in such a way that we regard ourselves as the origin of some of the inner light or satisfaction that this source has procured for us, from that moment we establish two centres of contemplation, two separate and rival principles, two bases which are not linked; lastly, we establish two *unities*, with this difference — that one is real and the other is apparent. (p. 2) [Then he adds:] But to divide being through the middle is to divide it into two parts; it is to pass from the whole to the quality of the part or the half, and it is here that the true origin of illegitimate twofoldness lies...this example is sufficient to show us the birth of the number *two* — to show us the origin of evil... (p. 3). (Louis Claude de Saint-Martin, *Des Nombres*, Nice, 1946, pp. 2-3)

Duality therefore signifies the establishment of two centres of contemplation, two separate and rival principles — one real and the other apparent — and this is the origin of evil, which is only illegitimate twofoldness. Is this the *only* possible interpretation of duality, twofoldness, the number two? Does there not exist a *legitimate twofoldness*?...a twofoldness which does not signify the *diminution* of unity, but rather its qualitative enrichment?

If we return to the conception of Saint-Martin of "two centres of contemplation" which are "two separate and rival principles", we can ask ourselves if they must *necessarily* be separate and rival? Does not the expression "contemplation" itself, chosen by Saint-Martin, suggest the idea of two centres which contemplate simultaneously—as would two eyes if they were placed vertically one above the other—the *two* aspects of reality, the phenomenal and the noumenal? And that it is by virtue of the two centres or "eyes" that we are—or are able to be—conscious of "that which is above and that which is below"? Could one, for example, enunciate the principal formula of the *Emerald Table* if one had only one "eye" or centre of contemplation instead of *two*?

Now, the *Sepher Yetzirah* says:

> Two is the breath which comes from the Spirit, and formed in
> it are twenty-two sounds... but the Spirit is first and above these.
> (*Sepher Yetzirah* i, 10; trsl. W. Wynn Westcott, London, 1893,
> p. 16)

Or, in other words, two is the divine Breath and its Reflection; it is the origin of the "Book of Revelation" which is the world as well as the Holy Scripture. Two is the number of con-sciousness of the breath of the Spirit and its "formed" (engraved) letters. It is the number of the reintegration of consciousness, signified by the Master to Nicodemus by the virginal Water and the Breath of the Holy Spirit.

Two is all this, and it is even more. Not only is the number two not necessarily the "illegitimate twofoldness" described by Saint-Martin, but also it is the number of love or the fundamental condition of love which it necessarily presupposes and postulates... because love is inconceivable without the Lover and the Loved, without ME and YOU, without One and the Other.

If God were only One and if he had not created the World, he would not be the God revealed by the Master, the God of whom St. John says:

> God *is* love; and he who abides in love abides in God, and God
> abides in him. (I John iv, 16)

He would not be this, because he would love no one other than himself. As this is impossible from the point of view of the God of love, he is revealed to human consciousness as the eternal Trinity—the Loving One who loves, the Loved One who loves, and their Love who loves them: Father, Son and Holy Spirit.

Do you not also experience, dear Unknown Friend, a feeling of discomfort each time that you encounter a formula stating the higher attributes of the Holy Trinity, such as "Power, Wisdom, Love" or "Being, Consciousness, Beatitude" (*sat—chit—ananda*)? Personally, I always experienced this discomfort, and it was only later, many years later, that I understood its cause. It is because God is love, that he admits of no comparison, that he surpasses all—power, wisdom, and even being. One can, if one wishes, speak of the "power of love" the "wisdom of love" and the "life of love" in order to make a distinction between the three Persons of the Holy Trinity, but one cannot put on the same level love on the one hand and wisdom, power and being on the other. For God is love and it is love—it is only love—which by its presence gives worth to power and to wisdom and to being itself. For *being* without love is deprived of all worth. Being without love would be the most appalling torment—the Inferno itself!

Does love therefore surpass being? How could one doubt this after the revelation of this truth through nineteen centuries by the Mystery of Calvary? "That which is below is like to that which is above"—and is not the sacrifice of His life, His terrestrial being, accomplished through love by God Incarnate, is this not the demonstration of the superiority of love over being? And is not the Resurrection the demonstration of the other aspect of the primacy of love over being, i.e. that love is not only superior to being but also that it engenders it and restores it?

The problem of the primacy of being or of love goes back to antiquity. Plato raised it when he said:

> The sun, I presume you will say, not only furnishes to visibles the power of visibility but it also provides for their generation and growth and nurture though it is not itself generation. . . In like manner, then, you are to say that the objects of knowledge not only receive from the presence of the good their being known, but their very existence and essence is derived to them from it, though the good itself is not essence but still transcends essence in dignity and surpassing power. (Plato, *The Republic* 509B; trsl. P. Shorey, 2 vols., London, 1930, 1935, vol. ii, p. 107)

And seven centuries later Sallustius, the friend of Emperor Julian, said:

> Now if the First Cause was soul, everything would be animated by soul, if intelligence, everything would be intellectual, if being, everything would share in being. Some in fact, seeing that all things possess being, have thought that the First Cause was being. This would be correct if things that were in being were in being only and were not good. If, however, things that are are by reason of their goodness and share in the good, then what is first must be higher than being and in fact good. A very clear indication of this is that fine souls for the sake of the good despise being, when they are willing to face danger for country or friends or virtue. (Sallustius, *Concerning the Gods and the Universe*, v; trsl. A. D. Nock, Cambridge, 1926, p. 11)

The primacy of good (good being the abstract philosophical notion of the *reality* of love) in relation to being has also been discussed by Plotinus (*Enneads* vi, 7, 23-24), by Proclus (*In Platonis Theologiam* ii, 4 = *On the Theology of Plato*), and by Dionysius the Areopagite (*De divinis nominibus*, iv = *On the Divine Names*). St. Bonaventura (*Collationes in Hexaemeron* x, 10) tried to reconcile this Platonic primacy of good with the Mosaic primacy of being: *Ego sum qui sum* ("I am that I am", Exodus iii, 14)—asserted first by John Damascenus (John of Damascus) and then by Thomas Aquinas. The latter states that amongst all the divine names there is one which is eminently suited to God, and this is *Qui est* ("He who is"), precisely because it signifies nothing other than being itself. Etienne Gilson, in harmony with St. Thomas, John Damascenus and Moses, writes concerning being:

> In this principle lies an inexhaustible metaphysical fecundity ...there is but one God and this God is Being, that is the corner-stone of all Christian philosophy, and it was not Plato, it was not even Aristotle, it was Moses who instituted it. (Etienne Gilson, *The Spirit of Mediaeval Philosophy*; trsl. A. H. C. Downes, London, 1950, p. 51)

Yet what is the full *significance* of the adoption of the primacy of being, instead of that of good, or according to St. John, that of love?

The idea of being is *neutral* from the point of view of the moral life. There is no need to have the experience of the good and the beautiful in order to arrive at it. The experience solely of the mineral realm already suffices to arrive at the morally neutral idea of being. For the mineral *is*. For this reason the idea of being is *objective*, i.e. it postulates, in the last analysis, the *thing* underlying everything, the permanent substance behind all phenomena.

I invite you, dear Unknown Friend, to close your eyes and to render an exact account of the image which accompanies this idea in your mental imagination. Do you not find the vague image of a substance without colour or form, very similar to water in the sea?

Whatever your subjective representation of being as such, the *idea* of being is morally indifferent and is, consequently, essentially naturalistic. It implies something *passive*, i.e. *a given or an unalterable fact*. In contrast, when you think of love in the Johannine sense or of the Platonic idea of good, you find yourself facing an essential *activity*, which is in no way neutral from the point of view of moral life, but which is the heart itself. And the image which accompanies this notion of pure actuality would be that of fire or of the sun (Plato compared the idea of good to the sun, and its light to truth), in place of the image of an indefinite fluid substance.

Thales and Heraclitus have two different conceptions. The one sees in *water* the essence of things and the other sees it in *fire*. But here, primarily, it is so that the idea of GOOD and its summit—LOVE—is due to the conception of the world as a *moral* process, whereas the idea of BEING and its summit—the God QUI EST—is due to the conception of the world as that of a fact of Nature. The idea of good (and of love) is essentially *subjective*. It is absolutely necessary to have had experience of psychic and spiritual life in order to be able to conceive of it, whilst—as we have already indicated—the idea of being, being essentially *objective*, presupposes only a certain degree of outward experience...of the mineral realm, for example.

The consequence of choosing between these two—I will not say "points of view", but rather "attitudes of soul"—lies above all in the intrinsic nature of the experience of practical mysticism which consequently derives from this choice. He who chooses being will aspire to true being and he who chooses love will aspire to love. For one only finds that for which one seeks. The seeker for true being will arrive at the experience of *repose* in being, and, as there cannot be *two* true beings ("the illegitimate twofoldness" of Saint-Martin) or two separate co-eternal substances but only *one* being and *one* substance, the centre of "false being" will be suppressed ("false being" = *ahamkara*, or the illusion of the separate existence of a separate substance of the "self"). The characteristic of this mystical way is that *one loses the capacity to cry*. An advanced pupil of yoga or Vedanta will for ever have dry eyes, whilst the masters of the Cabbala, according to the *Zohar*, cry much and often. Christian mysticism speaks also of the "gift of tears"—as a precious gift of divine grace. The Master cried in front of the tomb of Lazarus. Thus the outer characteristic of those who choose the other mystical way, that of the God of love, is that they have the "gift of tears". This is in keeping with the very essence of their mystical experience. Their union with the Divine is not the absorption of their being by Divine Being, but rather the experience of the breath of Divine Love, the illumination by Divine Love, and the warmth of Divine Love. The soul which receives this undergoes such a miraculous experience that it cries. In this mystical experience fire meets with FIRE. Then nothing is extinguished in the human personality but, on the contrary, everything is set ablaze. This is the experience of "legitimate twofoldness" or the union of two separate *substances* in one sole *essence*. The substances remain separate as long as they are bereft of that which is the most precious in all existence: free alliance in love.

I have spoken of "two *substances*" and "one *essence*". Here it is necessary to really grasp the significance of these two terms—substance (*substantia*) and essence (*essentia*), whose exact distinction is today almost effaced. However, at one time these two terms denoted two distinct categories not only of ideas but also of existence and consciousness itself.

Plato established the distinction between εἶναι (*einai*, being) and οὐσία (*ousia*, essence). *Being* signifies for him the fact of existence as such, whereas *essence* designates existence due to Ideas.

> Everything which has *existence* has *essence* through its share in Ideas, which are themselves essences. The term essence will therefore not designate for us abstract existence but the reality of the Idea. (A. J. E. Fouillée, *La philosophie de Platon*, 4 vols., Paris, 1888-89, vol. ii, pp. 106-7)

Essence (*essentia*, *ousia*) signifies the positive act itself by means of which being *is* (in the Cabbala one would speak of the act of *emanation* of the first Sephirah, KETHER—whose corresponding divine name is AHIH (*eyeh*), i.e. "I AM"—from AIN-SOPH, the Unlimited).

> . . . as if *esse* could generate the present participle active *essens*, whence *essentia* would be derived. (Etienne Gilson, *The Spirit of Mediaeval Philosophy*; trsl. A. H. C. Downes, London, 1950, p. 54)

Thus the term *essentia* properly belongs only to God alone; everything else enters into the category of *substantiae*. This is what the Church Father and Platonist, St. Augustine, says:

> . . . *manifestum est Deum abusive substantiam vocari, ut nomine usitatiore intellegitur essentia, quod vere ac proprie dicitur; ita ut fortasse solum Deum dici oporteat essentiam* (. . . hence it is clear that God is not properly called a substance, and that he is better called by the more usual term *essence*, which term is a right and proper one; so much so indeed that perhaps *God alone ought to be called essence*.) (St. Augustine, *De Trinitate* vii, 5, 10)

The distinction between substance and essence, between reality and the ideal, between being and love (or the idea of good), or between *He who is* and AIN-SOPH is also the key to the Gospel according to John:

> No one has ever *seen* God; the only Son, who is in the bosom of the Father, he has made him known. (John i, 18)

"No one has ever *seen* God", i.e. no one has ever contemplated God face to face while maintaining his personality. For "to see" signifies "to perceive while being in the face of that which one perceives". Before Jesus Christ there were, without doubt, numerous examples of the experience of God—being "seized by God" (experience of the prophets), being "immersed in God" (experience of yogis and mystics in antiquity), or seeing the revelation of His work, the world (experience of sages and philosophers in antiquity), but no one ever *saw* God. For neither the inspiration of the prophets, nor the immersion in God of the mystics, nor the contemplation of God in the mirror of the creation by the sages is equivalent to the new experience of the "vision" of God—the "beatific vision" of Christian theology. For this "vision" takes place in the domain of *essence* transcending all substance; it is not a fusion, but an *encounter* in the domain of essence, in which the human personality (the consciousness of self) remains not only intact and without impediment, but also becomes "that which it is", i.e. becomes truly itself—such as the Thought of God has conceived it for all eternity. The words of St. John, when thought of in this way, render intelligible those of the Master in the Gospel of St. John:

> All who came before me are thieves and robbers. (John x, 8)

There is a profound mystery in these words. Indeed, how may they be understood alongside numerous other sayings of the Master referring to Moses, David and other prophets, who were all before him?

Now, it is a matter here not of theft and robbery, but of the *principle of initiation* before and after Jesus Christ. The masters prior to His Coming taught the experience of God at the expense of the personality, which had to be diminished when it was "seized" by God or "immersed" in God. In *this sense* — in the sense of the diminution or augmentation of the "talent of gold" entrusted to humanity, the personality, which is the "image and likeness of God" (Goethe: *Das höchste Gut der Erdenkinder ist doch die Personlichkeit*, i.e. "The highest treasure of the children of earth is surely the personality") — the masters prior to Christ were "thieves and robbers". They certainly bore testimony to God but the way which they taught and practised was that of *depersonalisation*, which made them witnesses ("martyrs") of God. The greatness of Bhagavan, the Buddha, was the high degree of depersonalisation which he attained. The masters of yoga are masters of depersonalisation. The ancient philosophers — those who really lived as "philosophers" — practised depersonalisation. This is the case above all with the Stoics.

And this is why all those who have chosen the way of depersonalisation are unable to cry and why they have dry eyes for ever. For it is the personality which cries and which alone is capable of the "gift of tears". "Blessed are those who mourn, for they shall be comforted" (Matthew v, 4).

Therefore this is one aspect at least (there is also another more profound one, but I do not know if it will be possible to write about it in one of the following Letters) according to which we may say that the mysterious words relating to "thieves and robbers" can become a source of radiant light. When the Gospel speaks of those who came *before* Jesus Christ, it is not only time which the word "before" designates, but also the *grade* of initiation — they are thieves and robbers with respect to the personality, since they taught the depersonalisation of the human being. In contrast, the Master also says: "I have come that they (the sheep) may have *life*, and have it abundantly" (John x, 10); in other words, the Master has come in order to render *more living* that which is dear to him and which is menaced with dangers, i.e. the sheep as the image of the personality! This appears inconceivable in the presence of the ideal of the personality according to Nietzsche and his "superman" or the great historical personalities such as Alexander the Great, Julius Caesar, Napoleon... and the "great personalities" of modern times!

No, dear Unknown Friend, *possession* by the will-to-power or the will-to-glory makes neither the personality nor its greatness. The "sheep" in the language of love of the Master signify neither the "great personality" nor the "little personality", but simply the individual soul which lives. He wants the soul to live without danger and to have as intensive a life as God has destined for it. The "sheep" is the living entity, surrounded by dangers, which is the object of divine care. Doesn't this suffice? Is there too little brilliance and glory here? Is this too feeble an image to be able to arrive at, for example, a magician evoking good and evil spirits?

Here it is a matter of drawing attention to one thing, to one sole thing: the language of the Master is that of love and not that of psychology, philosophy, or science. The powerful magician, the artistic genius, the profound thinker, and the radiant mystic certainly merit all these qualifications and perhaps still greater ones, but they do not dazzle God. In the eyes of God they are dear sheep to him; in his consideration of them he desires that they shall never go astray and that they shall have life increasingly and unceasingly.

Before completing our reflections on the *problem of the number two*, the problem of legitimate twofoldness and illegitimate twofoldness, I should pay tribute to Saint-Yves d'Alveydre, who set this problem in motion with his passionate intellecuality. In his work *Mission des Juifs* ("Mission of the Jews", Paris, 1956), he concentrated on the comparison of the *complete* divine name (YOD-HÉ-VAU-HÉ) with the *incomplete* name (HÉ-VAU-HÉ). In the first case YOD, *essence*, is considered to be the supreme hierarchical principle; in the second case it is HÉ, *substance*, to which priority is attributed. It is in this way that spiritualism and naturalism originated—with all the consequences they entail in religious, philosophical, scientific and social spheres. The problem—as a *formula*—is therefore put with admirable exactness and precision, and it is this that I want to draw attention to. But I am at the same time obliged to say that exact and precise as it is, the material content that Saint-Yves gives to it leaves much to be desired. In particular he states that the principle of pure intellect is YOD, and to HÉ-VAU-HÉ as material content he attributes the principle of love and soul, or the "passionate principle". Thus, in attributing priority to the intellect as the masculine, spiritual principle, he subordinates love to it as the feminine, psychic principle. Now, the Master taught of the Father, who is love. The intellect being the reflection —or light—of the fire principle of love, can only be the feminine principle, Sophia or Wisdom, who *assists* the Creator in the work of creation, according to the Old Testament. The gnostic tradition also considers Sophia as the feminine principle. Pure intellect is that which reflects; love is that which acts.

The fact that man is usually more intellectual than woman does not signify that the intellect is a masculine principle. On the contrary, rather: man, being physically masculine, is feminine from the psychic point of view, whilst woman, being physically feminine, is masculine (active) in her soul. Now, the intellect is the feminine side of the soul, whilst the fertilising imagination is the masculine principle. The intellect that is not fertilised by imagination guided by the heart is sterile. It depends on impulses which it receives from the participation of the heart by means of the imagination.

With regard to the third principle, the Spirit, it is neither intellect nor imagination, but Love-Wisdom. In *principle* it ought to be androgynous, but in practice it is not always so.

This, therefore, is all that it seems to me necessary to say on the subject of the problem of two and its significance — the resolution of this problem being the key to the second Arcanum, the High Priestess. For this is the arcanum of the twofoldness underlying consciousness — spontaneous activity and its reflection; it is the arcanum of the transformation of the pure act into representation, of representation into memory pictures, of memory pictures into the word, and of the word into written characters or *the book*.

The High Priestess wears a three-layered tiara and holds an open book. The tiara is laden with precious stones, which suggests the idea that it is by way of three stages that the crystallisation of the pure act descends through the three higher and invisible planes before arriving at the fourth stage — the book. For the problems that the symbol implies are: *reflection*, *memory*, *word* and *writing*; or, in other words — *revelation* and *tradition*, spoken and written; or, to express it in a single word — GNOSIS (this is also the title given by Eliphas Lévi as a heading for the second chapter of his *Dogme et rituel de la haute magie*; trsl. A. E. Waite, *Transcendental Magic. Its Doctrine and Ritual*, London, 1968).

It is concerned with gnosis and not at all with science, since gnosis is exactly what the Card of the High Priestess expresses both in its entirety and in its details, namely the *descent* of revelation (the pure act or essence reflected by substance) down to the final stage — or "book". Science, on the contrary, begins with facts (the "characters" of the book of Nature) and ascends from facts to *laws* and from laws to *principles*. Gnosis is the reflection of that which is above; science, in contrast, is the interpretation of that which is below. The *last* stage of gnosis is the world of facts, where it becomes *fact* itself, i.e. it becomes "book"; the *first* stage of science is the world of facts which it "reads", in order to arrive at laws and principles.

As it is gnosis (i.e. mysticism become conscious of itself) that the Card symbolises, it does not present the image of a scientist or a doctor, but rather that of a priestess, the High Priestess — the sacred guardian of the Book of Revelation. As the High Priestess represents the stages of the descent of revelation, from the small uppermost circle on her tiara as far as the open book on her knees, her position is in keeping with this — she is *seated*. For, to be seated signifies a relationship between the vertical and horizontal which corresponds to the task of the outward projection (horizontal, book) of the descending revelation (vertical, tiara). This position indicates the *practical method of gnosis*, just as the standing Magician indicates the practical method of mysticism. The Magician *dares* — for this reason he is standing. The High Priestess *knows* — this is why she is seated. The transformation from *to dare* to *to know* consists in the change of position from that of the Magician to that of the High Priestess.

The essence of pure mysticism is creative activity. One becomes a mystic when one dares to elevate oneself — i.e. "to stand upright", then even more upright, and ever more upright – beyond all created being as far as the essence of Being, the divine, creative fire. "Concentration without effort" is burning without smoke or crackling fire. On the part of the human being it is the act of *daring* to aspire to the supreme Reality, and this act is real and effective only when the soul is serene and the body completely relaxed – without smoke and crackling fire.

The essence of pure gnosis is reflected mysticism. Gnosis signifies that that which takes place in mysticism has become *higher knowledge*. That is, gnosis is mysticism which has become conscious of itself. It is mystical *experience* transformed into higher knowledge.

Now, this transformation of mystical experience into knowledge takes place in stages. The first is the pure reflection or a kind of imaginative repetition of the experience. The second stage is its entrance into memory. The third stage is its assimilation in thought and feeling, in a manner where it becomes a "message" or inner *word*. The fourth stage, lastly, is reached when it becomes a communicable symbol or "writing", or "book"– i.e. when it is *formulated*.

The pure reflection of mystical experience is without image and without word. It is purely *movement*. Here consciousness is moved by the immediate contact with that which transcends it, with the trans-subjective. This experience is as certain as the experience belonging to the sense of *touch* in the physical world and is, at the same time, as much devoid of form, colour and sound as the sense of touch. For this reason one can compare it with this sense and designate it as "spiritual touch" or "intuition".

This designation is not quite adequate, but at least it has the merit of expressing the character of *immediate contact*, which is peculiar to the first stage of reflection of the mystical act. Here, mystical experience and gnosis are still inseparable and are as one.

If we want to establish the relationship between, on the one hand this state of consciousness and the three states which follow it, and on the other hand the sacred name יהוה (YOD-HÉ-VAU-HÉ; abbreviated YHVH), which is the summation of Jewish gnosis or the whole Cabbala, we cannot do otherwise than to attribute it to the first letter, YOD. The letter YOD is a point with the tendency of the indicated projection: י . This corresponds admirably to the experience of spiritual touch, which also is nothing other than a point signifying germinally within itself a world of potentialities.

Spiritual touch (or intuition) is that which permits contact between our consciousness and the world of pure mystical experience. It is by virtue of this that there exists in the world and in the history of mankind a real relationship between the living soul and the living God – which is true religion. Mysticism is the source and the root of all religion. Without it religion and the entire spiritual life of humanity would be only a code of laws regulating human thought and action. If God signifies for man something more than an abstract notion, it is thanks to spiritual touch or mysticism. It is the *seed* of all religious life – with its theology, rituals and practices. Mysticism is also the seed of gnosis, which is esoteric theology, just as magic is esoteric art and occultism or Hermeticism is esoteric philosophy. Now, mysticism is the YOD of the *Tetragrammaton*, just as gnosis is the first HÉ, magic is the VAU — or "child" of mysticism and gnosis — and Hermetic philosophy is the second (final) HÉ, i.e. the summation of what is revealed. The last HÉ or Hermetic philosophy is the "book" which the High Priestess holds on her knees, whilst the three layers of her tiara represent the stages of the descent of revelation from the mystical plane to the gnostic plane, then from the gnostic plane to the magical plane and, lastly, from the magical plane to the philosophical plane — to the plane of the "book" or the "doctrine".

Just as spiritual touch is the mystical sense, so there is a "gnostic sense", a "magical sense" and a special "Hermetic-philosophical sense". Full consciousness of the sacred name YHVH can only be attained by the united experience of these four senses and the practice of four different methods. For the fundamental thesis of Hermetic epistemology (or "gnoseology") is that "each object of knowledge demands a method of knowledge which is proper to it". This thesis or rule signifies that one ought never to apply the same method of knowledge on different planes, but only to different objects belonging to the same plane. A crying example of ignorance of this law is "cybernetic psychology", which wants to explain man and his psychic life by mechanical, material laws.

Each mode of experience and knowledge when pushed to its limit becomes a sense or engenders a special sense. He who dares to aspire to the experience of the unique essence of Being will develop the mystical sense or spiritual touch. If he wants not only *to live* but also to learn to understand what he lives through, he will develop the gnostic sense. And if he wants to put into practice what he has understood from mystical experience, he will develop the magical sense. If, lastly, he wants all that he has experienced, understood and practised to be not limited to himself and his time, but to become communicable to others and to be transmitted to future generations, he must develop the Hermetic-philosophical sense, and in practising it he will "write his book".

Such is the law that YOD-HÉ-VAU-HÉ expresses concerning the process of transformation of mystical experience into tradition; such is the law of the *birth* of tradition. Its source is mystical experience: one cannot be a gnostic or a magician or a Hermetic philosopher (or occultist) without being a mystic. The tradition is a living one only when it constitutes a *complete organism*, when it is the result of the union of mysticism, gnosis, magic and Hermetic philosophy. If this is not so, it *decays and dies*. And the death of the tradition manifests itself in the degeneration of its constituent elements, which become separated. Then, Hermetic philosophy separated from magic, gnosis and mysticism becomes a parasitic system of autonomous thought which is, truth to tell, a veritable psycho-pathological complex, because it bewitches or enslaves human consciousness and deprives it of its liberty. A person who has had the misfortune to fall victim to the spell of a philosophical system (and the spells of sorcerers are mere trifles in comparison to the disastrous effect of the spell of a philosophical system!) can no longer see the world, or people, or historic events, as they are; he sees everything only through the distorting prism of the system by which he is possessed. Thus, a Marxist of today is *incapable* of seeing anything else in the history of mankind other than the "class struggle".

What I am saying concerning mysticism, gnosis, magic and philosophy would be considered by him only as a ruse on the part of the bourgeois class, with the aim of "screening with a mystical and idealistic haze" the reality of the exploitation of the proletariat by the bourgeoisie. . . although I have not inherited anything from my parents and I have not experienced a single day without having to earn my living by means of work recognised as "legitimate" by Marxists!

Another contemporary example of possession by a system is Freudianism. A man possessed by this system will see in everything that I have written only the expression of "suppressed libido", which seeks and finds release in this manner. It would therefore be the lack of sexual fulfillment which has driven me to occupy myself with the Tarot and to write about it!

Is there any need for further examples? Is it still necessary to cite the Hegelians with their distortion of the history of humanity, the Scholastic "realists" of the Middle Ages with the Inquisition, the rationalists of the eighteenth century who were blinded by the light of their own autonomous reasoning?

Yes, autonomous philosophical systems separated from the living body of tradition are parasitic structures, which seize the thought, feeling and finally the will of human beings. In fact, they play a role comparable to the psycho-pathological complexes of neurosis or other psychic maladies of obsession. Their physical analogy is cancer.

With respect to autonomous magic, i.e. magic without mysticism and without gnosis, it necessarily degenerates into sorcery or, at least, into a pathological, romantic aestheticism. There is no "black magic", but rather sorcerers groping in the dark. They grope in the dark because the light of gnosis and mysticism is lacking.

Gnosis without mystical experience is sterility itself. It is just a religious ghost, without life or movement. It is the corpse of religion, animated intellectually by means of scraps fallen from the table of the past history of humanity. A "Universal Gnostic Church"! Good Lord! What can one say, what should be said, when one has a knowledge, however limited, of the laws of spiritual life governing all tradition?!

Passing on to mysticism which has not given birth to gnosis, magic and Hermetic philosophy—such a mysticism must, sooner or later, necessarily degenerate into "spiritual enjoyment" or "intoxication". The mystic who wants only the experience of mystical states without understanding them, without drawing practical conclusions from them for life, and without wanting to be useful to others, who forgets everyone and everything in order to enjoy the mystical experience, can be compared to a spiritual drunkard.

So tradition can only live—as with all other living organisms—when it is a complete organism of mysticism, gnosis and effective magic, which manifests itself outwardly as Hermetic philosophy. This means to say simply that a tradition cannot live unless the *whole* human being lives through it, in it, and for it. For the whole human being is at one and the same time a mystic, a gnostic, a magician and a philosopher, i.e. he is religious, contemplative, artistic and intelligent. Everyone *believes* in something, *understands* something, *is capable of* something and *thinks* something. It is human nature which determines whether a tradition will live or die. And it is also human nature which is capable of giving birth to a complete tradition and keeping it living. Because the four "senses"—mystical, gnostic, magical and philosophical—exist, be it in potentiality or in actuality, in each human being.

Now, the practical teaching of the second Arcanum, the High Priestess, relates to the development of the gnostic sense. What is the gnostic sense?

It is the *contemplative* sense. Contemplation—which follows on from concentration and meditation—commences the very moment that discursive and logical thought is suspended. Discursive thought is satisfied when it arrives at a well-founded *conclusion*. Now, this conclusion is the *point of departure* for contemplation. It fathoms the *profundity* of this conclusion at which discursive thought arrives. Contemplation discovers a world *within* that which discursive thought simply verifies as "true". The gnostic sense begins to operate when it is a matter of a new dimension in the act of knowledge, namely that of *depth*. It becomes active when it is a question of something deeper than the question: Is it true or false? It perceives more the *significance* of the truth discovered by discursive thought and also "why this truth is true in itself", i.e. it reaches to the mystical or essential source of this truth. How does it arrive at this? By listening in silence. It is as if one wanted to recall something forgotten. Consciousness "listens" in silence, as one "listens" inwardly in order to call to mind from the night of forgetfulness something that one formerly knew. But there is an essential difference between the "listening silence" of contemplation and the silence arising from the effort to recall. In this second situation, it is the *horizontal*—in time, past and present—which comes into play, whilst the "listening silence" of contemplation relates to the *vertical*—to that which is above and that which is below. In the act of recall, one establishes in oneself an inner mirror in order to reflect the past; when one "listens in silence" in the state of contemplation, one also makes consciousness into a mirror, but this mirror has the task of reflecting that which is above. It is the act of recall in the *vertical*.

There are, in fact, two types of memory: "horizontal memory", which renders the past present, and "vertical memory", which renders that which is above as present below, or—according to our distinction between the two categories of symbolism which were defined in the first Letter—the "mythological memory" and the "typological memory".

Henri Bergson is perfectly right when he writes of horizontal or mythological memory:

> The truth is that memory does not consist in a regression from
> the present to the past, but on the contrary in a progress from
> the past to the present. (Henri Bergson, *Matter and Memory*;
> trsl. N. M. Paul and W. S. Palmer, London, 1911, p. 319)

and also:

> ... pure memory is a spiritual manifestation. With memory we
> are in very truth in the domain of the spirit. (ibid., p. 320)

It is therefore the past which comes to us in the remembrance and this is why
the act of recollection is preceded by a state of empty silence which plays the role
of a mirror, where the past can be reflected or, according to Bergson, where

> the state of the brain continues the remembrance; it gives it a
> hold on the present by the materiality which it (acting as a mir-
> ror) confers upon it. (ibid., p. 320)

It is the same again for vertical or typological memory. Plato is also perfectly
right when he says of the memory of the transcendent Self which can confer
reminiscence upon the empirical self:

> Seeing that the soul is immortal and has been born many times,
> and has beheld all things both in this world and in the nether
> realms, she has acquired knowledge of all and everything...
> (thus) it would seem, research and learning are wholly recollec-
> tion. (Plato, *Menon* 81, c, d; trsl. W. R. M. Lamb, London, 1924,
> p. 303)

Here, likewise, that which is above, in the domain of the transcendent Self,
descends to the plane of the empirical self, when there is created in oneself the
empty silence which serves to mirror the revelation from above.

What is necessary, therefore, in order to obtain here in the realm of the state
of waking consciousness the reflection of that which is above in the mystical
domain?

It is necessary "to be seated", i.e. to establish an active-passive state of consciousness, or state of soul which listens attentively in silence. It is necessary to
be "woman", i.e. to be in the state of silent expectation, and not in that of the
activity which "talks". It is necessary "to cover with a veil" the intermediate planes
between the plane whose reflection is expected and the plane of the state of waking consciousness where the reflection becomes actualised. It is necessary "to cover
the head with a three-layered tiara", i.e. to apply oneself to a problem or ques-

tion of such gravity that it bears upon the three worlds and on that which is above. Lastly, it is necessary "to have one's eyes turned towards the open book on the knees", i.e. to carry out a complete psychurgical operation in the aim of objectifying one's result, in the aim of "continuing the book of the tradition", adding something to it.

Now, all these practical rules of gnosis are found clearly indicated in the Card, the High Priestess. Here is a *woman*, she is *seated*; she wears a *three-layered tiara*; a *veil* is suspended above her head to cover the intermediate planes that she does not want to perceive; and she is looking at an *open book* on her knees.

The gnostic sense is therefore spiritual hearing, just as the mystical sense is spiritual touch. This does not mean to say that the gnostic sense perceives sounds, but only that its perceptions are due to a consciousness analogous to that in the attitude of *expectation* and *attention* when one *listens*, and that the contact between the perceiver and the perceived is not so immediate as in spiritual touch or mystical experience.

It still remains to characterise the two other senses mentioned above, namely the magical sense and the Hermetic-philosophical sense.

The magical sense is that of *projection*, whilst the Hermetic-philosophical sense is that of *synthesis*. By "projection" is meant to put outwards, followed by detaching from oneself, the contents of the inner life — an operation similar to that which is produced on the psychic plane in artistic creation and on the physical plane in giving birth.

The talent of the artist consists in this: that he can render objective — or project — his ideas and feelings so as to obtain a more profound effect on others than that of the expression of ideas and feelings by a person who is not an artist. A work of art is endowed with a life of its own. When a woman gives birth to a child, she gives birth to a being endowed with a life of its own, which detaches itself from her organism in order to start an independent existence. The magical sense also consists in the faculty of projecting outwards the contents of the inner life, which remain endowed with a life of their own. Magic, art and giving birth are essentially analogous and pertain to the same category of projection or exteriorisation of the inner life. The Church dogma of the creation of the world *ex nihilo*, i.e. the projection from "nothingness" of forms and matter which are conferred with a life of their own, signifies the divine and cosmic crowning of this series of analogies. The doctrine of creation *ex nihilo* is the apotheosis of magic. Its essential statement is, in fact, that the world is a magical act.

In contrast, pantheistic, emanationist and demiurgic doctrines deprive creation of its magical sense. Pantheism denies the independent existence of creatures; they live only as parts of the divine life and the world is only the body of God. Emanationism attributes only a transitory, and therefore ephemeral, existence to creatures and the world. Demiurgism declares that *ex nihilo nihil* ("out of nothing comes nothing") and teaches that there must exist a *substance* co-eternal with God, which God uses as *material* for his work of craftmanship. God is therefore not the creator or magical author of the world, but only its craftsman—he only forms, i.e. regroups and recombines, the material elements which are given to him.

Here it is not a matter of considering the doctrine of creation *ex nihilo* as the *only* explanation of the world that we find around us, within us and above us. Because the world is vast and great, there is room and there are levels of existence for *all* modes of constructive activity which, taken all together, explain the world of our experience such as it is. What is it a question of here? It is to affirm with as much clarity as possible the thesis that the doctrine of creation *ex nihilo* is the highest possible expression of magic, namely divine and cosmic magic.

But if you ask me, dear Unknown Friend, if I believe that the creation of the world is only a magical act, without something preceding and without something following it, I reply to you: no, I do not believe this. A *mystical* act and a *gnostic* act "precede" in eternity the act of creation as a *magical* act; this is followed by the activity of formation by the demiurge, or the demiurgic hierarchies, who undertake the work of craftsmanship—work which is essentially that of executive or Hermetic-philosophical intelligence.

The classical Cabbala furnishes us with a marvellous example of the *peace* possible between apparently rival doctrines. In its doctrine of ten Sephiroth, it teaches first the mystery of eternal *mysticism*—AIN-SOPH, the Unlimited. Then it expounds the *gnostic* doctrine of eternal emanations from the womb of the Divine, which precede—*in ordine cognoscendi*—the act of creation. They are the ideas of God within God, which precede the creation—the latter being a conscious act and not impulsive or instinctive. Then it speaks of pure creation or creation *ex nihilo*—the act of the magical projection of the ideas of the plan of creation, i.e. the Sephiroth. This creative, magical act is followed—*in ordine cognoscendi*, always—by the activity of formation in which the beings of the spiritual hierarchies participate, including man. It is in this way that, according to the Cabbala, the world comes into being, that the world of facts or deeds known to us through experience becomes what it is.

Now, *'olam ha'assiah*, the world of facts, is preceded by *'olam ha yetzirah*, the world of formation or the demiurgic world; this is the product of *'olam ha beriah*, the world of creation or the magical world which is, in turn, the realisation of *'olam ha atziluth*, the world of emanations or the gnostic world, inseparate and inseparable from God, who in his true essence is the mystery of supreme mysticism —AIN-SOPH, the Unlimited.

It is therefore possible—and for us there is no doubt about it—to reconcile the diverse doctrines concerning the creation; it is only necessary to put each of them in its proper place, or to apply each to the plane which is proper to it. The Cabbala, through its doctrine of the Sephiroth, provides a wonderful proof that this is so.

Pantheism is true for the "world of emanations" (*'olam ha atziluth*), where there are only ideas—within God and inseparable from him; but theism is true when one leaves the domain of uncreated eternity to pass on to the creation, meaning the creation of the ancestors or archetypes of phenomena that we know through our experience. And demiurgism is true when we contemplate the world or plane of formation, or the evolution of beings with the aim of coming into conformity with their created prototypes.

But leaving aside the worlds or planes of formation, creation, emanation and divine-mystical essence, one can confine oneself solely to the plane of facts. Then naturalism becomes true—within the limits of this plane, taken in isolation.

The establishing of the hierarchic order of these doctrines concerning the creation, which appear to be rival, has led us right into the domain of activity of the Hermetic-philosophical sense—the sense of synthesis. This sense, corresponding to the second HÉ of the divine name YHVH, is essentially that of final summary or the vision of the *whole*. It differs from the gnostic sense—which corresponds to the first HÉ of the divine name—in that it summarises or gives the synthesis of the *differentiated whole*, whilst the gnostic sense gives the reflection of the *whole in its germinal state*. The gnostic sense produces the *first synthesis* or the synthesis before analysis. The Hermetic-philosophical sense, in contrast, produces the *second synthesis* or the synthesis after analysis. The work which is accomplished by means of this sense is not entirely creative. Rather, it is "demiurgic", a work of craftmanship, where one carries out the forming of a given material with the aim of giving it the form of its final manifestation.

Since one finds in the *Emerald Table* formulae summarising "the three parts of the philosophy of the whole world" (*tres partes philosophiae totius mundi*), and since these at the same time summarise the worlds of magical experience, gnostic revelation and mystical experience, we have given this sense the name "Hermetic-philosophical" sense, i.e. the sense of synthesis of the three worlds or higher planes in a fourth world or plane. It is the sense of synthesis operating in the *vertical* of the superimposed planes, i.e. it is "Hermetic". For Hermeticism is essentially the philosophy, based on magic, gnosis and mysticism, which aspires to the synthesis of the diverse planes of the macrocosm and microcosm. When one summarises facts on a single plane—for example those of biology—one uses the *scientific* sense and not the Hermetic-philosophical sense. The scientific sense—which is generally known and recognised—summarises the facts of experience *on a single plane*, in the *horizontal*. Hermeticism is not a *science* and will never be one. It can certainly *make use* of the sciences and their results, but by doing so it does not become a science.

Non-Hermetic contemporary philosophy summarises particular sciences with the aim of fulfilling the function of a "science of sciences"—and has this in common with Hermeticism. But, in itself, it differs from Hermeticism, which aspires to summarise experience in all planes, which varies according to the plane where the experience takes place. This is why we have chosen the term "Hermetic-philosophical" to designate the fourth sense, the sense of synthesis.

It goes without saying that the characterisation of the four senses—whose collaboration is necessary for a tradition to live and not to degenerate—is sketched here in a very incomplete manner. But the two following Arcana—the Empress and the Emperor—are of a nature such as to give greater depth and more concrete content to what we are setting forth, especially concerning the magical sense and the Hermetic-philosophical sense. For the third Arcanum of the Tarot, the Empress, is the Arcanum of magic and the fourth Arcanum, the Emperor, is that of Hermetic philosophy.

Meditation on the
Third Major Arcanum of the Tarot

THE EMPRESS

L'IMPÉRATRICE

Ecce ancilla Domini;
mihi fiat secundum verbum tuum.
Behold I am the handmaid of the Lord;
let it be to me according to your word.

(Luke i, 38)

LETTER III

THE EMPRESS

Dear Unknown Friend,

The third Arcanum, the Empress, is that of sacred magic. Now, there are three
kinds of magic: magic where the magician is the instrument of divine power—
this is sacred magic; magic where the magician himself is the source of the magical
operation—this is personal magic; lastly, magic where the magician is the instrument of elemental forces or other unconscious forces—this is sorcery. The teaching
of the third Arcanum—in view of the context of the Card and its place between
the second and fourth Arcana—refers to sacred or divine magic.

All magic, including sorcery, is the putting into practice of this: *that the subtle rules the dense*—force, matter; consciousness, force; and the superconscious or divine, consciousness. It is this latter rulership that the Empress symbolises. Her crown, sceptre and shield (coat-of-arms) are the three instruments of the exercise of this power. The crowned head indicates the power of the Divine over consciousness; the right arm (according to the viewer of the Card), which bears a sceptre topped by a cross mounted on a globe of gold, represents the power of consciousness over force; and the left arm, which carries a shield bearing an eagle, signifies the power of energy over matter or the volatile over the gross.

The crown is the *divine authorisation* of magic. It is only magic crowned from above which is not usurpatory. The crown is that which renders it legitimate. The sceptre is *magical power*. It is by virtue of the sceptre that she is not impotent. The shield bearing the eagle shows the *aim* of magical power; it is its emblem and its motto, which reads: "Liberation in order to ascend". And the steady throne on which the Empress is seated symbolises the indisputable and inalienable *place* which belongs to magic in spiritual, psychic and natural life—thanks to divine authorisation or the crown, to the reality of her power or the sceptre, and to that which she has as her objective or the shield. This is the *role* of magic in the world.

Let us now consider in a more thorough way the crown, the sceptre, the shield or coat-of-arms and the throne of the Empress, understood as the divine legitimacy, the power, the objective and the role of magic.

The *crown* of the Empress differs primarily from the tiara of the High Priestess of the second Arcanum in that it has *two* levels instead of three. The dignity or function that it signifies or confers therefore has bearing upon two planes. Gnosis has a tiara because she has the task of carrying revelation through three planes as far as the "book" or tradition. Magic is crowned, since her task is the sublimation of Nature, as indicated by the shield or coat-of-arms with the eagle in flight, that the Empress holds instead of the book of the High Priestess.

Joséphin Péladan defined magic as "the art of sublimation of man"; no other formula is superior to his (cf. *Comment on devient mage*, Paris, 1892 p. 135). This is exactly the emblem—or aim—of magic, if one understands by "sublimation of man" that of *human nature*. Péladan had a very profound understanding of the emblem of magic: the shield with the eagle in flight. All his works bear witness to this. Together they represent a magnificent flight; they aim, as a whole and each taken individually, at the ideal of the sublimation of human nature. It is because Péladan bore the emblem of magic: the flying eagle, that this is so. Isn't it to have the emblem of magic before one's eyes that one is invited "to throw the eagles of one's desires to the wind", because happiness "raised to the level of an ideal, freed from the negative aspects of oneself and of things . . . is the sole triumph of this world"? (J. Péladan, *Traité des antinomies*, Paris, 1901, p. 112). It is this same emblem—the shield with the eagle—that Papus had in mind, in actual fact, when he defined magic as:

The application of the strengthened human will to accelerate the evolution of the living forces of Nature. (Papus, *Traité méthodique de magie pratique*, Paris, 3rd edition, p. 10)

He preceded this definition by another:

Magic is the science of love. (ibid., p. 2)

For it is precisely "the accelerated evolution of the living forces of Nature" that the eagle of the *shield* of the Empress represents; "the science of LOVE" is the *sceptre* of the Empress, which represents the *means* by which the aim of magic is attained.

Now, if the shield signifies the "what?" and the sceptre the "how?" of magic, the crown represents here the "by what right?".

Although magic has disappeared from the criminal codes of our time, the question of its legitimacy still persists as a moral, theological and also medical question. One asks oneself today, just as in the past, if it is morally legitimate to aspire — without talking of exercising — to an exceptional power conferring us with dominion over our fellow beings; one asks oneself if such an aspiration is not due, in the last analysis, to vaingloriousness, and if it is compatible with the role that all sincere and believing Christians reserve for divine grace, be it immediate or be it acting through the intermediary of guardian Angels and the saints of God? One asks oneself, lastly, if such an aspiration is not unwholesome and contrary to human nature, religion and metaphysics, given the limits to which one can go with impunity towards the Invisible.

All these doubts and objections are well-founded. It is therefore a matter not of refuting them, but of knowing whether there exists a magic which is free from these doubts and objections or, in other words, whether there exists a *legitimate magic* from a moral, religious and medical point of view.

As a point of departure, we shall take these words from the New Testament:

> Now as Peter went here and there among them all, he came down also to the saints that lived at Lydda. There he found a man named Aeneas, who had been bedridden for eight years and was paralysed. And Peter said to him: Aeneas, Jesus Christ heals you; rise and make your bed. And immediately he rose. (Acts ix, 32-34)

Here is a spiritual act of healing whose legitimacy is beyond doubt: from a moral point of view, it is an act of pure charity; from a religious point of view, it is in the name of Jesus Christ and not the name of Peter himself that the healing is effected; from a medical point of view it is a perfect cure, without prejudice to physical or psychic health, that is denoted for the healer. That which establishes the indisputable legitimacy of the healing of Aeneas is, firstly, the *aim* of Peter's deed: to restore movement to the person who had been unable to move; secondly, it is the *means* by which the healing was accomplished: the word based on the essence of Jesus Christ; thirdly, it is the *source* of the deed: "Jesus Christ heals you!"

These are the three elements of sacred magic which render it legitimate and in which it is easy to recognise the three insignias of the Empress — the crown, the sceptre and the emblem. For to give movement to the motionless is the liberating action represented by the eagle on the shield; to realise the healing solely through the spoken word is to put into play the sceptre surmounted by the cross; to accomplish it in the name of Jesus Christ is to have the head crowned by the divine.

But, one could object, the healing of Aeneas has nothing to do with magic. It is a *miracle*, i.e. the action of God, and man is nothing here.

Was the apostle Peter there, therefore, for nothing? If this were true, why does *he* go up to Aeneas? Why is the divine action of healing not accomplished *directly*, without Peter as intermediary?

No, Peter was there for something. *His* presence and *his* voice were necessary in order that the healing could take place. Why?

This problem merits deep meditation, for it encloses the central mystery of the Christian religion, that of the *Incarnation*. Indeed, why must the Logos, the Son of the Father, incarnate and become God-Man in order to accomplish the supreme work of divine magic — the work of the Redemption?

In order to humble himself!? But, being God, he was humility itself. In order to participate in human destiny: human birth, life and death? But God who is love participated, participates, and will always participate in human destiny — he freezes with all those who are cold, he suffers with those who are suffering and he undergoes agony with all those who die. — You know that in monasteries in the Near East, at a time when hearts were still beating on the foundation of the divine Presence, the pronouncing of these words was taught as a miraculous cure for all afflictions and every suffering: "Glory to your long-suffering, Lord!"

No, the work of the Redemption, being that of love, requires the perfect union in love of *two wills*, distinct and free — divine will and human will. The mystery of the God-Man is the key of divine magic, being the fundamental condition of the work of the Redemption, which is an operation of divine magic comparable only to that of the creation of the world.

Thus miracles require *two* united wills! They are not manifestations of an all-powerful will *ordaining*, but are due to a new power which is *born* whenever there is unity between divine will and human will. Peter was therefore certainly there for something at the healing of Aeneas at Lydda. The divine will needed his will in order to give birth to the power which raised the paralysed Aeneas from his bed. Such an action, where there is simultaneously an accordance of divine will and human will, is exactly what we mean by "sacred magic" or "divine magic".

Should one speak of "magic" when it is a case of a miracle? Yes, because there is a *magus* and the participation of his will is essential for the realisation of the miracle. Peter goes up to Aeneas and it is he who utters the words which effect the healing. The participation of Peter is indisputable—he was there as a *human magus*. Consequently, the use of the word "magic" is quite justified, at least if one understands by "magic" the power of the invisible and spiritual over the visible and material.

But this was not "personal magic"; rather it was "divine magic" to which the healing of Aeneas was due. For Peter could do nothing if his will was not united with the divine will. He was fully conscious of this, and this is why he says to Aeneas: "Jesus Christ heals you". This means to say: "Jesus Christ really wants to heal you. Jesus Christ has sent me to you in order that I might do what he has said to me. As far as I am concerned, I am doubly happy to be able at one and the same time to serve my Master and to heal you, my dear brother Aeneas."

Here lies the meaning of the two-layered crown which the Empress wears. It is to be able to be "doubly happy" to serve that which is above and that which is below. For the crown, just as the tiara, represents the power of *service*. It is service rendered to that which is above and service rendered to that which is below which constitutes the legitimacy of sacred magic.

The magus in sacred magic plays the role of the last link in the magical chain which descends from above, i.e. in order to serve as the terrestrial *point of contact* and *point of concentration* for the operation conceived, willed and put into action from above. In fact, when one is this last link, one wears the *crown* of legitimate magic. And, let us say it again, all magic that is not crowned in this way is therefore illegitimate.

Is the legitimate exercise of sacred magic therefore reserved for the priesthood alone?

To this, I reply with another question: Is the love of God and of one's neighbour reserved for the priesthood alone? Sacred magic is the power of love, born of the union in love of divine will and human will. Now, Monsieur Philip of Lyons was neither priest nor doctor, but he healed sick people through a spiritual power which he said was not his but "from the Friend above".

The priesthood includes numerous thaumaturgists—St. Gregory, St. Nicholas and St. Patrick—which is sufficient to convince us that sacred magic is truly amongst the works of the priesthood. How could it be otherwise, given that the administration of the sacraments—these *universal* operations of sacred magic—constitute the principal responsibility of the clergy and that the *individual* operations "decided above" are entrusted above all to those living in the atmosphere of the universal sacraments? Is it not natural that he who participates each day in the mystery of the transubstantiation is called, in the first place, to sacred magic?

The life and work of the holy priest of Ars leaves no doubt that the response is affirmative. The life and work of the holy priest of Ars shows us the loftiness and splendour of individual sacred magic—*beyond* the universal sacraments—which is able to manifest itself in the life and work of a simple country parson.

But on the other hand, the life and work of Monsieur Philip of Lyons shows us the loftiness and splendour of individual sacred magic — *without* the universal sacraments — which is able to manifest itself in the life and work of a layman, born and raised in the country!

Love is active wherever it exists. It is everyone's vocation; it is no one's prerogative.

Thus, it is clear from the preceding that gnosis due to mystical experience must precede sacred magic. This is the meaning of the crown that the Empress wears. Sacred magic is the child of mysticism and gnosis.

If it were not so, magic would be the putting into practice of *occult theory*. This applies only to personal or usurpatory magic. Sacred or divine magic is the putting into practice of *mystical revelation*. The Master revealed to Peter what he had to do — inwardly and outwardly — in order to heal Aeneas at Lydda. It is here that the order of things in sacred magic is given: firstly, *real* contact with the Divine (mysticism), then the taking into *consciousness* of this contact (gnosis), and lastly the *putting into operation* or the execution of that which mystical revelation has made known as being the task to accomplish and the method to follow.

Personal or usurpatory magic follows, in contrast, the reverse order. Here it is the magician himself who studies occult theory and decides when and how to put it into practice. If he does so following the advice given by a master in magic, someone who has experimented in magic more than he has, the principle remains the same: it is always the human personality who decides the "what" and the "how". Thus Papus says:

> What differentiates magic from occult science in general is that the first is a *practical* science, whilst the second is above all theoretical. But to want to do magic without knowing occultism is to want to drive a locomotive without having passed through a special *theoretical* school. One can envisage the result (p. 4). Magic being a *practical* science demands preliminary theoretical knowledge, as with all practical sciences. (p. 5)

And lastly:

> Magic, considered as a science of application, limits its action almost solely to the development of relationships existing between man and Nature. The study of the relations existing between man and the higher plane, the divine plane, in all its variations, relates more to theurgy than to magic (p. 142). (Papus, *Traité méthodique de magie pratique*, Paris, 3rd edition, pp. 4-5, 142)

Here is an entirely characteristic definition, which leaves nothing more to desire, of what we have designated as "arbitrary" or "personal magic". Magic of this sort does not include that which is higher than man: the divine plane. Here man is the sole master — as he is elsewhere in all the practical sciences.

As a general rule, the principal director in every operation is the human will; the means of action, the implement used, is the astral or natural fluid, and the end to achieve is the realisation (generally on the physical plane) of the undertaken operation. (Papus, *La science des mages*, Paris, 1974, p. 69) [But] . . . regarding ceremonial magic and naturalism, we can only condemn them as much as for their uselessness as for the formidable dangers that they contain and for the state of soul which they suppose. . . In fact, one understands here, under this last designation (ceremonial magic), an operation where the *human will and intelligence* ALONE are active, without divine concurrence. (Papus, *Traité élémentaire de science occulte*, Paris, 1888 pp. 430-431)

The "formidable dangers" of arbitrary or personal magic have been described by all those who have had direct or indirect experience of this. Henry Cornelius Agrippa (*De Occulta Philosophia*, vol. iii), Eliphas Lévi (*Transcendental Magic. Its Doctrine and Ritual*) and Papus have said sufficient to prove that arbitrary or personal magic is most dangerous.

For sacred or divine magic, one risks only that it is inoperative, because of an error — which can be distressing — but it comprises no danger.

Before finishing here with the dangers of corrupt magic, I would like to add what is elaborated by Jean Herbert in his preface to the French edition of Arthur Avalon's *Serpent Power*, where he puts the reader on guard against the temptation of trying to practise the tantric method and evoking the "serpent power" (*kundalini*), raising it up to the head, to the *sahasrara* (crown) centre:

He who attempts this without being guided by an authentic master — which is almost certainly impossible in the Occident — will find himself in a situation quite analogous to that of a child whom one allows to play with all the drugs filling a pharmacy, or to walk with a lighted taper into a firework factory. Incurable heart problems, slow destruction of the spinal marrow, sexual disorders and madness await those who risk this. (Arthur Avalon, *La puissance du serpent*; trsl. J. Herbert, Lyons, 1959, Intro.)

Here is the bouquet of the "flowers of misfortune" which is offered to the beginner without a guru, or with a non-authentic guru!

Let us return to sacred magic. Having characterised its "crown" or divine legitimacy, we should now consider its "sceptre" or power.

The sceptre of the Empress comprises three parts: a cross, a globe and a staff topped by a little bowl or bulb. The staff is narrower below, beneath where the Empress holds it, than above, where it supports the globe surmounted by a cross. The globe is divided into two by a belt or "equatorial zone". Thus, it can be said that it is formed from *two cups*, one upside down, supporting the cross and turned downwards or "below", the other turned upwards and supported by the staff, is open towards the "above".

Now, the joining together of the cup surmounted by a cross and of another supported by a staff—which constitutes the sceptre of the Empress—is the symbolic expression of the method of the *realisation* of the potentiality represented by the crown. *It is the union of two potential wills in the crown, become actual in the sceptre.* The cup surmounted by the cross and turned downwards or "below" is the divine will, whilst the cup supported by the staff and turned upwards or "above" is the human will. Their active union is the sceptre or the power of sacred magic. This power results from the influx from the cross which flows from the upper cup into the empty lower cup and from there descends through the staff in order to be concentrated at its extremity as an "acorn" or a *drop*. Or to express it in other words: the Holy Blood from above concentrates itself and becomes a "drop" of human blood by the human word and action.

Perhaps you will say: but this is the Holy Grail, it is the mystical Eucharist of which you speak!

Yes, this is exactly to do with the Holy Grail or the mystical Eucharist. For it is there, and only there, that the power of sacred magic resides. This power is, in the last analysis, that of twofold *sincerity*—divine and human—united in the human word or action. Because not one word or action is *truly* sincere when it is only cerebral, and when it is only cerebral then it is not a flow of vital blood. The more sincerity there is in the human word or action, the more there is the vital essence of blood. When it happens—and the Angels fall down in adoration when this occurs—that the human wish is in accord with the divine, the Holy Blood is then united to the vital essence of the human blood and the *Mystery of the God-Man* is repeated, and also the miraculous power of the God-Man is reiterated. Here is the power of sacred magic—or its sceptre.

Dear Unknown Friend, do not think that I have only combined these things intellectually, after having read books on the Holy Grail and treatises of mystical theology on the sacrament of the Eucharist. No, I would never write of the mystery of blood as the source of sacred magic—even if I "knew" these things—if I had not visited and returned many times to the Chapel of Holy Blood at Bruges. There I have had the unsettling experience of the *reality* of the Holy Blood of the God-Man. It is this experience, with the effect of rejuvenating the soul—what am I saying!?—not only rejuvenating the soul, but even elevating it in the sense of the healing of Aeneas effected by St. Peter: "Rise, and make your bed!"—it is this experience, I say, which has revealed to me the mystery of the Holy Blood and the source of the power of sacred magic. Do not let the personal character of what

I am writing obscure this for you. I am an anonymous author and I remain so in order to be able to be more frank and sincere than is ordinarily permitted to an author.

The *aim* of sacred magic, as we have said, is represented by the shield that the Empress holds in place of the book which the High Priestess holds. Sacred gnosis has as its aim the communicable expression (or "book") of mystical revelation, whilst the aim of sacred magic is *liberating action*, i.e. the restoration of freedom to beings who have partially or totally lost it. The eagle in flight depicted on the shield signifies this emblem of sacred magic, which could thus be formulated: "Give freedom to he who is enslaved." And this includes all the works mentioned by Luke:

> Jesus cured many of diseases and plagues and evil spirits, and on many that were blind he bestowed sight. And he answered them: Go and tell John what you have seen and heard: the blind receive their sight, the lame walk, lepers are cleansed, and the deaf hear, the dead are raised up, the poor have good news preached to them. (Luke vii, 21-22)

This is the aim of sacred magic; it is nothing other than to give the freedom to see, to hear, to walk, to live, to follow an ideal and to be truly oneself—i.e. to give sight to the blind, hearing to the deaf, the ability to walk to the lame, life to the dead, good news or ideals to the poor and free will to those who are possessed by evil spirits. It never encroaches upon freedom, the restoration of which is its unique aim.

It is more than pure and simple healing which is the object of sacred magic; it is the restoration of freedom, including here freeing from the imprisonment of doubt, fear, hate, apathy and despair. The "evil spirits" which deprive man of his freedom are not at all beings of the so-called "hierarchies of evil" or "fallen hierarchies". Neither Satan, nor Belial, nor Lucifer, nor Mephistopheles have ever deprived anyone of his freedom. *Temptation* is their only weapon and this presupposes the freedom of he who is tempted. But *possession* by an "evil spirit" has nothing to do with temptation. It is invariably the same thing as with Frankenstein's monster. One engenders an elemental being and one subsequently becomes the slave of one's own creation. The "demons" or "evil spirits" of the New Testament are called today in psychotherapy "neuroses of obsession", "neuroses of fear", "fixed ideas", etc. They have been discovered by contemporary psychiatrists and are recognised as *real*—i.e. as "parasitic psychic organisms" independent of the conscious human will and tending to subjugate it. But the devil is not there to no avail—although not in the sense of direct participation. He observes the *law*—which protects human freedom and is the inviolable convention between the hierarchies of the "right" and those of the "left"—and never violates it, as stands out in the example of the story of Job. One need not fear the devil, but rather the perverse tendencies in oneself! For these perverse human tendencies can deprive us of our freedom and enslave us. Worse still, they can avail themselves of our imagination and inventive faculties and lead us to creations which can become the scourge of mankind. The atomic bomb and the hydrogen bomb are flagrant examples of this.

Man with the possible perversity of his warped imagination is far more dangerous than the devil and his legions. For man is not bound by the convention concluded between heaven and hell; he can go beyond the limits of the law and engender *arbitrarily* malicious forces whose nature and action are *beyond* the framework of the law...such being the Molochs and other "gods" of Canaa, Phoenecia, Carthage, ancient Mexico and other lands, which exacted human sacrifice. One has to guard against accusing the beings of the hierarchies of evil to their detriment of having played the role of Molochs, these being only creatures of the perverse collective human will and imagination. These are *egregores*, engendered by collective perversity, just as there exist the "demons" or "evil spirits" engendered by individuals. But we have said enough about demons; the problem of "evil spirits" will be treated in a more detailed and profound way in the fifteenth Letter, dedicated to Arcanum XV.

The *throne* on which the Empress is seated represents, as we have said, the role of sacred magic in the world. It is its place in the world and in the history of the world; it is, lastly, its basis. In other words, it is that which attends it, desires it and is always ready to receive it. What is this?

In view of the liberating function of sacred magic, it is all that which is deprived of liberty and is bound by necessity. Concerning this, St. Paul says:

> For the creation waits with eager longing for the revealing of the sons of God; for the creation was subjected to futility, not of its own will but by the will of him who subjected it in hope; because the creation itself will be set free from its bondage to decay and obtain the glorious liberty of the children of God. We know that the whole creation has been groaning in travail together until now; and not only the creation, but we ourselves, who have the first fruits of the Spirit, groan inwardly as we wait for adoption as sons, the redemption of our bodies. (Romans viii, 19-23)

It is therefore the mineral, plant, animal and human realms of Nature — in a word, Nature in its entirety — which constitute the domain of sacred magic. The reason for the existence of sacred magic stems from the Fall and the whole domain of the Fall — comprising fallen Nature, fallen man and the fallen hierarchies. These are the beings belonging to it who hope "with eager longing" to be "set free from its bondage to decay and obtain the glorious liberty of the children of God".

How does sacred magic operate towards this end? How, for example, does it deliver man?

The throne of the Empress has a back. It strongly resembles two wings, so that certain interpreters of the Tarot have seen the Empress as being winged. Others, however, see only a back. In view of the context of the Card, the meaning of the coat-of-arms bearing the eagle, the sceptre surmounted by the cross, and the two-layered crown, could one not see the back here in the form of two *petrified and immobilised* wings, but which had once been genuine wings and which are again potentially so?

If this interpretation is accepted, not only would it reconcile the two apparently opposing points of view but also it would agree with all that the Card teaches about the sphere, the aim, the power and the legitimacy of sacred magic. To give movement to the petrified wings. . .would this not be in accord with the liberating mission of sacred magic and with the words of St. Paul?

Whatever it may be, this interpretation comprises the answer to the question as to the concrete mode of the liberating action of sacred magic. It is in every way contrary to the action of constraint of false or personal magic. It sets in opposition to the action of hypnosis — the waking of the free will; and to suggestion — the deliverance from possession by fixed ideas and psychopathological complexes. It sets in opposition to evocation by necromancy — the ascent towards the deceased effected by the force of love; and to the means of constraint employed by ceremonial magic with respect to elemental beings (gnomes, undines, sylphs and salamanders) — the gain of their confidence and friendship by corresponding acts. It places in opposition to the procedures of the practical Cabbala which have the aim of subjugating "evil spirits" (in the sense of the fallen hierarchies — their transformation into servants through their own accord by resistance to the special temptations of each of them. For they also are waiting "for the revealing of the sons of God", and this revealing signifies for them, in the first place, inaccessibility to their temptations. Resist the devil, and the devil will be your friend. A devil is not an atheist; he does not doubt God. The faith which he lacks is faith in man. And the act of sacred magic with respect to such a devil is that of re-establishing his faith in man. The purpose of the trials of Job was not to dispel the doubts of God, but rather those of the devil. These doubts once dispelled, who was it then who laboured to give to Job all that he had lost, if not the same being who had formerly deprived him of everything? Job's enemy became his voluntary servant — and "voluntary servant" means to say *friend*. Sacred magic, finally — in place of the fluidic transfusion of magnetism — practises the taking upon oneself of the illnesses and infirmities of others, according to St. Paul's precept.

Bear one another's burdens, and so fulfill the law of Christ.

(Galatians vi, 2)

It is in this way that saints practise sacred magic. They would not project their forces, their vitality or their fluids into someone else, but on the contrary would rather *take* from him that which was unhealthy in him. St. Lidvina, for example,

who never left her bed or her room for many long years, once smelt strongly of
alcohol. At the same time the cure of an alcoholic was effected in the town
(Schiedam) where she lived.

Having advanced this list of contraries, I do not have the intention of judging,
still less of condemning—hypnosis, magnetism, suggestion, all evocation, ceremonial magic dealing with Nature, and practical Cabbala aspiring to the subjugation of "evil spirits". The sole aim here is to make clear that which differen-
tiates sacred magic from these practices. They *can* also serve the good. But sacred
magic can do nothing else than to serve the good.

Are there *grimoires* of sacred magic? Yes, if one understands by "*grimoire*" an
arsenal of arms or implements which one makes use of. This arsenal is composed
of formulae, gestures, and figures reproduced by the gestures. But one must not
choose them arbitrarily. The choice must be reserved either according to profound
knowledge *confirmed by revelation* or otherwise to *direct revelation* confirmed
subsequently by the knowledge of experience.

With regard to the arsenal of formulae, it is accessible almost entirely to everyone.
For the principal source of the formulae of sacred magic is the Holy Scripture,
the Bible, comprising the New and Old Testaments. The Gospel according to St.
John occupies a prominent place here, for it consists almost completely of magical
formulae. Then come the three other Gospels and the Apocalypse (Book of Revelation). One also finds magical formulae in the Epistles and in the Acts of the
Apostles. As for the Old Testament, one finds them above all in the Psalms, the
Book of Genesis (*Bereshith*), Ezekiel and the other prophets. There are also the
magical formulae in the liturgical ritual of the Church and in the written or oral
tradition leading back to the saints and to the great mystics. Equally, the text of
the *Emerald Table* belongs to the arsenal of formulae of sacred magic.

Concerning the "silent" part (i.e. the gestures and figures reproduced by gestures) of sacred magic, their choice must be in the same way either confirmed by
revelation or indicated by it. They consist, as a rule, of the ritual gestures employed
by the traditional Church (Roman or Greek-Orthodox) and of gestures reproducing
a certain number of geometrical figures. Thus it is necessary sometimes to kneel
down, sometimes to be upright, sometimes to prostrate oneself; sometimes it is
necessary to do the gesture of benediction, sometimes that of protection or that
of liberation, etc.

These formulae and gestures are not secret, but one should not *betray* them.
"To betray" does not signify to divulge them, to make them known to others; one
does not betray a magical formula which is known to nearly everyone solely by
the fact of making it known to others. But one betrays it when one uproots it
from its proper, sacred ground and from the sacred *context* of the magical operation to which it belongs and when one brings it down to a lower plane, i.e. when
one *abuses* it. It is the same as with the formulae by means of which consecration
operates in the Mass. Everyone knows them, but they operate only when they are
pronounced in the sacred context of the Mass by a person who is alone legitimately

authorised to do it. It is not secrecy which enables their operation; it is the *context* and it is the *niveau* of the operation, and it is the *legitimacy* of the operant or celebrant. Therefore one does not betray the formulae of consecration by printing them in the missals. But one certainly would betray them if one were to use them, as a layman, in an arbitrarily improvised or invented "mass".

The *mystery* is protected in another way than the *secret*. Its protection is its light, whilst the protection of a secret is its obscurity. As for an *arcanum* , which is a middle degree between the mystery and the secret, it is the twilight which protects it. For it reveals itself and hides itself at the same time by means of symbolism. Symbolism is a twilight for arcana. Thus the Arcana of the Tarot are formulae rendered visible and accessible to everyone. They were entertaining in the past for thousands of people; they were used for telling fortunes by hundreds of people; a few experienced in them a revelatory effect. Court de Gebelin was astonished by them; Eliphas Lévi was captivated by them; Papus was inspired by them; others followed them and became subject to the strange and almost irresistible attraction of the Tarot. They studied it, meditated and commented upon it, and interpreted it, being stimulated, inspired and illumined by "something" in the Tarot which simultaneously reveals itself and hides itself in the twilight of its symbols. And ourselves? Where do we stand in relation to the Tarot? We shall have a sure knowledge of this after the twenty-second Letter, dedicated to the Minor Arcana of the Tarot.

The throne on which the Empress is seated represents the second HÉ of the *Tetragrammaton* of sacred magic, i.e. its *manifested* entirety; her crown corresponds to YOD, the sceptre to the first HÉ and the coat-of-arms to the VAU of the *Tetragrammaton*. This is why we have defined the throne as "the role of sacred magic in the world and in history". One could equally say that it is the *phenomenon* of the whole of sacred magic as it has manifested itself, as it is manifesting itself, and as it will manifest itself in the history of mankind. It is its historical *body* which reveals its soul and spirit. By "body" I mean that which makes possible direct action in the world of facts. Thus the arsenal or store of magical formulae and gestures which one uses in the practical exercise of sacred magic are part of its body. The rituals of its universal operations, destined to serve the whole of mankind, and transcending space and time, i.e. the seven sacraments of the universal Church, in so far as they are rituals, are equally part of its body. Then those who have the mission or the ability to perpetuate the tradition of sacred magic are likewise part of it. This body is like a *tree* which has a certain number of branches which bear many leaves, but whose roots are in heaven and whose top is turned downwards. It has only one trunk and a sap which nourishes and vivifies all its branches with their innumerable leaves.

Is this the Tree of the Sephiroth of the Cabbala? Or rather the Tree of Knowledge of Good and Evil? Or, again, the Tree of Life?

The fruit of the Tree of Knowledge of Good and Evil has had a triple effect: toil, suffering and death. Toil or work took the place of mystical union with God, which union (without effort) is the teaching of the first Arcanum of the Tarot, the Magician. Suffering replaced the directly reflected revelation or gnosis, whose direct revelation is the teaching of the second Arcanum of the Tarot, the High Priestess. And death entered into the domain of life or creative, sacred magic, which is the teaching of the third Arcanum of the Tarot, the Empress. For sacred magic is that life which was before the Fall. The gnosis of the second Arcanum is that consciousness which was before the Fall. And the mystical spontaneity of the first Arcanum is that relationship between man and God which was before the Fall. This primordial spontaneity gave the impulse and direction to evolution and the development of the human being. It was not the struggle for existence, described by Charles Darwin a century ago, which was the fundamental directing impulse towards the ideal or aim of evolution before the Fall, but rather that state of being which we designate today by the term "mystical union". The principle of *struggle* or toil (effort) only came into play after the Fall. Similarly, suffering did not play the role of awakening consciousness before the time of the Fall; this role was then reserved for directly reflected revelation, or gnosis. Neither did death then play the role of liberating consciousness, through the destruction of the forms which enclose it, that it has played since the Fall. Instead of the destruction of forms, their continual *transformation* took place. This was operated by the perpetual action of life effecting the metamorphosis of forms, in conformity with changes in the consciousness using them. This perpetually liberating *constructive* action of life was — and still is — the function of sacred or divine magic. And it is this transforming function, opposed to the destructive function of death, that Moses' Genesis designates by the symbol of the Tree of Life.

For the Fall changed the destiny of humanity — so that mystical union became replaced by struggle or toil, gnosis by suffering and sacred magic by death. This is why the formula announcing the "good news" that the effects of the Fall can be overcome and that the *way* of human evolution can return to that of mystical union instead of struggle, that immediately reflected revelation or gnosis can replace the teaching of the *truth* through suffering, and that sacred magic or transforming *life* can take the place of destructive death — this is why, I say, this formula has the tenor of the following:

I AM THE WAY, THE TRUTH, AND THE LIFE. (John xiv, 6)

This formula is at the same time the summation of the first three Arcana of the Tarot, i.e. the arcanum of the true way or mystical spontaneity, the arcanum of revealed truth or gnosis, and the arcanum of transforming life or sacred magic.

Sacred magic is therefore the Tree of Life, inaccessible to arbitrary fool-hardiness, but manifesting itself in the whole history of mankind by the agency of those who know how to say, "*Ecce ancilla Domini, mihi fiat secundum verbum tuum*" (cf. Luke i, 38: "Behold, I am the handmaid of the Lord; let it be to me according to your word") or rather, "*Ecce servus Domini, faciam secundum verbum tuum*"

("Behold the servant of the Lord, I will do according to your word"). It manifests itself in human history by a miracle: namely, that human supra-biological *life* continues from century to century, from millennium to millennium, and its source does not dry up; that the sacred fire above the altars of hearts and the altars of stone is not extinguished from century to century, from millennium to millennium; that goodness, truth and beauty do not lose their attraction from century to century; that, in spite of all, there is faith, hope and charity in the world; that there are saints, sages, geniuses, benefactors, and healers; that pure thought, poetry, music, and prayer are not being engulfed by the void; that there is this universal miracle of human history; and *that the miraculous exists.* Yes, the miraculous does exist, for *life* is only a series of miracles, if we understand by "miracle" not the absence of cause (i.e. that it would not be caused by anyone or anything—which would be more the concept of "pure chance"), but rather the visible effect of an invisible cause, or the effect on a lower plane due to a cause on a higher plane.

Incomprehensibility is not at all the distinctive quality of a miracle; on the contrary, a miracle is often essentially more comprehensible than a so-called "natural" and "explained" phenomenon. It is, for example, more comprehensible that Teresa Neumann, in Bavaria, lived for decades without any food other than the host—in view of the fact that matter is only condensed energy and energy is only "condensed" consciousness—than the "well explained" fact of a single cell which, in multiplying itself by division, produces quite different cells for the brain, muscles, bones, hair, etc., which group themselves in such a way that the result is a complete human or animal organism. When someone tells me that all this is explained by heredity, that such are the "genes" contained within the first cell that it results in such an organism, then I nod in agreement, but I am completely hoodwinked.

The Tree of Life is the source of the miracles of generation, transformation, rejuvenation, healing and liberation. Conscious participation with it, *ad perpetranda miracula rei unius* as the *Emerald Table* expresses it, is the "great work" of sacred magic.

One can understand the idea of the "great work" when one compares it with the ideal of modern exact science. For the idea of science is *power*—practical technical power and intellectual technical power. The intellectual aspect of the scientific ideal is to reduce the multiplicity of phenomena to a limited number of laws and then reduce these to a single simple formula. It is a matter, in the last analysis, of mechanising the intellect in such a manner that it *calculates* the world instead of understanding it. Then one would attain intellectual technical power.

The practical aspect of the scientific ideal is revealed in the progress of modern science from the eighteenth century to the present day. Its essential stages are the discoveries and putting into man's service, successively, of steam, electricity and atomic energy. But as different as these appear to be, these discoveries are based only on a single principle, namely the principle of the *destruction of matter*, by which energy is freed in order to be captured anew by man so as to be put at his service.

It is so with the little regular explosions of petrol which produce the energy to drive a car. And it is so with the destruction of atoms, by means of the technique of neutron bombardment, which produces atomic energy. That it is a matter of coal, petrol, or hydrogen atoms, is not important; it is always a case of the production of energy as a consequence of the destruction of matter. For the practical aspect of the scientific ideal is the domination of Nature by means of putting into play the principle of *destruction* or *death*.

Imagine, dear Unknown Friend, efforts and discoveries in the opposite direction, in the direction of *construction* or *life*. Imagine, not an explosion, but rather the *blossoming out* of a *constructive* "atomic bomb". It is not too difficult to imagine, because each little acorn is such a "constructive bomb" and the oak is only the visible result of the slow "explosion" — or blossoming out — of this "bomb". Imagine it, and you will have the ideal of the *great work* or the idea of the *Tree of Life*. The image itself of the tree comprises the negation of the technical and mechanical element. It is the living synthesis of celestial light and elements of the earth. Not only is it the synthesis of heaven and earth, it constantly synthesises that which descends from above and that which ascends from below.

Now, the ideal of Hermeticism is *contrary* to that of science. Instead of aspiring to power over the forces of Nature by means of the destruction of matter, Hermeticism aspires to conscious participation with the constructive forces of the world on the basis of an alliance and a cordial communion with them. Science wants to *compel* Nature to obedience to the will of man such as it is; Hermeticism — or the philosophy of sacred magic — on the contrary wants to purify, illumine and change the will and nature of man in order to bring them into harmony with the creative principle of Nature (*natura naturans*) and to render them capable of receiving its willingly bestowed *revelation*. The "great work", as an ideal, is therefore the state of the human being who is in peace, alliance, harmony and collaboration with life. This is the "fruit" of the Tree of Life.

But does not the Bible say that the approach to the Tree of Life is defended and that "at the east of the garden of Eden God placed the Cherubim, and a flaming sword which turned every way, to guard the way to the Tree of Life" (Genesis iii, 24)? Yes, it is defended, but the defence is not absolute and general; it is *specific*. Read what the Bible says here: "Then the LORD God said: Behold, the man has become like one of us, knowing good and evil; and now, lest he put forth his hand and take also of the Tree of Life, and eat, and live for ever..." (Genesis iii, 22). Now, it is a matter here of defence against *putting forth the hand and taking* from the Tree of Life, and it is this and only this that the flaming sword at the garden of Eden prevents.

"Putting forth the hand and taking"— this is the motif, the method and the ideal of science. It is the will-to-power underlying the scientific attitude which is prevented by the flaming sword of the Guardian of Eden from repeating the act committed with respect to the Tree of Knowledge of Good and Evil. But the motif, method and ideal of Hermeticism is contrary to that of science. The will-to-serve underlies the fundamental Hermetic attitude. Instead of putting forward the hand to *take*, the human being opens his mind, his heart and his will to *receive* that which will be graciously bestowed upon him. The inspiration, illumination and intuition that he seeks are not so much conquests accomplished by his will; they are rather gifts from above, preceded by the efforts of the human will endeavouring to become worthy.

The flaming sword of the Guardian of Eden is a weapon of divine magic. This means to say that it is essentially a "yes" and not a "no". It is essentially constructive and not destructive. In other words, it invites, encourages and directs all those who are worthy, all that which is worthy in each person, to the benefits of the Tree of Life; and it forbids, discourages and sends away all those who are unworthy, and also all that which is unworthy in each person. The flaming sword is a *benediction* to those who seek the Tree of Eternal Love which is the Tree of Life, and at the same time, by the very fact that it blesses, the flaming force prohibits those who seek the Tree of Life in order to take possession of its fruits. The sword of the Holy Guardian of Eden is always active in the spiritual life of humanity. It calls to seekers and it repulses thieves. Thanks to it Hermeticism, the millennial-old tradition of uninterrupted pursuit of the ideal of the "great work", exists — in spite of all the chimera, all the illusions and all the forms of charlatanism, conscious and unconscious, which accompany this pursuit.

The sword of the Holy Guardian of Eden works the magical revelation of the Tree of Life — for everyone, without distinction. It is the magical word stirring ablaze in human souls ardent desire for the "great work", the miraculous life. It "will not break a bruised reed or quench a smouldering wick" (Matthew xii, 20), because its mission is divine; and it is characteristic of the Divine not only to save every droplet of sincerity and every spark of love, but also to make them grow and spread. Because in spite of all corruption that historical experience brings to the light of day, in totality nothing is corrupt. The traditional teaching of the Church that "Nature is wounded but not destroyed" (*natura vulnerata, non deleta*) is absolutely true.

The Tree of Life is the unity or synthesis of consciousness, force and matter. *Three* is its number. . . because it reflects the unity of the Holy Trinity. It is at the same time the unity of mysticism, gnosis and magic. This is why one should not separate them. The Empress, as a symbol of sacred magic, contains within itself gnosis and mysticism — or the High Priestess and the Magician. These Arcana are incomprehensible when one takes them separately. In general, all the Arcana of the Tarot are comprehensible only when considered as a whole.

But it so happens that in human consciousness one separates the inseparable — in forgetting the unity. One takes a branch of the tree and cultivates it as if it exists without the trunk. The branch can have a long life, but it degenerates. It is thus that in forgetting gnosis and mysticism, magic has been taken separately which, being a branch separated from its trunk, ceased to be sacred magic and became arbitrary or personal magic. This latter mechanised to a certain degree and became what one understands as "ceremonial magic", which flourished from the time of the Renaissance until the seventeenth century. It was *par excellence* the magic of the humanists, i.e. it was no longer divine magic, but *human* magic. It no longer served God, but man. Its ideal became the power of man over visible and invisible Nature. Later, invisible Nature was also forgotten. Visible Nature was concentrated upon alone, with the aim of subjugating it to the human will. It is in this way that technological and industrial science originated. It is the continuation of the ceremonial magic of the humanists, stripped of its occult element, just as the former is the continuation of sacred magic, but deprived of its gnostic and mystical element.

What I am saying here is perfectly in accord with what Papus (and Eliphas Lévi) thought, concerning which one cannot say that he was speaking without knowledge of the matter. For Papus said:

> Ceremonial magic is an operation by which man seeks, through the play of natural forces, to compel the invisible powers of diverse orders to act according to what he requires of them. To this end he seizes them, he surprises them, as it were, in projecting, through the effect of *correspondences* which suppose the unity of Creation, forces of which he himself is not master, but to which he can open extraordinary outlets . . . Ceremonial magic is of an order absolutely identical to our industrial science. Our power is almost nothing alongside that of steam, electricity and dynamite; but in opposing them by appropriate combinations to natural forces as powerful as themselves, we concentrate them, we accumulate them, we compel them to transport or to smash weights which would annihilate us . . . (Papus, *Traité élémentaire de science occulte*, Paris, 1888 pp. 425-426)

What more is there to say? One can, perhaps, add another statement by Papus, defining the relationship between the "scientific mage" or occultist and the sorcerer, as follows:

> The sorcerer is to the occultist as the worker is to the engineer.
> (Papus, *La science des mages*, Paris, 1974, p. 68)

The sorcerer is therefore only an amateur occultist.

Just as contemporary technological science is the direct continuation of ceremonial magic, contemporary profane art is merely a continuation of gnosis and magic which have lost sight of mysticism and become separated from it. Because art seeks to *reveal* and applies itself to do this in a *magical* manner.

The ancient mysteries were only sacred art — being in the background conscious of mysticism and gnosis. But after forgetting this background or, so to say, after this background receded too far into the background, there remained a gnosis (or a "revelationism") deprived at root of mystical discipline and experience. In this way "creative art" originated, and the mysteries became theatre, revelationary mantras became verses, hymns became songs, and revelationary "pantomimic" movements became dances, whilst cosmic myths gave way to *belles lettres*.

Art, being separated from the living organism of the unity of the *Tetragram-maton*, is necessarily removed from gnosis as well as from sacred magic—from which it springs and to which it owes its substance and the sap of its life. The pure revelation of gnosis has become more and more a game of the imagination and the power of magic has degenerated more and more into aesthetics. Richard Wagner understood this and wanted to remedy it. The work of Wagner followed the aim of the reintegration of art—to effect reunion with gnosis and mysticism so that it becomes sacred magic again.

Joséphin Péladan endeavoured to do the same in France. He even had dazzling success but this was short-lived—for reasons which he well understood subsequently. Silence is the indispensable climate for all revelation; noise renders it absolutely impossible.

The religious life, as everyone knows, is not exempt from decadence—when it ceases to be founded in mysticism, illumined by gnosis, and actuated by sacred magic. It grows cold without the fire of mysticism, it clouds over without the light of gnosis and becomes impotent without the power of sacred magic. There remains then only theological legalism supported by moral legalism—hence the origin of the religion of the scribes and Pharisees at the time of the New Testament. This is the twilight which precedes its night, its death.

FAITH is the experience of divine *breath*; HOPE is the experience of divine *light*; and LOVE is the experience of divine *fire*. There is no authentic and sincere religious life without *faith*, *hope* and *love*; but there is no faith, hope and love without mystical experience or, what is the same thing, without grace. No intellectual argument can awaken faith; what it can do, at best, is to eliminate obstacles, misunderstandings and prejudices, and thus help to establish the state of interior silence necessary for the experience of the divine breath. But faith itself is the divine breath whose origin is found neither in logical reasoning, nor in aesthetic impression, nor in human moral action.

The divine and flaming Word shines in the world of the silence of the soul and "moves" it. This movement is living faith—therefore real and authentic—and its light is hope or illumination, whilst all springs from the divine fire which is love or union with God. The three "ways" or stages of traditional mysticism—*purification, illumination and union*—are those of the experience of divine breath or faith, divine light or hope, and divine fire or love. These three fundamental experiences of the revelation of the Divine constitute the triangle of *life*—for no spirit, no soul and equally no body would be able to *live* if entirely deprived of all love, all hope and all faith. They would then be deprived of all vital élan (the vital élan advanced by Henri Bergson as the general impulse behind evolution). But what else could this be but some form of love, hope and faith operating at the basis of all life? It is because "in the beginning was the Word" and "all things were made through him" (John i, 1,3), and it is because the primordial Word still vibrates in all that lives, that the world still lives and has the vital élan which is nothing other than love, hope and faith inspired from the beginning by the creative Word.

In this sense Browning was right in having said, "Nature is supernatural". For its supernatural origin still manifests itself in its vital élan. To want to live! Good Lord, what a profession of faith, what a manifestation of hope and what ardour of love!

Love, hope and faith are at one and the same time the essence of mysticism, gnosis and sacred magic. FAITH is the source of magic power and all the miracles spoken of in the Gospels are attributable to it. The revelation — all the revelations of gnosis have only one aim: to give, to maintain and to increase HOPE. The book that the High Priestess holds on her knees is written so that hope may continue unceasingly. For all revelation which does not give hope is useless and superfluous. Mysticism is fire without reflection; it is union with the divine in LOVE. It is the primary source of all life, including religious, artistic and intellectual life. Without it, everything becomes pure and simple technique. Religion becomes a body of techniques of which the scribes and Pharisees are the engineers; it becomes legalistic. Art becomes a body of techniques — be they traditional or innovative — a field of imitation or experiences. Lastly, science becomes a body of techniques of power over Nature.

But the Arcanum of sacred magic, the Empress, calls to us to take another way. It calls us to the way of regeneration, instead of that of degeneration. It invites us to de-mechanise all that which has become solely intellectual, aesthetic and moral technique. One has to de-mechanise in order to become a mage. For sacred magic is through and through *life* — that life which is revealed in the Mystery of Blood. May our problems become so many cries of the blood (of the heart), may our words be borne by blood, and may our actions be as effusions of blood! This is how one becomes a mage. One becomes a mage by becoming *essential* — as essential as the blood is.

Eliphas Lévi puts as the sub-title to the chapter devoted to the third Arcanum of the Tarot in his *Transcendental Magic. Its Doctrine and Ritual: "Plenitudo Vocis"*. His choice is more than happy, it is inspired! Indeed! —"fullness of voice"— could one better describe the essence itself of sacred magic!? Yes, it is "fullness of voice" with which sacred magic is concerned; it is the voice full of blood; it is the blood which becomes voice. It is *being* in which there is nothing mechanical and which is entirely living.

The third Arcanum of the Tarot, being the arcanum of sacred magic, is by this very fact the arcanum of *generation*. For generation is only an aspect of sacred magic. If sacred magic is the union of two wills — human and divine — from which a miracle results, generation itself also presupposes the trinity of the generator, the generant and the generated. Now, the generated is the miracle resulting from the union of the principles of generator and generant. Whether it is a matter of a new idea, a work of art, the birth of a child, is not important; it is always the same law of generation which operates; it is always the same arcanum—that of fecundity—which is in play; and it is always the same mystery of the Incarnation of the Word which is the divine prototype here.

We have said above that sacred magic is life such as it was before the Fall. As life is always generative, the arcanum of sacred magic is at the same time that of *generation before the Fall—vertical* generation, from a higher plane to a lower one—instead of *horizontal* generation, which is accomplished on a single plane.

The formula of this mystery is well known: ET INCARNATUS EST DE SPIRITU SANCTO EX MARIA VIRGINE. It contains the trinity of the generator above, of the generant below, and the generated—or: the Holy Spirit, the Holy Virgin and the God-Man. It is at the same time the formula of sacred magic in general, because it expresses the mystery of the union of divine will and human will in the element of blood. The blood—in its triple sense, mystical, gnostic and magical—is the "sceptre" or power of sacred magic.

At this point, dear Unknown Friend, I shall withdraw and leave you alone with your Angel. It is not fitting that my human voice arrogates the right of uttering things which are a more profound continuation of what is outlined above.

Meditation on the
Fourth Major Arcanum of the Tarot

THE EMPEROR

L'EMPEREUR

Benedictus qui venit in nomine Domini.
Blessed is he who comes in the name
of the Lord.

(Luke xiii, 35)

LETTER IV

THE EMPEROR

Dear Unknown Friend,

The less superficial a person is — and the more he knows and is capable of — the greater is his authority. *To be* something, *to know* something and *to be capable of* something is what endows a person with authority. One can also say that a person has authority in proportion to what he unites within himself of the profundity of mysticism, the direct wisdom of gnosis and the productive power of magic. Whosoever has this to a certain degree can found a "school". Whosoever has this to a still higher degree can "lay down the law".

It is authority alone which is the true and unique power of law. Compulsion is only an expedient to which one takes recourse in order to remedy a lack of authority. Where there is authority, i.e. where there is present the breath of sacred magic filled by the rays of light of gnosis emanated from the profound fire of mysticism, there compulsion is superfluous.

Now, the Emperor of the fourth Arcanum of the Tarot does not have a sword or any other weapon. He rules by means of the *sceptre*, and by the sceptre alone. This is why the first idea that the Card naturally evokes is that of the *authority* underlying *law*. The thesis which proceeds from meditation on the three preceding Arcana is that all authority has its source in the ineffable divine name YHVH and that all law derives from this.

The implication here is that the human bearer of true authority does not replace divine authority but, on the contrary, cedes his place to it. He has to renounce something to this end.

The Card teaches us in the first instance that the Emperor has renounced compulsion and violence. He has no weapons. His right hand holds the sceptre forward, on which his gaze is fixed, and his left hand holds his tightly-fastened belt. He is neither standing nor sitting. He is simply leaning back against a lowered throne and has only one foot placed on the ground. His legs are crossed. The shield adorned with an eagle rests on the ground at his side. Lastly, he is wearing a large and heavy crown.

The context of the Card expresses active renunciation rather than the renunciation of constraint alone. The Emperor has renounced ease, being not seated. He has renounced walking, being in a leaning position and having his legs crossed. He may neither advance in order to take the offensive, nor move back in order to retreat. His station is by his seat and his coat-of-arms. He is on sentry-duty and as such he does not have freedom of movement. He is a guardian bound to his post.

What he guards is fundamentally the sceptre. Now the sceptre is not an implement with which one is empowered to do something or other. It is, from a practical point of view, a symbol serving nothing. The Emperor has therefore renounced all action having pledged his right hand to the sceptre that he holds before him, whereas his left hand holds his fastened belt. It is no longer free, because the Emperor restrains himself with it. It serves the function of holding the impulsive and instinctive nature of the Emperor in check, so that it does not intervene and divert him from his post as guardian.

The Emperor has therefore renounced *movement* by means of his legs and *action* by means of his arms. At the same time, he wears a large and heavy crown — and we have already meditated on the meaning of the crown with regard to that of the Empress, which has a double meaning. It is the sign of legitimacy, on the one hand, but it is also the sign of a task or a mission by which the crown is charged from above. Thus every crown is essentially a crown of thorns. Not only is it heavy, but also it calls for a painful restraint with regard to the thought and free or arbitrary imagination of the personality. It certainly emits rays outwards, but these same rays become thorns for the personality within. They play the role of nails piercing and crucifying each thought or image of the personal imagination.

Here true thought receives confirmation and subsequent illumination; false or irrelevant thought is riveted and reduced to impotence. The crown of the Emperor signifies the renunciation of freedom of intellectual movement, just as his arms and legs signify his renunciation of freedom of action and movement. He is deprived of the three so-called "natural" liberties of the human being—those of opinion, word and movement. Authority demands this.

But this is not all. The shield bearing an eagle rests on the ground at his side. The Emperor does not hold it with his hand, as the Empress does. The shield is certainly there, but it belongs rather to the *throne* than to the person of the Emperor. This means to say that the *purpose* for which the Emperor is on sentry-duty is not his but that of the throne. The Emperor does not have a personal mission; he has renounced this in favour of the throne. Or, in esoteric terms, he has no *name*; he is anonymous, because the name—the mission—belongs to the throne. He is not there in his own name but rather in the name of the throne. This is the fourth renunciation of the emperor—the renunciation of a personal mission or a *name*, in the esoteric meaning of the word.

It is said that, "Nature has a horror of emptiness" (*horror vacui*). The spiritual counter-truth here is that, "the Spirit has a horror of fullness". It is necessary to create a natural emptiness—and this is what renunciation achieves—in order for the spiritual to manifest itself. The beatitudes of the Sermon on the Mount (Matthew v, 3-12) state this fundamental truth. The first beatitude—"Blessed are the poor in spirit, for theirs is the kingdom of heaven"—means to say that those who are rich in spirit, who are filled with the "spiritual kingdom of *man*", have no room for the "kingdom of heaven". Revelation presupposes emptiness—space put at its disposal—in order to manifest itself. This is why it is necessary to renounce personal opinion in order to receive the revelation of the truth, personal action in order to become an agent for sacred magic, the way (or method) of personal development in order to be guided by the Master of ways, and one's personally chosen mission in order to be charged with a mission from above.

The Emperor has established in himself this fourfold emptiness. This is why he is "Emperor"; this is why he is *authority*. He has made a place in himself for the divine name YHVH, which is the source of authority. He has renounced personal intellectual initiative—and the emptiness which results is filled by divine initiative or the YOD of the sacred name. He has renounced action and movement—and the void which results is filled by revelationary action and magical movement from above, i.e. by the HÉ and VAU of the divine name. Finally, he has renounced his personal mission, he has become anonymous—and the emptiness which results is filled with authority (or the second HÉ of the divine name), i.e. he becomes the source of *law and order*.

Lao Tzu reveals the arcanum of *authority* in his *Tao Te Ching*. He says:

> Thirty spokes unite in one nave, and because of the part where
> nothing exists we have the use of a carriage wheel. Clay is mould-

ed into vessels, and because of the space where nothing exists we are able to use them as vessels. Doors and windows are cut out in the walls of a house, and because they are empty spaces, we are able to use them. Therefore, on the one hand we have the benefit of existence, and on the other, we make use of non-existence . . . [and again:] Be humble, and you will remain entire. Be bent, and you will remain straight. Be vacant, and you will remain full. Be worn, and you will remain new. He who has little will receive. He who has much will be embarrassed. Therefore the sage keeps to One and becomes the standard for the world. He does not display himself; therefore he shines. He does not approve himself; therefore he is noted. He does not praise himself; therefore he has merit. He does not glory in himself; therefore he excels. And because he does not compete; therefore no one in the world can compete with him. . . (Lao Tzu, *Tao Te Ching* xi and xxii; trsl. Ch'u Ta-Kao, London, 1953, p. 23 and p. 34)

. . . because he has authority.

God governs the world by authority, and not by force. If this were not so, there would be neither freedom nor law in the world; and the first three petitions of the Lord's Prayer (*Pater Noster*): "*Sanctificetur nomen tuum. Adveniat regnum tuum. Fiat voluntas tua sicut in caelo et in terra*", would lose all meaning. He who prays these petitions does so solely with the purpose of affirming and increasing divine *authority* and not divine power. The God who is almighty — not virtually but actually — has no need at all to be petitioned that his reign may come and that his will may be done. The meaning of this prayer is that God is powerful only in so far as his authority is freely recognised and accepted. Prayer is the act of such recognition and acceptance. One is free to be believing or unbelieving. Nothing and no one can compel us to have faith — no scientific discovery, no logical argument, no physical torture can force us to believe, i.e. to freely recognise and accept the *authority* of God. But on the other hand, once this authority is recognised and accepted, the powerless becomes powerful. Then divine power *can* manifest itself — and this is why it is said that a grain of faith is sufficient to move mountains.

Now, the problem of authority is at the same time of mystical, gnostic, magical and Hermetic significance. It comprises the Christian mystery of crucifixion and the "mystery of withdrawal" (*sod hatsimtsum*) of the Lurianic Cabbala. Here are some considerations which can help us to arrive at a most profound meditation upon this mystery.

The Christian world worships the Crucifix, i.e. the image expressing the paradox of almighty God reduced to a state of extreme powerlessness. And it is in this paradox that one sees the highest revelation of the Divine in the whole history of mankind. One sees there the most perfect revelation of the God of love. The Christian Creed says:

> Crucifixus etiam pro nobis sub Pontio Pilato, passus et sepultus est. (For our sake he was crucified under Pontius Pilate; he suffered death and was buried.)

The only Son of the eternal Father nailed to the cross *for our sake* — this is what is divinely impressed upon all open souls, including the robber crucified to the right. This impression is unforgettable and inexpressable. It is the immediate breath of God which has inspired and still inspires thousands of martyrs, confessors of the faith, virgins and recluses.

But it is not so that every human being finding himself facing the Crucifix may be thus divinely moved. There are those who react in the opposite way. It was so at the time of Calvary; it is so today.

> And those who passed by derided him, wagging their heads and saying: . . . If you are the Son of God, come down from the cross. (Matthew xxvii, 39-40)

The chief sacrificers, with the scribes and elders, also mocked him, saying:

> He saved others; he cannot save himself! If he is the king of Israel, let him come down now from the cross, and we will believe in him. He trusts in God; let God deliver him now, if he loves him! (Matthew xxvii, 42-43)

This is the other reaction. Nowadays we encounter exactly the same, for example, in Soviet radio broadcasts from Moscow. The argument from Moscow is always the same: if God exists, he must know that we, the communists, dethrone him. Why does he not give a visible sign, if not of his power, at least of his existence? Why does he not defend his own interests!? This is in other words the old argument: Come down from the cross, and we will believe in you.

I cite these well-known things because they reveal a certain dogma underlying them. It is the dogma or philosophical principle which states that *truth and power are identical*; that which is powerful is true and that which is powerless is false. According to this dogma or philosophical principle (which has become that of modern technological science) power is the absolute criterium and supreme ideal of truth. Only that which is powerful is of the Divine.

Now there are open and secret worshippers of the idol of power (for it *is* an idol and the source of all idolatry) — also in Christian factions or in religious and spiritual circles in general. I am not speaking about Christian or spiritually-minded

princes or politicians who covet power, but rather about the adherents to doctrines advancing the primacy of power. Here there are two categories: those who
aspire to the ideal of the "superman", and those who believe in a God that is *actually* almighty and therefore responsible for all that happens.

Amongst esotericists, occultists and magicians there are many—be it openly
or secretly—who aspire to the ideal of the superman. In the meantime, they often
pose as masters or high-priests worthy of the acclaim of the future superman. They
are, at the same time, singularly in agreement in that they raise God far, very far,
to the heights of Absolute Abstraction so that he does not discomfort them by
his too-concrete presence, and in order that they have room for themselves to be
able to develop their own greatness without the rival grandeur of the Divine to
discomfort them. They build their individual towers of Babel which fall, as a rule,
according to the law of all towers of Babel, and experience, sooner or later, a salutary
fall, as is the teaching of the sixteenth Card of the Tarot. They do not fall from
a *real* height into a *real* abyss; it is only from an *imaginary* height that they fall
and they fall only to the ground, i.e. they learn the lesson that we human beings
of today have all learned or have still to learn.

The worship of the idol of power conceived of as the superman, above all when
one identifies oneself with it, is relatively inoffensive—being, fundamentally, in-
fantile. But this is not so with the other category of power worshippers, namely
those who project this ideal onto God himself. Their faith in God depends only
on the *power* of God; if God was powerless, they would not believe in him. It
is they who teach that God has created souls predestined to eternal damnation
and others predestined to salvation; it is they who make God responsible for the
entire history of the human race, including all its atrocities. God, they say, "chas-
tises" his disobedient children by means of wars, revolutions, tyrannies and other
similar things. How could it be otherwise? God is almighty, therefore all that happens is only able to happen through his action or with his consent.

The idol of power has such a hold on some human minds that they prefer a
God who is a mixture of good and evil, provided that he is powerful, to a God
of love who governs only by the intrinsic authority of the Divine—by truth, beauty
and goodness—i.e. they prefer a God who is actually almighty to the *crucified God*.

However the father in the parable of the prodigal child had neither sent his
son far from his paternal home in order to lead a life of debauchery, nor had he
prevented him from leaving and forced him to lead a life which was pleasing to
him (the father). All he did was to await his return and to go and meet him when
the prodigal son was approaching his father's home. Everything which took place
in the story of the prodigal son, save for his return to the father, was clearly *contrary* to the will of the father.

Now the history of the human race since the Fall is that of the prodigal son.
It is not a matter of "the law of involution and evolution according to the divine
plan" of modern Theosophists, but rather of an abuse of freedom similar to that
of the prodigal son. And the key formula of the history of humanity is to be found

neither in the progress of civilisation nor in the process of evolution or in any other "process", but rather in the parable of the prodigal son, in the words:

> Father, I have sinned against heaven and before you; I am no longer worthy to be called your son; treat me as one of your hired servants. (Luke xv, 18-19)

Is mankind therefore solely responsible for its history? Without a doubt — because it is not God who has willed it to be as such. God is crucified in it.

One understands this when one takes account of the significance of the fact of human freedom, and likewise the freedom of the beings of the spiritual hierarchies — the Angels, Archangels, Principalities, Powers, Virtues, Dominions, Thrones, Cherubim and Seraphim. All these beings — including man (the *Ischim*) — have an existence that is either real or illusionary. If they have a *real* existence, if they are not a mirage, they are independent entities endowed not only with a *phenomenal* independence but also a *noumenal* independence. Now, noumenal independence is what we understand by *freedom*. Freedom, in fact, is nothing other than the real and complete existence of a being created by God. To be free and to exist are synonymous from a moral and spiritual point of view. Just as morality would not exist without freedom, so would an unfree spiritual entity — soul or spirit — not exist for itself, but would be part of another spiritual entity which is free, i.e. which really exists. Freedom is the spiritual existence of beings.

When we read in the Scripture that God created all beings, the essential meaning here is that God has given freedom — or existence — to all beings. Freedom once having been given, God does not take it back. This is why the beings of the ten hierarchies mentioned above are *immortal*. Death — not separation from the body, but *real* death — would be the *absolute* deprivation of liberty, i.e. complete destruction of the existence given by God. But who or what can take the divine gift of freedom, the divine gift of existence, from a being? Freedom, existence, is *inalienable*, and the beings of the ten hierarchies *are* immortal. The statement: freedom or existence is inalienable, can be understood as the highest *gift*, the very greatest value imaginable — then this would be a foretaste of paradise; or as *condemnation* to "perpetual existence" — then this would be a foretaste of hell. Because no one "sends" us anywhere — freedom not being a theatre. It is we ourselves who make the choice. Love existence, and you have chosen heaven; hate it, and there you have chosen hell.

Now, God is with respect to free beings either the ruling King (in the sense of authority such as that taught by the fourth Arcanum of the Tarot) or the Crucified. He is King with regard to those of his beings who voluntarily accept (who "believe") his authority; he is Crucified with respect to those beings who abuse their freedom and "worship idols", i.e. who replace divine authority by a substitute.

King and Crucified at one and the same time — this is the mystery of Pilate's inscription on the cross of Calvary: *Iesus Nazarenus Rex Judaeorum* (cf. John xix, 19: "Jesus of Nazareth, the King of the Jews"). Almighty and powerless, both at once—this is why miracles of healing in human history were able to be accomplished by saints whilst bloody wars and disasters raged around them!

Freedom—freedom is the true throne of God and is his cross at the same time. Freedom is the key to comprehension of the role of God in history—to comprehension of the God of love and the God-King, without the sacrilege of making him a tyrant and without the blasphemy of doubting his power or of doubting his very existence...God is all-powerful in history in as much as there is faith; and he is crucified in so far as one turns away from him.

Thus, divine crucifixion follows from the fact of freedom or the fact of the real existence of the beings of the ten hierarchies, when it is a matter of a world governed by divine authority and not by compulsion.

Let us turn now to the idea of *tsimtsum*—the "withdrawal of God"—of the Lurianic school of the Cabbala. The doctrine of *tsimtsum* reveals one of the "three mysteries" in the Cabbala: *sod hajichud*, the mystery of union; *sod hatsimtsum*, the mystery of concentration or divine withdrawal; *sod hagilgul*, the mystery of reincarnation or the "revolution of souls". The two other "mysteries"—the mystery of union and that of the revolution of souls—will be treated later, in other Letters (Letter X, for example). Concerning the "mystery of the divine withdrawal (or concentration)" which interests us here, it is a question of the thesis that the existence of the universe is rendered possible by the act of contraction of God within himself. God made a "place" for the world in abandoning a region interior to himself.

> The first act of *En-Soph*, the Infinite Being, is therefore not a step outside but a step inside, a movement of recoil, of falling back upon oneself, of withdrawing into oneself. Instead of emanation we have the opposite, contraction...The first act of all is not an act of revelation but one of limitation. Only in the second act does God send out a ray of His light and begin His revelation, or rather His unfolding as God the Creator, in the primordial space of His own creation. More than that, every new act of emanation and manifestation is preceded by one of concentration and retraction. (Gershom G. Scholem, *Major Trends in Jewish Mysticism*, London, 1955, p. 261)

In other words, in order to create the world *ex nihilo*, God had first to bring the void itself into existence. He had to withdraw within in order to create a mystical space, a space without his presence—the void. And it is in thinking this thought that we assist at the birth of *freedom*. For, as Berdyaev has formulated it:

> Freedom is not determined by God; it is part of the nothing out of which God created the world. (Nicolas Berdyaev, *The Destiny of Man*, London, 1937, p. 33)

The void — the mystical space from which God withdrew himself through his act of *tsimtsum* — is the place of origin of freedom, i.e. the place of the origin of an "ex-istence" which is absolute potentiality, not in any way determined. And all of the beings of the ten created hierarchies are the children of God and freedom — born of divine plenitude and the void. They carry within themselves a "drop" of the void and a "spark" of God. Their *existence*, their freedom, is the void within them. Their *essence*, their spark of love, is the divine "blood" within them. They are immortal, because the void is indestructible, and the monad proceeding from God is also indestructible. Further, these two indestructible elements — the *meonic* element (μὴ ὄν — void) and the *pleromic* element (πλήρωμα — plenitude) — are indissolubly bound to one another.

The idea of *tsimtsum*, the withdrawal of God in order to create freedom, and that of divine crucifixion on account of freedom, are in complete accordance. For the withdrawal of God in order to make a space for freedom and his renunciation of the use of his power against the abuse of freedom (within determined *limits*) are only two aspects of the same idea.

It goes without saying that the idea of *tsimtsum* (and that of divine crucifixion) is inapplicable when God is conceived of in the sense of pantheism. Pantheism, like materialism, does not admit the *real* existence of individual beings. Therefore the fact of freedom — not merely apparent freedom — is excluded. For pantheism and for materialism there is no question — and cannot be — of a divine withdrawal or a divine crucifixion. On the other hand, the Cabbalistic doctrine of *tsimtsum* is the only serious explanation that I know of concerning creation *ex nihilo* which is of a kind to act as a counterbalance to pure and simple pantheism. Moreover, it constitutes a deep link between the Old and New Testament, in bringing to light the cosmic significance of the idea of *sacrifice*.

Now, the reflection of the idea of divine withdrawal and divine crucifixion is found to be indicated, as we have seen, in the fourth Arcanum of the Tarot, the Emperor. The Emperor reigns by pure *authority*; he reigns over *free* beings, i.e. not by means of the *sword*, but by means of the *sceptre*. The sceptre itself bears a globe with a cross above. The sceptre therefore expresses in as clear as possible a manner the central idea of the Arcanum: just as the world (the globe) is ruled by the cross, so is the power of the Emperor over the terrestrial globe subject to the sign of the cross. The power of the Emperor reflects divine power. And just as the latter is effected by divine contraction (*tsimtsum*) and by voluntary divine powerlessness (crucifixion), so the power of the Emperor is effected by the contraction of his personal forces (the belt drawn tight by the Emperor) and by voluntary immobility (the crossed legs of the Emperor) at his post (the seat or throne of the Emperor).

The *post* of the Emperor. . .what an abundance of ideas concerning the post — its historical mission, its functions in the light of natural right, and its role in the light of divine right — of the Emperor of Christendom are to be found amongst mediaeval authors!

As it is suitable that the institution of a city or a kingdom be made according to the model of the institution of the world, similarly it is necessary to draw from divine government the order (*ratio*) of the government of a city—this is the fundamental thesis advanced on this subject by St. Thomas Aquinas (*De regno* xiv, 1). This is why authors of the Middle Ages could not imagine Christianity without an Emperor, just as they could not imagine the Universal Church without a pope. Because if the world is governed hierarchically, Christianity or the *Sanctum Imperium* cannot be otherwise. Hierarchy is a pyramid which exists only when it is complete. And it is the Emperor who is at its summit. Then come the kings, dukes, noblemen, citizens and peasants. But it is the crown of the Emperor which confers royalty to the royal crowns from which the ducal crowns and all the other crowns in turn derive their authority.

The *post* of the Emperor is nevertheless not only that of the last (or, rather, the first) instance of sole legitimacy. It was also *magical*, if we understand by magic the action of correspondences between that which is below and that which is above. It was the principle itself of authority from which all lesser authorities derived not only their legitimacy but also their hold over the consciousness of the people. This is why royal crowns one after another lost their lustre and were eclipsed after the imperial crown was eclipsed. Monarchies are unable to exist for long without the Monarchy; kings cannot apportion the crown and sceptre of the Emperor among themselves and pose as emperors in their particular countries, because the shadow of the Emperor is always present. And if in the past it was the Emperor who gave lustre to the royal crowns, it was later the shadow of the absent Emperor which obscured the royal crowns and, consequently, all the other crowns—those of dukes, princes, counts, etc. A pyramid is not complete without its summit; hierarchy *does not exist* when it is incomplete. Without an Emperor, there will be, sooner or later, no more kings. When there are no kings, there will be, sooner or later, no more nobility. When there is no more nobility, there will be, sooner or later, no more bourgeoisie or peasants. This is how one arrives at the dictatorship of the *proletariat*, the class hostile to the hierarchical principle, which latter, however, is the reflection of divine order. This is why the proletariat professes atheism.

Europe is haunted by the shadow of the Emperor. One senses his absence just as vividly as in former times one sensed his presence. Because the emptiness of the wound *speaks*, that which we miss knows how to make us sense it.

Napoleon, eye-witness to the French Revolution, understood the direction which Europe had taken—the direction towards the complete destruction of hierarchy. And he sensed the shadow of the Emperor. He knew what had to be restored in Europe, which was not the royal throne of France—because kings cannot exist for long without the Emperor—but rather the imperial throne of Europe. So he decided to fill the gap himself. He made himself Emperor and he made his brothers kings. But it was to the sword that he took recourse. Instead of ruling by the *sceptre*—the globe bearing the cross—he made the decision to rule by the sword.

But, "all who take up the sword will perish by the sword" (Matthew xxvi, 52). Hitler also had the delirium of desire to occupy the empty place of the Emperor. He believed he could establish the "thousand-year empire" of tyranny by means of the sword. But again—"all those who take up the sword will perish by the sword".

No, the post of the Emperor does not belong any longer either to those who desire it or to the choice of the people. It is reserved to the choice of heaven alone. It has become occult. And the crown, the sceptre, the throne, the coat-of-arms of the Emperor are to be found in the *catacombs*. . . in the catacombs—this means to say: under absolute protection.

Now, the Emperor on the fourth Card is alone, without a court or retinue. His throne is in no way to be found in a room of the imperial palace, but rather in the open—in the open in an uncultivated field, not located in a town. A meagre clump of grass by his foot is there as the whole imperial court—as all the witnesses of his imperial splendour. But the clear sky is spread above him. He is a silhouette on the background of the sky. Alone in the presence of the sky—this is how the Emperor is.

One could ask: Why is the astonishing fact that the Emperor is found with his throne in the open air (under the starry sky, if you wish) overlooked by so many authors on the Tarot? Why have they not stated the fact that the Emperor is alone, without a court or retinue? I believe that it is because it is rarely that one lets the symbol, the image of the symbol as such, say all that it has to say through its unique context. One lets it say a little, and one is suddenly more interested in one's own thoughts, i.e. in what one has to say oneself, rather than what the symbol has to say.

Yet the Card is specific: the Emperor is alone in open air in an uncultivated field and with a tuft of grass as his only company—save for the sky and the earth. The Card teaches us the arcanum of the *authority* of the Emperor, although it may be unrecognised, occult, unknown and unappreciated. It is a matter of the crown, the sceptre, the throne and the coat-of-arms being guarded, without any witnesses other than the sky and the earth, by a solitary man leaning against the throne, with his legs crossed, wearing a crown, holding the sceptre and clasping his belt. It is *authority* as such and it is the *post* of authority as such which is expressed here.

Authority is the magic of spiritual profundity filled with wisdom. Or, in other words, it is the result of magic based on gnosis due to mystical experience. Authority is the second HÉ of the divine name YHVH. But it is not the second HÉ taken separately; it is only when the *whole* divine name manifests itself. For this reason it is more correct to say that *authority is the completely-manifested divine name*. The completely-manifested divine name signifies at the same time a *post*, the post of the Emperor, or the state of consciousness of the complete synthesis of mysticism, gnosis and sacred magic. And it is this state of consciousness of complete synthesis which is *initiation*. . . initiation understood not in the sense of ritual nor in the sense of the possession of information held to be secret, but rather in the sense of *the state of consciousness where eternity and the present moment are one*. It is the simultaneous vision of the temporal and the eternal, of that which is below and that which is above.

The formula of initiation remains always the same:

> *Verum sine mendacio, certum et verissimum: Quod est inferius,*
> *est sicut quod est superius; et quod est superius, est sicut quod*
> *est inferius, ad perpetranda miracula rei unius. (Tabula*
> *Smaragdina*, 1-2)

This unity actualised, contemplated, practised and understood is initiation or "the sanctification of the divine name in man", which is the deeper meaning of the first petition of the *Pater Noster*: SANCTIFICETUR NOMEN TUUM.

The Emperor signifies the authority of initiation or of the initiate. It is due to the complete divine name, from the Cabbalistic viewpoint—to the "magical great arcanum", from the point of view of magic—and to the "philosopher's stone", from the standpoint of alchemy. It is, in other words, the unity and synthesis of mysticism, gnosis and magic. This unity or synthesis we have designated in the second Letter as "Hermetic philosophy", bound up with the Hermetic-philosophical sense. This Hermetic philosophy—it is necessary to repeat—does not signify a philosophy *derived* or disengaged from the organism of the unity of mysticism, gnosis and sacred magic. It *is* this very unity in manifestation. Hermetic philosophy is as inseparable from the unity, mysticism-gnosis-magic, as is the second HÉ from the divine name. It is *authority* or the manifestation of the unity, mysticism-gnosis-magic.

Hermetic philosophy corresponds to the stage of *verissimum* ("most true") in that which is *verum, sine mendacio, et certum* ("true it is, without falsehood, and certain") in the epistemological formula of the *Emerald Table*. For it is this which is the *summary* of all mystical experience, gnostic revelation and practical magic. It is spontaneous mystical experience which becomes "true" (*verum*), or reflected in consciousness (gnosis), and then becomes "certain" (*certum*) through its magical realisation—and which is then reflected a second time (the second HÉ, or the "second gnosis", of the divine name) in the domain of pure thought based on pure experience, where it is examined and finally summarised, and thus becomes "most true" (*verissimum*).

The formula: *verum, sine mendacio, certum et verissimum* therefore states the principle of epistemology (or "gnoseology") of Hermetic philosophy, with its triple touchstone. This principle can be formulated in several ways. Here is one: "That which is absolutely subjective (pure mystical experience) must objectivise itself in consciousness and be accepted there as *true* (gnostic revelation), then prove to be *certain* by its objective fruits (sacred magic) and, lastly, prove to be *absolutely true* in the light of pure thought based on pure subjective and objective experience (Hermetic philosophy)." It is a matter, therefore, of the four different senses; the mystical sense or spiritual touch, the gnostic sense or spiritual hearing, the magical sense or sense of spiritual vision and, lastly, the Hermetic-philosophical sense or sense of spiritual comprehension. The triple touchstone of Hermetic philosophy is therefore the *intrinsic value* of a revelation (*verum, sine mendacio*), its *constructive fruitfulness (certum)* and its *concordance* with earlier revelations, with the laws of thought and with all available experience (*verissimum*). In Hermetic philosophy something is absolutely true, therefore, only when it is of divine origin and bears fruit in conformity with its origin, and is in accordance with the categorical exigencies of thought and experience.

The Hermeticist is therefore a person who is at one and the same time a mystic, a gnostic, a magician and a "realist-idealist" philosopher. He is a *realist-idealist* philosopher because he relies as much on experience as on speculative thought, as much on facts as on ideas, because facts and ideas are for him only two aspects of the same reality-ideality, i.e. the same *truth*.

Hermetic philosophy, being the summary and synthesis of mysticism, gnosis and sacred magic, is not a philosophy among other philosophies, or a particular philosophical system amongst other particular philosophical systems. Just as the Catholic Church, being catholic or universal, cannot consider itself as a particular church among other particular churches, nor consider its dogmas as religious opinions among other religious opinions or confessions, so Hermetic philosophy, being the synthesis of all that which is essential in the spiritual life of humanity, *cannot* consider itself as a philosophy amongst many others. Presumption? It would be, without any doubt, a monstrous presumption if it were a matter of human invention instead of revelation from above. In fact, if you have a truth revealed from above, if the acceptance of this truth brings miracles of healing, peace and vivification with it, and if, lastly, it explains to you a thousand unexplained things — that are inexplicable without it — can you then consider it as an opinion among other opinions?

Dogmatism? Yes, if one understands by "dogma" the certainty due to revelations of divine worth which prove fruitful and constructive, and due to the confirmation that they receive from reason and experience together. When one has certainty based on the concordance of divine revelation, divine-human operation, and human understanding, how can one act as if one did not have it? Is it truly necessary "to deny three times before the cock crows" in order to be accepted into the good company of "free spirits" and "non-dogmatics", and to be chauffeured along with them by the fire of things relating to human creation? Heresy? Yes, if by "heresy" one understands the primacy of universal revelation, of good works universally recognised as such, and of the ideal of universality amongst philosophies.

Hermetic philosophy is not a particular philosophy amongst particular existing philosophies. It is not so already for the sole reason that it does not operate with univocal *concepts* and their verbal definitions, as do philosophies, but rather with *arcana* and their *symbolic* expressions. Compare the *Emerald Table* with *The Critique of Pure Reason* by Kant and you will see the difference. The *Emerald*

Table states the fundamental arcana of mystical-gnostic-magical-philosophical *work*; *The Critique of Pure Reason* elaborates an edifice composed of univocal concepts (such as the categories of quantity, quality, relation and modality) which, all together, portray the *transcendental method* of Kant, i.e. the method of "thinking about the act of thought" or "reflection about reflection". This method, however, is an aspect of the eighteenth Arcanum of the Tarot (The Moon), as we shall see, and this Arcanum, expressed by the symbol of the Card "The Moon", teaches in the *Hermetic way* the essence of what Kant taught in the *philosophical way* about the transcendental method.

So, is Hermetic philosophy only symbolism pure and simple, and has it nothing to do with the methods of philosophical and scientific reasoning?

Yes and no. Yes, in so far as Hermetic philosophy is of an esoteric nature, i.e. it consists of *arcana* orientated towards the *mystery* and expressed in *symbols*. No, in so far as it exercises a stimulating effect on the philosophical and scientific reasoning of its adherents. It is wrapped, so to say, in a philosophical and scientific intellectual penumbra, which is due to the activity of its adherents pursuing the aim of translating, in so far as it is possible to do so, the arcana and the symbols of Hermetic philosophy into univocal concepts and verbal definitions. It is a process of crystallisation, because the translation of multivocal concepts or arcana into univocal concepts is comparable to the transition from the state of organic life to the mineral state. It is thus that the occult sciences—such as the Cabbala, astrology and alchemy—are derived from Hermetic philosophy. These sciences are able to have their own *secrets*, but the *arcana* which are reflected in them belong to the domain of Hermetic philosophy. In so far as the intellectualisation of Hermetic philosophy is of the nature of *commentary* and *corollary*, it is legitimate and even indispensable. For then one will translate each arcanum into many univocal concepts—three for example—and, by this very fact, one will help the intellect to habituate itself to think Hermetically, i.e. in multi-vocal concepts or arcana. But when the intellectualisation of Hermetic philosophy pursues the aim of creating an *autonomous system* of univocal concepts without *formal* contradiction between them, it commits an abuse. For instead of helping human reason to raise itself above itself, it would set up a greater obstacle for it. It would captivate it instead of freeing it.

The occult sciences are therefore derived from Hermetic philosophy by way of intellectualisation. This is why one should not consider symbols—the Major Arcana of the Tarot, for example—as allegorical expressions of *theories* or *concepts* of these sciences. For it is the opposite which is true: it is the doctrines of the occult sciences which are derived from symbols—of the Tarot or other symbols—and it is they which are to be considered as intellectually "allegorical" expressions of the symbols and arcana of Hermetic esotericism. Thus, it would not do to say: the fourth Card "The Emperor" is the symbol of the astrological doctrine concerning Jupiter. One would rather say: the Arcanum of the fourth Card "The Emperor" is also revealed in the astrological doctrine concerning Jupiter. The correspondence as such remains intact, but there is a world of difference between these two statements here. Because in the case of the first statement, one remains an "astrologer" and nothing but an astrologer; whilst in the case of the second statement, one is thinking as a Hermeticist, although remaining an astrologer if one is one.

Hermetic philosophy is not composed of the Cabbala, astrology, magic and alchemy. These four branches sprouting from the trunk do not make the trunk, rather they live from the trunk. The trunk is the manifested unity of mysticism, gnosis and sacred magic. There are no theories; there is only experience, including here the intellectual experience of arcana and symbols. Mystical experience is the root, the gnostic experience of revelation is its sap and the experience or practice of sacred magic is its wood. For this reason its teaching—or the "body" of its tradition—consists of *spiritual exercises* and all its arcana (including the Arcana of the Tarot) are practical spiritual exercises, whose aim is to awaken from sleep ever-deeper layers of consciousness. Necessary commentaries and corollaries accompany this practice and constitute the "bark" of the trunk. Thus, the "key" to the Apocalypse of St. John is nowhere to be found. . . for it is not at all a matter of interpreting it with a view to extracting a philosophical, metaphysical or historical system. The key to the Apocalypse is to *practise* it, i.e. to make use of it as a book of spiritual exercises which awaken from sleep ever-deeper layers of consciousness. The seven letters to the churches, the seven seals of the sealed book, the seven trumpets and the seven vials signify, all together, a course of spiritual exercises composed of twenty-eight exercises. For as the Apocalypse is a revelation put into writing, it is necessary, in order to understand it, to establish in oneself a state of consciousness which is suited to receive revelations. It is the state of concentration without effort (taught by the first Arcanum), followed by a vigilant inner silence (taught by the second Arcanum), which becomes an inspired activity of imagination and thought, where the conscious self acts together with super-consciousness (teaching of the third Arcanum). Lastly, the conscious self halts its creative activity and contemplates—in letting pass in review—everything which preceded, with a view to summarising it (practical teaching of the fourth Arcanum). The mastery of these four psychurgical operations, symbolised by "The Magician", "The High Priestess", "The Empress" and "The Emperor", is the key to the Apocalypse. One will search in vain for another.

The Gospels, likewise, are spiritual exercises, i.e. one has not only to read and re-read them, but also to plunge entirely into their element, to breath their air, to participate as an eye-witness, as it were, in the events described there—and all this not in a scrutinising way, but as an "admirer", with ever-growing admiration.

The Old Testament also contains parts which are spiritual exercises. The Jewish Cabbalists—the author or authors of the *Zohar*, for example—made such use of it, and it is thus that the Cabbala originated and that it *lives*. The difference between Cabbalists and the other faithful depends only on the fact that the former drew spiritual exercises from the Scripture whilst the latter studied it and believed it.

The aim of spiritual exercises is *depth*. It is necessary to become deep in order to be able to attain experience and knowledge of profound things. And it is symbolism which is the language of depth—thus arcana, expressed by symbols, are both the means and the aim of the spiritual exercises of which the living tradition of Hermetic philosophy is composed.

Spiritual exercises in common form the common link that unites Hermeticists. It is not knowledge in common which unites them, but rather the spiritual exercises and the experience which goes hand in hand with them. If three people from different countries were to meet each other, having made the book of Genesis by Moses, the Gospel of St. John, and the vision of Ezekiel, the subject of spiritual exercises for many years, they would do so in brotherhood, although the one would know the history of humanity, the other would have the science of healing and the third would make a profound Cabbalist. That which one *knows* is the result of *personal* experience and orientation, whilst *depth*, the *niveau* to which one attains—disregarding the aspect and extent of knowledge that one has gained—is what one has *in common*. Hermeticism, the Hermetic tradition, is in the first place and above all a certain degree of depth, a certain *niveau* of consciousness. And it is the practice of spiritual exercises which safeguards this.

With respect to the knowledge of individual Hermeticists—and this is applicable to initiates also—it depends upon the individual vocation of each one of them. The task that one pursues determines the nature and the extent not only of knowledge but also of the personal experience upon which this knowledge is based. One has the experience and gains knowledge of that which is necessary for the accomplishment of the task which proceeds from one's individual vocation. In other words, one knows that which is necessary in order to be informed and to be able to orientate oneself in the domain relevant to one's individual vocation. Thus a Hermeticist whose vocation is healing would know things about the relationships existing between consciousness, the system of the "lotus flowers" or *chakras*, the nervous system and the system of endocrine glands, that another Hermeticist, whose vocation is the spiritual history of humanity, would not know. But this latter, in his turn, would know things ignored by the healer—facts of the past and of the present concerning relationships between the spiritual hierarchies and humanity, between that which took place or is taking place above and that which took place or is taking place below.

But this knowing, in so far as it is not a matter of *arcana*, consists of *facts*—though often of a purely spiritual nature—and not *theories*. Thus, for example, reincarnation is in no way a theory which one has to believe or not believe. In Hermeticism no one would dream of putting forward a case in order to persuade, or even to dissuade, people of the truth of the "reincarnationist theory". For the Hermeticist it is a fact which is either known through experience or ignored. Just as one does not make propaganda for or against the fact that we sleep at night and wake up anew each morning—for this is a matter of experience—so is the fact that we die and are born anew a matter of experience, i.e. either one has certainty about it or else one does not. But those who are certain should know that ignorance of reincarnation often has very profound and even sublime reasons associated with the vocation of the person in question. When, for example, a person has a vocation which demands a maximum of concentration *in the present*, he may renounce all spiritual memories of the past. Because the awakened memory is not always beneficial; it is often a burden. It is so, above all, when it is a matter of a vocation which demands an attitude entirely free of all prejudice, as is the case with the vocations of priest, doctor and judge. The priest, doctor and judge have to concentrate themselves in such a way on the tasks of the present that they must not be distracted by memories of former existences.

One can perform miracles without the memory of former lives, as was the case with the holy vicar of Ars — and one can also perform miracles, wholly in possession of this memory, as was the case with Monsieur Philip of Lyons. For reincarnation is neither a dogma, i.e. a truth necessary for salvation, nor a heresy, i.e. contrary to a truth necessary for salvation. It is simply a fact of experience, just as sleep and heredity are. As such, it is neutral. Everything depends on its interpretation. One can interpret it in such a manner as to make it a hymn to the glory of God — and one can interpret it in such a way as to make it a blasphemy. When one says: to forgive is to grant the opportunity to begin again; God forgives more than seventy-times-seven times, always granting us opportunities anew — what infinite goodness of God! Here is an interpretation to the glory of God.

But when one says: there is a mechanism of infinite evolution and one is morally *determined* by previous lives; there is no grace, there is only the law of cause and effect — then this is a blasphemous interpretation. It reduces God to the function of the engineer of a moral machine.

Reincarnation is in no way an exception in what is liable to a double interpretation. In fact, every pertinent fact is liable to it. Thus, for example, heredity can be interpreted in the sense of complete determinism, therefore excluding freedom, and thus also morality. Or rather it can be interpreted as a possibility for gradual improvement of the organism in order to render it a more perfect instrument to "vocations for posterity". Didn't Abraham receive the promise that the Messiah would come in his lineage? Wasn't this same promise given to David?

Nevertheless, whatever the personal interpretation of a fact may be, a fact remains a fact and it is necessary to know it when one wants to orientate oneself in the domain to which it belongs. Thus, Hermeticists have knowledge of diverse facts, according to their personal vocations, but Hermetic philosophy is nevertheless not the sum-total of knowledge acquired by individuals. It is an organism of arcana expressed in symbols which are at the same time both spiritual exercises and their resulting aptitudes. An arcanum practised as a spiritual exercise for a sufficient length of time becomes an aptitude. It does not give the pupil knowledge of new facts, but makes him suited to acquire such knowledge when he has need of it. Initiation is the capacity of orientating oneself in every domain and of acquiring there knowledge of relevant facts — the "key facts". The initiate is one who knows how to attain knowledge, i.e. who knows how to *ask, seek* and *put into practice* the appropriate means in order to succeed. Spiritual exercises alone have taught him — no theory or doctrine, however luminous, may in any way have rendered him capable of "knowing how to know". Spiritual exercises have taught him *practical sense* (and in Hermetic philosophy there is no other sense than the practical) and the infallible effectiveness of *the arcanum of the three united endeavours*, which is the basis of every spiritual exercise and every arcanum, namely:

> Ask, and it will be given you;
> seek, and you will find;
> knock, and it will be opened to you.
> (Luke xi, 9)

Thus, Hermetic philosophy does not teach what one ought to believe concerning God, man and Nature, but it teaches rather how *to ask*, *seek* and *knock* in order to arrive at mystical experience, gnostic illumination and the magical effect of that which one seeks to know about God, man and Nature. And it is after having asked, sought and knocked — and after one has received, found and gained access — that one *knows*. This kind of knowing — the certainty of the synthetic comprehension of mystical experience, gnostic revelation and magical effect — is the *Emperor*; this is the practical teaching of the fourth Card of the Tarot.

It is a matter here of the development and usage of the fourth spiritual sense, i.e. the Hermetic-philosophical sense, following the development and usage of the mystical, gnostic and magical senses. The aptitude for "knowing how to know" is the characteristic trait essential to this sense. We have defined it above (second Letter) as the "sense of synthesis". Now we are able to advance and to do so in a much more profound way in defining it as the "initiate sense" or the sense of orientation and acquisition of knowledge of essential facts in every domain.

How does this sense function? There is reason to indicate in the first instance that it is not identical with what one customarily designates as "metaphysical sense", since the metaphysical sense of metaphysicians is the taste and capacity for living in abstract theories, the liking for the abstract, whilst the Hermetic-philosophical sense is on the contrary due to the orientation towards the *concrete* — spiritual, psychic and physical. Whilst the metaphysical sense operates with the "concept of God", the Hermetic-philosophical sense is orientated towards the *living God* — the spiritual, concrete fact of God. The Christian Celestial Father and the Ancient of Days of the Cabbalists is not an abstract concept; it is not a notion, but rather a *being*.

The metaphysical sense works in such a manner as to deduce — by way of abstraction — the *laws* of facts and the *principles* of laws. The Hermetic-philosophical sense (or initiate sense), in contrast, perceives through the facts the *entities* of the spiritual hierarchies, and through them the living God. For the initiate sense the space between the "supreme Principle" and the domain of facts is not peopled with "laws" and "principles", but rather with living spiritual beings, each endowed with a manner, look, voice, way of speaking and name. For the initiate sense the

Archangel Michael is not a law or principle. He is a living being whose face is invisible because it has given place to the face of God. This is why he has the name MI-KHA-EL, i.e. "He who (MI) is as (KHA) God (EL)". No one could endure the vision of the face of Michael, because he is KHA-EL, i.e. "like unto God".

The Hermetic-philosophical sense (or initiate sense) is that of concrete spiritual realities. The Hermeticist explains facts not by laws obtained by abstraction nor, much less still, by principles obtained by active abstraction, but rather by proceeding from abstract facts to more concrete beings in order to arrive at that which is the most concrete, that alone in existence which is absolutely concrete, i.e. God. Because for the initiate sense God is that which is most real, and therefore most concrete. In fact, amongst all that exists, God is that alone which is absolutely real and concrete, whilst created beings are only relatively real and concrete; and what we designate as "concrete fact" is in reality only an abstraction from divine reality.

This does not mean to say that the Hermeticist is incapable of abstraction and that he necessarily neglects laws and principles. He is a human being and therefore also possesses the metaphysical sense. In possessing it he makes use of it like everyone, but what makes him a *Hermeticist* — in the sense of the Emperor of the Tarot — is the Hermetic-philosophical sense. He is as much a Hermeticist as he is endowed with the Hermetic-philosophical sense and makes use of it, whilst the metaphysical sense alone would never make a Hermeticist, in the proper sense of the word.

Is this not the tragedy of René Guénon who, being gifted with a developed metaphysical sense and yet lacking the Hermetic-philosophical sense, sought, always and everywhere, the *concrete* spiritual. And finally, tired of the world of abstractions, he hoped to find liberation from intellectualism by plunging himself into the element of fervour of the Moslem masses at prayer in a Cairo mosque. The last hope of a soul thirsty for mystical experience and languishing in the captivity of the intellect? If so, may divine mercy grant him what he sought so much.

There is room to remark here that the last orientation of René Guénon, i.e. towards the faith of simpler people adhering to a more simple religion, is not without reason. For the Hermetic-philosophical sense has more in common with the plain and sincere faith of simple people than abstract metaphysics has. For the common believer, God lives; likewise for the Hermeticist. The believer addresses himself to saints and Angels; for the Hermeticist they are real. The believer believes in miracles; the Hermeticist lives in the presence of miracles. The believer prays for the living and dead; the Hermeticist dedicates all his efforts in the domain of sacred magic to the good of the living and the dead. The believer esteems all that which is traditional; the Hermeticist does likewise. What more is there to say?. . . perhaps that the Emperor owes his *authority* not to his power — visible or invisible — over human beings, but rather because he *represents* them before God. He has *authority* not because he is superhuman, but rather because he is *very human*, because he represents all that which is human. King David was more human than all men of his time. This is why he was annointed by divine order by the prophet Samuel, and for this reason the Eternal gave him the solemn promise that his throne would be established for ever. The throne, the post of the representative of humanity, will therefore never perish. And it is this which is the post of the Emperor; it is this which is *true authority*.

Hermetic philosophy also has a human ideal to which it aspires. Its spiritual exercises, its arcana, follow the practical aim of realising the *man of authority*, the "father-man". This is the man who is more human than all others. . . the man worthy of "the throne of David".

The human ideal of practical Hermeticism is not the superman of Nietzsche, nor the superman of India plunged in contemplation of eternity, nor the superman-hierophant of Gurdjieff, nor the superman-philosopher of the Stoic and Vedanta philosophies—no, its human ideal is the man who is human to such a degree that he contains and bears in himself all that which is human, that he may be the guardian of the throne of David.

And the Divine? How is it here in that which concerns the manifestation of the Divine?

Practical Hermeticism is *alchemy*. The ideal of Hermeticism is essentially and fundamentally the alchemical ideal. This means to say: the more one becomes truly human, the more one manifests the divine element underlying human nature, which is the "image and likeness of God" (Genesis i, 26). The ideal of *abstraction* invites human beings to do away with human nature, to dehumanise. In contrast, the ideal of alchemical *transformation* of Hermeticism offers to human beings the way to the realisation of true human nature, which is the image and likeness of God. Hermeticism is the re-humanisation of all elements of human nature; it is their return to their true essence. Just as all base metal can be transformed into silver and into gold, so are all the forces of human nature susceptible to transformation into "silver" or "gold", i.e. into what they *are* when they share in the image and likeness of God.

But in order to re-become what they are in their essence, they must be submitted to the operation of *sublimation*. Now, this operation is crucifying for that which is base amongst them and, at the same time, it is the blossoming of that which is their true essence. The *cross* and the *rose*, the ROSE-CROSS, is the symbol of this operation of the realisation of the truly human man. Thus, the Emperor of the Tarot renounces the *four* arbitrary liberties of human nature. He is, in this sense, crucified. And as the *real* symbol of the emptiness which is established because of renunciation is the *wound*—one could say that the Emperor is he who has four wounds. It is by these four wounds that the manifestation of the divine image and likeness of human nature is accomplished in him.

The divine in human nature. . .and what of the Divine which transcends it?

In order for the latter to manifest, it is necessary to have one wound more. It is necessary to have *five* wounds. Now, it is the following Card "The Pope" which will teach us the Arcanum of the manifestation of the Divine transcending human nature by means of the five wounds.

Meditation on the
Fifth Major Arcanum of the Tarot

THE POPE

LE PAPE

At vero Malki-tzadek rex Salem, proferens
panem et vinum, erat enim sacerdos Dei
Altissimi, benedixit ei, et ait:
Benedictus Abram Deo excelso . . . et
benedictus Deus excelsus . . .
                              (Genesis xiv, 18-20)

(And Melchizedek king of Salem brought out
bread and wine; he was priest of God
Most High. And he blessed him and said:
Blessed be Abram by God Most High . . .
and blessed be God Most High . . .)

Ego sum via et veritas et vita: nemo
venit ad Patrem, nisi per me.
                              (John xiv, 6)

(I am the way, and the truth, and the life:
no one comes to the Father, but by me.)

De cetero nemo mihi molestus sit: ego
enim stigmata Domini Jesu in corpore
meo porto.
                              (Galatians vi, 17)

(Henceforth let no man trouble me:
for I bear on my body the marks of Jesus.)

LETTER V

THE POPE

Dear Unknown Friend,

The Card "The Pope" puts us in the presence of the *act of benediction*. It is essential to have this in mind when one undertakes the interpretation not only of the structure of the whole Card but also of each of its particular elements. One should therefore never lose from sight that in the first place it is a matter of *benediction* and everything associated with it — no matter who the Pope may be or who the acolytes kneeling before him are, and no matter what the two columns behind the Pope signify, and no matter what his tiara and the triple cross he is holding symbolise. What is benediction? What is its source and its effect? Who has the authority to bestow benediction? What role does it play in the spiritual life of humanity?

99

Now, benediction is more than a simple good wish made for others; it is also more than a magical impress of personal thought and will upon others. It is the putting into action of divine power transcending the individual thought and will of the one who is blessed as well as the one who is pronouncing the blessing. In other words it is an essentially *sacerdotal* act.

The Cabbala compares the role of prayer and benediction to a double movement, ascending and descending, similar to the circulation of the blood. The prayers of humanity rise towards God and, after having been divinely "oxidised", are transformed into benedictions which descend below from above. This is why one of the acolytes of the Card has his left hand raised and the other has his right hand lowered. The two blue columns behind the Pope symbolise *in the first place* this twofold current — rising and descending — of prayers and benedictions. At the same time the Pope himself holds aloft a triple cross on the side with the "column of prayer" and the praying acolyte, whilst his right hand — on the side with the "column of benediction" and the acolyte receiving (or "inspiring") benediction — makes the gesture of benediction.

The two sides of the Cabbala — the "right" side and the "left" side — and the two columns of the Sephiroth Tree, the pillar of Mercy and that of Severity, and similarly the two pillars of the Temple of Solomon, Jachin and Boaz, correspond exactly to the two columns of prayer and benediction on this Card. Because it is Severity which stimulates prayer and it is Mercy which blesses. The venous "blue blood" of Boaz ascends and the arterial oxidised "red blood" of Jachin descends. The "red blood" bears the vivifying benediction of oxygen; the "blue blood" rids the organism of the "severity" of carbonic acid. It is the same in the spiritual life. Spiritual asphyxia menaces he who does not practise *some form* of prayer; he who practises it receives vivifying benediction in some form. The two columns therefore have an essentially *practical* significance — as practical spiritually as respiration is for the life of the organism.

Thus, the first practical teaching of the fifth Arcanum — for the Major Arcana of the Tarot are spiritual *exercises* — relates to *spiritual respiration*.

There are two kinds of respiration: horizontal respiration which takes place between "outside" and "inside", and vertical respiration which takes place between "above" and "below". The "sting of death" or the essential crisis of the supreme agony is the abrupt passage from horizontal to vertical respiration. Yet he who has learnt vertical respiration whilst living will be spared from this "sting of death". For him the passage from the one form of respiration to the other will not be of the nature of a right angle but rather the arc of a circle: ⌐ ⌐ . The transition will not be abrupt but gradual, and curved instead of rectangular.

Now, the essence of vertical respiration is the alternation between prayer and benediction or grace. These two elements of vertical respiration manifest themselves in all domains of the inner life — mind, heart and will. Thus a relevant problem for the mind, which is not due to curiosity or intellectual collectionism, but rather to the thirst for truth, is fundamentally a prayer. And the illumination by which it may be followed is the corresponding benediction or grace. True suffering, also, is fundamentally always a prayer. And the consolation, peace and joy which can follow are the effects of the benediction or grace corresponding to it.

True effort of the will, i.e. one hundred percent effort, true *work*, is also a prayer. When it is intellectual work, it is prayer: Hallowed be thy name. When it is creative effort, it is prayer: Thy kingdom come. When it is work with a view to supplying for the material needs of life, it is prayer: Give us this day our daily bread. And all these forms of prayer in the language of work have their corresponding benedictions or graces.

The law of correspondence between the column of prayer (problems, suffering, effort) and that of benediction (illumination, consolation, fruits) is found expressed by the Master in the beatitudes of the Sermon on the Mount. The nine (for there are nine, and not eight) beatitudes can thus be understood as the formula of *vertical respiration*. They teach it to us.

This respiration is the state of soul that the apostle Paul designated as "freedom in God". It is a new way of breathing. One freely breathes the divine breath, which is freedom.

> The Lord is Spirit, and where the Spirit of the Lord is, there is freedom. (II Corinthians iii, 17)

The spiritual counterpart to horizontal respiration is the alternation from "extroversion" to "introversion" or from attention to the objective external life to the subjective inner life. The law of horizontal respiration is: "Love your neighbour as yourself" (Luke x, 27). Here is the equilibrium between these two directions of attention.

With respect to vertical respiration, its law is: "Love the Lord your God with all your heart, and with all your soul, and with all your mind" (Matthew xxii, 37). Here is the relationship between prayer and benediction or grace.

There are *three* levels of horizontal respiration, just as there are three stages of vertical respiration.

The three levels of horizontal respiration are:

> love of Nature;
> love of one's neighbour;
> love of the beings of the spiritual hierarchies (Angels, etc.).

The three stages of vertical respiration are:

> purification (by divine breath);
> illumination (by divine light);
> mystical union (in divine fire).

This is why the Pope holds aloft the *triple cross*. The triple cross has three cross-pieces which divide the vertical line into three parts. It is the *cross of complete and perfect spiritual respiration*, horizontal and vertical: ‡ It is the cross of triple love of neighbour (lower neighbour = Nature, equal neighbour = man, higher neighbour = beings of the hierarchies) and triple love of God (breath or faith, light or hope, fire or love).

It is the sceptre of the Pope's authority for this Card, just as the sphere formed from the double cup and topped by the cross is the sceptre of the Emperor. Just as the Emperor, guardian of the throne of David, represents towards heaven the human, i.e. the divine image and likeness in man, so does the Pope, guardian of the portal to the pillars of benediction and prayer, represent transcendental Divinity towards mankind. The two *posts*, that of Emperor and that of Pope, are two spiritual realities. They are as real as the head and the heart are in the life of the individual. The heart is the centre of respiration and blood circulation; the head is the centre of the nervous system and is the seat of thought.

And just as no parliament will replace the spiritual reality of the post of Emperor—the throne of David cannot be replaced by collectivity—so will no oecumenical council replace the spiritual reality of the post of Pope or the "throne of Melchizadek, king of plenitude (Salem)". Whether the "cannon shot" predicted in esoteric circles of the Occident be given or not, whether the sacerdotal throne remains visible or whether it be installed in the catacombs, it will *certainly* remain *present* for ever in the future history of humanity—despite what the prophets of its destruction may say.

Because history—as, moreover, the life of the individual—is "worked" by day and by night. It has a diurnal aspect and a nocturnal aspect. The former is exoteric, whilst the latter is esoteric. The silence and obscurity of the night is always full of events in preparation—and all that which is unconscious or superconscious in the human being belongs to the domain of "night". This is the magical side of history, the side of magical deeds and works acting behind the facade of history "by day". Thus, when the Gospel was preached by the light of day in the countries around the Mediterranean, the nocturnal rays of the Gospel effected a profound transformation of Buddhism. There, the ideal of individual liberation by entering the state of *nirvana* gave way to the ideal of renouncing *nirvana* for the work of mercy towards suffering humanity. The ideal of *mahayana*, the great chariot, then had its resplendent ascent to the heaven of Asia's moral values.

> *Dies diei eructat verbum et nox nocti indicat scientam.* Day to day pours forth *speech* (אמד — *'omer*) and night to night declares knowledge (רצת — *da'ath*) (Psalms xix, 1)

This is the formula of the twofold teaching—by the speech of day and by the knowledge of night; of the twofold tradition—by verbal teaching and by direct inspiration; of twofold magic—by the spoken word and by silent radiation; and lastly, of twofold history—"visible" history by day and "invisible" history by night.

Now, the posts of Emperor and Pope are realities beyond as well as on this side of the threshold which separates "day" and "night". And the Pope of the fifth Card is the guardian of this threshold. He is seated between the two pillars — the pillar of day or prayer and the pillar of night or benediction.

The Emperor of the fourth Card is the master of the day and the guardian of the blood or quintessence of the nocturnal reality of the day. The Pope is the guardian of respiration or of the reality of the relationship between day and night. That which he guards is the equilibrium between day and night, between human effort and divine grace. His post is founded on primordial cosmic deeds. Thus the first book of Moses says:

> . . . and God separated the light from the darkness. God called
> the light Day, and the darkness he called Night. (Genesis i, 4-5)

And the act of separation of the intelligible from the mysterious signifies at the same time the establishing of cosmic respiration, which is the analogy of "the Spirit of God moving above the face of the waters". For the divine breath (*ruach 'elohim*) *above* the profoundness of peace ("the waters" — it is this which is the psychological as well as the cosmic reality of *nirvana*) is the divine prototype of respiration. Therefore the "great chariot", the *mahayana* of Buddhism, raises itself towards the divine breath — the mercy which moves *above* the waters of the pre-cosmic peace of *nirvana*, whilst the "little chariot", the *hinayana*, aspires towards the end of respiration; its aim is to be drowned in the waters of peace — to enter into *nirvana* where there is no movement — neither change nor respiration.

But the divine breath (*ruach 'elohim*) is above the ocean of peace of *nirvana*; the divine breath moves it. And to renounce *nirvana*, after having arrived at its threshold, means to say: rise above *nirvana* and participate in the divine breath transcending it.

Now, primordial water penetrated by divine breath is the essence of *blood*; breath reflected by the water is *light*; the rhythmic alternation from absorption of the breath by water to its reflection by it is *respiration*. Light is the day, blood is the night, and respiration is plenitude (Salem). MELCHIZEDEK, king of Salem, *priest* of the Most High God (*kohen le'el 'elyon* — כֹּהֵן לְאֵל עֶלְיוֹן) is therefore appointed to plenitude, to *respiration*, whilst the *annointed king*, guardian of the throne of David, or the Emperor, is appointed to the day. Although he is appointed to the day, he is annointed by the night and he owes his authority to the night, whose mysterious presence during the day — the blood — he guards.

Dear Unknown Friend, you will probably ask yourself if there is a *third* post, a post for he who is appointed to the night?

Yes, the post of master of the night (he is also named "lord of the night") exists. We shall approach the various ideas relating to this post in the ninth Letter dedicated to the ninth Arcanum of the Tarot.

It suffices to indicate here that in Israel there were *three* higher posts — the posts of king, high priest and prophet. This is also the place to remark that it is a matter of *posts*, and not of persons; a single person can sometimes occupy two or even three posts.

But let us return to the post of the Pope, which is the subject of the fifth Arcanum of the Tarot. It relates to spiritual respiration, as we have seen. This is why the Pope represents another category of truth and another criterion of truth than the scientific truth and criterion. For him "true" is that which comprises *harmonious respiration*; "false" is that which upsets the harmony of spiritual respiration. Thus, the heliocentric system of modern astronomical science is true from the point of view of the science of phenomena, but it is at the same time fundamentally false from the viewpoint of spiritual respiration. The blood that issued from Christ onto the earth is precious to such a degree that he gave the earth the central position in the space of noumenal values. The *geocentric* cosmos is therefore *true* from the point of view of respiration, i.e. from the point of view of the life of prayer and benediction. And the heliocentric cosmos, although it has the support of all the facts of the phenomenal world, is *false* because it fails to recognise that which is truly central—the Incarnation of the Word—and replaces it by a centre situated more at the periphery, removed from the central value. The sun is only a centre in phenomenal space, and one commits the sin of idolatry in attributing to it the central role, which belongs to the sanctified earth—sanctified, and thus rendered central, by the Incarnation of the Word.

Here is another example, this time from the domain of esoteric experience. As we have already mentioned, reincarnation—successive lives of the same human individuality—is a fact of experience, as are the successive periods of wakefulness belonging to the day, which are interrupted by sleep at night. Buddha recognised the fact of reincarnation as such, but he considered it *regrettable*. This is why the aim of the eightfold path which he taught is to put an end to reincarnation. Because *nirvana* is the end of successive terrestrial lives.

Thus Buddha *recognised* and at the same time *denied* the fact of reincarnation. He recognised it as *fact* and he denied it as *ideal*. Because facts are transitory; they come and go. There was a time when there was no reincarnation; there will be a time when it will no longer be. Reincarnation commenced only after the Fall and it will cease with Reintegration. It is therefore not eternal, and therefore it is not an ideal.

There are therefore two truths: the one is actual or temporal and the other ideal or eternal. The first is founded on the *logic of facts*; the other on *moral logic*. Now, Psalm 85 designates actual truth (אֱמֶת.—*emeth*) by the word truth (*veritas*) and truth based on moral logic (חֶסֶד —*chesed*) by the word mercy (*misericordia*). The Psalm says:

> Mercy (*chesed*) and truth (*emeth*) will meet;
> Justice (*tsedek*) and peace (*schalom*) will embrace each other.

Truth (*emeth*) will spring up from the ground (*meeretz*).
And justice (*tsedek*) will look down from the heavens
(*mischamaim*).   (Psalm 85, 10-11)

Here is the problem of "double truth" in its entirety—and here is the moving
prophecy that the two truths, the factual and the moral, will at some time meet
and that their revelation in man—justice (*tsedek*) and peace (*schalom*)—will embrace each other! But they will meet only slowly and, given the actual state of
affairs, they often still contradict one another, at least in appearance. This is why
St. Paul had to say that "the wisdom of this world is folly with God" (I Corinthians iii, 19). And this is why also divine wisdom is often folly before this world . . .

Now, the Pope, being the guardian of *spiritual respiration* (and the letter ה,
Hé, the fifth letter of the Hebrew alphabet, has *breath* as its primitive hieroglyph),
is the representative of moral logic.

Benediction and prayer are the two pillars between which he is seated. It is only
that which is *ideal* which is true for him. Here is why, for him, marriage is
indissoluble—though there may be thousands of matrimonial catastrophes; here
is why confession and repentance efface every sin—though thousands of tribunals
only *punish* the guilty, whether they repent or not; here is why the Church is
guided by the Holy Spirit—though it practised or tolerated the practice of the
Inquisition for centuries; and here is why *a single life on earth suffices for eternal
salvation*—although souls reincarnate.

Thus, the Pope is always at the middle of a conflict between ideal truth and
actual truth, between mercy (*chesed*) and truth (*emeth*). And this conflict is a
wound—namely the fifth wound, *the wound of the heart*. For if the Emperor has
four wounds, the Pope has five.

If you are acquainted, dear Unknown Friend, with the symbolism of the Cabbala, you know that the wound spoken of here is due to the opposition between
the fourth Sephirah, CHESED (Mercy), and the fifth Sephirah, GEBURAH (Severity), on the Tree of the Sephiroth—and that this wound refers to the sixth Sephirah,
TIPHERETH (Beauty or Harmony), which is the synthesis of the two preceding
Sephiroth.

If, moreover, you occupy yourself with Christian esotericism, you will comprehend that the wound in question is that of the Sacred Heart, caused external-
ly by "one of the soldiers (who) pierced his side with a spear, and at once there
came out blood and water" (John xix, 34). And you will understand also that it
is mercy and truth (*chesed* and *emeth*) that came out as blood and water. This
is why the Evangelist emphasises the symbolic reality or the real symbolism of the
fact that the blood and water that came out of the wound *were not mixed* and
that it is in this fact that the spiritual sense of the wound is found expressed. The
wound is caused spiritually by the conflict between mercy and truth, between ideal
truth and actual truth, which are not united . . .

And the Evangelist goes on to say: "He who *saw* it has borne witness—his testimony is true, and he *knows* that he tells the truth—that you also may believe" (John xix, 35). He has therefore *seen* the fact, and he *knows* what he wants to say as a symbol of the spiritual reality of the wound.

But now we are in the realm of the esotericism of the five wounds, the flaming star, the pentagram, the quinternary or the number five. . .Louis Claude de Saint-Martin says that:

> As long as numbers are united and bound up with the decad, there is not one that presents the image of corruption or deformity. It is only when one separates them that these characteristics manifest themselves. Amongst the numbers thus specified, some are *absolutely evil*, such as *two and five*. These are also the only ones which divide the number ten. (Louis Claude de Saint-Martin, *Des nombres*, Nice, 1946, xxi)

According to Saint-Martin, the quinternary (with respect to the binary, we refer you to Letter II, where you may find a discussion of the statement of Saint-Martin concerning the evil nature of the number two) is therefore *absolutely evil* when it is not united and bound up with the decad. Thus he says:

> . . .the forms of animals must also be such as to serve as receptacles for the torments of the quinternaries, torments that we ourselves exert against them in imitation of these same quinternaries. (Louis Claude de Saint-Martin, *Des nombres*, Nice, 1946, xxxi)

Eliphas Lévi says, however, that:

> The Pentagram signifies the domination of the mind over the (four) elements; and the demons of air, the spirits of fire, the phantoms of water and ghosts of earth are enchained by this sign. Equipped therewith, and suitably disposed, you may behold the infinite through the medium of that faculty which is like the soul's eye, and you will be ministered unto by legions of angels and hosts of fiends (trsl., p. 63). [Then:] The empire of will over the Astral Light, which is the physical soul of the four elements, is represented in Magic by the Pentagram, placed at the head of this chapter (trsl., p. 67). [And further still:] On 24 July in the year 1854, the author of this book, Eliphas Lévi, made an experiment of evocation with the Pentagram, after due preparation according to the Ceremonies indicated in the thirteenth chapter of the *Ritual* (trsl., p. 69). [And lastly:] We must remark, however, that the use of the Pentagram is most danger-

ous for operators who are not in possession of its complete and perfect understanding. The direction of the points of the star is in no sense arbitrary, and may change the entire character of an operation, as we shall explain in the *Ritual* (trsl., p. 69). (Eliphas Lévi, *Dogme et rituel de la haute magie*; trsl. A. E. Waite, *Transcendental Magic. Its Doctrine and Ritual*, London, 1968, pp. 63, 67, 69)

In chapter five of *Transcendental Magic. Its Doctrine and Ritual* we find the following summary of Eliphas Lévi's doctrine concerning the pentagram:

The Pentagram, which in Gnostic schools is called the Blazing Star, is *the sign of intellectual omnipotence and autocracy.* (ibid., trsl. p. 237)

But in *The Key of the Mysteries* Eliphas Lévi says:

The quinary (or quinternary) is the number of religion, for it is the number of God united to that of woman. (Eliphas Lévi, *The Key of the Mysteries*; trsl. A. Crowley, London, 1969, p. 30)

And much later still, in his posthumous work *Le Grand Arcane ou l'occultisme dévoilé* ("The Great Arcanum, or Occultism Unveiled"), Eliphas Lévi writes:

The ancient rites have lost their effectiveness since Christianity appeared in the world. The Christian and Catholic religion, in fact, is the legitimate daughter of Jesus, king of the Mages. A simple scapular worn by a truly Christian person is a more invincible talisman than the ring and pentacle of Solomon. The Mass is the most prodigious of evocations. Necromancers evoke the dead, the sorcerer evokes the devil and he shakes, but the Catholic priest does not tremble in evoking the living God. Catholics alone have priests because they alone have the altar and the offering, i.e. the whole of religion. To practise high Magic is to compete with the Catholic priesthood; it is to be a dissident priest. Rome is the great Thebes of the new initiation . . . It has crypts for its catacombs; for talismen, its rosaries and medallions; for a magic chain, its congregations; for magnetic fires, its convents; for centres of attraction, its confessionals; for means of expansion, its pulpits and the addresses of its bishops; it has, lastly, its Pope, the Man-God rendered visible. (Eliphas Lévi, *Le Grande Arcane ou l'occultisme dévoilé*, Paris, 1921, pp. 67-68, 83-84)

And we conclude by citing Joséphin Péladan, who declared himself in agreement with the preceding:

> The Eucharist is the whole of Christianity; and through it Christianity has become living magic...Since Jesus there are still sorcerers, (but) there are no more mages. (Joséphin Péladan, *L'occulte catholique*, Paris, 1898, p. 312)

Well, after all these quotations, where are we now?

We have arrived at a very serious problem: that of the pentagram or *evil quinternary* and the Pentagram or *good quinternary*.

Because according to Saint-Martin—whose clear presentation of the problem lends itself better than any other in serving as a point of departure—the quinternary is *good* "as long as it is united and bound to the decad" and it is "absolutely *evil*" when it is separated and isolated from it. In other words, the pentagram, as the sign of *intellectual autocracy*, i.e. the emancipated human personality, is *good* when it is the expression of the personality whose will is united and bound to the fullness of the manifestation of Unity (the decad); and it is *evil* when it expresses the will of the personality separated from this Unity. Or, in other words again, the sign is good when it expresses the formula: *Fiat voluntas tua* ("Thy will be done"); and it is evil when the formula of the underlying will is: *Fiat voluntas mea* ("my will be done"). Here is the moral and practical meaning of Saint-Martin's statement.

With regard to the statements of Eliphas Lévi and Joséphin Péladan that we have quoted, they add their conviction that it is the Universal or Catholic Church which represents for humanity the decad or fullness of manifested unity. For them, the will united and bound to the essence of the Church is expressed by the good pentagram, understood in the sense of Saint-Martin, and the will that is purely and simply personal is expressed by the evil pentagram. This is why Madame Blavatsky accused Epiphas Lévi of Jesuit politics and why Joséphin Péladan's old occultist-friends regretted his relapse into Roman sectarianism.

But now, it is not a question of taking sides in the "war of the two roses", nor of accusing or regretting. Here it is a matter of the problem of personal arbitrary magic (the quinternary separated from the decad) and personal sacred magic (the quinternary united and bound to the decad). And this is the thesis that I put forward with regard to this problem, a thesis which is the fruit of forty-three years of experience in the esoteric domain: It is only the *pentagram of the five wounds* which is the effective sign of personal sacred magic, whilst the *pentagram of the five currents of personal will*, no matter how the points of this pentagram are turned, is the effective sign for the imposition of the personal will of the operator on beings weaker than him—it is always a fundamentally tyrannic act.

This is the thesis. Let us now proceed to its explanation.

A magical act presupposes an effect surpassing the normal power of the operator.

This surplus of power may be furnished by forces which are obedient to the operator, or by forces borrowed by him, or, lastly, by forces acting through the operator and which he obeys.

In the case of forces which are supplied to the operator by submission it is a matter of the operation of magic that we have designated (in Letter III) as "personal or arbitrary", i.e. an operation whose source of initiative, whose means and aim are found exclusively in the will and understanding of the personality of the operator. Such an operation can only make use of forces lower than the operator. For one does not command Angels. The operator here is alone and acts as a magical technician under his own responsibility and at his own risk and peril. One could also designate this type of magic as "Faustian".

In the case of forces borrowed by the operator, it is a matter of an act of collective magic. It is the "magic chain" which renders the operator more powerful; it "lends" him the forces which he then makes use of for the operation. In this case the operator is aided by forces which are equal to him (and are not lower than him as in the case of Faustian magic). The power and the effect depend here on the *number* of people belonging to the chain. One could designate this type of magic as "collective".

Lastly, in the case of forces acting through the operator as intermediary and which he obeys, it is also a matter of a "chain", but a *vertical and qualitative (hierarchical) chain* instead of a horizontal and quantitative chain, which latter is the case with collective magic. The operator here is alone in the horizontal sense, but he is not in the vertical sense: above him beings higher than him act with him and through him. This type of magic presupposes the fact of being in conscious relationship with higher spiritual beings, i.e. it assumes prior mystical and gnostic experience. We have designated this type of magic (in Letter III) as "sacred magic", because the forces active in operations of this magic are superior to the operator. However, its historical name is "theurgy".

The formulae expressing the fundamental attitude of the personal will corresponding to the three types of magic described above are:

> *Fiat voluntas mea* (Faustian magic);
> *Fiat voluntas nostra* (collective magic);
> *Fiat voluntas TUA* (sacred magic).

The first two forms of magic — Faustian and collective — make use of the method of which the pentagram of the five currents of personal and collective will is the sign. They are based on the principle that the strong dominates the weak. It is a matter here of the power of *compulsion*.

With respect to the third form of magic — sacred magic — the method it makes use of is not the *force* of the will, but rather its *purity*. But as the will as such is never entirely pure — for it is not the flesh which bears the stigmata of original sin, nor thought as such, but rather the will — it is necessary that the five dark currents inherent in the human will (i.e. the desire to be great, to take, to keep, to advance and to hold on to at the expense of others) are paralysed or "nailed". The *five wounds* are therefore the five vacuities which result in the five currents of the will. And these vacuities are filled by will from above, i.e. by absolutely *pure* will. This is the principle of magic of the pentagram of five wounds.

Before proceeding to the question of the way in which the five wounds of the will are produced and what the concrete practical method of the magic of the pentagram of five wounds is, it is necessary rather that we ponder on the concept itself of "wound".

A wound is a door through which the objective exterior world intrudes into the interior of the closed system of the subjective interior world. Speaking bio-logically, it is a breach in the walls of the fortress of the organism by which forces from outside the organism penetrate into its interior. A simple lesion of the skin, for example, signifies such a breach and for a certain time gives the air (and all that which is borne by the air) access into an interior region of the organism which would be barred to it if the skin were intact.

Now, the organ of sight, the eye, in comparison with the surface of the human body covered over with skin, is a *wound* which can be covered by mobile skin—the eyelids. Through this wound the objective outer world penetrates into our inner life with that much greater intensity, corresponding to the degree that sight reveals more of the outer world than the sense of touch. With the eyelids closed, the place where the experience of the world named "sight" takes place becomes again that reduced experience of the world—yet normal for the entire surface of the body—that we designate as "touch".

The eyes are open wounds which are so sensitive that they suffer with (i.e. react to) every nuance of light and colour. And it is the same with the other sense organs. They are *wounds*, i.e. it is they which impose on us the *objective* reality of the outer world. There where I would like to see beautiful flowers, my eyes make me see a pile of dung. I am *forced* to see what the objective world shows me by way of my eyes. It is like a nail from outside nailing my will.

The senses—given that they are sound and functioning normally—are wounds through which the objective world, without regard to our will, imposes itself on us. But the senses are organs of *perception*, not of action. Imagine that the five organs of action—the limbs, including the head in its function as a limb—were to have analogous wounds, i.e. that the five currents of will of which they are an expression were to give access to an *objective will* which would be to personal desires what sense perceptions are to the play of fantasy.

This is the esoteric concept of the wound. And this concept can become a spir-itual reality, then psychic, and eventually even physical with some people. The stigmatics—from St. Francis of Assisi to Padre Pio in Italy and Teresa Neumann in Germany during the present epoch—are people for whom the reality of the five wounds has reached to the physical plane. These are the *future organs* of the will in formation, the organs of action which taken together have the sacred pentagram as their sign—the quinternary united and bound to the fullness of the decad, according to Saint-Martin.

It is still necessary to specify the five wounds corresponding to the five dark currents of the will—the desire for personal greatness, to take, to keep, to advance and to hold on to at the expense of others—which correspond, in their turn, to the five limbs (including the head as a limb), although only four are allocated to the corresponding limbs. The desire to take or get hold of things is bound to the right hand; similarly, the desire to retain or keep belongs to the left hand; likewise, the desire to advance at the expense of others and the desire to hold onto at the expense of others correspond to the right foot and the left foot respectively; but it is not the case concerning the desire for personal greatness that it corresponds to the head. The head does not bear the fifth wound, for two reasons: firstly, because it bears the "crown of thorns" (to which we endeavoured to give an explanation in Letter IV), which is borne, in principle, by every person capable of *objective* thought—the "crown of thorns" being given to the human being since the beginning of human history. It is that subtle organ which is designated for us in the Occident as the "eight-petalled lotus", and which is designated in India as the "thousand-petalled lotus" or *sahasrara* (crown centre). This crown centre is a "natural gift", as it were, to each human being and every normal person possesses it. The "thorns" of the crown centre function as the "nails" of objectivity, which give conscience to thought. It is thanks to them that thought has not become wholly emancipated and as arbitrary, for example, as the imagination is. Thought *as such* is, in spite of all, the organ of truth, not of illusion.

Thus, it is not thought as such which allows the desire for personal greatness or the tendency towards megalomania, but rather *the will* which makes use of the head and which can take hold of thought and reduce it to the role of its instrument. And this constitutes the second reason as to why the fifth wound—that of *organic* humility, replacing the current of the will-to-greatness—is not found in the head, but rather in the heart, i.e. it reaches the heart, penetrating from the right-hand side. Because it is there that the will-to-greatness has its origin and it is there from whence it takes hold of the head and makes it its instrument. This is why many thinkers and scientists want to think "without the heart" in order to be objective—which is an illusion, because one can in no way think without the heart, the heart being the activating principle of thought; what one can do is to think with a humble and warm heart instead of with a pretentious and cold heart.

Thus, the fifth wound (which is the *first* in so far as its importance is concerned) is that of the heart instead of the head, the head being *from the point of view of the active will* an instrument or "limb" of the heart.

Let us now turn to the question concerning the origin of the five wounds—i.e. how they are produced—and to the concrete practical method of the magic of the sacred pentagram of five wounds.

How does one acquire the five wounds?

There exists only one single method, one sole means leading to this. And—no matter whether in full knowledge or whether instinctively—every esotericist, every mystic, every idealist, every spiritual-seeker and, lastly, every man of good will makes use of it, in Europe as in Asia, today as twenty centuries ago. This universal method of all ages and all cultures is nothing other than the practice of the three traditional vows, namely *obedience*, *poverty* and *chastity*.

Obedience rivets the will-to-greatness of the heart; *poverty* holds fast the desire to take and the desire to keep of the right hand and the left hand; *chastity* pins down the desires of the "Nimrodic hunter"—to advance and to hold on to at the expense of others or, in other words, to hunt and to trap game—of the right foot and the left foot.

The vow of *obedience* is the practice of silencing personal desires, emotions and imagination in the face of reason and conscience; it is the primacy of the ideal as opposed to the apparent, the nation as opposed to the personal, humanity as opposed to the nation, and God as opposed to humanity. It is the life of cosmic and human hierarchical ordering; it is the meaning and justification of the fact that there are Seraphim, Cherubim, Thrones; Dominions, Virtues, Powers; Principalities, Archangels, Angels; Priests, Knights and Commoners. Obedience is order: it is international law; it is the state; it is the Church; it is universal peace. True obedience is the very opposite of tyranny and slavery, since its root is the love which issues from faith and confidence. That which is above serves that which is below and that which is below obeys that which is above. Obedience is the practical conclusion to that which one recognises as the existence of something higher than oneself. Whosoever recognises God, obeys.

Such obedience as is practised in religious orders and the Catholic spiritual knighthood is a form of training—moreover, very effective—of the will, with a view to rivetting the will-to-greatness. The obedience that the *chela* has to his *guru* in India and Tibet follows, in principle, the same aim. This is true also of the absolute obedience that the *hassidim* have towards their *tzadekim* in the Jewish Hassidic communities, and similarly it is so with the obedience without reserve on the part of the disciples of the *startzy* (spiritual masters) in orthodox, pre-Bolshevist Russia.

The universal formula of obedience is: *Fiat voluntas tua*.

The vow of *poverty* is the practice of inner emptiness, which is established as a consequence of the silence of personal desires, emotions and imagination so that the soul is capable of receiving from above the revelation of the word, the life and the light. Poverty is perpetual active vigil and expectation before the eternal sources of creativity; it is the soul awaiting that which is new and unexpected; it is the aptitude for learning always and everywhere; it is the *conditio sine qua non* of all illumination, all revelation and all initiation.

The following is a short story which makes evident in a wonderful way the practical spiritual meaning of poverty:

Once upon a time four brothers went on a journey in order to seek the greatest treasure. After a week of travelling they arrived at a mountain of iron ore. "A whole mountain of iron ore!" cried one of the four. "Here is the treasure we have been seeking!" But the three others said: "This is not the greatest treasure," and continued their walk, whilst their brother remained by the mountain of iron ore. He was now rich and they were as poor as before. One month later they arrived at a field strewn with greenish and yellowish stones. "This is copper!" cried one of the three brothers. "This is certainly the treasure that we are seeking!" But the two other brothers did not share his opinion. Thus, he remained there, being the rich proprietor of a copper mine, whilst the two others continued on their way as poor as they were before. After a year they arrived at a valley full of stones shining with a whitish light. "Silver!" cried one of the two brothers. "This is at last the treasure that we are seeking!" But the other brother shook his head and continued on his way, whilst his brother remained there as the rich proprietor of a silver mine. Seven years later he arrived at a stony place in an arid desert. He sat down, being half-dead with fatigue. It was then that he noticed that the pebbles under his feet were gleaming. It was gold . . .

The vow of *chastity* means to say the putting into practice of the resolution to live according to solar law, without covetousness and without indifference. Because virtue is boring and vice is disgusting. But that which lives at the foundation of the heart is neither boring nor disgusting. The foundation of the heart is love. The heart lives only when it loves. It is then like the sun. And chastity is the state of the human being in which the heart, having become solar, is the centre of gravity.

In other words, chastity is the state of the human being where the centre named in occidental esotericism as the "twelve-petalled lotus" (*anahata* in Indian esotericism) is awakened and becomes the sun of the microcosmic "planetary system". The three lotus-centres situated below it (the ten-petalled, the six-petalled and the four-petalled) begin then to function in conformity with the life of the heart (the twelve-petalled lotus), i.e. "according to solar law". When they do this, the person is chaste, no matter whether he or she is celibate or married. Thus there are "virgins" who are married and mothers of children, and there are physical virgins who are not so in reality. The ideal of the Virgin-Mother that the traditional Church (Catholic and Orthodox) puts forward is truly worthy of reverence. It is the ideal of chastity which triumphs over sterility and indifference.

The practice of chastity does not concern solely the domain of sex. It bears equally on all other domains where there is choice between solar law and all sorts of dulling intoxications. Thus, for example, all fanaticism sins against chastity, because there one is carried away by a dark current. The French revolution was an orgy of perverse collective intoxication, just as the revolution in Russia was. Nationalism — such as in the Germany of Hitler — is likewise a form of intoxication drowning the conscience of the heart and is therefore incompatible with the ideal of chastity.

There are also forms of practical occultism which lend themselves to the pursuit of an unhealthy intoxication. Thus Joséphin Péladan acknowledged:

I do not conceal it; we have all at first been seduced by the aesthetic of occultism, and infatuated with the quaint and the strange; one has subscribed to the amusements of nervous females; one has sought thrills—the thrill of the invisible and of the beyond; one has asked for the excitement of the incorporeal.
(Joséphin Péladan, *L'occulte catholique*, Paris, 1898, p. 309)

The practice of chastity holds fast the leanings of the *hunter* in the human being, of which the male side is inclined to pursue game and the female side to set traps. The practice of poverty binds the tendencies of the *thief* in the human being, where the male side is inclined to seize and the female side to keep indefinitely, instead of waiting for the free gift or the merited fruit of work. The practice of obedience, lastly, rivets the will-to-greatness or the inclinations of the *usurper* in human nature, whose male side is inclined to estimate itself great in its own eyes and whose female side seeks to make itself estimated so in the eyes of others.

These three vows therefore constitute the sole known and indispensable method which leads to the five wounds, i.e. to the effective pentagram of sacred magic. It is still necessary to specify that it is not a matter of the *virtues* of humility, poverty and chastity being wholly realised—because no man in the flesh can possess these virtues totally—but rather of their *practice*, i.e. sincere efforts aimed at their realisation. It is the effort which counts.

Such is the answer to the question: How does one acquire the five wounds? Now follows the response to the question: How does the magic of the sacred pentagram of the five wounds operate?

As we have indicated above, it is the *purity* of the will and not its force which constitutes the basis of the magic of the sacred pentagram of five wounds. In this it corresponds to divine magic, which does not force but establishes (or re-establishes) freedom of choice through the *presence* of the true, the beautiful and the good. Now, it is a matter in the magic of the sacred pentagram of five wounds of accomplishing the *living presence* of the good alongside the consciousness of the subject of the operation. For good does not *fight* evil; it does not struggle against it. The good is only present, or it is not. Its victory consists in that it results in being present, its defeat in that it is forced to be absent. And it is the five wounds which assure the presence of the good, i.e. the presence of pure will from above.

The following is an episode which is found in the "Considerations on the Stigmata of St. Francis" (fifth consideration) and which is well suited to serve as a key to the problem with which we are occupied.

A Franciscan friar prayed for eight years following the death of St. Francis that the secret words which the Seraphim had spoken to St. Francis when he gave him the stigmata would be revealed to him. Now, one day St. Francis appeared to him and to seven other friars and, turning towards this friar, spoke to him thus:

Know, dearest friar, that when I was on Mount Alverna, all rapt in the contemplation of the Passion of Christ, in this Seraphic vision I was by Christ thus stigmatised in my body; and then Christ said to me, "Knowest thou what I have done to thee? I have given thee the marks of my Passion in order that thou mayst be My standard-bearer. And even as I, on the day of My death, descended into limbo and drew thence all the souls I found therein, by virtue of my stigmatas, and led them up to paradise, so do I grant to thee from this hour (that thou mayst be conformed to Me in thy death as thou hast been in thy life) that after thou hast passed from this life thou shalt go every year, on the day of thy death, to purgatory, and shalt deliver all the souls thou shalt find there of thy three Orders, to wit, Minors, Sisters, and Penitents, and likewise the souls of thy devoted followers, and this, in virtue of thy stigmatas that I have given thee; and thou shalt lead them to paradise." And those words I told not while I lived in the world. ("Considerations on the Glorious Stigmata of St. Francis" in *The Little Flowers of St. Francis*, book ii, ch. 9; trsl. T. Okey, London, 1963, pp. 129-130)

This said, St. Francis suddenly disappeared. Numerous friars subsequently heard this narrative from the lips of the eight friars who were present at this vision and revelation of St. Francis. And *"Frater Jacobus Blancus lector Romanus praedicavit hoc et dixit se audisse ab uno fratre de supradictis octo"* ("Brother Jacobus Blancus, lector Romanus, proclaimed this and said that he had heard it from one of the above-named eight") adds the manuscript of Saint-Isidore (discussed by Paul Sabatier) at the end of the narrative.

Let us now analyse the narrative from the point of view of the magic of the sacred pentagram of the five wounds.

It may be noted first of all that the stigmata given to St. Francis are of a spiritual as well as a corporeal nature, for their virtue (i.e. their magical power) continues after his death. Also, here it is indicated that the virtue of the stigmata of St. Francis, as well as those of Christ himself, is revealed in that he is able to lead back souls from limbo and purgatory and conduct them to paradise. Let us mention, lastly, that the narrative is quite categorical concerning the statement that it is only by virtue of his stigmata that Jesus Christ prior to his resurrection led souls out of limbo and conducted them to paradise, and similarly it is only by virtue of his stigmata that St. Francis, also, withdraws from purgatory each year on the day of his death all souls who are bound to him by a spiritual tie and leads them to paradise.

Take the terms "limbo", "purgatory" and "paradise" in their meaning as understood by analogy and you have a clear and precise formula for the working of the magic of the sacred pentagram of five wounds: it effects a change from the natural state ("limbo") and from the state of human suffering ("purgatory") to that of the blessedness of the divine state ("paradise"). The operation of the magic of the sacred pentagram of five wounds therefore consists in transforming the natural state into the human state and this latter into the divine state. This is the work of spiritual alchemy of the transformation from Nature ("limbo"), and from the Human ("purgatory"), into the Divine ("paradise"), according to the traditional threefold division—Nature, Man and God.

Let us now consider more closely the *practical* meaning of the terms "limbo", "purgatory" and "paradise", in so far as they are stages in the work of transmutation —or *liberation*—of the magic of the sacred pentagram of five wounds.

Their *practical* meaning is not spatial, i.e. referring to "places", but refers rather to *states* of the human being—in body, soul and spirit. When we understand it thus, we shall readily discover that the three states are known to us through experience and that experience supplies us with the *keys of analogy* to be able to understand the ideas of "limbo", "purgatory" and "paradise" as such, i.e. on all planes and at every level—psychological, metaphysical and theological—of their application.

Each of us has had the experience of a harmonious state of good health accompanied by a carefree state of soul and calmness of spirit. It is what one calls *joie de vivre*, pure and simple. If there were no serious illnesses, sorrows and problems, this would be permanently our natural state. It is what Nature, in so far as it is virgin and unfallen, offers us, which we could enjoy constantly if there were no fallen elements in Nature—no sickness and sin, no sorrow, fear and remorse in ourselves—and if, above all, life as a whole was not the field which death reaps unceasingly. But we have nevertheless from time to time moments, hours, perhaps even whole days, of the experience of the natural *joie de vivre*, without sorrows or cares. And this experience supplies us with the "key of analogy" for understanding what the meaning of "limbo" is. "Limbo" is the natural state of physical and psychic health that Nature—outside and within ourselves—can offer us from itself without the assistance of supernatural or divine grace. "Limbo" is the virginal part of Nature (human nature and outer Nature) according to the traditional doctrine *"natura vulnerata non deleta"* ("Nature is wounded but not destroyed"). Those who know the *Bhagavad-Gita*, or who have occupied themselves at all with the Hindu tradition, will easily recognise in the state designated by the term "limbo" the state or *guna* of Nature (*prakriti*) that is called *sattva* in India (the other two *gunas* being called *tamas* and *rajas*).

Concerning the experience relating to "purgatory", it comprises all purging— suffering—physical, psychic and spiritual. It is corporeal, moral and intellectual suffering which is our intermediate state between the experience of the natural innocence of "limbo" and the moments of heavenly joy when the rays of "paradise" reach us.

We already experience here below a foretaste of "purgatory" and of "paradise". We suffer and the consolations of heaven are given us. Human life is natural innocent joy, and its ruin is through sin; what ensues is suffering and it is the rays of benediction from heaven which console us. This is our life. It consists of experiencing the *reality* of "limbo", "purgatory" and "paradise".

Now, the magic of the sacred pentagram of five wounds "leads souls out of limbo and purgatory and conducts them to paradise". This means to say that it makes heaven present in "limbo" and "purgatory", that it enables it to descend into the domain of innocent and suffering Nature. This, in turn, means to say that it introduces the supernatural into the natural, heals sickness, illumines consciousness and enables participation in the spiritual life. "Purgatory" includes *all* sickness and *all* suffering. "To be led out of it" signifies liberation from it, i.e. to be healed, illumined and reunited with the spirit.

The magic of the five wounds operates by the *presence* of the reality of the superhuman spiritual world by means of the wounds, and accomplishes the transmutation from the states of "limbo" and "purgatory" to the state of union with the Divine, or "paradise". Concerning the ritual or technical side of the magic of the sacred pentagram with five wounds, this is to be found outlined in the third Letter, relating to the Arcanum "The Empress".

The quinternary "united and bound to the decad" of which Saint-Martin speaks is therefore the quinternary or pentagram of five wounds. The other quinternary, qualified by Saint-Martin as "absolutely evil", is separated from the *decad*, i.e. from the five currents (or "members") of the human will, endowed with five wounds from the divine will. (The five currents of the human will endowed with five wounds also correspond to the letters YHSVH of the name: יהשוה — IHSCHUH, Jesus — as is accepted symbolically by Khunrath, Kircher, Saint-Martin and others, although in Hebrew the name of Jesus is written: יהשואה — IHSCHUAH).

But I shall not say, as radically as Saint-Martin does, that the quinternary separated from the decad is absolutely evil. It is, rather, *arbitrary* — and it is evil only in so far as the human personality emancipated from the Divine and from Nature is evil.

In any case the pentagram, other than that of the five wounds, is not the sign of "black magic", but rather that of arbitrary magic, or "grey magic", if you wish. Because it is the sign of the power of the personality as such — which is inevitably a mixture of good and evil, even when it acts with the best intentions in the world. Oswald Wirth says concerning this:

> Common magic deceives itself about the power of this sign, which by itself confers no power. The individual will is powerful only in the measure to which it is in harmony with a more general power... Let us not seek to develop the will artificially and to transform ourselves into athletes of the will... (Oswald Wirth, *Le Tarot des imagiers du moyen âge*, Paris, 1927, p. 123)

Regarding the two forms of the pentagram — with the point above and with the point below—they do not in any way correspond to the division of magic into "white magic" and "black magic" (although the traditional masters—Eliphas Lévi, for example—teach this). You can certainly draw the head of a goat (as Eliphas Lévi does) in the "reversed pentagram"; it does not become through this the sign of black magic. The two forms of the pentagram refer to human electricity (i.e. the electricity of the human organism accompanying the movements of the will)— of the *head* and of the *legs*, which has nothing to do with horns. It is the same electricity in both cases, with the sole difference that in the case of the pentagram with the point turned above it is the will of the intellect which moves the electrical currents, whilst in the case of the pentagram with the point turned below, it is the intelligence of the will which does so. The two poles of the will can equally serve good or evil—although in fact both represent a mixture of the two principles. It is true, however, that there is more chance in the case of the sign of the pentagram with the point turned above for reason and conscience to make the best of the operation than in the case of the reversed pentagram, but all depends here on the intellectual and moral state of the operator. A perverse intellectuality would certainly make worse use of the upright pentagram than a sound will motivated by a good intention would of the reversed pentagram. Therefore, let us not be afraid of the reversed pentagram, or depend too much on the upright pentagram.

But let us return to the quinternary bound and united to the fullness of the decad, i.e. to the sacred pentagram of five wounds. Let us consider it now not as an individual affair but rather as one for the whole of mankind.

The history of mankind—seen from its "nocturnal" side—is at root the operation of a limited number of magical formulae and signs. Whatever you may do, you place yourself under the aegis of such a formula and sign. The cross, the pentagram and the hexagram are signs and formulae which operate in the history of mankind. The cross is the vow and virtue of obedience, i.e. the sign and formula of faith, as horizontal human respiration and vertical divine respiration united together. The pentagram is initiative; it is effort and work, i.e. the vow and virtue of poverty—or the sign and formula of hope as the effect of the presence of divine light here below. The hexagram is the vow and virtue of chastity, i.e. the sign and formula of love, as the unity of Father, Son and Holy Spirit, and Mother, Daughter and Holy Soul. The spiritual history of mankind is the way from the cross to the pentagram, and from the pentagram to the hexagram, i.e. it is the *school* of obedience, poverty and chastity, and it is at the same time the *divine, magical operation* where love is attained through faith by means of hope.

The Middle Ages erected the cross above the nations, societies, aspirations and thoughts of Europe. This was the epoch of obedience and faith—accompanied by every imaginable human abuse. This was followed by an epoch where the dawn of hope made itself felt. Humanism, with its flourishing of Renaissance art, philosophy and science, was born under the sign of hope. The sign of the pentagram began its ascent. It was then that opposition arose between the sacred pentagram of five wounds and the pentagram of the emancipated personality. A purely humanistic art, science and magic had its development under the sign of the pentagram of hope in man, as opposed to the sign of the pentagram of hope in God, i.e. the sacred pentagram of the five wounds, under which latter sign Christian esotericism — Christian-orientated mysticism, gnosis, sacred magic and Hermeticism — has its development.

The impulse of freedom — of hope in emancipated man — has built up and demolished a great deal. It has created a materialistic civilisation without parallel, but at the same time it has destroyed the hierarchical order — the order of spiritual obedience. A series of religious, political and social revolutions has ensued.

But the hierarchical order is eternal and obedience is indispensable. Now new hierarchical orders are beginning to be established, replacing obedience by tyranny and dictatorship. For he who sows the wind shall reap the whirlwind (cf. Hosea ix, 7) — this is a truth that we are learning with so much suffering today. The pentagram of hope in emancipated man has in former times sown the wind — and we and our contemporaries are now reaping the whirlwind.

Now, the post of Pope in the spiritual history of mankind is that of guardian of the sacred pentagram of the five wounds, i.e. he guards the one legitimate way of passing from the cross to the pentagram and from the pentagram to the hexagram. The function of the spiritual post of Pope is to see to it that it is only *after* the cross is taken up that the pentagram has its ascent and that it is only *after* the sacred pentagram of the five wounds is taken up that the raising of the hexagram takes place. The mission of the post of Pope is to take care that spiritual obedience, poverty and chastity — free and holy — do not disappear from the world and that there are always people in the world who embrace them and represent them. For these three practical vows constitute the preliminary condition for living faith, luminous hope and ardent love, i.e. for the *spiritual respiration* of humanity. Mankind would suffocate spiritually without faith, hope and love or charity. And it would be bereft of these if the practice of spiritual obedience, poverty and chastity — free and holy — were to cease.

The post of Pope or the Holy See is a formula of divine magic — just as the post of Emperor is — in the history of humanity. It is what is meant by the esoteric term *Petrus* (Peter). (Πέτρα *=petra=* rock). *Petrus* is the term in the Old and in the New Testament designating the divine, immovable ordinance or formula of divine magic. This is why the post of Pope was founded upon the quality of *Petrus* (Peter):

> And I tell you, you are Peter (*Petrus*), and on this rock (*petra*)
> I will build my Church, and the gates of hell shall not prevail
> against it. (Matthew xvi, 18)

The five "gates of hell" — the will-to-greatness, the desire to take and to keep, the desire to advance and to hold on to at the expense of others—being the counter-formula, shall not prevail against the formula of the five wounds. And these wounds are the "keys to the kingdom of heaven".

The divine magical power of these keys is such that whatever is bound by their virtue on earth will be bound in heaven and that whatever is loosened by their virtue on earth will be loosened in heaven. For that which is above is as that which is below and that which is below is as that which is above. And when disobedience, greed and unchastity prevail on the earth of such a kind that there never was before—then it is the virtue of the keys or the sacred wounds which can re-establish the unity of that which is above and that which is below, i.e. "to bind" and "to loosen", by an act which, put into words, would have the tenor of the following:

> May that which is above *be* as that which is below, and may that
> which is below *be* as that which is above.

Meditation on the
Sixth Major Arcanum of the Tarot

THE LOVER

L'AMOUREUX

She seizes him and kisses him,
And with impudent face she says to him:
I had to offer sacrifices,
And today I have paid my vows.
So now I have come out to meet you,
To seek you eagerly, and I have found you.

                    (Proverbs vii, 13-15)

I, Wisdom, dwell in prudence,
And I possess knowledge and discretion...
I love those who love me,
And those who seek me find me.

                    (Proverbs viii, 12, 17)

Set me as a seal upon your heart,
As a ring upon your arm;
For love is strong as death...
Its flashes are flashes of fire,
A flame of the Eternal.

                (Song of Songs viii, 6-7)

LETTER VI

THE LOVER

Dear Unknown Friend,

Here the whole composition of the sixth Card is translated from the visual language of the Tarot into that of the poetry of Solomon. For there a dark-haired woman with an impudent face clad in a red robe seizes the shoulder of the young man whilst another, with fair hair and dressed in a blue mantle, makes appeal to his heart with a chaste gesture of her left hand. At the same time, above, a winged infant archer, standing out against a white sphere emitting red, yellow and blue flames, is about to let fly an arrow directed at the other shoulder of the young man. Does one not hear, in contemplating the sixth Card of the Tarot, a voice which says: "I have found you", and another which says: "Those who seek me find me"? Does one not recognise the voice of sensuality and the voice of the heart, and likewise the flashes of fire from above of which king Solomon speaks?

The central theme of the sixth Arcanum is therefore that of the practice of the vow of *chastity*, just as the fifth Arcanum had *poverty* as its theme and the fourth *obedience*. The sixth Arcanum is at the same time the summary of the two preceding Arcana—chastity being the fruit of obedience and poverty. It summarises the three vows or methods of spiritual discipline in contrasting them with the three trials or temptations opposed to these vows. The choice before which the young man of the sixth Arcanum finds himself placed is of greater significance than that between vice and virtue. It is a matter here of choice between on the one hand the way of obedience, poverty and chastity and on the other hand the way of power, richness and debauchery. The *practical* teaching of the Arcanum "The Lover" has to do with the three vows and the three corresponding temptations. For this is the *practical* doctrine of the hexagram or sexternary.

The three vows are, in essence, memories of paradise, where man was united with God (obedience), where he possessed everything at once (poverty), and where his companion was at one and the same time his wife, his friend, his sister and his mother (chastity). For the real presence of God necessarily entails the action of prostrating oneself in the face of Him "who is more me than I myself am"— and here lies the root and source of the vow of obedience; the vision of the forces, substances and essences of the world in the guise of the "garden of divine symbols" (the garden of Eden) signifies the possession of everything without choosing, without laying hold of, or without appropriating any particular thing isolated from the whole—and here lies the root and source of the vow of poverty; lastly, total communion between two, between one and another, which comprises the entire range of all possible relationships of spirit, soul and body between two polarised beings necessarily constitutes the absolute wholeness of spiritual, psychic and physical being, in love—and here lies the root and source of the vow of chastity.

One is chaste only when one loves with the totality of one's being. Chastity is not wholeness of being in indifference, but rather in the love which is "strong as death and whose flashes are flashes of fire, the flame of the Eternal". It is *living unity*. It is three—spirit, soul and body—which are *one*, and the other three— spirit, soul and body—which are *one*; and three and three make *six*, and six is *two*, and two is one.

This is the formula of chastity in love. It is the formula of *Adam-Eve*. And it is this which is the principle of chastity, the living memory of paradise.

And the celibacy of monks and nuns? How does the formula of chastity "Adam-Eve" apply here?

Love is strong as death, i.e. death does not destroy it. Death can neither let one forget nor let one cease to hope. Those of us—we human souls of today—who bear within ourselves the flame of the memory of Eden cannot forget it, nor can we cease to hope for it. And if human souls come into the world with the imprint of this memory, and also with the impression of knowing that the meeting with the other will not take place for them in this life here below, they will then live this life as if *widowed*, in so far as they *remember*, and as if *engaged*, in so far as they *hope*. Now, all true monks are widowers and fiancés, and all true nuns are widows and fiancées, in the depths of their hearts. The true celibate bears witness to the eternity of love, just as the miracle of true marriage bears witness to its reality.

Yes, dear Unknown Friend, life is profound and its profundity is like an abyss of fathomless depth. Nietzsche *felt* this and knew how to express it in his "Song of the Night" (*Nachtlied* from *Thus Spake Zarathustra*, part iii, ch. 15):

> *O Mensch, gib acht,*
> *Was spricht die tiefe Mitternacht—*
> *Ich schlief, ich schlief—aus tiefem Traum bin ich erwacht—*
> *Die Welt ist tief, noch tiefer als der Tag gedacht,*
> *Tief ist ihr Weh,*
> *Die Lust—noch tiefer als das Herzeleid—*
> *Weh spricht—Vergeh,*
> *Doch alle Lust will Ewigkeit, will tiefe, tiefe Ewigkeit.*

> O man! Take heed!
> What saith deep Midnight, indeed?
> I lay asleep, asleep—
> I waked from my deep dream—
> The world is deep,
> And deeper than ever day may deem.
> Deep is its woe—
> Joy—deeper yet than woe is she:
> Saith woe: Hence, go!
> Yet Joy would have Eternity—
> Profound, profound Eternity!
>   (Friedrich Nietzsche, *Thus Spake Zarathustra*)*

Thus, it is the same arrow—"the arrow of fire, of the flame of the Eternal"—which brings about true celibacy as well as true marriage. The heart of the monk is pierced—and this is why he is a monk—just as is the heart of the fiancé on the eve of the wedding. Where is more truth or more beauty to be found? Who can say?

And charity, the love of one's neighbour...what is its relationship with the love whose prototype is given by the formula "Adam-Eve"?

We are surrounded by innumerable living and conscious beings—visible and invisible. But rather than knowing that they really exist and that they are as much alive as we ourselves, it nevertheless appears to us that they have a *less real exis-*

*Trsl. A. Tille, revised M.M. Bozman, Everyman Library, 1958, p. 284-285 *tence* and that they are *less living* than we ourselves. For us it is WE who experience the full measure of the intensity of reality, whilst other beings seem, in comparison with ourselves, to be less real; their existence seems to be more of the nature of a shadow than full reality. Our thoughts tell us that this is an illusion, that beings around us are as real as we ourselves are, and that they live just as intensely as we do. Yet fine as it is to say these things, all the same we feel ourselves at the centre of reality, and we feel other beings to be removed from this centre. That one qualifies this illusion as "egocentricity", or "egoism", or "*ahamkara*" (the illusion of self), or the "effect of the primordial Fall", does not matter; it does not alter the fact that we feel ourselves to be more real than others.

Now, to feel something as real in the measure of its full reality is to love. It is love which awakens us to the reality of ourselves, to the reality of others, to the reality of the world and to the reality of God. In so far as we love ourselves, we feel real. And we do not love—or we do not love as much as ourselves—other beings, who seem to us to be less real.

Now, two ways, two quite different methods exist which can free us from the illusion "me, living—you, shadow", and we have a choice. The one is to *extinguish* love of oneself and to become a "shadow amongst shadows". This is the equality of indifference. India offers us this method of liberation from *ahamkara*, the illusion of self. This illusion is destroyed *by extending the indifference that one has for other beings to oneself*. Here one reduces oneself to the state of a shadow equal to the other surrounding shadows. *Maya*, the great illusion, is to believe that individual beings, me and you, should be nothing more than shadows—appearances without reality. The formula for realising this is therefore: "me, shadow—you, shadow".

The other way or method is that of *extending the love that one has for oneself to other beings*, in order to arrive at the realisation of the formula: "me, living—you, living". Here it is a matter of rendering other beings as real as oneself, i.e. of loving them as oneself. To be able to attain this, one has first to love one's *neighbour* as oneself. For love is not an abstract programme but, rather, it is *substance* and *intensity*. It is necessary therefore that one radiates the substance and intensity of love with regard to *one* individual being in order that one can begin to ray it out in all directions. "To be able to make gold one has to have gold," say the alchemists. The spiritual counterpart of this maxim is that in order to be able to love everyone one has to love or to have loved someone. This someone is one's "neighbour".

Who is one's neighbour, understood in the Hermetic sense, i.e. meaning at one and the same time in a mystical, gnostic, magical and metaphysical sense? It is the being nearest to one at or since the beginning; this is the sister-soul for all eternity; this is one's twin-soul, the soul together with whom one beheld the dawn of mankind.

The dawn of mankind: it is this which the Bible describes as paradise. Now, this was at the stage of existence that God said: "It is not good that Adam should be alone" (Genesis ii, 18).

To be: this is to love. To be alone: this is to love oneself. Now, "it is not good (*tov*) that Adam should be alone" means to say: it is not good that man loves nobody but himself. This is why YHVH-Elohim said: I will make him a helper similar (corresponding) to him. And as Eve was part of Adam himself, he loved her as himself. Eve was therefore the "neighbour", the being nearest to Adam ("bone of my bones and flesh of my flesh"—Genesis ii, 23).

This is the origin of love, and it is common both to love which unites man and woman and to love of one's neighbour. In the beginning there was only one love and its source was one, since its principle was one.

All forms of love (charity, friendship, paternal love, maternal love, filial love, brotherly love) derive from the same unique primordial root of the fact of the couple Adam-Eve. For it is then that love—the *reality* of the other—issued forth and could subsequently branch out and diversify. It is the warmth of love of the first couple (and it does not matter if there was only one couple or if there were thousands of them—it is a question of the fact of the first qualitative issuing forth of love and not of the number of simultaneous or successive cases of this issuing forth) which is reflected in the love of parents for their children, reflected in turn in the love of children for their parents, reflected again in the love of children amongst themselves, reflected lastly in the love for all kinship of human beings and beyond immediate kinship, by analogy, for all that lives and breathes. . . Love once born as substance and intensity, tends to spread, ramify and diversify according to the forms of human relationships into which it enters. It is a cascading current which tends to fill and inundate all. This is why when there is true love between parents, the children love their parents, by analogy, and love each other; they love, by analogy—as their brothers and sisters by "psychological adoption"— their friends in school and in the neighbourhood; they love (always by analogy) their teachers, tutors, priests, etc., through reflection of the love that they have for their parents; and later they love their husbands and wives, as their parents once loved one another.

All this is clearly the inverse of Sigmund Freud's pansexual doctrine. For Freud it is "libido" or sexual desire which is the basis of all human psychological activity, which constitutes the motivating energy thereof, and which then becomes— through the process of sublimation or direction through channels other than the satisfaction of sexual desire—creative force: socially, artistically, in science and religion. However the whole of love, understood in the sense of the formula "Adam-Eve", is to sexual desire as white light containing the seven colours is to the colour red. "Adam-Eve" love includes the whole range of undifferentiated colours, whilst Freud's libido is only a single colour isolated and separated from the whole. And this separation from the whole—and the *whole* is the principle of chastity—is exactly the inverse of chastity; it is the very principle of unchastity. For unchastity is nothing other than the autonomy of carnal desire, so that the wholeness of the human being—in spirit, soul and body—is ruined. Sexual desire is only one aspect of love—the aspect reflected by that part of the physical and psychic organism which is the special domain of the "four-petalled lotus"—and it constitutes only *one-seventh* of the human psychic-physical organism. There are therefore *six more aspects*, whose significance is in no way less, and which Freud's doctrine ignores (or even denies their existence).

Just as Karl Marx, being impressed by the partial truth (reduced to its simplest basis) that it is first necessary to eat in order to be able to think, raised the economic interest to THE principle of man and the history of civilisation, so Sigmund Freud, being impressed by the partial truth that it is first necessary to be born in order to be able to eat and to think, and that sexual desire is necessary for birth, raised this latter to THE principle of man and the whole of human culture. As Marx saw *homo oeconomicus* (economic man) at the basis of *homo sapiens*, so Freud saw *homo sexualis* (sexual man) at the basis of *homo sapiens*.

Alfred Adler could not follow his master in the attribution of absolute primacy to sex—his experience on many occasions contradicting this doctrine. Thus this founder of another school of depth psychology was led to the discovery that it is the will-to-power which plays the leading role at the foundation of the human being. Adler then advanced the doctrine of *homo potestatis*—man motivated by the will-to-power—instead of the *homo sapiens* of eighteenth century science, the *homo oeconomicus* of Marx, and the *homo sexualis* of Freud.

However, Carl Gustav Jung, whilst admitting the partial truth of the doctrines of Freud and Adler, was led by his clinical experience to the discovery of a much deeper layer of the psyche than that studied by Freud and Adler. He had to admit the reality of a *religious* layer, which lies at a much greater depth than the layers of sex and of the will-to-power. Thus, thanks to the work of Jung, man is fundamentally *homo religiosus*, a religious being, though he may also be an economic entity, a sexual entity and an entity aspiring to power.

Now, Carl Gustav Jung re-established the principle of chastity in the domain of psychology—the other psychological schools mentioned being contrary to chastity, since they break down the unity of the spiritual, psychic and physical elements of the human being. He discovered the divine breath at the core of the human being.

At the same time the work of Jung constitutes the inauguration of a new method in the domain of psychology. It is the method of exploration of psychic layers in succession—corresponding to the layers of archaeology, palaeontology and geology. And just as archaeology, palaeontology and geology regard the layers with which they have to do as archives of the past (as time become space), so does the depth psychology of the school of Jung treat psychic layers as the living past of the soul, which is as distant as the layer in question is deep. The measure of depth here is at the same time that of the history of the soul's past, going back beyond the threshold of birth. One can well discuss whether the layers are collective or individual, whether their continuance is due to heredity or reincarnation—but one can no longer deny the reality of these layers or their value as a key to the psychic history of man and mankind. More than that: one can no longer deny the fact that, in the psychic domain, *nothing dies* and that the whole past *lives present* in the diverse layers of the depths of consciousness—the "unconscious" or sub-consciousness—of the soul. Palaeontological and geological layers contain only the imprints and fossils of the now dead past; psychic layers, in contrast, constitute a living witness to the actual past. They are the past which continues to live. They are *memory*—not intellectual, but psychically *substantial*—of the actual past. For this reason nothing perishes and nothing is lost in the domain of the psyche; *essential* history, i.e. *real* joy and suffering, real religions and revelations of the past, continue to live in us, and it is in we ourselves that the key to the essential history of mankind is to be found.

Now, it is in we ourselves that there is to be found the "Edenic" layer, or that of paradise and the Fall, of which an account is found in the book of Genesis of Moses. Do you doubt the essential truth of this account? Descend into the depths of your own soul, descend as far as the roots, to the sources of feeling, will and intelligence—and you will *know*. You will know, i.e. you will have *certainty* that the Biblical narrative is true in the most profound and authentic sense of the word —in the sense that you must deny yourself, deny the witness of the inner *structure* of your own soul, in order to be able to doubt the intrinsic truth of Moses' account. The descent into the depths of your own soul in meditating upon the account of paradise in Genesis will render you incapable of doubt. Such is the nature of the certainty that one can have here.

But, of course, it is not a matter of certainty with regard to the garden, its trees, the serpent, the apple or other forbidden fruit, but rather with regard to the vital psychic and spiritual *realities* that these images or symbols reveal. It is not the symbolic *language* of the account which gives certainty of its truth, but rather what it expresses.

It expresses in symbolic language the first layer (first in the sense of the *root* of all that is human in human nature) of human psychic life, or its "beginning". Now, knowledge of the beginning, *initium* in Latin, is the essence of *initiation*. Initiation is the conscious experience of the *initial microcosmic state* (this is the Hermetic initiation), and of the *initial macrocosmic state* (this is the Pythagorean initiation). The first is a conscious descent into the depths of the human being, to the initial layer. Its method is *enstasy*, i.e. experience of the depths at the foundation within oneself. Here one becomes more and more *profound* until one awakens within oneself to the primordial layer—or the "image and likeness of God"—which is the aim of enstasy. It is above all by means of the sense of spiritual touch that this experience of enstasy is effected. One can compare it to a chemical experiment undergone on the psychic and spiritual plane.

The second initiation experience—that we have designated "Pythagorean" from a historical point of view—is based above all on the auditory sense or sense of spiritual hearing. It is essentially *musical*, just as the first is substantial or *alchemical*. It is by *ecstasy*—or rapture, or going *out* of oneself—that the macrocosmic layers ("spheres" or "heavens") reveal themselves to consciousness. Pythagoras' "music of the spheres" was this experience, and it is this which was the source of the Pythagorean doctrine concerning the musical and mathematical structure of the macrocosm. For sounds, numbers and geometrical forms were the three stages of representing and mentally visualising the ineffable experience of the "music of the spheres".

It is only from a historical point of view that we have designated as "Pythagorean" the macrocosmic initiation by means of ecstasy. For it is in no way a prerogative of the epoch prior to Christianity. The following is what the apostle Paul says of his own experience of the "spheres" or "heavens" in ecstasy:

> I know a man in Christ who fourteen years ago was *carried up* to the third heaven—whether in the body or out of the body I do not know, God knows. And I know that this man was raised up into *paradise*—whether in the body or out of the body I do not know, God knows—and he *heard* ineffable words, which man is not allowed to express—(*et audivit arcane verba, quae non licet homini loqui—kai ekousen arreta remata, ha ouk exon anthropo lalesai*) (2 Corinthians xii, 2-4)

St. Paul was therefore *carried up* to the third heaven or the third macrocosmic sphere and he was then *raised up* into paradise where he *heard* ineffable words. His macrocosmic *initiation* through ecstacy therefore took place in the sphere of paradise, the conscious experience of which ("he *heard* ineffable words") is its aim, just as it is also the aim of initiation through enstasy, which latter is characterised by experience of the primordial layer at the root of the human being or microcosm. The macrocosmic sphere of paradise and the microcosmic layer of Eden are the *initia*, the "beginnings", to which one is initiated in the macrocosmic initiation as well as in the microcosmic initiation. Ecstasy to the heights beyond oneself and enstasy into the depths within oneself lead to knowledge of the same fundamental truth.

Christian esotericism unites these two methods of initiation. The Master has two groups of disciples—"disciples of the day" and "disciples of the night"—the first being disciples of the way of enstasy and the latter those of the way of ecstasy. He has also a third group of disciples "of day *and* night", i.e. who possess the keys to both doors at once, to the door of ecstasy and that of enstasy. Thus, the apostle John, author of the Gospel of the Word-made-flesh, was at the same time he who listened to the heart of the Master. He had the twofold experience—macrocosmic and microcosmic—of the Cosmic Word and the Sacred Heart, of which the litany says: "*Cor Jesu, rex et centrum omnium cordium*" ("Heart of Jesus, king and centre of all hearts"). It is thanks to this twofold experience that the Gospel which he wrote is at one and the same time so cosmic and so humanly intimate—of such *heights* and *depths* simultaneously. There, the macrocosmic solar sphere and the microcosmic solar sphere are united, which explains the singular magic of this Gospel.

For the *reality* of paradise is the unity of the macrocosmic solar sphere and the microcosmic solar layer—the sphere of the cosmic heart and the solar foundation of the human heart. Christian initiation is the conscious experience of the heart of the world and the solar nature of man. God-Man is the Initiator, and there is no other.

What we understand by the term "Initiator" is what the early Christians understood by the word *Kyrios* (*Dominus* or "Lord"). With this, Christian esotericism or Hermeticism is in full accord—with absolute sincerity, today as in the past—when the words of the Creed are recited in church:

> *Et in UNUM DOMINUM Jesum Christum, Filium Dei unigenitum,*
> *Et ex Patre natum ante omnia saecula,*
> *Deum de Deo, lumen de lumine,*
> *Deum verum de Deo vero,*
> *Genitum, non factum, consubstantialem Patri*
> *per quem omnia facta sunt;*
> *Qui propter nos homines, et propter nostram salutem descendit de coelis.*
> *Et incarnatus est de Spiritu Sancto ex Maria Virgine*
> *Et homo factus est.*

> We believe in *one Lord*, Jesus Christ, the only Son of God,
> eternally begotten of the Father,
> God from God, Light from Light,
> true God from true God,
> begotten, not made, of one Being with the Father.
> Through him all things were made.
> For us men and for our salvation he came down from heaven:
> by the power of the Holy Spirit he became incarnate from the Virgin Mary,
> and was made man.

We bow with respect and gratitude before all the great human souls of the past and present—the sages, the righteous, the prophets, the saints of all continents and all epochs throughout the whole of human history—and we are ready to learn from them all that they wish and are able to teach, but we have only one sole Initiator or Lord; we are obliged to reiterate this for the sake of certainty.

But let us return to the theme of paradise.

"Paradise" is therefore at one and the same time the fundamental layer of our soul and a cosmic sphere. One finds it just as well through enstasy as by ecstasy. It is the realm of beginning, and therefore of principles. Above we came across the principle of the three vows: obedience, poverty and chastity. Paradise, being the realm of beginning and principles, is at the same time that of the beginning of the Fall or the principle of *temptation*, i.e. the principle of transition from obedience to disobedience, from poverty to greed, and from chastity to unchastity.

The temptation in paradise was threefold, just as was the temptation of Jesus Christ in the wilderness. The following are the essential elements of the triple temptation in paradise, as it is described in the account of the Fall in the book of Genesis:

1. Eve *listened* to the voice of the serpent;
2. She *"saw* that the tree was good for food, and that it was a delight to the eyes" (Genesis iii, 6);
3. She *"took* of its fruit and ate; and she also gave some to her husband, and he ate" (Genesis iii, 6).

The voice of the serpent is that of the living being ("animal") whose intelligence is most advanced ("the most artful") amongst all living beings ("animals") whose consciousness is turned towards the horizonal ("animals of the *fields*"). Now, the intelligence of Adam-Eve was, before the Fall, *vertical*; their eyes had not yet been "opened", and they "were both naked, and were not ashamed" (Genesis ii, 25), i.e. they were conscious of everything vertically—from above to below or, in other words, in God, through God and for God. They were not conscious of "naked" things, i.e. things separated from God. The formula expressing their perception, their vision of things was: "That which is above is as that which is below, and that which is below is as that which is above" (*Tabula Smaragdina*, 2). Thus, although they "were both naked", they "were not ashamed". Because they saw divine ideality expressing itself through phenomenal reality. It was vertical con-sciousness (simultaneous knowledge of the ideal and the real), whose principles are found formulated in the Emerald Table. The formula of horizontal consciousness of the serpent (*nahasch*) would be that of realism, pure and simple: "That which is in me is as that which is outside of me, and that which is outside of me is as that which is in me." This is horizontal con-sciousness (simultaneous knowledge of the subjective and the objective), which sees things not in God, but separated from him or "naked"—within itself, through itself and for itself. And as the self here replaces God (horizontal consciousness being that of the opposition of subject and object), the serpent says that on the day when Adam-Eve (Adam and Eve) eat fruit from the tree which is in the middle of the garden, their eyes will open and they will be *as gods*, i.e. the self will replace the function previously filled by God and that they will know good and evil. If before they saw things in divine light, they will see them now in their own light, i.e. the function of illumination will belong to them, just as once it belonged to God. The *source* of the light will be transferred from God to man.

This was the temptation that Eve heard in listening to the voice of the serpent. Its essence is the principle of *power*, which is autonomy of the light of consciousness. And Eve *listened* to the voice of the serpent. This voice was as audible to her as the other voice bearing from above the single commandment: "You may eat of every tree of the garden; but of the tree of knowledge of good and evil you shall not eat, for on the day that you eat of it you shall die" (Genesis ii, 16-17).

She therefore heard *two* voices, two inspirations arising from contrary sources. Here is the origin and the principle of doubt. Doubt is twofold inspiration. Faith is a single inspiration. Certainty is vanquished doubt; it is faith regained.

Obedience, the principle of obedience, is devotion without reserve to the *sole* voice from above. Now, the very fact that Eve *listened* to another voice than that from above, that she *compared* the two voices, i.e. considered them as if they belonged to the *same plane* (and therefore she doubted), this very fact was an act of spiritual *disobedience* and was the root cause and beginning of the Fall.

It was then that she looked at the tree and saw that it "was good for food, and that it was a delight to the eyes"—this was the second phase of the temptation and the second stage of the Fall. For it was after having listened to the voice of the serpent that she looked at the tree. She looked at it in a new way—no longer as formerly, when the sole voice from above vibrated in her being, when she experienced not the least attraction for the tree, but rather now with the word of the serpent vibrating in her being—with a questioning, comparing, *doubting* look, i.e. *ready to have experience*. Because when one is in doubt, one is induced to make experiments in order to dispel it—if one does not surmount it by raising oneself to a higher plane.

It was in looking at the tree in this new way that it appeared to her "good for food, and a delight to the eyes". To be induced to seek experience is the beginning and the principle of greed, the principle opposed to poverty.

It was after having looked at the tree in a new way that Eve stretched forth her hand and "she took of its fruit and ate; and she also gave some to her husband, and he ate". Here is the third phase of the temptation and the third stage of the Fall: it is to escape from doubt by plunging into experience and making the other take part.

Here is the beginning and the principle of unchastity, contrary to the principle of chastity. Because to seek experiences or to make experiments *based on doubt* is the very essence of carnal, psychic and spiritual unchastity. For this reason one does not carry out experiments in Christian esotericism or Hermeticism. One would never take recourse to experiments with a view to dispelling doubt. One has experiences, of course, but one does not *make* experiments. Because it would be contrary to the holy vow of chastity to put forward a hand and to *take* from the tree of knowledge. The spiritual world does not in any way suffer experimenters. One seeks, one asks, one knocks at its door. But one does not open it by force. One waits for it to be opened.

The Christian doctrine and experience of *grace* expresses the very essence of chastity, just as it also contains the principles of poverty and obedience. It is the doctrine concerning chaste relationships between that which is below and that which is above. God is not an object and neither is he an object of knowledge. He is the *source* of illuminatory and revelatory grace. He cannot be *grasped*, but he can certainly reveal himself.

Here we have chastity, poverty and obedience underlying the Christian doctrine and experience of grace. Now, all Christian esotericism or Hermeticism, including here all its mysticism, gnosis and magic, is founded on the experience and doctrine of grace, one of the results of which is *initiation*. Initiation is an act of grace from above. It cannot be achieved or produced by any technical outer or inner procedures. One does not initiate oneself; one *becomes* initiated.

Grace...are we not tired of the age-old repetition of this subject in Sunday sermons in church, in theological treatises, in the writings of mystics and, lastly, in the pompous declarations of monarchs—be they "High-Christian", "Catholic", "Orthodox" or "defenders of the Faith"? Have we not heard and read about it to the point of satiety...whenever and wherever the perfume of incense is smelt and spiritual hymns are heard? Lastly, is not a disciple of modern Hermeticism—he who is getting ready to dare the great adventure of the quest for the Great Arcanum—in the right to ask that he be spared sermons on this mollifying and monotonous subject? Does it not presume too little of his character to invite him to renounce the magnificent magical quaternary—"to dare, to will, to be silent, and to know"—for the whining *Kyrie eleison*?

There is nothing more banal than the rising of the sun which repeats itself day after day throughout innumerable millions of years. Yet it is thanks to this banal phenomenon that our eyes—organs for the light of the sun—see all the new things that life brings. Just as the light of the sun renders us seeing with regard to things of the physical world, so does the light of the spiritual sun—grace—render us seeing with regard to what is brought about from the spiritual world. Light is necessary in order to be able to see there, as well as here.

Similarly, air is necessary in order to breathe and to live. Is not the air which surrounds us a perfect analogy for the *gratia gratis data*—for gratuitously bestowed grace? Because to live in the spirit, vivifying spirit is necessary, which is the air of spiritual respiration.

Can one produce artificially intellectual, moral or artistic *inspiration*? Can the lungs produce the air which they need for respiration?

Now, the *principle* of grace underlies earthly life as well as spiritual life. It is wholly—below and above—ruled by the *laws* of obedience, poverty and chastity. The lungs know that it is necessary to breathe—and they obey. The lungs know that they are in want—and they breathe in. They love purity—and they breathe out. The very process of breathing teaches the laws of obedience, poverty and chastity, i.e. it is a lesson (by analogy) in grace. Conscious breathing in of the reality of grace is Christian *Hatha-yoga*. Christian *Hatha-yoga* is the *vertical* breathing of prayer and benediction—or, in other words, one opens oneself to grace and one receives it.

With respect to the magnificent quaternary of traditional magic: "to dare, to will, to be silent and to know", it is formulated — *mutandis mutatis* — by the Master in the following way:

> Ask, and it will be given you;
> Seek, and you will find;
> Knock, and it will be opened to you.
> For everyone who asks receives,
> And he who seeks finds,
> And to him who knocks it will be opened.
> (Matthew vii, 7-8)

It is a matter of daring to ask, of the will to seek, of being silent in order to knock and of knowing when it is opened to you. For knowledge does not happen automatically; it is what is revealed when the door is opened.

This is the formula of the synthesis of effort and grace, of the principle of work and that of receptivity, and, lastly, of merit and gift. This synthesis enunciates the absolute law of all spiritual progress and, consequently, all spiritual discipline, whether it be practised by a solitary Christian Hermeticist, or by a community in a cloister or convent, or by a religious or mystical order, or by any esoteric or Christian-Hermetic fraternity. It is the law which every Christian disciple, of every Christian spiritual school, obeys. And Christian Hermeticism, i.e. the whole of traditional mysticism, gnosis, magic and occult philosophy, passed through baptism and transfiguration by the fire, light and life of Christianity, is in no way an exception here. Hermeticism without grace is only sterile erudite historicism; Hermeticism without effort is only superficial sentimental aestheticism. There is certainly THE WORK in Hermeticism, and this work is the child of grace and effort.

Dear Unknown Friend, if you have knowledge of theology, you will recognise here the pure and simple doctrine of the Catholic Church concerning the relationship between work and grace. You find here again the rejection of Pelagianism, according to which it is only work (or effort) which counts, and also of Luther's Protestantism, according to which it is only grace which counts. You find here the doctrine of the Catholic Church — *natura vulnerata, non deleta* — is also implied, i.e. that Nature is not entirely corrupt in consequence of the Fall, but that it preserves a virgin element and that consequently there is also an element in human nature which is therefore capable of effort and work which *counts*.

Thus, does Christian Hermeticism simply borrow the fundamental principles of its Hermetic-philosophical teaching from Catholic theology?

It should not be forgotten that Christian Hermeticism is not a religion apart, nor a church apart, nor even a science apart, which would compete with religion, with the Church, or with science. It is the connecting link (hyphen) between mysticism, gnosis and magic, expressed through symbolism — symbolism being the means of expression of the dimensions of *depth* and *height* (and therefore of enstasy and ecstasy), of all that is universal (which corresponds to the dimension of *breadth*), and of all that is traditional (corresponding to the dimension of *length*). Being Christian, Hermeticism accepts the cross of the universality, the tradition, the depth and the height of Christianity, in the sense of the apostle Paul when he said:

> That you, being rooted and grounded in love, may have power to comprehend with all the saints *what is the breadth and length and height and depth*, and to know the love of Christ which surpasses knowledge, that you may be filled with all the fullness of God. (Ephesians iii, 18-19)

This is the complete formula of initiation.

Now, in aspiring to knowledge and experience of the depth and height of Universal Christianity—i.e. Catholic and traditional, that is, of the Church—Hermeticism borrows nothing and cannot borrow anything from the Church, since it is nothing other, and *is unable* to be anything other, than an aspect of the Church itself, namely the aspect of its dimension of depth and height. It is therefore flesh of its flesh and blood of its blood; it does *not borrow* from the Church, since it *is part* of it. It is the *invisible* aspect of universality (in space) and tradition (in time), both of which become visible in the Church. For the Church is not only universal and traditional, but also profound and sublime. Now, Christian Hermeticism is only the *vertical aspect*, i.e. that of depth and height, of the Church. This in no way means to say that individual Hermeticists will be in possession of all that is profound and sublime (i.e. all the esotericism) of the Church; it means to say only that one is a Christian Hermeticist in so far as one has consciousness of the depth and height of the universal tradition of Christianity and that each person who has this experience and consciousness represents Christian Hermeticism. Then, are all the Church doctors who teach the way of spiritual experience beyond theoretical theology, and all the saints and mystics of the Church who have had this experience, at the same time Hermeticists? Yes, they are in so far as they are witnesses and representatives of the profound and sublime in Christianity. They all have much to say to modern Hermeticists, who have much to learn from them. Take for example *De triplici via* ("The Threefold Way") by St. Bonaventura; there you will read:

> Note, lastly, what the Truth must be:
> 1. In the first Hierarchy:
>   evoked by the utterance of prayer,
>   work of the Angels;
>   heard in study and reading,
>   work of the Archangels;
>   announced through example and preaching,
>   work of the Principalities.

2. In the second Hierarchy:
   joined with as refuge and place of indulgence,
     work of the Powers;
   apprehended through zeal and emulation,
     work of the Virtues;
   conjoined with in self-deprecation and mortification,
     work of the Dominions.
3. In the third Hierarchy:
   worshipped through sacrifice and praise,
     work of the Thrones;
   admired through ecstasy (going out of oneself)
   and contemplation,
     work of the Cherubim;
   embraced in kiss and dilection (*amplectanda per
   osculum et dilectionem*),
     work of the Seraphim.
Note diligently what I say here,
because this is a fountain of life.
> (St. Bonaventura, *De triplici via*, iii, 14)

Just a brief fragment to furnish material for years of meditation! Can one, being a Hermeticist, allow oneself to ignore such testimonies (and there are hundreds of them) of the spiritual world and its authentic experience? Fabre d'Olivet, Eliphas Lévi, Saint-Yves d'Alveydre, Guaita, Papus and Péladan certainly merit being studied — just as do so many others of Hermetic and occult movements — but studying them alone does not suffice. Are they the only authentic witnesses and are their works the only first-hand sources of the reality of the spiritual world and experience of it? Let us therefore take heed of *all* those who know through experience, and let us seek in the first place for the *authenticity* of the experience instead of for erudition and theoretical speculation.

But let us return to the theme of temptation. It is threefold, as we have seen. We are able therefore to speak of three fundamental temptations which relate to the three fundamental conditions of the state of grace from paradise, or to the three vows which form the basis of all spiritual culture following the Fall: obedience, poverty and chastity. This is the *practical* meaning of the hexagram or the seal of Solomon: ✡ . This seal is that of the memory of paradise and the Fall, i.e. it concerns the *Law* (Torah). For the Law is the child of paradise and the temptation.

Since the New Alliance is the fulfillment of the Old, the work of redemption began with the repetition of the three primordial temptations. But this time it was the Son of Man who was tempted, and the temptation took place not in the garden of Eden but rather in a terrestrial wilderness. And this time it was not the serpent ("the most artful amongst animals of the fields") who tempted him, but the "prince of this world", i.e. the "new man", the "superman" or the *other* "son of man"—who, if incarnated, would be the realisation of the promise of freedom made by the serpent.

Antichrist, the ideal of biological and historical *evolution without grace*, is not an individuality or entity created by God, but rather the *egregore* or phantom generated through the biological and historical evolution opened up by the serpent, who is the author and master of the biological and historical evolution that science studies and teaches. The antichrist is the ultimate *product* of this evolution without grace and not an entity *created* by God—the act of divine *creation* being always, without exception, an act of grace. He is therefore an *egregore*, an artificial being who owes his existence to collective generation *from below*.

Let us ponder, therefore, on the notion of *"egregore"* with a view to understanding better what the antichrist is—this important and enigmatic figure of esotericism and Christian Hermeticism, who is at the same time the source of the temptation in the wilderness.

To begin with, here is what Robert Ambelain says in *La Kabbale pratique*:

> One gives the name *egregore* to a *force* generated by a powerful spiritual current and then nourished at regular intervals, according to a rhythm in harmony with the universal life of the cosmos, or to a *union of entities* united by a common characteristic nature. (Robert Ambelain, *La Kabbale pratique*, Paris, 1951, p. 175)

This is a definition which leaves nothing more to be desired. It is unfortunately muddled up by the paragraph which immediately follows:

> In the Invisible, beyond the physical perception of man, exist artificial beings—generated by devotion, enthusiasm and fanaticism—that one names *egregores*. These are the souls of great spiritual currents, good or evil. The *Mystical Church*, *Heavenly Jerusalem*, the *Body of Christ* and all these synonymous names are the epithets that one commonly gives to the *egregore* of Catholicism. Freemasonry, Protestantism, Islam, Buddhism are *egregores*. Great political ideologies are other *egregores*. (ibid., p. 175)

Here is a singular mixture of truth and falsehood. What is true here is that invisible artificial collectively-engendered beings exist, i.e. that *egregores* are real; but what is false is the confusion of things which are of an entirely different nature (the "Body of Christ" and "political ideologies"!) without distinguishing the substance here. Because if one classifies the Mystical Church, the Body of Christ, Freemasonry and Buddhism as *egregores*, i.e. as "artificial beings generated by devotion, enthusiasm and fanaticism", why not consider God also as an *egregore*?

No, there are superhuman spiritual entities which are not artificially engendered, but which manifest themselves and *reveal* themselves. The confusion between that which descends from above and that which is engendered from below is, moreover, very widespread amongst materialistic scientists as also amongst occultists. Thus, many biologists consider the unity of consciousness—or the human soul—as the epiphenomenon or sum-product of millions of points of consciousness belonging to the cells of the organism's nervous system. For them the "soul" is only an *egregore* engendered collectively by millions of individual cells. But this is not so. The *egregore* of the cells certainly exists—this is the *phantom*, of an electromagnetic nature, which resists decomposition after death for some time and which can manifest in "haunted houses", etc. But this phantom has nothing to do either with the soul itself or with the subtle bodies (etheric or life body, and astral or soul body) with which the soul is clothed in addition to the physical body.

Now, to say that the Mystical Church or the Body of Christ, for example, is an *egregore* is to advance the thesis that it is a phantom engendered by millions of believers, just as the phantoms of the dead are engendered by millions of cells. The confusion of the *soul* and the *phantom* is a sufficiently serious error. No less serious is the case of confusion of *revelations* and *inventions*—of spiritual beings who reveal themselves *from above*, and *egregores* engendered artificially from below. Because *egregores*, as powerful as they may be, have only an ephemeral existence, whose duration depends entirely on galvanising nourishment on the part of their creators. However, it is the souls and spirits from above—forming, inspiring and directing communities of human beings—who nourish and vivify human souls: for example, Archangels (who are the spirits of nations); Principalities (Archai or "time spirits"); the spiritual entity which is behind Tibetan Buddhism; not to mention Christ, whose Flesh and Blood each day vivifies and unites the Church (Christ's Mystical Body). *Egregores* are therefore nourished by men, whilst the latter are nourished by souls and spirits from above.

Nevertheless, although God, Christ, the Holy Virgin, the spiritual hierarchies, the saints, the Church (or the Mystical Body of Christ) are real entities, there still exists also a phantom or *egregore* of the Church, which is its "double", just as every man, every nation, every religion, etc., have their "doubles". But just as he who sees in Russia, for example, only the bear, in France only the cock and in Germany only the wolf, is being unfair towards the country of the Heart, the country of Intelligence and the country of Initiative—so is one being unjust towards the Catholic Church when one sees, instead of the Mystical Body of Christ, only its historical phantom, the fox. In order to see rightly one has to look rightly. And to look rightly means to endeavour to see through the mists of the phantoms of things. This is one of the principal practical precepts of Christian Hermeticism. It is thanks to the effort to see through the phantoms that one arrives at knowledge of the depth and height spoken of by the apostle Paul, which is the very essence of Hermeticism.

Regarding the antichrist, this is the *phantom of the whole of mankind*, the being engendered through the whole historical evolution of humanity. He is the "superman" who haunts the consciousness of all those who seek to elevate themselves through their own effort, without grace. He appeared to Friedrich Nietzsche and showed him "in an instant all the kingdoms of the world" which have existed, exist and will exist, in the circle of eternal return (*die ewige Wiederkehr*); he invited him to cast himself down into the domain which is beyond good and evil (*jenseits von Gut und Böse*), and to embrace and announce the gospel of *evolution*, the gospel of the will-to-power (*Wille zur Macht*) — *this*, and this alone ("*Gott ist tot*. . .", i.e. "God is dead"), transforms stone (inorganic matter) into bread (organic matter), and organic matter into animal, and animal into man, and man into superman (*Uebermensch*), who is beyond good and evil and who obeys only his own will ("*O mein Wille, meine Notwendigkeit, du bist mein Gesetz*. .").

He appeared to Karl Marx and showed him "in an instant all the kingdoms of the world" where all the slaves of the past are transformed into sovereign masters who no longer obey either God, having dethroned him, or Nature, having subjugated her, and who eat their bread which they owe solely to their own knowledge and effort in transforming stone into bread.

And the phantom of humanity has appeared to many others. He appeared also to the Son of Man in the desert. This was the meeting of divine Law made flesh and the law of the serpent — biological and historical evolution — made soul.

Divine Law is grace; it is the activity descending from the Holy Trinity which was revealed forty days before the temptation in the wilderness, when the baptism of Jesus in the Jordan was accomplished by John the Baptist. The law of the serpent is the action of the will moving gropingly forward, snaking through epochs and layers of biological evolution, passing from form to form; it is the triad of the will-to-power, the "groping trial" and the transformation of that which is gross into that which is subtle.

Vertical trinitarian grace and the triadic spirit of horizontal evolution met, therefore, in the consciousness of the Son of Man forty days after the baptism in the Jordan. Then the three temptations of the Son of Man took place. And just as the baptism in the Jordan is the prototype of the Holy Sacrament of Baptism, so is the meeting of grace (received at the baptism in the Jordan) with the quintessence of the evolutionary impulse since the Fall the prototype of the Holy Sacrament of Confirmation. For it is then that grace from above is firmly established against the law from below. It is then that evolution gives way to grace.

The three temptations of the Son of Man in the wilderness were his experience of the directing impulses of evolution, namely the will-to-power, the "groping trial" and the transformation of the gross into the subtle. They signify at the same time the test of the three vows — the vows of obedience, chastity and poverty.

It is with the last trial that Matthew (ch. iv) begins his account of the temptation of Jesus Christ. For the celestial fullness (*pleroma*) which descended at the time of the baptism in the Jordan brought with it the corresponding terrestrial emptiness (*kenoma*), which is expressed in the Gospel account by the solitude, the wilderness and the fasting.

> Then Jesus was led up by the Spirit into the wilderness to be
> tempted by the devil. And he fasted forty days and forty nights,
> and afterward he was hungry. (Matthew iv, 1-2)

Hunger of the spirit, the soul and the body is the experience of *emptiness* or poverty. It is therefore the vow of poverty which is put to the test when "the tempter came and said to him: If you are the Son of God, command these stones to become loaves of bread" (Matthew iv, 3). "Command these stones to become loaves of bread"— this is the very essence of the aspiration of humanity in the scientific epoch, namely to victory over poverty. Synthetic resins, synthetic rubber, synthetic fibre, synthetic vitamins, synthetic proteins and...eventually synthetic bread!— When? Soon, perhaps. Who knows?

"Command these stones to become bread"— this is the formula of evolution in the sense of "transformism" belonging to the mentality of some academics, who teach that the plant kingdom (i.e. "bread") is only a transformation of the mineral kingdom (i.e. "these stones"), and that consequently organic matter ("bread") is only the result of the physical and chemical regrouping of little molecules into giant molecules ("macromolecules") in the process of "polymerisation". Polymerisation is therefore considered today by a number of scientists as the possible — even probable — equivalent of the operation proposed by the tempter in the wilderness, namely the transformation of stones into bread.

The operation proposed by the tempter is at the same time the dominant motif of the doctrines overrunning the world today which regard the economic life as primary and the spiritual life as its epiphenomenon or as an "ideological superstructure" upon the economic basis. That which is below is primary and that which is above is secondary, since it is matter which engenders spirit — such is the dogma commonly underlying "economicism" and "transformism", and the statement made by the tempter to the Son of Man. And this was his reply to this dogma: "Man shall not live by bread alone, but by every word that proceeds from the mouth of God" (Matthew iv, 4).

Let us ponder on this formula.

It expresses, in the first place, the essence of the vow of poverty. For the vow of poverty is to live as much from the word which comes from the mouth of God as from the bread which enters the mouth of man. Then it *adds* to the law of biological nourishment, where the kingdoms *lower* than man serve him food, the new law of grace, where it is the kingdom *higher* than man, the kingdom of heaven, which feeds him. This means to say that not only the spirit and the soul of man are able to *live*, i.e. to receive impulses, forces and substances from above, but also his body. The vivifying spiritual effect of divine magic or grace with respect to the spiritual and psychic life is the millennial-old common experience of sincere Christians, but it is less known that there were — and there are — cases where the body itself can go without any food for a lapse of time sufficient to cause death from biological hunger a hundred-fold. Thus, Teresa Neumann lived in our time at Konnarsreuth (Bavaria) solely from Holy Communion for decades; St. Catherine of Sienna lived nine years from Holy Communion alone; St. Lidvina of Schiedam (near Rotterdam, Holland) likewise lived for many years exclusively from Holy Communion—to cite only the cases that are well-verified.

This is the *significance* of the words: "Man shall not live by bread alone but by every word that proceeds from the mouth of God." Here is its principal implication: as the law of evolution, the law of the serpent, comprises the struggle for existence and as "bread" or food is the principal factor in the struggle for existence, the fact of the entry of grace into human history since Jesus Christ signifies at the same time the possibility of gradually abolishing the struggle for existence. It is therefore the vow of poverty which will abolish it.

> Then the devil took him to the holy city, and set him on the pinnacle of the temple, and said to him: If you are the Son of God, throw yourself down; for it is written, "He will give his Angels charge of you," and "On their hands they will bear you up, lest you strike your foot against a stone." Jesus said to him: Again it is written, "You shall not tempt the Lord your God!" (Matthew iv, 5-7)

This is the "groping trial", to which natural evolution owes much, which speaks this time. It is the *method* of so-called natural evolution which has replaced since the Fall the world created by God (i.e. "paradise"). Because evolution proceeds gropingly from form to form, trying and rejecting, then trying anew. . .The world of evolution from protozoa to vertebrates and from vertebrates to mammals and then to apes and to *pithecanthropus* is neither the accomplishment of absolute wisdom nor absolute goodness. It is rather the work of a really vast intelligence and a very resolute will pursuing a definite aim determined by the method of "trial and error". One could say that it is a matter more of a great scientific intellect and the will of an experimenter which is revealed in natural evolution (the existence of which one can no longer deny), rather than divine wisdom and goodness. The tableau of evolution that the natural sciences—above all biology—have at last obtained as the result of prodigious work reveals to us *without any doubt* the work of a very subtle, but imperfect, intellect and a very determined, but imperfect, will. It is therefore the serpent, "the most artful animal of the fields", that the world of biological evolution reveals to us, and not God. It is the serpent who is the "prince of this world", and who is the author and director of the purely biological evolution following the Fall. Read *The Phenomenon of Man* by Pierre Teilhard de Chardin, which gives the best summary and interpretation that I know of natural evolution; study this book and you *could not* arrive at any other conclusion than that the world of evolution is the work of the serpent of paradise, and that it is only since the prophetic religions (of which there were many) and

Christianity that the "good news" (*evangelion*) of *another way* than that of the evolution of the serpent exists.

Now, the tempter proposed to the Son of Man the method to which he owes his existence: the trial. "Throw yourself down and it will be seen if it is true that you are the Son of God and that you are not as I am, the son of evolution, son of the serpent." This was the temptation of chastity. For, as we have shown above, the spirit of chastity excludes all trial. The *trial* is the very essence of what the Bible designates as "fornication". Fornication — as, moreover, every other vice and also every virtue — is threefold: spiritual, psychic and carnal. Its root is spiritual; the region of its deployment and growth is that of the soul; and the flesh is simply the domain where it fructifies. It is thus that spiritual error becomes vice and vice becomes sickness.

For this reason the prophets of Israel stigmatised the spiritual fornication of the people of the Old Alliance each time that they let themselves be seduced by the cults of "strange gods"—Bel, Moloch and Astarte. These gods were only *egregores* — creatures of the collective human imagination and will — whilst the Holy One of Israel was the *revealed* God, unimaginable though he was, having no other relationship with the human will than that of the Law imposed upon it. This is why the "strange gods" had a singular attraction for the Israelites, being the gods of "this world" and not the transcendent God of revelation, obedience to which was to return to live in a *spiritual monastery* in relation to "this world and its gods". They were always being tempted to throw themselves from the height and isolation of the pinnacle of the temple above into the layers of collective instinct below, and to test whether there would be "Angels who will bear you up lest you strike your foot against a stone", i.e. to try to find in the near and dense layers of the forces of natural evolution directing and protecting forces with less effort than in the height and rare air surrounding the pinnacle of the revealed God's temple. The principle of spiritual fornication is therefore the preference of the subconscious to the conscious and superconscious, of instinct to the Law, and of the world of the serpent to the world of the WORD.

Just as the first two temptations are directed at the vows of holy poverty and holy chastity, so is the third temptation (according to the Gospel of Matthew) directed at the vow of holy obedience. This time it is a matter of the will-to-power, the Nietzschean *Wille zur Macht*.

> Again, the devil took him to a very high mountain, and showed him all the kingdoms of the world and their glory; and he said to him: All these I will give you, if you will fall down and worship me. Then Jesus said to him: Begone, Satan! for it is written, "You shall worship the Lord your God and him only shall you serve." (Matthew iv, 8-10)

Let us note the elements of this temptation: the very high mountain, all the kingdoms of the world and their glory, worship of he who has the power to rise to the top of the mountain and there to give possession of everything in the kingdoms of *his* world.

It is a matter, therefore, of accepting the ideal of the superman ("fall down and worship me"), who is the summit of evolution ("he took him to a very high mountain") and who, having passed through the mineral, plant, animal and human kingdoms, subjecting them to his power, is lord over them, i.e. he is their final cause or aim and ideal, their representative or their collective concentrated will, and he is their master, who has taken their subsequent evolution into his hands. Now, the choice here is between the ideal of the superman, who is "as God", and God himself.

Holy obedience is therefore faithfulness to the living God himself; revolt or disobedience is the decision taken in favour of the superman, who personifies the will-to-power.

The sixth Arcanum of the Tarot "The Lover", although it puts in relief only the temptation of chastity, evokes the whole range of ideas of the three temptations and the three vows—with the three temptations in paradise and those in the wilderness being inseparable in reality—just as the three vows are also. Because one cannot be "chaste" without being "poor" and "obedient", just as one cannot renounce the divine ideal in favour of the ideal of the superman without at the same time falling into the region of trial (experimentation), where there is no immediate certainty, and into the region of the law of the serpent formulated as follows: "You shall go upon your belly and you shall eat dust all the days of your life" (Genesis iii, 14), i.e. the region where there is no grace.

But what is the immediate consequence of resisting temptation? The Gospel account gives the answer here, as follows:

> Then the devil left him, and behold, Angels *came and ministered to him*. (Matthew iv, 11)

This response belongs to the range of ideas and facts of the seventh Arcanum of the Tarot "The Chariot", whose Card represents a man standing on a triumphal chariot drawn by two horses.

Meditation on the
Seventh Major Arcanum of the Tarot

THE CHARIOT
LE CHARIOT

Then the devil left him, and behold,
Angels came and ministered to him.
(Matthew iv, 11)

When the unclean spirit has gone out of
man, he passes through waterless places
seeking rest; and finding none he says: I
will return to my house from whence I
came. And when he comes he finds it
swept and put in order. Then he goes and
brings seven other spirits more evil than
himself, and they enter and dwell there;
and the last state of that man becomes
worse than the first.
(Luke xi, 24-26)

I have come in my Father's name, and you
do not receive me; if another comes in his
own name, him you will receive.
(John v, 43)

LETTER VII

THE CHARIOT

Dear Unknown Friend,

Like the preceding Arcana, the Arcanum "The Chariot" has a twofold aspect. It represents, from one side, he who—having triumphed over the three temptations —remains faithful to the vows of obedience, poverty and chastity; and it represents, from another side, the danger of the *fourth temptation*, which is the most subtle and intimate temptation, and is the invisible synthesis of the three temptations: the spiritual temptation of the victorious through his victory itself. It is the temptation to act "in one's own name", to act as master instead of as servant.

The seventh Arcanum is that of *mastership* understood in the sense of temptation as well as achievement. The three Gospel quotations which are found at the head of this Letter delineate the nature of the ideas here.

Paul Marteau says that the general and abstract meaning of the seventh Card is that it "represents *setting in motion in seven states*, i.e. in all domains" (*Le Tarot de Marseille*, Paris, 1949, p. 33), and it is exactly this that we have designated above as "mastership". For mastership is not the state of being moved, but rather that of being able to set in motion.

The Son of Man resisted being moved by the three temptations in the wilderness; consequently, it is he who set in motion the forces which served him. "Then the devil left him, and behold, Angels came and ministered to him."

Here, again, is a fundamental law of sacred magic. One could formulate it in the following way: *That which is above being as that which is below, renunciation below sets in motion forces of accomplishment above and the renunciation of that which is above sets in motion forces of accomplishment below*. What is the practical meaning of this law?

It is the following.

When you resist a temptation or renounce something desired below, you set in motion by this very fact forces of realisation of that which *corresponds above* to that which you come to renounce below. It is this that the Master designates by the word "reward" when he says, for example, that it is necessary to guard against practising righteousness before other people in order to gain their regard, "for then you will have no reward from your Father who is in heaven" (Matthew vi, 1). *Reward* is therefore the action that one sets in motion above by the renunciation of desire for things below. It is the "yes" from above corresponding to the "no" from below. And this correspondence constitutes a basis for magical realisation and for a fundamental law of Christian esotericism or Hermeticism. Let us guard ourselves from taking it lightly, for here is given to us one of the principal keys of sacred magic. It is not desire which bears *magical* realisation, but rather the renunciation of desire (that you have formerly experienced, of course). For renunciation through indifference has no moral — and therefore no magical — value.

Desire, and then renounce — here we have the practical magical meaning of the "law" of reward. To say that one has to renounce what one desires amounts to saying that one has to practise the three sacred vows — obedience, poverty and chastity. For the renunciation must be *sincere* in order for it to set in motion the forces of realisation from above, and it cannot be so when it lacks the air, light and warmth of the sacred vows. It is necessary therefore to understand once and for all that there is no true sacred magic — nor mysticism, gnosis or Hermeticism — outside of the three sacred vows, and that true magical training is essentially only the practice of the three vows. Is this hard? No, it is easy — it is the "concentration without effort" which was considered in the first of these Letters.

Let us now consider the text of the Gospel account concerning what happened immediately after the three temptations. "Then the devil left him" (*tote aphiesin auton ho diabolos*) says the Gospel according to Matthew, but the Gospel according to Luke adds "for a time" (Luke iv, 13). Now, these additional words give rise to the supposition that again a trial or temptation — the fourth, which is the most subtle and intimate—is to come. And it is this which forms part of the teaching of the seventh Arcanum, which represents a crowned man standing on a triumphal chariot drawn by two horses.

"And behold, Angels came. . .to him" (*kai idou angeloi proselthon*), i.e. now they *were able to* approach him, since a "space" necessary for their descent became free. Why and how?

Angels (ἄγγελοι *hoi angeloi*, in Greek) are entities which move *vertically*, from above below and from below above. "To move" signifies for them "to change respiration", and "distance" for them amounts to the number—and to the intensity of effort that it comprises—of changes from inhalation to exhalation. Thus, for example, when we say, "a distance of 300 miles from the earth", an Angel would say, "three successive changes from normal respiration in the sphere of the Angels". "To draw near" for Angels signifies a change in respiration; "to be unable to draw near" means to say that the "atmosphere" of the sphere which they want to draw near to is such that they can no longer breathe there, and that they would "faint" if they were to enter this sphere.

This is why the Angels were unable to approach the Son of Man during the time when the concentrated forces of terrestrial evolution—the forces of the "son of the serpent"—were active. They "occupied", so to say, the space around the Son of Man, so that the Angels were unable to breathe—and therefore they were unable to enter there without "fainting". But immediately that "the devil left him" and the atmosphere changed, they *were able to* approach him, and did so.

One can add, by way of a corollary, that the "law of presence" delineated above gives us a strong reason for acknowledging the necessity of churches, temples and consecrated or holy places in general. There are certainly other reasons again, but this would suffice, even if there were no other reasons, for us to defend the protection of all sacred places. Let us therefore protect through our thoughts, words and deeds, all churches, every chapel and, lastly, every temple, where one prays, worships, meditates and celebrates God and his servants.

". . .and they ministered to him" (*kai diekonoun auto*): the plural "they" indicates to us that it is a matter here of three Angels. Each temptation resisted corresponded to an Angel charged with the special mission of reward and who rendered a special service.

What, therefore, were these services?

He had refused—he, being famished—to command stones to become bread; now, it was "the word which comes from the mouth of God", become bread, which the Angel of poverty served him. He had refused to cast himself down from the pinnacle of the temple; now, it was breath from the height of the throne of God that the Angel of chastity brought to him. He had refused to accept the role of superman—to be king of the world at the price of worshipping the ideal of the world of the serpent; now, it was the royal crown of the world of God that the Angel of obedience presented him.

Just as the three mages offered their presents to the new-born Child—gold, frankincense and myrrh—so did the three Angels each offer a present to the Master, after his Baptism in the Jordan and his Confirmation in the wilderness: the crown of gold, the breath of incense from the throne of God and the divine word become food.

This is what happened *immediately* after the three temptations in the wilderness. This was the response from above to the threefold renunciation by the Son of Man below. But what was the effect of the vanquished temptations not only for the vanquisher himself and not only immediately, but also for the outside world of the so-called "four elements" and in the course of time?

The effect here was *mastership* of the world of the elements, and what took place in the course of time was the *seven archetypal miracles* described in the Gospel according to John, i.e. the miracle at the wedding of Cana, the miracle of the healing of the nobleman's son, the miracle of the healing of the paralysed man at the pool of Bethesda, the miracle of the feeding of the five thousand, the miracle of walking on the water, the miracle of the healing of the man born blind and the miracle of the raising of Lazarus at Bethany. And to the manifestation of these seven aspects of mastership or "glory" there corresponds the revelation of the seven aspects of the *name* of the Master: "I am the true vine", "I am the way, the truth and the life", "I am the door", "I am the bread of life", "I am the good shepherd", "I am the light of the world" and "I am the resurrection and the life". This is the rainbow of seven colours of the manifestation of "glory" or mastership and also the octave of the seven tones of revelation of the "name" or mission of the vanquisher of the three temptations. And this rainbow shone around the empty and sombre place in the wilderness where the temptations took place.

The seven miracles of the Gospel according to John are, in their totality, the "glory" (*doxa*) or splendour of the victory of the three sacred vows over the three temptations. Here there is at the same time a beautiful piece of qualitative mathematics: the threefold good, when it prevails over the threefold evil, *produces sevenfold good*, whilst when the threefold evil prevails over the threefold good it produces only threefold evil. For the good is only qualitative, and when it *is able to* manifest itself, it manifests itself *wholly*, in its indivisible fullness. This is what the number seven is—fullness (*pleroma*) or, when it manifests itself, "glory" (*doxa*), which St. John speaks of when he says: "And we have beheld his *glory* . . . and from his *fullness* we have all received grace upon grace" (John i, 14, 16). And the first miracle, that of the wedding at Cana, was the beginning of the manifestation of this fullness or "glory":

> This, the first of his signs, Jesus did at Cana in Galilee, and manifested his glory; and his disciples believed in him. (John ii, 11)

"His disciples believed in him" means to say that they believed in his *name*, or his *mission*, which was revealed in its seven aspects by the seven "I AM"-sayings quoted above from the Gospel according to John.

Now, the effect of the triumph over the temptation in the wilderness was the manifestation of the seven aspects of mastership or "glory" (the seven miracles) and the revelation of the mission or "name" of the Master. And all this was nothing other than the manifestation of the glory of the Father *through* the Son, and the revelation of the name of the Father *through* the name of the Son.

But the possibility of the *other* "glory", i.e. the manifestation of mastership in one's own name, also exists. The words of the Master at the head of this Letter—"I have come in my Father's name, and you do not receive me; if another comes in his own name, him you will receive" (John v, 43)—state it clearly. Experience in the domain of Occult, Esoteric, Hermetic, Cabbalistic, Gnostic, Magical, Martinist, Theosophical, Anthroposophical, Rosicrucian, Templar, Masonic, Sufi, Yogistic movements, and other contemporary spiritual movements, supplies us with ample proof that the words of the Master have in no way lost their actuality, even in the domain of science and in movements of a social, or national, or semi-scientific nature. Because for what other reason do the Theosophists, for example, prefer the Himalayan *mahatmas*, whose astral bodies through projection appear from a great distance (or who "precipitate" letters written in blue or red crayon), to the Master, who has never ceased to teach, inspire, illumine and heal, amongst us and near to us—in France, Italy, Germany, Spain, to name only the countries where there have been well-established cases of meetings with him—and who himself said: "I am with you always, to the end of time" (Matthew xxviii, 20)?

For what other reason does one seek a guru amongst the Hindu yogis or Tibetan lamas without giving oneself half a chance to seek for a teacher illumined through spiritual experience in our monasteries or spiritual orders, or amongst lay brothers and sisters who practise the Master's teaching and perhaps are quite near at hand? And why do members of secret societies or orders of the Masonic type consider the Sacrament of Flesh and Blood of the Lord insufficient for the work of building the new-man, and why do they seek special rituals to supplement it or even to replace it?

Yes, all these questions fall under the heading of the words of the Master: "I have come in my Father's name, and you do not receive me; if another comes in his own name, him you will receive." Why? Because for some the superman has more attraction than the Son of Man, and because he promises them a career of increasing power, whilst the Son of Man offers only a career of "foot washing".

Dear Unknown Friend, do not interpret what I am saying in the sense that I am opposed or even hostile to the above-mentioned societies, fraternities, and movements of a spiritual and initiatory nature, nor in the sense that I am accusing them of an anti-Christian attitude. Do not attribute me with a lack of respect for the *mahatmas* and *gurus* of India. It is a matter here only of the *purely psychological tendency* (that I have been able to observe something of everywhere) which prefers the ideal of the superman to the ideal of the Son of Man. There is room to add, in order to do justice to the societies and fraternities mentioned, that if this tendency shows up all over the place at the core of these societies and fraternities, it is also so that it is everywhere combatted in a more or less effective way. There is always an opposition to this tendency, although this opposition is sometimes only that of a minority.

Be that as it may, the charioteer of the Arcanum "The Chariot" is the victor over trials, i.e. the temptations, and if he is master, then it is thanks to himself. He is alone, standing in his chariot; no one is present to applaud him or to pay homage to him; he has no weapons—the sceptre that he holds not being a weapon. If he is master, his mastership was acquired in solitude and he owes it to the trials alone, and not to anyone or anything external to himself.

The victory achieved in solitude. . .what glory and what danger it comprises at one and the same time! It is the only *real* glory, for it in no way depends on human favour and judgement; it is *intrinsic glory*—the real radiance of the aura become luminous. It is, however, at the same time the most real and the most serious spiritual danger which exists. "Pride" and "vaingloriousness", the traditional names which one gives to it, do not suffice to characterise it in an adequate way. It is more than this. It is, rather, a kind of *mystical megalomania*, where one deifies the regulating centre of one's own being, one's ego, and where one sees the divine only within oneself and becomes blind to the divine above and outside of oneself. The "higher Self" is then experienced as the supreme and unique Self of the world, although it is only *higher* in relation to the ordinary, empirical self, and it is far from the *supreme* and unique being. . .far from being God, in other words.

It would be as well, now, to dwell on the problem of identification of the self with the higher Self and of the higher Self with God.

C. G. Jung who, after having explored the sexual or "Freudian" layer, and then that of the will-to-power or "Adlerian" layer, of the unconscious (i.e. *latent or occult consciousness*) of the human being, encountered a *spiritual* (mystical, gnostic and magical) layer during the course of his clinical and psychotherapeutic experience. Instead of drawing back from it or extricating himself from it through a corrosive "explanation", he had the courage and honesty to set himself to the laborious study of the phenomenology of this layer of the unconscious. Now, this work proved fruitful. Jung discovered here not only the causes of certain psychic disorders, but also the profound and intimate process that he designated as the "process of individuation", which is nothing other than the gradual birth of *another self* (Jung called it the "Self") higher to oneself or one's ordinary ego. The discovery of the process of the "second birth" prompted him to extend the range of his exploratory work considerably, notably to include symbolism, mystery rituals and the comparative study of contemporary and ancient religions.

Now, this broadening of his field of exploration also proved fruitful. Jung's arrival at his discovery (which at first racked him, preventing him from speaking of it to a living soul for fifteen years) had its train of consequences, including the knowledge and description of some dangers or temptations belonging to the way of initiation and the process of individuation which corresponds to it. One of these dangers—which are at the same time trials or temptations—is that which Jung designated by the term "inflation", which signifies the state of consciousness of the self inflated to excess, and which is known in psychiatry in its extreme manifestation by the term "megalomania".

Therefore, here we are concerned with a range of psychic phenomena, which to begin with show up in relatively innocent forms—such as a high opinion of oneself which is not entirely justified, or the somewhat exaggerated desire to have one's own way—which become quite dangerous when they manifest as a disparaging negativity towards everyone...the faculties of appreciation, gratitude and worship being concentrated upon oneself; and which eventually signify a catastrophe that is rarely curable, when they reveal themselves as obsession with easily recognisable illusions, or megalomania, pure and simple. Here, then, are the principal dangers of inflation: exaggerated importance attached to oneself, superiority complex tending towards obsession and, lastly, megalomania. The first degree signifies a practical *task* for work upon oneself; the second degree is a serious *trial*; whilst the third is a *catastrophe*.

What is it a question of in the process of inflation? Let us look first at what Jung himself says about it:

> The "superordinate personality" is the total man, i.e. man as he really is, not as he appears to himself. To this wholeness the unconscious psyche also belongs, which has its requirements and needs just as consciousness has...I usually describe the "superordinate personality" as the "self", thus making a sharp distinction between the *ego*, which, as is well known, extends only as far as the conscious mind, and the *whole* of the personality, which includes the unconscious as well as the conscious component. The ego is thus related to the "self" as part to the whole. To that extent the self is superordinate. Moreover, the self is felt empirically not as subject but as *object*, and this by reason of its unconscious component, which can only come to consciousness indirectly, by way of projection. (C. G. Jung and C. Kerényi, *Introduction to a Science of Mythology*; trsl. R. F. C. Hull, London, 1951, pp. 223-224)

Now, this "way of projection" is living symbolism—traditional symbolism as well as symbolism manifesting itself in dreams, "active imagination" and visions. Dreams, when observed in a series (often running into several hundreds), show that they obey a kind of *plan*. They seem to relate to one another and to be subject in a profound sense to a common goal:

> ...in the deepest sense...they seem....to be subordinated to a common goal, so that a long dream-series no longer appears as a senseless string of incoherent and isolated happenings, but

resembles the successive steps in a planned and orderly process of development. I have called this unconscious process spontaneously expressing itself in the symbolism of a long dream-series *the individuation process*.(C. G. Jung, *The Structure and Dynamics of the Psyche*; trsl. R. F. C. Hull, *The Collected Works of C. G. Jung*, vol. 8, London, 1972, pp. 289-290)

The process of individuation is "*the spontaneous realisation of the whole man*" (ibid., p. 292). For the formula that is henceforth valuable for the notion of the soul is: "psyche = ego-consciousness + unconscious" (C. G. Jung, *The Practice of Psychotherapy*; trsl. R. F. C. Hull, *The Collected Works of C. G. Jung*, vol. 16, London, 1954, p.90). With respect to the role of the unconscious in this formula, it is necessary to take account of the fact, principally,

> that in every child consciousness grows out of the unconscious in the course of a few years, also that consciousness is always only a temporary state based on an optimum physiological performance and therefore regularly interrupted by phases of unconsciousness (sleep), and finally that the unconscious psyche not only possesses the longer lease of life but is continuously present (i.e. *it assures the continuity of being*). (ibid., p.91)

Now, the process of individuation is that of the harmonisation of the conscious self and the unconscious in the psyche. But the "conscious and unconscious do not make a whole when one of them is suppressed and injured by the other." (C. G. Jung, *Conscious, Unconscious and Individuation*; trsl. R. F. C Hull, *The Collected Works of C. G. Jung*, vol. 9, part VI, London, 1959, p. 288). It is a matter of a harmonisation which is only realisable by way of the *re-centering* of the personality, i.e. the birth of a new centre of the personality, which participates in the nature of the unconscious as well as in the conscious self—a centre, in other words, where the unconscious is perpetually in transformation into consciousness. This is the aim of the process of individuation, which is at the same time a stage of initiation.

The process of individuation operates, as we have said, by establishing a collaboration between the unconscious and the conscious. The domain of *symbols* affords such a collaboration and it is here, consequently, that it can begin. In the process of individuation one meets—or rather one awakens—the symbol-forces that Jung designated, in consideration of their typical character, by the name "archetypes".

> The archetype—let us never forget this—is a psychic organ present in all of us. A bad explanation means a correspondingly bad attitude to this organ, which may thus be injured. But the ultimate sufferer is the bad interpreter himself. Hence the "explanation" should always be such that the functional significance of

the archetype remains unimpaired, i.e. that an adequate and appropriate relationship between the conscious mind and the archetypes is insured. For the archetype is an element of our psychic structure and thus a vital and necessary component in our psychic economy. . .There is no "rational" substitute for the archetype any more than there is for the cerebellum or the kidneys. (C. G. Jung and C. Kerényi, *Introduction to a Science of Mythology*; trsl. R. F. C. Hull, London, 1951, pp. 109-110)

Now, one must not take archetypes lightly. They are formidable psychic forces which can also invade, inundate and engulf consciousness. This is what happens in the case of the *identification* of consciousness with the archetype. Then it produces, more often than not, an identification with the role of the heroes (and, sometimes —when it is a matter of the archetype named "the wise old man" or "the great mother"—an identification with a cosmic figure).

At this stage there is usually another identification, this time with the hero, whose role is attractive for a variety of reasons. The identification is often extremely stubborn and dangerous to mental equilibrium. If it can be broken down and consciousness reduced to human proportions, the figure of the hero can gradually be differentiated into a symbol of the self. (ibid., p. 137)

And, let us add, if this does not succeed, the figure of the hero takes possession of consciousness. Then the "second identification"—or the "epiphany of the hero" —takes place:

The epiphany of the hero (the second identification) shows itself in a corresponding inflation: the colossal pretension grows into a conviction that one is something extraordinary, or else the impossibility of the pretension ever being fulfilled only proves one's own inferiority, which is favourable to the role of the heroic sufferer (a negative inflation). In spite of their contrariety, both forms are identical, because unconscious compensatory inferiority tallies with conscious megalomania, and unconscious megalomania with conscious inferiority (you never get one without the other). Once the reef of the second identification has been successfully circumnavigated, conscious processes can be cleanly separated from the unconscious, and the latter observed objectively. This leads to the possibility of an accommodation with the unconscious, and thus to a possible synthesis of the conscious and unconscious elements of knowledge and action. This in turn leads to a shifting of the centre of personality from the ego to the self. (ibid., pp. 137-138)

This is the aim of the process of individuation.

Now, inflation is the principal risk that attends each person who seeks the experience of *depth*, the experience of what is *occult*, which lives and works behind the facade of phenomena of ordinary consciousness. Therefore, inflation constitutes the principal danger and trial for occultists, esotericists, magicians, gnostics and mystics. Monasteries and spiritual orders have always known this, thanks to the immense pillar of experience which they have accumulated over millennia in the domain of the *profound life*. This is why their whole spiritual practice is based on the cultivation of *humility* by such means as the practice of obedience, the examination of conscience and the reciprocal brotherly help of members of the community. Thus, if Sabbatai Zevi (1625-1676) had been a member of a spiritual order with a discipline similar to that of Christian spiritual orders and monasteries, his illumination would never have led to his revealing himself (in 1648) to a group of disciples as the promised Messiah. Neither would he have had to become a Turk in order to save his life and continue his mission ("God has made me an Ishmaelite-Turk; he has commanded, and I have obeyed—the ninth day after my second birth", he wrote to his followers in Smyrna). Because he would have been spared *positive inflation*, just as he would have been spared the *negative inflation* of which Samuel Gandor, his disciple, gives the following description:

> It is said of Sabbatai Zevi that for fifteen years he has been bowed down by the following affliction: he is pursued by a sense of depression which leaves him no quiet moment and does not even permit him to read, without his being able to say what is the nature of this sadness which has come upon him. (Gershom G. Scholem, *Major Trends in Jewish Mysticism*, London, 1955, p. 290)

The history of the illumined Cabbalist Sabbatai Zevi is only an extreme case of the general dangers and trials which all practising esotericists have to face. Indeed, Hargrave Jennings expresses this danger and trial in a successful way concerning the Rosicrucians:

> They speak of all mankind as infinitely beneath them; their pride is beyond idea, although they are most humble and quiet in exterior. They glory in poverty, and declare that it is the state ordered for them; and this though they boast universal riches. They decline all human affections, or submit to them as advisable escapes only—appearance of loving obligations, which are assumed for convenient acceptance, or for passing in a world which is composed of them, or of their supposal. They mingle most gracefully in the society of women, with hearts wholly incapable of softness in this direction; while they criticise them with pity or contempt in their own minds as altogether another

order of beings from men. They are most simple and deferential in their exterior; and yet the self-value which fills their hearts ceases its self-glorifying expansion only with the boundless skies . . . In comparison with the Hermetic adepts, monarchs are poor, and their greatest accumulations are contemptible. By the side of the sages, the most learned are mere dolts and blockheads . . . Thus, towards mankind they are negative; towards everything else, positive; self-contained, self-illuminated, self-everything; but always prepared (nay, enjoined) to do good, wherever possible or safe. To this immeasurable exaltation of themselves, what standard of measure, or what appreciation, can you apply? Ordinary estimates fail in the idea of it. Either the state of these occult philosophers is the height of sublimity, or it is the height of absurdity. (Hargrave Jennings, *The Rosicrucians. Their Rites and Mysteries*, London-New York, 1887, pp. 30-31)

Let us say absurd as well as sublime, because *inflation* is always simultaneously sublime and absurd. This is what Eliphas Lévi says about it:

There is also a science which confers on man powers apparently superhuman. They are enumerated thus in a Hebrew manuscript of the sixteenth century:

ALEPH —He beholds God face to face, without dying, and converses familiarly with the seven genii who command the entire celestial army.

BETH —He is above all griefs and all fears.

GHIMEL —He reigns with all heaven and is served by all hell.

DALETH —He rules his own health and life and can influence equally those of others.

HÉ —He can neither be surprised by misfortune nor overwhelmed by disasters, nor can he be conquered by his enemies.

VAU —He knows the reason of the past, present and future.

ZAIN —He possesses the secret of the resurrection of the dead and the key of immortality.

(Eliphas Lévi, *Dogme et rituel de la haute magie*; trsl. A. E. Waite, *Transcendental Magic. Its Doctrine and Ritual*, London, 1968, p. 10)

Is it a matter here of a programme or of *actual* experience? If it is experience, it is one of inflation pushed very far. If it is a programme, he who takes its realisation seriously cannot fail to fall prey to inflation, be it positive (superiority complex) or negative (inferiority complex).

Whatever it may be, the experience or programme of this Hebrew manuscript of the sixteenth century quoted by Eliphas Lévi shows a remarkable similarity to the *experience* of John Custance, described by him in his book *Wisdom, Madness and Folly: the Philosophy of a Lunatic*. It is as follows:

> I feel so close to God, so inspired by His Spirit that in a sense I am God. I see the future, plan the Universe, save mankind; I am utterly and completely immortal; I am even male and female. The whole Universe, animate and inanimate, past, present and future, is within me. All nature and life, all spirits, are co-operating and connected with me; all things are possible. I am in a sense identical with all spirits from God to Satan. I reconcile Good and Evil and create light, darkness, worlds, universes. (John Custance, *Wisdom, Madness and Folly: the Philosophy of a Lunatic*, London, 1951, p. 51)

The state described by John Custance is characteristic of that of acute mania, and the author himself in no way denies it. But would he still look at it in this way, one can ask, if he knew that his experience is found described exactly in the *Brhadaranyaka Upanishad*, which says:

> He who has found and awakened to the Soul that has entered this conglomerate whole — he is the maker of everything, for he is the creator of all; the world is his: indeed, he is the world itself. (*Brhadaranyaka Upanishad* 4.4.13; trsl. R. E. Hume, *The Thirteen Principal Upanishads*, Oxford, 1962, p. 142)

Can one say with certainty that this text quoted from the Upanishads is based on an entirely different experience to that of John Custance?

Thirty-eight years ago I knew a tranquil man of mature age who taught English at the YMCA in the capital of a Baltic country. Now, he revealed to me one day that he had attained a spiritual state which manifests itself through "the eternal gaze" and which is that of consciousness of the identity of Self with the Eternal Reality of the world. The past, present and future — seen from the pedestal of eternity, where his consciousness had its abode — were an open book for him. He had no more problems, not because he had resolved them, but because he had attained the state of consciousness where they disappeared, having become of no importance. Because problems belong to the domain of motion in time and space; he who transcends this and arrives at the realm of eternity and infinity, where there is neither movement nor change, is free of problems.

When he spoke to me of these things, his beautiful blue eyes rayed out sincerity and certainty. But this radiance gave way to a dark and angry look as soon as I raised the question of the value of the "subjective feeling of eternity" when one is not aware of or one is unable objectively to do something more towards helping humanity, be it in spiritual (or other) progress, or in the alleviation of spiritual, psychic and bodily suffering. He did not forgive me this question and he turned his back on me, which was my last impression of him in this world (he made his way to India, where soon after he died as victim of an epidemic).

I recount this episode in my life only so that you may know, dear Unknown Friend, when and how the very serious problem of the forms of, and the dangers of, spiritual megalomania were awakened in me, and how I owe it to this objective experience that I began work on this problem, some of the outcomes of which I am in the process of showing.

Spiritual megalomania is as old as the world. Its origin is found well beyond the terrestrial world, according to the millennial-old tradition concerning the fall of Lucifer. The prophet Ezekiel gives a most moving description of this:

> You were the signet of perfection,
> You were full of wisdom, and perfect in beauty.
> You were in Eden, the garden of God;
> You were covered with every kind of precious stone:
>   Sardonyx, topaz, and diamond,
>   Chrysolite, onyx, and jasper,
>   Sapphire, carbuncle, emerald, and gold,
>   With which you were adorned,
>   And which were prepared for you
>   On the day that you were created.
> You were a guardian Cherubim, with outspread wings;
> I placed you, and you were, on the holy mountain of God;
> You walked in the midst of the stones of fire . . .
> Your heart was proud because of your beauty,
> You corrupted your wisdom for the sake of your splendour.
> I cast you to the ground,
> I exposed you before kings, to feast their eyes on you . . .
>
> (Ezekiel xxviii, 12-17)

Here is the higher (i.e. celestial) origin of inflation, superiority complex and megalomania. And since "that which is below is as that which is above", it is repeated below in human earthly life from century to century and generation to generation. It is repeated above all in the lives of those human beings who are detached from the ordinary earthly setting and the state of consciousness belonging to it, and who transcend it, be it in the sense of height, in the sense of breadth, or, lastly, in the sense of depth. He who aspires to a plane *higher* than that of the terrestrial setting risks becoming haughty; he who seeks *breadth* beyond the normal circle of earthly duties and pleasures risks considering himself to be more and more important; he who is in search of the *depth*, beneath the surface of the phenomena of terrestrial life, runs the greatest risk: that of inflation, of which C. G. Jung speaks.

The abstract metaphysician, who arranges worlds according to an order that he has chosen, can lose all interest for the particular and for the individual, in such a way that he comes to consider human beings to be almost as insignificant as insects. He regards them only from above. Seen from his metaphysical height, they lose all proportion and become for him small or almost insignificant—whilst he, the metaphysician, is great, since he participates in great metaphysical things, which clothe him in grandeur.

The reformer who *wants* to correct or save humanity easily falls victim to the temptation of considering himself as the active centre of the passive circle of humanity. He feels himself as the bearer of a mission of universal significance; therefore he feels himself to be more and more important.

The *practising* occultist, esotericist or Hermeticist (if he is not practising, he is only a metaphysician or reformer) experiences the higher forces which work beyond his consciousness and which make their entrance there. At what price?. . . Either at the price of worshipping on his knees—or otherwise at the price of the identification of self with these higher forces, which results in megalomania.

One speaks often of the dangers of occultism. Black magic is usually the supreme danger against which the beginner is put on guard by the "masters"; others (above all those who know more or less about medicine) see it as disorders of the nervous system.

But experience during forty-three years of practical occultism (or esotericism) has taught me that the danger of occultism is neither black magic nor nervous disorder—at least, these dangers are met no more often amongst occultists than amongst politicians, artists, psychologists, believers and agnostics. I am not able to cite by name any black magician amongst the occultists that I know, whereas it would not be too difficult to name some politicians who, for example, have nothing to do with occultism—and who would even be hostile to it—but whose influence and impact agree very well with the classical concept of that of the "black magician". Indeed, is it difficult to name politicians who have exercised a deadly, suggestive influence on the popular masses, blinding them and inciting them to acts of cruelty, injustice and violence, of which each individual, taken separately, would be incapable. . .and who, through their semi-magical influence, have deprived individuals of their freedom and rendered them *possessed*? And is not this action to deprive men of their moral freedom and to render them *possessed* the aim and very essence of black magic?

No, dear Unknown Friend, occultists—including those amongst them who practise ceremonial magic—are neither masters nor disciples of black magic. Truth to tell, they are amongst those who have least of all in common with it. It is true that they—above all the adepts of ceremonial magic—often fall prey to illusions and mislead themselves and others, but is this black magic? Besides, where can one find a class of human beings who never make mistakes? Even Doctor Faust—who made a pact with the devil (and this concerns all "pact-makers" of this kind, ancient and modern)—was only the naive victim of a prank on the part of Mephistopheles (who is a rogue well-known to all those who have knowledge of the "occult world"), because how can you "sell" something which in no way belongs to you? It is his soul which would have been able to sell Doctor Faust, but never would Doctor Faust be able to give away his soul, however solemn his pact was and no matter whether he wrote and signed with blood or with ordinary ink.

It is Mephistopheles' way of giving a lesson to those who want to be "supermen"; he brings to light the puerility of their pretensions. And whilst wholly deploring the naivety of poor Doctor Faust, one is led to consider the "method of roguishness" of Mephistopheles as, in the last analysis, salutary. Because what Mephistopheles does (and other examples of this method of a more recent date could be cited) is to show the ridiculousness and absurdity of the aspirations and pretensions of so-called "supermen". "Of all Spirits who deny, the rogue is the least burden to me," says God concerning Mephistopheles in Goethe's *Faust* ("Prologue in Heaven", *Faust*, part I).

Let us therefore not condemn the rogue of the spiritual world, and above all let us not be afraid of him. Nor let us condemn Doctor Faust, our brother, by accusing him of black magic—it is, rather, childish credulity of which he can be accused, if he must be accused. In any case, he was one-hundred times more innocent with respect to mankind than our contemporaries who have invented the nuclear bomb...as good citizens and scientists.

No, neither black magic nor nervous disorders constitute the special dangers of occultism. Its principal danger—of which, however, it has no monopoly—is designated by the three terms: superiority complex, inflation, megalomania.

In fact, an occultist (who is not a beginner) who has not attained this moral illness, or who has not at some time in the past undergone it, is rare. The tendency to megalomania shows up all over the place amongst occultists. Decades of personal relationships, as well as reading occult literature, have taught me this. There are many levels of this moral defect. It manifests at first as self-assurance and a certain informality with which one speaks of higher and sacred things. Then it expresses itself as "knowing-better" and "knowing-all", i.e. as the attitude of a master towards everyone. Lastly, it manifests as implicit or even explicit infallibility.

I do not want to cite passages from occult literature, nor to name names, nor to mention biographical facts concerning known occultists, in order to prove or illustrate this diagnosis. It would not be difficult for you, dear Unknown Friend, to find them yourself in abundance. What my intention is here is to refute the false accusations concerning occultism, on the one hand, and on the other hand to show up the real danger that occultism presents—so that one is put on guard against it. But what should one do against this danger, in order to guard one's moral well-being?

The ancient saying "*ora et labora*" ("work and pray") constitutes the only answer that I have been able to find. *Worship* and *work* constitute the only curative as well as prophylactic remedy that I know against megalomaniacal illusions. It is necessary to worship what is above us and it is necessary to participate in human effort in the domain of objective facts in order to be able to hold in check the illusions concerning *what one is* and *what one is capable of*. For whoever is aware of raising his prayer and meditation to the level of pure worship will always be conscious of the *distance* which separates (and at the same time unites) the worshipper and the worshipped. Therefore he will not be tempted to worship himself, which is in the last analysis the cause of megalomania. He will always have in sight the difference between himself and the worshipped. He will not confuse *what he is* with *what the worshipped being is*.

On the other hand, he who *works*, i.e. who takes part in human effort, with a view to objective and verifiable results, will not easily fall prey to illusion with respect to *what he is capable of*. Thus, for example, a practising doctor inclined to overestimate his power of healing will soon learn to know the real limits of his ability through experience of his failures.

Jacob Boehme was a shoemaker, and was illumined. When he had had the experience of illumination (". . . the Door became opened to me, so that in a quarter of an hour I observed and knew more than if I had attended a university for many years. . ." he wrote in a letter to the tax collector Lindner), where he "recognised the Being of Beings, the firmament and the abyss. . ." (same letter), he in no way concluded from it that he, in so far as he was a shoemaker, could henceforth do more than his colleagues in the trade, or that he himself could do more than before his illumination. On the other hand, through his illumination he learned to know the greatness of God and the world (". . . of which I was highly astounded, without knowing how it happened to me, and thereupon my heart turned to praise of God"— same letter), and this filled him with *worship*.

Therefore, it was work and the worship of God which protected the moral wellbeing of Jacob Boehme. And I allow myself to add here that my experience in the domain of esotericism has taught me that what was salutary in Boehme's case is also so, without exception, regarding all those who aspire to supersensible experiences.

Worship and work— *ora et labora*— therefore constitute the *conditio sine qua non* for practical esotericism in order to hold in check the tendency towards megalomania. This is in order to hold it in check, yet in order to obtain *immunity* from this moral illness, more than this is necessary. One has to have the real experience of concretely meeting a being higher than oneself. I mean by "concretely meeting" neither the feeling of "higher Self", nor the more or less vague feeling of the "presence of a higher entity", nor even the experience of a "flood of inspiration" which fills one with life and light— no, what I mean by "concretely meeting" is nothing other than a true and really concrete meeting, i.e. face to face. It can be spiritual— face to face in vision— or more physically concrete. Thus, St. Teresa of Avila (in order to cite only *one* of many known examples) met the Master, conversed with him, asked and received from him advice and instruction on an objective spiritual plane (yes, spirituality is not exclusively subjective— it can also be objective). And certainly Papus and his group of occultist friends met Monsieur Philip of Lyons on the physical plane. Here are two examples of the concrete meeting that I mean.

Now, he who has had the experience of a concrete meeting with a higher being (a saint or righteous individual, an Angel or another hierarchical being, the Virgin Mary, the Master. . .) becomes through this very fact immune with respect to the tendency towards megalomania. The experience of having been face to face with a Great One necessarily comprises complete healing and immunity from any tendency towards megalomania. No human being who has *seen and heard* will be able to make an idol of himself. More than this: the true and ultimate criterion for the reality of these so-called "visionary" experiences, i.e. with respect to their authenticity or falsity, is given in the moral *effect* of these experiences, notably whether they make the recipient more humble or more pretentious. The experience of her meetings with the Master made St. Teresa more and more humble. The experience on the terrestrial plane of the meeting with Monsieur Philip of Lyons also made Papus and his occultist friends more humble. Now, these two experiences — quite different though they are with respect to subject and object — were *authentic*. Neither Papus was thereby mistaken about the spiritual greatness of he who he recognised as his "spiritual master", nor was St. Teresa any less mistaken about the reality of the Master, whom she saw and heard speak.

Dear Unknown Friend, read the Bible and you will find there a great number of examples of this law, which may be expressed as follows: *authentic experience of the Divine makes one humble; he who is not humble has not had authentic experience of the Divine*. Take the apostles who "saw and heard" the Master and the prophets who "saw and heard" the God of Israel — you will not find amongst them any trace of tendencies towards pride such as you can certainly find amongst many gnostic teachers who (*consequently*) had not "seen and heard".

But if it is true that it is necessary to have "seen and heard" in order to thoroughly learn the lesson of humility, what is there to say about people who are "naturally" humble and who have not "seen and heard"?

Without prejudice to other good and valuable answers, the answer which seems right to me is that all those who are humble *have certainly seen and heard* — no matter where or when, and no matter whether they remember or not. Humility can be the result of the real (i.e. non-intellectual) memory of the soul of the spiritual experience prior to birth, or it can be due to memory of nocturnal experience undergone during sleep and which remains in the domain of the unconscious or, lastly, it can be the effect of experience that is present consciously or unconsciously but is unacknowledged by oneself or others. For humility, like charity, is not a natural quality of human nature. Its origins can in no way be found in the domain of *natural* evolution, since it is not possible to conceive of it as the fruit of the "struggle for existence", i.e. natural selection and the survival of the fittest at the expense of the weak. Because the school of the struggle for existence does not produce humble people; it produces only strugglers and fighters of every kind. Humility is therefore a quality which must be due to the action of grace, i.e. it must be a gift from above. Now, the "concrete meetings, face to face" of which it is a question here are always, without exception, events due to grace, being *meetings* where a higher being voluntarily draws near to a lower being. The meeting which made Saul, the Pharisee, into Paul the apostle was not due to his efforts; it was an act of the One whom he met. It is the same with all meetings "face to face" with higher beings. Our part is only "to seek", "to knock" and "to pray", but the decisive act comes from above.

Let us now return to the Arcanum "The Chariot", whose traditional meaning is "victory, triumph, success".

> This meaning is derived naturally from the bearing of the personage (the charioteer) and presents no difficulty. (J. Maxwell, *Le Tarot*, Paris, 1933, p. 87)

Now, there is all the same a difficulty that it presents, namely that of answering the question: Does this Card signify a warning or an ideal, or rather both at once?

I am inclined to see in all the Arcana of the Tarot simultaneously both warnings and aims to be attained—at least, this is what I have learnt through forty years of study and meditation on the Tarot.

Thus the Magician is a warning against the intellectual jugglery of the metaphysician, heedless of experience, and against charlatancy of every kind—and at the same time it teaches "concentration without effort" and the use of the method of analogy.

The High Priestess warns us of the dangers of gnosticism in teaching the discipline of true gnosis.

The Empress evokes the dangers of mediumship and magic in revealing to us the mysteries of sacred magic.

The Emperor warns us of the will-to-power and teaches us the power of the cross.

The Pope confronts us with the humanistic cult of personality and the magical pentagram in which this culminates, and opposes to this holy poverty, obedience to the Divine, and the magic of the five wounds.

The Lover warns us of the three temptations and teaches us the three sacred vows.

The Chariot, lastly, warns us of the danger of megalomania and teaches us the *real triumph* achieved by the Self.

The real triumph achieved by the Self—this means to say the successful outcome of the "process of individuation", according to C. G. Jung, or the successful outcome of the work of true liberation, which is the fruit of *catharsis* (purification) and which precedes *photismos* (illumination), and which is followed by *henosis* (union), according to the occidental initiation tradition.

The "triumpher" on the Chariot can therefore signify either a sick person suffering from megalomania or a man who has passed through *catharsis* or purification, the first of the three stages on the way of initiation.

The thesis that I am advancing here is this: that, just as with all the other Cards of the Arcana of the Tarot, the Card of the seventh Arcanum also expresses a double meaning. The personage on this seventh Card signifies at one and the same time the "triumpher" and the "Triumpher"—the megalomaniac and the integrated man, master of himself.

The integrated man, master of himself, conqueror in all trials—who is he?

It is he who holds in check the four temptations—i.e. the three temptations in the wilderness described in the Gospels as well as the temptation which synthesises them: the temptation of pride, the centre of the triangle of temptations—and who is, therefore, master of the four elements which compose the vehicle of his being: fire, air, water and earth. Master of the four elements—that is to say: *creative* being in clear, fluid and precise thought (*creativity*, *clarity*, *fluidity* and *precision* being the manifestations of the four elements in the domain of thought). It means to say, moreover, that he has a warm, large, tender and faithful heart (*warmth*, *magnanimity*, *sensitivity* and *faithfulness* being the manifestations of the four elements in the domain of feeling). There is, lastly, to add that he has ardour ("man of desire"), fullness, flexibility and stability in his will (where the four elements manifest themselves as *intensity*, *scope*, *adaptability* and *firmness*). To summarise, one can say that a master of the four elements is a man of initiative, who is serene, mobile and firm. He represents the four natural virtues of Catholic theology: prudence, strength, temperance and justice; or rather Plato's four cardinal virtues: wisdom, courage, temperance and justice; or yet again the four qualities of Sankaracharya: *viveka* (discernment), *vairagya* (serenity), the "six jewels" of just conduct, and the desire for deliverance. Whatever the formulation may be of the four virtues in question, it is always a matter of the four elements or projections of the sacred name יהוה —the *Tetragrammaton*—in human nature.

The four columns supporting the canopy on the chariot drawn by two horses, in the Card of the seventh Arcanum, therefore signify the four elements taken in *a vertical sense*, i.e. in their analogous meaning through the three worlds—the spiritual world, the soul world and the physical world.

And what is signified by the canopy itself that the four columns support?

The function of a canopy, taken as a material object, is to *protect* the person who is found beneath it. It therefore serves as a roof. Taken in its spiritual sense, at which one arrives by way of analogy, the canopy above the man wearing a yellow royal crown expresses two contrary things: that the crowned man is a megalomaniac in the condition of "splendid isolation", separated from heaven by the canopy, or else that the crowned man is an initiate in the mystery of spiritual well-being and that he does not identify himself with heaven, *being conscious of the difference* which exists between himself and that which is above him. In other words, the canopy indicates the facts and truths underlying humility as well as megalomania. Humility, being the law of spiritual health, implies consciousness of the difference and distance between the centre of human consciousness and the centre of divine consciousness. He has a "skin"—or a canopy, if you wish—in his consciousness (just as the human body has a skin), which separates the human from the Divine, at the same time uniting them. This "spiritual skin" protects the spiritual well-being of man by not allowing him to identify himself *ontologically* with God, or to say "I am God" (cf. *Brhadaranyaka Upanishad* 1.4.10: *"aham brahmasmi"* = "I am Brahma"), but at the same time allowing him the *relationship of breathing*, coming together and separating (which is never *alienation*!), which together constitute the life of *love*. The life of love consists of coming together and separating always with the consciousness present of *non-identity*: this is analogous to the process of breathing which consists of inhalation and exhalation. Is this not found expressed in an unparalleled way in the extract from Psalm 43, which is the sixth phrase in the Mass: *"Emitte lucem tuam, et veritatem tuam: ipsa me deduxerunt, et adduxerunt in montem sanctum tuum, et in tabernacula tua"*? ("Oh send out thy light and thy truth; let them lead me, let them bring me to thy holy hill and to thy tabernacles"—Psalm 43, 3). Yes, the *light* of your presence (*drawing near*) and the *truth* that I receive in me through reflection (*separating*), this leads us towards the *tabernacle*.

Tabernacles...are these not tents, baldachins, *canopies* under which man is united in love with the Divine, without identifying himself with it or being absorbed by it? Aren't these tabernacles made of the "skin of humility", which alone protects us against the danger of killing love through ontological identification — i.e. the identification of the human being with divine being ("this soul is God" —*"ayam atma brahma"*, *Mandukya Upanishad*, 2; "consciousness is God"— *"pragnanam brahma"*, *Aitareya Upanishad*, 5.3)—and therefore protects us from the danger of spiritual megalomania (i.e. from arrogating to ourselves the very being of God instead of his image)?

There are three forms of mystical experience: the experience of union with Nature, that of union with the transcendental human Self, and that of union with God. The first kind of experience is that of the obliteration of the differentiation between the individual's psychic life and surrounding Nature. It is this which Lévy-Bruhl calls "mystical participation", which notion he coined whilst studying the psychology of primitive peoples. This notion designates the state of consciousness where the separation between the conscious subject and the object of the outside world disappears, and where subject and object become one. This kind of experience underlies not only shamanism and the totemism of the primitives but also the so-called "mythogenous" consciousness, which is the source of natural myths, as well as the ardent desire of poets and philosophers for union with Nature (e.g. Empedocles threw himself into the crater of the volcano on Mount Etna in order to unite himself with the elements of Nature). The effect of peyote, mescalin, hashish, alcohol, etc., can sometimes (but not always, and not with everyone) produce states of consciousness analogous to that of "mystical participation". The characteristic trait of this form of experience is *intoxication*, i.e. the temporary fusion of oneself with forces exterior to one's self-consciousness. The Dionysian orgies of antiquity were based on the experience of "sacred intoxication" due to the obliteration of the differentiation between self and non-self.

The second form of mystical experience is that of the transcendental Self. It consists in separating the ordinary empirical self from the higher Self, which is above all motion and all that which belongs to the domain of space and time. The higher Self is therefore experienced as immortal and free.

If "Nature mysticism" is characterised by intoxication, that of the Self, in contrast, has the characteristic trait of progressively "coming to one's senses", with the aim of *complete sobriety*. A philosophy based on the mystical experience of the Self, which represents it in the purest way and is least distorted by the addition of hazardous intellectual speculations, is that of the Indian school of Sankya. There the individual *purusha* is experienced in its separation from *prakriti* (i.e. all movement, space and time) as immortal and free. Although the same experience is found at the basis of the Vedanta philosophy, its followers are not satisfied with the immediate experience which teaches nothing more, and nothing less, than that the true Self of man is immortal and free, but they add the postulate that the higher Self *is* God ("this soul is God"—*"ayam atma brahma"*, *Mandukya Upanishad*, 2). The Sankya philosophy, in contrast, remains within the limits of the experience of the higher Self as such and in no way denies the plurality of *purushas* (i.e. the plurality of immortal and free higher Egos), nor does it raise the individual *purusha* to the dignity of the Absolute—which has resulted in it being considered an atheistic philosophy. It is so, if one understands by "atheist" the frank confession: I have not had *experience* of anything higher than the immortal and free Ego; abiding by the experience, what can I say in good faith? Sankya is not a religion and therefore does not merit being classed as "atheistic" any more than, for example, the modern psychological school of Jung does. On the other hand, can it be considered as proof of belief in God to attribute to the higher Self of man the dignity of the Absolute?

The third sort of mystical* experience is that of the *living God*, the God of Abraham, Isaac and Jacob in the Judaeo-Christian tradition, the God of St. Augustine, St. Francis, St. Teresa and St. John of the Cross in the Christian tradition, the God of the Bhagavad-Gita, Ramanuja, Madhva and Caitanya in the Hindu tradition. Here it is a matter of union with God in love, which implies a substantial duality being essentially at one.

This experience has as its principal characteristic trait the *synthesis* of the intoxication of Nature mysticism and the sobriety of mysticism of the higher Self. The term coined by tradition to express the state where ardent enthusiasm and profound peace manifest themselves simultaneously is that of "beatitude", or "beatific vision" (i.e. *beatitudo*, or *visio beatifica*). *Beatific vision* implies the duality of the seer and the seen, on the one hand, and their union or intrinsic oneness in love, on the other hand. This is why this term expresses in a wonderfully clear and precise way the essence of theistic mystical experience: the meeting of the soul with God, face to face, in love. And this experience is all the more elevated the more complete the differentiation is, and the more perfect the union is. For

---

*The term "mystical" used here comprises mystical experience proper *and* gnostic experience, as united.

this reason the Holy Cabbala puts at the centre of spiritual experience that of the Holy Face (*arich anphin*) of the Ancient of Days, and this is also why it teaches that the supreme experience of the human being—as well as the highest form of death for a mortal—is attained when God embraces the human soul. This is what the *Sepher Yetzirah* says:

> And after that our father Abraham had perceived, and under-
> stood, and had taken down and engraved all these things, the
> Lord most high (*adon hakol*) revealed Himself, and called him
> His beloved, and made a Covenant with him and his seed...
> (*Sepher Yetzirah* vi, 4; trsl. W. Wynn Westcott, London, 1893,
> pp. 26-27)

And St. John of the Cross spoke of his experiences of the divine Presence in the tabernacles of love only in the language of love.

The three forms of mystical experience have their "hygienic laws", or their "taber-nacles" or "skins". They fall under the law of temperance or *measure*. Otherwise the rage of acute mania, megalomania and complete alienation from the world (ἰδιοτία) menace, respectively, their adepts. The *breast-plate*, the *canopy* and the *crown* are the three symbols for the salutary measures pertaining to the domains of experience of Nature mysticism, human mysticism, and divine mysticism.

Now, the "triumpher" of the seventh Arcanum wears a breast-plate, stands under a canopy and is crowned. This is why he does not lose himself in Nature, why he does not lose God in the experience of his higher Self and why he does not lose the world in experiencing the love of God. He holds in check the dangers of rage, megalomania and exaltation. He is *sane*.

The "triumpher" of the seventh Arcanum is the true adept of Hermeticism, i.e. an adept of mysticism, gnosis and magic—divine, human and natural. He is not running. He stands upright. He is not seated, deep in meditation. He holds a sceptre which serves him to bridle the two horses (one blue and one red) which draw his chariot. He is not absent, plunged into exalted ecstasy. He is on his way and he goes forward, standing upright all the while in his vehicle. The two horses, the one blue and the other red, have relieved him of the effort of walking. The instinctive forces of "yes" and "no", attraction and repulsion, arterial blood and venous blood, trust and mistrust, faith and doubt, life and death and, lastly, "right" and "left"—symbolised by the pillars of Jachin and Boaz—have become motive forces in him, obedient to his sceptre. They serve him voluntarily as he is their true master. He trusts them and they trust him—this is mastership according to Hermeticism. For in Hermeticism mastership does not signify the subjugation of the lower by the higher, but rather the alliance of superconsciousness, consciousness and instinctive—or sub-consciousness. This is the Hermetic ideal of peace in the microcosm—the prototype of peace within a humanity divided into races, nations, classes and beliefs.

This peace is equilibrium or justice, where each particular force playing its part in the life of the microcosm is assigned its rightful place in the life of the entire psychic and physical organism.

Equilibrium or justice is the subject of the following Arcanum—the eighth Arcanum, Justice—which will be the theme of the next Letter.

Summarising the practical teaching (for it is always the practical aspect which occupies us in the first place) of the seventh Arcanum of the Tarot, one can say that the "triumpher" is a "convalescent", i.e. that the "triumpher" has triumphed over sickness or imbalance—spiritual, psychic and physical—which means to say that he is at the same time "righteous", or the one who has triumphed over the four temptations by remaining faithful to the three sacred vows as well as to their root and synthesis: humility. In turn, this means to say that he is a "liberated man" or "master". He is free of astrological planetary influences—rediscovered in our time by C. G. Jung in the guise of the "collective unconscious" with its seven (!) principal psychic forces or "archetypes". He is master of the "archetypes" (astrological planetary influences, or *archontes* of the ancient gnostics), i.e. the "shadow", the "persona", the "animus", the "anima", the "wise old man" or "father", the "mother" and even the "self", above which is the "Self of Selves" or God.

In other words, he holds in check the influences, in so far as they are baleful, of the moon, Mercury, Mars, Venus, Jupiter, Saturn and even the sun, above which he knows there exists the "Sun of suns" or *God*. He is not *without* the planets, archetypes or *archontes* (just as he is not without earth, water, air and fire) for these are what comprise that which is called the "astral body" (or psychic body) in occultism. The psychic body is a *body* in so far as it is composed of unconscious, collective or "planetary" psychic forces. It is the astrological planets (or Jung's archetypes) which form the "stuff" of the psychic or astral body. The "triumpher" of the seventh Arcanum is therefore the master of the astral body. . . master of the astral body—this means to say master of the *seven* forces which it comprises, holding them in equilibrium.

What is the eighth force which puts the seven forces of the astral body in equilibrium?

It is the eighth Arcanum of the Tarot, Justice, which gives the answer to this question.

Meditation on the
Eighth Major Arcanum of the Tarot

JUSTICE

LA JUSTICE

The Son and the Spirit—this is all that is
granted to us. With respect to absolute
unity or the Father, no one has been able
to see him nor will see him in this world,
if this is not within the *octenary*—which
is, in fact, the only way whereby one could
attain to him.

(Louis Claude de Saint-Martin,
Des nombres)*

Quis custodiat custodes? (Who will guard
the guards? . . . The fundamental problem
of jurisprudence)

LETTER VIII

JUSTICE

Dear Unknown Friend,

The seventh Arcanum taught us how inner equilibrium is attained; the teaching of the eighth Arcanum is how this equilibrium, once reached, is maintained; and the ninth Arcanum shows us the method or way which opens up to he who knows how to attain and maintain equilibrium. In other words, the seventh Arcanum tells us how to attain equilibrium (or *health*), the eighth Arcanum shows us the "mechanism" of microcosmic and macrocosmic equilibrium and the ninth Arcanum teaches us the "way of peace" or the "middle way"—that of balanced spiritual development—which is proper to Hermeticism, taken as the synthesis of mysticism, gnosis, magic and science.

*Nice, 1946, xiv.

173

The Card of the eighth Arcanum represents a woman seated on a yellow seat between two pillars, dressed in a red tunic and covered with a blue mantle. She holds a yellow sword and a yellow balance in her hands. On her head she wears a three-part tiara mounted by a crown.

Now, the totality of the Card evokes the idea of law interposed between the free action of the individual will and the essence of being. Man can act from his own free will—law *reacts* to his action through visible and invisible effects. But behind this reaction is found the essential ground of ultimate reality (the *ens realissimum* of St. Thomas Aquinas), which confers universality, regularity and immutability to the reactions of law. Law is interposed between the freedom of man and the freedom of God. She is seated between two pillars: that of will (Jachin) and that of providence (Boaz). She does not act; she can only react. This is why she is represented as a woman and not as a man. The crown which she wears indicates that she derives her dignity and mission from above—from the supreme Being, from providence. The balance and the sword that she holds in her hands indicate what she guards (equilibrium) and how she guards it (the sanction of equilibrium) in the domain of the free will of individuals. Thus she says: "I am seated on the seat which is between the individual will of beings and the universal will of the supreme Being. I am the guardian of equilibrium between the individual and the universal. I have the power to re-establish it each time that it is violated. I am order, health, harmony, *justice*."

It is the balance which indicates equilibrium—or order, health, harmony and justice—and it is the sword which signifies the power to re-establish it each time that the individual will sins against the universal will.

This is the general meaning of the Card which, so to say, captures our attention from the very beginning of our meditation on the eighth Arcanum. Yet the general meaning—although many consider it as the goal of their efforts towards knowledge—is only the antechamber to the Hermetic meaning. For this latter does not lie in the *generality* obtained by the method of *abstraction*, but rather in the *depth* obtained by the method of *penetration*. The general answers obtained by means of abstraction are, in reality, only so many questions and tasks assigned for penetration. Because the more a general idea is abstract, the more superficial it is. The most general and most abstract idea which exists in philosophy is that of the "Absolute" (cf. Hegel), but it is at the same time the most superficial idea in the world. In signifying all, it expresses nothing. You can certainly die—and even live—for God, but you would never die as a martyr for the Absolute. Because to die for the Absolute amounts to dying for nothing. The idea of the Absolute is only a shadow of shadows, whilst the living God is the prototype of prototypes...the prototype of prototypes, this means to say: the universal Father.

One of the meanings of the first commandment—"Thou shalt have no other gods before me" (Exodus xx, 3)—is that one should not substitute an intellectual *abstraction* of God for the spiritual *reality* of God. One therefore sins against the first commandment when one substitutes for the fiery, luminous and vibrant Being of life the abstractions of a "principle" or "idea"—be it the "First Cause", or the "Absolute"—which are, truth to tell, only mentally "graven images" or mental *idols* created by the human intellect.

Therefore, let us not sin against the first commandment and let us not substitute mentally graven images or abstract ideas for the reality of Justice. But, on the other hand, let us also not embrace the cause of intellectual iconoclasts who want to see only idols in every concept and abstract idea. For all concepts and abstract ideas *can* become *icons* or "sacred images" when one considers them not as the *end*, but rather as the *beginning* of the way of knowledge of spiritual reality. In the domain of the intellectual life, *hypotheses* do not play the role of idols, but rather that of sacred images. Because no one accepts a hypothesis as absolute truth, just as no one worships a sacred image as absolute reality. Yet hypotheses are fruitful in that they lead us to the truth, in guiding us to it within the totality of our experience—just as icons or sacred images are also fruitful in leading us to experience the spiritual reality that they represent. An icon is the beginning of the way to spiritual reality; it does not replace it—as in idolatry—but gives an impulse and direction towards it. Similarly, a concept or abstract idea does not replace spiritual reality, but rather gives an impulse and direction towards it. Therefore, let us avoid the Scylla of idolatry and the Charybdis of the intellectual iconoclastic attitude, and let us take abstract ideas as *hypotheses* leading to the truth, and images or *symbols* as our guides to reality. Let us therefore not commit the error of wanting to "explain" a symbol by reducing it to a few general abstract ideas. Let us also avoid the error of wanting to "concretise" an abstract idea by clothing it in the form of an allegory. Rather, let us seek *practical spiritual experience* of reality and the truth by means of concrete images as well as abstract ideas. For the Tarot is a system or organism of spiritual exercises; in the first place it is *practical*. If this were not so, it would be hardly worthwhile to occupy oneself with it.

Therefore, let us take the Arcanum "Justice" as an invitation towards an effort of consciousness with the intention of arriving at an experience of the reality it represents and an understanding of the truth that it expresses. First of all, the fact may be stated that it is in the domain of *judgement* that the reality and truth of justice manifests itself. Because to pronounce judgement with respect to anything whatsoever amounts to an action having as its aim the finding of justice. It is not only the judges at tribunals who judge; everyone judges in the degree to which he *thinks*. All of us, in so far as we are thinking beings, are judges. Because every problem, every question that we try to resolve, gives way in reality to a session for our inner tribunal, where the "pros and cons" are confronted and weighed before judgement is pronounced. We are all judges, good or bad; we are so, and we exercise the functions of a judge almost unceasingly from morning 'til night. The commandment—"Thou shalt not judge" (Matthew vii, 1)—would therefore amount to the renunciation of thought. For to think is to judge. "True" and "false", "beautiful" and "ugly", "good" and "bad" are judgments that we pronounce many times each day. Nevertheless, it is one thing to judge and another thing to condemn. One judges *phenomena* and *actions*, but one cannot judge *beings* as such. Because to do so would exceed the competence of the judgement of thought. Therefore one should not judge *beings*, because they are inaccessible to the judgement of thought which is founded only on phenomenal experience. Thus, negative judgement concerning beings, or their condemnation, is in reality impossible. And it is in this sense that there is a ground for understanding the Christian commandment: "Thou shalt not judge"—i.e. do not judge *beings*, do not *condemn*. For he who condemns assumes a function of which he is not capable. He *lies* in presenting as truth and justice a judgement which is devoid of any foundation. It is therefore better to say to one's neighbour, "You are acting like a madman", since whoever says, "You *are* mad", deserves to be punished by the fire of hell (cf. Matthew v, 22).

Therefore, one has to know the extent of one's knowledge and ignorance when one makes a judgement. And one is always ignorant of the noumenal being (or the soul) of another. This is why no human judgement has bearing on the soul.

And *intuition*? Is it there for nothing? Certainly it exists and is there for something. Nevertheless, intuition being perception due to sympathy and love never accuses. It always plays the role of the defence, the advocate. As it perceives the soul of beings, it sees only the image of God in them. Seeing and knowing that the soul of the offender is always the first victim of all sin or crime that he could commit, intuition can play no other role than that of the advocate. The saying "to know all is to forgive all" refers to understanding "from within"—that is to say, "intuitive"—and not to external understanding, i.e. phenomenal and discursive understanding. A moving formula for the role of intuition in the exercise of justice is given to us in the prayer of the Master as he was being crucified: "Father, forgive them; for they know not what they do" (Luke xxiii, 34). This formula indicates three facts:

1. what they are doing, from a phenomenal point of view, is
   criminal;
2. judgement is handed over to the Father;
3. this is accompanied by the plea "forgive them", based on the
   certainty due to intuitive perception that "they know not
   what they do".

It is thanks to recognition of the role of intuition in intelligence, as distinct from the role of research and the establishment of facts due to understanding, that the strict justice of the latter faculty has been supplemented by *equity* in the exercise of justice in countries which have accepted the principles of Roman and Anglo-Saxon law. Common law is what is found through understanding after it has compared the facts with the letter of the law. Equity is what intelligence finds necessary to modify within common law after comparison with the results of efforts to arrive at an intuitive perception of the human being whose lot is at stake. It is for the sake of equity, or the judgement of intuition within intelligence, that the jury became instituted in the exercise of justice within Christian civilisation. Before Christianity the institution of the jury did not exist. Neither the wife of Pilate nor "the great multitude of people and women who bewailed and lamented him" (Luke xxiii, 27) had a voice at Pilate's tribunal. The "jury" (the women of Jerusalem) could then only weep or converse in secret with the "judge" (the wife of Pilate). Then it was equity which cried in the streets of Jerusalem and it was the intuition within intelligence which whispered warnings in Pilate's ear through the mouth of his wife. And it was the absence of a jury as a judicial organ of equity which forced the judge, Pilate, to resort to a monstrous deed of justice — abdicating the function of judge, washing his hands of it and transferring it to the prosecutor.

Now, justice is done only in the case when *all* the pertinent facts for and against the accused are established, then weighed by understanding, and then submitted to the judgement of intelligence. The three functions of justice — instruction, debate, and decision — correspond to the three degrees of knowledge — hypothetical, argumentative, and intuitive — designated by Plato as " δόξα " (*doxa*) or "hypothetical opinion", "διάνοια" (*dianoia*) or "conclusion based on arguments" and "ἐπιστήμη"(*episteme*) or "intuitive perception". In fact, the facts established and presented by the instruction serve as the basis both for the prosecution and the defence for their respective *hypotheses*: "guilty" and "innocent". The debates which follow pursue the aim of arriving at a *conclusion* based on arguments advanced in favour of one or the other hypothesis. The decision taken by the jury is understood in principle as the result of an effort of consciousness to rise above the appearance of facts and the formalism of logical arguments with a view to an intuitive perception of the matter from a human point of view. It is therefore equity which has the last word.

One can say, therefore, that the process of the exercise of human justice consists in the total exertion of all three cognitive faculties of the human being: the faculty of forming hypotheses on the basis of data supplied by the senses (*doxa*), the faculty of logical discursion or intellectual weighing for and against these hypotheses (*dianoia*) and, lastly, the faculty of intuition (*episteme*).

Now, the structure of "fair human justice" is only — and *can* only be — an "image" or analogy of the structure of divine cosmic justice. The Jewish Cabbala brings this out more clearly than any other current of tradition that I know of.

There the system known as the "Sephiroth Tree" consists of three pillars: the right, the left and the middle. The right pillar or that of Mercy comprises the Sephiroth *Chokmah* (Wisdom), *Chesed* or *Gedulah* (Grace/Mercy or Magnificence/Majesty) and *Netzach* (Victory or Triumph). The left pillar or that of Severity is composed of the Sephiroth *Binah* (Intelligence), *Geburah* or *Pachad* (Severity or Fear) and *Hod* (Glory or Honour). The Sephiroth of the middle pillar are *Kether* (Crown), *Tiphereth* (Beauty), *Yesod* (Foundation) and *Malkuth* (Realm or Kingdom).

The right pillar is often designated as the "pillar of Grace (Mercy)", whilst the left pillar bears the name the "pillar of Severity". Now these two pillars (which the *Zohar* regards as those of metaphysical GOOD and EVIL) correspond, from the point of view of justice, to *defence* and *prosecution*, whilst the middle pillar corresponds to *equity*. The system of ten Sephiroth is based on mobile *equilibrium*, with the tendency to re-establish it in an instance where a momentary dissymmetry is produced. *It is a system of balance*.

> In its most simple form a balance consists of a fixed axis (a column in the middle), which is generally vertical, a beam which forms a T or a + (cross) with this axis and, lastly, two scales suspended at the ends of the beam. The balance gives rise to three fundamental relationships: (i) the equilibrium between the two scales establishes a relationship of correlation; (ii) the common suspension of the scales at a point of balance and the propping up of the whole system by a support evokes a relationship of subordination; and (iii) the different roles of the two scales in the weighing introduces between the opposite ends a differentiation by virtue of which an orientation or current is produced. (Francis Warrain, *La théodicée de la Kabbale*, Paris, 1949, p. 50)

In the system of Sephiroth it is a matter of a system of balance established simultaneously in four worlds, or on four planes: the world of emanation (*ôlam ha-atziluth*), the world of creation (*ôlam ha-beriah*), the world of formation (*ôlam ha-yetzirah*) and the world of action (*ôlam ha-àssiah*), both in a vertical sense, i.e. the balance establishes and re-establishes equilibrium between that which is above and that which is below, as well as in a horizontal sense, i.e. the balance maintains equilibrium between the right side and the left side, the pillars of Grace and Severity. Therefore, weighing is effected on the one hand by means of scales on the right and left and on the other hand by scales above and below. The working of the "right-left" balance is the law of justice which maintains equilibrium between the individual freedom of beings and universal order. In the last analysis it is KARMA which is the law governing the adjustment of mutual debts between beings. But the working of the "heaven-earth" balance surpasses the justice of karma; it is that of the justice of grace.

"*Gratia gratis data . . .*" The sun shines on the good and wicked alike. Is this morally right? Is it the justice of grace here which is higher than the protective, distributive and punitive justice of the law? This is so. There is the sublime "other justice" of grace, which is the meaning of the New Testament. For the Old Testament is to the New Testament as karma is to grace. Grace also makes use of the balance, i.e. justice. It is the balance whose one scale is on the earth and whose other scale is in heaven. The Lord's prayer reveals to us the principle of the justice of grace and the operation of weighing by means of the "heaven-earth" balance. There it is said: "Forgive us our trespasses, as we forgive those who trespass against us." And then the Master adds: "For if you forgive men their trespasses, your heavenly Father also will forgive you; but if you do not forgive men their trespasses, neither will your Father forgive your trespasses" (Matthew vi, 12, 14-15).

The Master is explicit with respect to the balance operating between earth and heaven—". . . if you do not forgive men their trespasses, neither will your Father forgive your trespasses"—this is the law, this is the infallible and implacable operation of the "heaven-earth" balance. That this balance governs not only forgiveness but also the entire domain of gifts from above, understood as the Holy Spirit, is evident in the words of the Master concerning the Lord's prayer in the Gospel of Luke: "If you then, who are evil, know how to give good gifts to your children, how much more will the heavenly Father give the Holy Spirit to those who ask him!" (Luke xi, 13)

The sun shines on the good and wicked alike. But it is certainly necessary to open the windows of a dark room in order for light to be able to enter there. The *light* of the sun is in no way created or merited by us. It is a gift, pure and simple — *gratia gratis data*. Nevertheless, it is necessary to open our windows in order for it to enter into our abode, just as it is necessary to open our eyes in order to see it. The practical meaning of the "heaven-earth" balance is that of *cooperation* with grace. Human effort is therefore not for nothing in the domain of the working of grace. Neither election alone from above (Calvinism) nor faith alone below (Lutheranism) suffice for the requirements of the "heaven-earth" balance. Chosen or not chosen, having faith or not, it is necessary for us, for example, to "forgive those who trespass against us" here below in order for our trespasses to be forgiven above. There is a correlation — not in *measure*, but rather in *nature* — between the scale below, "effort", and the scale above, "gift", of the "heaven-earth" balance. The correlation between effort below and gift from above is not, I repeat, one of measure or *quantity*, but rather one of substance or *quality*. It can be that the forgiveness on my part of one single offence by another can produce the forgiveness of a thousand or so offences of the same nature by me. The "heaven-earth" balance does not weigh *quantity*; its working belongs entirely to the domain of *quality*. This is why there is no quantitative justice in the relationship between efforts below and gifts from above. The latter always surpass the measure of quantitative justice. This is important to understand above all with regard to the glaring injustice of eternal hell, that one life — or more, it does not matter — which is limited in time can bring about. Eternal hell is unjust, however, only from a purely quantitative point of view. One compares the limited number of years of life — or lives — on earth with the unlimited number of years of eternity and thus one arrives at the conclusion that the measure of chastisement is out of all proportion with the measure of the transgression and that, consequently, there is no justice. But let us consider the problem of eternal hell not from the point of view of quantity (which is absurd, as time does not exist in eternity), but rather from that of quality.

How is it with this problem, then?

The following is the answer we arrive at when we abandon a quantitative correlation between time and eternity: whoever enters the region of eternity without an ounce of love, enters it without an ounce of love, i.e. he enters eternal hell. For to live without love—this is hell. And to live without love in the region of eternity—this is to live in eternal hell.

> Hell is the state of the soul powerless to come out of itself, absolute self-centredness, dark and evil isolation, i.e. final inability to love. (Nicolas Berdyaev, *The Destiny of Man*, London, 1937, p. 351)

This subjective state of soul is neither long nor short—it is as *intense* as eternity is. Similarly, the blessedness that a saint experiences in the vision of God is as intense as eternity—although it could not so last, since someone present at the ecstasy of a saint would time it as a few minutes. The "region" of eternity is that of *intensity*, which surpasses the measures of quantity that we employ in time and space. "Eternity" is not a duration of infinite length; it is the "intensity of quality" which, if compared with time and thus translated into the language of quantity, is comparable with an infinite duration. Concerning this, Nicolas A. Berdyaev says:

> In our life on earth it is given to us to experience torments that appear to us to go on for ever, that are not for a moment, for an hour or a day, but seem to last an infinity...Objectively this infinity may last a moment, an hour, or a day, but it receives the name of everlasting hell...When Origen said that Christ will remain on the cross so long as a single creature remains in hell, he expressed an eternal truth. (Nicolas Berdyaev, *The Destiny of Man*, London, 1937, p. 342 and p. 347)

What can one add to this, if not "amen"? Eternal hell is the state of a soul imprisoned within itself, where the *soul* has no hope of coming out. "Eternal" means to say "without hope". All suicides committed through desperation bear witness to the reality of eternal hell as a state of soul. Before committing suicide, the person who commits it experiences a state of complete despair, i.e. *eternal* hell. This is why he prefers nothingness to the state of despair. Nothingness is therefore his last hope.

Eternal bliss—"heaven"—is, in contrast, the state of soul which is filled with boundless hope. This is not a blissfulness which lasts for an infinite number of years; it is the *intensity* of hope which gives the quality "eternal". Similarly, it is the intensity of despair which imparts to the state of soul designated "hell" the quality "eternal".

The anguish of Gethsemane which gave rise to perspiration of blood was *eternal*. This night, the night of Gethsemane, was not measured in hours. It was—it *is*—immeasurable, therefore eternal. It is due to its eternity that he sweated blood, and not because of the temporary, and therefore passing, trial. He knew eternal hell through experience, and as he came out of it, we have the "good news" that not only death is vanquished by the Resurrection, but also that hell is—through Gethsemane. The majesty of the victory over hell announced by the words "I am he" caused many to prostrate themselves on the ground, from amongst the band of soldiers and officers from the chief priests and Pharisees who had come to arrest him (John xviii, 5-6). The soul of Origen was also prostrated in the face of the victory over eternal hell and moved by the revelation contained in the words: "It is I," spoken by He who had just come out from eternal hell. This is why Origen himself knew with certain knowledge that there would be no "damned" at the end of the world and that the devil, also, would be saved. And whoever meditates on the sweat of blood in Gethsemane and on the words "It is I" (or "I am he"), announcing the eternal victory over eternal hell, also will know with certain knowledge that eternal hell *exists* as a reality, but that it will be *empty* at the end of time. The sweat of blood in Gethsemane is the source of "Origenism"; here is the source of its inspiration.

But the "good news" of the eternal victory over eternal hell has not been understood by the "Greeks" (those seeking wisdom), nor by the "Jews" (those wanting miracles). It can be understood only by *Christians*. For "Greeks" deny the reality of eternal hell as being incompatible with the idea of God who is at one and the same time good and all-powerful. "Jews" abide by eternal damnation, i.e. they insist on a *populated* eternal hell, because otherwise God (as the judge) would be lacking the absolute power of punishment. They deny the infinity of divine love. And it is Christians alone who accept and understand the "folly and weakness" of the cross (cf. 1 Corinthians i, 22-25), i.e. the work of infinite love achieved by no other means than by love itself. For them, not only do the means not sanctify the aim, but also the means must be identical with the aim. They know that love will never be taught and understood through severity and fear. They apprehend hearts directly through goodness, beauty and truth, whilst the fear of hell and eternal damnation has not given birth to love in any human heart hitherto—and will never do so. And it is not the severity of strict justice which teaches us the love of the father for the prodigal son, but rather the joyous feast with which the son was welcomed home by him.

Nevertheless, the "Greeks" would say that the father knew in advance that the son would come back, since the son had, in fact, no other choice, and everything is only a *drama in appearance*. The father's way of acting was only a "clever ruse" (Hegel's "*List der Vernunft*"). And the "Jews" would say that it was the power of the father which acted within the soul of the prodigal son and commanded him to return to his father's home, which irresistible power he could only obey.

Thus, the *joy* and the *feast* of welcome from the father remain incomprehensible both to the worshippers of God's wisdom ("Greeks") and the worshippers of God's power ("Jews"). The meaning of both is understandable only to the worshippers of the love of God ("Christians"). They understand that the story of the prodigal son is a real drama of real love and real freedom, and that the joy and celebration of the father are genuine, just as the suffering of the father and also that of the son, which preceded their reunion, was genuine. Moreover, they understand that the story of the prodigal son is the history of the whole human race, and that the history of the human race is a real drama of real divine love and real human freedom.

"Greeks", "Jews", and "Christians"—worshippers of the wisdom, power and love of God! There are always plenty of "Greeks" and "Jews" in the lap of the Church, and within Christianity in general. It is they who are responsible for all heresies of faith and all moral heresies, and it is they who cause the scissions and schisms in the universal community of Christians. Thus the central fact of divine love, the Incarnation of the Word and the person of the God-Man, was from the beginning the special object of efforts by "Jews" and "Greeks" with a view to transforming it into a deed of power or a fact of wisdom. "Jesus Christ is only the Messiah, the chosen and annointed man *sent* by God" taught the "Jews" (Ebionites and Cerinthians), who denied the divine Incarnation as being incompatible with the omnipotence of God. "The Word incarnated, but is not God: the Word is his creation", taught the "Jews" of the fourth century, disciples of Arius, inspired by the idea that the power of God is sufficient to create a being of such perfection that he could accomplish the work of salvation without himself incarnating.

"There are two persons in Jesus Christ, one divine and the other human," said the "Greeks" known under the name of "Nestorians", who saw an impassable abyss between absolute divine wisdom and relative human wisdom, and who were unable to admit that the former united itself with the latter without diminution and obscuration. On the contrary: "There is only a single nature in Jesus Christ," taught the "Jews" known under the name of "Eutychians" who—being blind in that which concerns the union of the two natures, divine and human, through *love*, without either losing itself in the other or the two losing themselves in giving birth to a third nature—believed that the union of two natures could only be *substantial*, and that divine omnipotence could certainly accomplish this alchemical miracle of the fusion of two natures *substantially*. Later "Jews" known as "Monophysites" and "Jacobites" took over the doctrine of Eutychianism and founded their own churches.

At the same time "Greeks", convinced that there is only wisdom or ignorance—the former being pure spirit and the latter being matter—denied the reality of the two natures in the God-Man, and therefore the *Incarnation* itself, since the *incarnation* of wisdom would amount to its reduction to a state of ignorance. This is why the "Doceta" (the name that is attributed to them) taught that the human nature of the Word was only apparent, and that the body of Jesus Christ was only a phantom.

The "Greek" Apollinaris (fourth century) believed it necessary to change the proportion between the two natures and to reduce the presence of human nature in Jesus Christ by a third. He taught that the complete human nature consists of three principles: body, soul (*psyche*) and spirit (*pneuma*), whilst the human nature in Jesus Christ consisted only of two principles — body and soul — his human spirit having been replaced by the divine Word. Here one can see again the same "Greek" scruple of wanting to preserve divine wisdom intact and unobscured by the human element.

Thus, the "Greeks", devoted to the cause of the supremacy of wisdom, and the "Jews", devoted to that of the supremacy of the power of God, have endeavoured through the course of centuries to de-throne the principle of love in favour either of the principle of wisdom or that of power.

The struggle for the principle of love commenced in antiquity, and continued during the Middle Ages and after; it still continues today around the Church, at the heart of the Church, and within the soul of every Christian individual. For what was the struggle between the extreme "realists" and the extreme "nominalists" at the heart of the mediaeval and modern Scholastic School, if not the struggle between the "Greeks" ("realists") and the "Jews" ("nominalists")?. . . and the struggle between the "rationalists" ("*ratio nobilior potestas*") and the "voluntarists" ("*voluntas nobilior potestas*") at the heart of the same School? For the "realists" and "rationalists", ideas were objective realities and God's faculty of reason was higher than his will, whilst for the "nominalists" and "voluntarists" ideas were only names under which one classes phenomena — useful *abstractions* with a view to the classification of phenomena — and it was will which was higher than the faculty of reason within God. For the latter God is, in the first place, all-powerful will, whilst for the former he is, above all, reason — infinite wisdom.

And the *love* of God? It is this third, essentially Christian, principle which has held the *balance* through the course of the centuries, and holds it still in preventing the complete scission and disintegration of Christianity. In so far as there is peace at the heart of Christianity, it is due only to the principle of the supremacy of love.

For the complete victory of "realism", with its faith in that which is *general* at the expense of that which is individual, would have drowned Christianity in severity and cruelty. This is manifested with sufficient certainty in the historical fact of the inquisition — this latter being the practical conclusion of the fundamental dogma of realism: "the general is superior to the individual", which was consequently acted upon.

And the complete victory of "nominalism" would have drowned Christianity in the element of the relativity of the individual and personal opinions, beliefs and revelations of a kind such that it would have disintegrated to dust. The hundreds of Protestant sects and modes of belief at the core of these sects proves this with absolute certainty.

No, in so far as there is unity in space (the Church) and in time (tradition) for Christianity, this is due neither to "realist" severity nor to "nominalist" indulgence, but rather to the peace of equilibrium between the "Greek" and "Jewish" tendencies that the "Christian" tendency of love has succeeded in establishing and maintaining. If this were not so, the whole Christian world would now be divided into two spheres: a sphere where one would suffocate under "puritanical severity", "Huguenot boredom" and a kind of Calvinism (Calvin himself was a "realist"); and a sphere where each family or even each person would have a small religion and a little private church (Luther himself was a "nominalist") of a kind where *Christianity* as such would be only an abstraction, only a *name* or *word* (*mere vox* or *flatus vocis*).

Hence, these are the things at work when one evokes the problem of *balance*.

One generally encounters the same things that are in Christianity also at the heart of the Hermetic tradition or "occult movement". Here also there are "Greeks", "Jews" and "Christians". The "Jews" seek for miracles, i.e. deeds of magical realisation, and the "Greeks" aspire to an absolute theory which would be to exoteric philosophies as algebra is to arithmetic. Thus, Martinez de Pasqually and the circle of his disciples practised ceremonial magic with the intention of bringing about the evocation of the Risen One himself. Hoené-Wronski, in contrast, elaborated an absolute system of the "philosophy of philosophies", the purpose of which was to understand within its framework, and to put in its proper place within it, every philosophy of the past, present and future.

Fabre d'Olivet (author of *The Philosophical History of the Human Race*) and Saint-Yves d'Alveydre (author of *Archeometry or the System of Principles and Criteria for all Philosophical, Religious and Scientific Doctrines of the Past, Present and Future*) represent the "Greek" tendency *par excellence* within the framework of the Hermetic or occult movement. Eliphas Lévi and authors on magic and the practical Cabbala who have continued his work from the nineteenth century to the present day represent, in contrast, the "Jewish" tendency.

Louis Claude de Saint-Martin, after having collaborated with the intimate circle of disciples of Martinez de Pasqually, dissociated himself from this circle and the work of its master. He did so as a friend, not as an adversary, and in no way doubted the reality of the magic practised in this circle. He did so because he had found the "inner way", the experiences and realisation of which surpass in value the experiences and realisations of magic, theurgy, necromancy and artificial magnetism:

> This sort of clarity (issuing from the practice of the rites of high
> theurgy) must belong to those who are called directly to make
> use of it, by the order of God and for the manifestation of his
> glory. And when they are called there in this way there is no

uneasiness about their instruction, for then they receive, without
any darkening, a thousand times more notions, and notions a
thousand times more sure than those that a simple amateur such
as myself could give them on all these fundamentals.

Wanting to speak to others, and above all to the public (via
books), is to want—to no purpose—to stimulate and to work
up a vain curiosity, rather for the vanity of the writer than for
the benefit of the reader. Now, if I have made errors of this sort
in my earlier writings, I would continue to do so if I were to persist in marching on the spot. Thus, my recent writings speak
much more about this central initiation which, through our
union with God, can teach us all that we must know, and there
is very little about the descriptive anatomy of those delicate
points concerning which you would like me to disclose my view.
(Louis Claude de Saint-Martin in a letter dated 1797; cf. Robert
Ambelain, *Le Martinisme*, Paris, 1946, p. 113)

He found the "true theurgy" in the domain of the inner spiritual life and consequently abandoned outer or ceremonial theurgy. On the other hand, Saint-Martin
did not take up the "Greek" way: the grandiose intellectual adventure of creating
an absolute philosophical system. He remained *practical*; he only changed the
form of the practice, namely the practice of ceremonial magic for that of sacred
or divine magic, which is founded on mystical experience and gnostic revelation.
Thus Saint-Martin represents the third tendency in the occidental Hermetic movement—the Christian tendency.

Just as with Christianity in general, Hermeticism has not entirely disintegrated
—thanks to the "Christians" at its core, who maintain equilibrium between the
"Jews" and the "Greeks". If this were not so, we would now have two divergent
literatures and movements, which would have in common only a few vestiges of
a once common terminology. One current, the "Greek" current, would perhaps
at some time arrive at the "Archeometry of past, present and future Archeometries"
and the other current, the "Jewish" current, would perhaps attain to the "zodiacal
operation of the evocation of the twelve Thrones".

However, the *source* of the life and viability of the entire Hermetic current
through the course of the ages is to be found neither in intellectual theory nor
in magical practice. It is quite precisely stated by Hermes Trismegistus, the pre-
Christian sage, in the dialogue *Asclepius*:

For speaking as a prophet speaks, I tell you that in after times
none will pursue philosophy in singleness of heart. Philosophy
is nothing else than striving through constant contemplation
and saintly piety to attain to knowledge of God; but there will
be many who will make philosophy hard to understand, and
corrupt it with manifold speculations...philosophy will be

mixed with diverse and unintelligible sciences, such as arithmetic, music and geometry. Whereas the student of philosophy undefiled, which is dependent on devotion to God, and on that alone, ought to direct his attention to the other sciences only so far as he may. . . be led to revere, adore, and praise God's skill and wisdom. . . For to worship God in thought and spirit with singleness of heart, to revere God in all his works, and to give thanks to God, whose will, and his alone, is wholly filled with goodness—this is philosophy unsullied by intrusive cravings for unprofitable knowledge. (*Asclepius* i; trsl. Walter Scott, *Hermetica*, vol. i, Oxford, 1924, pp. 309 and 311)

Let us now place this statement of pre-Christian Hermeticism into the Christian epoch, with all the transformations that this transference entails, and we have the eternal foundation of Hermeticism—the source of its life and viability.

The text quoted, considered from the point of view of its value in advancing *knowledge*, appears quite banal; it appears as banality itself. Any pious Cistercian monk of the twelfth century—proud of his pious ignorance—would have been able to be the author of this text. But let us consider it from the point of view of the *will*, taking it as a programme of action—action through millennia, from the past and into the future. What does it then say to us?

At first it tells us that there are three basic diverse impulses underlying this kind of human endeavour (the endeavour of aspiration to knowledge) which aim at building the edifice of the body of philosophy and the sciences. These are: *curiosity*, where one wants to know for the sake of knowledge, according to the principle of "art for art's sake"; *usefulness*, where one is led to the work of research, experimentation and invention through the needs of human life, so as to make labour more fruitful, to preserve health and to prolong life; and, lastly, the *glory of God*, where there is neither curiosity nor practical utility but, as the great palaeontologist of our time, Pierre Teilhard de Chardin, said: ". . . the tremendous power of the divine attraction. . . the specific effect of which is. . . to make man's endeavour holy" (Pierre Teilhard de Chardin, *Le Milieu divin. An essay on the interior life*, London, 1964, p. 65).

Thus, there is knowledge for the sake of knowledge, knowledge for the sake of better serving one's neighbour, and knowledge in order to better love God. Knowledge for the sake of knowledge comes down in the last analysis to the promise of the serpent in paradise: "You shall be as gods, knowing good and evil" (Genesis iii, 5). Therefore, it is for his own glory that man takes up this way. This is why ancient Hermeticism, Jewish Cabbalistic Hermeticism and Christian Hermeticism unanimously condemn curiosity or knowledge for the sake of knowledge as vain, foolhardy and baneful. Thus, it is said in an extract from the sacred book of Hermes Trismegistus entitled *Kore Kosmu* ("The Virgin of the World", or "The Eye-Pupil of the World"):

Hermes, you are doing a rash thing in making man; for he is like to be a creature that sees with inquisitive eyes, and hears things he has no right to hear, and indulges greedily his sense of taste, and makes voluptuous use of his sense of smell, and misuses to all extremes his sense of touch. Tell me, you that are the author of his being, is it your settled purpose to leave him free from care, this being that is going to look with audacious gaze upon the beauteous mysteries of Nature?. . .They will dig up roots of plants, and investigate the properties of stones. They will dissect the lower animals—yes, and one another also— seeking to find out how they have come to be alive, and what manner of thing is hidden within. . .They will dig mines, and search into the uttermost darkness of the depths of the earth. And all this might be borne, but they will do yet more: they will press on to the world above, seeking to discover by observation the laws of movement of the heavens. Are they then to meet with no impediment? Shall they never be overpowered by the cruel stings of fear, and shall they luxuriate in a life exempt from cares?. . .that they may fail to get the things they hoped for, and be subdued by the pangs of grief. Let their presumptuous eagerness be disappointed of its expectations. (*Kore Kosmu*; trsl. Walter Scott, *Hermetica*, vol. i, Oxford, 1924, p. 483)

Such is the *accusation* of the demon Momus—"a mighty spirit. . .who had a body of enormous bulk, and a mind of surpassing power" (ibid., p. 481)—the spirit inquisitor of the human race quoted in *Kore Kosmu*. But here follows Hermes' defence of man's cognitive faculty in the discourse dedicated to his son Tat, entitled *The Key*:

For man is a being of divine nature; he is comparable, not to the other living creatures upon earth, but to the gods in heaven. Nay, if we are to speak the truth without fear, he who is indeed a man is even above the gods of heaven, or at any rate he equals them in power. None of the gods of heaven will ever quit heaven, and pass its boundary, and come down to earth; but man ascends even to heaven, and measures it; and what is more than all beside, he mounts to heaven without quitting the earth; to so vast a distance can he put forth his power. We must not shrink then from saying that a man on earth is a mortal god, and that a god in heaven is an immortal man. (*Corpus Hermeticum*, book x, "A discourse of Hermes Trismegistus. The Key"; trsl. Walter Scott, *Hermetica*, vol. i, Oxford, 1924, p. 205)

Here we have accusation (prosecution) and defence. The judgement which ensues is that knowledge for the sake of knowledge, which Momus, the prosecutor, has in mind, is to be condemned, since Momus is right in so far as his accusation is applied to the impulse which aspires to knowledge for the sake of knowledge. On the other hand, the defence advanced by Hermes Trismegistus, in so far as it is applied to the use of the cognitive faculty either for the glory of God or for the service of one's neighbour, is well-founded and just. There is, therefore, a legitimate — even glorious — knowledge, and an illegitimate, vain, indiscreet and foolhardy knowledge.

Now, Hermeticism — in its life and soul — is the millennial-old current in human history of *knowledge for the sake of the glory of God*, whilst the corpus of today's official sciences is due either to utility or to the desire for knowledge for the sake of knowledge (curiosity).

We Hermeticists are theologians of that Holy Scripture revealing God which is named "the world"; similarly, theologians of the Holy Scriptures revealing God are Hermeticists in so far as they dedicate their effort to the glory of God. And just as the world is not only a material body but is also soul and spirit, so is the Holy Scripture not simply the "dead letter" but is also soul and spirit. This is why our threefold knowledge (mystical-gnostic-magical) of the world has dedicated itself through the course of the centuries to the glory of the Holy Trinity, just as the threefold knowledge of divine revelation through the Holy Scripture (i.e. through the Old Testament, the New Testament, and the Apocalypse) does. Are we not called, we theologians of the world, and you, theologians of the Holy Scripture, to watch at the same altar and to fulfill the same task of not letting the lamp illumined to the glory of God be extinguished in the world? Is it not our common duty to provide for it, to provide the holy oil of human endeavour so that its flame is never extinguished, so that it always bears witness to God by the very fact of its existence, and so that it continues to burn from century to century? Has not the time finally arrived when we Hermeticists shall take account of the incontestable fact that it is thanks to the Church that we have air to breathe and that we have a place of shelter and refuge in this world of materialism, imperialism, nationalism, technologism, biologism and psychologism? It is in so far that the Church lives that we live. The church bells once reduced to silence, all human voices desiring to serve the glory of God will also be reduced to silence. We live and we die with the Church. Because in order to live, we need air to breathe; we need the atmosphere of piety, sacrifice, and appreciation of the invisible as a higher reality. This air, this atmosphere in the world, exists in the world only by grace of the Church. Without it Hermeticism — indeed, every idealistic philosophy and all metaphysical idealism — would be drowned in utilitarianism, materialism, industrialism, technologism, biologism and psychologism. Dear Unknown Friend, imagine to yourself a world without the Church. Imagine a world of factories, clubs, sports, political meetings, utilitarian universities, utilitarian arts or recreations — in which you would hear not a single word of praise for the Holy Trinity or of benediction in its name. Imagine to yourself a world in which you would never hear a human voice say: "*Gloria Patri, et Filio, et Spiritui Sancto, sicut erat in principio, et nunc, et semper, et in saecula saeculorum*", or "*Benedicat vos omnipotens Deus, Pater, Filius et Spiritus Sanctus"*. A world without worship and without benediction. . . how deprived of ozone the psychic and spiritual atmosphere would then be, and how empty and cold it would be! Do you think that Hermeticism could exist and live for a single day?

Therefore make use of the balance of Justice and judge impartially. When you have done so, you will no doubt say: Never will I throw stones – in thought, or through word or deed – against the Church, since it is she who makes possible, and stimulates and protects, human endeavour for the glory of God. And as Hermeticism is such an endeavour, it could not exist without the Church. We Hermeticists have only one choice: either to live as parasites (for it is thanks to the Church that we are able to live), if we are strangers to, or are hostile to, the Church; or to live as her faithful friends and servants, if we understand what we owe to her and so begin to love her.

Now is the time for the Hermetic movement to make true Christian peace with the Church and to cease to be her semi-illegitimate child, leading a half-tolerated life more or less in the shadow of the Church – and to become eventually an adopted child, if not a recognised legitimate child. But "it takes two to love". And there is many a pretension to be abandoned in order to accomplish this. What is sure, however, is that if the two parties in question have at heart only the glory of God, all obstacles to this peace will evaporate in smoke.

May the pretension of certain Hermeticists evaporate in smoke – namely to have the authority to found small churches under their own leadership and to set up altar against altar and hierarchy against hierarchy.

On the other hand, may the pretension of certain theologians evaporate in smoke – namely to be a supreme tribunal, without recourse to further appeal, concerning all planes of existence beyond the five senses. The lesson learnt through Copernicus and Galileo by theologians who arrogated to themselves the authority of a supreme tribunal for the perceptible world can also be repeated on higher levels of the world – in case of a relapse into the arrogant spirit of Galileo's judges concerning other planes of existence. The revealed, and therefore absolute, truths of salvation – yes, these are entrusted to the magisterium of the Church, and therefore to the work of interpretation, explanation and presentation of competent theologians. But the immense domain where salvation operates – the physical, vital, psychic and spiritual worlds: their structure, forces, beings, their reciprocal relationships, their transformations and the history of these transformations – aren't all these aspects of the macrocosm and microcosm, and many others, the field of work to be accomplished for the glory of God and for the benefit of one's neighbour, for all those who want to do so and who do not want to bury in the earth the talents given to them by the Master (cf. Matthew xxv, 14-30) and thus to be unprofitable servants?

Let us therefore appeal to the balance of Justice – which is at the same time the balance of peace – let us take recourse to it, let us dedicate ourselves to it, let us serve it! Then we shall operate with the universal and eternal magic of Justice, for universal and general good. Since he who invokes the balance of Justice—who takes it as a method of practical training in thinking, feeling, and the will—such a one, I may say, falls under the title of the fourth beatitude of the Sermon on the Mount: "Blessed are those who hunger and thirst after justice, for they shall be satisfied" (Matthew v, 6). "Satisfied"—this means to say: justice will be done.

Let us therefore be just towards the theologians, and they will be just towards us. Let us recognise our just debts towards the Church, and she will recognise our just rights. And then there will be *peace*, i.e. the operation of the balance of Justice.

We who are occupied with the way of the spiritual exercise of the balance of justice (for *all* the Arcana of the Tarot are, in the first place, spiritual exercises) have to do so thoroughly and completely—which would not be the case if we were to fail to put to work the balance of Justice in our thought and in our hearts with respect to another domain where there is no peace, and where justice is yet to be established: this is the sphere of relationships existing between Hermeticism and official science.

Just as it is time that Hermeticism made peace with the Church and finds its rightful place within its heart, so is it time that it made true peace with Academia, and finds its rightful place there. Because, until now, Hermeticism in the eyes of Academia is only an illegitimate child: the fruit of an obscure liaison between a religion unfaithful to its own vocation and a science that is likewise untrue to its own vocation. In other words, Hermeticism is a badly-coined alloy of false religiosity with a false scientific spirit. In the eyes of Academia, Hermeticists are only a clique, which makes its recruits amongst mistaken believers and misguided scientists.

Now let us again make use of the balance of Justice. Is the above-mentioned criticism valid?—Yes it is.

It is well-founded, because Academia as well as the Church is based on the three sacred vows—obedience, poverty and chastity—whilst we Hermeticists behave as pontiffs, without the sacraments and the discipline that this entails, and as academics, without due experience and discipline. We do not want to *obey* either religious or scientific discipline. At the same time, it is obedience or *discipline* which underlies the moral greatness of the Church and the intellectual greatness of Academia.

The "asceticism" of Academia entails, as well as obedience to the authority of facts, strict rules for proofs and for collaboration, and chastity in the guise of complete sobriety, and also poverty in the form of ignorance, postulated as the basis of all research work. A true scientist is an objective man—sober and open to all experience or new thought.

The fact that true scientists are as rare as saints in the Church does not at all alter the fact that it is they who represent science. Because it is not the sick and deformed who represent a family, but rather its healthy members.

Now, true science is the discipline of objectivity, sobriety and diligence or, in other words, the discipline of the vows of obedience, chastity and poverty. For one cannot be diligent if one is not poor; richness always entails idleness. One cannot be sober without having a dislike of all that intoxicates; and this is chastity. Lastly, one cannot be objective without obedience to experience and the strict rules of research.

It is by virtue of the practice of these three sacred vows that science makes true progress. Thanks to this practice it advances in the direction of *depth*, i.e. into the same domain as Hermeticism. Science has made three great discoveries in the domain of depth: it has penetrated in the depths of the sphere of biology to discover the *law of evolution*; it has penetrated into the depths of matter and has found *pure energy*; it has dared to penetrate into the realm of psychic depth, to discover the world of *occult consciousness*. The three great discoveries of science—evolution, nuclear energy and the unconscious—have certainly made science a collaborator, if not a rival, of Hermeticism, by the fact of having entered the domain which is proper to Hermeticism, the domain of depth.

Therefore Hermeticism now shares its hereditary domain with science...as a sister or as a rival? This is the question upon which everything depends.

All depends on our decision, we Hermeticists of today, to take either the part of *service* towards science in its endeavour to explore the realm of depth or that of *rivalry* with it. The decision to serve implies and entails renunciation of the role of representing an esoteric and sacred science different from exoteric and profane science. It is a matter of renouncing the desire to set up "chair against chair", just as with respect to the Church it is a matter of renouncing the desire to erect "altar against altar". Hermeticism, in pretending to be science—i.e. a body of doctrines of general validity, and generally demonstrable—can only cut a poor shape. For, being essentially *esoteric*, i.e. intimate and personal, it cannot with any appreciable success play the role of a science of general validity demonstrable to everyone. The esoteric character of Hermeticism and the general validity of science are mutually exclusive. One cannot—and must not—present what is intimate and personal, that is to say *esoteric*, as having a general validity, that is to say *scientific*.

Yes, I know with one-hundred per cent certainty that there are great truths in Hermeticism, but these truths are not *scientific*, i.e. of general validity. They are valuable only for *personalities*, each individually, who have the same hunger and the same thirst as I, the same ideal as I, and perhaps the same memories from past recall as I have. They are valuable only for members of "my family"—the people whom I call my "Unknown Friends" to whom these Letters are addressed.

Hermeticism is not a science which differs from other sciences or which even opposes itself to them. No more is it a religion. It is a uniting—in the inner forum of personal and intimate consciousness—of revealed truth with truth acquired through human endeavour. Being a synthesis—intimate and personal for each person—of religion and science, it cannot rival either the one or the other. A hyphen does not have the function of replacing the two terms that it unites. The true Hermeticist is therefore one who applies to himself a *double discipline*—that of the Church and that of Academia. He prays and he thinks. And he does so with the fervour and sincerity of a son of the Church, concerning his praying, and with the discipline and diligence of an academic, concerning his thinking. *Ora et labora*—"pray and work"—is certainly his formula, where "and" is the legitimate place of Hermeticism. It is an open door, in the inner forum of his consciousness, between the oratory and the laboratory. It is the *door* between the two —and not *another* laboratory or *another* oratory.

Ora et labora...oratory and laboratory united in the inner forum of the personality...what is this, in the last analysis, if not the practice of the balance of Justice?

Hermeticism, understood as the balance *ora et labora*, implies a great deal of readjustment with respect to habits of thought which have taken root amongst Hermeticists since the second half of the nineteenth century. The following is an example that I have chosen because of its great spiritual significance.

Christian Hermeticists are unanimous concerning the pre-eminence of the mission and the person of Jesus Christ in the spiritual history of mankind. For them, Jesus Christ is to other spiritual masters of mankind (Krishna, Buddha, Moses, Orpheus, etc.) as the sun is to the other visible planets in the heavens. In this they distinguish themselves from modern Theosophists of the school of Blavatsky and from oriental occultists and esotericists, e.g. Yoga, Vedanta, Sufi, Mazdaznan, Gurdjieff's school, etc. They are Christian, therefore, in the sense that they recognise the uniqueness of the divine Incarnation who is Jesus Christ.

At the same time, the tendency is certainly accentuated, if not prevalent, amongst contemporary Hermeticists to occupy themselves more with the "Cosmic Christ" or the "Logos" than with the human person of the "Son of Man", Jesus of Nazareth. More importance is attributed to the divine and abstract aspect of the God-Man than to his human and concrete aspect.

Therefore, let us once again take recourse to the balance of Justice and weigh up the alternatives: "cosmic principle" and "concrete personality of the Master".

Firstly, let us look at results or fruits in the domain of experience of aspiration to knowledge of the Logos, and those of aspiration to contact with Jesus Christ, the Master.

It must be pointed out, in the first place, that it was not the revelation or knowledge of the cosmic Logos which gave rise to the new spiritual impulse that manifested itself in the apostles, martyrs and saints—which we call "Christianity"— but rather the life, death and resurrection of Jesus Christ. It was not through the name of the Logos that demons were exorcised, the sick were healed, and the dead were brought back to life, but rather through the name of Jesus (cf. Acts iv, 12; Ephesians i, 21).

> Therefore God has highly exalted him and bestowed on him the
> name which is above every name, that at the name of Jesus every
> knee should bow, in heaven and on earth and under the earth,

> and every tongue confess that Jesus Christ is Lord, to the glory
> of God the Father. (Philippians ii, 9-11)

It was contact with the person of Jesus Christ which opened up the current of miracles and conversions. And it is the same even today.

With respect to the cosmic Logos, the idea was neither new nor activating at the beginning of Christianity. Hellenistic Hermeticists (cf. *The Divine Pymander of Hermes Trismegistus*), Stoics and Philo of Alexandria had said almost everything there is to be said on it in philosophical, gnostic and mystical terms. Consequently St. John did not have in mind the advancement of a new doctrine of the Logos in his Gospel, but rather to bear witness to the fact that the Logos "became flesh and dwelt among us" (John i, 14).

Now, it was Jesus Christ who gave to the idea of the Logos the warmth and life which created living Christianity, whilst the idea of the Logos held by the sages of antiquity, although it was true, was lacking this warmth and life. It had light, but *magic* was lacking here. And it is the same even today.

Monsieur Philip of Lyons (1849-1905), the Thaumaturgist, attributed all his miraculous healings and other prodigies to the *friend*: "All I do is to ask him on your behalf, this is all" (Dr. Philippe Encausse (Papus), *Le Maître Philippe de Lyon*, Paris, 1958, p. 146). Now, Monsieur Philip's friend was Jesus Christ.

Monsieur Philip was Papus' "spiritual master". Papus had yet another master, who was his "intellectual master". This was Marquis Saint-Yves d'Alveydre, the author of *Mission des Juifs* ("Mission of the Jews") and *Archéomètre* ("Archeometry"). The latter gave himself up entirely to the endeavour to understand, and to make understood, the Logos or the Cosmic Christ. At the same time, Monsieur Philip of Lyons, the "father of the poor", served the work of Jesus Christ in healing, comforting and illumining people from all social classes (e.g. both the Russian imperial family and the workers of Lyons), by making himself an instrument of Jesus Christ. The one brought about the invention of an *intellectual* instrument — archeometry — which he (Saint-Yves d'Alveydre) used to comprehend and express the cosmic logic of the work of the Logos in the history of mankind; the other (Monsieur Philip) made *himself* an instrument of the divine magic of Jesus Christ in order to serve his neighbour.

Papus found himself between a master of universal logicism and a master of divine magic. He found himself faced with a choice between the way of logicism exemplified by Fabre d'Olivet, Hoené-Wronski and Saint-Yves d'Alveydre, and the way of divine magic — of individual contact with Jesus Christ — represented by Eliphas Lévi (in his maturity), Monsieur Philip, and all the Christian saints. Did he make a choice between these two ways? Yes and no. *Yes*, he made one in the sense of having understood the superiority of the magic of love over ceremonial magic, and the superiority of contact with the Master to all theoretical knowledge of the cosmic Logos and to contact with any "magical chain". *No*, in the sense that he did not turn his back on Saint-Yves d'Alveydre and his work, but remained faithful to him until his death and even after his death—which, to its glory, will turn the eyes of all people of heart to the fact that the way of acting according to the principle "the feast is over, goodbye to the saint" can only distress. Nevertheless, the attitude taken by Papus, faced with the two ways and two masters, was not only noble in a human sense. It divulges something more.

It is the faithfulness of Papus to Hermeticism which it discloses. For Hermeticism is an *athanor* ("alchemical furnace") erected in the individual human consciousness, where the mercury of intellectuality undergoes transmutation into the gold of spirituality. St. Augustine acted as a Hermeticist in transmuting Platonism into Christian thought. Similarly, St. Thomas Aquinas acted as a Hermeticist in doing the same thing with Aristotelianism. Both of them accomplished the sacrament of baptism with respect to Greece's intellectual heritage.

Now, this is precisely what Papus did—or was in the process of doing—with regard to the logicism of Saint-Yves d'Alveydre and his precursors after meeting his spiritual master, Monsieur Philip of Lyons. It was neither a compromise nor hesitation to take sides, but rather the Hermetic hope of achieving a synthesis of intellectuality and spirituality. Papus took upon himself this inner work, whose beginning is a rending conflict between two contraries. We cannot say with certainty if, or how far, his endeavour was crowned with success—a premature death having deprived us of the possibility of being witness to the mature fruits of Papus' spiritual life. With respect to his endeavours in the outer world of serving as a link between Monsieur Philip and Saint-Yves d'Alveydre, Papus was not successful. As proof of this lack of success is the fact that Saint-Yves did not want to see Monsieur Philip at Lyons, nor did he invite him to see him. Concerning other people, Papus' endeavours were crowned with success: notably, it was Papus who procured for Monsieur Philip a circle of intelligent people—mainly occultists and doctors—which was important for both parties.

Papus' work has remained unfulfilled, at least on the visible plane. This work is the synthesis of intellectuality and spirituality, of the cosmic Logos and the Logos made flesh—or, briefly, *Christian Hermeticism* as such. For Christian Hermeticism is a task—it is not a fact of history. This means to say that it is not a matter of "renaissances" of Hermeticism (such as those of the Hellenistic epoch which took place in the twelfth century, the fifteenth century, the seventeenth century and the nineteenth century) but rather of the *resurrection* of Hermeticism. Renaissances are only reminiscences of the past which surge up to the surface from the depths of human souls from time to time, whilst *resurrection* signifies an appeal to present and future life, to the accomplishment of a mission for the future, addressed to what was of eternal value in the past by the same voice which called Lazarus back to life.

The spiritual history of Christianity is the history of successive resurrections of that which is valuable from the past, worthy of eternity. It is the history of the magic of love reviving the dead. It was thus that Platonism became resuscitated and will go on living for ever—thanks to the vivifying breath of he who is the resurrection and the life ("*Ego sum resurrectio et vita*"—John xi, 25). It is thus that Aristotelianism will participate in eternal life. And it is thus that Hermeticism, also, will live until the end of the world and, perhaps, beyond the end of the world.

Moses and the prophets will live on for ever, for they have acquired their place in the eternal constellation of the Word of resurrection and life. The magical poetry and songs of Orpheus will be resuscitated and will live for all eternity as colour and sound of the Word of resurrection and life. The magic of Zarathustra's mages will be revived and will live as the eternal human endeavour of aspiration towards light and life. The truths revealed by Krishna will join the retinue of the "recalled to eternal life". The ancient cosmic revelations of the Rishis will live again and will awaken in humanity anew a sense for the marvels of the "blue, white and gilded..."

All these souls of mankind's spiritual history will be resuscitated, i.e. will be called to join the work of the Word that became flesh, that died and rose again from the dead—so that the truth of the promise—"I have come so that *nothing* should be lost but that *all* should have eternal life" (John vi, 38-40)—will be accomplished.

Hermeticism also is called to live—not only as a reminiscence, but also as a resuscitation. This will take place when those who are faithful to it—i.e. in whom reminiscences of its past are living—comprehend the truth that man is the key to the world, and that Jesus Christ is the key to man, and that Jesus Christ is the key to the world, and that the world—such as it was before the Fall and such as it will be after its Reintegration—is the Word, and that the Word is Jesus Christ, and that, lastly, Jesus Christ reveals God the Father who transcends both the world and man.

Through Jesus Christ one arrives at the Word or Logos; through the Word or Logos one understands the world; and through the Word and the world, whose unity is the Holy Spirit, one arrives at an eternally-increasing knowledge of the Father.

This is one of the teachings of the balance of Justice taken as a spiritual exercise. But it can give us many other teachings relating to such problems as: karma, or the law of equilibrium in mankind's history and in the history of the human individuality; the problem of the relationships between fate (historical, biological and astrological), freedom and providence; the problem of the three swords (of the Cherubim of Eden, the Archangel Michael and the Angel of the Apocalypse) or the problem of sanction in the work of cosmic justice; and lastly, the gnostic problem of the *ogdoad* ("eightfoldness"). All these problems certainly merit treatment under the title of—or better, by means of—the balance of Justice. Truth to tell, they not only merit it, but they badly *need* it. I certainly know this to be so, but I must renounce doing it, because I cannot write an entire volume on the eighth Arcanum alone, let alone twenty-two volumes on the twenty-two Arcana of the Tarot—having undertaken to write only *letters* on the Arcana. A letter must not become a volume. I must therefore renounce many—yes, the majority—of the things that I would very much like to put into writing. But I hope that the *method* of using the balance of Justice (that I want only to *illustrate* in this Letter) will find an active and sympathetic reception and that you, dear Unknown Friend, will set to work with weighing the problems not dealt with here, by means of the balance of Justice.

In doing this, you will have, perhaps, not only the satisfaction and the joy of fresh enlightenment but also that of breathing the air of the honesty and moral courage of impartial justice. Perhaps, moreover, you will have an experience which will be a conclusive answer to the question posed at the end of the preceding Letter, namely: What is the *eighth* force which puts the seven forces of the astral body in equilibrium? For it is this eighth force which works in judging and weighing up by means of the balance of Justice, in the inner forum of consciousness. It is the "eighth planet" or the unknown factor upon which so much depends in the interpretation of a traditional astrological horoscope, with seven planets, and in the interpretation of the traditional characterological formula of the composition and proportions of the psychic organism or "character".

Whether it is a matter of an astrological horoscope or of a characterological formula is not important, there is always an X-factor upon the *use* of which astrological or characterological data depends. It is the factor of *free will* which underlies the traditional astrological rule: *Astra inclinant, non necessitant* ("the stars incline, they do not compel"). The same rule is valuable for "microcosmic astrology" or characterology. There also free will is the indeterminable factor which does not allow the part that a man with a well-determined character will take in some circumstances or other to be predicted with certainty. For it is not *character* which is the source of judgement and conscious choice, but rather this force in us which weighs and judges by means of the balance of Justice. *Freedom* is a fact which one experiences when someone judges not by his temperament ("etheric body") or by his character ("astral body"), but rather by the balance of Justice—or by his own *conscience*. The word *conscience* ("con-science") contains the idea of balance, for it implies "simultaneous knowing", i.e. knowledge of the facts of the *two scales* suspended at the extremities of the beam of the balance. Conscience is neither a product nor a function of *character*. It is above it. And it is here—and only here—that there begins and there is found the domain of *freedom*. One is not at all free when one judges or acts according to character or temperament; but one certainly is when one judges and acts according to the balance of Justice, or *conscience*. But Justice, the practice of the balance, is only the beginning of a long path of the development of conscience—and therefore of the growth of freedom.

The following Arcanum, the Hermit, invites us to a meditative endeavour dedicated to the path of conscience.

Meditation on the
Ninth Major Arcanum of the Tarot

THE HERMIT
L'HERMITE

Isis: "Give heed, my son Horus; for you shall
hear the secret doctrine, of which our
forefather Kamephis was the first teacher.
It so befell that Hermes heard this teaching
from Kamephis, the eldest of all our race;
I heard it from Hermes,
the writer of the records,
when he initiated me
in the rite of Black (Perfection).
(ὁπot' ἐμὲ καί τῳ τελέιῳ μελάνι ἐτίμησε,
Words of Isis from the sacred book
of Hermes Trismegistus entitled *Kore Kosmu*).*

For Trismegistus who, I do not know how,
has completed the discovery of virtually the
entire truth, has often described the power
and the majesty of the Word, as illustrated by
the foregoing quotation, where he (Hermes)
proclaims the existence of an ineffable and
holy Word, whose pronunciation is beyond
the power of man
(*quo fatetur esse ineffabilem quendem*
sanctumque SERMONEM, cuius enarratio
modum hominis excedet,
Lactantius, *Divinae institutiones* iv, 9,3)

For the gate is narrow and the way is hard,
that leads to life,
and those who find it are few.
(Matthew vii, 14)

LETTER IX

THE HERMIT

Dear Unknown Friend,

The Hermit! I am pleased to have arrived, in the series of these Letter-Meditations, at this venerable and mysterious figure of a solitary itinerant dressed in a red robe under a blue mantle, holding in his right hand a lantern — alternately yellow and red — and leaning on a staff. For it is the venerable and mysterious Hermit who was master of the most intimate and most cherished dreams of my youth, as moreover he is the master of dreams for all youth in every country, who are

*("The Virgin of the World"); trsl. Walter Scott, Hermetica, vol. i, Oxford, 1924, p. 457; cf. also French trsl. by A. J. Festugière, Corpus Hermeticum vol. iv, Paris, 1954, p. 10, whose translation reads: "...when he honoured me with the gift of Perfect Night".

enamoured by the call to seek the narrow gate and the hard way to the Divine. Name for me a country or a time for which the youth—who are truly "young", i.e. living for the Ideal—has not had its imagination haunted by the figure of a wise and good father, a spiritual father, a hermit, who has passed through the narrow gate and who walks the hard way—someone whom one could trust without reserve and whom one could venerate and love without limit. Which *young* Russian man, for example, would not have undertaken a journey, no matter how long and of what duration, in order to meet a *staretz*, i.e. a wise and good father, a spiritual father, a *hermit*? Which *young* Jewish man from Poland, Lithuania, White Russia, Ukraine or Romania would not have done as much to meet a Hassidic *tsadik*, i.e. a wise and good father, a spiritual father, a *hermit*? Which *young* man in India would refuse to make every possible effort to find and meet a chela or *guru*, i.e. a wise and good father, a spiritual father, a *hermit*?

And was it otherwise with the youth around Origen, Clement of Alexandria, St. Benedict, St. Dominic, St. Francis of Assisi, St. Ignatius of Loyola? Was it otherwise, also, with the pagan youth of Athens around Socrates and Plato?

It was the same in ancient Persia around Zarathustra, Ostanes and other representatives of the spiritual dynasty of the mages that was founded by the great Zarathustra. It was also so in Israel with the schools of the prophets, and with the Nazorenes and Essenes. It was the same in ancient Egypt, where the figure of the founder of the dynasty of "wise and good fathers"—that of Hermes Trismegistus—became, not only for Egypt but also for the entire Graeco-Roman world, the prototype of the wise and good father, the *hermit*!

Eliphas Lévi certainly sensed the universal historical meaning of the Hermit. This is why he stated the admirable formula:

> The initiate is he who possesses the lamp of Trismegistus, the mantle of Apollonius, and the staff of the patriarchs. (Eliphas Lévi, *Dogme et rituel de la haute magie*; trsl. A. E. Waite, *Transcendental Magic. Its Doctrine and Ritual*, London, 1968, p. 92)

In fact, the Hermit who haunts the imagination of "young" youth, the Hermit of legend and the Hermit of history was, is, and always will be the solitary man with the lamp, mantle and staff. For he possesses the gift of letting light shine in the darkness—this is his "lamp"; he has the faculty of separating himself from the collective moods, prejudices and desires of race, nation, class and family— the faculty of reducing to silence the cacophony of collectivism vociferating around him, in order to listen to and understand the hierarchical harmony of the spheres—this is his "mantle"; at the same time he possesses a sense of realism which is so developed that he stands in the domain of reality not on two feet, but rather on three, i.e. he advances only after having *touched* the ground through immediate experience and at first-hand contact without intermediaries—this is his "staff". He creates light, he creates silence and he creates certainty—conforming to the criterion of the *Emerald Table*, namely the triple concordance of that which is *clear*, of that which is *in harmony with the totality* of revealed truths and of that which is the object of *immediate* experience:

> *Verum, sine mendacio, certum et verissimum* (*Tabula Smarag-dina*, 1).
> *Verum, sine mendacio*—this is clarity (the lamp);
> *Certum*—this is the concordance of that which is clear and the totality of other truths (the "lamp" *and* the "mantle");
> *Verissimum*—this is the concordance of that which is clear, the totality of other truths, and authentic and immediate experience (the "lamp", the "mantle" *and* the "staff").

The Hermit therefore represents not only a wise and good father who is a reflection of the Father in heaven, but also the method and essence of *Hermeticism*. For Hermeticism is founded on the concordance of three methods of knowledge: the *a priori* knowledge of intelligence (the "lamp"); the harmony of all by analogy (the "mantle"); and authentic immediate experience (the "staff").

Hermeticism is thus a threefold synthesis of three antinomies:

1. the synthesis of the antinomy "idealism—realism";
2. the synthesis of the antinomy "realism—nominalism";
3. the synthesis of the antinomy "faith—empirical science".

In so far as it is a synthesis—a personal one, of course, in the inner forum of the consciousness of each—in which the three antinomies above supply each time a third term, its number is nine, and it is the ninth Arcanum of the Tarot which teaches us about the three syntheses of the three antinomies.

Let us now look at how Hermeticism is the synthesis of the above three antitheses or antinomies.

1. *The antinomy "idealism—realism"*

This reduces to two opposite formulae, namely:

> "Consciousness or the idea is prior to everything"—this is the formula of idealism; and
> "The thing (*res*) is prior to all consciousness or ideas"—this is the basic formula of realism.

The idealist (e.g. Hegel) considers everything as so many forms of thought, whilst the realist (e.g. Spencer) affirms that objects of knowledge have an existence which is independent of thought or consciousness on the part of the subject of the knowledge.

The realist says that notions, laws and ideas are *derived*—by way of abstraction—from *objects* of knowledge. The idealist says, on the contrary, that notions, laws and ideas are *projected*—by way of "concretisation"—from the *subject* of knowledge into objects.

The realist advances the so-called "correspondence" theory of truth, i.e. that "truth is the correspondence between object and intellect". The idealist relies on the so-called "coherence" theory of truth, i.e. that "truth is coherence—or absence of contradictions—in the handling of ideas, notions and objects (objects being only notions) by the intellect".

Truth is, according to realism, that which in the intellect corresponds with the object. According to idealism, truth is that which constitutes a *coherent system* in the intellect.

The entire world exactly reflected in the intellect—this is the ideal of knowledge for realism. The entire world exactly reflecting the postulates and categories of the intellect as a unique coherent system—this is the ideal of knowledge for idealism. It is the world which bears the word and it is the human intellect which listens, says realism. It is the intellect which bears the word and it is the world which is its reflection, says idealism.

"*Nihil in intellectu quod non prius fuerit in sensu*" ("nothing is in the intellect which has not had prior existence in the sense world") is the millennial-old formula of realism. "*Nihil in sensu quod non prius fuerit in intellectu*" ("nothing is in the sense world which has not had prior existence in the intellect") is the counter-formula of idealism.

Which is right? Realism with its idol, i.e. the "thing" (*res*) prior to thought, and its Mazdean dualism, i.e. darkness (the thing) and light (thought), which latter proceeds from or is born from the former? Or idealism with its idol of the human intellect which it sets on the throne of God, and its pan-intellectual monism where there is room neither for the "gift of Perfect Night", i.e. the superhuman wisdom mentioned in the sacred book of Hermes Trismegistus entitled *Kore Kosmu*, nor for the shadows of evil, ugliness and illusion that we experience every day?

No, let us not prostrate ourselves either before the world or before the intellect, but let us prostrate ourselves in adoration of the common source of both the world and the intellect—God: God whose Word is at one and the same time the "true light that enlightens every man coming into the world" (John i, 9) and the creator of the world—"all things were made through him, and nothing that was made was made without him" (John i, 3).

The thing, the world—it is the Word which is its source. The intellect, the light of thought—it is again the Word which is its source. This is why Christian Hermeticism of the present as well as the pagan Hermeticism of the past is neither merely realistic nor simply idealistic. It is "logoistic" ("of the Logos"), being founded neither on the thing nor on the human intellect, but rather on the Logos, the Word of God, whose *objective* manifestation is the world of prototypes underlying the phenomenal world, and whose *subjective* manifestation is the light or prototype of human intelligence. "The light shines in the darkness, and the darkness receives it not" (John i, 5), which means to say that there is darkness both in the world and within consciousness which has not received—i.e. is not penetrated by—the light, and that consequently evil, ugliness and illusion certainly exist in the world and in consciousness.

But the darkness of the world that is not penetrated by the Word is not the source of consciousness, and the human intellect that is not illumined by the Word is not the principle of the world. In the phenomenal world there are "objective illusions", i.e. "things which are *not real*" which have not been made by the Word, but which have arisen for an ephemeral existence from the sub-strata of darkness. In the domain of subjective consciousness there are illusions, i.e. notions, ideas and ideals which are *not real*, which have not been engendered by the light of the Word, but which have arisen for an ephemeral existence from the depths of darkness in the subconscious.

Now, the correspondence between an illusory object and a notion of it in the intellect would not be truth, but rather a double illusion. Realism should be aware of this when it advances its so-called "correspondence" theory of truth. And the inner coherence of an intellectual system based on illusions would not be a criterion of its truth, but rather an indication of an obsession that is so much the deeper the more the coherence is complete. Idealism should be aware of this when it advances its so-called "coherence" theory of truth.

Objects are only *real*, in the sense of realism, when they are real in the Word. And intellectual constructions are only *true*, in the sense of idealism, when they are true in the Word. The human intellect, as such, is not the producer of truth after the fashion of a spider producing its web. A fact of the outer or inner world, in so far as it is a fact, need not instate truth when it can just as well point to an illusion or the history of an illusion, be it in Nature (e.g. antediluvian monsters) or be it human (e.g. many idols of the past or present).

Now, the "world" of our experience is the phenomenal manifestation of both the world created by the Word and the evolutionary world of the serpent. The "intellect" of our experience, also, is the manifestation both of the light of the Word and of the "ruse" (to take the Biblical term for the method where darkness *imitates* light without receiving it) of the serpent. This is why it is still necessary to distinguish, before one professes to realism, between the World and the world. Similarly, before one embraces idealism, one has to distinguish between cosmic Intelligence and the human intellect.

But once this distinction is made, one can without hesitation embrace idealism and realism at one and the same time—which would be the "idealism—realism" or the *logoism* of ancient and contemporary Hermeticism.

Then the method of correspondence becomes the staff in the hand of the Hermit and the method of coherence becomes the mantle which covers him. This is thanks to the light of the Hermit's lamp, which is the holy instrument where the light of the Word is united with the oil of human intellectual endeavour.

2. *The antinomy "realism — nominalism"*

In this antinomy the term "realism" has nothing in common with the "realism" of the antinomy "realism — idealism". Realism here signifies the school of occidental thought which attributes objective reality to general notions that are now usually designated as "abstract" but which mediaeval philosophy designated *"universalia"* ("universals"). The current of occidental thought which denies the objective reality of universals and which admits reality only in "particulars" is that of nominalism.

Now "realism", as a current of occidental thought opposed to nominalism, differs from realism opposed to idealism in the sense that it is a matter here of the objective reality of universals (types and species) and not of the correspondence between notions of the intellect and the reality of objects (as *the* criterion of truth). Therefore it is a question of a totally different problem. "Realists", in that which concerns the problem of the reality of universals, are in fact extreme "idealists" in that which concerns the problem of the priority of the intellect or the object.

The problem underlying the antinomy "realism — nominalism" was posed for the first time in the history of ideas in an explicit manner by Porphyry (A.D. 234-ca. 304) in his *Isagoge* (or *Introduction by Porphyry the Phoenecian, disciple of Plotinus of Lycopolis*, to give the complete title of this little work). The problem is posed from the beginning, with all desirable clarity, as follows:

> . . . I shall put aside the investigation of certain profound questions concerning genera and species (i.e. universals), since such an undertaking requires more detailed examination: (1) whether genera or species exist in themselves or reside in mere concepts alone; (2) whether, if they exist, they are corporeal or incorporeal; and (3) whether they exist apart or in sense objects and in dependence on them. (Porphyry, *Isagoge* i, 9-14; trsl. E. W. Warren, *Mediaeval Sources in Translation*, vol. 16, Toronto, 1975, pp. 27-28)

In fact, from Boethius to the Renaissance — and even to our own time — there has been given to this problem the "more detailed examination" which Porphyry believed that it merited. For the mediaeval doctors, having clearly seen that the problem of universals is at the very centre of philosophy, treated it as the central problem, which gave rise to the division of the world of philosophers into "realists" (types and species exist in themselves, above and beyond individuals) and "nominalists" (types and species do not exist beyond individuals; they are only "names", i.e. words useful for the purpose of classification). A third school — that of the "conceptualists" or, according to the case, "moderate realists" or "moderate nominalists" (general ideas certainly exist, but they exist only in the mind of he who conceives them)—originated during the controversy and played a role, not of synthesis, but rather one similar to the role of Lorraine which the Emperor Lothar I assigned to it, namely that of intermediary between France and Germany.

The passionate controversy between realism and nominalism lasted a millennium and, not restricting itself to learned debates, it took diverse forms, including the decisions of Church councils, as for example the council of Soissons, which condemned nominalism in 1092.

The thesis of the "realists" leads back to Plato, to his doctrine of ideas. That of the "nominalists" is associated with Antisthenes: "I see a horse, but I don't see horseness" (cf. W. K. C. Guthrie, *A History of Greek Philosophy*, vol. iii, Cambridge, 1969, p. 214). Now, the essence of the problem is whether "horseness" is anterior to the individual horses (*universale ante rem*), whether it is immanent in the individual horses (*universale in re*) or whether it is, lastly, posterior to the individual horses and is only derived from them by way of abstraction (*universale post rem*). According to Plato, "horseness" exists as an idea *before* the horses; according to Aristotle, "horseness" exists only *in* the horses as the principle of their form; according to the conceptualists (e.g. Kant), "horseness" is a concept formed by the mind by way of summarising the common features of all horses, abstracting from the particular characteristics (*universale post rem*).

The problem whether "horseness" is anterior to the real horses, whether it is the formative principle in them or, rather, whether it is only a notion of the mind derived from the experience of the senses is, truth to tell, not passionate when it is a matter only of "horseness". Nevertheless, it becomes so when it is a question of mankind or the world. For then it becomes a problem of *creation*, which differs from *genesis*. In creation the idea or "plan" of the world is anterior to the act of its realisation, whilst in genesis or evolution there is not an idea or plan anterior to the fact, but rather a *force* immanent in substances and individual beings, which pushes them to seek through trial and error a way of progressing. With respect to humanity, it becomes a problem of the prototype man or celestial *Adam*, i.e. a problem of the *creation* of man or his evolutionary *genesis*.

Let us now examine more closely the fundamental theses of realism and nominalism.

> "The general is anterior to the particular"—is the formula at the basis of realism.

> "The particular is anterior to the general"—is the counter-formula of nominalism.

These two contrary theses imply that for realism the general is more real and of higher objective value than the particular, and that for nominalism the particular is more real and of higher objective value than the general. In other words, for realism *humanity* is more real and is of higher value than the individual man. In contrast, for nominalism it is the *individual man* who is more real and has a higher value than humanity.

For realism, there would be no human beings if there were no humanity. For nominalism, on the contrary, there would be no humanity if there were no human beings. Human beings compose humanity, says the nominalist. Humanity engenders, from its invisible but real womb, individual human beings, says the realist.

Who is right? Realism with its idol of collectivity anterior to the individuality, the individual soul, which, through the mouth of Caiaphas enunciated the justification for condemning Jesus Christ to death, in having said: "It is expedient for you that one man should die for the people, and that the whole nation should not perish" (John xi, 50)?...which through the tribunals of the Inquisition annihilated "noxious individuals" in sacrificing them for the interests of humanity or the Church?...Realism which, lastly, setting the race above individuals or the class above individuals, exterminated millions of Jews and gipsys at the hands of the Nazis, and also millions of *koulaks* or well-to-do peasants and individuals of the higher classes at the hands of the Bolsheviks.

And nominalism?

Nominalism is blind to ideas and principles, which are only words as far as it is concerned. Truth, beauty and goodness do not exist for it as objective realities, and are only a matter of taste. No serious science or philosophy worthy of its name would be able to exist if nominalism were the only intellectual terrain in which it could live. For instead of aspiring to the universal, it would go in search of the particular. It would collect only particular facts and, far from setting any value on their common traits from which it would be able to derive laws and principles, would only result in a kind of museum of particular facts. This museum would wait in vain for the advent of scientific and philosophical thought in order for it to be useful to mankind in a general way: nominalism itself would not produce it. For it is the opposite of science.

Instead of science or philosophy, it would give rise to a multitude of sects of subjective tastes. Each would think and believe in its own way. One would only adhere to that which pleased one. This is precisely why the Church condemned nominalism as a doctrine and why science banished it as a method. It would have atomised the Church into a mass of small religions according to the personal taste of each individual, and it would have reduced science to sterile collectionism and an infinite number of private opinions.

Therefore we cannot dispense with realism if we attach any value to the existence of objective truth (science) and trans-subjective truth (religion). Objective and trans-subjective truth must therefore be admitted if one aspires to a union of mankind in the universal objective truth of science and trans-subjective truth of religion.

But can we do without nominalism?

No, for nominalism is a vision of the world consisting of individual, unique and irreplaceable beings. It is a vision of the world as a great community of entities, instead of a world of laws, principles and ideas. It is the vision of a world where Father, Son and Holy Spirit, true and living persons, united by the eternal bonds of paternity, filiality and fraternity, reign — surrounded by Seraphim, Cherubim, Thrones, Dominions, Virtues, Powers, Principalities, Archangels, Angels, human beings and beings of Nature, visible and invisible. How can one say, with all sincerity of the heart, in prayer addressed to the Father in heaven: "Hallowed be thy *name*", without believing that it is the unique and holy name of a living being — unique and holy, and not a designation for the supreme idea or the "first cause" or the "absolute principle"? Can one *love* an invisible world of impersonal "first causes", a world populated by laws and principles?

If general intellectual knowledge of the world as such (i.e. science) and as the work of God (i.e. philosophy) is not possible without idealistic realism, intuitive individual knowledge — through love — of particular beings (i.e. mysticism, gnosis and magic) is no more so without realistic nominalism.

Now, one can neither embrace idealistic realism or realistic nominalism without reserve, nor dispense with one or the other. For love (which demands realistic nominalism) as well as the intellect (which demands idealistic realism) are structural faculties of human nature. Human nature itself is realist, in so far as thought is concerned, and it is nominalist, in so far as social communion or love is concerned.

The "problem" of universals was resolved in the spiritual history of mankind by the *fact* of the Incarnation, where the fundamental universal of the world — the Logos — became Jesus Christ, who is the fundamental particular of the world. Here, the universal of universals, the very principle of intelligibility, the Logos, became the particular of particulars, the very prototype of the personality, Jesus Christ.

It is above all the Gospel according to St. John which portrays in an explicit and clear way the fact of the union of the principle of universal knowledge with the Being of individual love, from heart to heart. This Gospel describes the work of divine alchemy, where water is united with fire — where water became living water, and tongues of fire became the Pentecostal tongues understandable to everyone individually. The substance of baptism — vivified water and fire not consuming the particular but enabling it to participate in eternity — is the outcome of the work of redemption that began with the Incarnation. Baptism is — in the domain of the history of the spirit — also the union of realism and nominalism, the union of the head and the heart in the human being, which union is only the reflection of the fact of the Incarnation, where "the Word became flesh".

Christian Hermeticism is the friend of realistic nominalism, in so far as this form of nominalism aspires to mystical experience of the communion of beings through love, as well as of idealistic realism, in so far as the latter aspires to the

Logos. Christian Hermeticism itself can only be knowledge of the universal which is revealed in the particular. For Hermeticism there are no "principles", "laws" and "ideas" which exist *outside* of individual beings, not as structural traits of their nature, but as entities separated and independent from it. For Hermeticism there is neither a "law of gravitation" nor a "law of reincarnation"; there is only the attraction and repulsion of beings (atoms are beings also) in so far as gravitation is concerned, and only the attraction of beings to earthly life, with its joys and sorrows, in so far as reincarnation is concerned. But on the other hand, if there were no such entities in the world as the laws of gravitation and reincarnation, there is certainly the universal desire of beings — great and small — to associate with one another, to form together molecules, organisms, families, communities, nations. . . It is a desire or universal *structural* need which manifests itself as "law". "Laws" are *immanent* in beings, as logic is immanent in thought, being part of the very nature of thought. And true progress, true evolution, is the advance of beings from life under one law to life under another law, i.e. the structural change of beings. It is thus that the law "an eye for an eye, and a tooth for a tooth" is in the process of being gradually replaced by the law of forgiveness. It is thus again that the law "the weak serve the strong, the people serve the king, the disciple serves the master" will one day give way to the law shown by the Master through the act of the Washing of the Feet. According to this higher law, it is the strong who serve the weak, the king who serves the people, the master who serves the disciple — just as it is in heaven, where Angels serve human beings, Archangels serve Angels and men, Principalities serve Archangels, Angels and human beings, and so on. And God? He serves all beings without exception.

Thus the "law" of the *struggle for existence* that Darwin observed in the domain of biology will one day cede its place to the law of *cooperation for existence* which exists already in the cooperation of flowering plants and bees, in the cooperation of different cells in an organism, and in cooperation in the human social organism. The end of the "law" of the struggle for existence and the future triumph of the law of cooperation for life has been foretold by the prophet Isaiah:

> The wolf shall dwell with the lamb,
> And the leopard shall lie down with the kid,
> And the calf and the lion and the fatling together,
> And a little child shall lead them.
> (Isaiah xi, 6)

This will be, because the new "law" — i.e. a profound change in the psychic and physical structure of beings — will replace the old "law", firstly in consciousness, then in desires and affections, then lastly in the organic structure of beings.

"Laws" succeed one another and change. They are not immutable metaphysical entities. It is the same with respect to "principles" and "ideas". "The sabbath was made for man, not man for the sabbath; so the Son of Man is lord even of the sabbath" (Mark ii, 27-28)—here is the relationship between beings, on the one side, and laws, principles and ideas, on the other.

Are laws, principles and ideas therefore not real?

They are certainly real, but their reality is not that of an existence separate from beings, i.e. that of metaphysical entities populating a world or plane—a world of laws, principles and ideas—proper to themselves. The spiritual world is not a world of laws, principles and ideas; it is a world of spiritual beings—human souls, Angels, Archangels, Principalities, Powers, Virtues, Dominions, Thrones, Cherubim, Seraphim and the Holy Trinity: the Holy Spirit, the Son and the Father.

What, then, is the reality of laws, principles and ideas?

It is in their structural *kinship*—spiritual, psychic and corporeal. All beings manifest a universal kinship and bear witness to their common origin and their common archetype. Now, this common archetype—that the Cabbala calls "Adam Kadmon"—is the law, the principle and idea of all beings. "The image and likeness of God" in Adam is the law by virtue of which God "let them have dominion over the fish of the sea, and over the birds of the air, and over the cattle, and over all the earth, and over every creeping thing that creeps upon the earth" (Genesis i, 26). Adam is the law, the principle and the idea of all the beings of Nature, because he is their prototype-synthesis.

Realism is right when it affirms the reality of universals, for they are the structural features of the archetype for all particular beings. Also, nominalism is right when it teaches that there are no other realities in the world than individual beings and that universals are not to be found amongst these beings.

Hermeticism regards the Logos who became man as the archetypal universal become the perfect particular being. The controversy between realism and nominalism does not exist for Christian Hermeticism.

3. The antinomy "faith—empirical science"

"For truly, I say to you, if you have faith as a grain of mustard seed, you will say to this mountain: Move hence to yonder place—and it will move; and nothing will be impossible to you" (Matthew xvii, 20-21)—these are the words of the Master.

"And science takes a grain of hydrogen and releases the energy imprisoned in this grain, and reduces the mountain to dust"—replies the twentieth century.

This is where we are with respect to the antinomy of faith and empirical science. Our faith does not transport mountains, but the energy that we have learnt to wield through science is quite capable of reducing them to dust.

Is it because we do not have a mustard-grain of faith?

Is it because we have concentrated all our efforts on the task of penetrating the secret contained in a grain of hydrogen instead of the task of acquiring faith as in a grain of mustard?

In order to be able to answer these questions we must first take account of what faith is and what empirical science is.

Faith:

Faith which can — when it is as a grain of mustard seed — transport mountains: Is this faith identical with faith-belief, with the feeling of certainty with regard to a doctrine?. . . Is it identical with faith-confidence, with the absence of doubt with respect to the sureness of the authority of a witness or testimony?. . . Is it, lastly, identical with faith-hope, with optimism as opposed to pessimism? Briefly, is it sufficient that we have no doubt at all in order to realise "nothing will be impossible to you"?

Many mad people certainly display a complete absence of doubt with regard to their illusions or fixed ideas. They would therefore be able to do miracles, if faith was nothing other than *intensity* of belief, confidence and hope, due to the absence of doubt. Because mad people certainly have this intensity. However, the intensity of belief, confidence and hope alone is not the faith that the Gospel has in view. There it is evidently a question not only of the intensity of certainty, but rather the intensity of the certainty of the *truth*. If this were not so, mad people would be thaumaturgists and madness would be the ideal.

A force which can move a mountain must be equal to that which piled it up. Therefore, the faith which can move mountains can neither be an intellectual opinion nor a personal feeling, no matter how intense. It must be the product of the union of the thinking, feeling and desiring human being with cosmic being — with God. The faith which moves mountains is therefore complete union — even if only for an instant — of man and God.

This is why illusion can in no way engender faith; and this is also why miracles due to faith are testimonies of the *truth* — and not only of sincerity — of belief, confidence and hope of the person through whom they are operated. Miracles are *fruits* of the union of the whole, concentrated human being with cosmic truth, beauty and goodness — with *God*. They are operations of divine-human magic which is, and always will be, based on the spiritual constellation "God-Man" — or, in other words, they always operate "in the *name* of Jesus Christ", conforming to the formula:

My Father is working still, and I am working (John v, 17).
(ὁ πατήρ μου ἕως ἄρτι ἐργάζεται, κἀγώ ἐργάζομαι — *Pater meus usque modo operatur, et ego operor*).

The faith for which "nothing is impossible" is the state of soul where "God works, and the soul also works". It is the state of soul concentrated on the truth to which God adds the intensity of certainty and the power which renders miracles possible. It is magic due to the union of two mages: God and man.

It is therefore neither logical certainty, nor the certainty of authority, nor the acceptance of a testimony worthy of faith — it is the union of the soul with God, attained through effort of thought, through confidence in that which is worthy of confidence, through accepting testimonies worthy of faith, through prayer, meditation, contemplation, through practising moral endeavour, and through many other ways and endeavours which help the soul to open to the divine breath.

Faith is divine breath in the soul, just as hope is divine light and love is divine fire in the soul.

Empirical science:

Heat, steam, magnetism, electricity, nuclear energy—such are the powerful forces harnessed by man thanks to the prodigious work of empirical science! It is thanks to science that we are able to converse with our friends across the ocean, to see what takes place thousands of miles away, to visit a sick friend in another country within an hour, to call to our aid, when we are in distress at sea, in the mountains or in the desert, life-saving expeditions: planes, boats, ambulances. It is again thanks to science that we are able to hear the voice of someone who has been dead for years, that we are able to walk despite having lost a leg, that we are able to see far although being myopic, that we are able to hear whilst being almost deaf, and that we have the capacity for many other things, all of which are thanks to empirical science.

To what may the fabulous success which science achieves be attributed? What is the basic principle which can explain it?

It is *doubt* in the first place. For it is thanks to doubting the experience of the senses that science has been able to establish that it is not the sun which moves across the sky but rather the earth which moves around it. It is thanks to doubting all-powerful fate that remedies and methods of treatment for healing formerly incurable illnesses were sought for and found. It is again thanks to doubting past traditions that empirical science discovered biological evolution, hormones, enzymes, vitamins, the structure of the atom, and subconscious consciousness...

For doubt is at the very root of every question, and questions are the basis of every quest and all research. Doubt is therefore the father of the scientific method. It is this which is the *primus motor*, the principle which once set in motion the whole prodigious machine consisting of laboratories, observatories, libraries, museums, collections, universities, scientific academies and associations.

Doubt set it all in motion. But is the *fruitfulness* of the motion to be attributed to doubt alone? Does doubt alone suffice for discoveries? Is it not necessary to *believe* in the possibility of such discoveries before one sets out on the route which leads to them?

Evidently this is necessary. The father of empirical science is doubt and its mother is faith. It owes its fruitfulness to faith, just as it owes its motivating force to doubt. Just as there is "scientific doubt" underlying empirical science as a method, so there is a "scientific faith" which underlies science as the principle of its fruitfulness. Newton *doubted* the traditional theory of "gravity", but he *believed* in the unity of the world, and therefore in cosmic *analogy*. This is why he could arrive at the cosmic law of gravitation in consequence of the fact of an apple falling from a tree. Doubt set his thought in motion; faith rendered it fruitful.

What, therefore, are the dogmas of scientific faith? The following is the scientific creed:

> I believe in a single substance, the mother of all forces, which engenders bodies and the consciousness of everything, visible and invisible.
>
> I believe in a single Lord, the Human Mind, the unique son of the substance of the world, born from the substance of the world after centuries of evolution: the encapsulated reflection of the great world, the epiphenomenal light of primordial darkness, the real reflection of the real world—evolved through trial and error, not engendered or created, consubstantial with the mother-substance—and through whom the whole world can be reflected. It is he who—for we human beings, and for our use—has ascended from the shadows of the mother-substance.
>
> He has taken on flesh from matter through the work of evolution, and he has become the Human Brain.
>
> Although he is destroyed with each generation that passes, he is formed anew in each generation following, according to Heredity. He is summoned to ascend to comprehensive knowledge of the whole world and to be seated at the right of the mother-substance, which will serve him in his mission as judge and legislator, and his reign will never end.
>
> I believe in Evolution, which directs all, which gives life to the inorganic and consciousness to the organic, which proceeds from the mother-substance and fashions the thinking mind. With the mother-substance and the human mind, evolution receives equal authority and importance. It has spoken through universal progress.
>
> I believe in one diligent, universal, civilising Science. I acknowledge a single discipline for the elimination of errors and I await the future fruits of collective efforts of the past for the life of civilisation to come. So be it.

These are the twelve articles of scientific faith, which is based not only on scientific effort throughout the centuries but also on the martyrdom undergone by numerous human beings in the name of science. Compare this creed with the traditional Christian Creed, article by article, and the whole significance of the antinomy "faith—empirical science" will be evident.

The Synthesis:

The *unique substance* at the basis of the multiplicity of phenomena; the *human mind* capable of reducing this multiplicity to a unity; the *evolution* to which the human mind owes its existence, and the collaboration with which it promises to the human mind its future development until it becomes master of evolution;

the *collective and organised effort*, according to the method of doubt and empirical verification continued from century to century—these are the four principle dogmas of scientific faith. Substance, the human mind, evolution and the scientific method constitute the four "letters" of the *tetragrammaton* of the "ineffable name" of science.

Eliphas Lévi made much of a case for the role which the name HVHY (*Havajot*)—which is an inversion of the sacred *Tetragrammaton* YHVH—plays in being used in black magical evocations. As the *Tetragrammaton* is the law of causality (the sequence: active principle, passive principle, neutral principle—and their manifestation; or again: effective cause, material cause, final cause—and the phenomenon) and consequently of reason, he concluded that the inversion of the *Tetragrammaton* is the magical formula for chaos and irrationality.

Yet it is precisely the inverted *tetragrammaton* which is the arcanum of empirical science. Because it is the passive principle of substance or matter which empirical science considers as first, as the "principle" *par excellence*, whilst the neutral principle (the human mind) follows, and the active principle (the method) concludes the series. In fact, in the name YOD-HÉ-VAU-HÉ (יהוה), if YOD is the active principle (effective cause), the first HÉ is the passive principle (material cause), VAU is the neutral principle (final cause) and the second HÉ is the whole phenomenon which results from it, then the inverse name HÉ-VAU-HÉ-YOD (הוהי) would be the series: "passive principle—neutral principle—passive principle—active principle" or "matter, reason, evolution, scientific method".

The series HVHY means to say that nothing precedes matter; that nothing moves it; that it moves from itself; that mind is the child of matter; that evolution is matter which engenders mind; and that, lastly, mind, once born, is the activity of matter in evolution, which becomes conscious of itself and takes evolution in its hands. The inverted *tetragrammaton* is without doubt the formula-synthesis of empirical science.

Is it that of chaos and irrationality?

No. It is the mirroring of the formula spirit-matter-evolution-individuality of the sacred name YHVH. It is not the formula of irrationality, no more than it is that of intelligence—it *is* the formula of *cunning* ("ruse"), i.e. of reflected intelligence.

It is not a logoical formula, a formula of the Logos, but rather it is that of the serpent of Genesis "who was the most cunning of all living creatures" (Genesis iii, 1), and whose aspiration is the expansion of consciousness in the horizontal ("the fields"). The ultimate aim of the logic of cunning, that of the serpent, is not to become God but to become "*like* God". "To become *like*"—this is the essence of cunning and is also the meaning of scientific faith, the scientific creed, which is at the same time only a paraphrase and development of the promise of the serpent: "your eyes will be opened, and you will be like gods, knowing good and evil" (Genesis iii, 5).

To open your eyes, to be like gods, knowing good and evil—this is the great arcanum of empirical science. This is why it is dedicated to the cause of enlightenment ("open your eyes", for the horizontal); this is why it aspires to absolute power for man ("be like gods"); and this is why, lastly, it is intrinsically amoral or *morally neutral* ("knowing good *and* evil").

Does it deceive us? No. It opens our eyes *in fact*, and thanks to it we see *more* in the horizontal; it gives us power over Nature *in fact*, and makes us sovereign over Nature; it is useful to us *in fact*, no matter whether for good or for evil. Empirical science in no way deceives us. The serpent has not lied — *on the plane where its voice and promise were audible*.

On the plane of *horizontal expansion* ("the fields" of Genesis) the serpent certainly keeps its promise . . . but at what price with regard to other planes, and with regard to the vertical?

What is the price of scientific enlightenment, this "opening of the eyes" in the horizontal, i.e. for the *quantitative* aspect of the world? It is at the price of the obscuration of its *qualitative* aspect. The more one has "open eyes" for quantity, the more one becomes blind to quality. Yet all that one understands by "spiritual world" is only quality, and all experience of the spiritual world is due to "eyes that are open" for quality, for the *vertical* aspect of the world. Thus number has only a qualitative meaning in the spiritual world. "One" signifies unity, "two"— duality, "three"— trinity, and "four"— the duality of dualities. The *vertical* world, the spiritual world, is that of *values* and, as the "value of values" is the individual being, it is a world of individual beings or entities. Angels, Archangels, Principalities, Powers, Virtues, Dominions, Thrones, Cherubim and Seraphim are so many individualised values or entities. And the *supreme value* is the supreme Entity— *God*.

Science reduces quality to quantity. This is what it calls "knowledge". Thus the prismatic colours — red, orange, yellow, green, blue, indigo and violet — lose for science their quality of redness, orangeness, etc., and become quantities, i.e. numbers expressing different frequencies or wavelengths of the vibration that one calls "light". Light, also, is reduced to quantity. It is only a formula expressing quantitative factors of the vibration of something deprived of all quality.

Is it necessary, therefore, to turn one's back on empirical science because it accomplishes the promise of the serpent — in opening our eyes to the quantitative world at the price of making us blind to the qualitative world?

What should one do, confronted with the choice between science and religion?

But is it necessary to chose? Does it not suffice to give each of these two aspirations its place — not that which they arrogate to themselves, but that which is their proper place?

In fact, if there is not a religious empirical science or a scientific religion, there are religious scientists and scientific believers. In order to be a religious scientist or a scientific believer honestly, i.e. without compromising one's conscience, it is necessary to *add* to the definite horizontal aspiration the definite vertical aspiration, i.e. to live under the sign of the cross:

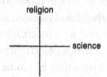

This means to say that one separates the quantitative and qualitative aspects of the world in a clear way, and that one takes account of the precise difference between the function of a mechanism and the action of a sacrament. For the whole world has its mechanical side and its sacramental side. Moses describes the sacramental world in the book of Genesis; modern astronomy is in the process of describing the world-machine. The one speaks to us of the "what" and the other of the "how" of the world. The "how" is the mechanism; the "what" is the essence. The mechanism is knowable through quantity; the essence is revealed by quality.

And the scientific creed? How does one reconcile it with the Christian creed? . . . because it is not the expression of belief in quantity alone, but it is also — and above all — that of belief in *values* contrary to those of the Christian creed.

I have no other answer than the following:

Crucify the serpent. Put the serpent — or the scientific creed — on the cross of religion and science, and a metamorphosis of the serpent will follow. The scientific creed then becomes what it *is* in reality: the mirroring of the creative Word. It will no longer be *truth*; it will be *method*. It will no longer say: "in the beginning was substance or matter", but it will say: "in order to understand the mechanism of the *made* world, it is necessary to choose a method which takes account of the origin of matter and of that which set it in motion from above". And it will no longer say: "the brain produces consciousness", but it will say: "in order to understand the function of the brain, it is necessary to consider it in such a way *as if* consciousness is caused by it".

The first metamorphosis of scientific faith will therefore be the transformation of its metaphysical dogmas into methodological postulates. Its denial of God, of the creation, and of ante-phenomenal spirit, will become the method of the "ignorant scientist" (or *docta ignorantia*, to use the expression of Nicolaus Cusanus), which is nothing other than concentration on the domain which is proper to it.

This metamorphosis will be followed sooner or later by another, namely that of changing the very will which manifests itself in scientific faith. The *will-to-power*, aspiring to the unlimited growth of man's domination of Nature, no matter whether for good or evil, will gradually lose its moral indifference and will become more and more inclined to good — it will be transformed into the *will-to-service*. It is thus that scientific faith will undergo an alchemical transmutation and that empirical science will cease to be amoral or morally indifferent. It will side with what is constructive, with what serves the health, life and well-being of humanity. After this, it will be open to all the innovations in its method that particular tasks call for, and it will one day, finally devote itself to the constructive vital forces of the world with the same zeal and intensity that today it devotes to forces of destruction (heat due to combustion, electricity due to decomposition or friction, nuclear energy due to the destruction of atoms. . .). This in its turn will call for changes in scientific method in the sense that wishful ignorance of the spiritual world will be abandoned as out of date.

But all this will not be able to take place until a number of scientists have "set the bronze serpent on a pole", i.e. to add, first of all in the inner forum of consciousness, the *vertical* of religion to the horizontal of empirical science. This will neutralise the poison of scientific faith and transform it into a servant of life.

It is the divine counsel that was given to Moses in the desert, between Mount Hor and the land of Edom, that I am referring to here:

> Moses made a bronze serpent, and set it on a pole; and if a ser-
> pent bit any man, he would look at the bronze serpent and live.
> (Numbers xxi, 9)

It is also we, who are in the desert of the present day, who have need of the bronze serpent set on a pole, in order to look at it and thus save our spiritual life. The synthesis of science and religon is not a theory, but rather the inner act of consciousness of adding the spiritual vertical to the scientific horizontal or, in other words, *the act of erecting the bronze serpent*.

It should be said that this is not only Biblical advice or the pious desire of a solitary man afflicted by the ravages that scientific faith, supported by the success of empirical science, has brought to bear upon mankind's spiritual life, but rather it is already an accomplished fact. And it is France which has had the honour of giving birth to and contributing to the education of the great contemporary scientist Pierre Teilhard de Chardin (who is at the same time Father Pierre Teilhard de Chardin) who, knowing the situation from both sides, has erected high the bronze serpent in our time. His *Phenomenon of Man*, just as with all his works (published in five volumes), is the realised synthesis of the antinomy "faith—empirical science", in the sense that a true scientist who was a true believer succeeded through his life's work in uniting the horizontal of science (and what a horizontal!) with the vertical of religion (and what a vertical!). It should still be added that he is not alone, and that there are many others who look at the bronze serpent and who thereby *conserve* LIFE.

With respect to ourselves—Hermeticists—here we are brought up against a work which would have been due to be accomplished by us, but which was not because we have not wanted to embrace wholeheartedly either the cause of science and its discipline or that of religion and its discipline. We insisted upon a science for ourselves and a faith for ourselves. This is why no one amongst us was able to fully erect the bronze serpent for our age. Because to be able to do this he would have to be simultaneously a true scientist according to the rules of Academia and a true believer according to the criteria of the Church.

Who amongst us has not — at least in his youth — applauded the maxim boldly stated by Papus: "Neither Voltaire, nor Loyola!". . .which means to say: neither doubt nor faith?

Well, the result is that we doubt a little and we believe a little. We do not have enough critical spirit where we ought to have it, and yet we have enough to render our faith lame when it is a matter of accepting without reserve the spiritual values offered for our appraisal. In practice, "neither Voltaire, nor Loyola" means to say "a little Voltaire and a little Loyola", because one cannot do entirely without doubt and faith. And there is one — I still have Father Pierre Teilhard de Chardin in mind — who had the courage to say "both Voltaire and Loyola", and to be a true scientist at the same time as being a Jesuit. He heroically accepted the cross of "Voltairian" doubt and "Ignatian" faith. The result is a light-filled vision of the world evolving through the impulse of the serpent towards a final aim set by providence.

Let us also not fear, therefore, to become like the Hermit of the Tarot, who is clothed in the habit of faith and whose doubt fathoms the ground — with his staff! The light of the lamp which he holds is that which is emitted from the opposition of faith and doubt!

The Gift of Black Perfection (or The Gift of Perfect Night).

The Arcana of the Tarot, I must stress, are spiritual exercises. And the ninth Arcanum, the Hermit is one of them.

For this reason the preceding meditations on the three antinomies aim not so much at a solution of the antinomies that will please everyone, but more to encourage spiritual endeavour orientated towards the solution of these antinomies. You can certainly resolve them in a more profound and satisfying way. It is a matter, in the case of the solutions that I have proposed above, above all of a *concrete illustration* (which is, I know, far from being the best) of an individual endeavour by way of a special spiritual exercise. This consists in setting before you a thesis and an antithesis, both as clearly as possible — I should say: as crystallised light — in such a way that all intellectual light which is at your disposal may then be consumed by these two opposing theses. You will then arrive at a state of mind in which all that you know and clearly perceive is put into the thesis and its antithesis, so that they may be like two rays of light, whilst your mind itself is plunged into darkness. You know and see nothing more than the light of these two contrary theses; beyond them there remains only darkness.

And it is then that one undertakes the essential thing about this exercise, namely *the endeavour to draw light from darkness*, i.e. an effort aiming at knowledge which appears to you to be not only unknown but also unknowable.

In fact, every serious antinomy signifies psychologically: "the light that I possess is polarised at two poles; between these two luminous poles there is only darkness". Now, it is from this darkness that the solution to the antinomy, the synthesis, must be drawn. It is necessary to *create* light from darkness. One could say that it is a matter of an act analogous to the *Fiat lux* ("Let there be light", Genesis i, 3) of the first day of creation.

Experience teaches us that there are two kinds of darkness in the domain of consciousness. One is that of ignorance, passivity and laziness, which is "infra-light" darkness. The other, in contrast, is the darkness of higher knowledge, intense activity and endeavour still to be made—this is "ultra-light". It is a question of this latter "darkness" in instances where it is a matter of resolving an antinomy or finding a synthesis.

Modern Hermetic literature (of the nineteenth and twentieth centuries) takes account of the "neutralisation of binaries", i.e. the method where one finds the *third* term, or neutral term, for the two terms ("binary") corresponding to the active and passive principles. Thus you will find in Papus' *Traité élémentaire de science occulte* (Paris, 1888, p. 121) the following examples of this "neutralisation":

Father (+)   —   Mother (–)   —   Child (n)

Light (+)   —   Darkness (–)   —   Twilight (n)

Sun (+)   —   Moon (–)   —   Mercury (n)

The method of the "neutralisation of binaries" (the term was in use in Russia; I am not sure if it is used in France) is generally considered by Hermetic and occultist authors as the traditional method of Hermeticism.

Now, a binary can be "neutralised" in *three* different ways: (1) above (synthesis); (2) in the horizontal (compromise); and (3) below (mixture). Neutralisation above takes place when one finds the neutral term on a plane higher than the plane of the binary itself:

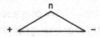

Horizontal neutralisation is accomplished by finding the median term between the two terms of the binary on the plane of the binary itself:

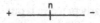

Neutralisation below is effected when one reduces the binary to a third term on a plane lower than that of the binary, by way of mixing:

In order to illustrate the three ways of "neutralisation" of binaries, the "coloured body" of the German scientist Wilhelm Ostwald (cf. *Die Farbenfibel*, Leipzig, 1916) will serve us as an example. Ostwald's coloured body is formed by two cones:

north pole

equator

south pole

This body therefore has a "north pole", a "south pole" and an "equator".

The "north pole" is the *white point* which is the synthesis of all colours. It is this white light which is more and more differentiated as it progressively descends towards the "equator". There the colours attain their maximum differentiation and individual intensity. Thus, for example, red is only present in potentiality at the point of the "north pole", then it becomes pinkish as it comes a degree lower, then rose, then reddish, before becoming bright red when it reaches the "equator". The "equator" therefore consists of seven colours (the seven colours of the visible spectrum) at their maximum intensity.

These same colours, in continuing their descent from the "equator" towards the "south pole", gradually lose their chromatic light and become darker. When they reach the "south pole" they lose all distinction and become equally *black*. The "south pole" is therefore the *black point* of the coloured body, just as the "north pole" is the *white point*. The "white point" is the synthesis of all the colours; it is their "neutralisation above", in the light. The "equator" is the region of maximum distinction between the colours. It is there that the transition from one colour to another can be established. It is the region where "horizontal neutralisation" can be effected. The "black point", lastly, is that of the confusion of all colours, where they are lost in darkness. It is the region of "neutralisation below".

Ostwald's coloured body, invented by its maker towards useful ends in the coloured fabrics and textile industry, allows the "latitude and longitude" of every nuance and degree of intensity of each colour to be shown precisely, and can therefore be useful — certainly without the knowledge of its inventor — for Hermetic meditations as an important basis for a chain of analogies.

We are able by analogy, therefore, to conceive of the "white point" or "north pole" of the coloured body as that of *wisdom*, the "equator" as that of the family of particular sciences of human knowledge, and the "black point" or "south pole" as that of *ignorance*. Now, wisdom is the synthesis above of all the particular sciences of human knowledge. It contains them simultaneously, undifferentiated within itself, as white light contains the seven prismatic colours. The "neutralisation" or synthesis of the binary "yellow—blue", for example, can therefore be effected by rising towards the "white point" of wisdom.

Another method of finding a third term for the binary "yellow—blue" is that of finding the point of transition from yellow to blue on the scale on the equator of prismatic colours, which is exactly at the middle of the distance separating the "most yellow point" from the "most blue point". This would be the *green* point.

Lastly, there is the third method of "neutralisation"—that in the direction beneath the equator. This is the direction towards the "black point", where the particular colours disappear into darkness. The "neutralisation" of the binary "yellow—blue" is therefore effected, according to this method, when a point on the scale of the reversed cone of the coloured body is found, where yellow and blue cease to be discernible in the dark brown which they become.

If we now take instead of the binary "yellow—blue" that of "mathematics—descriptive science" or "mathematics—phenomenalism", and apply the three methods of "neutralisation" here, we obtain a formula of transcendental synthesis, another that is a compromise or equilibrium, and a third that is indifferent, as follows:

1. Transcendental synthesis: "God geometrises; numbers are the creators of phenomena" (the formula of Plato and the Pythagoreans);
2. Equilibrium: "The world is order, i.e. phenomena display limits due to the equilibrium that we call measure, number and weight" (the formula of Aristotle and the Peripatetics);
3. Indifference: "Our mind reduces phenomena to numbers so as to make it easier for the work of the mind to handle them" (formula of the sceptics).

We see, therefore, that Platonism is orientated towards the "white point" of wisdom, Aristotelianism moves in the "equatorial" region of precise distinctions, and scepticism tends towards the "black point" of nihilism.

With respect to Hermeticism, the Hermit holds the lamp which represents the "luminous point" of transcendental synthesis; he is wrapped in a mantle, hanging in folds, for deploying the particular qualities which have their place in the region of the "equator"; and he supports himself with a staff for feeling his way in the domain of darkness, in the region of the reversed cone culminating in the "black point". He is therefore a Peripatetic Platonist (en route around the "equator"), making use of scepticism (his "staff") while he walks. This is why the traditional interpretation of the ninth Arcanum is *prudence*.

Prudence is constant awareness of being between two darknesses—the darkness of the "white point" of absolute synthesis above, which is dazzling and which demands a slow and gradual spiritual preparation in order to be able to bear its light without being blinded, and the darkness of the black point, that of the subconscious below. Prudence is at the same time "mobile concentration" proceeding from one particular colour to another in the "equatorial" region between the two opposite poles. It is wrapped in the mantle of their "synopsis" not as a knowledge that is ever-present in the mind, but rather as the background of each particular branch of knowledge—as the certainty of *faith* in the unity which certainly envelops it and with which it is clothed, but which is open at the front to make room for the use of the lamp (*orientated vision*) and the staff (*concentrated touch*).

Prudence does not entail a vision that is always present in the mind, either of the "white point" of synthesis, or of the "synopsis" of the rainbow of colours. It is an enveloping presence, as the subconscious envelops the conscious, and is present only as a force of orientation, as a directing inclination and fundamental impulse in relation to the conscious. Prudence never elaborates an "absolute system" for synthesising all knowledge. It is occupied only with particular problems on the basis of their synthesis present at deeper levels of consciousness. A general all-embracing synthesis is formed on another level of consciousness than that where the conscious self performs intellectual work. It is thus that the prudent Hermit would be able to offer you dozens of answers to dozens of questions, giving them spontaneously and without apparent care for their mutual agreement, and you would have the impression that each particular answer is absolutely *ad hoc* and that it is in no way due to a preconceived intellectual system. You will ask, perhaps, if this is not a matter of "intellectual poetry", such that each particular answer appears spontaneously and ingenuously, although it may certainly be appropriate and conclusive.

This would be the first impression. However, after thought and reflection, you would find that all these spontaneous and well-intentioned *ad hoc* answers disclose a "whole", an organism of synthesis behind them, and that they are *in essence* prodigiously married, and *in essence* constitute only a single articulated "word".

Then you will understand the role played by the mantle enveloping the Hermit, when he employs his lamp for seeing clearly into particular problems, and when he employs his staff for probing his terrain. The "mantle" is the presence at a deeper level of consciousness of the *whole truth*, and it is this which envelops and inspires all intellectual work relating to particular problems that is carried out by the conscious self with its lamp and staff. It is this which gives the conscious self direction and style, and sees to it that each solution to each particular problem is in harmony with the whole. The whole truth lives at this deeper level, and is present there as the certainty of *absolute faith*, as the certainty of the *imprint* of truth from above.

The initiate is not someone who knows everything. He is a person who bears the truth within a deeper level of his consciousness, not as an intellectual system, but rather as a level in his being, as a "mantle" which envelops him. This truth-imprint manifests itself as unshakeable certainty, i.e. as *faith* in the sense of the *voice of the presence of truth*.

Truth attained through synthesis is present at a deeper level of consciousness than that of the consciousness of self. It is found in darkness. It is from this darkness that the rays of light of particular branches of knowledge are emitted, as a result of efforts aspiring to the "neutralisation of binaries" or the "solution of antinomies". These efforts are nothing other than excursions into the region of this deeper level of consciousness; they are contacts established with the inner darkness, which is full of revelations of truth.

The knowledge and power drawn from this dark and silent region of luminous certainty can be well described as the "gift of Perfect Night", the " τέλειον μέλαν " mentioned in *Kore Kosmu*, the sacred book of Hermes Trismegistus.

The "gift of Perfect Night" manifests itself in consequence of such spiritual endeavours as are implied by the "neutralisation of binaries" or the "solution of antinomies". It is, one can say, the very essence of Hermeticism and constitutes at one and the same time the method which is proper to it and the faculty of knowledge to the exercise of which its very existence is due.

The Hermit is the spiritual image of he who follows the method and exercises the faculty of the "gift of black perfection" (or the "gift of Perfect Night"). As this method comprises true impartiality, i.e. the search for the synthesis of antinomies and the third term of binaries, the Hermeticist must necessarily be solitary, i.e. a hermit. *Solitude* is the method itself of Hermeticism. For one has to be profoundly alone in order to be able to exercise the "gift of Perfect Night" in the face of contraries, binaries, antinomies and parts which divide and rend the world of truth. He who seeks synthesis, i.e. true *peace*, can never take part for or against opposing things. And since it is precisely "taking sides" which groups people into communities and divides them into sections, he is necessarily alone. He can neither embrace any human cause without reserve, nor be opposed to any human cause, being loyal to the cause of *truth*, which is synthesis and peace. This is why he is condemned, whether he wants it or not, to profound solitude. He *is* a hermit in his inner life, whatever his outer life may be. He will never be given the joy of plunging himself in national, social or political collectivity. He will never have the blissful experience of having shared out the weight of responsibility with the multitude, and he can never fit in at festivals—or orgies—in the sense implied in the words "we French", "we Germans", "we Jews", "we Republicans", "we Royalists", or "we communists". The intoxication of plunging into collectivity is not given to him. He must be sober, i.e. *alone*. Because the pursuit of truth through synthesis—which is peace—implies prudence, and prudence is solitude.

This is why the Gospel puts the peacemakers in the same list as those who are poor in spirit, those who mourn, those who hunger and thirst for righteousness and those who are persecuted for righteousness' sake, assigning them another blessing than that of which they are deprived. "Blessed are the peacemakers, for they shall be called sons of God" (Matthew v, 9) is what is said in the Sermon on the Mount for those who refuse to take sides in the face of partial truths and prejudices, being dedicated to the cause of the whole truth which unites the world and bears *peace* to it.

The itinerant Hermit—with his mantle, his lamp and his staff—is a "travelling salesman" of peace. He makes his way from opinion to opinion, from belief to belief, from experience to experience — and traces his route so that he traverses the way of peace between opinions, beliefs and experiences, being always equipped with his mantle, lamp and staff. He does so alone, because he *walks* (and no one can walk for him) and because his work is peace (which is prudence, and therefore solitude).

However, there is no need to take pity on him. For he has his joys, and these are intense. When, for example, he meets another itinerant hermit on the way, what joy and what happiness there is in this meeting of two solitary travellers! This joy has nothing in common with that of the intoxication of feeling free from the burden of responsibility which plunging into collectivity brings about. On the contrary, it is the joy of responsibility encountering the same responsibility, which together share and alleviate the responsiblity of a *third* — one who said of his earthly life:

> Foxes have holes, and birds of the air have nests; but the Son
> of Man has nowhere to lay his head. (Matthew viii, 20)

For it is the Master whom all itinerant hermits follow and serve. It is then the joy of two who meet one another in his name, and where he is "present".

Then there are the joys of profound silence, full of revelations, and those of the starry heaven, whose solemn presence speaks in the language of eternity, and the joys of the constellations of stars, and those of thoughts, and those of breathing air full of spirituality! No, one need not take pity on the Hermit. Although, like his Master, he has nowhere to lay his head, he is already blessed with the good fortune that the Master promised to those who are peacemakers. He has the good fortune to participate in the work of the Son of God, in taking part in the solitude of the earthly life of the Son of Man.

Those who are peacemakers — hermits — do not in any way procure peace "at any price" and without distinction in kind. For one can achieve peace in various ways, and it is still necessary to distinguish between peace and Peace. Ostwald's coloured body can again help us in the solution of this problem. The "white point", the "equator of living colours" and the "black point" of this body can serve as a basis, by analogy, for the problem of the different types of peace and the different ways of realising it.

Peace is unity in diversity. There is no peace where there is no diversity, and there is no peace when there is only diversity.

Now, unity where diversity disappears is not peace. For this reason, although the "white point" of the coloured body, where all colours are drowned in light, is certainly that which renders peace possible, it is not peace as such, taken by itself. Similarly, the "black point" of the body, where all colours disappear into darkness, is not the point of peace, but rather the point of death of diversity and the conflicts that diversity can produce. It is therefore the "equator of living colours" which is the region proper to peace. The living colours of the rainbow that appear in the sky are the visible manifestation of the idea of peace, because the rainbow causes us to see unity in the diversity of colours. There the whole family of colours presents itself to us as seven sisters who join their hands. For this reason the rainbow is the sign of peace (or alliance) between heaven and earth, as in Moses' Genesis:

> And God said: This is the sign of the covenant which I make between me and you and every living creature that is with you, for all future generations—I set my bow in the cloud, and it shall be a sign of the covenant between me and the earth. (Genesis ix, 12-13)

Now, four types of peace, understood as the elimination of conflict or opposition, are possible: transcendental peace ("nirvanaic"), immanent peace ("catholic"), the peace of predominance ("hegemonic") and the peace of death ("nihilistic").

Transcendental or "nirvanaic" peace corresponds to the "white point" of the coloured body. Immanent or "catholic" peace is the simultaneous living manifestation of *all* colours of the rainbow and corresponds to the "equator" of the coloured body. The peace of predominance, or "hegemonic" peace, corresponds to the result of the tendency of a particular colour to eclipse other colours in the region of the "equator of colours", and to engulf them so that there remains only a single colour. The peace of death, or "nihilistic" peace, corresponds to the "black point" of the coloured body, and signifies an absolute levelling-out of all diversity. Of these four kinds of peace, it is only the peace that we have designated "immanent" or "catholic" (universal) which is real and true peace. It is the peace of *brotherhood* and mutual *complement*.

As it is this peace that the Hermit has for an ideal, he is not presented on the Card in the *padmasana* posture of Buddhist or yogic meditation aiming at the transcendent peace of *nirvana*, nor is he presented *seated* on the throne of power making a commanding gesture, nor lying asleep or dead on the ground, but rather he is presented as *walking*. He walks, i.e. he goes round the "equator of living colours" of the coloured body, and his way is that of peace in the sense of unity in diversity.

It follows from the foregoing that the Hermit, i.e. the serious Hermeticist, is in no way a "neutralist"—although he applies himself to the "neutralisation" of binaries or polarities, to the solution of antinomies or opposites, and to the peace of the rainbow or unity in diversity. He knows how to say "no" to the tendencies aiming at false peace—those of transcendental indifference, subjugation and nihilism—just as he knows how to say "yes" to everything which aims at the true peace of unity in diversity.

He knows how to say "yes" and "no"—these two magical words of the will, by means of which the will is strong, and without which it goes to sleep. "Yes and no"— this is the very life of the will, its supreme and unique law. The will does not know of a third term between, beyond, above or below "yes and no". "Amen" and "anathema" are not only the solemn formulae of liturgy summarising ultimate affirmation and negation, but also those of the will which lives and keeps awake. The will as such is never impartial, neutral or indifferent.

Now we have arrived at a further antinomy— a *practical* antinomy: "wisdom— will", or "universal synthesis— particular action" or, also, "knowledge— will". One *must* know, i.e. see unity in diversity, and one *must* will, i.e. cut through contemplated unity, with a sharp sword that cuts both ways— the "yes" and the "no" of the will. To become contemplative is to turn to inactivity. To become active is, in the last analysis, to turn to ignorance.

One can certainly choose to live a contemplative kind of life, but at what price? The following analogy illustrates the price of choosing contemplation as the principal way and central preoccupation of life:

A boat carries passengers and a crew consisting of a captain, officers and sailors. It is the same with the boat as with human society, which voyages from century to century. The latter also bears crew and passengers. The members of crew are vigilant so that the boat follows its route and the passengers are healthy and safe. Now, to take the part of living a contemplative life implies the decision to become a passenger on the boat of human society and to leave the responsibility for the boat's route, and for the well-being of the other passengers as well as oneself, to the crew— the captain, and the officers and sailors. One therefore becomes a passenger on the boat of human history, when one chooses a life of the contemplative kind. This is the moral price of this choice.

Nevertheless, one must guard against the direct— but superficial— conclusion that all "hermits" and "contemplatives" in the various religious orders are passengers. Nothing could be further from the truth. Because amongst these "contemplatives" are often found not only sailors and officers of the crew but also even captains. It is because their work and aim is essentially *practical*, although spiritual, that this is so. *Prayer*, divine service, study, and a disciplined and austere life constitute a very active and effective endeavour, having in view the route and destiny of the boat of mankind's spiritual history. Truth to tell, it is the "contemplatives" who bear consciously and voluntarily the bulk of the responsibility for the spiritual route of the boat and for the spiritual well-being both of its crew and its passengers. "Contemplative", for these orders, signifies spiritual endeavour and spiritual responsibility, whilst "contemplative" in the sense of choosing the pole of contemplation at the expense of the pole of will within the human being means that one prefers the *enjoyment* of contemplation to the *effort* of will and action (spiritual or outward) that the latter entails. In fact, one can meet a fair number of people who enjoy the contemplative life. They are almost never from religious orders or orders of so-called contemplatives, but above all are lay-amateurs who are so on their own authority. One can meet them amongst dilettante yoga-practitioners, would-be Cabbalists, make-believe Sufis, and metaphysicians in general.

One can, on the other hand, decide for the pole of will within the human being and want to occupy oneself only with what relates to action and practical aim. One can certainly choose a life of action of some kind, but at what price! The price is inevitably narrow-mindedness. "What is the good of occupying myself with Eskimos, with whom I have nothing to do, when I do not even know sufficient people in my street and colleagues in my office?"—says one who has chosen action at the expense of knowledge. If he is a believer, he will ask: What is the good of all these vain spiritual occupations—philosophies, sciences, and social and political doctrines—if the sound precepts of the Gospels (or the Bible, the Koran, the Dhammapada, etc.) are sufficient for my salvation and that of humanity? Action demands concentration and this inevitably entails the limitation of the spirit to cross-sections of life and the loss of perspective of its totality.

Now, the prudence taught by the Arcanum "The Hermit" can also give the solution to the practical antinomy "knowledge—will".

The Hermit is neither deep in meditation or study nor is he engaged in work or action. *He is walking*. This means to say that he manifests a third state beyond that of contemplation and action. He represents—in relation to the binary "knowledge —will" or "contemplation—action" or, lastly, "head—limbs"—the term of synthesis, namely that of *heart*. For it is the *heart* where contemplation and action are united, where knowledge becomes will and where will becomes knowledge. The heart does not need to forget all contemplation in order to act, and does not need to suppress all action in order to contemplate. It is the heart which is simultaneously active and contemplative, untiringly and unceasingly. It *walks*. It walks day and night, and we listen day and night to the steps of its incessant walking. This is why, if we want to represent a man who lives the law of the heart, who is centred in the heart and is a visible expression of the heart—the "wise and good father", or the Hermit—we present him as *walking*, steadily and without haste.

The Hermit of the ninth Card is a man of heart, a solitary man who is walking. Therefore he is a man who has realised in himself the antinomy "knowledge—will" or "contemplation—action". For the heart is the solution here.

The "heart" that we have in mind here is not that of emotion and the faculty of being passionate that one generally understands by "heart". It is the middle centre of the seven centres of man's psychic and vital constitution. It is the "twelve-petalled lotus" or *anahata* centre of Indian esotericism. This centre is the most *human* of all the centres or "lotus flowers". For if the eight-petalled lotus or crown centre is that of the revelation of wisdom, the two-petalled lotus is that of intellectual initiative, the sixteen-petalled lotus (the larynx centre) is that of the creative word, the ten-petalled lotus is that of science, the six-petalled lotus is that of harmony and health, and the four-petalled lotus is that of creative force, then the twelve-petalled lotus (the heart centre) is that of *love*. This is why it is the most human of the centres, and it is the ultimate criterion not of what a human being possesses — what he can do and what he knows — but rather of what he *is*. For the human being is fundamentally what his heart is. It is here that the humanity of the human being resides and is revealed. The heart is the sun of the microcosm.

For this reason Christian Hermeticism — in common with Christianity in general — is "heliocentric", i.e. it attributes to the heart the central place in all its practices. The great work of spiritual alchemy or "ethical Hermeticism" is the transmutation of the substances ("metals") of the other lotuses into the substance of the heart ("gold"). "Ethical Hermeticism" (a term employed in Russia for spiritual alchemy) aims at the transformation of the whole system of lotuses into a system of seven hearts, i.e. to transform the human being entirely into heart. In practice, this means to say the *humanisation* of the whole human being and the transformation of the system of lotuses into a system functioning by love and for love. Thus the wisdom revealed by the eight-petalled lotus will cease to be abstract and transcendental: it will become full of warmth, as the fire of Pentecost. The intellectual initiative of the two-petalled lotus will become "compassion-filled insight" into the world. The creative word of the sixteen-petalled lotus will become magical: it will have the faculty of illumining, consoling and healing.

The heart itself, or the twelve-petalled lotus, which alone of the centres is not attached to the organism, and which can go out of it and live — by the exteriorisation of its "petals", which can be rayed outwards — with and in others, will become a traveller, a visitor and anonymous companion of those who are in prison, those who are in exile, and those who bear heavy loads of responsibility. It will be an itinerant Hermit, traversing ways leading from one end of the earth to the other, and also ways through spheres of the spiritual world — from purgatory to the very feet of the Father. Because no distance is insurmountable for love and no door can prevent it from entering — according to the promise which says: "and the gates of hell shall not prevail against it" (Matthew xvi, 18). It is the heart which is the marvellous organ called to serve love in its works. It is the structure of the heart — simultaneously human and divine, a structure of love — which by way of analogy can open our understanding to the significance of the meaning of the following words of the Master: "And lo, *I am with you* always, to the end of time" (Matthew xxviii, 20).

The science of the ten-petalled lotus will then become conscience, i.e. the servant of God and neighbour. The six-petalled lotus, the centre of health, will become that of holiness, i.e. harmony between spirit, soul and body. The creative force of the four-petalled lotus will then serve as a source of energy and inexhaustible élan for the long way of the itinerant hermit, who is a man of heart, i.e. a man who has regained his humanity.

The disciple of Hindu yoga and tantra meditates on, or inwardly recites, "seed-mantras" (*bija mantra*) in order to arouse and advance the development of these centres or chakras. He inwardly vibrates the syllable OM for the centre between the eyebrows (the two-petalled lotus), the syllable HAM for the larynx centre (the sixteen-petalled lotus), the syllable YAM for the heart centre (the twelve-petalled lotus), the syllable RAM for the umbilical centre (the ten-petalled lotus), the syllable VAM for the pelvic centre (the six-petalled lotus) and the syllable LAM for the centre at the base of the spine (the four-petalled lotus). Concerning the crown centre (the eight-petalled lotus), there is no *bija mantra* for it — this centre being not the means but rather the aim of yogic development. It is the centre of liberation.

Now, the following "mantras" or Christian formulae are those which relate to these centres:

> I am the resurrection and the life — the eight-petalled lotus;
> I am the light of the world — the two-petalled lotus;
> I am the good shepherd — the sixteen-petalled lotus;
> I am the bread of life — the twelve-petalled lotus;
> I am the door , — the ten-petalled lotus;
> I am the way, the truth and the life — the six-petalled lotus;
> I am the true vine — the four-petalled lotus.

Here is the difference in the choice of method: It is a matter, dear Unknown Friend, of choosing between the method of vibrating particular syllabic sounds — Om, Ham, Yam, Ram, Vam and Lam — and the method which has in view spiritual communion with the seven rays of the "I AM" or the seven aspects of the perfect SELF, who is Jesus Christ. The first method aims at awakening the centres *such as they are*; the second aims at the *Christianisation* of all the centres, i.e. their *transformation* in conformity with their divine-human prototypes. It is a matter here of the realisation of the words of the apostle Paul: "Therefore, if anyone is in Christ, he is a new creation" (II Corinthians v, 17).

The work of Christianisation of the human organisation, i.e. the transformation of the human being into a man of heart, is accomplished in the *inner* life of man, the lotus-flowers being only the field where the *effects* of this purely inner work are manifested. Now, the domain where this transformation is immediately effected consists of three pairs of contraries (practical "antinomies") and three "neutralisations of binaries" — nine factors in all — as follows:

When we speak of the practical antinomy "knowledge — will" and its solution — the "heart" — this is only a general view of the task of integration of the human being. In *practice* we have to do with "will and the heart of knowledge", "knowledge and the will of the heart" and "knowledge and the heart of the will", for there is feeling and will in the domain of thought, thought and will in the domain of feeling, and thought and feeling in the domain of the will. There are therefore three triangles of "knowledge — heart — will" in practising the inner work of integrating the human being.

Now, the distinctly practical teaching of the ninth Arcanum is that it is necessary to subordinate the directing intellectual initiative, as well as the flowing spontaneous movement of thought, to the "heart of thought", i.e. to the profound feeling that is found at the basis of the thinking that one sometimes designates "intellectual intuition" and which is the "feeling for truth". It is also necessary to subordinate both spontaneous imagination and actively directed imagination to the direction of the heart, i.e. to the profound feeling of moral warmth that one sometimes designates "moral intuition" and which is the "feeling for beauty". Lastly, it is necessary to subordinate spontaneous impulses and designs directed from the will to the profound feeling which accompanies them that one sometimes designates "practical intuition" and which is the "feeling for the good".

The Hermit of the ninth Card is the Christian Hermeticist, who represents the "inner work of nine", the work of realising the supremacy of the heart in the human being—in familiar, traditional terms: the "work of salvation"—because the "salvation of the soul" is the restoration of the reign of the *heart*.

Meditation on the
Tenth Major Arcanum of the Tarot

THE WHEEL OF FORTUNE
LA ROUE DE FORTUNE

Vanity of vanities! All is vanity. . .
What has been is what will be,
And what has been done is what will be done;
And there is nothing new under the sun.
                              (Ecclesiastes i, 2, 9)

Qui propter nos homines et propter nostram
salutem descendit de coelis. Et incarnatus est
de Spiritu Sancto ex Maria Virgine, et homo
factus est. . .et ascendit in coelum, sedet ad
dexteram Patris.

(For us men and for our salvation he came
down from heaven: by the power of the Holy
Spirit he became incarnate from the Virgin
Mary, and was made man. . .he ascended into
heaven and is seated at the right hand of the
Father)
                              (from the Creed)

And I applied my mind to know wisdom
And to know madness and folly.
I perceived that this also is
    but a striving after wind.
For in much wisdom is much vexation,
And he who increases knowledge increases
sorrow.
                              (Ecclesiastes i, 17-18)

Blessed are those who mourn,
For they shall be comforted.
                              (Matthew v, 4)

LETTER X

THE WHEEL OF
FORTUNE

Dear Unknown Friend,

We have before us a wheel which rotates, and three figures in animal form of
which two (the monkey and the dog) turn with the wheel, whilst the third (the
sphinx) is beyond the movement of the wheel: he is seated on a platform above
the wheel. The monkey descends in order to rise again; the dog rises in order to
descend again. First one and then the other pass before the sphinx. Simple and
natural questions, which arise spontaneously when one looks at the Card, are:

> Why do the monkey and the dog turn with the wheel? Why is
> the sphinx there?
> How many times will the monkey and the dog pass before the
> sphinx? And why are there these meetings with the sphinx?

233

Once having posed these simple questions, we find ourselves already at the heart of the tenth Arcanum, plunged into the very sphere of notions and ideas which it is called to awaken.

In fact, the wheel alone, without its two passengers and without the sphinx seated above it, evokes only the idea of a circle or, at most, that of circular movement. The wheel with the two animals, the one rising and the other descending — without the sphinx above it — evokes the idea of a vain and absurd game. But the wheel turning with its two passengers *and* the sphinx dominating the whole makes the onlooker ask himself if this is not an *arcanum*, i.e. a key that one has to know in order to be able to orientate oneself, in this case in the domain of problems and phenomena relating to the circular movement of living beings. It is especially the sphinx above the wheel which gives us an intellectual shock and which impels us to seek out the Arcanum of this Card.

Now, there are two categories of ideas concerning the genetic relationship and the general genesis of the four kingdoms of Nature — the mineral realm, the plant realm, the animal realm and the human realm — which have their root in the intellectual life of humanity. The one is based on the idea of the *Fall*, i.e. degeneration and descent from above below. According to this class of ideas, it is not the monkey who is the ancestor of man, but rather, on the contrary, it is man who is the ancestor of the monkey, which latter is a degenerate and degraded descendant. And the three kingdoms of Nature below the human kingdom are, according to this set of ideas, the projected residue or exteriorisation of the comprehensive being of primordial man, or Adam, who is the original prototype and synthesis of all the entities comprising the four kingdoms of Nature.

The other class of ideas comprises the idea of *evolution*, i.e. progress transforming from below above. According to this category of ideas, it is the most primitive entity — from the point of view of consciousness as well as biological structure — which is the origin of all beings in the four kingdoms of Nature and which is their common ancestor.

The Card of the tenth Major Arcanum of the Tarot represents a monkey — i.e. an animal with a face still preserving features that one cannot fail to recognise as human — who is falling. For it is not the monkey who is climbing down, but rather it is the movement of the wheel which carries him along. In descending, the monkey raises his head because he is not descending of his own accord. From where does he descend — this animal with a head bearing human features?

He descends from the place where the sphinx is sitting. The crowned and winged sphinx, with a human head and an animal body, and holding a white sword, represents the plane and the stage of being from which the monkey is moving away and towards which the dog is approaching.

Now, if you had had the task of portraying the idea of the Fall in the sense of degeneration from the comprehensive being — the prototype of all Nature — wouldn't you have shown the sphinx crowned above, as the only possible figure representing the unity of the human and the animal kingdom, the latter in turn being the synthesis of the plant and mineral kingdoms? And wouldn't you have portrayed one figure descending in the course of animalisation, deprived of the crown, the sword and the wings, but yet still with features bearing witness to its origin, i.e. would you not have chosen the monkey to represent the transition from the prototype state of comprehensive being to the state of reduced and specialised being? Does not the monkey lend itself marvellously to serve as a symbol of the animalisation which is effected at the expense of the Angelic and human elements of the prototype being?

On the other hand, if you had wanted to give visual expression to the nostalgia of fallen and fragmented beings for the lost state of fullness and integration, would you not choose the dog, the animal most passionately drawn and attached to the human element, as a symbol of the aspiration of animals towards union with human nature, i.e. the aspiration towards the *sphinx*, where animal nature is united to human nature?

The Card of the tenth Arcanum therefore teaches, through its actual context, an organism of ideas relating to the problem of the Fall and the Reintegration, according to Hermetic and Biblical tradition. It portrays the *whole* circle, including ascent as well as descent, whilst the "transformism" of modern science is occupied with only *half* of the circle, namely the half of ascent or evolution. The fact is that certain eminent scientists (such as Edgar Daqué in Germany and Pierre Teilhard de Chardin in France) advance the postulate of the pre-existence — be it only potentially — of a prototype for all beings, which is the ultimate as well as the effective cause of the whole process of evolution, and this postulate alone renders evolution intelligible. However, it in no way changes the fact that science *works* on the basis of the fundamental supposition that the minimum is the ancestor of the maximum, the simple is the ancestor of the complicated, and that it is the primitive which produces the more developed organism and consciousness, although for thought (i.e. reason) this is absolutely unintelligible. This basic scientific presupposition renders evolution unintelligible because it disregards half of the circle, namely all that which precedes — be it only *in ordine cognoscendi* — the state of primitivity from which science takes its point of departure. Because one has to renounce thought and reduce it to lethargy in order to be able to sincerely believe that man evolved from the primitive and unconscious particles of a primordial mist which was once our planet, without this mist bearing within itself the seed of all possibilities for future evolution, which is the process of "eclosion", i.e. the process of transition from a potential state to an actual state. Thus Arnold Lunn, editor of the book *Is Evolution Proved?*, writes that he would certainly like to believe in evolution and accept it as proved, if he could surmount four difficulties, including the following:

> . . . for the fact (is) that no evolutionist had produced a plausible *guess*, much less a theory supported by evidence, to suggest how a purely natural process could have evolved, from the

> mud, sand, mists and seas of the primeval planet, the brain that
> conceived Beethoven's Ninth Symphony and the reactions to the
> beauty of music, of art, and of Nature. (*Is Evolution Proved?*
> A debate between D. Dewar and H. S. Shelton, ed. Arnold
> Lunn, London, 1947, p. 333)

It is my painful duty to have to add to the above quotation the reply by William S. Beck, author of *Modern Science and the Nature of Life*, to the difficulty to which Arnold Lunn draws attention. He says:

> It seems that the argument against evolution is pure meta-
> physical brocade, artfully draped so as to obscure the cogent
> evidence of science. (William S. Beck, *Modern Science and the
> Nature of Life*, London, 1961, p.133)

Metaphysical brocade or not, it does not matter, the fact of the unintelligibility for human thought of the *theory* (not the facts!) of evolution advanced by science nevertheless remains a fact. It is and always will be unintelligible in so far as it takes consideration of only half of the whole circle of evolution, and refuses to accept the other half of the circle, that of *involution*, or the Fall, which would make it intelligible.

Now, the tenth Major Arcanum of the Tarot represents a *circle*, a wheel comprising both the descent or departure from the comprehensive prototype being and the ascent towards this being.

The doctrine of the circle of involution and evolution is generally a platitude in occult literature, but it is not so when it is a matter of involution understood as the *Fall* and evolution understood as *salvation*. There is a world of difference between the orientalistic doctrine concerning the semi-automatic "process" of involution and evolution, and the Hermetic, Biblical and Christian doctrine concerning the Fall and salvation. The former sees in the circle of involution-evolution only a purely natural process, similar to the process of respiration in a living organism—animal or human. The Hermetic, Biblical and Christian tradition, in contrast, sees here a cosmic tragedy and drama full of the supreme dangers and risks that the traditional terms "perdition" and "salvation" imply.

Fall, perdition, redemption, salvation are words which, truth to tell, are devoid of meaning, both for a spiritually-orientated evolutionist and for an evolutionist who is scientifically orientated. The former sees in cosmic evolution the eternal circular movement of exteriorisation and interiorisation—the exhalation and inhalation of divine cosmic respiration. What Fall, then? What risk, what perdition!? What redemption, and of what!? What salvation!? The whole inventory of fundamental Judaeo-Christian ideas is inapplicable in a naturally (i.e. *inevitably*) evolving world.

Who is right? Those for whom evolution is an organically determined process in which descent and ascent are only two successive phases of a single cosmic vibration? Or those who see in evolution a cosmic tragedy and drama whose essence and *leitmotiv* correspond to the parable of the prodigal son?

What is it to be right? Are the passengers on a boat who have tickets for the voyage mistaken in considering the boat and its crew together as their means of navigation—transporting them following a determined route to the place of destination? For the travellers, the sea voyage is a "natural process", something which happens by itself, provided that the ticket for the passage is paid.

But can the captain, officers and other members of the crew consider the passage over the sea in the same way as the passengers? Evidently not. For those who are responsible for the voyage, the passage signifies work, watches, manoeuvring and orientation in order to follow the route and bear the load of responsibility for everything. For the crew, therefore, the voyage is in no way a kind of "natural process", something which happens quite by itself. On the contrary, for them it is effort, struggle and risk.

It is the same with evolution. One sees it as a "natural process" when one looks at it through the eyes of the passengers, and one sees it as a "tragedy and drama" when one looks at it through the eyes of members of the crew. All determinism and fatalism—including naturalism and pantheism—places the responsibility somewhere beyond the moral human being: in Nature, in God, in the stars...This is because all determinism or fatalism is a manifestation of the mentality and psychology of a passenger.

Evolution seen through the eyes of a passenger, i.e. seen as something which works by itself, is nevertheless not an illusion. That is, one can indeed find and prove the existence of a "process of evolution" or a "progressive process" which, on a phenomenological level, takes place by itself. But what effort, what sacrifices, what errors and what transgressions hide behind the phenomenological facade of the "process of evolution" and "universal progress"—established and yet to be established. Here we have arrived at the heart of the "exotericism—esotericism" problem. Exotericism lives in "processes", esotericism in tragedies and dramas. The ancient mysteries were tragedies and dramas—it is here where their esoteric character lies. Exotericism corresponds to the mentality and psychology of a passenger, esotericism to that of a member of the crew.

But I repeat: exotericism is not purely and simply an illusion. For if ten righteous men had been found in Sodom and Gomorrah, God would have spared these cities. And their inhabitants would have continued the "process of evolution" of their civilisation and its customs. It is true that they would not have surmised Abraham's prayer nor the role that the ten righteous men would have played in the possibility for them to continue the "process of their evolution", but they would have continued this process in fact.

It is similar for the whole of evolution. For there is natural selection and there is spiritual selection—or election. The inhabitants of Sodom and Gomorrah had sinned against Nature and had been rejected by natural selection, but they would have been able to survive if ten righteous men had been found amongst them. Then spiritual selection would have spared them, owing to the ten righteous men. The fact of having evolved and of having given shelter to ten righteous men among them would have been sufficient to justify the continuance of their existence, although their customs were contrary to Nature. "Spiritual selection" would have prevailed, therefore, over "natural selection" or, in other words, esotericism would have determined and saved the exoteric life.

Esotericism is therefore not a life and activity which seeks secrecy. It is based on the mentality and psychology of the crew, and its "secrets" are secrets only in so far as the mentality and psychology of the passengers is such as to refuse to participate in responsibility. At the same time there is no more serious error than that of wanting to "organise" a community or fraternity which would be called to play either the role of an instrument of spiritual selection or election, or even the role of a spiritual élite. For one can neither assume the function of election nor consider oneself as elect. It would be morally monstrous if a group of people were to say: "We shall choose ten righteous men for our time", or "we are the righteous of our time". *Because one does not elect; one is elected.* Knowledge of the fact of "spiritual selection", or election, and of the role that it plays in the history of mankind and in evolution in general can therefore certainly give rise to the birth of a false esotericism, i.e. to the formation of groups, communities or fraternities which believe themselves authorised to elect, or believe themselves to be elect. "False prophets" and "false elects (Christs)"—of which the Gospel speaks—are, and will be, produced by false esotericism cultivated by those who assume the right of election or "spiritual selection". It may be added that no Christian saint has ever considered himself otherwise than as a great sinner, and that there was no righteous man or prophet of the Old Testament who was not called or chosen from above.

But let us return to the subject of evolution.

Evolution, as understood exoterically, is a cosmic process—biological or spiritual, this is not important—whilst esoterically understood it is a drama or "mystery" in the sense of the ancient mysteries. And it is only for evolution thus understood that the ideas of the Fall, perdition, redemption and salvation become not only applicable but also necessary.

First let us take the ideas "perdition" and "salvation" and try to understand them on the level of cosmic evolution—or cosmic drama.

Do not be shocked, dear Unknown Friend, and do forgive me, for I am going to relate a myth—a cosmic myth from the gnosis—not ancient or modern, but from the eternal gnosis; because the cosmic drama is in reality a myth made flesh, and it must first be seen as such before one draws principal intellectual lessons from it. Therefore I am going to relate the myth in order to draw from it some ideas, which are related to the Arcanum of the Tarot with which we are occupied.

When the Father had accomplished his work on the seventh day of creation, that he had made through his Word, he rested on the seventh day from all his work that he had made. And the Father blessed the seventh day, and he sanctified it, because on this day he rested from all his work that he had created.

Thus the seventh day is blessed and sanctified, because it is the day not of the world and the movement of the world, but rather of the Father himself alone. It is the seventh part of the circle of movement of the world, when he withdraws and becomes immobile and silent.

Thus it was that the circle of movement of the world was not closed, but remained open. And the seventh day was sanctified and blessed as the open part of the circle of movement of the world, in such a way that the beings of the world had access to the Father and the Father had access to them.

But the serpent said: There is no freedom for the world, in so far as the circle of the world is not closed. Because freedom is to be in oneself, without interference from outside, especially from above, on the part of the Father. The world will always follow the will of the Father, and not its own, in so far as there is an opening in the circle of the world, in so far as the sabbath exists.

And the serpent took his tail in his mouth and thus formed a closed circle. He turned himself with great force and thus created in the world the great swirl which caught hold of Adam and Eve. And the other beings, upon whom Adam had impressed the names that he gave them, followed them.

And the serpent said to the beings of the world moving on this side of the closed circle, that he formed by taking his tail in his mouth and setting himself in rotation: Here is your way—you will commence by my tail and you will arrive at my head. Then you will have traversed the length of the circle of my being and you will have within you the entire closed circle, and thus you will be free as I am free.

But woman guarded the memory of the world opened towards the Father and the holy sabbath. And she offered herself for the rending of the closed circle in herself in order to give birth to children issuing from the world beyond it, from the world where there is the sabbath. Thus originated the suffering of her pregnancy, and thus originated sorrow on this side of the world of the serpent.

And hostility came between woman and the serpent, between the generations of woman, giving birth with pain, and the generations of the serpent, giving birth with pleasure. The former will crush the head of the serpent and the serpent will wound the heel of the woman. For woman moves in a contrary sense to the movement of the serpent, and her head reaches to the tail of the serpent, and her heels touch the head of the serpent. This is because in the world (which is the current of the serpent) suffering is its counter-movement. It was through the counter-movement of suffering that there originated the counter-current (of the sons of woman) which is the thought born from suffering and from memory of the world of the sabbath.

Thus the sons of woman set up altars to the Father, this side of the world of the serpent. And Enosh, son of Seth, not only worshipped the Father, but even came to know his Name. He began to invoke the Name of the Father. But Enoch, a descendant of Seth, went still further: he "walked with god" (Genesis v, 22). He did not pass through the bitterness of death which, for living beings on this side of the circle of the serpent, is the way out of the closed circle of the serpent, for he was "taken up" by the Father (Genesis v, 24). For about that time thought aspiring to the Father succeeded in piercing the circle of the serpent and in accomplishing an opening in the closed circle.

Thus initiation and prophecy could be established on this side of the world of the serpent. Initiation kept living the memory of the world of the sabbath, and prophecy nourished the hope of deliverance from the circle of the serpent and the future re-establishment of the world of the sabbath.

Buddhas taught the way of going out from the world of the serpent and of arriving at the repose of the sabbath.

But the prophets proclaimed the transformation of the world of the serpent from within it by the coming of the Word which will live in the world of the serpent and will re-establish within the world of the serpent not only the sabbath but also the other six days of creation such as they were before a third of the beings from each of them were uprooted and swept down by the closed whirlwind of the serpent (cf. Revelation xii, 4).

This came to be. The Woman-Virgin who is the soul of the counter-movement to the serpent, and of suffering since the beginning of the world of the serpent, received, conceived and gave birth to the Word of the Father. "And the Word became flesh and dwelt amongst men in the world of the serpent, full of grace and truth" (cf. John i, 14).

This is the cosmic myth, the esoteric drama which underlies the exoteric "process of evolution". It sets forth, in the first place, the idea of the *open circle* and the *closed circle*. The open circle—or the spiral—is the world before the Fall of the six days of creation crowned by the seventh day, the cosmic sabbath, which corresponds to what one designates in mathematics as the "step of the spiral". It suggests the idea of unlimited growth and advancement, being through its form only the introduction or antechamber to eternity. It promises unlimited progress.

The closed circle, in contrast, is in principle only a *prison*, whatever its extent may be. It is a wheel which turns on itself and therefore suggests no advancement beyond its circle. The idea that the closed circle — or wheel — suggests, is that of *eternal repetition*.

Three historical personalities have vividly portrayed the idea of the cosmic wheel, although each of them did so in a different way. These are: Gautama Buddha, Solomon and Friedrich Nietzsche.

The first told of the "wheel of incarnations", where birth, sickness, old age and death repeat themselves endlessly. The illumination that the Buddha had under the Bodhi-tree revealed three truths to him: that the world is a wheel of births and deaths, that its movement is fundamentally nothing other than suffering, and that there is a way towards the centre of the wheel, which is at rest.

King Solomon had experience of the wheel — not as that of incarnations, as with Buddha — but rather as inexorable fate, rendering all human hope and endeavour in vain:

> Vanity of vanities! All is vanity. What does man gain by all the toil at which he toils under the sun? A generation goes, and a generation comes, but the earth remains for ever. The sun rises and the sun goes down, and hastens to the place where it rises anew. The wind blows to the south, and goes round to the north; round and round goes the wind, and repeats the same circuits. All streams run to the sea, but the sea is never full; the streams continue to flow, to the place where they flow again...What has been is what will be, and what has been done is what will be done; and there is nothing new under the sun. (Ecclesiastes i, 2-7, 9)

> I have seen everything that is done under the sun; and behold, all is vanity and a striving after the wind. What is crooked cannot be made straight, and what is lacking cannot be numbered ...I have applied my mind to know wisdom and to know madness and folly. I perceived that this also is but a striving after wind. For in much wisdom is much vexation, and he who increases knowledge increases sorrow. (Ecclesiastes i, 14-15, 17-18)

This is the wheel of existence under the sun of which Solomon, the wise and sorrowful king of Jerusalem, had a vision. And what practical advice does he give for posterity? That of supreme despair, as follows:

> There is nothing better for a man than that he should eat and drink and find enjoyment in his toil...
> Rejoice, O young man, in your youth, and let your heart cheer you in the days of your youth; walk in the ways of your heart and the sight of your eyes. But know that for all these things

God will bring you into judgement. Remove vexation from your mind, and put away pain from your body; for youth and the dawn of life are vanity. (Ecclesiastes ii, 24; xi, 9-10)

It is Solomon's despair which made him into an Old Testament prophet and gave his work a place between the psalms and the books of the prophets. For Solomon portrays the emptiness—which he calls "vanity"—of the world of the serpent and thus sets in relief the dilemma: either suicide, or salvation on the part of God, for above the turning wheel of vanity there is GOD.

Solomon's despair certainly belongs to the Holy Scripture. He portrays the world without Christ—which, moreover, the Buddha did also. Solomon's sadness is the sighing of creation for deliverance, having become conscious in him.

Thus Buddha rightly diagnosed the world of the serpent before Christ; Solomon wept over it; but Nietzsche—how monstrous!—*sang* of it. Yes, Nietzsche saw and understood the wheel, the closed circle with no outlet, of the world of the serpent, and he said "Yes" to it. He had the vision of eternal repetition, the "eternal return" ("*ewige Wiederkunft*")—and he identified it with eternity, although it is the very opposite of eternity:

—Oh! how should I not burn for Eternity, and for the marriage ring of rings—the Ring of Recurrence? Never yet found I the woman by whom I would have children, save it be by this Woman that I love: for I love thee, O Eternity!
  For I love thee, O Eternity!
            (Friedrich Nietzsche, *Thus Spake Zarathustra*)*

—so he sings of the wheel that Buddha diagnosed as the great misfortune and that Solomon estimated as the vanity of vanities.

Poetical lyricism? It is more than this! Nietzsche certainly gave a poetic form to what he took to be his illumination. But this was only a summary of the last consequences drawn from modern science—not as method, but rather as mode of world-outlook. In fact, according to the positivistic science of the end of the nineteenth century, the world is the sum-total of innumerable combinations of simple particles, atoms. The combinations change endlessly, but at some time the number of possible combinations of atoms must necessarily reach its limit and the number of new combinations must be exhausted. Then the previous combinations must repeat themselves. Therefore there will be sometime in the future a day which will be the exact repetition of today. This is the scientific basis of the "eternal return".

Belief in the eternal return has a basis not only in the calculation of possible atomic combinations but also in the scientific dogma of the quantitative constancy

---

*Trsl. A. Tille, rev. M. M. Bozman, Everyman Library, 1958, p. 204.

of matter and energy in the world. Nothing disappears, nothing appears in the world. The sum-total of matter and energy in the world is constant. It is impossible for it to be either augmented or diminished. One can add nothing to it, nor take anything from it. The world is a closed circle from which nothing escapes and into which nothing enters.

Now, given that the world is a determined quantity, it is calculable. In the last analysis, it is only a determined number of particles and/or units of energy. Therefore the number of combinations of these particles is no longer unlimited. The limit must be reached sometime. And then past combinations will be repeated...The "eternal return" of everything is therefore an inevitable conclusion in a world understood as a closed circle.

In a world which is a closed circle, whose matter and energy are a constant quantity, there are no miracles. Because the cosmic notion of a "miracle" entails inconstancy of the quantity of matter and energy in the world. A miracle takes place when the energy of the world undergoes either an increase or a diminution. This presupposes an *opening* in the circle of the world. For a miracle to be possible, the world must be an open circle, the world must be a spiral, i.e. it must have an "uncreated" sphere or a "sabbath", according to the cosmic myth narrated above.

Now religion—all advanced religion—teaches that the world is an open circle. For this reason it insists upon the reality of miracles. Miracles ("the supernatural") are a reality of action from beyond the circle of Nature, which appears to be closed. This is the reality of the cosmic sabbath.

The "good news" of religion is that the world is not a closed circle, that it is not an eternal prison, that it has an exit and an entrance. There is an entrance, which is why Christmas is a joyous festival. There is an exit, which is why Ascension is a festival. And that the world can be transformed, such as it is, into such as it was before the Fall—this is the "good news" of the festival of festivals, the festival of the Resurrection or Easter.

The world as a closed circle, the world of the eternal return, the world where "there is nothing new under the sun"—what is this in reality?

It is nothing other than *cosmic hell*. For the idea of hell can be understood as eternal existence in a closed circle. The closed circle of egoism would then be subjective and individual hell; the closed circle of a world of constant energy would then be objective and cosmic hell.

Now we have the cosmic meaning of the terms "salvation" and "perdition". "Perdition" is to be caught up in the eternal circulation of the world of the closed circle, the world without a sabbath; "salvation" is life in the world of the open circle, or spiral, where there is both exit and entrance. "Perdition" is existence in the closed circle of the "eternal return"; "salvation" is life under the open sky, where each day is new and unique—a miracle in the infinite chain of miracles...For God is not unknowable, but rather, knowable—through inexhaustible and infinite knowledge. The infinite "revelationability" and "knowability" of God: this is the essence of the eternal sabbath, the seventh day of creation. The seventh day of creation is that of eternal life and the source of miracles. For it is laden with possibilities of new things, and from it "energies" can be added to the so-called "constant" quantity of the phenomenal world, just as energies of this world can disappear into it.

The two other terms in the cosmic drama of evolution are "the Fall" and "redemption". It is now easier to understand them after having drawn out to a certain extent the cosmic meaning of the terms "salvation" and "perdition". For "the Fall" is a cosmic event, a whirlwind set in motion by the closed circle of the serpent "biting" his tail and "sweeping down part of the created world" (cf. Revelation xii, 4). And "redemption", to say it directly, is the cosmic act of the Reintegration of the fallen world, first in creating an *opening* in its closed circle (religion, initiation, prophecy), then in instituting a *path* of exit (Buddhas) and entrance (Avatars) through this door, and lastly in transforming the fallen world from within by the radiation of the incarnated Word (Jesus Christ).

This is the meaning of these two terms on a level of generalisation carried to a high degree. Let us now look at the meaning of these two terms more closely, so that the essential details can stand out from the totality.

Firstly, the Fall . . . here we are confronted with the Biblical account of paradise and the six days of creation; with the impressive tableau of natural evolution that science advances; with the contours of a majestic outline by the genius of ancient India of *kalpas*, *manvantaras* and *yugas*—a world of periodicity and rhythm, a world dreamt periodically by cosmic consciousness; with the exposition (following the "Stanzas of Dzyan") of cosmogony and anthropogony according to the Indo-Tibetan tradition, given by H. P. Blavatsky in the three volumes of her *Secret Doctrine*; with the grandiose tableau of the spiritual evolution of the world through seven so-called "planetary" phases that Rudolf Steiner has bequeathed to the dumbfounded intellectuality of our century; lastly, with the cosmogonies and eschatologies—explicit or implicit—of Hermes Trismegistus, Plato, the *Zohar* and diverse gnostic schools of the first centuries of our era.

May I be permitted to say straight away that, although I have had actual experience of comparing the whole range of these ideas and documents for more than forty years, I cannot make use of them here in the sense of the treatment which they merit, i.e. to classify them, to extract the essential points of similarity or contrast, to make relevant quotations, etc. If I were to do so, I would drown the essential theme in a sea of secondary elements (secondary with regard to the main theme). Therefore I have to proceed in the following way: the *spirit* of all the various ideas and documents enumerated above will be present as a general background, but it will be necessary to refrain from any explicit use of the material which they comprise. Having said this, let us return to the problem of the cosmic Fall.

Firstly, one can ask: What is this problem? How does it arise?

Let us look at the totality of our experience of the world—personal, historical, biological, etc. What does it say to us?

Leibnitz, the philosopher of optimism, said that the given world is the most perfect of possible worlds. Schopenhauer, the philosopher of pessimism, said that in the given world the sum of suffering outweighs that of joy, and that the world of our experience is therefore not only imperfect but also, in the last analysis, evil. Both Leibnitz and Schopenhauer looked at the totality of experience of the world, as we are now seeking to, and what a difference in what they saw!

From the point of view of *pure thought*, which is that of Leibnitz, the totality of the world shows up without any doubt a perfect arrangement of equilibrium, a harmonious functioning of its essential parts and — despite what may take place in its more obscure nooks and crannies — the totality of the world taken in its great outlines, in its *essential* outlines, is harmony itself.

From the point of view of *pure will*, which is that of Schopenhauer, the experience of each individual being in the world confirms the diagnosis of the world given by Gautama Buddha, which diagnosis is therefore to be accepted as true.

And from the point of view of the *heart*, which is that of Hermeticism and the Judaeo-Christian tradition, what can one say about the world?

The heart says to us: the cosmos, this marvel of wisdom, beauty and goodness, suffers. It is ailing. This great organism which *cannot* have been born out of sickness, whose birth *must* have been due to perfect health, i.e. to perfect wisdom, beauty and goodness, the totality of which was its cradle — this great organism is ailing. The continents — and the planets — grow ever-more hard, petrifying: this is the "sclerosis" of the cosmos. And on the surface of its land-masses in the process of petrification, and in the deeps of the seas, and in the air, there reigns the struggle for existence — this is the fever of inflammation in the world.

But sick as it is, the world still retains — everywhere and always — characteristics of its primordial health, and shows the working of forces of its new health, its convalescence. Because alongside the struggle for existence there is cooperation in order to live, and alongside the mineral petrification, there is the succulent and breathing cover of the plant kingdom. The world can therefore be lauded and wept for at the same time.

This is the origin of the problem of the Fall: that the world is worthy of being sung for and wept for at the same time.

The world is not what it should be. There is a contradiction between the totality and the details. For whilst the starry heavens represent a harmony of equilibrium and perfect cooperation, animals and insects devour one another and innumerable legions of infectious microbes bear sickness and death to men, animals and plants.

It is this contradiction which the term "the Fall" alludes to. In the first place, it designates a state of affairs in the world which gives the impression that the world is composed of two independent, if not opposed, worlds, as if in the organism of the great world of the "harmony of the spheres" there is interpolated another world with its own laws and evolution — as if a cancerous outgrowth has taken place in the otherwise healthy organism of the great world.

Science takes the two worlds together and considers them as inseparably united, and names this totality "Nature"—Nature with two faces: Nature, benign and cruel, at one and the same time; Nature both stubborn and astonishingly cooperative; wise and blind Nature; Nature, the loving mother and the cruel stepmother, full of malice. With all due respect to science, it is necessary to draw attention to a quite simple error of thought that it commits. Notably, it commits the same error that a doctor would commit if he were to consider a state of sickness (e.g. cancer) as normal or "natural", and if he were to declare that the cancerous process as well as the circulation of the blood were two aspects of the *nature* of the organism of the sick person. This would be something monstrous, if the doctor refused to distinguish between nature and *counter-nature* (sickness) in the organism of the patient—yet this is precisely what science does with regard to the world-organism. It refuses to distinguish between Nature and counter-Nature, health and sickness, natural evolution and evolution contrary to Nature.

The ancients always knew that there is an anomaly in the state of the world. Whether they attributed it to the principle of ignorance ("*avidya*") as in ancient India, or to the principle of darkness (Ahriman) as in ancient Persia, or again to the principle of evil (Satan) as the ancient Semites did, is not important; it is always a matter of distinction between the natural world and the unnatural world, between the natural and the perverse, between health and sickness.

It goes without saying that Hermeticism, in accordance with the Judaeo-Christian tradition, regards the "Nature" of science not as the world created by God, but rather as the *field* where the created world meets with the world of the serpent.

The world of the serpent: this is the "world within the World" which gave rise to the dualism of Zoroastrianism, Manichaeism and certain gnostic schools. These kinds of dualism fall under the title of "heresy", i.e. they sin against the essential truths of salvation, because they commit the same error as modern science, but in an inverse sense. Just as science refuses to distinguish in "Nature" between the Nature of orthogenesis and cooperation on the one hand, and the Nature producing genetic impasses and parasites on the other hand, so did the Manichaeans, Cathars, Albigenses, etc., refuse to distinguish between virginal Nature and fallen Nature. But whilst science considers its "Nature"—although Nature is a contradiction in herself—as the sovereign queen of evolution, who has managed to lead evolution from the albuminous cell to the developed brain of *homo sapiens*, the radical dualists considered their "Nature" as being evil through and through. In other words, science considers Nature, in the last analysis, good; the Manichaeans regarded Nature as evil. Science refuses to see Satan there; the radical dualists wanted to see nothing but Satan there.

But let us return to the world of the serpent. The most general characteristic feature of this world is *enfoldment*, whilst the most general characteristic feature of the created world is unfoldment, blossoming and *radiation*. Thus the brain and intestines in the animal kingdom are due to enfoldment; foliage, branches and flowers are expressions of the contrary tendency in the plant kingdom. Thus, for example, foliage is the "lung" of the plant, unfolded and open to the air whilst the animal or human lung is enfolded foliage. Or another example: the sun is in a state of radiation, whilst the planets are in a state of condensation, i.e. enfoldment.

These two tendencies have their traditional designations. They are "light" and "darkness", i.e. radiation and enfoldment, respectively. This is why the Gospel according to John, in describing the cosmic drama, says: "Light shineth in the darkness, and the darkness apprehendeth it not" (John i, 5)—(*kai to phos en te skotia phainei, kai he skotia auto ou katelaben*; *et lux in tenebris lucet, et tenebrae eam non comprehenderunt*). *Ou katelaben*...*non comprehenderunt*—this expresses that the light was not caught up in the whirlwind of enfoldment and is not obscured by it, but *shines in the darkness*. This is the quintessence of the Gospel, the "good news".

Thus the sun and the stars are to the planets (including the earth) as light is to darkness. And in the microcosm, the system of "lotus flowers" is to the system of endocrine glands as light is to darkness. For the "lotus flowers" are, fundamentally, blossoming glands, whilst the glands are enfolded "lotus flowers". The endocrinal glands are *precipitates* of the "lotus flowers" in the microcosm, just as the planets are precipitates of the "planetary spheres" in the macrocosm or planetary system.

Now, the world of the serpent is that of enfoldment. The serpent biting his tail and thus forming a closed circle is its symbol. Completely successful enfoldment would be hell or the state of complete isolation.

But complete enfoldment or accomplished isolation has in no way succeeded in the world. The history of so-called "natural" evolution traces for us a tableau of successive attempts—none of which have been successful—aiming at establishing through complete enfoldment a viable organism with an absolutely autonomous consciousness, without falling prey to madness. Is not the atom an entity produced by enfoldment, which is autonomous and independent? But atoms *associate* themselves with one another in molecules! Is the molecule, therefore, not an autonomous entity? Well, molecules associate themselves into mysterious fraternities of life that we name "organic cells". Then there are the innumerable associations of molecules in the organism...the history of the evolution of living organisms is that of the triumph of the principle of association and cooperation over that of dissociation and isolation. The latter has succeeded in forming only non-viable monsters, e.g. the dinosaurs and giant reptiles which overran the earth and which had their uncontested reign for a hundred million years of the mesozoic or reptile era. Where are they now? They were only a great biological impasse, therefore they perished. Their reign gave way to that of mammals and birds. The former also produced many forms of impasse before an upsurge of vertebrates came, during the advance of which form after form was rejected, condemned either to a rapid or a slow extinction, until the primates, from which one subdivision— that of *homo sapiens*— took possession of the earth, and now rules without rival.

Thus our planet, which was in the mesozoic era the "planet of reptiles", has now become the "planet of human beings". Is the human being the grand-daughter of the reptile? Or, in Biblical terms, are human beings the "children of the serpent", the "children of darkness", the product of enfoldment—or are they "children of the light" (Luke xvi, 8)?

Man has the most developed brain. Now the brain is—as Henri Bergson has shown—an organ which plays the role of a *sieve* with respect to consciousness: it is an instrument of knowledge and ignorance at one and the same time. Its function is to admit on behalf of consciousness what is appropriate to it and not to admit—"to forget"—what is not appropriate to it from the point of view of action, or the will aspiring to action.

The brain is therefore an organ of *selection*—the epitome of the process of evolution! For what the brain does is essentially what took place during millions of years of biological evolution. The whole of evolution is the process of the sequence "creation-selection-rejection-forget", repeated incessantly. The "proper" forms are chosen, the others are rejected. There is an invisible sieve at work. Now, this sieve has become visible; it has become flesh. It is the brain. Henri Bergson says concerning the brain:

> In the work of thought in general, as in the particular case of memory, the brain appears to be charged simply with the task of impressing on the body the movements and attitudes which *act* what the mind thinks, or what the circumstances invite it to think. I have expressed this by saying that the brain is an "organ of pantomime". . . Indeed, the cerebral phenomena are to the mental life just what the gestures of the conductor are to the symphony: they mark out the motor articulations, they do nothing else. In other words, we should find nothing of the higher workings of the mind within the cerebral cortex. Except its sensory functions, the brain has no other part than to *mime*, in the full meaning of the term, the mental life. (Henri Bergson, *Mind-Energy*; trsl. H. W. Carr, London, 1920, pp. 74-75)

The brain is therefore an organ effecting mimicry, choosing what it is going to mime. It mimes accordingly.

Now, relevant mimicry is precisely what the Book of Genesis understands by *cunning* when it says that "the serpent was more cunning (*arum*—עָדוּס) than any other wild creature that the LORD God had made" (Genesis iii, 1). It is, as it were, the "psychological" principle of the serpent, just as enfoldment and movement in a closed circle is its "dynamic" principle. To be cunning is to mime wisdom, after having eliminated the essential—its light—and then to make use of it for one's own ends. This is why it is said that "the devil is the ape of God", that he apes God.

The brain is therefore due to the serpent. It is the work of the serpent; and mankind, as the animal species endowed with the most developed brain, is certainly a grand-daughter of the serpent. Human beings, as cerebral beings, are indeed "children of the serpent" or "children of darkness".

This is why there exists a kind of brotherly piety with which the serpent is venerated in various places in the world—Egypt, India (the "sacred *nagas*"), Mexico, central America and, lastly, China, where the sacred reptile is venerated in its flying form, that of the dragon. Even Moses erected a bronze serpent on a pole in the desert, and it was only in the time of the reign of Hezekiah, son of Ahaz, king of Judah, that worship of the serpent was put to an end—notably when Hezekiah "broke in pieces the bronze serpent that Moses had made, for until those days (i.e. during all the centuries of Judges and Kings, until Hezekiah!) the people of Israel had burned incense to it; it was called Nehushtan" (II Kings xviii, 4). But many centuries later a gnostic sect, the Naasenes (Nahashenes), worshipped the serpent in the same region—and this was after Jesus Christ!

Even in the nineteenth and twentieth centuries, several occultist writers have striven to restore the cult of the serpent, this time in an intellectual form. Thus H. P. Blavatsky did much in her *Secret Doctrine* to honour the serpent as the philosophical idea of ancient wisdom. She interpreted it as the principle of universal energy, *fohat*, which has a unique and indispensable place between the universal intellect, *mahat*, and universal matter, *prakriti*. She evoked the ancient legends and traditions of the teachers of childlike humanity, who were the creators of civilisation—the "sons of the serpent"—the benefactors of mankind at the dawn of its history.

Eliphas Lévi presented the serpent as the "great magical agent", i.e. the intermediary principle between consciousness and the world of objective facts. According to him, the serpent is the principle of realisation, i.e. that which in practice translates the will into events, that which objectifies the subjective.

Stanislas de Guaita dedicated his unfinished work to the serpent by giving it the title *Le serpent de la Genèse*. In this book he portrays the reality of the role of the "great magical agent" in history.

As to the Theosophical Society, the serpent biting its tail with a hexagram and Egyptian tau within the closed circle of the serpent was chosen as its symbol and seal, accompanied by the motto of the Maharajas of Benares: *satiyat nasti paro dharmah*—"there is no religion higher than truth".

Yes, the serpent is indeed the "great magical agent", that is to say, the principle which mimes consciousness and which is therefore the link between the subjective and the objective, just as the brain is the link between consciousness and action. Yes, the first representatives of cerebral intellectuality, the "sons of the serpent" of ancient legends, were certainly the first masters of new-born civilisation. It is certainly they who taught the rudiments of the arts and sciences to childlike humanity.

Having admitted this, I nevertheless ask myself: Is the serpent, as the "great magical agent", the *only* magical agent, and is he the magical agent of *all* magic? Does divine or sacred magic (which we have referred to in the Letters relating to the third and fifth Arcana of the Tarot) make use of the same agency as that of fakirs, hypnotists, magnetic healers and necromancers?

Now, centuries of experience show that there is not only *another agent* and *another magic*, but also that there is another consciousness and experience than that due to the brain. It was not the serpent that John the Baptist saw descend upon the Master of sacred magic, the greatest thaumaturgist of history, but rather a *dove*.

> John bore witness: I saw the Spirit descend as a dove from heaven, and it remained on him. (John i, 32)

...several days later the miracle of the wedding at Cana was accomplished.

The seven miracles—the wedding at Cana, the healing of the nobleman's son, the healing of the sick man at the pool of Bethesda, the feeding of the five thousand, the walking on water, the healing of the man born blind, and the raising of Lazarus—did not have the serpent as their agent, nor was the brain the instrument of their accomplishment, nor was cerebral intellectuality the source of their initiative. The agent here is the dove, i.e. the Spirit which is above the brain, above the head, and which *descends* upon the head and remains there—the Spirit which *transcends* cerebral intellectuality. This Spirit is the source of initiative and, simultaneously, is the agent and instrument of divine or sacred magic.

Therefore I ask myself—and I ask you, dear Unknown Friend—why occultist-authors have not directed their zeal, fervour and ability to serve the cause of the dove, instead of that of the serpent? Why have they not recognised the *great agent* of sacred magic, which has certainly demonstrated that it is called to illumine, heal and transform the world? Why did the Theosophical Society, which values truth above all belief, not choose the dove of the Holy Spirit as its standard? Why was the dove of the Holy Spirit, which is the very principle of universal spirituality, not chosen instead of the serpent biting its tail? Why did Stanislas de Guaita not write a book entitled *The Dove of the Gospel*? Why did Eliphas Lévi not refer to the *new* great magical agent, the dove, which is called to replace the ancient magical agent, the serpent? Why did H. P. Blavatsky refuse to see that there are two principles of cosmic energy, that of *fohat* or the energy of the serpent, and that of the Holy Spirit or the energy of salvation? Even if the *Stanzas of Dzyan* do not make any mention of it, are they to be taken as the only source of truth? And is the testimony of prophets, apostles and saints for over three thousand years for nothing!?

I am perplexed, I repeat, not because the interpretation of the serpent according to the above-mentioned occultist-authors is not true, in what it essentially concerns, but because the subject of the serpent is treated by them with a strange exclusiveness, even partiality, that is difficult to explain by objective facts referring to the problem as such, without recourse to psychological factors.

Be that as it may, there is a rather pronounced tendency in occult literature to present the serpent as the sole principle of realisation, and even as the sole principle of knowledge, including occult knowledge.

Now, with respect to ourselves, we are able, in the first place, to see in the serpent only the principle of cerebration, cerebral intellectuality, and the principle of enfoldment, the tendency to form closed circles—or, in other words, the principle of the *Fall*. I say: *in the first place*, because, thanks to the work of salvation, which has a millennial-old history, a gradual spiritualisation of the work of the serpent—including cerebral intellectuality—has taken place, and because intervention from above not only frustrates the formation of completely closed circles, but also gives to the tendency of enfoldment a direction towards *solidarity* through stages such as the family, the nation and the community of civilisation. In other words, providence sees to it that the circles formed by the serpent are not entirely closed, and that the series of its circles is changed into a series of as many *spirals*.

But the benefits of this gradual metamorphosis of the work of the serpent are not due to the serpent, but rather to the other principle—the contrary principle— that of the *"light which shines in the darkness"*. For the reality and entirety of *evolution* consists on the one hand of the enfolding activity of the serpent, which has formed the brain and produced cerebral intellectuality, and on the other hand of the activity of the light from above, which *opens* the enfolded and illumines cerebral intellectuality. The serpent and the dove: these are, in the last analysis, the factors underlying the *whole* process of evolution.

If you were to ask me, dear Unknown Friend, if one has to choose and take the side of either the serpent or the dove, my reply would be in the framework of the Master's counsel:

Be wise as serpents and innocent as doves (Matthew x, 16),

i.e. that one should try to unite cerebral intellectuality with spiritual spontaneity. It is certainly necessary to think in articulated thoughts and in a discursive manner, but above this process of discursive thought there always soars the ideal! It is in the light of the ideal that one should think.

But let us return to the question: Are human beings "children of the serpent" or "children of the light"? We have said that human beings, as the animal species endowed with the most developed brain, are children of the serpent. Now, it is necessary to add that as beings aspiring to the ideal of the good, the beautiful and the true, human beings are children of the light. Because, whatever may be said in the contrary sense, there is no reason—nor is there anything given in the whole domain of biological evolution culminating in the formation of the human brain—which explains and makes the human aspiration towards truth, beauty and goodness appear necessary. Every monastery and convent is, moreover, a direct contradiction to the thesis that mankind is only the product of biological evolution. All renunciation of concrete things—such as wealth, power, health and even life—for an ideal, bears witness to the trans-evolutionary and trans-cerebral reality of the nucleus of the human being.

If the excavations carried out by palaeontologists supply skulls and skeletons as evidence of the biological evolution leading to the human brain, the martyrs throughout history bear witness at the same time to the fact of the transcendence of the nucleus of human nature with respect to biological evolution. This is because complete evolution is the intersection of biological evolution and spiritual evolution. The fact of the intersection of these two quite different domains is the reality of the Fall.

The other term of the cosmic drama with which we are occupied, and which is linked to that of the Fall, is *redemption*.

We have said above that redemption is the "cosmic act of the Reintegration of the fallen world, first in creating an *opening* in its closed circle (religion, initiation, prophecy), then in instituting a path of exit (Buddhas) and entrance (Avatars) through this door, and lastly in transforming the fallen world from within by the radiation of the incarnated Word (Jesus Christ)".

Thus, the thesis that we are advancing here is that the work of salvation leading to actual redemption is *universal* concerning both *time* and *space*. For it has acted since the cradle of mankind's history and it extends to all groups and all religions of mankind. The centuries are its stages and the whole of mankind was—and is—its field. The work of salvation is *catholic* in the literal, Hermetic, magical, gnostic and mystical sense of the word. This means to say that the history of the suffering, militant and triumphant Church is as long as that of humanity, and that it is as vast as humanity itself. For the Word is the "true light that enlightens every man coming into the world" (John i, 9), i.e. every human being, always and everywhere.

There is therefore only a single work of salvation, which includes all human endeavour truly aiming at transcending the brain and cerebral intellectuality, and which includes all true revelations from above, throughout all the ages of the history of mankind. It operates in stages. . . From the first altar erected somewhere on a hill or in the corner of a field, to the great cathedrals of Europe aspiring to heights of consciousness above the sphere of cerebral intellectuality; it has been in stages.

The stages of the work of universal salvation constitute the spiritual history of mankind, which is the great universal Bible of which the historical Bible is a part. It can be summarised in two ways according to two different points of view: from the point of view of *revelation*, and that of *operation*.

According to the first point of view, mankind's spiritual history could be summarised—as the Cabbala does—by giving the various aspects of God that are revealed successively in the spiritual history of mankind. The ten *names of God* of the Cabbala, which correspond to the ten Sephiroth of the Sephiroth Tree, represent a summary of mankind's spiritual history from the point of view of the gradual *revelation* of God. For, from the aspect represented by the name ADONAI (LORD), to the aspect indicated by the name EYEH (I AM), there is a long road, the former name being a term for the superiority of power, pure and simple, whilst the latter name signifies intuition of the Being who is the essence of being, or "He who is".

According to the point of view of the operation of the work of salvation, one could summarise mankind's spiritual history by describing its stages from the first opening of the closed circle of the serpent to the advent and blossoming of the "reign of God" within this circle. The stages in question are, therefore, the *opening* of the closed circle, the *path* of exit and entrance through this door, and the *Incarnation of the Word*. The first stage, that of the opening of the closed circle, makes way for the entrance of *faith* into incarnated mankind; the second brings it *hope*; the third kindles *love* within it, which is the active *presence* of divine life at the heart of the circle of the serpent. All that mankind had been believing, had been hoping, has become reality in the present—this is the essence of the whole spiritual history of mankind in a single phrase.

But this summary comprises a world of events. It includes: the first awakening of memories of paradise in souls immersed in the darkness of the struggle for existence; the institution of worship (cult) to guard these memories and to protect them from being forgotten; the arising of priests charged with this cult, and of seers and prophets who keep it alive and develop it; the arising of schools of individual effort aspiring to trans-cerebral experience; the glorious news that such endeavour is not in vain, that there is a path of exit; the teachings of the Buddhas, the masters of this path; the revelations of the Avatars, Rishis, great masters and "men of God"—demonstrating the reality of the path of entrance, manifestation and incarnation; the spiritual preparation in the whole world, and the real preparation in a chosen people—Israel—of the Incarnation prefigured by the incarnations and manifestations of Avatars and Boddhisattvas (on the path to "Buddhahood"); then the Incarnation itself, and lastly all that is implied in St. Paul's words:

> Great indeed, we confess, is the mystery of our religion: He was manifested in the flesh, vindicated in the Spirit, seen by Angels, preached among the nations, believed on in the world, and taken up in Glory. (I Timothy iii, 16)

Now, what is generally understood by "evolution" is due to the concurrence of two principal lines of operation—that of the serpent and that of the work of salvation. Principal, I say, because there are also secondary lines which play an intermediary role between the principal lines—such as, for example, the line of evolution of individual souls by way of repeated incarnations. This subject has been considered in a preceding Letter (Letter IV) and will be considered again in the thirteenth Letter. We draw attention here, in the context of general evolution, only to the following fact.

Science is at present confronted with the problem of the transmission by way of heredity of characteristics acquired through experience. This problem, such as it is presented today, is due to the paradoxical contradiction between what is known of the law of heredity and what is known about evolution and progress in general. Notably, it has been found that acquired characteristics do not transmit themselves by heredity and, on the other hand, the sum-total of facts concerning general evolution provides evidence of progress. In order to resolve the contradiction between heredity, which only *reproduces*, and general evolution, which demonstrates *creativity*, it is necessary to have recourse to a further dimension, i.e. to add the vertical dimension to that of horizontal continuity in time — the latter dimension being that of heredity, which connects successive generations. It has to be admitted that acquired characteristics are accumulated *somewhere else* other than by way of the mechanism peculiar to heredity, and that between "heredity" and "acquired characteristics" (which latter do not disappear but are simply relegated "somewhere else") there is an active tension which manifests itself in education and self-education, as well as in the arising of intellectual and moral geniuses as fruits of a mediocre line of forefathers. This tension between the mechanism of heredity and characteristics acquired through experience — and accumulated "somewhere else"— leads in the long run to the prevalence of the latter, and a kind of "eruption" of acquired characteristics takes place in the hereditary mechanism. The fruits of past experience, so to say, "reincarnate".

It is thus that one is led to postulate the principle of reincarnation. And when modern depth psychology of the school of Jung adds sufficient material concerning the resurgence of past experiences in dreams, vision, and in the life of fantasy, of people who — in their normal consciousness — know nothing about it (and thus, for example, the rituals and symbols of the ancient mysteries reappear in the full light of day of the twentieth century), then the postulate necessary to explain the possibility of progress ceases to be solely a postulate, but becomes a conclusion, based on experience and endowed with a high degree of probability.

It is true that Jung designated the realm where past experiences are buried as the "collective unconscious". But why *collective*? Why not individual unconscious? Is it simply because experiences of the past, which arise from the depths of consciousness, have much in common?. . .that they resemble one another?

But it is *human beings* in whom these experiences of the past arise. It is therefore quite natural that they have much in common — in fact, as much in common as human beings have in common. For this reason alone, is it necessary to postulate the *collectivity* of subconscious (or superconscious) memory that spans millennia? Is it not more simple and natural to conclude that the one who remembers an experience is also the one who experienced it?

But to do justice to Jung it should be pointed out that he did not insist on a *substantial collectivity* to his "collective unconscious". As a true scientist, he leaves open the question whether the collective unconscious is a reservoir common to mankind, or whether it is a totality derived by synthesising *characteristics common to individuals*. The "metaphysic", so to say, of the collective unconscious was but little elaborated by Jung. Be that as it may, the *facts* that Jung assembled and presented lend themselves *at least* as easily to interpretation in terms of reincarnation as in terms of a collective unconscious.

But for the inner forum of consciousness — and I remind you, dear Unknown Friend, that these Letters are addressed only to your inner forum, and that on principle they do not aim to advance doctrines of general, i.e. scientific, validity — it is the experience within the depths of your own soul which has the last word on the problem of individual reincarnation, and it is to this that the task falls of transforming the possibility and probability of reincarnation into certainty...certainty in the inner forum of consciousness, of course.

There are, therefore, three "continuities" in evolution: biological or hereditary continuity, psychic continuity or reincarnation, and spiritual continuity or the work of salvation. Note that these three lines of continuity correspond to the dynamic triangle to which Fabre d'Olivet reduced the history of the human race — the triangle: destiny, will, providence. Heredity corresponds to destiny (fate), reincarnation to will (freedom) and the work of salvation to providence. This is what he says concerning this triangle:

> But if man is, at first...only a power in germ which civilisation must develop, whence will come to him the indispensable principles of this culture? I reply that it will be from the two powers to which he finds himself linked and of which he must form the third...These two powers, between which he finds himself placed, are destiny and providence. Beneath him is destiny, *natura naturata* (necessitated Nature); above him is providence, *natura naturans* (free Nature). He is himself, as kingdom of man, the mediatory will, the effective force, placed between these two Natures to serve them as a link, a means of communication, and to unite two actions, two movements, which would be incompatible without him.
> The three powers which I have just named...constitute the universal ternary. Nothing escapes their action; all in the universe is subject to them; all except God himself who, enveloping them in His unfathomable unity, forms with them the sacred tetrad of the ancients, that immense quaternary, which is all in all and outside of which there is nothing. (Fabre d'Olivet, *L'histoire philosophique du genre humain*; trsl. N. L. Redfield, *Hermeneutic Interpretation of the Origin of the Social State of Man and of the Destiny of the Adamic Race*, London-New York, 1915, intr., pp. xl-xli)

I permit myself to add to this quotation from Fabre d'Olivet that during my whole life I have not succeeded in finding a more lucid formula and a more effective general key for understanding the evolution and history of mankind than that given by Fabre d'Olivet. However, the century and a half which has elapsed since his work and the growth of knowledge concerning mankind's history which has been achieved in this lapse of time—and also the unfortunate bias of Fabre d'Olivet, which blinded him with respect to certain mysteries of Christianity—has forced me to revise the *application* by Fabre d'Olivet of his praiseworthy general principles concerning concrete problems and details of the history of mankind. The same remark is applicable also to Saint-Yves d'Alveydre, above all to his work *Mission des Juifs* ("The Mission of the Jews"), excepting the anti-Christian bias, which is not to be found with him.

Heredity, reincarnation and the work of salvation—reincarnation being the intermediary principle between the other two—therefore together constitute the cosmic drama of evolution.

The tenth Card of the Tarot, in evoking this whole problem, gives a cross-section through the *middle* of the problem of evolution by portraying the aspect of most practical significance, i.e. the relationship between "animality" (animal nature) and "humanity" (human nature). The sphinx above the wheel represents animality and humanity united—either *still* not differentiated, or *already* reintegrated. The enigma of the sphinx is therefore that of the humanisation of animality and the animalisation of humanity. The dog ascending towards the sphinx represents animality aspiring to union with humanity; the monkey descending represents the process of the animalisation of humanity.

It is a matter, therefore, of the Arcanum of the practical solution of the problem: How to accomplish, without eradication or ejection, a wholeness of the human and animal elements in the human personality without the former animalising (becoming "monkey") or the latter falling under the tyrannical domination (becoming "dogs") of the former? Or, in other words: How to descend into the animal element without becoming animalised and how to make an ascent without the coercion of animality to the human element?

Now, the tenth Arcanum is also strictly practical. It is a spiritual exercise which has the aim of awakening an "arcanum", i.e. skilled knowledge of a certain "know-how". And the "know-how" of which it is a matter with the tenth Arcanum is the right way of handling on the one hand the elements of animalised man, which proceed away from a centre, and on the other hand those elements of animality aspiring to humanity, which strive towards a stable centre. This stable centre is the sphinx, placed above the wheel of animality, i.e. above the *automatic* movement in man's psychic nature.

The wheel and the sphinx above it. . .what practical task does this context suggest? The following:

There is "created" animality and there is "evolved" animality. The former had its origin before the Fall and the latter owes its existence to evolution since the

LETTER X THE WHEEL OF FORTUNE 257

Fall, i.e. to the work of the serpent. There is the animality created by the divine Word of which the Gospel of John says that "all things were made through him, and nothing that was made was made without him" (John i, 3), and of which Moses' Book of Genesis speaks in terms of the creation of animals "according to their kinds" (Genesis i, 24) on the fifth and sixth days of the creation.

The animality of divine origin is summarised by the four prototypes or kinds of the holy *Hayoth* (Cherubim). These are: the Bull, the Lion, the Eagle and the Angel or Man. And if one unites these four prototypes in one sole being, one obtains the *sphinx*. The sphinx is therefore the prototype-synthesis of holy animality, i.e. divine instinctivity, or the principle of spontaneous obedience to God. For "holy animality" means nothing other than "spontaneous obedience to God" or "divine instinct".

The *other* instincts are due to the evolution of the serpent. They are summarised by the term *bestiality*. Therefore, there are instincts of divine origin and there are bestial instincts. Thus, the instinct which leads to elevation of the spirit and of the heart is symbolised by the Eagle, which iconographic tradition represents as the inspirative principle — or channel of divine inspiration — of John the Evangelist. At the same time, the eagle as the prototype of the bird of prey represents the instinct of aggression and lightning attack. It is the eagle as the instinct of rapaciousness which figured, as the inspiring principle, on the standards of the Roman legions.

Similarly, the Lion symbolises the instinct that can be designated as "moral courage". The martyrs were representatives of the Lion, and it is the Lion as "moral courage" which is associated with the evangelist Mark in Christian iconography. But just as there is the Eagle and the eagle, so there is the Lion and the lion. Ferociousness is to moral courage as the lion is to the Lion. The former is a degeneration of the latter.

The Bull is the symbol of the instinct of productive concentration. It underlies the propensity to deep meditation. It is the channel of divine inspiration of the evangelist Luke. It is the Bull in this sense which has given rise to the cult of the sacred Cow (the female aspect of the Bull) in India. The worship of the cow in India is simply a popular counterpart to the Hindu propensity for meditation. But again there is the Bull and the bull. The latter is a degeneration of the former. It is concentration of the will on a single thing, rendering the subject blind to everything else. In sacrificing the bull in the Mithraic mysteries, it was not intended that the propensity to meditation be killed, but rather that impetuosity — rage which blinds — be slain.

The evangelist Matthew, according to iconography, has the Angel or Man as inspiring companion, who represents the propensity to objectivity, which is manifested, for example, in the truthfulness of an epic narrative made by an annalist or chronicler. But there is objectivity and "objectivity". One can be objective, i.e. impartial, in taking everything equally to heart. And one can be "objective" ("impartial") in assuming an attitude of equal indifference towards everything. The former is Angelic objectivity; the latter is its degeneration—it is that of cold and heartless observation. The former manifests itself by means of the instinct that we call *conscience*; the latter is manifested in what many take to be the "scientific spirit" and which, truth to tell, is only the propensity towards *cynicism*.

Thus we have a comparative array of the principle instincts of divine origin and those that have originated since the Fall.

Now, the practical task which follows from this is that of inner alchemy: the transmutation of fallen instincts into their non-fallen prototypes, i.e. the transmutation of "eagle" into Eagle, of "lion" into Lion, of "bull" into Bull, and of "man" into Angel—or, in other words, the task is to establish, or re-establish, the *sphinx* above the wheel of instinctivity, to transform the "wheel" of psychic automatism into the sphinx. How is this to be done?

By way of metamorphosis, i.e. by alternating contraction and expansion . . . just as the growth of a plant is the manifestation of two tendencies—a vertical tendency and a horizontal tendency—operating alternately, so that the former pushes upwards and the latter effects its blossoming out, so does psychic metamorphosis operate by restriction of the expansive tendency, which results in elevation, followed by expansion on the new plane attained by elevation which, in turn, will be followed by restriction, resulting in a new elevation, and so on. This is the law of metamorphosis which Goethe ascertained and studied in the plant realm, and it is also the law of transmutation of psychic forces—the narrow way, or the way of the Cross—in the human kingdom. For human beings and plants live under the law of the Cross—the latter organically, the former spiritually. For this reason the plant is a "manual" of practical Hermeticism, where one can read the immutable laws of spiritual discipline. Schiller, the "brother" of Goethe, understood this, which is why he said:

> Dost thou seek the highest, the greatest?
> The plant can show it thee.
> What the plant is unconsciously,
> Be thou intentionally
> —That's it!

> *(Suchst du das Höchste, das Grösste?*
> *Die Pflanze kann es dich lehren,*
> *Was sie willenlos ist, sei du es wollend—das ist's!)*

This is because the plant kingdom is the most virginal realm of Nature following the Fall, and because man is on the way to the Reintegration. Every garden therefore preserves something of the garden of Eden, and can serve as a living library for someone aspiring to salvation.

Now, it is a matter of extending the law of the Cross, which rules the plant realm organically and the human kingdom spiritually, to the *animal kingdom* also. And this must be done not by training dogs, horses and parrots, but rather by apply-ing the law of the Cross to the inner animality in man's psychic life. It is necessary to restrain the bull in us in order to elevate it to the Bull. This means to say that the instinctive desire which shows itself as rage concentrated upon a single thing, and which blinds one to everything else, is to be restrained and thus elevated to the propensity for profound meditation. This entire operation is summarised in Hermeticism by the words "to be silent". The precept "to be silent" is not, as many authors interpret it, solely a rule of prudence, but it is moreover a *practical method* of transforming this narrowing and blinkering instinct into a propensity towards depth and, correspondingly, an aversion towards all that is of a superficial nature.

The winged Bull is therefore the result obtained by the procedure of "being silent". This means to say that the Bull is elevated to the level of the Eagle and is united with it. A marriage of the impetus towards the heights and the propen-sity towards depth is effected by this union. The marriage of opposites—this tradi-tional theme of alchemy—is the essence of the practice of the law of the Cross. For the Cross is the union of two pairs of opposites, and the practice of the Cross is the work of conciliation of four opposites—two horizontal and two vertical op-posites. The Eagle and the Bull are vertical opposites: they are the tendencies towards the heights and the depths, towards the general and the particular, towards a comprehensive overview and towards the minutiae of points of detail.

The Angel and the Lion constitute the other pair of opposites on the cross of man's instinctivity. Here it is a matter of the transformation of combative courage into moral courage—into the courage of *conscience*. For the instinct that we call "moral conscience" is the effect of inspiration on the part of the Angel, and it is by elevating instinctual courage, i.e. the desire for heroism, adventure and strug-gle, that the latter is united with conscience and becomes the moral courage that we admire in martyrs and saints.

The *winged Lion* is the result to be obtained by the procedure signified by the term "to dare", which implies moral courage. Just as the Bull becomes winged through its conjunction with the Eagle by the practice of "to be silent", and just as the Eagle acquires the constancy and perseverance of the Bull thanks to the practice of "to will"—so does the Lion acquire wings through its conjunction with the Angel by the practice of "to dare", and the effect of the inspiration of the Angel, which one's "daring" produces, becomes spontaneous certainty by the practice signified by the term "to know". These are therefore the four lines of endeavour with a view to achieving the task symbolised by the sphinx: to be silent, to will, to dare and to know.

"To be silent" is the restriction of the will which elevates itself, following the law of the Cross, as a consequence of this restriction. Then it has its expansion on another plane. There it becomes the true "to will".

Constant attention to conscience restrains impulsiveness and this latter is therefore raised to a new plane, where it has its expansion. The disciplining of impulsiveness by conscience is the practical sense of "to dare" and "to know". For it is only in harmony with knowledge due to conscience that impulsiveness becomes a "legitimate daring" or moral courage.

Here is the principle of Hermetic asceticism over the millennia. It is based on the law of the Cross; its aim is the sphinx, which is animality united with humanity. It is clear that this is a very ancient teaching and that the tenth Arcanum goes back to ancient Hermeticism before our era; we are put into contact with the ideas of those who erected the sphinx and the pyramids. It is *intrinsic* evidence — not iconographic and historical evidence — which leads us to this conclusion.

And what reinforces this, moreover, is what is missing from the tenth Card. It presents us the wheel of animality and the sphinx as the solution to the practical problem of animality. Now, a more profound and sustained analysis of the sphinx and of the whole context of the Card leads us inevitably to *four* animals and to all that this comprises: divine and fallen animality, the Fall and the Reintegration, the principle of practical asceticism, etc. All this can be amplified by the facts and knowledge that modern history, biology and psychology supply us with. But one essential thing is lacking from this Card — this is the *quinta essentia*, the "fifth essence"—which would make the sphinx a reality for us, *but which is not the sphinx itself*. The active principle of the Cross — the "fifth essence", without which the whole operation cannot be practised and would remain only knowledge and a hope — is not to be found indicated here. The sphinx figures here as the last solution or, rather, as the last *enigma*.

The absence of a *direct* indication (for indirectly the whole Card relates to the enigma of the sphinx and, through this very fact, to the "fifth essence") in the context of the Card of the principle of the *New Adam*, who is the "fifth essence"— as we know today equally in esotericism and exotericism — indicates the *pre-Christian* origin of the tenth Card. From the point of view of iconography it is clearly mediaeval (of the *late* Middle Ages), as all the other Cards are, but *intrinsically* it is older, notably pre-Christian.

Is it the oldest or is it simply the *least evolved* of the twenty-two Cards of the Major Arcana of the Tarot?

The twenty-two Cards of the Major Arcana of the Tarot being an *organism*, a complete whole, it is not a question of diverse and disparate origins of particular Cards, but rather of the degrees of their evolution or transformation. For the Tarot, also, is *not a wheel*, a closed circle, but rather a *spiral*, i.e. it evolves through tradition and. . . reincarnation.

The authors who saw in the Tarot the "Sacred Book of Thoth" (Thoth = Hermes) were both right and wrong at the same time. They were right in so far as they traced back the history of the *essence* of the Tarot to antiquity, notably to ancient Egypt. And they were wrong in so far as they believed that the Tarot had been *inherited* from ancient Egypt, i.e. that it had been *transmitted* from generation to generation subject to minor iconographic changes. As support for their thesis the ingenious story or legend (that you probably know) is recounted concerning the council of Egyptian priests who deliberated on the problem of the preservation of the essence of their wisdom for the generations to come, after the extinguishing of the light of Egypt. Proposition after proposition was rejected — whether to commit the wisdom to paper, stone, metal, etc. — and at last it was decided to entrust the wisdom to a less destructible and more stable agent than paper, stone and metal, i.e. to human *vice*. Thus a game of cards, the Tarot, was devised, which has come down to us.

But from an iconographic point of view, the Tarot is definitely mediaeval. And from a historical point of view, there is no evidence that it existed before the end of the fourteenth century (cf. Gérard van Rijnberk, *Le Tarot*, Lyons, 1947, pp. 48ff.). Therefore if it is a matter of a popular game — designed to be as such by Egyptian sages — we would have to have a lot of material concerning the Tarot (as a card-game) during the fourteen, or at least ten, preceding centuries during which there is a complete silence concerning the Tarot.

No, the Tarot is *not inherited*, it has *reincarnated*. It has "reincarnated" in conformity with the experience of modern depth psychology of the school of Jung, who ascertained the upsurge of ancient and even archaic mysteries and cults from the depths of the unconscious of people in the twentieth century. The Tarot is the "Sacred Book of Thoth" — not inherited or transmitted — but reborn.

In support of this thesis, let us make a quotation — this time not from a modern legend, but from the text of a Greek Hermetic treatise of considerable antiquity. This is *Kore Kosmu*, or Isis teaching her son Horus the mysteries of heaven. Here it is a matter of the "Sacred Book of Thoth", concerning its nature and origin. The following is the relevant text:

> As long as the Craftsman who made the universe willed not to be known, all was wrapped in ignorance. But when he determined to reveal himself, he breathed into certain godlike men a passionate desire to know him, and bestowed on their minds a radiance ampler than that which they already had within their breasts, so that they might first will to seek the yet unknown God, and then have power to find him. But this, Horus my wondrous son, it would not have been possible for men of mortal breed to do, if there had not arisen one whose soul was responsive to the influence of the holy Powers of heaven. And such a man was Hermes, he who won knowledge of all. Hermes saw all things, and understood what he saw, and had power to explain to others what he understood... *for what he had discovered he inscribed on tablets, and hid securely what he had inscribed*, leaving the larger part untold, *that all later ages of the world might seek it*... And thus did Hermes speak: "...And now I must deposit hard by the secret things of Osiris these holy symbols of the cosmic elements, and after speaking over them a prayer, depart to heaven." It is not fitting, my son, that I should leave this report unfinished; I must tell you all that Hermes said

when he was depositing his books. Thus did he speak: "Ye holy
books, which have been written by my perishable hands, but
have been annointed with the drug of imperishability by Him
who is master over all, *remain ye undecaying through all ages*,
and be ye unseen and undiscovered by all men who shall go to
and fro on the plains of this land, until the time when heaven,
grown old, shall beget organisms (those that the Creator has
named *souls*) worthy of you." Having spoken this prayer over the
works of his hands, *Hermes was received into the sanctuary of
the everlasting zones*. (*Kore Kosmu*; trsl. Walter Scott, *Hermetica* vol. i, Oxford, 1924, pp. 459-461)

This is the Graeco-Egyptian version of the nature and origin of the "Sacred Book
of Thoth". According to this version the books comprising it were engraved by
"perishable hands, but have been annointed with the drug of imperishability"
and remain deposited "undecaying through all ages" in the "sanctuary of the
everlasting zones" belonging to Hermes, so "that all later ages of the world might
seek them. . ." They are therefore "inscribed" magically in a region *between heaven
and earth*, close enough to the earth to be reached by the souls of seekers on the
earth and to awake in them the spirit of quest through their attraction, and far
enough removed, on the other hand, so as never to be seized by cerebral intellectuality, i.e. to be taken hold of, analysed and exploited by it. The *original* of the
"Sacred Book of Thoth" is to be found in the "trans-cerebral" region. For this reason
it is necessary to seek for it not in crypts, manuscripts or stone inscriptions, nor
even in secret societies or fraternities, but rather in the "sanctuary of the everlasting
zones" belonging to Hermes. It is necessary to *elevate oneself* above the zone of
cerebral intellectuality, because the "sacred books" were written, according to the
Hermetic treatise that we have quoted, *before* the formation of the brain. They
make an appeal—magically effective across time, "throughout all ages"—to transcend cerebral intellectuality, and to raise "the organisms worthy of them, those
that the Creator has named *souls*", to the region where they remain deposited.

This region, this garden of the "holy symbols of the cosmic elements", planted
between earth and heaven—these magical formulae, gnostic symbols and mystic
fires of the primordial revelation, which constitute the "sanctuary" above cerebral
intellectuality and below heaven—is the *reality* of Hermeticism. It is an incentive across the ages, stimulating human souls to aspire to the vision of "all things"
and, having seen this totality, to comprehend it, and having comprehended it,
to attain the power of revealing it and showing it. The *totality of things* (*ta sympanta*, in Greek)—this is the soul of Hermeticism across time, "throughout all
ages". And as the brain is the organ of practical specialisation, the appeal and
aspiration to the totality of things (*ta sympanta*) amounts to an appeal and aspiration to transcend the brain and cerebral intellectuality.

Hermeticism haunts mankind from century to century. Is this because of a pleiad of brilliant writers? Or because of secret societies, or again because of the attraction towards what is secret in general? It could be . . .

But why are there always writers, and in every epoch? And why are there secret societies? Why, lastly, does the secret itself exercise such an attraction?

Because in the depths of the unconscious—which knocks at the door and wants to become conscious—there is present the "sanctuary of the everlasting zones", where the "Sacred Book of Thoth" remains deposited, from whence symbolic and Hermetic works are born, or reincarnate. The Tarot is such a work.

The Tarot has its invisible prototype, and the function and mission of the Tarot is to elevate the soul to this original. This is why it is a system of spiritual exercises. It gives direction and an impulse to transcend cerebral intellectuality for the *soul* to penetrate into the "sanctuary of the everlasting zones" where the "holy symbols of the cosmic elements" remain.

The totality of things. . . intuition transcending cerebral intellectuality. . . Hermeticism. . . But why Hermeticism? Is this not the aspiration of every metaphysical philosophy and all religious mystical practice?

Certainly the mystical practice of religion transcends cerebral intellectuality. But it does so in order to attain *heaven*, and not the intermediary zone between heaven and earth, where the primordial revelation of the "mysteries of heaven" are found deposited. Saints *live* the light, warmth and life of heaven. Celestial gold, blue and white radiate into their lives and through their lives.

With respect to Hermeticists, they are called—or should I say "condemned"?—to live neither for the day of earth nor for the Day of heaven, but rather are immersed in the Night, in the profound darkness of the mystery of relationships between heaven and earth. The thinking which unites heaven and earth, which is immanent equally in every earthly phenomenal structure and every celestial noumenal entity, is that which is the vision and comprehension of the totality of things, as the power to reveal it and show it.

Saints do not aspire to cosmic *thought*, to a comprehension of the totality of things, but rather to divine *life*.

And metaphysicians? Do not idealist philosophers aspire to the totality of things, to grasp it through thought?

Plato, the father of metaphysical philosophy, had had the experience of trans-cerebral thinking, of thought that is not *conceived*, but *seen*. This is why he was able to teach the method of gradual elevation beyond cerebral intellectuality: the elevation from an opinion (*doxa*) which is possible, to a conclusion (*dianoia*) which is probable, by way of dialectical argument and, lastly, from a probable conclusion to the certainty of immediate perception (*episteme*). It is through *episteme*, through immediate perception, that he had had the experience of *objective* thought, cosmic thought, that he named the "world of ideas". Having had the experience of ideas that are not conceived or invented through subjective cerebral intellectuality, but perceived and contemplated through *episteme*, Plato committed an error—moreover, quite understandable—of peopling the higher sphere of the spiritual world with ideas, although no "world of ideas" as a separate world or sphere exists. The whole world is peopled only by *individual beings*, and ideas live and exist only in them, through them and in relationships between them. Ideas are certainly real, but as an *immanent* reality, not as a separate reality. Ideas live only in a given consciousness—be it that of God, or of the Angelic hierarchies, or of man.

But they can also be projected outwards (or "engraved", as our ancient treatise expresses it), incarnated in symbols and formulae, and thus conserved in the objective spiritual world. This entire operation of the projection, incarnation and conservation of ideas is called in Hermeticism "writing the book". It is of such a "book" that the Apocalypse speaks when it says:

> And I saw in the right hand of Him who was seated on the throne a book written within and without, sealed with seven seals. (Revelation v, 1)

Such, also, is the "Sacred Book (or Books) of Thoth" of which *Kore Kosmu* speaks.

Now, Plato, in elevating himself above cerebral intellectuality, had a meeting with the "Sacred Book of Thoth", with the "holy symbols of the cosmic elements", which are "imperishable and undecaying", and which are in the "sanctuary of the everlasting zones" belonging to Hermes. As the Hermeticist that he was, he attained to the "sanctuary", but as the speculative philosopher that he was also, he failed to appreciate the magical fact of a *living spiritual monument* and he gave it an interpretation—which was later declined by his disciple Aristotle—which is not magical but "rational", in postulating a "world of ideas" beyond the world of phenomena.

Here is the fundamental error of all metaphysical philosophy, from Plato to the present time. It hypostatises ideas. Ideas live only in the consciousness of individuals or are present *in potency* in books—in visibly written books, such as the Holy Scripture, in invisible books, which are living spiritual monuments due to the operation of divine magic and, lastly, in the whole world, which is also a great book containing *in potency* the ideas of its creation and destiny expressed through the *symbolism of facts*.

This is, therefore, how Hermeticism differs from religious mysticism and metaphysical philosophy. Hermeticism as the aspiration to the *totality of things* is neither a school, nor a sect, nor a community. It is the *destiny* of a certain class or group of souls. For there are souls who *must* necessarily aspire to the "totality of things", and who are impelled by the river current of thought, which never stops, flowing always forward and always further on, without cease. . .There is no stopping for these souls; they cannot, without renouncing their own lives, leave this river of thought, which pours without cease—equally during youth, mature age and old age—without halting, from one darkness needing to be illumined to another darkness needing to be penetrated. Such was, is, and will be my destiny. And in addressing these Letters to the *Unknown Friend*, I address myself to he who shares this destiny with me.

Monsieur Professor, forgive me this arrogant and immodest (if not puerile, in your eyes) aspiration — the aspiration to personal certainty with respect to the totality of things — that you, in the industrious and fertile work that you do, hope to attain only after centuries of the collective endeavour of generations of scientists. But at least know that I am infinitely grateful to you, and that you have in me a disciple always eager to learn from you, with respect and gratitude, and who would never presume to teach you, whatever it may be.

Monsieur Priest, pardon me concerning what you think to be human pride which wants to penetrate into the mysteries of God, instead of bowing before divine wisdom and goodness and accepting with humility, as befits a Christian, the revealed truths of salvation — which, in so far as they are practised, suffice absolutely for the well-being, happiness and salvation of the soul. I say this to you now as if at confession: *I am unable not to* aspire to the depth, the height and the breadth of comprehensive truth, to comprehension of the *totality of things*. I have made the sacrifice of the intellect (*sacrificium intellectus*) in all sincerity and without reserve, but what an intensification of the life of thought, what increased ardour in the aspiration to spiritual knowledge, that has followed! I know that the truths of salvation revealed and transmitted by the Council of the Holy Church are both necessary and sufficient for salvation, and I have no doubt whatever that they are true, and I strive to do my best to practise them; but *I am unable* to arrest the current of the river of thought which bears me towards mysteries that perhaps are meant only for saints — perhaps only for Angels — in any case, that I know without doubt are reserved for beings more worthy than me. Father, will you grant me absolution?

Come what may, I can only echo Jacob's words:

I will not let you go until you have blessed me.
(Genesis xxxii, 26)

FORCE
—————
LA FORCE

Haec est totius fortitudinis
fortitudo fortis:
quia vincet omnem rem subtilem
omnemque solidam penetrabit.

(This thing is the strongest of all powers,
the force of all forces,
for it overcometh every subtle thing
and doth penetrate every solid substance.)
                    (*Tabula Smaragdina*, 9)

Virgo potens
Virgo clemens
Virgo fidelis

(Powerful Virgin
 Merciful Virgin
 Faithful Virgin)
     (Lauretanian Litany)

LETTER XI

FORCE

Dear Unknown Friend,

In the preceding Letter the transformation of fallen animality into holy animality was discussed, where the latter is spontaneous obedience to God, without the hindrance of reflection, doubt or motives of interest. Such obedience is basically an instinct. This is why holy animality is represented in the Hermetic tradition, in the vision of Ezekiel, in the Apocalypse of St. John, and in Christian iconography, by four holy animals, whose synthesis — the sphinx — is divine instinctivity, or the kingdom of God in and through the unconscious. For God reigns — i.e. he is worshipped, obeyed and loved — not only through explicit theologies and philosophies, or through explicit prayer, meditation and cult-acts, but also in general through the "hunger and thirst for righteousness", for truth, and for beauty, and likewise through each act of generosity and every expression of respect, admiration and adoration...Yes, the world is full of implicit religion, and the inspired saints and poets, who say that the birds "praise God" when they sing, are in no way mistaken. Because it is their tiny life itself which sings the "great life" and makes heard, through its countless variations, the same news which is as old as the world and new as the day: "Life lives and vibrates in me." What homage to the source of life is expressed by these small streams of life: the birds which sing!

Religio naturalis, natural religion, certainly exists and fills the world. Its waters emanate from the throne of God because – in filling beings, great and small, with the prodigious hope and faith which underlies vital élan – they *cannot* flow out from anywhere else other than the immediate presence of God. The cascades of hope and faith which are revealed by the great "yes" that all living beings say, by the very fact that they are living and that they prefer life to death, these cascades cannot bear in themselves anything else other than certain testimony of the fundamental Presence of God, i.e. the meaning and purpose of being alive.

The waves of this testimony reach the unconscious nature of beings and take effect there as this prodigious conviction which underlies vital élan. The "primal revelation", which is refered to by theology and to which natural religion is due, is the hope and faith, which vibrates both in the whole world and in each particular being (generally as a *subconscious* conviction), that life proceeds from a holy source, that it flows towards an end of supreme worth, and that it is "gift, benediction and vocation".

The mystery of natural religion, which is at the same time that of vital élan, is found expressed with remarkable clarity in the Apocalypse of St.John:

> Before the throne there is as it were a sea of glass, like crystal. And round the throne, on each side of the throne, are four living creatures, full of eyes in front and behind: the first living creature like a lion, the second living creature like an ox, the third living creature with the face of a man, and the fourth living creature like a flying eagle. And the four living creatures, each of them with six wings, are full of eyes all round and within, and day and night they never cease to sing: Holy, holy, holy, is the Lord God Almighty, who was, and is, and is to come!
> (Revelation iv, 6-8)

This gives a tableau of the working of natural religion, and its structure and elements. It is the Presence which is reflected in the limpid sea "like crystal", and it is Holy Animality, which never ceases to sing: "Holy, holy, holy, is the Lord God Almighty, who was and is and is to come!"

The "sea of glass" is the eye of the whole of Nature for God; the four creatures "full of eyes all round and within"– what they are and what they do – represent the natural *reaction* to the divine Presence. *Perception* and *reaction* — here is the essence of the natural religion which fills the unconscious core of creatures and which manifests itself through vital élan. Because all that lives participates in the collective perception of the "sea of glass", and in the collective reaction of the chorus: "Holy, holy, holy. . .", for this participation is the Life of life and the source from which the Élan of vital élan springs forth.

The saying "Nature is fundamentally supernatural" is therefore profoundly true. For natural and supernatural *life* always originate from the same source. The source of *all* life is religion, conscious or unconscious, i.e. *perception* of the Presence and *reaction* to the Presence.

In so far as my heart beats, that I breathe, that my blood circulates — in so far, in other words, that faith and hope work in me — in so far do I take part, thereby, in the great cosmic ritual in which all beings participate, all the hierarchies from the Seraphim down to butterflies. . . namely, in natural religion's "sacrament of baptism", which is immersion in the waters of the "sea of glass", and natural religion's "sacrament of confirmation", which takes place day and night through the chorus of choirs of animated Nature: "Holy, holy, holy. . ." All beings are baptised and confirmed in natural religion. Because, in so far as they live, they have faith and hope. But the baptism and confirmation with "fire and Spirit", the sacraments of love, surpass those of natural religion. They bear forgiveness and healing to *fallen* Nature.

Fallen Nature also has its unconscious mystery, i.e. its collective instinctivity of *perception* (its "waters") and its collective instinctivity of *reaction* (its "creatures"). Again, it is the Apocalypse of St. John which reveals this. The following is the origin of the "sea" of fallen Nature according to the Apocalypse:

> The serpent poured water like a river out of his *mouth* after the woman, to sweep her away with the flood. But the earth came to the help of the woman, and the earth opened its mouth and swallowed the river which the dragon had poured from his mouth. (Revelation xii, 15-16)

The difference between the waters of the "sea of glass" before the throne and the waters poured forth by the serpent is that the former are the calm, peace and stability of contemplation, or pure perception — they are "as glass", "like crystal" — whilst the latter are in movement, "poured forth", "like a river", *in the pursuit of an aim*, namely that of sweeping away the woman.

In the world there are therefore two different kinds of arriving at a conviction: one can be illumined by the serene clarity of contemplation, or one can be *swept away* by an electrifying flood of passionate arguments aiming at a desired end. The faith of the illuminated is full of tolerance, patience and calm steadfastness — "like crystal"; the faith of those who are swept away is, in contrast, fanatical, agitated and aggressive — in order to live it needs conquests without end, because it is conquest alone which keeps it alive. The faith of those who are swept away is greedy for *success*, this being its reason for existence, its criterion and its motivating force. Nazis and communists are of this faith, i.e. that of those who are swept away. True Christians and true humanists can only belong to the other faith, i.e. that of the illuminated.

In the world there are therefore two kinds of faith, two kinds of instinctivity, two different ways of *seeing* the world, two different ways of *looking* at it. There is the open and innocent look which desires only to reflect the light—i.e. which wants only *to see*—and there is the scrutinising look, which seeks to find and lay hold of its desired prey. There are spirits whose thought and imagination are put to the service, without reserve, of that which is true, beautiful and good—and there are spirits whose will, infatuated with an aim, make use of thought and imagination so as to win others to their cause, so as to sweep them away by the river of their *will*. A Plato has never had success as a revolutionary and will never do so. But Plato himself will always live throughout the centuries of human history—he has lived there for twenty-three centuries—and will be in each century the companion of the young and old who love pure thought, seeking only the light which it comprises. Karl Marx, in contrast, has had one century of astonishing success, and has revolutionised the world. He has swept away millions—those who went to the barricades and trenches in civil wars, and those who went to the prisons, either as jailers or as prisoners. But you, as a solitary human soul, a soul of depth and sobriety, what do you owe to Karl Marx? You know quite well that despite the intellectual fracas and the blood and dust provoked by Marx, when once appeased it will be Plato, anew, to whom the young will turn, and also the old, who will love the light of thought in centuries to come. For Plato *illumines*, whilst Marx *sweeps away*.

Can you imagine a *Christian Hermeticist* in Moscow's Red Square on the first of May or on the anniversary day of the October Revolution, the great socialist revolution!

But let us return to our Tarot Arcana, seeing that we are still neither swept away by any kind of "mass-movement", nor forced to march in columns and shout with the crowd . . .

Now, the waters which pour out of the mouth of the serpent sweep away, whilst those of the "sea of glass" like crystal, before the throne, illumine. And just as the collective perception of virgin Nature (the "sea of glass" before the throne) is accompanied by the collective reaction to this perception (perpetual adoration by the four holy creatures), so also there is in fallen Nature a reaction to the waters of the serpent swallowed up by the earth, namely the *beasts* of the Apocalypse. The Apocalypse does not designate them by the term "living creature" (*to dzoon*), which it uses to designate the four before the throne, but rather by the term "beast" (*to therion*; Latin, *bestia*). Thus it opposes *animality* and *bestiality*. Genuine animality is holy; bestiality is degenerate.

Besides the "red dragon with seven heads and ten horns" (Revelation xii, 3), which is the primordial serpent, the Apocalypse speaks of the beast "with ten horns and seven heads, with ten diadems upon its horns and a blasphemous name upon its heads" (Revelation xiii, 1). St. John saw this beast rising out of the sea: "It was like a leopard, its feet were like a bear's, and its mouth was like a lion's mouth" (Revelation xiii, 2). St. John goes on to describe "another beast which rose out of the earth; it had two horns like a lamb and it spoke like a dragon" (Revelation xiii, 11). The Apocalypse speaks also of "a scarlet beast, which was full of blasphemous names, having seven heads and ten horns" upon which the woman Babylon is seated (Revelation xvii, 3). Finally, it speaks of the "false prophet who, in the presence of the two-horned beast, worked signs by which he deceived those who had received the mark of the beast and those who worshipped its image" (Revelation xix, 20).

There are therefore four* beasts (including the "false prophet" who is a *human* beast), which correspond to the four *Hayoth*, the holy living creatures before the throne.

Since it is a matter here (in the two "tableaus" above) of the mystery of Force (*shakti* in the tantric tradition), namely that which moves non-fallen Nature and that which moves fallen Nature, and since the notion "force" comes down to the principle of *reaction*, which implies the *perception* preceding it, the two tableaus are summarised in two feminine figures:

> . . . a woman clothed with the sun, with the moon under her feet, and on her head a crown of twelve stars; she was with child and she cried out in her pangs of birth, in anguish for delivery. . . (Revelation xii, 1-2); [and] . . . a woman sitting on a scarlet beast. . . arrayed in purple and scarlet, and bedecked with gold and jewels and pearls, holding in her hand a golden cup full of abominations and the impurities of her fornication. . . (Revelation xvii, 3-4).

The former is the soul of cosmic non-fallen Nature (sun, moon, stars) and the latter is the soul of terrestrial fallen Nature (gold, jewels, pearls and beast). The first is a mother; the second is a prostitute. The one is *perception* of that which is above and *reaction* to that which is thus perceived—through its realisation ("childbirth"); the other is *horizontal perception* ("fornication") and *reaction* to that which is thus perceived—through sterile enjoyment (the "cup full of abominations and the impurities of her fornication"). The one is the Virgin-Mother and the other is the great prostitute of Babylon.

The Virgin-Mother. . . the soul of natural virgin Nature, i.e. non-fallen Nature, which is in the anguish of perpetual childbirth, until the Birth which is the ideal of all births is accomplished.

Evolution. . . orthogenesis. . . natural selection. . . mutations in the hereditary

---

*If the red dragon is not included (ed.)

mechanism...Avatars...Advent...Christmas...so many problems and ideas referring to the one great expectation and the one great hope for evolution to attain its ultimate level of flowering and to give its flower: for orthogenesis to produce *the being of the culmination of evolution*, for natural selection to result in the future superman, for the mechanism of heredity to bring its optimum to the light of day, for what we worship above to manifest amongst us below, for the Messiah to come, for God to become man! Evolution, progress, genealogies, prophecies, hopes throughout the centuries—what do they signify *at root* if not the "anguish of childbirth" across the ages and the constant expectation of the Birth in question? What other ideal could be present—radiating into the depths of all motherhood? What other aim could animate free Nature (*natura naturans*) throughout the millennia of her activity of generation?

This is therefore what is conveyed by the "good news": "The Word *became* flesh and *dwelt* among us" (John i, 14). Free Nature, natural religion, the "woman clothed with the sun, with the moon under her feet and on her head a crown of twelve stars"—the Virgin-Sophia—was present in Mary and it is thus that the soul of non-fallen Nature gave birth to the divine Word.

Free Nature has therefore accomplished her task. She has surpassed herself, and since then the epoch of the supernatural—the epoch of divine magic—has begun. Natural religion is now flooded in the radiance ("glory") of supernatural religion, and non-fallen Nature has become a dispensator and cooperator in the miracles of the new evolution, the "evolution" of the *Second Birth*.

Nevertheless, the Virgin is the principle of Force, i.e. the principle cooperating in the realisation of supernatural acts of the Holy Spirit. This means to say that divine magic not only does not act *against* non-fallen Nature but also that the latter *cooperates* with it. The sun, moon and stars therefore lend their assistance to acts of divine magic aspiring to the Resurrection. If this were not so, if virgin Nature did not participate in acts of divine magic (miracles), then these latter would always be new creations *ex nihilo*, and not transformations, transmutations and healings. Yet the wine at the wedding of Cana was not *created* from nothing, but rather it was *water* which was changed into wine. Let us also note the fact that the Virgin-Mother was not only present at the wedding but also that she took part in an explicit manner in the miracle of changing the water into wine—since it was thanks to her initiative that the miracle took place.

The multiplying of bread in the desert was a miracle of the *multiplying* of loaves, and not of the *creation* of bread from nothing. Here also the *cooperation* of Nature is evident. And the man born blind had to wash in the pool of Siloam in order to be healed by the words of the Master and by the clay made with the Master's saliva that was applied to his eyes. Here the participation of Nature is apparent.

Even the miracle of miracles, the Resurrection itself, was not the creation of a new body, but rather the transformation of the crucified body: the latter had to *disappear* from the tomb in order that the Resurrected One could *appear* to Mary Magdalene and the others. And the Resurrected One himself indicated the *continuity* of his body by inviting Thomas to put his finger in the marks of the nails and his hand in the wound on his side.

Virgin Nature therefore has her part in all the miracles. And it is virgin Nature participating actively in the miracles of divine magic which is the subject of the eleventh Arcanum of the Tarot, Force, representing a woman victorious over a lion, holding its jaws open with her hands. The woman does so with the same apparent ease—without effort—with which the Magician of the first Arcanum handles his objects. Moreover, she wears a hat similar to that of the Magician—in the form of a lemniscate. One could say that the two stand equally under the sign of rhythm—the respiration of eternity—the sign ∞ ; and that the two manifest two aspects of a single principle, namely that effort signifies the presence of an obstacle, whilst natural integrity on the one hand, and undivided attention on the other hand, exclude inner conflict—and therefore every obstacle, and therefore all effort. Just as perfect concentration takes place effortlessly, so does true Force act without effort. Now, the Magician is the Arcanum of the wholeness of consciousness, or concentration without effort; Force is the Arcanum of the natural integrity of being, or power without effort. Because Force subdues the lion not by force similar to that of the lion, but rather by force of a higher order and on a higher plane. This is the Arcanum of Force.

What, therefore, does the eleventh Arcanum of the Tarot teach?

Through the very tableau that it represents, it says: the Virgin tames the lion and thereby invites us to leave the plane of *quantity*—for the Virgin is evidently weaker than the lion concerning the quantity of physical force—and to raise ourselves to the plane of *quality*, for it is evidently there that the superiority of the Virgin over the lion is to be found.

What is it, therefore, that the lion obeys? What is it that he spontaneously yields to? Is he *hypnotised*? He is not, because the Virgin does not even look at him; her gaze is turned elsewhere, far from the lion whose jaws she opens. The lion is subjected to no constraint—either physical or hypnotic—therefore he obeys nothing beyond his own nature, and therefore it is his true nature which acts in him. It is the Lion before which the lion yields; it is holy animality which bestial animality obeys.

Now, the Force which the Card invokes is that of natural religion—that of non-fallen Nature. It is the magic of virgin Nature which awakens the virgin nature in the lion, and it is this Force that the eleventh Arcanum is called to reveal.

There are two principles which one has to understand and distinguish when one wants to go deeply into the Arcanum of Force. The one is the principle of the serpent, and the other is that of the Virgin. The former is *opposition* from which there proceeds friction which produces energy. The other is *concordance* from which comes fusion which engenders force.

Thus, enormous energies of a psychic nature are released into the world through a war due to a conflict of interests and pretensions; and energies of an intellectual nature pass from a virtual state to one of actuality when there is a controversy. It is said: "Truth springs forth from the clash of opinions", but actually it is not the truth which springs forth, but rather combative intellectual energy, for truth is revealed through the *fusion* of opinions and not through a clash. A clash certainly produces intellectual energy, but hardly ever discloses the truth. Quarrelling will never lead to the truth, as long as one does not give it up and seek for peace. Certainly minds can be electrified by polemic, which can cause a veritable intellectual storm in the world; but polemic cannot make the clouds disappear, nor is it given to making the sun shine.

I must confess, dear Unknown Friend, that during my long quest for truth I have been truly enriched by the fruits of the constructive work of many scientists, and by the spiritual endeavour of many mystics and esotericists, and also by the moral example of many human beings of good will—but I owe nothing to polemics or polemicists. I owe nothing to early Christian authors who attack paganism, nor to pagan authors who attack Christianity. I owe nothing to the learned Protestant doctors of the sixteenth century; and the academics of the Enlightenment and the Revolution of the eighteenth century have not taught me anything. Also, I owe nothing to the *militant* savants of the nineteenth century; and the revolutionary spirits of our century, such as Lenin, have not given me anything.

What I want to say is that the polemicists enumerated above have given me a lot in the way of *objects* of knowledge—and it is thanks to them that I have understood the intrinsic sterility of the spirit of opposition as such—but they have given me nothing in the way of *sources* of knowledge. In other words, I have learnt much *through them*, but I have learnt nothing *from them*. I owe them what they *do not want* to be owed, and I owe them nothing of what they *want* one to owe them.

Now, it is through the fusion of opinions that truth lights up. *Con-versation*—the process of *"together-versing"* (flowing together)—is the very opposite of *controversy*, the process of *"contra-versing"* (flowing against). Conversation is the operation of the fusion of opinions; it is a work of synthesis. True conversation always has in principle the underlying statement from the Gospel: "Where two or three are gathered in my name, there am I in the midst of them" (Matthew xviii, 20). For all true conversation calls upon the transcendent Centre, who is the way, the truth and the life.

The *Zohar* is a historical document which, amongst other things, supplies perhaps the best example of the creative role that conversation can play. There the Rabbis—Eleazar, Simeon, José, Abba and others—join their efforts and experiences with the aim of arriving together at a deeper, loftier and greater comprehension of the TORAH. And these Rabbis weep and embrace one another when this happens! From page to page the reader of the *Zohar*—this remarkable document of spirituality experienced in common, aspired to in common and appreciated in common—learns to understand, appreciate, and love more and more the conversation which aims at the fusion and synthesis of opinions.

Now, the force which is at work here is that of the Virgin (which the doctors of the *Zohar* call SHEKINAH), whilst the energy which electrifies polemicists is that of the serpent.

The force of life, and electrical energy: Are these not the most clear manifestations of these two principles?

Life and electricity must be clearly distinguished. Thus, today there is a tendency to confuse them, and to reduce them to electricity alone. However, electricity is due to the antagonism of opposites, whilst life is the fusion of polarities. Empedocles (ca. 490–ca. 430 B.C.) certainly saw this difference and taught that the motion of the four elements—earth, water, air and fire—is due to two opposite causes: friendship (love) and strife (enmity). The Apocalypse of St. John speaks of the war between the celestial armies of the Archistrategist Michael and the red dragon with his hordes, on the one hand, and the wedding of the Lamb and his Bride (*hieros gamos*), on the other hand.

The dragon (or "serpent of old") *opposes* himself to the higher spheres—here is the origin of "terrestrial electricity"; the hierarchies, represented by the Archistrategist Michael, have to resist the dragon—here is the origin of "celestial electricity". It is celestial electricity which was the means of the miracles of divine anger in the Old Testament: the flash of fire that came out of the tabernacle and consumed Nadab and Abihu, the sons of Aaron (Leviticus x, 1-2); the fire of the Lord which burned in the camp at Taberah and consumed some outlying parts of the camp (Numbers xi, 1-3); the earth which "opened its mouth and swallowed up" Korah and all his men (Numbers xvii, 32); Uzzah struck down on the spot, having taken hold of the ark, because the oxen stumbled and made it tilt (II Samuel vi, 6-7); the fire from above which consumed Elijah's burnt offering before the prophets of Baal (I Kings xviii, 38); the fire which descended twice and both times consumed fifty soldiers and their captains, near the hill at the top of which Elijah was sitting (II Kings i, 10-12); the miracles of Elishah (II Kings), etc. And it is terrestrial electricity of which we make use not only in the technical field of our civilisation but also in hypnosis, in demagogic propaganda, in movements of revolutionary masses...for electrical energy has its analogous forms on various planes—physical, psychic and even mental.

With respect to life, it is like the water of the "sea of glass, like crystal" coming from the throne; it is Force, natural religion, the soul of non-fallen Nature, the Virgin.

Virginity is obedience to the Divine, and is therefore in harmony and cooperation with the Divine. The Virgin is therefore the soul of life, i.e. *Force*, which exercises no constraint, but moves all. And the lion of the eleventh Card is obedient to the Force of its own life, to the profound impulse at the very depths of its own being, when it obeys the Virgin who opens its mouth.

Scripture has two different terms in Greek for "life" : *Zoe* and *bios*. The first signifies "vivifying life" and the second "derived life". *Zoe* is to *bios* as free Nature (*natura naturans*) is to necessitated Nature (*natura naturata*) (cf. also the philosophy of John Scotus Erigena). *Zoe* is therefore the source and *bios* is that which flows, having come from the source. It is *bios* which flows from generation to generation; and it is *Zoe* which fills the individual in prayer and meditation, in acts of sacrifice and participation in the sacred sacraments. *Zoe* is vivification from above in a *vertical sense*; *bios* is vitality which, although it once issued from the same source above, passes in the *horizontal* from generation to generation.

Now *bios*, biological life, flows in the domain of the serpent. For this reason it is mingled with electrical energy in an inextricable way; biological processes cause electrical currents and the latter influence the former in living organisms. But it is not *bios* which drains the resources of the organism—rather, it is electricity. For electricity is generated through chemical decomposition and by the opposition of contrary forces, i.e. by internal friction in the organism. This is what causes fatigue, exhaustion, senility and death. *Bios*, as such, is never tired or exhausted, and never grows old or dies. The heart and respiration do not need any rest, whereas the remainder of the organism—above all the *brain*—is plunged into a state of rest each night, through sleep, having been drained during the preceding day. Then it is *bios* which, during sleep, repairs the damage done to the organism by electricity. Sleep is the time when electrical activity is reduced to a minimum and when *bios* prevails.

A *tree*, where *bios* always prevails—which "sleeps" continually, so to speak—is in principle *immortal*. For it is not the exhaustion of its interior vitality, but rather mechanical destruction from outside which puts an end to its life. A tree does not *die* of old age; it is always *killed*—uprooted by a storm, struck by lightning, dragged down by the force of gravity, or cut down by man.

The fruit of the Tree of Knowledge of Good and Evil—the fruit of the *polarity* of opposites—is therefore electricity; and electricity entails fatigue, exhaustion, *death*. Death is the price that is paid for the knowledge of good and evil, i.e. the price of life amidst opposites. For it is electricity—physical, psychic and mental— which was introduced into the being of Adam-Eve, and thereby into the whole of life-endowed Nature, from the moment that Adam-Eve entered into communion with the *tree of opposites*, that is to say with the *principle of electricity*. And it is thus that death entered into the domain of life-endowed Nature.

Nevertheless, life-endowed Nature is not a uniform and integral entity. It is divided. There is above all division according to the preponderant roles played by *bios*, electricity and *Zoe*. The soul of life-endowed Nature in which *bios* is subordinated to electricity is the "woman Babylon" of the Apocalypse. Life-endowed Nature in which *bios* and electricity are in equilibrium is the "suffering creation" of which St. Paul said that it "sighs for deliverance" (Romans viii, 19-23). And, lastly, life-endowed Nature in which *bios* dominates electricity—and therefore is itself dominated by *Zoe*—is non-fallen Nature. Its soul is the celestial Virgin— the high priestess of natural religion. This is what constitutes the Arcanum of the eleventh Card of the Tarot.

One could formulate it as follows: *Force is virginity*.

What is virginity?

The state of virginity is that of the consonance of three principles—the spirit, the soul and the body. A being in whom spirit, soul and body are in consonance is in a state of virginity. In other words, it is the principle of the unity of three worlds: heaven, purgatory and earth. From the point of view of the earth, it is complete *obedience* of the body to the soul. From the point of view of purgatory, it is complete obedience of the soul to the breath of eternity—or *chastity*. From the point of view of heaven, it is absolute receptivity to the Divine—or *poverty*.

Virginity is therefore the unity of that which is above and that which is below, and it is this which is *Force*, i.e. the action of three worlds in harmony. Because Force—"the strongest of all powers, the force of all forces" (*Tabula Smaragdina*, 9) —is the unity of three worlds in action, that is to say in action where the divine spirit, the heart and the body are united.

It is the Virgin speaking through Solomon when he writes:

> Before his works of old
> I was set up from everlasting,
> From the beginning,
> or ever the earth was.
> When there were no depths I was brought forth,
> when there were no springs abounding with water.
> Before the mountains had been shaped,
> before the hills, I was brought forth;
> before he had made the earth with its fields,
> or the first of the dust of the world.
> When he established the heavens, I was there,
> when he drew a circle on the face of the deep,
> when he made firm the skies above,
> when he established the fountains of the deep,
> when he assigned to the sea its limit,
> so that the waters might not transgress his command,
> when he marked out the foundations of the earth,
> then I was at work beside him.
> (Proverbs viii, 22-30)

"When he marked out the foundations of the earth, then I was at work beside him"—is a clear statement of the role of the Virgin, who cooperates with the Divine not only in the miracles of redemption but also in those of creation.

Co-creatrix, Co-redemptrix, Co-sanctificatrix, Virgo, Mater, Regina...this formula summarises the thoughts relating to the principle of virginity. Here is the place to point out that principles do not exist separately from the beings who incarnate and manifest them. Principles as such are always *immanent*. This is why the reality of the principle of the Divine is God; the reality of the principle of the divine Word is Jesus Christ; and the reality of the principle of fertile and productive virginity is Mary-Sophia. Mary-Sophia represents, i.e. incarnates and manifests, the principle of virginity, that of non-fallen Nature, that of natural

religion, and that of Force. . .She is the central individuality—the "queen"—of
the whole domain in question. She is the conscious individual soul who is the
concrete ideal—the "queen"—of virginity, motherhood, and creative-productive
or queenly wisdom (queenly = regnal from *regina* = queen).

There is not a shadow of doubt for anyone who takes the spiritual life of mankind
seriously, even if he is short of authentic spiritual experience, that the Blessed Virgin
is not an ideal only, nor a mental image only, nor an archetype of the unconscious
(of depth-psychology), nor, lastly, an occultistic *egregore* (a collective astral creation of believers), but rather a concrete and living individuality—like you or I—
who loves, suffers, and rejoices. It is not only the children of Fatima, the child
Bernadette at Lourdes, the children of La Salette-Fallavaux, and the children of
Beauraing in Belgium, who have witnessed the "Lady", but also innumerable adults
across the centuries, including our own. Numerous meetings still remain intimate
and undivulged (I know of three series of such meetings, including one in Tokyo,
Japan), but one series of meetings with the Blessed Virgin took place recently in
Amsterdam in the Netherlands, where the Blessed Virgin manifested herself as
the "Lady of all nations" (*de Vrouwe van alle Volkeren*) and inaugurated a prayer-
movement with a special prayer, with a view to saving all nations from "degeneration, disaster and war" (*verwording, rampen en oorlog*).* I may add that I went
to Amsterdam in order to make as scrupulous an investigation as possible, and
the result of this investigation there (confirmed subsequently by experiences of
a personal nature) was complete certainty not only with respect to the authenticity of the experiences of the seer (a woman forty years of age) but also with respect
to the authenticity of the *subject* of these experiences.

In writing of these things, I can only agree with the sentiment expressed by
Rabbi Simeon in the *Zohar*, who exclaimed:

> Woe to me if I tell and woe to me if I do not tell! If I tell, then
> the wicked will know how to worship their master; and if I do
> not tell, then the companions will be left in ignorance of this
> discovery! (*Zohar* 11b; trsl. H. Sperling and M. Simon, 5 vols.,
> London-Bournemouth, 1949, vol. i, p. 48)

Be that as it may, meetings with the Blessed Virgin are so numerous and so
well-attested that one must certainly at least admit their objective reality. I say
"at least", because this does not satisfy the demands of my conscience. In fact,
I would not be entirely honest or frank with you, dear Unknown Friend, if I were

*Translator's note: The prayer revealed by the Blessed Virgin—the "Lady of All Nations"—in Amster-
dam on February 11, 1951, has been translated into English as follows:
"Lord Jesus Christ, Son of the Father,
Send now your Spirit over the earth.
Let the Holy Spirit live in the hearts of all peoples,
That they may be preserved from degeneration, disaster and war.
May the Lady of All Nations, who once was Mary,
Be our Advocate. Amen"
(Cf. *The Messages of the Lady of All Nations* Amsterdam, 1971)

not to say what is an absolutely sure result (in the inner forum of my consciousness) of more than forty years of endeavour and experience. It is the following:

One meets the Blessed Virgin inevitably when one attains a certain intensity of spiritual aspiration, when this aspiration is authentic and pure. The very fact of having attained a spiritual sphere which comprises a certain degree of intensity and purity of intention puts you in the presence of the Blessed Virgin. This meeting belongs to a certain "sphere"—i.e. to a certain degree of intensity and purity of spiritual aspiration—of spiritual experience, just as the experience of having a mother belongs naturally to human family life on earth. It is therefore as "natural" for the spiritual domain as the fact of having a mother is natural in the domain of one's terrestrial family. The difference is that on earth one can certainly be motherless, whilst in the realm of the spiritual this can never happen.

Therefore, the thesis that I am advancing with one hundred per cent conviction is that every Hermeticist who truly seeks authentic spiritual reality will sooner or later meet the Blessed Virgin. This meeting signifies, apart from the illumination and consolation that it comprises, protection against a very serious spiritual danger. For he who advances in the sense of depth and height in the "domain of the invisible" one day arrives at the sphere known by esotericists as the "sphere of mirages" or the "zone of illusion". This zone surrounds the earth as a belt of illusory mirages. It is this zone which the prophets and the Apocalypse designate "Babylon". The soul and the queen of this zone is in fact Babylon, the great prostitute, who is the adversary of the Virgin.

Now, one cannot pass by this zone without being enveloped by perfect purity. One cannot traverse it without the protection of the "mantle of the Blessed Virgin"— the mantle which was an object of worship and of a special cult in Russia (*Pokrov Presvyatyya Bogoroditsy* —"Mantle of the Very Holy Mother of God"). It is therefore the protection of this "mantle" which is absolutely necessary in order to be able to traverse the "sphere of mirages" without falling prey to the influence of its illusions.

The way of Hermeticism, solitary and intimate as it is, comprises authentic experiences from which it follows that the Roman Catholic Church is, in fact, a depository of Christian spiritual truth, and the more one advances on the way of free research for this truth, the more one approaches the Church. Sooner or later one inevitably experiences that spiritual reality corresponds—with an astonishing exactitude—to what the Church teaches: that there are guardian Angels; that there are saints who participate actively in our lives; that the Blessed Virgin *is* real, and that she is almost precisely such as she is understood, worshipped and portrayed by the Church; that the sacraments *are* effective, and that there are seven of them—and not two, or three, or even eight; that the three sacred vows—of obedience, chastity and poverty—constitute in fact the very essence of all authentic spirituality; that prayer is a powerful means of charity, for beyond as well as here below; that the ecclesiastical hierarchy reflects the celestial hierarchical order; that the Holy See and the papacy represent a mystery of divine magic; that hell, purgatory and heaven *are* realities; that, lastly, the Master himself—although he loves everyone, Christians of all confession as well as all non-Christians—abides with his Church, since he is always present there, since he visits the faithful there and instructs his disciples there. The Master is always findable and meetable there.

Let us return to the Arcanum of Force.

It is said that "union makes force", and one understands by this the alliance of individual wills with a view to achieving a common aim. It is the formula for the *quantitative* increase of force. With respect to qualitative force, it would be appropriate to say that "unity is force", because one is strong only in so far as there is unity of spirit, soul and body, i.e. in so far as there is *virginity*. It is inner conflict that renders us weak: the fact that we serve two or even three masters at the same time.

The *Emerald Table* of Hermes states not only the principle of universal analogy, but also that of universal force: "to *accomplish* the miracles of one thing". It teaches concerning the "strongest of all powers, the force of all forces, for it overcometh every subtle thing and doth penetrate every solid substance" (*Tabula Smaragdina*, 9). The force taught by the *Emerald Table* is the unity in action of heaven and earth, for *thelema* (the fundamental will) "doth ascend from earth to heaven; again it doth descend to earth, and uniteth in itself the force from things superior and things inferior" (*Tabula Smaragdina*, 8).

Let us now examine the two aspects of Force which the *Emerald Table* speaks of, namely:

> that it "*overcometh every subtle thing*"
> and "*doth penetrate every solid substance*".

1. "*It overcometh every subtle thing*"

The deeper meaning—mystical, gnostic, magical and Hermetic—of "overcoming" is to change the enemy into a friend. To render him impotent only is not yet victory. Thus the Germany of 1914 was certainly rendered impotent in 1918, but was not overcome—as the year 1939 proves. But after the defeat of 1945, Germany was certainly *overcome*—in so far as she is sincerely allied to her old adversaries. The same applies to Japan as a state.

On another plane, it is likewise true that the devil will be overcome only at the moment when his voice—no matter whether it is rough or smooth—will be heard in chorus with the choirs of celestial hierarchies praising God.

Saul of Tarsus was the very soul of the persecution of Christians; Paul the apostle was the very soul of the work of conquest of the so-called "pagan" world for Christianity. Here is a case of authentic victory in the true sense of the word.

And it is authentic victory that one must hope for and wait for in the conflict that tradition represents as the struggle between the Archistrategist Michael and the dragon. The day when it is achieved will be the day of a new festival—the festival of the coronation of the Virgin *on earth*. For then the principle of opposition will be replaced on earth by that of collaboration. This will be the triumph of life over electricity. And cerebral intellectuality will then bow before Wisdom (SOPHIA) and will unite with her.

"To overcome every subtle thing" is therefore equivalent to changing opposing forces — mental, psychic and electrical — into friendly and allied forces. The "subtle things" to overcome are the intellectual forces of temptation based on *doubt*, the psychic forces of temptation based on sterile *enjoyment*, and the electrical forces of temptation based on *power*.

In the last analysis, the "subtle things" meant here are therefore equivalent to temptations. However every temptation is similar to a two-way flow of traffic. Because when evil tempts good, it is itself at the same time "tempted" by the latter. Temptation always entails *contact*, and therefore an exchange of influence. Every beautiful temptress, in attempting to tempt a saint, risks finishing up by "wetting his feet with her tears, wiping them with the hair of her head, kissing them, and annointing them with ointment" (Luke vii, 38). Do we not have prefigured here the victory over the "great prostitute Babylon"? Have we not discovered the root and core of the much celebrated and lamented "fall of Babylon", described in chapters 17 and 18 of the Apocalypse?

Doubt, sterile enjoyment, power — these constitute together the "technology" of temptation.

First of all, doubt. . . it is the principle of division and opposition, and therefore of illness. For just as intellectual doubt divides the intellect by confronting it with two contrary tableaus, and reduces it to the impotence of indecision, so is bodily illness a "doubt" in the organism, i.e. two tendencies, opposed to one another, reducing it to impotence and constraining it to remain in bed.

Doubt is to faith as the sight of eyes suffering from astigmatism is to normal eyesight. Just as normal eyes either do not see or see *together*, so does faith see — whether more or less is not important — with the "higher eye" and the "lower eye" *together*. For *certainty* is due to the coordinated vision of the higher or transcendent Self — this is the "higher eye" — and the lower or empirical self, which is the "lower eye". Doubt appears when the "higher eye" and the "lower eye" do not see together. There is then a spiritual astigmatism, a lack of coordination between the two "seers" in man. Doubt is a beast with two horns, since it only bifurcates.

However, doubt that is mastered, under the control of the will and put into its service, proves to be prodigiously useful, as the whole history of science shows. There doubt is utilised as the instrument of scientific faith; there one doubts within the precise limits of the scientific method, being guided by — and in — the interests of scientific faith. If Pasteur had not doubted spontaneous generation on the one hand, and if he had not had faith in observation and experimentation, on the other hand, we would not now benefit from the fruits of the "Pasteurian revolution" in biology and medicine.

Productive though it is in the scientific domain, doubt nevertheless entails expenses that must be paid. Its practice, be it only by using it as a method, results in partial blindness; it renders us *one-eyed*. For the fact of regularly turning away from the "higher eye", from its message and testimony, and confining oneself to the "lower eye" (the five senses plus cerebral intellectuality), cannot fail, sooner or later, to have its effect, i.e. to render one-eyed he who assiduously practises the use of one eye instead of two.

And exactly as the great doctors of theology, metaphysics and mysticism of the Middle Ages proved to be sterile in what concerns medicine, biology, physics, physiology and other sciences—the help of which saves, in France alone, 69,000 human lives each year from the bane of tuberculosis, and has reduced mortality due to typhoid fever by more than 97 percent, mortality due to diptheria also by 97 percent, that due to scarlet fever by 98 percent, etc. (cf. Dr. Étienne May, *La médecine, son passé, son présent, son avenir*, Paris, 1957, pp. 336-337)—so are the doctors of the sciences of our time sterile in what concerns the vital spiritual needs of mankind. The former had an eye only for the spiritual; the latter have an eye only for the temporal.

Is it necessary to be one-eyed in order to produce something of value—whether scientific or spiritual? No. Individual examples, including the recent example of the author of *The Phenomenon of Man* and *Le Milieu divin*, prove it. And esoteric Hermeticism, i.e. Hermeticism cultivated within the inner forum of consciousness, is called to play a role—whether visible or invisible is of little importance—as a link in each individual's inner forum of consciousness, between what is given by the *two* "eyes". It can certainly be an agent in establishing coordination of the two "eyes", between culture and civilisation, between spirituality and progress, between religion and science. It can act as a healing agent in this singular contemporary illness (which is a kind of schizophrenia) of the dissociation between spirituality and intellectuality—but it can do so only in the inner forum of each individually, in order to guard against arrogating functions of general significance belonging properly to Church and Academia. Briefly, the role which it is called to play is anonymous and intimate, and is not provided with the means of the armoury of collectives, such as pamphlets, press, radio, television and congresses where a great din is made. The magic of the constant work of service done in silence—this is what it is a matter of.

A secret, then? Not at all, for a private thing is not a secret thing. The private life is not a secret life. Silence as the essential condition for intimate work is in no way equivalent to a jealously guarded secret. Just as Trappist monks maintain silence without anyone suspecting them of wanting to keep secrets, so is the community composed of Hermeticists scattered in the world in the right to be silent, in order to maintain the atmosphere of privacy essential for its work, without it being suspected of dark secrets. Authentic spiritual life requires the inviolable sanctuary of privacy—which has nothing in common with "initiation secrets" or those of "secret societies", whose secrets, furthermore, inevitably become "open secrets".

Let us now consider sterile enjoyment. The role that certain schools of philosophy and psychology assign to *pleasure* as the final cause of all human activity—including moral activity—is well known. According to them, man would not have any desire to act if he did not have the promise of real or imaginary pleasure.

What is pleasure? It is the lowest constituent of the scale: pleasure — joy — blissfulness — beatitude. It is only the psycho-physical signal announcing accord between what one desires and what one attains. Being only a signal, it does not have moral value in itself; it is desire, whose satisfaction it signals, which falls under the moral qualification of good or evil. This is why pleasure can be followed by joy or disgust, according to the case. Pleasure is therefore a reaction — at the surface of man's psychic being — to objective events. In other words, a life dedicated to the pursuit of pleasure alone would be the most superficial that one could imagine for a human being.

Joy is more profound than pleasure. It is still an index, but what it indicates is deeper than the relationship between a desire and the event of its being satisfied. Joy is the *state* of soul which participates most intensely in *life* and experiences it in appreciating its value. Joy is the spreading of the soul beyond the limits of conscious awareness. It signifies an augmentation of the soul's vital élan.

Blissfulness is the state of the human being where spirit, soul and body are united in a comprehensive *rhythm*. It is the rhythm of the spiritual, psychic and bodily life brought into harmony.

Lastly, beatitude transcends blissfulness in so far as the state which it comprises is higher than that in which the rhythm of the human spirit, soul and body holds sway; it is the state of the actual Presence of the "Fourth" — of God. It is therefore the state of the "beatific vision" (*visio beatifica*) of Christian tradition.

Pleasure is therefore most peripheral and superficial on the scale of blessedness. Yet in the technique of temptation it plays the same role with regard to the soul as doubt does with regard to the spirit. For just as doubt reduces the spirit to impotence, so does pleasure (or sterile enjoyment) reduce the soul to impotence, to a state of passivity. It enslaves it and changes it from the subject into an object of action.

Lastly, *power*. . . here again schools of philosophy and psychology have erected the "will-to-power" as the supreme principle of human activity. According to them man aspires only to power; and religion, science and art are only means to this end.

Now, it is true that no one desires powerlessness as such. And if we worship the Crucifix, which is the symbol of complete outer powerlessness, we do so because it is at the same time the symbol of supreme inner power. For there is power and Power. The one enslaves and the other liberates. The one constrains; the other inspires.

True power always appears as powerlessness. For it is always due to a kind of crucifixion. False power, however, crucifies others. This is because it knows of no other growth than that at the expense of others. An autocrat is powerful only when he has reduced to impotence all other candidates — all the independent elements in his country; a hypnotist is powerful in so far as the number of people who resist his hypnosis is small; a philosophical system is powerful in so far as it *compels* minds to accept it by the weight of the totality of its arguments (Fichte attempted to *compel* the reader to understand — *Ein Versuch, die Leser zum Verstehen zu zwingen*); lastly, a machine is powerful in so far as it is capable of rendering powerless the obstacles which prevent it from functioning.

Now, the technique of temptation in the domain of power consists in substituting false power for the true—in the substitution of the power of compulsion or "electricity" for that of freedom of inspiration and healing or "life" (*Zoe*).

Sacred magic has nothing in common with the power which compels. It operates only with currents of "life" or *Zoe*—spiritual, psychic and physical. Even its "armoury"—such as the "swords" of the Archangel Michael and the Holy Cherubim who guards the gate of Eden—are showers of rays of "life" whose intensity is such as to repulse or put to flight anyone who is either opposed to "life", or who cannot support its intensity, and on the other hand it attracts and vivifies anyone who aspires to "life" and who can support its intensity. Who knows how many people otherwise ill or despairing owe the re-establishment of their physical or psychic health to the "sword" of the Archangel Michael? There are no statistics of this kind, but if there were, one would probably be astonished at the number of "victims" of the flaming sword!

Be that as it may, the "swords" in question are powerful arms of true power. They are the fruits of outer powerlessness, i.e. they are forces due to *crucifixion*. For the guardian of freedom is, by this very fact, the victim of freedom; he has also to endure the age-old abuse of the freedom that he protects. It is the age-old powerlessness towards the abuse of freedom—therefore it is an age-old crucifixion—which is the source of power concentrated in the "sword" of the Archistrategist Michael...

It is the same with the "flaming sword" of the Cherubim "set in the east of Eden". Here again it is divine impotence in relation to human freedom, which latter chose the way of the Fall—impotence which nourished and concentrated the "sword".

Thus, here is the choice which each of us is called to make: the choice between the power of crucifixion and that of compulsion. To pray or to order: Which would we prefer?

"Electricity" in its triple form—physical, psychic and mental—is an instrument which lends itself prodigiously to the service of the will-to-power, i.e. to the desire to order and subjugate. For this reason it is a temptation for mankind. Mankind is confronted by the choice between the power of sacred magic and that of mechanics—a choice which, in the last analysis, amounts to one between life (*Zoe*) and electricity.

These are therefore the three principle "subtle things" which are overcome by Force or virginity.

2. "*It doth penetrate every solid substance*"

Solidity is the experience of an obstacle to our freedom of movement. Air is certainly not it, whilst a wall of stone certainly is. Similarly, mistrust towards you can erect a veritable psychic wall which can be an insurmountable obstacle to your movement aiming at contact and the communication of ideas. Similarly, again, a well-defined and rigid intellectual system can render you dumb with regard to the person who is held under its power. It would be impossible, for example, to reach the inner organ of comprehension of an orthodox Marxist or a Freudian psychoanalyst in speaking to them of authentic mystical experience. The one would *hear* only what lends itself to interpretation by the concept of "narcosis", remaining quite deaf to the rest, and the other would have an open ear only for that which lends itself to interpretation by the concept of "sublimation of libido", i.e. for what lets itself be reduced to the play of sexuality. Therefore, here again there is a wall.

Now, there is physical, psychic and mental "solidity". All three forms of solidity have in common that they are experienced as obstacles to our movement. They are experienced as *impenetrable*. Nevertheless, the *Emerald Table* affirms that "every solid substance", i.e. each physical, psychic and mental obstacle, is certainly penetrable for Force or virginity.

How?

By action opposite to that of explosion, i.e. by *emollient action*. With regard to a mental obstacle presented by a rigid intellectual system, Force will not occupy itself with the mental formation itself, but will admit its breath into the heart of the person concerned. The heart having tasted life (*Zoe*), the creative movement of life will pass its breath to the head and will breathe movement into the mental formation. This latter, having been set in motion—*not by doubt, but rather by creative élan*—will lose its rigidity and will become fluid. It is thus that the liquification of crystallised mental formations is effected.

With respect to psychic obstacles, it is again emollient action which effects the transformation of a psychic complex from rigidity into sensitivity. Here again it is the breath of life which dissolves the complex, by way of the heart so that the mistrust, fear or hate, concentrated in the complex is dispersed and the soul is left free of the blinding influence of the psychic complex.

Lastly, physical obstacles exist for Force, i.e. for the radiation of life, only in so far as they are due to morbid processes of crystallisation in living organisms. If we give them a common comprehensive name, it is "sclerosis"; this constitutes the obstacle in general. Sclerosis is the process of gradual alienation of the body from the soul and spirit. A corpse is the limit and end of this, because the corpse is a body completely alienated with regard to the soul and spirit.

This is what Dr. Étienne May says in making an assessment from the standpoint of modern day medicine:

> With regard to arterio-sclerosis, it is to a certain extent a natural
> modification of the arteries with age. And thus, pushing this
> to an absurd extreme, one could almost say that, all other ill-
> nesses being suppressed, sclerosis of the arteries—in the long
> run obligatory—would alone prevent us from becoming im-
> mortal. (Dr. Étienne May, *La médecine, son passé, son présent,
> son avenir*, Paris, 1957, p. 341)

Sclerosis is therefore death itself, which is at work during life in modifying, little by little, the living body into a corpse. At least, this is what it appears to be, seen in the light of modern medicine and biology.

There are, nonetheless, two different ways of dying. The one is where the body refuses to serve as the instrument for the soul—which is the case with sclerosis. The other is that where the principle which vivifies and animates the body retires and thus is missed by the body; it is then the *soul* which quits the body.

In the first case, it is the body which expels the soul; in the second case, it is the soul which refuses to make use of the body any longer. One dies, therefore, because the body becomes unserviceable for life or, otherwise, because life itself retires from the body. In the latter case one certifies from a clinical point of view a generally increasing lapse of biological functions which advances to the point where the activity of respiration and circulation halts, i.e. where clinical death takes place. This can happen in the state of deep sleep, at the hours when vitality is normally at its minimum—between two and four o'clock in the morning. Then one says that death was due to old age, pure and simple—without any specific ailment, including sclerosis, being the cause. With respect to hardening of the arteries or arterio-sclerosis, this process has long been considered as an inevitable consequence of advancing age. "But one knows nowadays that there is arterio-sclerosis in young people and that there are old people whose arteries (without speaking of the brain and nervous sytem) remain supple" (Dr. Étienne May, *La médecine, son passé, son présent, son avenir*, Paris, 1957, p. 346). One can therefore die with supple arteries, without cancer and without being the victim of pathological viruses. One can depart entirely, just as one departs partially when one falls asleep.

Now, there are several modes of sleeping. There is sleep and Sleep. You can believe, or not believe, in the testimony of the Cabbala, which describes what is said to happen during the sleep of the righteous, during the sleep of ordinary people, and during the sleep of sinners. (It is described how at the hour of midnight the Ancient of Days draws near to the earth and arrives at the gate of Eden, where the souls of the righteous meet him, etc.) However there is no one who does not know from sure experience what arises during sleep at night, in diverse states not only of health but also of the soul. The overwhelming cares of one day can be changed during sleep into things of secondary importance and can even appear insignificant, whilst insignificant things of the day before, which skated almost imperceptibly across the screen of your memory before sleep, can acquire in dream a singular importance which was not at all surmised the preceding day. How many different ways of awakening! How moods, states of mind, desires, general states of soul, differ when you awake, for example, after a Christmas night or an Easter night, or some night in November or February. . . If the ways of awakening are as different as black and white, it is because there are as many different kinds of *sleep*.

Just as there are several modes of sleeping, so there are several modes of dying.

It is again the Cabbala which makes mention of this and which describes a whole scale of ways of dying, the summit of which would be death due to the kiss of the Eternal One. According to the Cabbala, conscious or unconscious *ecstasy* would therefore be the most sublime cause of death.

Must an ecstatic rapture necessarily be sudden or can it be slow and gradual as well? Consider the process of death where it is not the body which refuses to serve the soul, but rather where it is the soul itself which gradually quits the body—could this not be the visible manifestation of invisible ecstasy, of the increasing attraction of the Divine working in the very depths of the soul? Would not increasing *nostalgia* suffice to explain the gradual departure of vital élan that is recorded in the case of general decline resulting in death?

Be that as it may, this is not only what the Cabbala teaches, but also contemporary Christian Hermeticism. The Hermetic teaching is as follows:

During the period of preparation for so-called "natural" death—i.e. caused neither by the unserviceability of the organism, nor by violent interference from outside, nor by poisoning—a well-defined process takes place in the "vital body" (the "etheric body", or *nephesch* according to the Cabbala). There the vital forces concentrate little by little in the region of the eight-petalled lotus, which is the crown centre. To the extent that this concentration in the crown region of the head (in fact, even above the head, if one understands by "head" the physical brain) takes place, vital activity diminishes—at first in the lower region of the organism, i.e. the genital and intestinal region, then in the region of the stomach, and lastly in the central region in the neighbourhood of the heart. At the moment when the concentration of vitality at the crown centre is complete, the heart and also the circulatory and respiratory system cease their activity—this is the moment of death.

Now, the process here corresponds to the ecstasy to which one aspires in the practice of yoga. For the state of *samadhi*, or yogic ecstasy, is realised, in terms of esoteric physio-psychurgy, by the concentration of energy—arising from the lower region of the body—in the crown region, in the region of the "thousand-petalled lotus" (*sahasrara*). The eight-petalled lotus is designated in India as "thousand-petalled" because of its intense scintillation, which gives the impression of a multitude of petals (a "thousand"). Once the energy is concentrated in the crown region the body is reduced to a state of stupor, and the consciousness of the self departs and is united with the consciousness of the transcendent Self—which is the state of *samadhi* or ecstasy. *Samadhi* or yogic ecstasy is a temporary or artificial death.

Although the Christian ecstasy of *sursum corda* ("elevation of the heart") differs essentially from *samadhi*, there is no reason to deny the reality of yogic ecstasy or the fact that it is an authentic ecstasy, albeit not the only possible one.

It is therefore quite justifiable to say that so-called "natural" death is fundamentally a natural ecstasy—notably, a natural *samadhi*, where the transcendent Self accomplishes union with the personal self, in withdrawing it from the body and uniting with it. It is, again, a case where Force "doth penetrate the solid substance" when one dies a natural death, having supple arteries and a normal nervous system. It is then Force (*Zoe*) which keeps the blood vessels supple through its emollient action, and which renders natural death possible as a result of "natural ecstasy" or the gathering of vital forces above.

These, therefore, are some of the facts and thoughts which can contribute to an understanding of the statement from the *Tabula Smaragdina*:

It doth penetrate every solid substance.

The concept of Force is that of an intermediary between pure consciousness and manifestation. It is the link between the idea and the phenomenon.

Force has two aspects—that of electricity and that of life (or struggle on the one hand, and cooperation, on the other). These two aspects correspond to the serpent (*nahash*) and the Virgin. Occultists of the school of Eliphas Lévi considered the serpent as the "great magical agent" *par excellence* and did not much occupy themselves with the Virgin, who bears the principle of sacred magic. They interested themselves above all in the psychic and mental aspect of the principle of electricity, called by them the "mobile astral agency", thus desiring to extend the domain of science—which is occupied only with the physical aspect of electricity—to the psychic and mental realms. They wanted to win over to science, i.e. for that understanding which makes use of the method of observation and experimentation, the *whole* domain of electricity—physical, psychic and mental.

Their dominant preoccupation was therefore to demonstrate that the tradition of ancient and mediaeval magic contains many a truth—due to observation and experimentation—ignored by science, and that the "great magical agent" can certainly be placed in the service of human intelligence and will just as is the energy of electricity and magnetism. The fact is that they enveloped their essential message in a cloud of verbal romanticism, evoking the mild shivers that accompany allusions to "secret initiations", to the "mysteries" of age-old secret fraternities of adepts who know and accomplish all that is worth the trouble of knowing and accomplishing, to mysterious communities of sages and mages who possess, across the ages, the knowledge and power for the occult government of the world, secretly fashioning the destiny of mankind. The fact of this romanticism—quite understandable and excusable, moreover—does not at all prevent an understanding of the true task that they were pursuing in establishing facts and in sifting out laws and principles from the totality of occult traditions and experiences. What they were doing in reality—disregarding the romanticism—was elaborating a *modern science* from the raw material of occult traditions and experiences.

May at long last the whisperers be silent—all those who spread rumours about the work of these occultists, placing them under suspicion of "satanism" and "dark practices"! They are no more—nor less—"satanists" than the people who, for example, treat mental patients with electric shocks, and they are without doubt innocent angels in comparison with the physicists who discovered nuclear energy and put it in the service of destruction!

It is time, once and for all, that an end is made to the foolish and unpleasant accusations—concerning contemporary doctors of occultism—of "satanism" or "black magic". They are, if the worst comes to the worst, romantics infatuated with the ideal of an absolute science of a glorious past, and they are, in so far as they are doing their best, pioneers of a science of the ignored or neglected domain of magic, i.e. a science of the dynamic relationships which exist between subjective consciousness and objective phenomena.

But, whilst wholly rejecting with indignation all the suspicions and accusations of "satanism" with regard to the classical authors of contemporary occultism, I regret nonetheless that they preferred science to Hermeticism, and consequently dedicated their efforts, in preference, to the study of the principle of the serpent, that of psychic and mental *electricity*, instead of devoting themselves to the task of rendering themselves capable of participating consciously in the principle of the Virgin, that of psychic and mental *life*. If they had chosen Hermeticism—i.e. the spiritual life which comprises the totality of mysticism, gnosis, magic and the perennial philosophy—they would have "written" collectively a modern Christian *Zohar* (or "Book of Splendour"), and they would have poured out into the world a flow of wisdom and spiritual life which would have been able to accomplish a true spiritual renaissance in the western world. *Satis scientiae, sapientiae parum* ("lots of knowledge, but too little wisdom")—this is what must be said to the representatives of occult science of our time. It is not the scholars and experimenters who are called to realise a spiritual springtime in the western world, but rather those participating in authentic sources of the profound life—the deeper life of thinking, feeling and the will. In order for this to take place, thought must become meditative, feeling—contemplative, and the will—ascetic. For in order to attain authentic sources of the profound life, one must seek profound thought—which is meditation; one must seek profound feeling—which is contemplation; and one must seek the primal will (beyond desires and longings)—which is asceticism. It is thus that conscious participation in authentic spiritual life is gained, and it is thus that the sources of this life are opened.

The Virgin, the Force of our Arcanum, is the principle of springtime, i.e. that of creative spiritual élan and spiritual flourishing. The prodigious flourishing of philosophy and the arts in ancient Athens took place under the sign of the Virgin. Similarly, the flourishing of the Renaissance at Florence was under the vernal sign of the Virgin. Also, Weimar at the beginning of the nineteenth century was a place where the breath of the Virgin perceptibly moved hearts and minds.

In ancient Egypt the domain of the mysteries of death was attributed to Osiris, and that of life—including language, writing, law and the arts—was attributed to Isis. Thus, Isis was the soul of the civilisation of ancient Egypt, which we are still admiring after more than twenty centuries.

The sickness of the West today is that it is more and more lacking creative élan.

292   MEDITATIONS ON THE TAROT

The Reformation, rationalism, the French revolution, materialistic faith of the nineteenth century, and the Bolshevik revolution, show that everywhere mankind is turning away from the Virgin. The consequence of this is that the sources of creative spiritual élan are drying up, one after the other, and that an increasing *aridity* is showing up in all domains of the spiritual life of the West. It is said that the West is growing old. But why? Because it lacks creative élan, because it has turned away from the source of creative élan, because it has turned away from the Virgin. Without virginity there is no springtime; there is neither freshness nor youth.

For this reason, it is regrettable that most of the authors and doctors of contemporary occultism also side with the "dethroners" of the Virgin. Thus, they turn towards "scientism", i.e. towards knowledge which unveils and undresses, and they turn away from wisdom, i.e. from knowledge which is veiled and dressed with symbols, which is due not to *scrutinising observation* but rather to *revelatory worship*. For there is a world of difference between a scientific scrutiniser of the "naked truth" and a worshipper of the truth which is revealed through symbols. The former is inevitably an *iconoclast*; the latter is an *iconodule*. The former seeks nudity; the latter prepares himself for revelation through the fullness of symbolism.

Now, the Hermeticist is essentially an *iconophile*. For him symbols are not obstacles that must be eliminated in order to arrive at knowledge of the truth, but rather means for receiving revelation. The "clothes"—the symbols—of truth are for him not what *hides* it, but rather what *reveals* it. The entire world, in so far as it is a series of symbols, does not hide, but reveals the Word. The divine commandment: *Thou shalt not kill*, is also applicable to the domain of knowledge. He who *denies* the life of symbols, kills them in his thought. For to deny that which reveals means to kill that which lives in the domain of thought. The iconoclast is an intellectual murderer. The Hermeticist is, in contrast, an iconophile and traditionalist. This means to say that he does not side with the successive waves of iconoclasm—the waves named "reformation", "enlightenment", "scientific faith"—which set fire to forests of symbols protecting the intellectual sun of humanity against barrenness and erosion. This means to say, also, that he has as a basic principle not only the commandment "Thou shalt not kill", but also the commandment which is the foundation of all tradition—i.e. all continuity in progress, growth, development and evolution—the commandment: *Honour thy father and thy mother*.

To honour "father" and "mother" is the spirit and soul of *tradition*, of constructive continuation from the past to the present, of true progress across the ages of the path of the life of mankind towards truth. It is still more—it is the very essence of the life of the spirit and the soul. Because it is the experience of honoured paternal love which renders us capable of raising our gaze to heaven and saying with sincerity and authenticity: *Pater noster qui es in coelis* ("Our Father who art in heaven"). And it is the experience of honoured maternal love which underlies our prayer: *Sancta Maria, Mater Dei, ora pro nobis* ("Holy Mary, Mother of God, pray for us").

The source of spiritual life is in this experience of the two aspects of love: the virile love which provides for and directs our steps towards what is good for us, and the tender love which assuages all our tears. Now, when care and tenderness manifest themselves amongst human beings on earth, it is unthinkable that this unparalleled treasure is not also to be found at the very depths of the world from which mankind has arisen. Here is the foundation of *natural religion* in human consciousness—and therefore of all confidence in divine order, all worship of the invisible, and all aspiration towards the invisible. And this aspiration proves to be well founded—the invisible is in fact neither deaf nor mute. This latter fact is the foundation of *supernatural religion* in the experience of human consciousness which experiences the action of grace and revelation from above. Grace and revelation are the manifestation of paternal love from above, just as it is said in the Sermon on the Mount:

> What man of you, if his son asks him for bread, will give him a stone? Or if he asks for a fish, will give him a serpent? If you then, who are evil, know how to give good gifts to your children, how much more will your Father who is in heaven give good things to those who ask him! (Matthew vii, 9-11)

Hermeticism, in so far as it is a living tradition—for more than thirty centuries—owes its life to the commandment "Honour thy father and thy mother". For this commandment brings longevity with it—as, moreover, is said in the text: "Honour thy father and thy mother, *that thy days may be long* in the land which the LORD God gives thee" (Exodus xx, 12). It is in honouring the transcendent God ("Our Father who is in heaven") and the soul of non-fallen Nature ("the Virgin Mother") that Hermeticism—in spite of numerous temporary aberrations on the part of its representatives who at one time have given themselves up to pagan "philosophism", at another time to "cabbalism" without Christ, or to "alchemism" in order to make material gold, or lastly to modern "scientism"—has survived Egyptian decadence, Graeco-Roman pagan decadence, the organised "theologism" of the Middle Ages, the iconoclasm of the Reformation, the rationalism of the Enlightenment and, lastly, the "scientism" of the nineteenth century. Even though Hermeticism has every reason to regret, to repent, to expiate and make good a lot of its past, in this it is no exception, as all man's spiritual traditions have sinned a lot. Its longevity, however, is due to the fact that, fundamentally, it has honoured its celestial and terrestrial parents. It is not true—as its adversaries would have it—that its longevity is due to the persistence in human nature of the vices of morbid curiosity and arrogant presumption, which latter refuses to bow before a mystery. No, Hermeticism lives and survives from century to century thanks to its essential faithfulness to the divine commandments "Thou shalt not kill" and "Honour thy father and thy mother".

As a Hermeticist, I honour all the spiritual "fathers and mothers" of earthly mankind's past who have contributed to its spiritual life, including all the ancient sages, the patriarchs, Moses, the prophets, Greek philosophers, Cabbalists, apostles and saints, the masters of the Scholastic School, Christian mystics, and many others besides. Is this, therefore, syncretism? No, but thanks should be accorded to those to whom it is due. To deny is to kill; to forget is to bury. To honour and appreciate is to preserve living; to restore to memory is to recall to life. In honouring much, Hermeticism participates in the life of much; therefore it has much life. It is to this that Hermeticism owes its longevity.

In writing all these things, I am concerned all the time with the subject of Force, the eleventh Arcanum of the Tarot. For Force is life, and longevity is an important aspect of it. The Virgin is not only the source of creative élan, but also of spiritual longevity. This is why the West, in turning away more and more from the Virgin, *is growing old*, i.e. it is distancing itself from the rejuvenating source of longevity. Each revolution which has taken place in the West—that of the Reformation, the French revolution, the scientific revolution, the delirium of nationalism, the communist revolution—has advanced the process of aging in the West, because each has signified a further distancing from the principle of the Virgin. In other words, Our Lady *is* Our Lady, and is not to be replaced with impunity either by the "goddess reason", or by the "goddess biological evolution", or by the "goddess economy".

The adulation of all these "goddesses" bears witness to the unfaithfulness of so-called "Christian" mankind; it very much resembles the sort of spiritual adultery which the Biblical prophets gave so much utterance to. It is, still more, a sin against one of the commandments of faithfulness to the principle of non-fallen Nature, the Virgin Mother, namely the commandment: *Thou shalt not commit adultery*.

Every living spiritual tradition ought to be faithful to its original impulse, to the essence and substance of the cause that it espouses, and to the ideal aim that it pursues. In other words, it will preserve its identity only by remaining faithful to its effective cause, to its formal and material causes, and to its final cause. The four modes of causality of the traditional school of logic—*causa efficiens*, *causa formalis*, *causa materialis*, and *causa finalis*—also constitute the logic of causality for all living spiritual tradition. For every spiritual tradition has its original impulse, its principle and its method, as well as its ideal. It is always the *Tetragrammaton* YOD-HÉ-VAU-HÉ which underlies the reality of life as well as logical causality. The effective cause, the original impulse, is the YOD of the *Tetragrammaton*; the formal cause is the first HÉ; the material cause is the VAU; and the final cause is the second HÉ. Source, law, method and aim constitute the "*Tetragrammaton*" of every living spiritual tradition.

A spiritual tradition of universal significance—whose effective cause was God, whose formal cause was the Law, whose material cause was the community of Israel (or the *Shekinah*) and whose final cause was the Christ—was founded, or rather engendered, in the desert at Mt. Sinai. This tradition was an *alliance* in the manner of a marriage. And the conditions of durability of this tradition—or alliance, or marriage—are found expounded in the ten commandments received on Mt. Sinai. Their totality is, so to say, a "portrait" of the Virgin, the *Shekinah*, i.e. non-fallen Nature or divine Force. The Cabbalists of the *Zohar* certainly understood this, namely that the soul of the Torah (the Law) is the Virgin Mother.

> The Torah is situated between two houses, one recondite and on high, and the other more accessible. The one on high is the "Great Voice" referred to in the verse, "a great voice which did not cease" (Deut. v, 22). This voice is in the recesses and is not heard or revealed, and when it issues from the throat it utters the aspirate without sound and it flows on without ceasing, though it is so tenuous as to be inaudible. From this issues the Torah, which is the voice of Jacob. The audible voice issues from the inaudible. In due course speech is attached to it, and through the force of that speech it emerges into the open. The voice of Jacob, which is the Torah, is thus attached to two females, to this inner voice which is inaudible, and to this outer voice which is heard. Strictly speaking there are two which are inaudible and two which are heard. The two which are not heard are, first, the supernal Wisdom which is located in the Thought and is not disclosed or heard; and secondly the same Wisdom when it issues and discloses itself a little in a whisper which cannot be heard, being then called the "Great Voice", which is very tenuous and issues in a whisper. The two which are heard are those which issue from this source—the voice of Jacob and the articulation which accompanies it. This "Great Voice" which cannot be heard is a "house" to the supernal Wisdom (the female is always called "house"), and the articulation we have mentioned is a "house" to the Voice of Jacob, which is the Torah, and therefore the Torah commences with the letter *beth*, which is, as it were, a "house" to it. (*Zohar* 50b; trsl. H. Sperling and M. Simon, 5 vols., London-Bournemouth, 1949, vol. i, pp. 160-161)

Now, the written Law is the "house" of the oral Law, and the oral Law is the "house" of the Voice which whispers, which, in its turn, is the "house" of the silent Voice which is Thought or the "house" of transcendent Wisdom.

It is in this sense that the ten commandments "whisper" their message of the integral being of the Virgin, who was the instrument of realisation of the aim of the Sinai alliance—the Incarnation of the Word. The ten commandments represent the formal cause (the principles, or the Law) of realisation of the final cause (the Incarnation of the Word) of the tradition founded at Mt. Sinai. At the same time, they suggest, by way of whispering, the Virgin, who is the material cause of this realisation.

Here, therefore, is the "*Tetragrammaton*" of the tradition inaugurated by the patriarchs and founded anew by Moses: the *revelation* of God through words and deeds—this is its YOD, its effective cause; the revealed *Law*—this is its first HÉ, its formal cause; the Virgin present in the Law and in the community of Israel as its Force-life—this is its VAU, its material cause; the Messiah, lastly, whose birth is the final cause of the tradition-alliance-marriage of Israel—this is the second HÉ.

The spiritual tradition of Israel being of universal significance, every particular spiritual tradition falls under the law of its origin, life and work. In other words, no spiritual tradition can live or accomplish its mission in the world without conforming to the essential conditions of the origin, life and mission of the tradition of Israel. In other words again, there are no true traditions other than those modelled on the tradition of Israel. For it is *the* spiritual tradition *par excellence*—the model, the prototype and the law of all viable spiritual traditions which have missions to accomplish.

The following are the essential conditions to which every viable spiritual tradition must adhere: it must be founded from above; it must observe the ten commandments and be inspired by the ideal of virginity; and its aim must be implied in the will which founded it, with every human "programme" withdrawn from it.

1. *It must be founded from above.*

This means to say, in the first place, that the original impulse of a viable spiritual tradition must be given either by explicit revelation or by direct action from above acting with moral irresistibility. It is in this way that the living traditions represented by the Benedictine, Dominican, Franciscan, Jesuit, and also other orders, were founded. An explicit revelation or an irresistible vocation was the source of their origin. Thus the Benedictine order still flourishes after fifteen centuries, Dominican and Franciscan orders after seven centuries, and the Jesuit order after four centuries. Even though it would be easy to draw up a long list of their imperfections and their sins, these orders nonetheless furnish examples of a remarkable longevity. And what they have in common is above all the fact that the origin of the initiative of their foundation was from above.

2. *It must observe the ten commandments and be inspired by the ideal of virginity.*

The ten commandments signify much more than simply a moral code of daily life. They signify, further, the hygiene, the method and the conditions of fructification of the spiritual life, including all forms and degrees of practical esotericism. In this sense, they may be formulated as follows (cf. Exodus xx, 1-17):

i   surrender to the living God ("thou shalt have no other gods before me");
ii non-substitution of products of the human mind, or those of Nature, for the reality of the living God ("thou shalt not make for thyself a graven image, or any likeness");

iii   activity in the name of God without making use of his name in order to adorn oneself with it ("thou shalt not take the name of the Lord thy God in vain");

iv   practice of meditation ("remember the sabbath day, to keep it holy");

v   continuity of effort and experience ("honour thy father and thy mother");

vi   constructive attitude ("thou shalt not kill");

vii   faithfulness to the alliance ("thou shalt not commit adultery");

viii   renunciation of the desire to accept merit which is neither the fruit of one's own work nor the gift of grace ("thou shalt not steal");

ix   renunciation of an accusatory role towards others ("thou shalt not bear false witness against thy neighbour");

x   respectful consideration for the private and personal life of others ("thou shalt not covet thy neighbour's house").

These constitute the ten foundations not only for a healthy moral life but also for all mystical, gnostic, magical and Hermetic practice.

In fact, mysticism is the awakening of the soul to the reality of the presence of God. This awakening is possible only towards the living God, only towards the divine Person, whereas pantheism offers only the perspective of letting oneself be lulled by the undulation of the ocean of deified Nature, and atheism offers only nothingness. Gnosis is what reflected consciousness apprehends of mystical experience and revelation from above. The fundamental law of gnosis is not to substitute imagery drawn from the human mind, or from Nature, for divine intuition. Magic is the bringing into play of that which consciousness has received from mysticism and gnosis. Now, the fundamental law of sacred magic is to act in and through the name of the Divine, whilst guarding against making the name of the Divine an instrument of one's own will. Hermeticism is the life of thought *within* the whole organism of mysticism, gnosis and magic. Its fundamental law is meditation, i.e. the practice of "remembering the sabbath day, to keep it holy". Meditation is "sanctified rest", where thought is turned towards that which is above.

This, then, is the role of the first four commandments in spiritual practice. The other six commandments state the fundamental laws of spiritual culture or discipline serving as a basis for the spiritual practice to which the first four commandments relate.

In truth, in order to advance one has to learn. In order to learn, one has to appreciate the experience of the past and one has to *continue* it. All progress presupposes continuity—coherence between the past, present and future. This is stated by the fifth commandment: *Honour thy father and thy mother*. There only is real progress within a living *tradition*. For life—spiritual as well as biological—is always tradition, i.e. continuity. Therefore, one has to abstain from all action that

298 MEDITATIONS ON THE TAROT

breaks continuity, cutting the current of life. It is the fundamental law of a *constructive* attitude, which is essential in spiritual life, that is stated by the sixth commandment: *Thou shalt not kill*. Continuity—or tradition and life—implies faithfulness to the cause that is espoused, to the direction taken, to the ideal that one has as a guide, and to all alliances with entities above and with human beings below, for the sake of the continuity of life. This is what is stated by the seventh commandment: *Thou shalt not commit adultery*. There is carnal adultery, psychic adultery and spiritual adultery. The Biblical prophets spoke of this in relation to the unfaithfulness to the alliance of Sinai on the part of the kings and people of Israel, who on many occasions gave themselves up to cults of Canaanite divinities. This is today also the case when one embraces, for example, the Vedanta or Buddhism, whilst having been baptised and sufficiently instructed in order to have access—given good will—to experience of the sublime Christian mysteries. I am speaking neither about the *study* nor the adoption of the *technical methods* of yoga, Vedanta or Buddhism, but only about the case where one changes *faith*, i.e. where one substitutes the ideal of liberation for that of love, an impersonal God for the personal God, return to the state of potentiality (or *nirvana*) for the *kingdom of God*, a wise instructor for the Saviour, and so on. However, there is no element of spiritual adultery in the case of J. M. Déchanet, for example; he is the author of *La Voie du silence* (trsl. R. X. Hindmarsh, *Christian Yoga*, London, 1960), who adapted the technical methods of yoga to Christian spiritual practice. For nothing is more natural and legitimate than to learn and make use of the benefits of *experiences* accumulated in the East or West. If western medicine saves the lives of millions in the East, why should not oriental yoga help millions in the West, those engaged in spiritual practice, to attain the equilibrium and psycho-physical health that the technical methods of yoga render possible in such an effective way? Exchange of the fruits of experience between the various cultural realms of mankind is simply an expression of the fact of human brotherhood. It expresses reciprocal help between members of a single family, and has nothing in common with spiritual adultery, i.e. with unfaithfulness to the spiritual alliance or faith to which one belongs or to which one is called to belong.

All the fruits of human experience merit being studied and examined—and, according to their merit, accepted or rejected. But experience is one thing and faith, or metaphysical ideal, is another. With the latter what is at stake are the *moral values* that one cannot change without either essential ruin or gain in the life of soul and spirit. One cannot change faith without gaining or losing. A Negro fetishist who embraces Islam gains; a Christian who is converted to Islam loses. The former gains new moral values for his soul; the latter loses moral values from his soul. Regrettable or not, it is a fact that religions constitute a scale of moral and spiritual values. They are not equal—being stages of mankind's evolution over millennia, on the one hand, and successive revelations from above, on the other hand. There is therefore no religion without value, or that is even intrinsically false or "diabolical" ; but, on the other hand, there is no religion of higher value than that of love.

Spiritual adultery is therefore the exchange of a higher moral and spiritual value for a lower moral and spiritual value. It is, for example, the exchange of: the living God for an impersonal divinity; Christ crucified and resurrected for a sage deep in meditation; the Holy Virgin-Mother for Nature in evolution; the community of saints, apostles, martyrs, monks, confessors, church doctors and virgins for a "community of geniuses" of philosophy, art, science, etc.

We have said that all the fruits of human experience merit being studied and examined — and, according to their merit, accepted or rejected. In speaking of spiritual experience, there are certainly fruits of experience that must be rejected. These are those that are due to *theft*, i.e. where there is the desire to obtain without effort or sacrifice results whose worth implies effort and sacrifice. Thus Gurdjieff, the master of P. D. Ouspensky (the author of *Tertium Organum*), taught that there are three ways of coming out of the confinement of ordinary experience and consciousness — the way of the yogi, the way of the monk and that of the "artful man" (*put' khitrogo cheloviek* in Russian). What the yogi and the monk achieve after long endeavours of discipline and sacrifice, the "artful man" (*khitryi cheloviek*) can achieve without effort, without sacrifice, and almost immediately, taking a pill containing quite assorted elements.

There are indeed people who seek transcendental experience by means of the cactus peyote (*Echinocactus Williamsii*, or *Anhalonium Williamsii*, or even *Lophophora Williamsii Lemaire*), whose usage towards the end of evoking visions was widespread amongst tribes of Red Indians from Mexico to Canada, which led to the foundation of a "Native American Church", an indigenous American church (cf. Oliver La Farge, *A Pictorial History of the American Indian*, London, 1962). What is understandable and quite excusable with respect to American Indians — seeing their desperate situation — is not so with respect to people of European origin, the heirs of the Christian civilisation of the West. Those seeking transcendental experience by such means evidently want to dispense with the costs of the way of regular spiritual development, in order to obtain cheaply what others obtain only after much effort and sacrifice.

The commandment: *Thou shalt not steal* is still of fundamental importance for the spiritual life. Every school of authentic spirituality owes its continuation to the commandment which preserves its authenticity and which, for the spiritual domain, comes down to a fundamental rule of agricultural labour: you will harvest only after having tilled the earth, only after having sown, and only after having waited for the time when the fruit will be ripe for harvesting. All "tricks" of a technical nature, having as their aim the dispensing with the effort and sacrifice required for normal spiritual growth and development, thus fall under the heading of sinning against the eighth commandment.

There still remain two commandments as indispensable for the spiritual life as the eight commandments already discussed: *Thou shalt not bear false witness against they neighbour*, and *Thou shalt not covet thy neighbour's house*.

These two commandments relate to the spirit of *rivalry*, which manifests itself either as negative criticism or as envy. This means to say that every spiritual movement, every spiritual tradition, every school of spirituality, and every disciple or so-called "master" of a school of spiritual life, should in no way be motivated by a spirit of rivalry, but rather by love for the cause and ideal.

Thus St. Teresa of Avila, enamoured by the cause and ideal of a life entirely devoted to God, accomplished a profound reform of the Carmelite order without destroying the unity of the Church, and without accusing or condemning anyone. At the same time the Augustinian monk Martin Luther, given up to the spirit of criticism, thought out a reform of the whole Church and, carried away by the desire to do better, founded a rival church, whilst declaring Rome as "the seat of the antichrist" and its faithful either as "poor strays" or as "wolves in sheep's clothing". Therefore St. Teresa, St. John of the Cross, St. Peter of Alcantara, St. Julian of Avila and other contempories of the same spiritual stature would, according·to Luther, be "strays" or "ravishing wolves in sheep's clothing", i.e. either deceived or deceivers. Here is a clear case of "bearing false witness against thy neighbour" due to the spirit of criticism and rivalry. Anyone who takes on himself the mission of judge can act only in the sense of destruction. Anyone who begins to criticise before long passes to censure and sooner or later ends up by condemning, which leads inevitably to division into hostile camps and to other forms of destruction.

Criticism and polemicism are mortal enemies of the spiritual life. For they signify the substitution of destructive electrical energy for constructive vital force. A complete change of the inspiring and motivating source takes place when a person or spiritual movement becomes engaged in the way of rivalry—with the criticism and polemicism that it comprises. Once carried away by electricity, "bearing witness against thy neighbour" will always be essentially and intrinsically false.

Now, there is no authentic spirituality which owes its origin and existence to opposition or rivalry. "To be *against* something" is sterile and is never capable of engendering a viable tradition or giving birth to a school of spiritual life, whilst "to be *for* something" is fertile and is an indispensable condition for all constructive activity. This includes every tradition or viable school of spirituality.

The spirit underlying "bearing false witness against thy neighbour" and "coveting thy neighbour's house" is spiritually sterile and destructive. Particular spiritual schools and traditions should not, in order to live, be rivals, but should live in consciousness of the *kinship* of their cause and ideals, if there *is* kinship; or, if there is not, they should respect the domain of freedom of the other—the "house" proper to it—without mixing this with envy or criticism. If there is no cooperation resulting from kinship of causes and ideals, then spiritual traditions and schools should live and let live in peace!

Be that as it may, the totality of the ten commandments constitutes the law of life, progress and fertility for spiritual traditions and schools, just as it is that of the life, progress and fertility of each individual engaged on a path of spiritual practice. For the ten commandments—when comprehended and practised— signify harmony with non-fallen Nature, with the Virgin and the principle of virginity, i.e. with the Force of the eleventh Arcanum of the Tarot.

Haec est totius fortitudinis
fortitudo fortis:
quia vincet omnem rem subtilem,
omnemque solidam penetrabit.
     (*Tabula Smaragdina*, 9)

Meditation on the
Twelfth Major Arcanum of the Tarot

THE HANGED MAN
LE PENDU

Truly, truly, I say to you,
unless one is born anew,
he cannot see the kingdom of God...
Truly, truly, I say to you,
unless one is born of water and the Spirit,
he cannot enter the kingdom of God...
The wind blows where it wills,
and you hear the sound of it,
but you do not know whence it comes
   or whither it goes;
so it is with everyone who is born of the Spirit.
                              (John iii, 3, 5, 8)

Foxes have holes, and birds of the air have nests;
but the Son of man has nowhere to lay his head.
                              (Matthew viii, 20)

Then the righteous will shine like the sun
in the kingdom of their Father.
                    (Matthew xiii, 43)

That which I had to say
about the operation of *sol*
is completed.
   (*Tabula Smaragdina*, 13)

LETTER XII

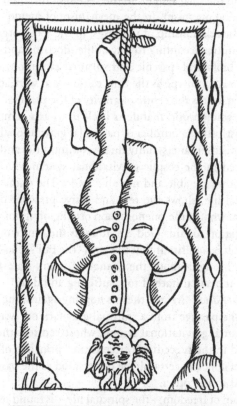

THE HANGED MAN

Dear Unknown Friend,

Here before us is the Card of the twelfth Arcanum of the Tarot, the Hanged Man. It represents a young man suspended by one foot between two trees, with branches cut close to the trunk, from a transversal beam that they support, thus forming a porch.

The position of the man—upside down, head below, hanging by one foot in a porch, with his free leg folded back at the knee and his arms bound behind his back—at first naturally evokes ideas of gravitation and of the torture that conflict with it can inflict on man. Therefore, our first impression of the Card plunges us into the heart of the problem of the relationship between man and gravitation, and the conflicts that this relationship entails.

Gravitation—physical, psychic and spiritual—occupies a central place as a regulating factor in the solar system, in the system of the atom, in the biological cell, in the biological organism, in the mechanism of memory and the association of ideas, in the relationship of the sexes, in the social organism, in the formation of communities according to way of life, doctrine and ideal, and, lastly, in the process of biological, psychic and spiritual evolution, where a centre of gravity—or universal prototype as the final cause—is at work across the ages, just as the sun, in so far as it is the centre of gravity of the planetary system, operates across space. The whole world manifests itself to us as a comprehensive system of gravitation constituting a number of particular gravitational systems—such as atoms, cells, organisms, planets, individuals, communities and hierarchies. Each one of us is placed in the cosmic gravitational system which determines our freedom, i.e. what we are able and not able to do. The domain of our freedom itself, our spiritual life, shows the real and active presence of gravitation of a spiritual order. For what is the phenomenon of religion if not the manifestation of spiritual gravitation towards God, i.e. towards the centre of spiritual gravitation of the world? It is significant that the term "the Fall"—chosen for the primordial event which brought about the change of man's state from that named "paradise" to the terrestrial state of toil, suffering and death—is borrowed from the domain of *gravitation*. In fact, there is nothing against the conception of the Fall of Adam as the passage from a spiritual gravitational system, whose centre is God, to a terrestrial gravitational system, whose centre is the serpent (that we have characterised in the preceding Letter as the "principle of electricity"). The Fall, as a phenomenon, can certainly be understood as the passage from the one gravitational field to the other.

Now, the domain of freedom—the spiritual life—is found placed between two gravitational fields with two different centres. The Gospel designates them as "heaven" and "this world", or as the "kingdom of God" and the "kingdom of the prince of this world". And it designates those whose will follows or is submitted to the gravitation of "this world" as "children of this world", and those whose will follows the gravitation of "heaven" as the "children (or the sons) of light".

The Manichaeans straight away drew the conclusion from this that the invisible world, or heaven, is good and the visible world of Nature is bad, wholly forgetting the fact that evil is of spiritual origin, and is therefore invisible, and that good is impressed into created Nature, and is therefore also visible. Although the two gravitational fields are interpenetrating and one could not, or should not, identify them simply with visible Nature and the invisible spiritual world, they are nevertheless certainly real and *morally* quite discernible. For just as there is a "discernment of spirits", of which the apostle Paul speaks, so there is a discernment of the phenomena of Nature, which manifests, for example, in medical diagnosis, in the choice of remedies from the kingdoms of Nature, in the domain of physical and psychic hygiene, etc.

The human being participates in these two gravitational fields, as the apostle Paul had in mind when he said:

> For the desires of the flesh are against the Spirit, and the desires of the Spirit are against the flesh; for these are opposed to each other, to prevent you from doing what you would. (Galatians v, 17)

These "opposing desires" are the tendencies through which the two gravitational fields manifest themselves. The man who lives in the grip of gravitation of "this world" at the expense of the gravitation of "heaven" is the "carnal man"; he who lives in equilibrium between the two gravitational fields is the "psychic man"; and, lastly, the one who lives under the sway of the gravitation of "heaven" is the "spiritual man".

It is this latter who constitutes the subject of the twelfth Arcanum of the Tarot, for it is an upside-down man that the twelfth Card represents. The Hanged Man represents the condition of one in the life of whom gravitation from above has replaced that from below.

Firstly, it should be said that attraction from above is as real as that from below, and that the condition of a human being who has passed, whilst living, from the field of terrestrial gravitation into that of heaven is indeed comparable to that of the Hanged Man of the Card. This is at one and the same time a benefaction and a martyrdom; both are very real.

The history of the human race bears witness to the reality of attraction from above. The exodus into Egyptian, Palestinian, Syrian and other deserts inaugurated by St. Paul of Thebes and St. Anthony the Great were nothing other than the manifestation of irresistible attraction from above. The desert fathers, pioneers of this exodus, had no programme or plan to found any communities or schools of Christian spirituality comparable to the schools of yoga in India. No, what happened to them was the irresistible appeal from above to solitude and a life given up entirely to spiritual reality. Thus, St. Anthony the Great said:

> As fish who remain on dry land die, so do monks who linger outside of the cell, or who pass time with people of the world, slacken the tension of solitude. Therefore it is necessary — as fish do to the sea — that we return to the cell, so as not to forget, through dallying outside, our interior vigil. (St. Anthony the Great, *Apophthegmata*, x)

Thus, the "tension of solitude" is the element proper to souls under the sway of attraction from above. It was "as fish seeking the sea" that they sought solitude where they found the "tension", i.e. the relationship between the gravitation of heaven and that of earth, which was as right for them as water is for fish. It was in solitude that they could *live*, i.e. develop spiritual temperature, breathe spiritual air, quench their spiritual thirst and satisfy their spiritual hunger. Outside of the solitude and tension that the "interior vigil" meant to them, the desert fathers felt cold, were unable to breathe, and suffered spiritual hunger and thirst.

This, therefore, is really something quite different from programmes and plans: the reality of the attraction of heaven at work in the lives of the desert fathers.

They were pioneers. Before long, still during their lifetime, the deserts of Thebais, Neutra and Ceuta were peopled with anchorites. Then, in Upper Egypt, St. Pachomius founded cenobites, the prototypes of the monasteries that we know, where several hermits lived together under a superior or abbot. This form of life was, much later, adapted and perfected by St. Basil in the East, and by St. Augustine, St. Cassian and St. Benedict in the West.

Although all this immense subsequent development was present in germ in the solitary lives of St. Paul of Thebes and St. Anthony the Great, this was not at all the conscious motive for their retreat into the desert. This motive was solely the desire for solitude caused by the irresistible attraction of heaven.

The attraction of heaven is so real that it can take hold of not only the soul but also the physical body. Then the body is carried up and no longer touches the ground. The following is what St. Teresa of Avila, who had this experience, wrote in her "Life" (her autobiography):

> Then the cloud rises to heaven taking the soul with it, and begins to show it the features of the kingdom He has prepared for it. I do not know whether this is an accurate comparison, but in point of fact that is how it happens. In these raptures, the soul no longer seems to animate the body; its natural heat therefore is felt to diminish and it gradually gets cold, though with a feeling of very great joy and sweetness. Here there is no possibility of resisting . . . rapture is, as a rule, irresistible. Before you can be warned by a thought or help yourself in any way, it comes as a quick and violent shock; you see and feel this cloud, or this powerful eagle rising and bearing you up on its wings. You realise, I repeat, and indeed see that you are being carried away you know not where. . . We have to go willingly wherever we are carried, for in fact, we are being borne off whether we like it or not. In this emergency very often I should like to resist, and I exert all my strength to do so, especially at such times as I am in a public place, and very often when I am in private also, because I am afraid of delusions. Sometimes with a great struggle I have been able to do something against it. But it has been like fighting a great giant, and has left me utterly exhausted. At other times resistance has been impossible; my soul has been carried away, and usually my head as well, without my being able to prevent it; *and sometimes it has affected my whole body,*

which has been lifted from the ground. . .It seemed to me when I tried to resist that a great force, for which I can find no comparison, *was lifting me up from beneath my feet*. It came with greater violence than any other spiritual experience. . .I confess that in me it aroused a great fear, at first a very great fear. One sees one's body being lifted from the ground; and though the soul draws it up after itself, and does so most gently if it does not resist, one does not lose consciousness. At least I myself was sufficiently aware to realise that I was being lifted. . .(*The Life of St. Teresa of Avila*; trsl. J. M. Cohen, London, 1957, pp. 136-138)

This is a simple and veracious testimony of the reality of the irresistible attraction from above and of the passage from the field of terrestrial gravitation to the field of celestial gravitation. St. Teresa had the experience where the body was "drawn up after the soul" which was, in its turn, under the sway of attraction emanating from the centre of spiritual attraction which was, for her, the Lord.

But when the centre of spiritual attraction, when the Lord himself, is clothed in a body—which was the case in the earthly life of Jesus Christ—what happens then? There is then no question of being carried off in a rapture, because to what place could the Humanity of the Lord be carried off—the "rapturing" and "carrying off" principle, the centre of spiritual gravitation, being in itself?

Now, the Gospel clarifies this point for us. It says:

When evening came, his disciples went down to the sea, got into a boat, and started across the sea to Capernaum. It was now dark, and Jesus had not yet come to them. The sea rose because a strong wind was blowing. When they had rowed about three or four miles, they saw Jesus walking on the sea and drawing near to the boat. They were frightened, but he said to them: It is I; do not be afraid. (John vi, 16-20)
And Peter answered him: Lord, if it is you, bid me come to you on the water. He said: Come! So Peter got out of the boat *and walked on the water and came to Jesus*. But when he saw the wind, he was afraid, and beginning to sink he cried out: Lord, save me! Jesus immediately reached out his hand *and caught him*, saying to him: O man of little faith, why did you doubt? (Matthew xiv, 28-31)

The key to the answer is found above all in the words, "It is I; do not be afraid". The accepted translation of *ego eimi, me phobeisthe* in Greek, or *ego sum, nolite timere* in Latin, is: "It is I; do not be afraid". This is right and there is nothing to be said against it—*ego eimi* and *ego sum* mean literally "I am", but in the given *context* signify "It is I". The context bears this out. This is why the translation "It is I" is not only justified, but also—in view of the context—necessary. It is however legitimate, without questioning the rightness of the accepted translation, to *understand* the words *ego eimi* (*ego sum*) more literally, and, at the same time, more profoundly. For *two* questions are implied in the fear and confusion of the disciples. "*Who* is the one who we see walking on the water?" and "*How* is he able to walk on the water?"

Now, "It is I" is the answer to the first question, and "*I am*" is the answer to the second. For "I am" reveals an esoteric truth (i.e. profound and not immediately obvious), whilst "It is I" is an exoteric or factual answer. It *hides* and *contains*, as its kernel, the esoteric answer. What is, therefore, the esoteric truth that the words "I am; do not be afraid" reveal?

"*I am*" is the formula of revelation in the world of the *existence* of the divine *essence* of Jesus Christ. The whole Gospel is the history of this gradual revelation, the stages of which it summarises through the diverse aspects of the comprehensive "*I am*", such as "*I am* the true vine", "*I am* the way, the truth and the life", "*I am* the door", "*I am* the bread of life", "*I am* the good shepherd", "*I am* the light of the world" and "*I am* the resurrection and the life".

Now, the words "I am; do not be afraid" spoken by the one walking on the water amount to the statement: "*I am gravitation*, and he who holds to me will never sink or be engulfed". Because *fear* is due to the menace of being engulfed by elemental forces of gravitation of a lower order, i.e. of being carried away by the play of blind forces from the agitated "sea" of the "electrical field" of *death*. "*I am*; do not be afraid" is therefore the message of the centre, or Master, of celestial gravitation, demonstrated by the action of support with regard to Peter, who was saved from sinking. Thus, there is another field of gravitation than that of death, and he who unites himself with it can *walk on water*, i.e. transcend the agitated element of "this world", the electrical gravitational field of the serpent. This message contains not only the invitation to have recourse to the "kingdom of heaven", but also the solemn declaration of the *immortality* of the soul, in so far as the soul is capable of transcending the engulfing gravitation and "walking on the water".

Peter, who "got out of the boat and walked on the water and came to Jesus", experienced the same elevating rapture that St. Teresa describes. He *got out* of the boat, which means — in view of all the laws of reason and memory — that he was taken out of the domain of ordinary consciousness, i.e. that of reason, memory and sense perception, and he walked on the water, *drawn by Jesus*. He experienced, therefore, the same elevation of the soul which draws the body up after it as spoken of by St. Teresa. He even experienced the same fear which St. Teresa confessed took hold of her in seeing "one's body being lifted from the ground". And just as she was drawn by a hand extended from above, so did Peter have the experience of help from the same hand.

Now, St. Teresa and St. Peter — the one and the other — had the same experience of psycho-somatic ecstasy (as, moreover, many other saints have had). But the question which occupies us is that of the state of Jesus Christ himself, walking on the water. Was it an ecstasy for him also?

No. And this is why: ecstasy is the going out of the soul from the domain of the powers of discursive reason, memory and imagination — sometimes followed by the body. Both Peter and St. Teresa passed in their rapture through the stages: "*You are*"; "I draw near to *You*"; "It is not I, but *You* who lives and acts in me". It is therefore the attraction of the *divine You*, resulting in union with him, which constitutes the essence of their psycho-somatic ecstasy, whilst Jesus Christ walked on the water not by virtue of *ecstasy* — not by going out of his Humanity — but rather by virtue of *enstasy*, i.e. centering in himself, which is the active virtue of the formula "*I am*; do not be afraid". The Humanity of Jesus Christ walking on the water did not lead to a *You* attracting and supporting it, but rather to the *divine I* of the Son of the eternal Father present in itself.

EGO SUM; nolite timere — means to say therefore: I am gravitation; just as the sun in the visible world bears itself and attracts the planets, so am I the true sun of the invisible world who bears himself and attracts and supports other beings. "*Do not be afraid, for I AM*."

Yet Jesus Christ walking on the water reveals still another mystery than that of the sun of the spiritual world, the centre of celestial gravitation. For not only did he *stand* on the water — which would suffice to reveal and demonstrate this truth — but he also *walked* on the water, i.e. he moved in a quite definite direction in the horizontal sense. He walked towards the boat in which his disciples rowed. There, in his walking towards the boat, is already contained in germ — essentially revealing it — his whole work, temporal and eternal, i.e. his sacrifice, his resurrection, and all that is implied in his promise: "Lo, I am with you always, until the end of the world" (Matthew xxviii, 20).

The boat with his disciples is, therefore, and will be until the end of the world, the aim of the *I am* walking on the water. His enstasy, his profound centering in himself, does not distance him from the navigators on the agitated sea of history and evolution, and does not make him disappear into the other sea — the calm sea of *nirvana* — but rather, on the contrary, it entails that he walks, until the end of the world, after the boat with his disciples.

The hermits of the desert, the psycho-somatic ecstasy of St. Teresa and St. Peter, Jesus Christ walking on the water — the totality of these facts should bring to the light of our minds the spiritual and manifest *reality* of celestial gravitation. At least, it is to this end that we have dwelt upon these things.

It is necessary, nevertheless, to add here a consideration of facts which appear to belong to the sphere of celestial gravitation but which are, in reality, of a contrary nature. The facts that I have in mind are those of "levitation", i.e. instances of elevation of the body from the ground, which one could be tempted to regard as being of the same nature as the psycho-somatic raptures of St. Teresa and St. Peter, or even as the walking of Jesus Christ on the water.

Thus, legend attributes to Simon Magus that he could elevate himself physically in the air. Cases of the elevation of spiritualist mediums are also known in our time. It is characteristic that even Gérard van Rijnberk, who truly ought to have known better, did not distinguish the levitation of mediums from that which accompanies the rapture of saints. This is what he says concerning the "levitation of mediums":

> The phenomenon of levitation has been affirmed for several holy personages of the Hindu, Buddhist and Christian religions. They raised themselves in the air several feet and hovered for some time without any means of support. This fact has been established for a number of saints of the Catholic Church.* I restrict myself to naming the great Teresa (sixteenth century), her contemporary John of the Cross, Peter of Alcantara, also of the same period, then a little later Joseph of Copertino (1603-1623), who was seen flying through the air several times...This phenomenon has been related also of several mediums, but unfortunately almost without exception this has taken place in complete darkness. Home alone accomplished it once in the full light of day. It is necessary to reserve judgement on these facts which certainly seem quite incredible. (Gérard van Rijnberk, *Les métasciences biologiques — métaphysiologie et métapsychologie*, Paris, 1952, pp. 154-155).

This is all that this author "who for half a century studied occultism with profound respect" (Gérard van Rijnberk, op. cit., p. 205) had to say on the subject of levitation.

There is room here, however, to say something more. There is in the first place a distinction between elevation of the body due to *celestial attraction* and elevation of the body effected by electrical *repelling action* directed from below. The difference as such is comparable to that between the flight of a balloon filled with warm air and the flight of a rocket due to repulsion effected by the current that it emits. An example of the second kind of levitation is known to me at first hand:

> A middle-aged gentleman (he was American) was talking with a travelling companion in a compartment on an international train in Europe. The conversation revolved around the diverse currents and methods of comtemporary occultism. The American advanced the radical thesis that there is a practical occultism and a literary or verbal occultism, and that the latter is hardly

---

*In fact, one finds the following cases of levitation cited in Joseph von Görres, *Die Christliche Mystik* (5 vols.; Regensburg, 1836-1842): St. Ambrosius Sensedonio (i, p. 324); St. Philip of Néri (ii, p. 9); St. Teresa of Avila (ii, p. 122); St. Thomas Aquinas (ii, p. 208); St. Saviour of Horta (ii, p. 214); St. Thomas of Villanova (ii, p. 253); St. Catherine of Sienna (ii, p.426); Joan of Carniola (ii, pp. 493-494); St. Mary of Agréda (ii, p. 520); St. Peter of Alcantara (ii, pp. 523, 529); Christine the Admirable (ii, p. 535); Adelaide of Adelhausen (ii, p. 536); Esperance of Brenegalla and Agnes of Bohemia (ii, p. 537); St. Colette, Dalmatius of Gerona, Anthony of St. Reine, St. Francis of Assisi, Bernard of Courléon and St. Joseph of Copertino (ii, p. 539); Joan Rodriguez (ii, p. 548); St. Dominique of Jesus-Maria, the Blessed Gerardesca of Pisa and Elisabeth of Falkenstein (ii, p. 549); Damian of Vicari, Agnes of Chatillon, Michael Lazar and Peter of Regolada (ii, pp. 551-552).

to be taken seriously, and that it is only the former kind of occultism that is worthy of its name. As his interlocutor would not
let himself be convinced that facts of visible realisation are the
sole criteria of truth and value, the American believed it right
to convince his interlocutor by a demonstration of fact—which
he announced. Having announced it, he stretched out on his
couchette (there were only these two people in the compartment) and started to breathe deeply, keeping complete silence.
In one or two minutes his body, extended as it was on the
couchette, slowly rose in the air to a height of several inches and
remained hovering for close to a minute. This demonstration
having evoked in his interlocutor only a profound disgust, the
anonymous master of levitation left the compartment before
long and did not show himself again.

What merits drawing attention to—other than the fact of levitation effected
by the will—is that the thing was done through a considerable effort. The experimenter had to be silent and concentrate himself entirely on a centre in his
organism in order to make a current of energy emanate which, acting in consecutive
waves, repulsed him from the couchette and thus made him rise in the air. He
did not elevate himself very high, because, it seems, elevation to a greater height
would require an excessive effort. The demonstration having been made, the experimenter had a fatigued look and had no further desire to converse. A loss of
energy in him was quite evident.

With respect to spiritualist mediums—no matter whether their levitation takes
place in darkness or in the full light of day, visibility being in no way the sole
means of control—there is nothing, from the Hermetic point of view, against admitting the possibility and even reality of their levitation. If there are cases of levitation of objects such as tables, attested through photography, why should it not
be possible for mediums themselves to be able to be elevated in the air, as physical
objects, by the same force which works for other physical objects? It is said that
the driving energy producing physical phenomena at mediumistic seances
emanates from the medium. But why should this energy, once exteriorised from
the medium, not be able to elevate the medium himself—or herself? Why can
it not also support the body of the medium?

Human electricity coming out from the organism of the medium can certainly
make it the object of its action—which, moreover, "is narrated of several mediums"
(Gérard van Rijnberk, op. cit., p. 155). But what is important to draw attention
to in the case of the levitation of mediums is that the agent that levitates mediums
is the same as that which effects the levitation of tables and other physical objects
and that, consequently, it is not—and cannot be—a matter of the effect of the
spiritual or "celestial gravitation" which acts in the case of the rapture of saints.

There are therefore *three* categories of levitation of the human body: rapture
due to "celestial gravitation", levitation due to a current of human electricity

emitted wilfully (arbitrary magic), or involuntarily (mediumistic levitation). According to tradition, Simon Magus—whom St. Peter, through prayer, caused to fall—is attributed with levitation achieved through arbitrary magic. Levitation through arbitrary magic and mediumistic levitation have this in common, that both are effected by electrical force emanating from the human organism and acting by repulsion; in this they differ from the levitation of saints, which is due to attraction from above.

Concerning the centre from which is made to emanate the current necessary for "Simonian" levitation, it is that of the "four-petalled lotus" (*muladhara chakra*), where the "serpent power" (*kundalini*)—latent electrical force—is found. Now, this "serpent power" can be awoken and directed either above (yoga) or below and outside (arbitrary magic). In the latter case it serves as the agent in levitation. It is thus that the American occultist, whose demonstration of levitation we recounted above, accomplished this phenomenon. One can, without going into details, mention in this context the excursions in the countryside of witches and sorcerers, of whom it is said that they make use of "broomsticks" for this end. Now, the repulsing current emanating from the centre at the base of the spine certainly produces the impression of a beam in the form of a broomstick; sorcerers, when splitting themselves off from, and leaving behind, their physical body, move after the fashion of modern rocket reactions. Thus in Estonia, people in the country possess a special term for this phenomenon which, moreover, is more adequate than "broomstick", namely *tulehänt*, which means to say "beam of fire".

It follows, therefore, from the foregoing, that one must not cast all in the same mould: the levitation of saints, "Simonian" levitation, and that of mediums. It is truly not something superhuman to distinguish them with sufficient clarity so that they are in no way confused, provided that one takes the trouble.

Returning to the subject of the man who lives under the law of celestial gravitation—the Hanged Man—let us see what it is to live on the earth whilst being, at the same time, under the sway of the "celestial gravitational field".

The law of terrestrial gravitation, evolution and earthly life in general is *enfoldment*, i.e. the coagulation of mental, psychic and physical stuff around relative centres of gravitation, such as the earth, the nation, the individual, the organism—whilst the law of celestial gravitation, evolution, and spiritual life in general is *radiation*, i.e. the extension of mental, psychic and physical stuff rising up to an absolute centre of gravitation. "Then the righteous will shine like the sun in the kingdom of their Father" (Matthew xiii, 43)—this is a precise and comprehensive characterisation of the law of celestial gravitation.

The corresponding formula expressing the essence of the law of terrestrial gravitation is found in chapter six of Genesis: "The *giants* were on the earth in those days, and also afterward, when the sons of God came into the daughters of men, and they bore children to them. These are the heroes who were famous in antiquity" (Genesis vi, 4).

The "sons of God" (*bene ha-elohim*), i.e. entities who lived in the field of divine gravitation, changed gravitational field in giving way to the attraction of *possession* or *enfoldment*, and gave birth to beings endowed with a great *force of enfoldment*—the "giants" (*nephelim*). They exchanged radiation (the state of the sons of God) for enfoldment (the state of the giants on earth). And since this time the world of enfoldment has tended to produce the *strong hero* (*gibbor*), whilst the world of radiation has tended to give birth to the herald of radiation, the *righteous man* (*tsaddik*), on the earth. It was not so long ago that Friedrich Nietzsche loudly proclaimed himself champion of the ideal of the *gibbor* or "superman" (*Uebermensch*). Moreover, having once birched the Righteous One, Nietzsche wove a crown of thorns, placed it on His head, and affronted and mocked Him in his books *Ecce Homo* and *Antichrist*.

The world is divided. There are those who worship the *gibbor*, the strong hero—Nietzsche manifested with force and talent that this is so—and there are those who love the *tsaddik*, the righteous man.

Yes, indeed, this is so. Terrestrial gravitation, "the flesh", pushes mankind towards the ideal of enfoldment, i.e. possession, power and enjoyment, whilst celestial gravitation, "the spirit", draws mankind towards the ideal of radiation, i.e. poverty, obedience and chastity.

May occultists, esotericists and Hermeticists take account of this state of things and may they understand that the only side they can take without betraying the soul of the Hermetic tradition is that of ranging themselves resolutely and without reserve on the side of radiation, i.e. to take the side of the righteous man, the Hanged Man! May they abandon the dreams and phantoms having to do with the "superman", which still haunt certain esoteric fraternities and societies either in the guise of a "Grand Master", or a "Great Initiate", or an "Arch Mage"! May our communities become those of people who learn from everyone instead of teaching everyone! May they recruit people who live in consciousness of having behaved wrongly towards God, neighbour and the world, rather than those who think they are in the right. In a word, may they be subject to celestial attraction, which acts in awakening the inclination towards and love for poverty, obedience and chastity!

We must not only see and think clearly, but also *will clearly*. For one cannot serve two masters at once.

I have moved away from the subject of the concrete state of the man who lives under the law of celestial gravitation. Let us return to this.

Two things characterise the state of the *spiritual man*: that he is *suspended* and that he is *upside down*. Here is what St. Teresa says about the first characteristic trait:

> The soul seems to me to be in this state when no comfort comes
> to it from heaven and it is not there itself, and when it desires
> none from the earth and is not there either. Then it is as if
> crucified between heaven and earth, suffering and receiving no

help from either. (*The Life of St. Teresa of Avila*; trsl. J. M. Cohen, London, 1957, p. 140)

The soul is suspended between heaven and earth; it experiences complete *solitude*. For here it is no longer a matter of ordinary solitude where one is alone *in* the world, but rather of complete solitude where one is alone because one is *outside* of the world — the celestial as well as the terrestrial world.

> Transported thus into this desert it seems that the soul can cer-
> tainly, in all truth, say with the Royal Prophet, "I lie awake, I
> am like a lonely bird on the housetop." (Psalm 102, 7) It is possi-
> ble that King David was experiencing this same loneliness when
> he wrote these words. This verse comes to my mind at these times
> in such a way that it seems to be fulfilled in me. It is a comfort
> to me to know that others have felt these extremes of loneliness,
> and an even greater comfort that they have been people of such
> quality. (*The Life of St. Teresa*; trsl. J. M. Cohen, London, 1957,
> p. 139)

This is the "zero point" between the fields of terrestrial and celestial gravitation. It is from there that the soul either is elevated in contemplation of divine and celestial things, or descends to act in the human and terrestrial domain, but this "zero point" is certainly the place of its permanent sojourn. After elevation or after the accomplishment of an act, it returns there. The solitude of the desert between the two worlds is its abode.

The other characteristic trait of the *spiritual man* is that he is upside down. This means to say, firstly, that the "solid ground" under his feet is found above, whilst the ground below is only the concern and perception of the head. Second-ly, it means to say that his *will* is connected with heaven and is found in immedi-ate contact (not by the intermediary of thought and feeling) with the spiritual world. This is in such a way that his will "knows" things that the head — his think-ing — still does not know, and so that it is the *future*, the celestial designs for the future, which work in and through his will rather than experience and memory of the past. He is therefore literally the "man of the future", the *final cause* being the element activating his will. He is the "man of desire", in the sense of the book of Daniel and in the sense of Louis Claude de Saint-Martin, i.e. the man whose will is set high, above the powers of the head — above thought, imagination and memory.

Now, the normal relationship between thought, feeling and the will for a civilised and educated man is such that his thought awakens feeling and directs the will. Thought plays a stimulating role, by means of imagination, towards feel-ing, and an educative role, by means of imagination and feeling, towards the will. Having to act, one thinks, one imagines, one feels, and — lastly — one desires and acts.

This is not so for the "spiritual man". For him it is the will which plays the stimulating and educative role towards feeling and thought. He acts first, then he desires, then he feels the worth of his action, and lastly he understands.

Abraham left his country of birth and went — in crossing the desert — into a strange country where, centuries later, a people descended from him was to find its native land and where, several centuries later on, the work of mankind's salvation was to take place. Did he know all this? Yes and no. Yes, in the sense that *he acted as if he knew* — his *will* being enamoured with these future things, and by their greatness and significance. No, in the sense that he did not have in his thoughts and imagination a plan or clear programme concerning how, when and through what stages, precisely, these things would be realised.

The certainty which in the first place takes hold of the will, from whence it takes its effect on feeling and thought, is precisely what the apostle Paul understood by the expression "faith" (*pistis, fides*). According to him:

> Faith is the firm assurance of things hoped for, the conviction of things not seen . . . By faith Abraham obeyed when he was called to go out to a place which he was to receive as an inheritance; *and he went out, not knowing where he was to go*. (Hebrews xi, 1, 8)

Abraham had therefore had "the *firm assurance* of things hoped for" after having experienced "the conviction of things not seen", i.e. his will knew, whilst his mind and imagination "did not see" or did not have the kind of assurance proper to them. All the same, he *obeyed* and left without knowing where he was going, i.e. he *acted* before his thought and imagination had understood the whole world implied in his action. When he left, therefore, his head followed his feet; his feet were then "above", in so far as they experienced the commandment of heaven, and his head obeyed them and was turned "below", in so far as it saw nothing but the privations, risks and perils of the enterprise. Abraham therefore found himself precisely in the condition of the Hanged Man of our Arcanum.

"By faith Abraham obeyed when he was called . . ." Here is the key to the mystery of faith, or knowledge of the will: ". . . *obeyed when he was called* . . ."

The will is an active force; it is not naturally an organ of perception. In order for it to be able to perceive it should not — it must not — become passive, for then it would fall asleep or fade away, because its very nature is activity, and in ceasing to be active it would cease to be will; no, it should change centre of gravitation, i.e. to transform "*my* will" into "*thy* will". It is the inner act of love alone which can accomplish the change of centre that the will uses or around which it gravitates. Instead of gravitating around the centre "me", it can orientate itself towards the centre "you". This transformation, effected by love, is what one calls "obedience".

Now, it is through obedience that the will is able to *perceive*. What it is able to perceive or be infused with is revelation from above, which inspires, directs and strengthens. It is thus that the will of a martyr can sustain anything and that the will of a thaumaturgist can accomplish everything.

Abraham's *divine call* was such an act of infused revelation. "And he obeyed", says the apostle. It is nevertheless necessary to add here that he obeyed even before his departure. For the *divine call* itself presupposes obedience — the transcentralisation of the will which renders the will capable of receiving a divine call from above. For the will must already be in a state of obedience in order for it to be able to perceive the inspiration or intuition from above and to receive the imprint of the divine call, i.e. *the gift of faith*.

Faith, as a supernatural gift, which is the case here, is not the same thing as the natural, rational and morally founded confidence that one has in an authority. The confidence that one puts in a doctor, judge or priest is only natural. In fact, it is rational and in accordance with human justice to recognise the authority of experienced experts, and hence to place one's trust in them. St. Teresa had complete confidence in her confessors, who nevertheless were mistaken about the serious question of the source of her mystical, gnostic and magical experiences, notably whether they had their origin from God or from a demon. But in the conflict between supernatural faith and natural confidence — which took place in her when her confessors, and also theologians of authority, declared that her spiritual experiences originated from a demon — it was faith which prevailed. For it was a conflict between the immediate-and-authentic divine action on the will, and the confidence of human thought and feeling in an authority, who is only a second-hand source. It was not only in her that the authentic divine revelation prevailed, but also it brought the confessors and theologians in question to recognise its authenticity.

The raptures of St. Teresa were those of faith, i.e. the union of the *will* with God, which left behind the other powers of the soul, namely thought and imagination. Here is what she says concerning this:

> I can only say that the soul conceives itself to be near God, and that *it is left with such a conviction that it cannot possibly help believing*. All the faculties (thought, imagination, memory) are in abeyance, and so suspended, as I have said, that their operations cannot be followed. If the soul has previously been meditating on any subject, it vanishes from the memory at once, as completely as if it had never been thought of. If it has been reading, it is unable to remember it or dwell on the words; and it is the same with vocal prayer. So the restless little moth of memory has its wings burned, and it can flutter no more. The will must be fully occupied in loving, but does not understand how it loves. If it understands, it does not understand how it understands, or at least, cannot comprehend anything of what it understands. I do not think that it understands at all, because,

as I have said, it does not understand itself. Nor can I myself understand this. . .Let it be observed too that however long the soul may enjoy this suspension of the faculties, the actual time is, in my opinion, very short. Half an hour would be a very long period of rapture, longer, I think, than any I ever experienced. Actually, it is very difficult to judge the time, since the senses are in abeyance. But I do not think that it can ever be long before one of them recovers. *It is the will that maintains the contact.* But the other two faculties soon begin to trouble it once more. But, as the will is calm, they become suspended again, and they are quiet for a little longer. But eventually they spring into life again. In this way some hours may be — and are — spent in prayer. For once the two faculties have begun to grow drunk on the taste of this wine, they are very ready to give themselves up again in order to enjoy some more. *Then they keep company with the will*, and the three rejoice together. (*The Life of St. Teresa*; trsl. J. M. Cohen, London, 1957, pp. 126-127)

The will united with God and the two other faculties suspended is the state of the soul in receiving the supernatural gift of faith, and it is certainly the faith thus experienced which triumphed for St. Teresa over scruples due to the confidence that she bore towards the theologians.

The state of soul described by St. Teresa corresponds overall still more to the condition of the Hanged Man of our Arcanum. For, like him, the soul of St. Teresa was "upside down", i.e. where the will precedes the head (understanding and memory) and is raised above it. The will then receives the divine imprint that the head at some time will understand — or not.

Now, practical Hermeticism has the aspiration that the two other powers keep company with the will at the moment when this latter is in the state of complete obedience towards the Divine, i.e. it aspires to the realisation of the last sentence of the above-quoted text:

> Then they (the two other powers) keep company with the will,
> and the three rejoice together.

Let us add: the three rejoice together in the joy of *union*, *knowledge*, and the future *realisation* of this experience — Hermeticism being a totality comprising mysticism, gnosis and divine magic.

Practical Hermeticism therefore applies itself to educating thought and imagination (or memory) to keep in step with the will. This is why it requires constant effort of thought and imagination combined in order to think, meditate and contemplate in *symbols* — symbolism being the sole means of rendering thought and imagination capable of not being suspended when the will submits to revelation from above and enabling them to unite with it in its act of receptive obedience, so that the soul not only has a revelation of faith but also participates in this revelation with its understanding and memory.

This is the principal point of practical Hermeticism and, at the same time, its contribution to Christian mysticism. I say Christian mysticism and not Christian mystical theology, because theology rationalises the material of mystical experience in deriving rules and laws, whilst Hermeticism wants thought and imagination to participate in this experience. Its aim is found in the experience itself, not in the domain of explaining it or accounting for it.

Meanwhile, the Hermeticist is also a "Hanged Man". For him, too, faith predomiantes at the beginning and for a long time subsequently. This is because it is a difficult task, exacting inner asceticism for a long time, to render thought and imagination capable of being present and upright by the altar where the fire of faith is kindled and burns. But with time the gap between the certainty of faith and that of knowledge becomes narrower and narrower. Thought and imagination become more and more capable of participating in the revelation of faith to the will—until the day arrives when they participate in it on equal footing with the will. This is then the spiritual event that is designated *Hermetic initiation*.

Thus, I know a man who, being a soldier in the White Army and having been unjustly accused by two officers of the allied marines, "understood" in the space of an instant of time the relationship which exists between eternity and the instant. This was a lightning flash received from above both through the will and through thought and imagination. The three powers of the soul were taken hold of and illumined by it simultaneously.

Authentic Hermeticism can therefore never be in contradiction with authentic faith. It can contradict only the opinions of theologians, i.e. not the *faith* but the *confidence* that is borne towards the statements of theologians. The strange thing is that theologians are as a rule very modest and even humble people, but from the moment that they sit in the chair of their science and drape themselves with the mantle of its "primary and secondary conclusions"—and, above all, the "general consensus"—they change and are no longer recognisable. From the modest people that they are, they change all of a sudden into sources of divine oracles. This is because their science is the most pretentious of all sciences that exist, being interpretative of the absolute truth of revelation. In contrast, the representatives of the natural sciences are, as a rule, very pretentious people, but the discipline of their science renders them modest. This is because their science is modest, being interpretative of the relative truth of experience.

Thus we have a paradox: modest people become pretentious thanks to their science, and pretentious people become modest, again thanks to their science. The danger for the one is knowing too much; the danger for the others is to know nothing. Thus, from the mouth of one of its conscientious representatives, the physiologist Du Bois-Reymond, empirical science declared itself *ignoramus et ig-*

norabimus ("we do not know and we shall never know") with regard to the seven "enigmas" (*Welträtsel*) of the world:

1. the essence of matter and energy;
2. the origin of motion;
3. the origin of the senses (sense-perception);
4. the question of free will;
5. the origin of life;
6. the purposeful organisation of Nature;
7. the origin of thought and language.
(E. H. Du Bois-Reymond, *Ueber die Grenzen des Naturerkennens. Die sieben Welträtsel*, Leipzig, 1882)

On the other hand, there is complete certainty for certain theologians not only with regard to the above enigmas but also with respect to the destiny of the soul after the death of the body, and to what then is—or is not—possible. Thus we read:

> At its departure from the body, the soul is no longer in a position to change its moral orientation, nor to go back on its previous adherence to sin but, on the contrary, it *fixes itself* in the disposition of will found at the precise instant of death; it becomes henceforth inflexible, and rebels against every idea of retraction, conversion or repentance (p. 392); [and], Eternal punishment exists only in the function of the eternal perseverance of the perverse disposition of unrepentants on departing from the present life (p. 394) (Cardinal Louis Billot, *Études*, Paris, 1923, pp. 392, 394).

Accordingly, it is therefore the body and not the soul which bears within it the possibility of changing its moral orientation, going back on adherence to sin, being converted, and repenting; it is therefore the precise instant of death and not the totality of earthly life which determines for all eternity the moral disposition of the soul and therefore its eternal destiny; the body dying, the soul at the instant of death is thus made to depart like a rocket with a pre-fixed programme (a pre-set rocket programme) for eternity. The mercy of God therefore acts only at the instant of death of the body, the destiny of the soul subsequently being only a semi-mechanical deployment of the soul's disposition at the instant of its departure from the body.

These are undoubtedly monstrous conclusions. It is evident, however, that if the conscientious Du Bois-Reymond is too timid and, in consequence of this fact, opens the doors to scepticism, the zealous theologian is, in contrast, rash and, as a consequence of this fact, opens the doors to unbelief. For it is impossible to believe simultaneously Cardinal Billot's statement and that of the Gospel which says:

If a man has a hundred sheep, and one of them has gone astray,
does he not leave the ninety-nine on the hills and go in search
of the one that went astray?. . . So it is the will of my Father who
is in heaven that not one of these little ones should perish.
(Matthew xviii, 12, 14)

One is bound to believe either that the mercy of God is limited, i.e. that it
extends only to the instant of bodily death, or that it is infinite and never ceases,
i.e. that it possesses the means of acting also after the instant of the soul's separation from the body. Here the love — no, the very justice — of God is in question.

Du Bois-Reymond ought to have said: "Being given the methods of contemporary science and the faculties of knowledge known up to the present time, the
seven great world enigmas *seem to be insoluble*; but if the methods and faculties
of knowledge change at some time without losing their scientific character, it could
be otherwise with the enigmas in question." And would it not be better if Cardinal Billot had said: "In the Scriptures there are passages relating to the love of
God and to the chastisement of sin which, given the present character of our reasoning and moral sentiment, seem to be contradictory. As it is impossible for them
to be really contradictory, I have formed a personal opinion which seems to me
to reconcile them in a satisfactory way. But I do not know if it is the only possible
solution to the problem, or whether there are other and better ones. What is nevertheless certain is that freedom exists and that it entails the risk of eternal hell,
whatever the exact sense of the word 'eternal' may be, this being a dogma of the
faith. With respect to the mechanism of the realisation of this truth, I have the
following opinion:" (and then he could give his opinion that earthly life is the
domain of freedom, whilst the other world is that of fate — an opinion that he
would still have to defend against pertinent arguments in favour of the contrary
thesis).

Now, practical Hermeticism is — like Christian mysticism — based on the experience of authentic faith, i.e. the experience of the human being upside down, where
the will is above intellectuality and imagination. Its practical aim is nevertheless
to render the intellect and imagination equal companions of the will favoured
by revelation from above. And here is how this is to be achieved:

One *moralises* thought in substituting *moral logic* for formal logic. One makes
an entrance for moral warmth in the domain of "cold thought". At the same time,
one intellectualises the imagination by disciplining it and submitting it to the
laws of moral logic. This is what Goethe understood by "exact imagination" (*exakte
Phantasie*), i.e. dispensing with imagination which *plays* according to free and
arbitrary association, and instead applying it to *work* in accordance with the associations dictated by moral logic — in harmony with the laws of *symbolism*. It is thus
that thought and imagination become capable of being attentive to and participating in the experience of the will receiving favours from above.

The statement: "One moralises thought in substituting moral logic for formal logic" could be said to be very concise, and calls for an amplification. It means to say that formal logic — whether explicitly or implicitly operating with syllogistic forms is not important — cedes its function as the supreme court of appeal to the moral logic of conscience. (Syllogistic logic operates with forms of syllogisms, where two suppositions together constitute a common implication, and where the conclusion comprises that which is implied.) Thus the logic of Caiaphas' argument, which persuaded the assembly of the Sanhedrin to make a decision against Jesus Christ, was impeccable from the point of view of formal logic, but was at the same time a great violation of moral logic. "It is expedient for you that one man should die for the people, and that the whole nation should not perish" (John xi, 50) — this was Caiaphas' argument. This argument is based on the logical principle that the part is less than the whole, the part being "one man" and the whole being "the nation". Being faced with the alternative — "If we let him go, all will believe in him, and the Romans will come to destroy our city and nation" — the decision was taken to sacrifice the part for the whole.

For moral logic, however, the *quantitative* principle that the part is less than the whole is not valid in a general sense; there are distinctions to be made. For already in a living organism where it is not the *size* but rather the importance of the vital *function* which counts, the principle in question would be: "the part is equal to the whole". Because, for example, the heart, which is only a small part of the whole human organism, cannot be sacrificed without sacrificing the life of the whole organism.

And in the moral and spiritual domain, where it is only quality which counts, *one* righteous man is worth more than the whole nation, if it is a question not of voluntary sacrifice but rather of the one who must be sacrificed. Thus in the spiritual and moral domain the above logical principle can be transformed into its opposite formula: "the part is greater than the whole".

Here is an example, therefore, of the operation of "moral logic" or *concrete and qualitative* logic, quite different from *formal and quantitative* logic. It is the conflict between the logic of the Logos and that of "this world", which the apostle Paul spoke of when he said:

> . . . they went about in skins of sheep and goats, destitute, afflicted, ill-treated — *of whom the world was not worthy* — wandering over deserts and mountains, and in dens and caves of the earth. (Hebrews xi, 37-38)

"Moral logic" is the human analogy of that of the Logos "that enlightens every man coming into the world" (John i, 9). It is the logic of faith, i.e. the logic of thought which participates in the revelation accorded to the will. "Moral logic" introduces warmth into the light of thought, so that the latter becomes *solar*, instead of lunar, which is what it is when it has only light alone and is cold, without warmth.

324   MEDITATIONS ON THE TAROT

"One intellectualises the imagination by disciplining it and submitting it to the laws of moral logic." This means to say that a kind of *asceticism* should be applied to the life of imagination in order to transform its arbitrary *play* into *work* inspired and directed from above. Here symbolism plays the leading role—one which is both preparatory and educational. For symbolism is simultaneously imaginative and logical, i.e. logical according to "moral logic".

Thus the Arcana of the Tarot with which we are occupied constitute a practical school of education for the imagination, with a view to rendering it capable of participating on an equal footing with "solarised" thought and "zodiacalised" will in the revelation from above. It is then intellectualised, i.e. it loses the feverish warmth which is normal for it and becomes luminous; it is "selenised" and becomes "lunar", just as the intellect was before its "solarisation" by moral logic. The prayer that is made for souls in purgatory—*locum refrigerii, lucis et pacis dona eis Domine* ("give to them, O Lord, a place of refreshment, light and peace")—expresses well that it is necessary for the imagination to become reflecting instead of fantasising.

The "zodiacalisation" of the will, the "solarisation" of thought and the "selenisation" (or "lunarisation") of imagination—we have chosen these three terms to signify the voluntary sacrifice of the soul's powers to *heaven*—means to say: that the will becomes an organ of perception and execution towards God, as the zodiac is in the macrocosm; that thought becomes both warm and luminous, as the sun is in the macrocosm; that, lastly, the imagination becomes reflecting towards truth, as the moon is towards the sun in the macrocosm.

It is a matter, therefore, of sacrificing the three powers of the soul to heaven. This sacrifice is nothing other than the three traditional and universal vows—that of obedience or the sacrifice of the will, that of poverty or the sacrifice of thought, and that of chastity or the sacrifice of imagination. It is thus that the will, thought and imagination become reflectors of the revelation from above, instead of being instruments of human arbitrariness.

This means to say, in terms of esoteric psycho-physiology, that the disposition of the crown centre (the "eight-petalled lotus")—which is always beyond the reach of human arbitrariness and which is constantly in a state of "divine repose", i.e. which is always at the disposal of heaven—extends to the other centres or "lotuses". One after the other they withdraw from the influence of human arbitrariness and immerse themselves in "divine repose", i.e. they become organs of pure revelation. The entire human psycho-physiological organisation thus becomes a divine instrument. *Saintliness* is achieved when all seven (or eight—in rare cases) centres are entirely at the disposal of heaven. The degrees of saintliness—from the point of view of the human psycho-physiological organisation—depend on how many and which centres are at the disposal of heaven.

With respect to Hermeticists, they do not as a rule attain to complete saintliness, where all seven centres are put at the disposal of the divine, since their work and mission—if there is a mission—entails and exacts efforts and labours which presuppose the preservation of human *initiative*, i.e. that at least the frontal centre (the "two-petalled lotus") remains at the disposal of the freedom (should the case arise) of human arbitrariness. I say *at least* the "two-petalled lotus" remains at the disposal of the individual because it is the centre of *intellectual initiative*. It can certainly be taken hold of by revelation from above for some time — instants, minutes, even hours — but, as a rule, for the Hermeticist this must remain at his discretion. Indeed, it would be very distressing for him to be able to think only what is caused from above and to turn his intellectual gaze only towards what is determined from above.

I know a man who had thus "lost" the use of his centre of intellectual initiative, which is at the same time that of the direction of attention, and who — being a Hermeticist — suffered very much from this. He was able to comprehend very many great things — above all things of general significance — but he was as if paralysed concerning *his* personal problems. He was not able to think about what he wanted to, nor to direct his attention to what he wanted to see and understand. This lasted some time until use of the centre in question was "restored" to him by the intervention of a benefactor from above. I would recommend people who have similar or identical difficulties to address themselves to the Holy Archangel Michael who is, it seems to me, a very special friend and protector of the kind of Hermeticists that I have in view in these Letters, i.e. people who want to unite saintliness and initiation, or who aspire to a Hermeticism that is holy and blessed from above.

The Card of the twelfth Arcanum of the Tarot, the Hanged Man, represents in the first place the man whose will is "zodiacalised", because here it is this which is the decisive spiritual event — the "solarisation" of thought and the "selenisation" of imagination being only consequences. The two trees, between which the Hanged Man is balanced, bear twelve scars left by their cut branches. They are twelve — these branches — because the zodiac has a twelvefold action and influence; and they are cut, because the Hanged Man is beyond their action and influence, and because their essence is *in him*. The twelve branches are cut and inactive outwardly, having become the *will* of the Hanged Man — the "zodiacalised" will, as we have said. The Hanged Man has absorbed the zodiac; he has himself *become* the zodiac. He is the *thirteenth*, in whose will the *twelve servants of God*, who are the twelve channels of His will, are present.

For *twelve* is the number of modalities of the will and its action; *seven* is the number of basic modalities of feeling and imagination; *three* is the numerical law of thought and word; and *one*, lastly, is the number of the Self who thinks, feels and wills. The monad therefore reveals itself through the *trinity* underlying thought and word, through the *septenary* underlying feeling and imagination, and through the *duodenary* underlying will and action.

The sum of the numbers of reality — one, three, seven and twelve — is twenty-two.* This is the true reason for the fact that there are *twenty-two* Major Arcana of the Tarot, and no more or no less. Because the author — or authors, if we think

---

*Translator's note: In the German translation of this book the following explanation is given: "The sum of the numbers of reality — one, three, seven and twelve — is *twenty-two* (and not twenty-three, since One transcends the other and includes them in itself)." (*Die grossen Arcana des Tarot. Meditationen*, Basel, 1983, p. 353)

in terms of collaboration from the vertical dimension of three superimposed worlds—of the Tarot proposed to give articulated symbolic expression only to things which count. And how could he count less or more than twenty-two!? Could he omit the monad—the fundamental unity behind the worlds of the macrocosm or God, and the fundamental unity behind the states of consciousness of the microcosm, or the soul? Could he pass by the Holy Trinity of God the Creator, Saviour and Sanctifier? Or could he pass by the trinity of the human being, who is by analogy an image of God in his spiritual, soul and corporeal being? After that, could he neglect or remain blind to the action of the trinity in the four elements—radiation, expansion, mobility and stability, or fire, air, water and earth? And after having taken account of the action of the trinity *in* the quaternary of elements, how could he not pay attention to the real manifestation of the action of the trinity *through* the quaternary, i.e. the three times four (or twelve) modalities of action, being the three modalities of action of the trinity through the four means of realising it?

Not being able to suppress any of the four members of the sacred name or *Tetragrammaton*—which comprises four members or numbers: one, three, seven and twelve—the author of the Tarot conceived and designed the twenty-two Arcana. But twenty-two is four, and four is three revealing one. The Tarot is therefore unity elucidated in twenty-two symbolic ways.

Concerning the Hanged Man, the twelve branches of the two trees between which he balances are cut. This means to say—or indicate—that he has reduced the twelve to one and that it is himself, the Hanged Man, who is the sole manifestation of it. He has, so to say, "swallowed" the zodiac, which amounts to the fact that his will has become identical with the will of the Divine, which manifests itself in three times four ways.

He bears in himself—or rather, he is borne by it—the *synthesis* of the twelve modalities of action of divine and fundamental will. This is what is meant by "reducing the twelve to one". It is to be hanged; it is to be upside down; and it is to live under the sign of celestial gravitation instead of that of terrestrial gravitation.

We have said: the Hanged Man is the *thirteenth*. Now, to be the thirteenth can signify two things: either the reduction of the twelve to one—and then the Hanged Man represents the *fundamental unity* of the twelve modalities of will—or else the crystallisation of a *thirteenth* synthetic element. In the latter case, it would be a matter of a *skeleton*, which is the last synthetic crystallisation of "zodiacal" will, and which is both the principle and concrete image of *death*. As death and its relationship to the skeleton will be the subject of the following Letter on the thirteenth Arcanum of the Tarot, "Death", I ask you, dear Unknown Friend, to remember the context of the two problems—as indicated here—namely the problem of the identity of individual will with divine will and the problem of attraction from above in its double aspect of ecstasy and death. For it is both in ecstasy and in the case of natural death that the "zodiacalisation" of the will takes place.

With respect to the Hanged Man, he represents the first alternative, i.e. the fundamental unity of the twelve modalities of divine will, which are the effective and final causes of radiation, expansion, mobility and stability—spiritual, psychic and material.

One finds a profound and breathtaking feeling of these cosmic depths in the cosmogonic hymn of the *Rigveda*. It awakens in the meditant at least a feeling of the profundity of the fundamental cosmic incentive towards, or feeling for, "zodiacality". The hymn is as follows:

> At first there was neither Being nor non-Being,
>   no kingdom of air, no sky beyond it.
> Who straddled what, and where? who gave shelter?
>   was water there, unfathomed depth of water?
> There was no death then, nor immortality,
>   no sign of stirring, no curtain of day or night.
> Only one thing, Breath, breathed, breathing without breath,
>   nothing else, nothing whatsoever.
> Also, there was Darkness, darkness within darkness,
>   the darkness of undiscriminated chaos.
> Whatever existed then was void and formless.
>   Then came the stirring of warmth, giving shape...
> Then rose Desire, primal Desire,
>   the primal seed, the germ of Spirit.
> The searching sages looked in their hearts, and knew:
>   Being was a manner of non-Being.
> And a line cut Being from non-Being transversely:
>   What was above it, and what below it?
> Only mighty makers, mighty forces,
>   action flowing freely and a fund of energy...
>
> (*Rigveda* x, 129; trsl. P. Lal, "The Song of Creation"
> in *The Golden Womb of the Sun*, Calcutta, 1965)

This is what a Hindu soul felt one starry night more than thirty centuries ago, in beholding the universe. Is it not a commentary on the natural mysticism—*fiat lux* ("Let there be light")—of Genesis?

It is this profound sphere, from whence the anonymous author of the Vedic hymn drew his inspiration, in which the Hanged Man participates through his will. He is the link between being and non-being, between darkness and created light. He is found suspended between the potential and the real. And it is the potential which is more real for him than the real properly said. He lives by authentic *faith*—what the Hermetic book *Kore Kosmu* designates as "the gift of black perfection" or "the gift of Perfect Night", i.e. the gift of perfect certainty drawn from the night of ultra-luminous darkness. For there is darkness and Darkness. The former is that of ignorance and blindness; the latter is that of knowledge going beyond natural human cognitive powers; it reveals itself to intuitive seeing. It is ultra-luminous in the same sense that ultra-violet rays go beyond the human eye's scale of natural visibility.

The following is a passage from the *Vita Antonii* (*Life of St. Anthony*) by St. Athanasius, bishop of Alexandria, relating to this subject:

> And indeed, after this still others came. They were of those who among the pagans are supposedly wise. They asked him to state an argument for our faith in Christ . . . (Anthony said to them through an interpreter) . . . "since, of course, you pin your faith on demonstrative proofs and this is an art in which you are masters, and you want us also not to worship God without demonstrative arguments — do you first tell me this: How does precise knowledge of things come about, especially knowledge about God? Is it by verbal proof or by an act of faith? And which comes first, an active faith or verbal proof?" When they replied that the act of faith takes precedence and that this constitutes accurate knowledge, Anthony said: "Well said! Faith arises from the disposition of the soul, while dialectic comes from the skill of those who devise it. Accordingly, those who are equipped with an active faith have no need of verbal argument, and probably find it even superfluous. For what we apprehend by faith, that you attempt to construct by arguments; and often you cannot even express what we perceive. The conclusion is that an active faith is better and stronger than your sophistic arguments . . ." (St. Athanasius, *The Life of Saint Anthony*; trsl. R. T. Meyer, Westminster, 1950, pp. 81, 83-84)

Here we have a clear comparison of the certainty due to "active faith" and that due to the demonstration by reasoning. The difference between them is the same as that between a photograph of a person and a meeting with this person. It is the difference that there is between image and reality, between an idea that one makes of the truth and the truth itself, present and acting.

The certainty of faith springs from the actual meeting with truth and its persuasive and transforming action, whilst that of certainty due to sound reasoning is only a degree — raised to a greater or lesser extent — of *semblance of the truth*, because it depends on the validity of our reasoning, and on the completeness and exactness of the elements which serve as its basis. A new item of information can turn the whole edifice of our reasoning upside down, just as an item of information which is proved false or inexact can have the same consequence. This is why all conviction founded on reasoning is intrinsically *hypothetical* and implies the following reservation: "Provided that the items of information that I possess are complete and exact, and that there arise no others to contradict them, I am led by the following arguments to the conclusion that . . ." At the same time, the certainty of faith has nothing hypothetical about it: it is absolute. The Christian martyrs did not die for hypotheses, but rather for the truths of faith of which they were absolutely certain.

May I be spared the objection that communists also sometimes die for their Marxist-Leninism! Because if they do so voluntarily, it is not for the dogmas (concerning the supremacy of the economy, the ideological superstructure, etc.) that they have, but rather for the grain of Christian truth which takes hold of their hearts, namely that of human brotherhood and social justice. Materialism as such does not have—and cannot have—martyrs; and if it seems so, then those whom materialism accounts as such, truth to tell, bear witness *against* it. For their testimony is as follows: "There are values higher than economics, higher even than life, because we sacrifice not only material goods but also our very lives." Such is their testimony against materialistic Marxism. Now follows their testimony against Christianity: "We have lost the fullness of faith; there remains to us only a grain. But even this grain which remains is so precious that we give our lives for it. And you who have fullness, what is your sacrifice for it?" Such is their testimony against Christianity. . . in so far as the latter is also materialistic. For there is doctrinal materialism alongside the will influenced by faith, and there is on the other hand doctrinal spiritualism alongside the will influenced by materialistic interests.

It is this duality which produces heresies and sects. Thus the adherents to Arianism denied the divinity of Jesus Christ not because of it being contrary to reason, but rather because it seemed to them contrary to reason as a consequence of the fact that their *will* was opposed to it. The Messiah that they *wanted* was the Messiah wanted by Jewish orthodoxy. For this reason, just as this latter rejected the Christ and had him crucified, accusing him of having "made himself the Son of God" ("The Jews answered Pilate: We have a law, and by that law he ought to die, because he has made himself the Son of God"–John xix, 7), so did the followers of Arius advance the same accusation against the Church in declaring that it had made him the Son of God. The Arianists were in no way less instructed or less intellectually endowed than the orthodox believers. What they were lacking was the will illumined by revelation from above, i.e. authentic faith. It remained such as it was before Jesus Christ, such as it lived and acted in Jewish orthodoxy. In fact, the Arianists *wanted* another Messiah and, being Christian, they applied themselves to changing the Messiah so as to conform to their pre-Christian will.

Yet in the case where the will perceives the revelation from above and understanding follows this up, as in the case of the *Hanged Man*, certainty is absolute and no heresy could result, if we understand by "heresy" doctrines or maxims of prejudice to the cause of salvation or incompatible with the truths of faith. The Hanged Man can certainly be *accused* of heresy, but he can never be its perpetrator. His element is authentic faith—and how could authentic faith, or divine action in the human will, engender things contrary to itself?

Do you know what the *ex cathedra* infallibility of the pope in matters of doctrine and morality is? It is that he finds himself in the condition of the Hanged Man when he makes a declaration *ex cathedra* (i.e. in the condition of the Hanged Man) concerning things of faith and morality. It is the condition in which the apostle Peter was when he was able to say, "You are the Christ, the Son of the living God," and of which the Lord said in reply, "Flesh and blood has not revealed this to you, but my Father who is in heaven" (Matthew xvi, 16-17). And just as a stone does not have its own motion, and can only be a moved object, so is the will of he who is found in the condition of the Hanged Man deprived of its own movement and can only be moved from above.

This is one side of the mystery of infallibility in things of faith and morality. It is the arbitrary paralysed and reduced to nothing—the state of the stone—which safeguards the infallibility of judgement in this domain. It is above all a matter of the elimination of the source of errors—for, as a rule, the Roman pontiff making an *ex cathedra* statement does not do so as a prophet but as a pontiff.

The whole mystery of infallibility has, without doubt, still other aspects, including what we discussed in the fifth Letter on the fifth Arcanum of the Tarot, "The Pope", and still greater depths, but the aspect which is presented in the light of the Arcanum "The Hanged Man" is of a nature to bring to bear the most clarity on the problem in question—this Arcanum being that of authentic faith.

Now, authentic faith brings with it absolute certainty, above all when it is not limited to the will alone but succeeds in making understanding and imagination also participate in its experience. Then the soul becomes the seat of a kind of Christian faith-wisdom symbolism similar to the faith-wisdom symbolism of the *Zohar*, i.e. that of the Jewish Cabbala. The latter is then to the former as the Old Testament is to the New. And just as the Old Testament and the New Testament together comprise the Holy Scripture, so do the Jewish Cabbala and Christian faith-wisdom symbolism together constitute Christian Hermeticism. Just as in Christian theology one would not dispense with the Old Testament, similarly in Christian Hermeticism one would not dispense with the Cabbala. This is the law of continuity of the living tradition, or the commandment: "Honour thy father and thy mother". The mother of Christian Hermeticism is the Cabbala and its father is Egyptian Hermeticism, the Hellenistic writings of which we have received under the title *Corpus Hermeticum*—comprising twenty-nine (or more) treatises. The *Corpus Hermeticum* (works attributed to or inspired by Hermes Trismegistus) is the Egyptian-Hellenistic counterpart to the Jewish *Zohar* and the Jewish Cabbala in general.

Certainly, it is not a matter of "borrowing"—which is, moreover, always sterile—the method of historical and philological science, because although "Moses was instructed in all the wisdom of the Egyptians" (Acts vii, 22), he nevertheless had a real and authentic meeting with "the Angel of the LORD who appeared to him in a flame of fire out of the midst of a bush" (Exodus iii, 2). It is this meeting which was the commencement of his mission.

No, things actually experienced cannot be borrowed. They follow one another, as human generations follow one another and are linked only by the profound ties of heredity, i.e. the continuity of the *life* of tradition through effort, problems, aspirations, suffering. Just as one generation passes to another the *organs* of knowledge and the *vital impulse* with respect to their use, so the stages in a spiritual tradition such as that of Egypt-Israel-Christendom are, so to say, incarnations of new souls who inherit only the organs and the impulse (body and blood) of their predecessors. Israel is a new soul in comparison with Egypt, and Christendom is a new soul in comparison with Israel. But Egypt aspired to the God of gods and succeeded in achieving a high knowledge — even authentic faith — of God, as the writings of the *Corpus Hermeticum* prove; Israel had intercourse with this God through the intermediary of Moses and the prophets; lastly, concerning Christianity, God was made flesh. From the sanctuaries of Egypt, through the desert of Sinai, to the cross of Calvary, there is a way — the way of divine revelation, on the one hand, and the historical way of monotheism in human consciousness, on the other hand. Christianity in no way "borrowed" the "idea of the Messiah" from Judaism, for Jesus Christ was not an "idea", but rather the Incarnation of the Word and the fulfillment of the hope of Israel. And the God of Moses and the prophets was no more "borrowed" from the sanctuaries of Egypt, for the clouds, the lightning and thunder on Mt. Sinai where He was revealed are not things that can be borrowed. And the vision of creative God in the Egyptian sanctuary, described in the Hermetic treatise *Poemander* is not "borrowed" from anyone. Its introduction is as follows:

> My thoughts being once seriously busied about the things that are, and my understanding lifted up, all my bodily senses being exceedingly holden back, as it is with them that are very heavy of sleep. . . me thought I saw one of an exceedingly great stature, and an infinite greatness call me by my name, and say unto me, "*What wouldest thou hear and see*? Or what wouldest thou understand to learn and know?" (*Poemander* i, book II in *The Divine Pymander of Hermes Mercurius Trismegistus*; trsl. Doctor Everard, London, 1884, p. 7)

It is therefore evident that it is a matter of a spiritual *experience* and not of any teachings transmitted by word of mouth. A living tradition is not a current of word of mouth but rather a series of revelations and endeavours. It is the "biography" of *authentic faith*.

Authentic faith — the condition of the Hanged Man of our Arcanum — thus differs from knowledge due to reasoning in that it possesses absolute certainty, whilst reasoning results only in relative certainty. However, reasoning is not the only method of knowledge. There are also so-called occult or super-normal methods of knowledge. I have in mind the diverse forms of clairvoyance — corporeal, psychic and spiritual. What is the relationship, therefore, between authentic faith and the experiences of clairvoyance?

It is necessary to say first of all that the whole domain of super-sensory experiences is divided into two intrinsically different parts, namely into that of perception of what is *outside of* the soul (horizontal perception) and that of revelation of what is *above* the soul (vertical revelation). The latter is trans-subjective and the former is extra-subjective or objective. St. Teresa called them "imaginary vision" (i.e. "imaged") and "intellectual vision" (i.e. non-"imaged"). The following is an example of "intellectual vision":

> One day when I was at prayer — it was the feast day of the glorious St. Peter — I saw Christ at my side — or, to put it better, I was conscious of Him, for I saw nothing with the eyes of the body or the eyes of the soul. He seemed quite close to me and I saw that it was He. As I thought, He was speaking to me. Being completely ignorant that such visions were possible, I was very much afraid at first, and could do nothing but weep, though as soon as He spoke His first word of assurance to me, I regained my usual calm, and became cheerful and free from fear. All the time Jesus Christ seemed to be at my side, but *as this was not an imaginary vision* I could not see in what form. But *I most clearly felt* that He was all the time on my right, and He was witness of everything that I was doing. Each time I became a little recollected, or was not entirely distracted, I could not but be aware that He was beside me.
>
> In great trouble, I went at once to my confessor to tell him about this. He asked me in what form I had seen Him, and I replied that I had not seen Him. He asked me how I knew it was Christ, and I replied that I did not know how, but that I could not help being aware that He was beside me, and that I had plainly seen and felt it. . . I had no way of explaining myself except by using comparisons; and no comparison, I think, can help one much to describe this kind of vision, for it is one of the highest possible kinds. This was told me afterwards by a holy man of great spirituality called Friar Peter of Alcantara. . .and other men of great learning have told me the same thing. It is, of all the kinds of vision, the one with which the devil can least interfere. . .For if I say that I do not see Him with the eyes of the body or the eyes of the soul, because this is no ordinary vision, how then can I know and affirm that He is beside me with greater certainty than if I saw Him? If one says that one is like a person in the dark who cannot see someone though he is beside him, or that one is like somebody who is blind, it is not right. There is some similarity here, but not much, because a person in the dark can perceive with other senses, or hear his

neighbour speak or move, or can touch him. Here this is not so, nor is there any feeling of darkness. On the contrary, He appears to the soul by a knowledge brighter than the sun. I do not mean that any sun is seen, or any brightness, but there is a light which, though unseen, illumines the understanding so that the soul may enjoy this great blessing, which brings very great blessings with it . . .

Then my confessor asked me: Who said that it was Jesus Christ? I answered: He often tells me so Himself, but before ever He said it, *it was impressed on my understanding that it was He*, and even before that He used to tell me He was there when I could not see Him . . . The Lord is pleased to engrave it so deeply on the understanding that one can no more doubt it than one can doubt the evidence of one's eyes. (*The Life of St. Teresa* trsl. J. M. Cohen, London, 1957, pp. 187-189)

And the following is an example of "imaginary vision":

One day when I was at prayer, He was pleased to show me His hands only; their beauty was beyond description. This put me in great fear. . . A few days later I saw that divine face also, which seems to leave me completely entranced. I could not understand why the Lord was revealing Himself to me gradually like this, since He was afterwards to grant me the favour of seeing Him whole . . . Once when I was at Mass on St. Paul's Day, there stood before me the most sacred Humanity, in all the beauty and majesty of His resurrection body, as it appears in all the paintings . . . Although this vision was imaginary, I never saw it or any other with the eyes of the body, but only with the eyes of the soul. Those who know better than I say that my previous vision was more perfect than this one, while this in its turn is much nearer to perfection than those that are seen with the eyes of the body . . . if I were to spend many years imagining how I could invent anything so beautiful, I could not do it. I should not know how to begin. For in its whiteness and radiance alone it exceeds anything that we can imagine. It is not a dazzling radiance but a soft whiteness and infused radiance, which causes the eyes great delight and never tires them; nor are they tired by the brilliance which confronts them as they look on this divine beauty . . . it does not matter whether they (the eyes) are open or closed; if the Lord wishes us to see it, we shall do so even against our will. . . (Ibid., 196-198).

These examples suffice to give a clear idea of the nature of the *trans-subjective* experience or "intellectual vision"—as St. Teresa calls it—and of the *extra-subjective* experience or "imaginary vision". The former is the projection in the soul of a spiritual experience which takes place above it; the soul itself perceives nothing—it can only *react* to what the spirit experiences, which makes it participate in the fruits of its experience. It is *trans-subjective* because the revelation itself takes place neither outside nor within the soul but, rather, above it, i.e. in the spirit. In this way it happens that the soul has certainty as if it had seen, without having seen, and as if it had heard, without having heard. It is the spirit which projects into it certainty of its certain experiences. It is the spirit which "sees", "hears" and "touches" in its own way and which infuses the soul with the fruits of its experience—a certainty equal to, or even higher than, that which the soul would have if it had "seen", "heard" and "touched" itself.

With respect to the extra-subjective experience, or "imaginary vision", it is the soul itself which "sees", "hears" and "touches". It "sees" outside of itself, but with the "eyes of the soul", i.e. *not* as a hallucination of the bodily senses, but rather as imagination moved *from outside* instead of being moved by its own arbitrariness. Now the images caused from outside of the soul can be neither sensed nor defined other than as *perceptions*. And as they are not corporeal perceptions, one experiences and describes them as "perceptions of the soul". This is why St. Teresa speaks of vision with the "eyes of the soul".

The "eyes of the soul" of which St. Teresa speaks are what we call in modern Hermeticism the "lotus flowers" or simply "lotuses", and what Hindu yoga names "chakra centres" or "chakras".

The higher lotuses—the eight-petalled, two-petalled and sixteen-petalled—are organs which are made use of by the spirit (i.e. either the human spirit alone, or the human spirit united with the divine Holy Spirit, or, lastly, the human spirit united with another human or hierarchical spirit through and in the Holy Spirit) in the case of revelation from above, i.e. in the case of St. Teresa's "intellectual vision".

The lower lotuses—the ten-petalled, six-petalled and four-petalled—are the organs of horizontal perception, i.e. St. Teresa's "imaginary vision".

Concerning the *heart*, i.e. the twelve-petalled lotus, it participates in the two kinds of vision or, if you wish, it possesses a *third* kind of clairvoyant perception, which is the synthesis of the other two. For the "heart" is the centre or lotus of *love*—where, truth to tell, it is no longer a question of "above" or "outside" or even of "above" and "below", because love abolishes all distances and all distinctions of space (even distinctions of spiritual space) and has the power to make all things present. It is thus that God is present in a heart glowing with love.

The heart perceives diverse presences as impressions and nuances of spiritual *warmth*. It is thus that the hearts of the two disciples going to Emmaus recognised the One who went on the way with them before their eyes and their understanding did, and who said to one another after their eyes opened and they recognised him: "Did not our hearts burn within us while he talked to us on the road, while he opened to us the scriptures?" (Luke xxiv, 32). The heart burning in diverse ways—this is the kind of "vision" and spiritual knowledge which is proper to the heart.

Dear Unknown Friend, be attentive to your heart and towards the nuances of intimate warmth which arises from its depths! Who knows who may go on his way with you without your eyes and your understanding surmising it?

Now, the three higher lotuses are above all those of *infused certainty* or "imperceptible light", and these are the principal instruments (*instruments* and not *sources*) of "intellectual vision" or trans-subjective revelation.

The three lower lotuses are those of *certainty of experience at first hand*; they render us "eye-witnesses" to invisible things. They manifest them to us in "perceptible light" as forms, movements, colours, sounds and breath—concrete and objective—although incorporeal in the sense of the physical world.

And the central centre, the heart or twelve-petalled lotus, gives us the *certainty of authentic faith*—that which was born in the "fire of Emmaus"—through which the immediate presence of entities who want to go on the way with us is manifested. This fire contains at the same time both the "imperceptible light" of "intellectual vision" and the "perceptible light" of "imaginary vision", in their synthesis, which we call here the "fire of Emmaus".

In addition to these two—or three—kinds of supersensible experience there is still another which often passes for spiritual, but which in reality is not. I have in mind the kind of clairvoyance which is due either to over-refinement of the senses or to their halluncinatory function. St. Teresa of Avila also mentions it in the text of her autobiography, from which we have quoted above. She says, notably, that "those who know better than I say that my previous vision ("intellectual") was more perfect than this one ("imaginary"), while this in its turn is much nearer to perfection than *those that are seen with the eyes of the body...*" (Ibid., p. 197).

It seems that it was generally admitted amongst "those who know" from the sixteenth century that there are, in addition to "intellectual vision" and "imaginary vision", visions "that are seen with the eyes of the body", i.e. visions due either to over-refinement of the senses or to hallucination. Therefore the fact was known then, as it is today, that there are people who can read a letter put in an envelope, see a playing-card of which only the reverse is shown to them, see coloured light around people, animals and plants ("auras"), etc. On the other hand, it was known—as it is known today—that the senses can function in two directions: that they can receive *impressions* from outside and that they can project *expressions* of the soul outside. In the latter case it is a matter of hallucinations.

Now, there are illusory hallucinations and revelatory hallucinations. All depends on what the soul exteriorises through the channels of the corporeal senses. It is therefore quite possible—and in fact happens from time to time—that the soul transforms authentic and true perceptions into hallucinations, i.e. that it projects from the psychic—and even spiritual—plane onto the physical plane. It is then an illusion with respect to the physical plane, but it is at the same time a revelation with respect to the higher plane to which the original of the hallucinated copy belongs.

"Hallucination" and "illusion" are not synonyms. When Martin Luther, as it is recounted, threw an inkpot at the figure of a demon (or the devil himself, as tradition would have it) which appeared to him, without doubt he acted under an illusion with respect to the plane — the inkpot not being on the same plane as the demon — but should one conclude from this that the demon was in no way present?. . .that there was nothing there and that it was all only a trick of the imagination, without cause or reason?

No, just as there is hysteria due to illusion and hysteria based on truth — as, for example, is the case with stigmatas and wounds from the crown of thorns, which manifest themselves on the bodies of people who have had spiritual experience of the Lord's Passion — so also there are illusory hallucinations, due to fears or immoderate desires, and revelatory hallucinations, i.e. "hallucinations of the truth".

Let us now return to the question concerning the relationship between authentic faith and the experiences of clairvoyance, between the condition of the Hanged Man and the condition of the "seer". It follows from the preceding that authentic faith is above all the burning fire of the heart, which thus bears a witness to spiritual reality. The light which accompanies it is due to *revelation* from above by means of the three higher lotuses, which is, following St. Teresa, the grace and favour of "intellectual vision".

Concerning "imaginary visions"— and still more strongly so for visions due to over-refinement of the senses or to their inverse functioning (not in the normal direction "external world — brain", but in the reverse direction "brain — external world"), which takes place in the case of hallucination — they are in no way sources of authentic faith, and possess no more value than what authentic faith, moral conscience and (should it arise) reasoning are able to attribute to them. In any case: authentic faith precedes them, if they signify a revelatory contribution to the spiritual life of the soul; moral conscience precedes them, if they bring about an enrichment of the moral life of the soul; and reasoning precedes them, if they result in an increase of knowledge for the soul or the acquisition of new items of information of value to the soul.

For what one sees or hears must be understood. And one cannot understand without the revelatory "imperceptible light" and "Emmaus fire". One can also not understand and appreciate their value without the work of reasoning, if it is a matter of gaining items of information of a kind to augment knowledge. Reasoning is bound to compare the items of information furnished by clairvoyant experience, to classify them, and to look for relationships between them in order, lastly, to draw conclusions from them. Clairvoyant or not, all empirical experience is necessarily hypothetical. It is only *authentic faith* which has absolute certainty.

Thus, dear Unknown Friend, important above all else is the authentic faith of the "fire of Emmaus", then the same faith illumined by the "imperceptible light" from above of "intellectual vision"—*after which* all will profitably serve your soul: both "imaginary visions" and visions due to over-refinement of the senses, experience of the senses, moral and logical reasoning, the study of all the sciences, and even hallucinations if they happen without you having arbitrarily sought and provoked them. Do not scorn anything or reject anything, if you have authentic faith. It is this, and this alone, which renders everything truly useful and which gives them value which they would not have without it.

This is the essential message of the Hanged Man, the upside-down man, whose feet are above and whose head is below, whose zodiacalised will is an authentic witness of the truths of the *twelve articles of faith*, and who lives suspended between two opposed fields of gravitation—heaven and earth.

Who is the Hanged Man? Is he a saint, a righteous man, an initiate?

He can certainly be regarded as all three, for all three have in common that their will is an organ of heaven, but what he is most especially, what he represents individually, is neither sanctity, nor righteousness, nor initiation, but something which is their synthesis. The Hanged Man is the *eternal Job*, tried and tested from century to century, who represents humanity towards God and God towards humanity. The Hanged Man is the *truly human man* and his lot is a truly human one.

The Hanged Man is the representative of humanity who is found between two kingdoms—that of this world and that of heaven. For that which is truly human in man and in humanity is the Hanged Man. And it is the Hanged Man who said, thousands of years ago:

> Has not man a hard destiny upon earth,
> and are not his days like the days of a hireling?
> Like a slave who longs for the shadow,
> and like a hireling who looks for his wages...
> Oh that my words were written!
> Oh that they were inscribed in a book!
> Oh that with an iron pen and lead
> they were graven in the rock for ever!
> My foot has held fast to his steps;
> I have kept his way and have not turned aside...
> For I *know* that my Redeemer lives,
> and at last he will stand upon the earth.
> And after my skin has been thus destroyed,
> then from my flesh I shall see God,
> whom I shall see on my side,
> and my eyes shall behold, and not another.
> *My heart faints within me in expectation*!
>   (Job vii, 1-2; xix, 23-24; xxiii, 11; xix, 25-27)

This is the discourse of the Hanged Man across the centuries.

Meditation on the
Thirteenth Major Arcanum of the Tarot

DEATH

——————

LA MORT

And the woman said to the serpent,
"We may eat of the fruit of the trees of the garden;
but God said, 'You shall not eat of the fruit of the
tree which is in the midst of the garden,
neither shall you touch it, lest you die.' "
But the serpent said to the woman,
"You will not die.
For God knows that when you eat of it
your eyes will be opened,
and you will be as gods,
knowing good and evil."

(Genesis iii, 2-5)

O dry bones, hear the word of the LORD.
(Ezekiel xxvii, 4)

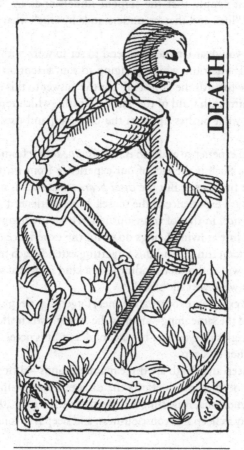

Dear Unknown Friend,

Have you ever been struck by the contrary statements concerning death made by God and the serpent in the narrative in Genesis on the Fall? Because God says there, "You shall not eat of the tree of knowledge of good and evil, for on the day when you eat from it you will die", and the serpent says, "You will not die". Here God is categorical; the serpent is just as much so.

Did the serpent quite simply lie? Or is it a matter of a fundamental error on the part of the serpent? Or again, did he state a truth from the range of truths proper to the domain of the serpent which are untruths in the domain of truths for God? In other words, are there *two* immortalities and *two* different deaths—one from the point of view of God, the other from the point of view of the serpent? Thus, is it simply that the serpent understands by "death" what God understands by "life" and that he understands by "life" what God understands by "death"?

Now, I invite you dear Unknown Friend to set to work with a view to finding an answer to this question, whilst bringing to your attention fruits of the work that I have made towards the same end. For the answer to this question is the Arcanum of the thirteenth Card of the Tarot, "Death", which represents a skeleton who reaps only what pushes up from the black soil and rises above it—hands, heads, etc.

Our empirical experience of death is the *disappearance* from the physical plane of living beings. Such is the fact of our experience from without, that we have by means of our five senses. But the *disappearance* as such is not confined to the domain of outward experience of the senses. It is experienced also in the domain of inner experience, in that of consciousness. There the images and representations disappear just as living beings do so for the experience of the senses. This is what we call "forgetting". And this forgetting extends each night to the totality of our memory, will and understanding—of a kind such that we forget *ourselves* entirely. This is what we call "sleep".

For our whole experience (outer and inner) forgetting, sleep and death are three manifestations of the same thing—namely the "thing" which effects disappearance. It is said that sleep is the younger brother of death. It is necessary to add: forgetting is the brother of sleep.

Forgetting, sleep and death are three manifestations—differing in degree—of a sole principle or force which effects the disappearance of intellectual, psychic and physical phenomena. Forgetting is to sleep as sleep is to death. Or again: forgetting is to memory as sleep is to consciousness, and sleep is to consciousness as death is to life.

One forgets, one goes to sleep, and one dies. One remembers, one awakes, and one is born. Remembering is to forgetting as awakening is to falling asleep, and awakening is to sleeping as birth is to death. One forgets oneself when one goes to sleep, and one remembers oneself when one awakes. It is also the mechanism of forgetting which is at work when one dies, and it is the mechanism of remembering which works at birth. When Nature forgets us, then we die; when we forget ourselves, then we fall asleep; and when we lose active interest in something, then we forget it.

Nevertheless, it must not be forgotten that the respective domains of forgetting, sleep and death are more vast and more profound than intellectual forgetting, organic sleep, and clinical death. Apart from intellectual forgetting there is also forgetting in the domain of the soul (psychic forgetting) and a forgetting in the domain of the will, just as there is memory in the domain of the soul and memory in the domain of the will—beyond intellectual memory. Thus, for example, one can retain a clear and precise intellectual memory of a friend from the past but at the same time have completely forgotten him psychically. One recalls, but without the living friendship of former times. Similarly, one can remember a person intellectually and psychically, i.e. with vivid feeling, but at the same time have forgotten him in the domain of the will. One remembers him with tenderness perhaps, but one *does nothing* for him.

Beyond organic sleep, i.e when one is in bed and oblivious of everything including oneself, there is psychic sleep and a sleep of the will. During the sixteen or eighteen hours that we are in the waking state there are layers of our psychic being which are asleep. During the waking state one is "asleep" to many things — facts, people, ideas, God . . .

And if the Buddha is considered — and venerated — as "fully awake" to the facts of human life such as sickness, old age and death, it is because those who are not Buddhas know that they are asleep with regard to these facts — not intellectually, but psychically and in their will. They "know" it and they *do not know* it at the same time. For one *knows* truly when one *understands* what one knows, when one *feels* what one has understood, and when one has *put into practice* what one has understood and felt.

Similarly, beyond clinical death there is a psychic death and a moral death. During our seventy or eighty years of life we bear within us layers of death in our psychic being. There are things which are missing from our psychic and moral being. The *absence* of faith, hope and love cannot be remedied either by arguments or by exhortations or even by a living example. An act of divine magic — or grace — is necessary to accomplish the *infusion* of life into that which is dead. And if Christ is worshipped as the Risen One, it is because those who bear death within them know that it is only divine magic which can raise what is dead within them and that the risen Christ is the guarantor of this.

Forgetting, sleep and death — like remembering, waking and birth — have imaginary and symbolic expressions proper to them. Thus *black* is the image of forgetting, *tufts of grass* are the image of sleep, and a *skeleton* with a scythe is the image of death . . . Black is the symbol both of involuntary and natural forgetting and of that voluntary and supernatural forgetting of which St. John of the Cross speaks — this threefold night of the senses, the understanding and the will, in which the union of the soul with God is accomplished. Tufts of grass or leaves are the symbol of sleep, because deep sleep is the state where we live a vegetative life. Organic life — breathing, circulation, digestion and growth — continue during sleep without "animality" and "humanity" being present. We are "plants" when we are deep in sleep. And the skeleton is the symbol of death because it reduces the phenomenon of the conscious, mobile, living and material man to that which is *mineral* in him — the skeleton.

Natural forgetting reduces man to *animality*; natural sleep reduces him to *vegetality*; and natural death reduces him to *minerality*. The whole problem of death, comprising three degrees — forgetting, sleep and death proper, or the *Arcanum of death* — must therefore be presented to us as the image of a black sphere, beneath which there are tufts of grass and above which there is a skeleton.

And it is precisely the thirteenth Card of the Tarot which presents us this image. The *context* of the Card is that of the threefold manifestation of the *principle of subtraction* by way of forgetting, sleep and death. We have here the black soil, the blue and yellow tufts of grass, and also the skeleton mowing. The Card contains still a fourth element, represented on the Card by the human heads and hands, and one foot, to which we shall return later.

The thirteenth Arcanum of the Tarot is therefore that of the *principle of subtraction* or death, and is the opposite of the *principle of addition* or life. It is necessary to *subtract* the Self from the astral body, the etheric body and the physical body in order to understand the mechanism of *forgetting*; it is necessary to subtract the Self and the astral body, from the etheric body and the physical body in order to obtain the state of *sleep*; and it is necessary to subtract the Self, the astral body and the etheric body from the physical body in order to obtain the corpse, i.e. the fact of *death*. These three degrees of subtraction in their totality constitute the process of *excarnation*, just as the corresponding three degrees of addition constitute the totality of the process of *incarnation*. For incarnation is the addition of an astral body to the Self, the addition of an etheric body to the astral body and the Self, and lastly the addition of a physical body to the etheric body, the astral body and the Self.

Now, the *scythe* which is held by the skeleton of the Card represents the work of subtraction. It is this which symbolises the force of excarnation, i.e. that which severs the ties between the Self and the astral body (forgetting), the ties between the astral body and the etheric body (sleep), and the ties between the etheric body and the physical body (death).

What are the ties between the soul and the body — rather, the soul and the *bodies* — that the scythe of the threefold principle of subtraction severs? What is it that unites the Self to the astral body, the astral body to the vital or etheric body, and the vital body to to the physical body? In other words, how and why do we remember the past, how and why do we wake in the morning, and how and why do we live several decades?

In the first place, let us disregard the enormous literature where these questions are dealt with and endeavour to undertake a *meditative* work, i.e. to think *directly* about the subject which occupies us, without the intermediary of what may be borrowed from sources other than our immediate experience and understanding. To meditate is to think with a view to attaining certainty in the inner forum of consciousness, renouncing all pretension of arriving at things of general validity (i.e. things which may be a contribution to *science*). In meditation — and these Letters are only meditations — it is a matter above all of the question, posed in all honesty to our own conscience and answered in all honesty by our own conscience: "What do I *myself* know?", and not the question: "What is generally known?"

Let us disregard for the moment, dear Unknown Friend, *what is generally known and said* on the subject of the ties between the soul and the body, and let us endeavour to take account — just for ourselves — of what *we* know and are able to know about it.

Firstly, let us consider the domain of forgetting and remembering — the memory. Memory is the magic, in the subjective domain, which effects the evocation of things from the past. It renders past things present. Just as a sorcerer or necromancer evokes the spirits of the dead by making them appear, so does memory evoke things of the past and make them appear to our inner mental vision. The present *remembrance* is the result of a magical operation in the subjective domain, where one has succeeded in evoking from the black void of forgetfulness a living image from the past. A living image from the past. . . imprint? symbol? copy? phantom? It is all of these at once. It is an imprint in so far as it reproduces an impression received in the past; it is a symbol in so far as it makes use of my imagination to represent a *reality* which goes beyond its imaginary representation; it is a copy in so far as it only aims at reproducing the original from the past; it is a phantom in so far as it is an apparition from the black abyss of forgetfulness and in so far as it recalls to life the past in making it present to my inner vision.

What is the force at work in the subjective magical operation of remembering?

There are four types of memory that one experiences: mechanical or automatic memory, logical memory, moral memory and vertical or revelatory memory.

Mechanical or automatic memory hardly makes any demand on the act of recall. The remembrance simply *happens*. It takes place in an automatic way according to the laws of association — i.e. resemblances, affinities and alliances between things — which effect recall without my taking any other part than that of an observer. This sort of memory supplies me, on the occasion of each impression that I receive, with a host of images of the past from which I can choose. Thus when I see a pipe, I can choose between images of the past which present themselves to my mind, e.g. "an old sea-dog whom I saw at B. in 19. . ."; "a book on Red Indians where it was a matter of the peace-pipe ritual", "my friend S. who used to put everyone to flight when he lit his pipe of tobacco cultivated and prepared by himself at the time of the last war when there was no tobacco for sale", etc.

In so far as logical memory is concerned, I am more active than in the case of automatic memory. Here I have *to think* in order to remember things. Thus, for example, if I want to remember the Hindu Trinity, amongst whom I have forgotten one of the three terms, I ask myself: If there is a Creator and a Destroyer, Brahma and Shiva, which third principle *ought* to be found between the Creator and the Destroyer? I concentrate on the empty place between the two and I make an effort to fill it logically. "Ah, it is the Conserver principle — this is Vishnu — of course!" I say to myself. In logical memory there is less automatism and more conscious effort.

With respect to moral memory, there is hardly any automatism. Here the remembrance is no longer something which happens but rather it is an authentic magical act, although subjective. It is love which is at work in moral memory when it recalls things from the past. Here it is admiration, respect, friendship, gratitude, affection and a thousand other things which have deeply moved you, which render things from the past *unforgettable*, i.e. evocable at each instant. The more one has loved, the more one remembers through moral memory.

As a general rule young people possess a very strong mechanical memory. It becomes feebler with age and it is logical or intellectual memory which comes to its assistance. This demands an effort to think, an intellectual effort. People who have failed to develop a taste for thinking and intellectual effort will have difficulties with their memory in mature age. Mechanical memory will fail them more and more, and logical memory, called to supplement it, will also be lacking.

With respect to moral memory, it is above all in old age that it replaces more and more not only mechanical memory but also logical and intellectual memory. It is the heart then which supplies the energy which nourishes and maintains memory and which supplements the growing lapse of mechanical memory and intellectual memory. Senile lapse of memory is due to the fact that the person who suffers from it failed to replace in time the functions of intellectual memory—without mentioning mechanical memory—by those of moral memory. People who know how to and are able to give everything a moral worth and to see a moral sense in everything will not forget anything; they will have a normal, if not excellent, memory to a very advanced age.

Moral memory—which can comprehend everything without exception—is all the more effective the less one is morally indifferent. Indifference, a lack of moral interest, is the fundamental cause of the lapse of memory which often takes place in old age. The less one is indifferent, the more one remembers of the past and the more one is capable of learning new things.

Beyond the three types of memory—mechanical, logical and moral—of which it is a matter here, there is still the kind of memory that we have designated as "vertical or revelatory memory". It is not a memory of the past in the sense of the horizontal line: today, yesterday, the day before, etc., but rather in the sense of the vertical line: here, higher, still higher, etc. It is a "memory" which does not link the present to the past on the plane of physical, psychic and intellectual life, but which links the plane of ordinary consciousness to planes or states of consciousness higher than that of ordinary consciousness. It is the faculty of the "lower self" to reproduce the experience and knowledge of the "higher Self" or, if you like, the faculty of the "higher Self" to imprint its experience and knowledge upon the consciousness of the "lower self". It is the link between the "higher eye" and the "lower eye", which renders us authentically religious and wise, and immune to the assaults of scepticism, materialism and determinism. It is this also which is the source of certainty not only of God and the spiritual world with its hierarchical entities but also of the immortality of our being and reincarnation, wherever it is a matter of reincarnation. "Dawn is the friend of the muses" and similar

popular proverbs—such as *Die Morgenstunde hat Gold im Munde* ("the morning hour has gold in its mouth"), or *Utro vechera mudreye* ("morning is wiser
than the evening"), or even *De morgenstond heeft goud in den mond* (the Dutch
version of *Die Morgenstunde hat Gold im Munde*)—relate to the benefits of vertical memory from which one benefits in the morning, after the return of consciousness from the plane of "natural ecstasy" or sleep.

Vertical memory is the more effective to the extent that the three sacred vows—
obedience, poverty and chastity—render the lower man capable of listening to,
perceiving and receiving things from above without distortion. Vertical memory
is fundamentally only moral memory carried in its development to a still higher
degree. This is why it is only moral purification, which the practice of the three
sacred vows entails, that counts in the case of vertical memory. Intellectual interests,
as such, do not count here.

This is an outlined inventory of the domain of memory. Let us now return to
the question: What is the force at work in the subjective magical operation of recall?

It is necessary, firstly, to take account of the fact that in the scale that we have
established: "mechanical memory"—"intellectual memory"—"moral memory"—
"vertical memory" it is a matter of degrees of *remoteness and proximity*, concerning an immediate and lucid understanding of the evidence as to "how" and "why"
memory functions through consciousness. In fact, the more something is mechanical, the more it is removed from immediate understanding through consciousness,
and the more it is removed from the latter, the more it is mysterious and incomprehensible. A purely mechanical explanation is, truth to tell, not at all an explanation, because it removes the object to be explained from the domain where
understanding takes place—by shifting it from the domain of comprehensibility, i.e. from "thinkability" and "feelability"—into the domain of the unconscious
and therefore of incomprehensibility. He who wants to explain the phenomenon
of smiling, for example, by the contraction of muscles in the region of the mouth
and cheeks, and this latter through electrical impulses transmitted through the
nerves from the centre called the "brain", will in no way give an explanation of
the phenomenon of "smiling", even if he correctly describes the entire mechanical
process in the muscles and nerves, for the simple reason that he disregards the
joy of which the smiling is a manifestation and which set in motion both the
muscles of the mouth and the electrical impulses of the nerves. For it is not nerves
and muscles which are manifested in smiling, but rather joy.

And just as the description of the mechanical process of the muscles and nerves
is in no way a reply to the question: What is smiling?, so is every mechanical explanation of whatever it may be in no way an explanation of the whole, but rather
it reduces questions to silence by shifting the subject of the questions from the
domain of comprehensibility to that of incomprehensibility—from the light of
consciousness to the darkness of the unconscious. For what we call "mechanical"

is in reality only the unconscious (or rather "that which is deprived of consciousness") and is therefore inaccessible to consciousness, and therefore incomprehensible, unthinkable and unfeelable. "Mechanicalism" is therefore not at all the realm of answers, but rather the graveyard for real questions.

This is why in the scale of memory under discussion we must not—and in fact cannot—seek to understand the working of recall in the domain where it is unknowable and incomprehensible, i.e. in that of "mechanical memory". On the contrary, we must seek it at the other end of the scale—where it is least embedded in the darkness of "mechanicalism" and where it most reveals its essence in the light of consciousness, i.e. in the domain of "moral memory" and "vertical memory". For it is the stage of complete development which illumines and explains the previous stages, and not vice versa. The minimum is only the reduced maximum and it is through the maximum that one understands the minimum, and not vice versa. It is consciousness which renders the mechanical and unconscious comprehensible, the latter being only consciousness reduced to a minimum, and not vice versa. It is man who is the key to the biological evolution of Nature and not the primitive organic cell.

We must therefore seek for the key to the operation of recall in memory at the highest degree of memory's development—"moral memory" and "vertical memory". Therefore, what is the force at work in the subjective magical operation of remembering, such as it is revealed in "vertical memory" and in "moral memory"?

The following reveals it to its highest conceivable degree—other degrees being only its analogous, weakened manifestations:

> Now Jesus *loved* Martha and her sister and Lazarus. . .when Jesus came, he found that Lazarus had already been in the tomb four days. . .Jesus wept. . .Then Jesus, deeply moved again, came to the tomb; it was a cave, and a stone lay upon it. Jesus said: *Take away the stone*. . .So they took away the stone. . . Jesus *cried with a loud voice: Lazarus, come out*. The dead man came out, his hands and feet bound with bandages, and his face wrapped with a cloth. (John xi, 5-44)

Here is the *force of recall* in its most complete, most strong and most elevated manifestation. It is *love*, for "Jesus loved Martha and her sister and Lazarus".

The operation of *recall* to life—or resurrection—comprises *three* stages: that of *coming*, that of *taking away the stone* and that of *recall*, i.e. "crying with a loud voice".

Firstly, coming: "To come and to arrive" is the activity which seeks and finds the *last door* which separates the recaller from the recalled. The "about two miles" between Bethany and Jerusalem that the Master went in order to arrive at the tomb of Lazarus represent the first effort in the whole operation of recall: that which aims at arriving at the point of maximum approach to the subject of recall.

Then, the taking away of the stone: this is the effort which vanquishes doubt, depression, fatigue and, lastly, despair, which bar the way to the recalled, like the stone placed before the tomb. By analogy, one is powerless to recall in the domain of vertical memory and moral memory things that one believes are lost for ever, or regarding which one believes that it is impossible to call them to the light of consciousness. This doubt and lack of faith paralyses the effort to recall and is like the stone placed before the tomb. This stone is often — if not always — the cause for many people of the absence of all living feeling and conviction, without speaking of precise and concrete remembrances, of former lives, i.e. of reincarnation. The remembrances have knocked at the door in vain, the stone placed before it not allowing them to come out from their depths and enter into the light of consciousness.

Lastly, recall: "To cry with a loud voice" is the culminating — and the supreme — effort of the operation of recall through the force of love, whether to life, as was the case with Lazarus, or whether to memory, as is the case of recall with vertical and moral memory.

A voice is louder, i.e. more audible, in the physical world, the more intense the vibrations are that it produces in the air. It is otherwise in the spiritual world. There a voice is more audible, i.e. "louder", the more it expresses underlying *effort* and *suffering*. *Work* and *suffering* are the things which render our voices audible to the spiritual world and in the spiritual world. These are the factors which create "vibrations" sufficiently "loud" in the spiritual world in order to render our voices audible. This is why the rosary-prayer repeats the *Ave Maria* one hundred and fifty times and the *Pater Noster* fifteen times. For if it is suffering which renders audible the ejaculative prayer of a single word —"Jesus!", for example — it is *effort* which renders the rosary-prayer audible. I would lack respect for the truth if I did not say that the *effort* of the rosary-prayer founded on *suffering* makes it a powerful means — sometimes almost all-powerful — in sacred magic.

Now, the "cry with a loud voice", which is the decisive act in the whole operation of recall, must be strong both in effort and in suffering: "Jesus wept...Then Jesus, deeply moved again, came to the tomb...Jesus cried with a loud voice: Lazarus, come out." It is love which wept and which strove to accomplish the miracle of recall from death to life — which is also the case in recall from forgetfulness to memory.

Is recall therefore a miracle?

...yes, a miracle. But allow me, dear Unknown Friend, to say something concerning the miracle that I believe to be of the highest significance, of which every Christian Hermeticist and every Cabbalist should take account: it is that *there is no freedom outside of the miraculous* and that man is man only in so far as he lives from the miracle, through the miracle and for the miracle.

All that is not mechanical — physical, psychic and intellectual — is miraculous, and all that is not miraculous is only mechanical — physical, psychic and intellectual. Freedom is a miracle and man is only free in so far as he is not a machine — physical, psychic and intellectual. We have no other choice than between the machine and slavery, on the one hand, and the miracle and freedom, on the other hand.

The human machine *functions* according to the determined programme "maximum pleasure at minimum cost" in a way so as to lend itself to precise prediction in its reactions to given circumstances. In the intellectual domain it rejects every notion and every idea which does not harmonise with the intellectual system established in it; in the psychic domain it rejects all that does not harmonise with the complex of "happiness" established in it; and in the physical domain it automatically follows the orders transmitted by the complex "instinct" established in it.

It is only the *functioning* of the human machine when a rich man declares himself anti-communist and a poor man declares himself pro-communist. But it is a *miracle* — that is to say an act of freedom — when a rich man abandons his possessions and embraces poverty, as did St. Anthony the Great and also many other saints, and also Carmelites, Franciscans, Dominicans, etc., who took the vow of poverty. The *miracle* of St. Francis is not only the healing of a leper but also the love of St. Francis for "Lady Poverty". Did not the miracles of Jesus Christ, after the resurrection of Lazarus, culminate in the cross on Calvary where, in the full agony of torture, he said: "Father, forgive them, for they know not what they do" (Luke xxiii, 34)?

All that one *does* is miraculous; all intellectual, psychic and physical *functioning* according to "nature", i.e. according to human automatism, is mechanical. The *Sermon on the Mount* is the teaching of *doing* and of the triumph over *functioning*.

> Love your enemies, do good to those who hate you, bless those
> who curse you . . . and pray for those who persecute you, so that
> you may be sons of your Father who is in heaven. (Luke vi, 27-28;
> Matthew v, 44-45)

Is this not a teaching which aims at the liberation of the machine, i.e. of all *functioning*, and which is a school for the miraculous?

Because to bless those who curse you is a miracle from the point of view of the "normal and natural" functioning of the reactions of the human machine. This does not just happen, it is *done* (it is created); and I repeat, one only *does* miracles, and all that is *done* is a miracle, and nothing is *done* without it being a miracle. All that which is not a miracle is not really *done* — it happens, as part of automatic functioning. It is only through the miracle that true being expresses itself, that the creative Word is revealed.

It is wrong, therefore, to interpret the phrases at the beginning of the Gospel according to John as the teaching of a kind of cosmic rationalism, analogous to the Stoic doctrine of *nous* ("mind"). No, the phrases at the beginning of the Gospel according to John openly declare the cosmic role of the *miracle*, and that the world is due to a miracle, i.e. that it was *made* by the creative Word, and not that it was due to any functioning, to any automatic — even highly intellectual — process:

> All things were made through the Word, and nothing that was
> made was made without him. (John i, 3)

This is what the Evangelist says; and what we have said above concerning the miracle and the machine — i.e. concerning "doing" and "functioning"— is only the microcosmic analogy to the statement of macrocosmic significance from the Gospel according to John.

Now, "all things made through the Word" includes also *recall* in vertical and moral memory. The act of recall belongs to the sphere of "doing" and therefore to that of the miraculous, and not to the sphere of "functioning". Recall in "logical memory" is a mixture of doing and functioning. Lastly, recall in mechanical memory is only functioning, i.e. the act of moral recall reduced to a minimum.

If recall is an act analogous to the resurrection of Lazarus, then what is *forgetting*?

Forgetting outlines a scale analogous to that of recall. It can take place automatically, semi-automatically, and in a free and conscious way, according to the category of memory in which it is placed. In mechanical memory one forgets automatically; things are just forgotten. In logical memory things become distant and are effaced little by little if one does not recall them from time to time to the field of conscious attention. In moral memory and in vertical memory *nothing is forgotten*; forgetting here is a moral act of will.

Let us follow the same procedure as is the case in recall, i.e. let us begin at the end of the scale where forgetting is an act of consciousness and where it is understandable — where it takes place in the light of consciousness.

Now, there is no one who does not know through experience that all conscious effort entails concentration or contemplation, and that concentration and contemplation signify conscious and willed *forgetting* of many things which do not relate to the subject of concentration or contemplation. One knows that when one prays the *Pater Noster* one forgets not only one's daily affairs but also all other prayers for the time that one prays the *Pater Noster*.

It is the same with spiritual and divine *values*, and those of the phenomenal world. The three stages on the way towards the soul's union with God — those of purification, illumination and union — are simply the history of a single growing effort of concentration of the entire soul upon God. St. John of the Cross says of the effect of the experience of actual union of the soul's powers with God:

> . . . all the powers of the soul together, because of the union in
> the inner cellar, drink of the Beloved . . . This draught of God's
> most deep wisdom makes the soul forget all the things of this
> world, and consider all its previous knowledge, and the know-
> ledge of the whole world besides, as pure ignorance in com-
> parison with this knowledge. (St. John of the Cross, *A Spiritual
> Canticle* xxvi, 7, 10; trsl. D. Lewis, London, 1909, pp. 204-205)

And again:

> . . .the more the memory is united to God the more it loses all
> distinct knowledge, and at last all such fades utterly away, when
> the state of perfection is reached. In the beginning, when this
> is going on, great forgetfulness ensues, for these forms and
> knowledge fall into oblivion. . .the memory is lost in God. But
> he who has attained to the habit of union does not forget, in
> this way, that which relates to moral and natural reason; he per-
> forms in much greater perfection all necessary and befitting ac-
> tions, though by the ministry of forms and knowledge, in the
> memory, supplied in a special manner by God. (St. John of the
> Cross, *The Ascent of Mount Carmel* III, i, 5; trsl. D. Lewis, Lon-
> don, 1906, pp. 244-245)

I may add that the masters of Raja-yoga, Bhakti-yoga and Jnana-yoga teach the
practice of complete forgetting of the phenomenal world with a view to attaining
perfect contemplation. The teaching of forgetting is found also in the mystical
Cabbala and in Mohammedan mysticism, e.g. that of Sufism.

Now, forgetting is the means of transition from one state of consciousness to
another. Even in the case of *sleep*, which can be considered as a "natural ecstasy",
one has to forget the world of the day in order to be able to pass into the world
of the night. In order to fall asleep one has to be able to forget. Insomnia is due
to the inability to forget.

And awakening? Awakening is simultaneously an act of recall of the world of
the day and an act of forgetting the nocturnal world. Awakening would be incomplete—which it, moreover, often is—if one did not forget the experiences of the
nocturnal world. The night would then be mingled with the day and human consciousness would be hindered in its capacity with respect to the tasks and duties
of the day—its concentration being hampered by the haunting memory of nocturnal remembrances.

And birth and death?

If the soul's mystical union with God is forgetting of the phenomenal world
and recall of God, death is simultaneously the *call* from above and *forgetting* below.
The three stages of the way leading to the soul's union with God—purification,
illumination and union—are repeated after death: *purgatory* is purification
(*catharsis*), which precedes illumination or *heaven*, and heaven is the state of the
soul when it arrives at union with God, analogous to that experienced by mystics
during their terrestrial life. This union, there as here, becomes habitual—which
is a sovereign good for the soul—and then it remembers anew the earth and its
trials. Memory then manifests a "greater perfection" (says St. John of the Cross
concerning the resuscitated functions of memory in the case of the soul which
has the *habit of union*) in all its action—let us add, actions directed towards the
earth.

This is the motivation for the blessed work of saints. Saints are souls who possess the "hàbit of union" and are therefore in possession of the higher spiritualised memory spoken of by St. John of the Cross. They *do not seek* union with God; they *are* united with God. This is why they act — their faces being turned towards the earth and not towards God — in the name of God on earth. They act, *being united* with God, in the guise of organs of his will.

It is the same with the celestial hierarchies — with *Angels*, for example. Guardian Angels could never be guardians of human beings if their looks were turned towards God, if they were absorbed in contemplation of God. It is thanks to their *habitual* union with God, i.e. thanks to the *accomplished fact* of the union of their will with the divine will, that they are able to fulfill their task as guardians of men. They know the divine will in a "blind" way — through the dim intuition of their own will, i.e. through perfect *faith* — whilst what they *see* is the earth and human life on earth. Their faces, as are those of the saints, are turned towards the earth. This is the motivation for devotion to the guardian Angels.

With respect to birth, it can, also, be either "holy" or "natural", i.e. it can either be an act of obedience to divine will or rather it can be effected as a consequence of a "call from the earth". A soul can be *sent to* the earth or it can be *attracted by* the earth. In the first case it is an *act* analogous to the recall of vertical and moral memory, i.e. analogous to the miracle of the resurrection of Lazarus. In the latter case it is an event that is half-voluntary and half-involuntary, where the soul falls — often without realising it — into the sphere of terrestrial attraction, which bears it to birth, and thereby it is made little by little to forget its experiences above. Birth is then a forgetting of heaven and simultaneously a recall to the earth.

This is not so with "holy birth". Here it is the remembrance of the divine which is the force which accomplishes incarnation. It is not thanks to forgetting of the divine that the soul is then incarnated, but rather thanks to its remembering. It is in the state of "habitual union" with God that the soul is incarnated. Then its will does not lose memory of the divine. This memory acts in it, imprinted as it is in the soul's will, during the whole terrestrial life which follows a "holy birth". One could then speak of a "mission", or an "election". . . and rightly, because such a mission is the only one which really exists. For the true mission is not what the *human being* proposes to do on the earth according to his tastes, his interests and even his ideals, but rather what God wants him to do. Arbitrary "missions", although due to the best intentions in the world, have only contributed confusion to human history. It is to these inopportune "missions" that we owe many crises upsetting the life of mankind's living traditions — interrupting, in the guise of passing comets, the peaceful and constructive flow of true progress.

A true mission on the earth serves the cause of the ennoblement and spiritualisation of *that which is*, i.e. of what lives as tradition. It brings an impulse effecting the rejuvenation and intensification of tradition. Arbitrary missions, on the contrary, aim at revolutionising the course of mankind's history and substituting specific innovations for what lives as tradition. In pushing this to the extreme one could say: a true mission brings to greater perfection everything human on the earth—the family, civilisation, culture, religion, etc., whilst arbitrary missions can result in summoning the intervention of Martians or Venusians so that they rule affairs on the earth!

Now, birth, awakening and recall, on the one hand, and death, falling asleep and forgetting, on the other hand, constitute, so to say, the two "pillar-forces" of reality. They manifest in remembering and forgetting, in the rhythm of sleeping and waking and in that of birth and death—as well as in the respiration of organisms, in the circulation of blood, and in alimentation. They are the "yes" and "no" in every domain—mental, psychic and physical.

The Gospel maxim, "Let what you say be simply 'Yes' or 'No'; anything more than this comes from evil" (Matthew v, 37) reveals its significance in this context. The "yes" and the "no"—this is the essential of reality, i.e. the *truth*, pure and simple, whilst the "surplus" comes from evil, i.e. it belongs to the sphere of the serpent. For the serpent of Genesis has his own word—the word which is the "surplus" over "yes" and "no". He is in possession of a *third* term.

And here we return to the question that we posed at the beginning of this Letter, namely: Has the serpent, having said, "You will not die", simply told a lie, or has he stated a truth from the range of truths proper to the domain of the serpent? In other words: What is the "surplus" that the serpent adds to the "yes" and "no" understood as *life* and *death*?

If you accept, dear Unknown Friend, what we have said in the preceding Letters on the difference in principle that there is between *life* and *electricity*, between the principle of the Virgin and that of the serpent, you will certainly be able to penetrate more deeply the secret of the "surplus" offered and promised by the serpent to humanity concerning the "yes" and "no" understood as life and death.

Here is this secret: the serpent offers and promises such a *crystallisation*, according to the principle of enfoldment, that the human being will resist death and become, so to say, "death-proof", immune to death. This crystallisation is effected through *friction*, i.e. by the electrical energy which is produced by the struggle between "yes" and "no" in man.

Without doubt you know, dear Unknown Friend, that there are schools—occult or other—which teach and practise *crystallisation* and that there are other schools which teach and practise *radiation*, i.e. the complete de-crystallisation of the human being and his transformation into a "sun", into a centre of radiation. "Then the righteous will shine like the sun in the kingdom of their Father" (Matthew xiii, 43)—this is the practical aim of "schools of radiation", to which that of Christian Hermeticism belongs.

The "schools of crystallisation" are quite numerous and widespread. There are those which are entirely secret, with very serious intentions; there are also those which are known in the guise of almost popular movements for "health, rejuvenation and longevity". I shall not speak here of the practices of entirely secret schools, the secret not being mine but that of others. Also I shall not speak about the almost popular movement, because it will certainly be easy to understand their aim and methods after having understood the aim and method of an occult school that I have chosen as an illustrative example. I have chosen this particular occult school as an example, because it is something between the secret schools and the almost popular movements and because it has itself taken the decision to show itself in broad daylight, thus authorising me to speak of it and to cite its documents, accessible to everyone.

I have in mind the school of G. I. Gurdjieff, and I am going to cite the work In Search of the Miraculous by P. D. Ouspensky. Now, the following is the teaching of Gurdjieff, such as it has been understood and formulated by Ouspensky, concerning the practical task of survival:

> On one occasion, at one of these meetings, someone asked about the possibility of reincarnation, and whether it was possible to believe in cases of communication with the dead. "Many things are possible," said G. (Gurdjieff). "But it is necessary to understand that man's being, both in life and after death, if it does exist after death, may be very different in quality. The 'man-machine' with whom everything depends upon external influences, with whom everything happens, who is now one, the next moment another, and the next moment a third, has no future of any kind; he is buried and that is all. *Dust returns to dust.* This applies to him. In order to be able to speak of any kind of future life there must be a certain crystallisation, a certain fusion of man's inner qualities, a certain independence of external influences. If there is anything in a man able to resist external influences, then this very thing itself may also be able to resist the death of the physical body . . . But even if something survives, its future can be very varied. In certain cases of fuller crystallisation, what people call 'reincarnation' may be possible after death, and, in other cases, what people call 'existence on the other side'. In both cases it is the continuation of life in the 'astral body', or with the help of the 'astral body'. You know what the expression 'astral body' means. But the systems with which you are acquainted and which use this expression state that *all* men have an 'astral body'. This is quite wrong. What may be called the 'astral body' is obtained by means of fusion, that. is, by means of terribly hard inner work and struggle. Man is not born with it. And only very few men acquire an 'astral body'. If it is formed it may continue to live after the death of the physical body, and it may be born again in another physical body . . . Fusion, inner unity, is obtained by means of 'friction', by the struggle between 'yes' and 'no' in man. If a man lives without inner struggle, if everything happens in him without

opposition, if he goes wherever he is drawn or wherever the wind blows, he will remain such as he is. But if a struggle begins in him, and particularly if there is a definite line in this struggle, then, gradually, permanent traits begin to form themselves, he begins to 'crystallise'...Crystallisation is possible on any foundations. Take for example a brigand, a really good, genuine brigand. I knew such brigands in the Caucasus. He will stand with a rifle behind a stone by the roadside for eight hours without stirring. Could you do this? All the time, mind you, a struggle is going on in him. He is thirsty and hot, and flies are biting him; but he stands still. Another is a monk; he is afraid of the devil; all night long he beats his head on the floor and prays. Thus crystallisation is achieved...Such people can become immortal." (P. D. Ouspensky, *In Search of the Miraculous*, London, 1969, pp. 31-32)

Let us now take account of the essential points in the quoted text. Firstly, it is the *physical body* which gives birth to what is called in the quotation the "astral body" which will be the bearer of survival. Then, according to the text, immortality is neither a birthright of the human soul nor a gift of divine grace — *it is made* by means of the crystallisation of a new body within the physical body which can resist death and survive the destruction of the physical body. That is to say, the soul created by God does not exist; it must be created by the human being from within the human physical body. Thus it is a quantity of energy crystallised within the human physical body and engendered through this latter, produced by friction or the struggle between "yes" and "no" in man. For both the robber and the monk, and also the occultist, can become immortal through the *energy* that they produce by their efforts.

It is a matter of a plan of construction, from within the physical body, of a tower or a "house of four rooms" or levels (Ouspensky, ibid., p. 44), rising from the sphere of mortality to that of immortality, from earth to heaven. Now, the Bible knows of the method of building "a tower with its top in the heavens" and of making "a name for ourselves lest we be scattered abroad upon the face of the whole earth" (Genesis xi, 4). It is the ideal and millennial-old method of construction of the *tower of Babel*. The "tower of Babel" is a very ancient method. The following is what Gurdjieff says about it:

According to an ancient teaching, traces of which may be found in many systems, old and new, a man who has attained the full development possible for man, a man in the full sense of the word, *consists of four bodies*. These four bodies are composed of substances which gradually become finer and finer, mutually interpenetrate one another, and form four independent organisms, standing in a definite relationship to one another but capable of independent action. The reason why it is possible for four bodies to exist is that the human organism, that is, the physical body, has such a complex organisation that, under certain conditions, a new independent organism can grow in it, affording a much more convenient and responsive instrument for the activity of consciousness than the physical body. . . In this second body, under certain conditions, a third body can grow, again having characteristics of its own. . . In the third body, under certain conditions, a fourth can grow, which differs as much from the third as the third differs from the second and the second from the first . . . (p. 40)

An Eastern teaching describes the functions of the four bodies, their gradual growth, and the conditions of this growth, in the following way: Let us imagine a vessel or a retort filled with various metallic powders. The powders are not in any way connected with each other and every accidental change in the position of the retort changes the relative position of the powders . . . It is impossible to stabilise the interrelation of powders in a state of mechanical mixture. But the powders may be fused; the nature of the powders makes this possible. To do this a special kind of fire must be lighted under the retort which, by heating and melting the powders, finally fuses them together. Fused in this way the powders will be in the state of a chemical compound . . . The contents of the retort have become indivisible, "individual". This is a picture of the formation of the second body. The fire by means of which fusion is attained is produced by "friction", which in its turn is produced in man by the struggle between "yes" and "no". . .

The process of imparting new properties to the alloy corresponds to the process of the formation of the third body. . . The process of fixing these acquired properties corresponds to the process of the formation of the fourth body. And only the man who possesses four fully developed bodies can be called a "man" in the full sense of the word. This man possesses many properties which ordinary man does not possess. *One of these properties is immortality*. (P. D. Ouspensky, *In Search of the Miraculous*, London, 1969, pp. 40, 43-44)

Now, the "special fire lit under the retort" is due to friction which is, in its turn, the product of the struggle between "yes" and "no". This fire is therefore what we understand by "electricity". It is therefore thanks to electricity, or energy produced by friction, that the process of crystallisation works.

The architects of the tower of Babel also made use of *fire* for the preparation of its materials of construction. " 'Come, let us make bricks, and *burn them thoroughly.*' And they had brick for stone, and bitumen for mortar" (Genesis xi, 3).

The essence of the method of "construction of the tower of Babel" is *inverse crystallisation*. Normal crystallisation—the "stone"—is the final state of the process of transition from the gaseous to the liquid state and from the liquid to the solid state. Thus vapour becomes water (liquid) and water becomes ice. Ice is crystallised vapour. Similarly, a general but warm intention becomes a current of discursive thought which, in its turn, results in a well-defined formula. Or in still other terms: the spiritual becomes psychic and the psychic becomes corporeal.

The process of normal crystallisation is therefore one of concretisation from above below:

| Spirit
| Soul
↓ Body

The process of crystallisation designated as the "construction of the tower of Babel", takes place, in contrast, from below above:

↑ Spirit
| Soul
| Body

With regard to this latter process, it is a matter of transformation into "body" of the psychic and spiritual. And it is thus that one can conquer death and realise immortality. . .corporeal immortality. For if the spiritual and the psychic, in becoming corporeal, become mortal, would it not be possible that the corporeal, in rising to the psychic and spiritual, becomes immortal?

Is this scheme realisable or is it simply an illusion, pure and simple? Although this question belongs to the framework of problems of the sixteenth Major Arcanum of the Tarot, and although it will be treated in the sixteenth Letter, let us nonetheless consider some facts with a view to coming to an answer.

The facts that I have in mind are those of *corporeal survival*, i.e. *physical manifestations* that one attributes—rightly or wrongly—to dead people or to "ghosts". Ghosts exist. This is not a question of belief; it is a matter of fact. There is an immense literature, without speaking of facts that one can find in the sphere of personal experience, which bears witness to the existence of ghosts. Now it is no longer a matter of believing or denying; now it is a matter only of understanding and explaining. Ghosts exist therefore. Thus it happens from time to time after someone's death that this person or "something" of him or similar to him manifests in an outward and physical way (noises, movements, etc.) in the guise of an active *energy*. It is as if a certain quantity of energy, freed through death, but remaining condensed and not dispersed, manifests as an entity or as an individual "body".

An analysis of the manifestations of ghosts has enabled me to extract from them the following characteristic traits:

1. a ghost is an entity made up of psycho-physiological electrical energy, with an inferior consciousness in comparison with that of a normal human person;

2. the consciousness which is revealed by the actions of a ghost, and by its way of acting in general, is very limited and extremely specialised—one is tempted to characterise it as "maniacal", since it manifests itself as the crystallisation of a single passion, a single habit, or a single fixed idea;

3. the energy of which the ghost is constituted becomes weakened with time—provided that it is not nourished by an affirmative and favourable attitude from its human entourage; it fades away. One can make it disappear through the Church ritual of exorcism, or by individual prayer, or lastly by a special action which demands courage and which consists in *clasping and breathing in* the ghost, in such a way as to receive it into oneself and of oneself to make the electrical energy of the ghost dissipate. I dare not recommend this latter method because it entails the experience of an electric shock —which can be excessive—at the moment when the energy of the ghost passes into your organism. I may add, however, that it is this experience of an electric shock which gives absolute certainty with respect to the electrical nature of the "body" of the ghost. At the same time it can also supply proof—in the inner forum of consciousness, it goes without saying—that the ghost is not the soul of the departed one, and that it is a burden to him, being bound to the soul of the departed by a heavy link of responsibility. In the case that I have mentioned, soon after the dissipation of the ghost's electrical energy through its reception into oneself, the departed one hastens to make acknowledgement of his gratitude, by means of a very vivid and clear dream, for his deliverance from this heavy burden.

What, then, is a ghost? It is exactly what Gurdjieff teaches concerning the product of psychic crystallisation effected from within the physical body, and which can resist the death of the latter. This is the "astral body" of which Gurdjieff said that, "if it is formed it may continue to live after the death of the physical body. . . if it is not re-born, then, in the course of time, it also dies; it is not immortal but it can live long after the death of the physical body" (Ouspensky, op. cit., p. 32). Of course, the "astral body" spoken of by Gurdjieff has nothing to do with the "astral body" of Hermeticism, which latter is, truth to tell, simply the totality of the soul's *psychic* memories.

A ghost is always constituted as a consequence of *crystallisation*, i.e. crystallisation of a desire, a passion, or a purpose of great intensity, which produces a *complex* of energy in the human being. Thus, a "genuine brigand" who stands "with a rifle behind a stone by the roadside for eight hours without stirring" or "a monk. . .(who) is afraid of the devil (and) all night long he beats his head on the floor and prays" (Ouspensky, op. cit., p. 32) in fact crystallise within them a *complex* of energy, a psycho-electrical *double*, which would be able, as a dense *complex*, to resist death.

And the same thing that *happens* with human beings who are possessed by strong desires, passions and intentions can be *achieved* methodically by making use of the scientific method of the "construction of the tower of Babel". Then one could not only animate the double crystallised from a desire, a passion or a dominant intention, but also equip it with an intellectual apparatus of very developed functioning and a mechanical memory in which all the facts of experience on the physical plane are accumulated. The "self" of such an occultist would then be allied to this double, who is the bearer of his memory and intellect, and could incarnate himself anew — avoiding purgatory and the whole path of purification, illumination and union which is the lot of the human soul after death.

It is therefore not purely and simply a matter of an illusion in the case of the ideal and method of the "construction of the tower of Babel". Rather, it is a matter of *another kind of immortality*, notably that which the serpent of Genesis had in mind when he said, "*You will not die* if you eat of the fruit of the Tree of Knowledge of Good and Evil". For the fruit of the Tree of Knowledge of Good and Evil produces the inner friction in man of the struggle between "yes" and "no", and this friction in its turn produces the electrical fire which effects the crystallisation whose product will resist death. This is the meaning of the promise — or rather the *programme* — of the serpent. This programme underlies the millennial-old method of the "construction of the tower of Babel", and it constitutes the esoteric kernel or the hidden secret of *materialistic science in general*.

We have chosen Gurdjieff (and Ouspensky) to exemplify the ideal and the method of the "construction of the tower of Babel", but Gurdjieff — being openly materialistic in the true sense of this word, and being deprived of all mystical sense — only spoke on behalf of the multitude. All he did was to give forth clearly what animates and impels — in an unconscious or semi-conscious way — millions and millions of scientists devoted to the cause of *longevity*, i.e. to the victory over death through human science, without God and without mysticism: the universal cause of the *construction of the tower of Babel*.

Gurdjieff is simply a representative of the cause of materialistic science; he knew what it wants in reality and he also knew what he wanted himself. He was, moreover, a good-natured man, endowed with an exquisite sense of humour, a good son, a good friend, and very intelligent with respect to common sense — to indicate only the qualities that he possessed which leap out at one. It would therefore be wrong to see in him a "prophet of darkness" or an instrument of a special "Satanic mission". No, he was simply a good representative of the "wisdom of this world", i.e. of good sense and empirical experience *without any mystical inclination*. Gurdjieff was not any more a "Satanist" than the celebrated Russian physiologist Pavlov or any other representative of materialistic science.

Assuredly, his practical and theoretical teaching of crystallisation from below above is not compatible either with Carl Jung's process of individuation or with Christian Hermeticism or with the Cabbala. For Hermeticism also teaches a crystallisation but it is a crystallisation from above below, i.e. the crystallisation of which Hermeticism itself—in so far as it is philosophy and knowledge—is the product: crystallised mysticism being gnosis, crystallised gnosis being magic, and crystallised magic being this philosophy and knowledge which passes under the name of "Hermeticism". Thus if one disregards the intermediary stages, one could · say that Hermeticism is crystallised mysticism, whilst Gurdjieff's materialistic occultism replaces—and abolishes—mysticism by crystallised materialistic science.

In returning to the question posed at the beginning of this Letter: Did the serpent of Genesis simply lie?—we are now able to answer: no, he did not lie. He opposed to divine immortality another immortality: that of crystallisation from below above, or the "tower of Babel". He advanced the bold programme—but real and realisable—aiming at a mankind which would be composed of the living and of ghosts, with the latter reincarnating almost without delay and avoiding the way which leads through purgatory to heaven.

You see now, dear Unknown Friend, *why* the Church was hostile to the *doctrine* of reincarnation, although the *fact* of repeated incarnations was known—and could not remain unknown—to a large number of people faithful to the Church with authentic spiritual experience. The deeper reason is the danger of reincarnation by way of the ghost, where one avoids the path of purification (in purgatory), illumination and celestial union. For humanity could succumb to the temptation of preparing for a future terrestrial life, instead of preparing for purgatory and heaven, during earthly life. To prepare for a future terrestrial life, instead of preparing for the confrontation with Eternity, amounts to crystallisation in the sense of the formation of an electric double—the body of the ghost—which could, in its turn, serve as the bridge from one incarnation to another and be the means of evading purgatory and the confrontation with Eternity. One ought during earthly life to prepare for this meeting with a fully awakened consciousness, which is purgatory, and for the experience of the presence of the Eternal, which is heaven, and not to prepare for a future terrestrial life, which would amount to the crystallisation of the "body" of a ghost. It is worth a hundred times more to know nothing of the fact of reincarnation, and to deny the doctrine of reincarnation, than to turn thoughts and desires towards the future terrestrial life and thus to be tempted to resort to the means offered through the promise of immortality made by the serpent. This is why, I repeat, the Church was, from the beginning, hostile to the idea of reincarnation and did all that it could so that this idea would not take root in consciousness—and above all in the human will.

I confess that it is only after hesitation, due to objections of a very serious moral order, that I have decided to write of the danger that the doctrine of reincarnation entails, and above all of that abuse that can be—and is, in fact—made of it. It is the faith that you, dear Unknown Friend, understand the weight of responsibility that weighs on each person who sees himself treating reincarnation not as belonging to the domain of esoteric (i.e. intimate) experience, but as an exoteric teaching to popularise—called to convince everyone—which has determined me to speak of the practical abuse of the fact of reincarnation. I *implore* you therefore, dear Unknown Friend, to have the good will to examine, in the light of moral conscience, the question whether the way of treating reincarnation in exoteric teaching that has been adopted and is practised in general both by representatives of the French occult movement of the nineteenth and twentieth centuries and by Theosophists, Anthroposophists, Rosicrucians, etc., is justified and desirable.

I may add that in the last analysis it is a matter not only of the moral danger of evading purgatory and the experience of Eternity, but also of *replacing one immortality by another*, namely that of God by that of the serpent. For there are *two* deaths and *two* immortalities.

The "death" of which the father speaks in the parable of the prodigal son— "my son was dead, and is alive again; he was lost, and is found" (Luke xv, 24)—is *remoteness from the Father and his house*, whilst the death of the physical body means remoteness from the physical plane and the electrical field of terrestrial gravitation (which was the matter in question in the twelfth Letter, concerning the Arcanum "The Hanged Man"). Now, the refusal to take the way of purgatory and heaven amounts to refusing to return to the house of the Father, i.e. the decision to remain *remote* from the Father. And it is precisely this which is *death* in a divine sense. *Complete crystallisation* is therefore complete death from the divine point of view, whilst complete life is the state of "radiating as the sun", i.e. that of *complete de-crystallisation*. Thus the divine words, "You shall not eat from the Tree of Knowledge of Good and Evil, for on the day when you eat of it you will die", state simply that "the day when you eat from the Tree of Knowledge of Good and Evil, *you will remove yourself from Me*". And the promise of the serpent, "You will not die", means to say, "You will live remote from God and it will be I who shall attend to the uninterrupted continuation of your life in the horizontal, for I shall make up for the lack of divine wisdom and love by replacing them with the intellect and with psycho-physical electricity, which will be the source of your life". Therefore the serpent understands by "life" what God understands by "death"—and vice versa. Now, Hermeticism—Christian Hermeticism as well as ancient and pre-Christian Hermeticism—has always advanced the fundamental thesis of all true mysticism, true gnosis, and true sacred magic, that there is *vertical* Life and Death and that there is *horizontal* life and death. For Christian Hermeticism the Cross of humanity—the Cross of Calvary—is that of two opposed lives and deaths. Resurrection is not only the triumph of Life over Death, but is moreover the triumph of Life over life.

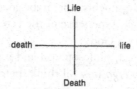

It is the victory of the vertical over the horizontal, of radiation over crystallisation. This is why when the women who went to the tomb at the break of day did not find the body of Lord Jesus, the two men who appeared to them in resplendent apparel said to them, "Why do you seek the living *among the dead*?" (Luke xxiv, 5). Therefore, let us no longer seek amongst the dead for he who is living, and above all let us not seek for immortal Life in the domain of death—in the domain of the intellect borne by electricity or, to employ an image borrowed from the Cabbala, in the domain of Samael mounted on the dragon.

It is not phantoms and ghosts which are the source of certainty of survival or immortality. The source of this certainty is found elsewhere. Where, then?. . . in the experience of the kernel of the human being and his relationship with the breath, light and warmth of God.

Certainty of immortality issues from the participation experienced in that which is intrinsically indestructible and imperishable, and therefore immortal. He who has had experience of the kernel of his being, i.e. he who has once been *truly himself*, permeated by the divine breath, bathed in divine light and ardent with divine warmth, he *knows* what immortality is and that he is immortal. You will have beautifully explained to him the "epiphenomenal nature" of consciousness, i.e. that consciousness is only the functioning of the brain and nervous system and that it is like the rainbow—a play of colours resulting from the refraction and reflection of solar rays on the clouds—you will have beautifully said all this, and he will have not even a little grain of doubt that all this is false and the contrary is true. Perhaps he would not be able to find valid arguments *for you* against epiphenomenalism, but as for *him*, he has no need of them. For it is not to arguments that he owes his certainty, but rather to experience.

Imagine the reaction of a St. John of the Cross or a St. Teresa of Avila to a discourse, armed with all the arguments of modern science, addressed to them so as to prove to them that the soul is only a mirage produced by chemical and electrical reactions of the organism! To prove this to them!—they who many times went out of the body, left in a state of complete insensibility, and returned full of life and light drawn not only from beyond all chemical and electrical reactions but also from beyond all sense imagery and all intellectual activity! I think that they would have sent the author of such remarks either to a psychiatrist or to an exorcist!

Certainty in immortality can thus be *absolute*, i.e. in no way dependent on the validity or invalidity of arguments, nor on the good or bad attestation of outer facts. It is when man has had experience of the kernel of his own being and of his essential relationship with God.

I certainly know the logical, philosophical and psychological criticism of the Cartesian argument, *cogito ergo sum* ("I think therefore I am"), and I accept it without reserve *in foro scientiae*, but it was not the force of this argument in the tribunal of science which gave René Descartes certainty of his transcendent Self, the kernel of his being, but rather the *experience* in the tribunal of consciousness (*in foro conscientiae*) where, whilst thinking in the admirable way which was characteristic of him, he went out of discursive thought and found himself suddenly as the *thinker* of thoughts! It was therefore not a logical *argument* but a real and intimate experience of *thought*—in the process of thinking—which gave Descartes complete certainty of the reality of the "I am" which manifests itself in the "I think".

The German philosopher Immanuel Kant (a soul of childlike purity, endowed with a remarkable honesty and diligence) made Descartes' spontaneous experience a new method of inner effort aspiring to knowledge, namely the *transcendental method*.

This method amounts to the effort to transcend the thinking in which the thinker is ordinarily immersed, by going out from it and elevating himself above it, in order to *observe* thought—or "to think about thought"—from a point of observation taken *above discursive thought*. Kant's "Copernican discovery" consists above all in detaching the thinker from "naive thought", i.e. from the state where the thinker is lost in the process of thought, being immersed in it, so as to occupy a point situated above thought, from where the thinker can examine what is thought in an entirely detached way and with implacable and incorruptible truthfulness—this is the "transcendental criticism" of Kant. His works *Critique of Pure Reason* and *Critique of Judgement* are the fruits of the application of this method in the sense of the *revision* of the totality of our knowledge, and in the sense of a clear investigation of the pretensions of the intellect and of the senses to being able to judge things belonging to the metaphysical domain—for example, God, the immortality of the soul, and moral freedom. With respect to his *Critique of Practical Reason* we find here, beyond the results of the critical look of the thinker turned towards the domain of discursive thought and sense perceptions in which he had been immersed before, in addition what the thinker, this kernel of the human being, has to say himself. This can be summarised as follows:

> I would have to alter the foundation of my very being, or to annihilate myself, if I were to say that God does not exist, that I am not free, and that I am not immortal. The very structure of my being is such that it postulates categorically the *existence of God* or infinite perfectibility, *freedom* or morality as such, and the *immortality of the soul* or the possibility of infinite perfectioning.

It goes without saying that just as René Descartes' argument "I think therefore I am" became the object of the annihilating criticism of logicians, philosophers and psychologists, so is the fundamental argument advanced by Immanual Kant in his *Critique of Practical Reason* the subject of a no less severe criticism — and no less founded *in foro scientiae* — than in the case of Descartes' argument. But here also it is necessary to say that it was not a *logical conclusion* or an argument of discursive thought which gave Kant certainty of God, freedom and immortality, but rather the real and intimate *experience* that he had when he practised his transcendental method. This latter evidently proved itself to be an *authentic spiritual exercise*, which led Kant to arrive at experience of the kernel of his being — just as Descartes arrived there — and from which he drew the threefold certainty: the reality of *God*, the reality of *moral freedom* and, lastly, the reality of the *soul's immortality*.

Similarly, in Hindu Jnana-yoga the yogi arrives at the transcendent Self by critically observing firstly his body and arriving at the experience, "This body is not the Self", then critically examining his psychic life — desires, feelings, memory images, etc. — to arrive at the experience, "This psychic life is not the Self", and, lastly, critically examining his thinking itself, from which he detaches himself, and experiences the thinker — just as Descartes and Kant arrived at the experience of the transcendent Self by rising from thought to the thinker. From this comes their certainty of "I am" (Descartes) and "I am free, I am immortal (and) I am in the presence of God" (Kant).

May the criticism of Descartes and Kant eventually become silent, restraining itself through understanding; may it *no more interfere with* that at which these two spirits arrived, namely the *intimate experience* of the kernel of their being, the transcendent Self. May it one day cease from being repeated to satiety that Kant "proved himself to be unfaithful to his own method and to have betrayed his own principles" and that, in growing old and becoming senile, he "sank into the fideism of his youth". For the truth is that Kant betrayed nothing and did not sink into anything, but that he arrived at the ripe fruit of his life and work. Or would one wish that he had not arrived anywhere, and that he had finished his life as a master of criticism and doubt only?. . .that the honest and assiduous effort of his life had not brought any experience, and therefore any certainty, with regard to things belonging to the metaphysical sphere? Instead of rejoicing in and celebrating the fact of his certainty, one speaks of his lapse and one accuses him of unfaithfulness! Good Lord! How petty!

You see therefore, dear Unknown Friend, that the great thinkers of the West — just as the Hindu yogis — have arrived at the experience of the kernel of the human being, the transcendent Self, the experience of which gave them certainty of immortality.

Christian Hermeticism, being a synthesis of mysticism, gnosis and sacred magic, offers humanity *three* methods of experience, beyond the "philosophical method" outlined above, for arriving at the certainty of immortality.

There is in the first place the traditional mystical way of purification, illumination and union, which is the voluntary and conscious experience of the three stages of the way of the human soul after death—through purgatory to heaven, and from heaven to God. You will find this not only with the great Christian mystics such as Dionysius the Areopagite, Bonaventura, Teresa of Avila, and John of the Cross ...not only in the pre-Christian teachings of the Hermetic treatises attributed to Hermes Trismegistus, such as *The Divine Pymander*, but also in the great mysteries of pagans, Egyptians, and others, where the three stages of *catharsis* (purification), *photismos* (illumination) and *henosis* (union, or identification with the Divine) give consciousness of the *post-mortem* states and certainty of immortality. Jean Marques-Rivière says concerning this:

> (This is) the essential teaching of Egyptian esotericism as well as that of the Greeks: the knowledge of states after death, in order to overcome fear of this death, psychological and human fear. The initiate had knowledge of what awaited him; what could he be afraid of? (Jean Marques-Rivière, *Histoire des doctrines ésotériques*, Paris, 1950, p. 90)

Just as the practice of *concentration* is the "art of forgetting" and the practice of profound communion, or *meditation*, is the mastering of the "art of sleeping", so does the *contemplation* of authentic initiation signify the mastering of the "art of dying". It is through mastering forgetting, sleep and death that one arrived in the past, that one arrives today, and that one will arrive in the future, at the mystical experience of the soul united with God, and therefore at the absolute certainty of immortality. And one arrived there, one arrives there, and one will arrive there through the three stages of the eternal mystical way: those of purification, illumination and union. St. John of the Cross shows that it is authentic *faith* which is revealed, acts, and increases in purification; that it is *hope* which is simultaneously both the agent and the fruit of illumination; and that, lastly, it is *charity* which achieves union of the soul with God (cf. John of the Cross, *The Ascent of Mount Carmel* II, v).

This is the eternal way, and no one can invent or find another. One can certainly divide it into thirty-three stages—or even into ninety-nine, if one wished; one can re-clothe it in intellectual vestments, or beautiful and simple symbolism; one can present it in diverse terminology—Sanscrit, Cabbalistic, Greek, Latin, etc. But one will always have to do with the sole way—and always the same way—of eternal mysticism: the way of purification, illumination and union. Because there is no other, and there has never been another, and there never will be any other.

Hermeticism, also, has no other way to offer than that of eternal mysticism— the gnostic, magical and philosophical methods being founded on it. In other words, one cannot dispense with purification in order to become a gnostic or a mage or even a philosopher (in the true and original sense of this word). Nor can

one any more dispense with illumination in gnosis, in sacred magic and in philosophy (again in the true and original sense of this word). For a non-illumined
gnostic would not be a gnostic, but rather an "oddball"; a non-illumined mage
would be only a sorcerer; and a non-illumined philosopher would be either a complete sceptic or an amateur at "intellectual play". And with respect to the primary
source from whence the gnostic draws his revelation, the mage his power, and the
philosopher his enlightenment—there is only one: the more or less immediate
contact of the soul with God. It is therefore always the same *way* on which one
advances, without regard to whether one employs the mystical, gnostic, magical
or philosophical method.

There are many tracks, but there is only one way. This means to say that whatever
one does, one advances and grows only in the sense of purification, illumination
and union; and that whatever one knows and whatever experience one has, the
criterion of true progress is solely progress in purification, illumination and union.
One judges a tree by its fruits; one judges the mystic, gnostic, mage and philosopher
by their faith, hope and charity, i.e. by their progress in purification, illumination and union.

Spiritual greatness, the calibre of a soul, is measured only through faith, hope
and charity (love). Buddha certainly saw that the world is sick—and, considering
it incurable, he taught the means to leave it. Christ, also, saw that the world is
sick unto death, but he considered it curable and set to work the force for healing
the world—that which manifests itself through the Resurrection. Here is the difference between the faith, hope and love of the Master of Nirvana and that of
the Master of the Resurrection and the Life. The former said to the world, "You
are incurable; here is the means for putting an end to your suffering—to your
life." The latter said to the world, "You are curable; here is the remedy for saving
your life." Two doctors with the same diagnosis—but a world of difference in the
treatment!

Tradition teaches—and every serious esotericist and occultist knows that it is
so—that the Archangel Michael is the archistrategist, i.e. that he directs the celestial
army. Why is he in charge? Because his faith, hope and love are such that they
have put him in charge. For "to be in charge" signifies in the spiritual world to
be less subject than others to doubt, despair and condemning judgement.

Tradition teaches that the Archangel Michael represents the sun, and similarly
the Archangel Gabriel—the moon, the Archangel Raphael—Mercury, the Archangel Anael—Venus, Zachariel—Jupiter, Oriphiel—Saturn, and Samael—Mars.
Why the *sun*? Because the sun is the visible symbol, the image itself of faith, hope
and love. It sheds light on the good and the wicked, without leaving or quitting
its central post.

Yes, the greatness of God himself, i.e. of what is *divine* for us in him, is not
his power in the sense that he is stronger than the totality of forces in the universe,
nor his foreknowledge in the sense that he foresees, as a perfect engineer, the future
functioning of the forces of the "world machine", pre-calculated and pre-

determined, nor even the fact that he is absolutely indispensable as the centre of all gravitation—spiritual, psychic and physical—of the universe. No, what is truly *divine* in God, i.e. what makes every knee bow before him, is his faith, his hope and his love. For just as we believe in God, so also does God believe in us—but with a divinely greater and more elevated faith; his hope with regard to this immense community of free beings that we call the "world" is infinite, just as his love for these beings is infinite.

We do not worship God because he is able to do more than us, or because he knows more than us, but rather because he has more faith, more hope and more love than us. Our God is infinitely *noble and generous*, and not only all-powerful and all-informed! God is great through his faith, hope and love—and the fear of God is basically that of offending such nobleness and generosity!

Now, Christian Hermeticism is based on the way of eternal mysticism; with regard to its practice, this is its basis and its point of departure. Point of departure—where?...in the domain of gnosis and in that of sacred magic, just as in the domain of Hermetic philosophy.

Gnosis—which, it goes without saying, has nothing to do with any method borrowed from the teachings of gnostic sects or with their articles of faith—is the contribution of mystical experience to understanding and memory. It is distinguished from pure mysticism in that the latter amounts to the experience in which the *will*—purified and illumined—is in union with the Divine, whilst understanding and memory are excluded from it and remain outside of the threshold of mystical experience. And it is precisely the fact of the non-participation of understanding and memory in mystical experience which renders it inexpressible and incommunicable. Gnosis, on the other hand, is the same mystical experience *with the participation of understanding and memory*, which pass the threshold together with the will and remain in a state of wakefulness. It is schooling by means of *symbolism* which renders them capable of participating in the mystical experience of the will without lapsing. They participate only as *witnesses*, i.e. they maintain complete silence and only play the role of a *mirror*. But the result of their presence as witnesses to the mystical experience of the will is the *ability to express and communicate* this experience. This is because understanding and memory have received an impression of it. And this impression is what we understand here by "gnosis". A mystic is a gnostic in so far as, and as much as, he can express and communicate to others his experiences. "God is love, and he who abides in love abides in God, and God abides in him" (I John iv, 16)—this is a mystical statement. "God is the Trinity: Father, Son and Holy Spirit"—this is a gnostic statement. Or, "I and the Father are one" (John x, 30)—mystical statement; "In my Father's house are many rooms" (John xiv, 2)—gnostic statement.

Gnosis is therefore the fruit of the silent participation of understanding and memory in the mystical experience of the will. I say "*silent* participation" because otherwise, i.e. in the case of *active* participation, it would no longer be a matter of revelation, but rather of a statement produced by the understanding and imagination. For in order to apprehend one has to listen, and to listen one has to be silent. The faculty of understanding and that of memory / imagination must be silent if they want to apprehend, i.e. to receive a revelation from above.

Just as gnosis is the fruit of the participation of understanding and memory in the mystical union of the will with God, so is sacred magic the fruit of the participation of the three forces of the soul in mystical union with God *with regard to one's neighbour and to Nature*. When the soul, having had the experience of union with the Divine, turns towards its neighbour and towards Nature, not in order to contemplate but in order to act—then the soul becomes that of a *mage*. Every mystic is a mage in as much as and in so far as he *acts*, being inspired by his mystical experience. Sacred magic is the putting into action of what the mystic contemplates and what the gnostic apprehends through revelation.

Hermetic philosophy, lastly, draws its conclusions from mystical, gnostic and magical experiences and works with a view to setting these in accord with the experiences of terrestrial life and with the sciences which are occupied therewith. It is thus that Hermeticism can give *trismegistic* ("thrice greatest") certainty of immortality, i.e. the threefold certainty of mystical, gnostic and magical experience.

As you see, this certainty is produced in three—or four—stages of *descending* revelatory movement, from above below. It is what tradition calls the "descent of the heavenly Jerusalem", as opposed to the method outlined above of the "construction of the tower of Babel". Christian (*and* pre-Christian) Hermeticism therefore belongs decidedly to the extended tradition which practises the method of the "descent of the heavenly Jerusalem", which works in the history of mankind with a view to preparing the whole of mankind for the future spiritual event of the "descent of the heavenly Jerusalem" on a universal scale. For the "descent of the heavenly Jerusalem" is at the same time a practical method of spiritual schools. The totality of inner mystical, gnostic, and magical experiences of individuals, the gradual transformation of the whole of human civilisation into a "celestial city", i.e. where the laws are those of heaven, and, lastly, the Reintegration of the whole of Nature, which is a work of cosmic significance, together comprise the realisation of a "new heaven and a new earth" (Revelation xxi, 1), where the world is *healed*. The "descent of the heavenly Jerusalem" therefore comprises the most intimate experiences of individual souls as well as the history and evolution of our planet—according to the law: ". . . nothing is covered that will not be revealed, or hidden that will not be known" (Matthew x, 26), for everything that takes place in subjective intimacy will one day become objective reality. It is the *magical* law of history that the subjective at some time becomes objective, that the aspirations, thoughts and feelings of today become the events of history tomorrow. "For they sow the wind, and they shall reap the whirlwind" (Hosea ix, 7).

This leads me to return to the Card of the thirteenth Major Arcanum of the Tarot. Here we see that Death reaps hands, feet, and lastly heads, *which appear above the level of the black soil*. He does not reap growing grass or whole human figures—which, moreover, are not to be found here.

Death acts as the guardian of a determined *level*, and cuts off every member of the human body which appears above this level. It acts as a surgeon rather than as an exterminator. . . but what kind of surgeon is it?

We have spoken above of the method and ideal of the "construction of the tower of Babel", i.e. the method and ideal where one makes electrical energy *ascend*, after having animated and intellectualised it, from the physical organism to higher planes—firstly to the vital or etheric plane, the plane where "grass grows", according to the Card of the thirteenth Arcanum.

This ascent, provided that it is not effected methodically and in full knowledge of its action, i.e. within an occult school, in practice takes place partially—sometimes it is only the "electric hands" which succeed in ascending to the vital or etheric plane, sometimes it is the "feet", and sometimes it is only the "head". Now, Death on our Card sees to it that the vital world is not invaded by "emissaries" from the physical world. It *cuts off*, as a true surgeon, the electrical "members" of the physical body which appear above the level—which is the threshold of the two worlds—where the realm of the vital world begins. It therefore accomplishes *amputations* of sick members—"sick" in the sense that they have usurped a domain of existence which does not legitimately belong to them—before the sickness becomes irremediable. What Death does in this Card is therefore to act as a guardian of the threshold between the two worlds and, correspondingly, to apply a kind of surgery.

Now, in general, is not Death the principle of surgery in the world? Is it called to *kill*, to destroy, or does it not have a mission to *heal* through surgery?

The answer that I propose, dear Unknown Friend, is that Death is certainly the principle of surgery in the world. It effects the amputation of members that become unusable—even the totality of unusable members, i.e. the whole physical body—so as to free the whole human being.

Just as there is natural medicine which re-establishes health through the rules and habits of a sound life—diet, sleep, breathing, exercises, etc.—and just as there is homeopathic medicine which heals by helping the *whole organism* to overcome the sickness, and just as there is allopathic medicine, which combats sickness through opposites, and just as, lastly, there is surgery which saves the life of the organism by sacrificing part of it, so there is in the world a healing "mechanism" analogously hierarchical to the hierarchical scale of natural, homeopathic, allopathic and surgical medicine.

Death corresponds to surgery in the "cosmic hospital". It is the last expedient to save life. Beyond it there are three further principles for maintaining and re-establishing health in the world and in individual beings. These correspond to *mysticism*, *gnosis* and *magic*. Thus, in paraphrasing a slogan from the French revolution, one could say:

Mysticism, gnosis, magic—or death.

Meditation on the
Fourteenth Major Arcanum of the Tarot

TEMPERANCE

TEMPÉRANCE

Exaudi nos, Domine sancte,
Pater omnipotens, aeterne Deus,
et mittere digneris sanctum Angelum tuum de coelis,
qui custodiat, foveat, protegat,
visitat atque defendat
omnes habitantes in hoc habitaculo.

(Hear us Lord, holy Lord,
almighty Father, eternal God,
and deign to send your holy Angel from heaven,
to guard, cherish, protect, visit and defend
all who are gathered together in this place.)
  (Liturgical prayer of the introductory
    service preceding the solemn Mass)

Everyone who drinks of this water
will thirst again, but whoever
drinks of the water that I shall give him
will never thirst;
the water that I shall give him
will become in him a spring of water
welling up to eternal life.
  (John iv, 13-14)

Truly, truly, I say to you,
unless one is born anew,
he cannot enter the kingdom of God.
  (John iii, 3)

By upbringing and intellectual training,
I belong to the "children of heaven";
but by temperament, and by my professional studies,
I am a "child of the earth".
Situated thus by life at the heart of two worlds
with whose theory, idiom and feelings
intimate experience has made me familiar,
I have not erected any watertight bulkhead inside myself.
On the contrary, I have allowed
two apparently conflicting influences full freedom to
react upon one another deep within me.
  (Pierre Teilhard de Chardin)*

LETTER XIV

TEMPERANCE

Dear Unknown Friend,

The Card of the fourteenth Major Arcanum of the Tarot places us in the presence of an Angel in a robe which is half red and half blue, who is accomplishing—or presiding over the accomplishment of—a strange act, where he is pouring colourless water from one vase into another, or rather he is making it gush almost horizontally between the two vases, at an angle of about 45 degrees, the vases being held at a considerable distance from one another.

An intellectual shock!...and therefore an *arcanum*—something which one has

Comment je crois Intr.; trsl. R. Hague, *How I Believe*, London, 1969, p. 7.

to take hold of and apprehend beyond the usual plane of experience and thought. This invites us, therefore, to profound meditation—to a spiritual exercise. Let us follow this invitation.

What is the problem that the Card—its whole context—arouses spontaneously in the mind of he who looks at it attentively? What is the *message* of the Angel with two wings, in the red and blue robe, holding two vases, one red and one blue, and making water gush in a mysterious way from one vase to the other? Is he not the one who bears the good news that beyond the duality of "either-or" there is—or is possible—still that of "not only-but also" or "both-and"? Does not the totality of the Card, the Angel of the Card, suggest the problem of *cooperating polarity*, or *integrated duality*? Does it not first of all suggest the presentiment or suspicion that perhaps it is thanks to the two wings, the two arms, the two colours of the robe, the two vases, that the water pours forth?. . .that this water is the fruit and the gift of the "both-and" of integrated duality, which jumps to one's attention as one looks at the Card?

Thus the idea which is presented first of all to the mind, in the presence of the Card of the fourteenth Arcanum, belongs to the range of ideas relating to *polarity* and what this latter offers in possibilities for the spiritual knowledge and realisation—mystical, gnostic and magical—of the Hermeticist.

In preceding Letters there has already been the question, in diverse connections, of a *twofold polarity*—that of "polemic" (war), which produces energy of an "electrical" kind, and that of cooperation or "peace", which releases force of a "vital" nature. Now, the Angel of the Card of the fourteenth Arcanum invites us to return to the problem of this double polarity and twofold dynamic, in promising to throw new light on this subject. Let us therefore return to this.

An expert of the first order in spiritual life and authentic spiritual experience, St. Bernard of Clairvaux, has bequeathed to posterity a doctrine of fundamental importance. This is his doctrine of the *divine image and likeness* of man. This doctrine lends itself admirably to serve as a point of departure for a thoroughgoing investigation of this twofold polarity. The following are its essential points:

God made man "in his image and likeness" (Genesis i, 26). The divine image and the divine likeness coincided in the first man, before the original sin. But their coincidence did not persist after the Fall. The image has remained intact, but the initial likeness has been lost. Man is, following the original sin, in the "disfigurement of unlikeness", whilst conserving the image.

> Man was made in the image and likeness of God: in image he possesses freedom of will, and in likeness he possesses virtues. The likeness has been destroyed; however, man conserves the image. The image can be burnt in hell, but not consumed. It is damaged but not destroyed. Through fate as such it is not effaced, but subsists. Wherever the soul is, there also will be the

image. It is not so with the likeness. This remains in the soul which accomplishes the good; in the soul which sins it is wretchedly transformed. The soul which has sinned ranks with beasts devoid of intelligence. (St. Bernard of Clairvaux, *Sermon on the Annunciation of the Blessed Virgin Mary*; French trsl. M. M. Davy, *Oeuvres de Saint Bernard*, vol. i, p. 106)

According to St. Bernard, the image is therefore the *essential structure* of the human being and the likeness in him is the totality of functions or the *functional structure*. It is the essential structure of the human being, the image, which is indestructable and which establishes freedom in an inalienable and irremovable way.

Man *is* free, and remains so through all eternity—on earth, in hell, in purgatory, in heaven—always and everywhere. Freedom is therefore an *absolute fact*. As such, it entails immortality—the argument that one finds again in Immanuel Kant's *Critique of Practical Reason*, for what is his "categorical imperative" if not the divine image in man?

With respect to the likeness or totality of *functions* of the human being, a hotbed of sin, with its attractions towards evil, has taken root there. And it is immortal only in proportion to the measure that it conforms again to its image. Its immortality is optional.

This is the essence of St. Bernard's doctrine. It gives rise to the question: If the divine image in man has not undergone any weakening and if the divine likeness in him has partly abrogated and has had to make way for inclinations and habits tending towards evil, is there something in human life which counterbalances the bad inclinations in man's functional organism, opposing good inclinations to them? Yes. There is certainly something added to man's functional organism to play in it the role of a counterweight to the leverage of vicious inclinations and habit which have become established since the primordial Fall. *This is the guardian Angel*.

The guardian Angel accompanies as a faithful ally the divine image in man, just as vicious inclinations have made their way into the human functional organism which was, before the Fall, the divine likeness. The guardian Angel undertakes the functions, destroyed by original sin, in the likeness, and fills the breach wrought by them. He substitutes himself for functions destroyed through the Fall.

As the prayer of the service of aspersion (that I have put at the head of this Letter) states it, in praying to God "to deign to send from heaven his holy Angel to *guard*, *cherish*, *protect*, *visit* and *defend* all those who are gathered together in this place", the Angel acquits his charge in five ways: he guards, cherishes, protects, visits and defends. He is therefore a "flaming star", a luminous pentagram, above man.

He *guards* memory, i.e. the continuity of the great past in the present, which is the preparation for the great future. It is the guardian Angel who takes care that there is a connection between the great "yesterday, today and tomorrow" of the human soul. He is a perpetual "memento" with regard to the primordial likeness, with regard to the eternal mission assigned to the soul in the cosmic symphony, and with regard to the special room for the soul "in my Father's house, where there are many rooms" (John xiv, 2). If it is necessary, the guardian Angel awakens recollections of the soul's previous earthly lives, in order to establish continuity of endeavour — of the quest and aspiration of the soul from life to life — so that particular lives are not merely isolated episodes but constitute the stages of a single *path* towards one sole end.

The guardian Angel *cherishes* the endeavour, quest and aspiration of the soul engaged on this way. This means to say that he fills in the breaks in the psychic functional organism due to the disfigurement of the likeness, and makes up for its failings — given the soul's good will towards it. For *support* never signifies substitution of the Angel's will for that of man. The will remains free, always and everywhere. The guardian Angel never touches on man's free will and resigns himself to await the decision or choice made in the inviolable sanctuary of free will — in order to lend his assistance immediately if it is just, or to remain a passive observer reduced alone to prayer if it is not.

Just as the guardian Angel is sometimes constrained not to participate in the soul's activity — this activity not being in accord with the divine image of the soul — so also he can sometimes take a greater part in human activity than usual — this activity being of a nature not simply permitted but also called for. Then the guardian Angel descends from the point of his ordinary post into the domain of human activity. He then *visits* the human being.

Such "visits" of the guardian Angel do sometimes take place — when their possibility and necessity coincide. But what the guardian Angel does unceasingly is to *protect* the human being. Here he makes up for the failings of the human senses, which are deprived of their clairvoyance from before the original sin. He is the clairvoyant helping the non-clairvoyant with respect to psychic and physical temptations and dangers. He warns, informs and helps to appreciate. Nevertheless, what he never does is to suppress the occasions themselves of temptation. For, as St. Anthony the Great said, "without temptation there is no spiritual progress". Temptation belongs as an integral part to the exercise of human free will, which is inviolable — both for an Angel and for a demon.

With respect to the last of the five functions of the guardian Angel concerning man, namely his *defence*, it differs from the others in that it is turned above, towards heaven, and is no longer directed below or horizontally. In dealing with the question of the defence that the guardian Angel accords to his protégé, we approach the holy mystery of the very heart of the guardian Angel. For the nature of Angelic love is revealed here, of which the following are some indications.

Guardian Angels remain above their protégés. This means to say, amongst other things, that they *screen* him from heaven, from the look directed below from above. The fact that human beings on earth are screened by their guardian Angels from

Divine Justice signifies—other than guarding, supporting, protecting and con-tacting—that guardian Angels are the *defenders*, the advocates, of man before Divine Justice. Just as Moses said to the LORD, when the children of Israel had committed the mortal sin of having preferred a god made of gold to the Living God, ". . . but now, if thou wilt forgive their sin—and if not, blot me, I pray thee, out of thy book which thou hast written" (Exodus xxxii, 32), so do guardian Angels "cover" their protégés before the face of Divine Justice. This amounts to the declaration—whether explicit or implicit is not important—"Forgive them their sins. If not, efface us from the Book of Life that you have written." This is the defence of guardian Angels for their protégés.

The guardian Angel covers his protégé with his wings, in conferring on him his own merits before the eyes of Divine Justice and also in taking on himself the faults of his protégé before the eyes of Divine Justice. It is as if he says, "If the lightning of divine wrath must strike my protégé, my child, may it strike me in-stead of him—or if he must be struck, may it strike both of us together!"

The guardian Angel defends his protégé like a *mother* defends her child, without regard to whether he may be good or bad. It is the mystery of maternal love which lives in the heart of the guardian Angel. Not all Angels are guardian Angels; there are others who have diverse missions. But guardian Angels, in so far as they are guardian Angels, are "mothers" of their protégés. This is why traditional art presents them as winged females. And this is why the Card of the fourteenth Ar-canum of the Tarot also openly presents the Angel as a winged female, dressed in a woman's robe, half-blue and half-red.

Guardian Angels—or should I use the feminine form, "Angelines"?—are the manifestation of high and pure maternal love. For this reason the Holy Virgin and Mother of God bears the liturgical title *Regina Angelorum*—"queen of the Angels". It is the maternal love in her that she has in common with the guardian Angels and which, in surpassing theirs, makes her their queen.

There are, as I said above, other Angels who are not guardian Angels. I am not speaking of the eight celestial hierarchies above that of the Angels; I am speaking solely of the hierarchy of the Angels, i.e. of the *ninth* celestial hierarchy. There are Angels who are "messengers", i.e. "Angels" (*angeloi*—"messengers" in Greek) in the proper sense of the word; there are Angels with special missions and tasks— Angels of the Father, the Son, the Holy Spirit, the Virgin, Death, Life, Karma, Relationships (between different spheres), Revelations of Wisdom, Knowledge, Ascetic Discipline—and many others. Many of them represent paternal love, or rather fraternal love.

Here I do not want to say anything either for or against what Swedenborg says concerning the sex of Angels, but what I would like to portray here is the mater-nal love of guardian Angels, and that there are other Angels who represent pater-nal love and also fraternal love. And it is in *this sense*—and only in this sense— that I would like you, dear Unknown Friend, to think of the Angels as entities in whom prevails either the tenderness of maternal love or the justice of paternal love. For what it is a matter of is not to project earthly sexuality upon heaven, but rather, on the contrary, to see in the former a reflection—although often disfigured—of the polarity from above. I may add that the Jewish Cabbala—above all the *Zohar*—teaches admirably the lesson of thinking of things here below as the reflection of things from above, and not inversely. The *Zohar* is truly one of the better schools of purity and chastity concerning all that relates to husband and wife, father and mother, son and daughter, fiancé and fiancée, at one and the same time in the spiritual, soul and physical worlds. For true chastity is not to refuse to look at and to see, or even to deny, but rather to see the celestial proto-types through and beyond things here below. And it is this chastity that one finds and apprehends in the *Zohar*, the Book of Splendour of the Jewish Cabbala.

But let us return to guardian Angels. The Angels, including guardian Angels, live and move exclusively in the *vertical*. Ascent and descent constitute the law of their life, their respiration. They ascend towards God; they descend towards mankind.

It is said that the Angels are in perpetual contemplation of God. They are, if one understands by contemplation the state of being in permanent contact with the Holy Trinity and of being blinded by its light. It is the "dark contemplation" of which St. John of the Cross spoke which is that of the Angels. They do not *see* God; they are united to him substantially. With respect to guardian Angels, neither do they see one another, nor do they see entities of the other hierarchies—Archangels, Principalities, Powers, Virtues, Dominions, Thrones, Cherubim and Seraphim. For the presence of transcendental divine light in them envelops in darkness their perception of the intermediary spheres between God and mankind.

It is the latter sphere that they see, or rather the "spheres" of their protégés. It is here that they make use of this clairvoyance, which the human being—who has lost it—has need of for the protection it affords. It is here also that the Angels display the geniality of synthetic and profound understanding—without parallel—which has merited them, on the part of human beings, with the attribute of "omniscience". They are not omniscient, but the facility with which they orien-tate themselves in human things and grasp them—at contact with which their "dark" divine wisdom becomes resplendent—has so impressed human beings who have had the experience of consciously meeting with them that they have been led to consider them as omniscient. It is to this impression that has been gained of Angels that the word "genius" owes its original meaning, namely that of superhuman intelligence.

But—and this is the tragic side of Angelic existence—this geniality shows up only when the human being has need of it, when he makes room for the flashing forth of its illumination. The Angel depends on man in his creative activity. If the human being does not ask for it, if he turns away from him, the Angel has no motive for creative activity. He can then fall into a state of consciousness where all his creative geniality remains in potential and does not manifest. It is a state of vegetation or "twilight existence", comparable to sleep from the human point of view. An Angel who has nothing to exist for is a tragedy in the spiritual world.

Therefore, dear Unknown Friend, think of your guardian Angel, think of him when you have problems, questions to resolve, tasks to accomplish, plans to formulate, cares and fears to appease! Think of him as a luminous cloud of maternal love above you, moved by the sole desire to serve you and to be useful to you. Do not allow the scruple to arise in you, however noble it may be, that when you appeal to your guardian Angel you are allowing an entity to come between you and God who is not God, and that therefore you abandon the aspiration to *immediate* contact between your soul and God — to the direct and authentic touch of God, without intermediary! For the guardian Angel will never interpose himself between your soul and God in any way, even to an infinitesimal degree, to impede the occurrence of the "song of songs" of your soul and God! He has no other concern than to make these immediate and authentic contacts possible, to render your soul disposed to them — and he withdraws as soon as his Lord and yours draws near to your soul. The guardian Angel is the friend of the bride at the spiritual marriage of the soul and God. Just as the friend of the husband who "prepared the way of the Lord and made his paths straight" was obedient to the law of the friend of the husband —"He must increase, but I must decrease" (John iii, 30) — so does the friend of the bride, who prepares the way of the Lord and makes his paths straight, obey the same law. The guardian Angel withdraws before the approach of One who is greater than he.

There is what is called in Christian Hermeticism the "freeing of the guardian Angel". The guardian Angel is freed — often in order to be able to acquit new missions — when the soul has acquired the disposition of its part of "likeness" in order to experience the Divine more intimately and more immediately, which corresponds to another hierarchical degree. Then it is an *Archangel* who replaces the freed guardian Angel. Human beings whose guardian is an Archangel have not only new experiences of the Divine in their inner life, but also, through this very fact, receive a new and objective vocation. They become *representatives* of a human group — a nation or a human karmic community — which means to say that from this time onwards their actions will no longer be purely personal but will at the same time have significance and value for those of the human community that they represent.

It was so for Daniel, who in praying the following, was acting not only in his name but also — and above all — in the name of the people of Israel:

> ...*we* have sinned and done wrong and acted wickedly and
> rebelled, turning aside from thy commandments and ordinances
> ...Now, therefore, O our God, hearken to the prayer of thy servant and to his supplications, and for the love of the Lord, cause
> thy face to shine upon thy sanctuary, which is desolate. O my
> God, incline thy ear and hear! Open thy eyes and behold our
> desolations, and the city which is called by thy name... (Daniel
> ix, 5, 17-18)

And it was the *Archangel Gabriel* who "came to him in swift flight at the time of the evening sacrifice...he came to give him wisdom and understanding" (Daniel ix, 21-22). Here we have an example of the freeing of the guardian Angel and of the assumption of his responsibility by an Archangel—in this case the Archangel Gabriel.

It also happens sometimes that the Archangel is freed as well. Then it is an entity from the hierarchy of Powers or Elohim which replaces the Archangel. The human being then becomes a representative of the future of humanity. He lives in the present what mankind someday is due to experience in future centuries.

It is thus that Moses, Elijah and David, for example, were under the protection of the wings of an Elohim—and not only their words but also their *lives* themselves were *prophetic*.

But one could make the objection that it is *God* himself who was revealed and spoke to Moses, Elijah and David, and not an entity of the hierarchy of Powers or Elohim. There is reason to reply to this objection that just as there were human prophets through whose mouths the Holy Spirit spoke, so also there were hierarchical entities through whom the Holy Spirit, the Son and the Father spoke and acted. Thus the three Angels who appeared to Abraham in the heat of the day (Genesis xviii) spoke and acted as the Holy Trinity—Father, Son and Holy Spirit. It was the Holy Trinity who spoke—through them—to Abraham.

Similarly, Jahve-Elohim was the "bearer" or "representative" of God—of his word and his power—in the accomplishment of the mission with which he was charged by the Holy Trinity, namely that of preparation for the Incarnation of Christ. In so far as he was an "authorised agent" representing God, Jahve-Elohim brought the providential design of the Incarnation to realisation; in so far as he was an Elohim or Power, he acted as guardian entity of Moses, Elijah and David.

Lastly, a guardian Elohim—and there are many of them—can also be freed. Then it is an entity of the first hierarchy, a *Seraphim*, who replaces him. It was so for St. Francis of Assisi. The Seraphim who gave him the teaching of the Crucifixion whereby he gained the stigmata—the Seraphim in the vision of St. Francis—was his guardian. This is why St. Francis represents more than mankind; what he represents is "divinised humanity"—this is the God-Man, Jesus Christ himself. However, stigmata are not always visible. There are stigmata, so to say, "turned outside", and there are stigmata "turned within"—but all those who are under the guardianship of a Seraphim bear the stigmata, visible or invisible. For they represent the Christ.

With respect to stigmata, this subject has been treated from a *practical* point of view in the fifth Letter on the Arcanum "The Pope". It is not fitting to treat it theoretically. Respect forbids me.

The following is what St. John of the Cross said concerning the stigmata of St. Francis:

> It will happen that while the soul is inflamed with the love of
> God...it will feel that a Seraphim is assailing it by means of

an arrow or dart which is all afire with love. And the Seraphim
pierces and cauterises this soul which, like a red-hot coal, or better a flame, is already enkindled. And then in this cauterisa-
tion, when the soul is transpierced with that dart, the flame
gushes forth, vehemently and with a sudden ascent. . . And being wounded by this fiery dart, the soul feels the wound with
unsurpassable delight. . .God sometimes permits an effect to
extend to the bodily senses in the fashion in which it existed
interiorly, the wound and sore (then) appears outwardly, as happened when the Seraphim wounded St. Francis. When the soul
is wounded with love by the five wounds, the effect extends to
the body and these wounds are impressed on the body and it
is wounded, just as the soul is wounded with love. God does
not usually bestow a favour upon the body without bestowing
it first and principally upon the soul. (St. John of the Cross,
The Living Flame of Love ii, 9, 11; trsl. K. Kavenaugh and O.
Rodriguez, *The Collected Works of St. John of the Cross*, London, 1966, pp. 598-599)

You see therefore, dear Unknown Friend, how it is with regard to the guardian
Angel and the union of the soul with God. There is no reason to fear that the
least hindrance to this union can ever arise on the part of the entities who are
spiritual guardians of the human soul. On the contrary, rather, it is they who make
it at all possible — and even beyond the possible — for the soul to be united with
God in complete intimacy and with perfect authenticity and freedom. The friend
of the wife only leads the wife to the husband — then she withdraws. Her joy is
that of herself diminishing and of seeing that of the wife increase.

The Card of the fourteenth Arcanum represents a *winged* female. What do the
wings that she has — and the wings of hierarchical entities in general — signify?

Tentacles, paws, arms, wings — are they not simply diverse forms manifesting
a common prototype or principle? They are in so far as they express the desire
to bear the sense of touch further, to be able to touch things more removed than
those in the immediate neighbourhood of the surface of the body. They are *active extensions* of the passive and receptive sense of touch which is spread out over
the surface of the organism. In making use of them, the sense of touch makes
"excursions" from its usual orbit circumscribed by the skin which covers the body.

The organs of action are simply crystallised will. I walk not because I have legs
but rather, on the contrary, I have legs because I have the will to move about.
I touch, I take and I give not because I have arms, but I have arms because I have
the will to touch, to take and to give.

The "what" of the will engenders the "how" of the action (the organ), and not
inversely. The arms are therefore the expression of the will to bear touch further
than the surface of one's own body. They are the manifestation of extended touch,
due to the will to touch things at a distance.

It is similar with *wings*. They are also an exteriorised will — a will become organ.

This is the will to go out from the usual orbit not only in the horizontal but also in the vertical, not only to bear touch *forward*, but also to bear it *above*. Wings express the will for movement according to a cross, i.e. not only that of *expansion* on a plane but also that of *elevation* to another plane.

All this is related to the *whole* corporeal organism, i.e. the etheric and astral bodies as well as the physical body. Therefore there are physical wings (as with birds), etheric wings and astral wings. The wings of the subtle bodies (the vital body and the soul body)—like the physical wings of birds with regard to the air—are organs of active contact with the "air", i.e. with the substance and currents of the spiritual world. Just as the bird, whose body is solid and liquid, elevates itself by means of wings from the solid and liquid regions into that of the air, so does the Angel elevate itself by means of currents of vital and psychic energy—which correspond to wings—into the spiritual world higher than vital and astral elements.

Here the analogy stops. For there is also an essential difference between the functioning of the physical wings of a bird, and the operation of the wings—currents of vital and psychic forces—of an Angel. It is as follows:

The bird, in flying, *supports* itself on the air in order to overcome terrestrial gravitation. Its flying results from its effort—it *beats* the air with its wings—directed against terrestrial gravitation. However, it is the opposite for an Angel. Its "flying" is not a mechanical operation of "sculling in the air", as is the case with a bird, but it is a *magical operation* of the establishing of contact with "celestial gravitation", i.e. with divine attraction. He does not use his wings *against* terrestrial gravitation, but rather he employs them *in order* to put himself in contact with "celestial gravitation". It is the *touch* of divine love that the Angel seeks and finds by means of his wings, and which raises him in ecstasy to a higher sphere.

One could thus say in a concise way: the bird flies by *beating* its wings against the air, by resting on the air; the Angel "flies" by *immobilising* its wings after having touched God. The bird flies thanks to the air; the Angel "flies" thanks to God. In other words, the Angel's wings constitute semi-organic links with God.

Links—for there are two: one wing holds him in contact with divine understanding, and the other with divine memory / imagination. The two wings are therefore related to the contemplative and creative aspects of God which, in their turn, correspond to the divine *image and likeness* in man of which Genesis speaks. For the image is the analogous *structural* relationship of the kernel of the human being—his higher Self or, according to Leibnitz, his "monad"—with God at rest, whilst the likeness is the analogous *functional* relationship of the human being, i.e. his three powers—understanding, imagination and will—with God in action.

Now, the two Angelic wings are the Angel's links with the eternal sabbath and the eternal creativity of God—or, in other words, with *divine gnosis* and *divine magic*. It is by means of the "gnostic" (or "left") wing that the Angel is in contemplation of divine wisdom, and it is by means of the "magical" (or "right") wing that he is active in his capacity as messenger or "Angel".

This is the *principle* of polarity underlying the duality of the wings. The principle remains valid also for Angels—and for entities from other spiritual hierarchies—who have more than two wings (sixteen, for example). It will be the task of a future science of "Angelology" to grasp the reason or reasons for the plurality of wings of certain Angelic entities. This future science will develop—as there is reason to hope—within the heart of mystical theology, the first layer of which was given by St. Dionysius the Areopagite, or "pseudo-Dionysius", as the learned take pleasure in designating the founder of mystical theology. With respect to us, we have to restrict ourselves to a general explanation of the *two* wings of Angels, in reminding ourselves that it is a matter here of a meditation on the fourteenth Arcanum of the Tarot, whose Card represents an entity with *two wings*—which constitutes, consequently, the problem which occupies us here.

From tradition we know that there are also human beings endowed with wings. Thus the right panel of a triptych forming the circle of a deesis, a Russian icon from the hand of Nicephorus Savine, shows St. John the Baptist as winged (beginning of the seventeenth century, school of Stroganoff, at present in Tretiakoff Gallery, Moscow; cf. T. Talbot Rice, *Icons — Ikonen — Icones*, London, 1959, plate 63). Similarly, in place of the Hermit of the Marseille Tarot, the Bologna Tarot shows a winged patriarch, who walks laboriously, bent double on two crutches, having a pillar behind him (cf. Oswald Wirth, *Le Tarot des imagiers du moyen age*, Paris, 1927, p. 145). This is *not* Saturn as Oswald Wirth interprets this Card of the Bologna Tarot, but rather the *Hermit*, i.e. the very essence of the *way* of practical Hermeticism. For the winged old man before a pillar, supporting himself on two crutches has nothing—iconographically—to do with Saturn, save for the advanced age, whilst the context (the pillar, wings, and crutches) of the Card portrays all that is essential, both as fulfilment and as trial, of the spiritual way of Hermeticism. To become a *pillar* is the *aim* of the Hermit or Hermeticist; the *means* of raising oneself as a pillar are *wings*; and what becomes more and more difficult for one who becomes a pillar is horizontal movement. The contemplation which is established as a more-or-less permanent state in the soul, by means of wings, renders horizontal movement more and more difficult—the powers of the soul (understanding, imagination and will) being immersed in contemplation. The Hermit of the Bologna Tarot is therefore a Hermeticist (and iconographically the patriarch represents Hermes Trismegistus rather than Saturn, the oriental covering of his head and his dress being traditionally those of the aged Hermes Trismegistus). The Hermeticist, as portrayed in the Card "The Hermit" of the Bologna Tarot, lives in the vertical, immobilised; he has become a "spiritual stylite" at the expense of movement in the horizontal. Here it is not a matter of ancient mythology, but rather of the Arcanum of the practical and spiritual way of Hermeticism.

The astral and etheric wings of a human being signify a more-or-less advanced degree of recovery of the divine likeness in him. For certainly it was the lot of man before the original sin to have wings. He lost them subsequently. How are they recovered?

Wings are organs of the subtle bodies—astral and vital—and not any kind of activities of the conscious self. It is therefore a matter of the domain of the *unconscious* when it is a question of wings. It is a matter of the task of rendering spiritual endeavours turned towards God, such as prayer and meditation, semi-*organic*, i.e. to transform *conscious acts* of the self into psycho-vital currents of the subtle bodies.

The apostolic counsel "Pray constantly" (I Thessalonians v, 17) is the key here. It is impossible to pray unceasingly in full consciousness, but it is certainly possible to carry over prayer from consciousness into the unconscious, where it can operate unceasingly. The astral and vital bodies can pray unceasingly—which is not possible for the conscious self. The latter can certainly, through its initiative, establish a current of unceasing prayer in consciousness at first, then carry it over into the psychic unconscious (astral body) and into the vital unconscious (etheric body). Yes, it can even carry it as far as the physical body, as is evident from the "sincere accounts of a pilgrim to his spiritual father" (*otkrovennye rasskazy strannika dukhovnymn svoimu ottsu*)—a Russian book from an anonymous author of the past century on the practical training of the school of unceasing prayer. I have seen translations of this book in English, German, Dutch and French (English translation: *The Way of a Pilgrim*; trsl. R. M. French, London, 1954). It is described how the pilgrim—who is the author of the book—in waking up during the night, hears his heart beating distinctly the words of the prayer: "Lord Jesus Christ—Son of God—have mercy on me—a sinner" (*Gospodi Iisuse Khriste—Syne Bozhiy—pomiluy mya greshnego*).

Now, it is "unceasing prayer", established in the psychic and vital bodies, which forms the currents directed above in these bodies, and which *can* lead to the formation of wings. I say "can", because the formation of wings demands something still further, namely a current from above which moves to meet that from below. *Wings* are formed only when the two currents—that of human endeavour and that of grace—meet and unite. The Devil of the fifteenth Arcanum of the Tarot also has wings. But his wings consist only of energy engendered from below. They are deprived of grace from above. Angelic wings, on the contrary, are due to the union of effort and grace, just as are those of the divine likeness to-be-recovered in man. It is divine grace which plays the decisive role here. In the last analysis, wings are a *gift* of divine grace.

Pure humanism can create only the wings of Icarus. And the lot of Icarus is known: his wings of "wax" melted in the warmth of the sun, and the unfortunate Icarus fell to the earth. Regarding demonism, it can develop only the wings of a bat, i.e. those of darkness which are organs by means of which one can *plunge* into the depths of darkness.

The presence of authentic and legitimate wings in the human subconscious (i.e. the psychic and vital bodies) is not without effect on the consciousness of the human being. It manifests itself above all, and in general, as a constant orientation of consciousness towards God. Then man always has the feeling of the presence of God and the spiritual worlds and nothing can take this feeling away from him or suffocate it in him.

This feeling (that the Bible designates as "walking with God" or "walking before the face of God") crystallises itself into two unshakeable convictions: that one can endure all for God and that one can accomplish everything with God. *Martyrdom* and *thaumaturgy* are the two pillars on which faith rests and through which it conquered the old world. Now, it is the "gnostic wing" which disposes consciousness towards martyrdom and it is the "magical wing" which disposes it towards thaumaturgy. A winged human being is therefore disposed towards the heroic and towards the miraculous.

This is the essential of the problem of wings. They are the opposite of legs, because they are organs of contact with heaven, whilst legs are those of contact with the earth. The former put us in relationship with "celestial gravitation"; the latter put us in relationship with terrestrial gravitation.

With respect to *arms* — and the Angel of the Card of the fourteenth Arcanum has arms — they are related to the *horizontal*, i.e. to the fields of mutual attraction of beings who meet one another. If the law of wings is the love of God, that of arms is the love of neighbour. And the law of legs is the love of terrestrial Nature.

The Angel of the Card holds two vases united by a current of water. Thus we find ourselves right in the *problem of fluids*.

The problem of fluids is that of the dynamic functioning of the *whole* human being, i.e. corporeal, psychic and spiritual. In reality, it amounts to that of *life* — understood as a comprehensive spiritual, psychic and corporeal process. For just as there exists a system of physical circulation, so also there exists a system of vital and astral circulation, which in its turn is simply a reflection of the system of circulation comprising spirit, soul and body — the threefold body — as a living unity. The principle underlying this total system of circulation is the divine *likeness*. And as it is this which has undergone the disfiguring effect of original sin, it is the mission of the guardian Angel to see to it that the total system of circulation functions in as healthy a way as possible. The guardian Angel therefore watches over the functioning of the system of spiritual-psychic-corporeal circulation, i.e. the *health* and the *life* of the whole human being. This is why the Card of the fourteenth Arcanum represents him to us as engaged in the accomplishing of his office of regulating the system of circulation, or the human being's fluidic system. The system in question comprises several active centres — the "lotuses", the nerve centres, the glands, to name only the principal ones — but the harmonious functioning of all these centres depends on a single thing, a single action which takes place at the key position: this is the current which constitutes the relationship between the *image* and the *likeness* in man. The monad (the image) should not exist for nothing nor should it inundate the system of circulation (the likeness).

In the first case, the human being would be deprived of the stimulation to live a truly human life, that is to say he would not be orientated towards the aim of human existence. In the latter case, the human being would be shattered by the additional impulse coming from the monad (the image)—which would be an irreparable catastrophe. Now, it is a *just measure* in the relationship between the image and the likeness which has to be guarded and which is, in fact, guarded by the guardian Angel.

This is why tradition has given the name *Temperance* to the fourteenth Arcanum of the Tarot. For it is a matter here of the *measure* in the fluidic relationship between the image and the likeness which is necessary for *life* and *health*.

Just measure in the fluidic relationship between the absolute radicalism of the monad (the image) and the relativism of the phenomenal personality (the likeness) constitutes the fundamental principle of spiritual, psychic and corporeal health. This measure amounts to an always changing equilibrium between eternity and the moment, between the absolute and the relative, between contemplation and action, between the ideal and the phenomenal. Many relevant things can be said concerning the polarity of Mary and Martha—and have indeed been said—but we, all of us, live a healthy life only in as much as the two sisters in us are present and active as *sisters*, i.e. that they *collaborate*, having in view the Third.

No one can dispense with the Mary in himself—nor, equally, with the Martha in himself—and remain healthy in spirit, soul and body. "Pray and work" cannot be replaced by any other formula. For one cannot live either without contemplation or without action. This is what Krishna made Arjuna understand in the Bhagavad-Gita: ". . .performing all actions, always depending on me, he (man), through my favour, obtains the imperishable and eternal seat" (Bhagavad-Gita xviii, 56; trsl. K. T. Telang, *Sacred Books of the East* viii, Oxford, 1882, p. 128).

And, equally, this is what St. Bernard showed to advantage through his monastic reform, where contemplation and work were united, as also through his affirmation of Christian chivalry in his sermon on the second Crusade and in the rules that he gave to the Templar Order. Nowadays many criticise the saint for his intervention sanctioning and encouraging the Crusade, but what he did was simply to make an appeal to "Christian Arjunas" on the new field of *Kurukshetra*, where the two armies of Islam and Christianity had *already* been assembled for a battle without mercy some centuries before him. The battle had commenced in the seventh century of our era, when the Arabs invaded the eastern Christian countries. Charles Martel repulsed them at Poitiers in France, and through this victory (in 732) saved Christian civilisation and the West from Mohammedan conquest. Should one have been content with having saved the kernel of the West and have taken only a defensive attitude—in the manner of the Byzantine empire, which subsequently, little by little, became entirely conquered by the Mohammedans? The great battle of the twelfth century was still not achieved; it was always in process. Can one demand of St. Bernard that he should have preached the necessity of abandoning the Holy Land to the Mohammedans and of beginning a "peaceful co-existence", at the expense of the country where the cradle of Christianity is to be found?

Be that as it may concerning the crusades, St. Bernard advanced not only active contemplation for the monks but also contemplative activity for the knights—just as Krishna did more than fifteen centuries before him. The one and the other did so because they knew that man is at one and the same time a contemplative and an active being, that "faith without works is death"—and that, equally, works without faith are death. All this as *theory* is as clear as the day. But with respect to practice, it is not thus so. Practice entails an *arcanum*—an intimate *savoir-faire*—which is the fourteenth Major Arcanum of the Tarot, Temperance.

Temperance, as a spiritual exercise, signifies the task of knowing the relationship between the image or monad, the likeness or phenomenal personality, and the guardian Angel or individual grace. This means to say that one should find the source, current and direction of inner *life*—in grasping its nature and role—and work and live in conformity with this knowledge.

Firstly, the relationship between image and likeness: What is the intimate experience of this, and how does it reveal itself? The following is a straightforward answer:

The contact established between image and likeness is experienced as inner *weeping*. Weeping is the reality of the fact that the two sisters—the image and the likeness—*touch*. The usual experience rendered by the expression: "I am moved to tears" is only a reflection of what happens when image and likeness touch. They then mingle their tears—and the inner current which results from this is the *life* of the human soul.

Tears, sweat and blood are the three substances of the threefold mystical-gnostic-magical Mystery of man. To be touched from above is "tears"; the effort to conform to that which is above is "sweat"; and the consummated marriage of grace from above and effort from below is "blood". Tears announce the engagement of the eternal and the temporal; sweat is the trial that this entails; and blood is the region where the wedding of eternity and the moment is celebrated and where their marriage is consummated.

The Mystery (i.e. it is more than an arcanum) is whole and indivisible: tears, sweat and blood. But certain people seek and would grasp the Mystery only in tears. Others hope to find it only in sweat. Still others have a presentiment that, beyond all inner experiences and endeavours, the alliance exists through the blood and in the blood, and they do not want to know or recognise the other two aspects of the Mystery.

Here we have the inner reasons for the three principal heresies (for every serious heresy is a truth over-accentuated at the expense of the whole truth, i.e. at the expense of the *living organism of truth*). For those who seek only tears are inclined to quietism or illuminism; those who prefer sweat, i.e. effort of will, easily fall into the Pelagian heresy of denying grace; and those who seek the Mystery only in the blood often arrive at the Lutheran heresy where work, i.e. effort, counts for nothing. But the Mystery, I repeat, is whole and indivisible: tears, sweat and blood—engagement, trial and wedding—faith, hope and love.

Concerning tears...this is what flows between the two vases—that of the image and that of the likeness—which are held by the guardian Angel of the Card of the fourteenth Arcanum of the Tarot. The fourteenth Arcanum therefore teaches the spiritual exercise dedicated to the *mystery of tears*.

"Tears"—like "sweat" and "blood"—signify, both as an expression and as a fluidic substance, more than the physical body-fluid secreted by glands in the eyes. They signify also the subtle fluid of a spiritual and psychic nature which emanates from the heart, i.e. the "twelve-petalled lotus" of man's super-physical organisation. The expression "to have tears in one's voice" already points to inner tears, and the expression "to lament one's weaknesses" goes further in the same direction.

The fact that there are tears of sorrow, joy, admiration, compassion, tenderness, etc., signifies that tears are produced by the *intensity* of the inner life. They flow— whether inwardly or outwardly is not important—when the soul, moved by the spirit or by the outer world, experiences a higher degree of intensity in its inner life than is customary. The soul who cries is therefore more *living*, and therefore fresher and younger than when it does not cry.

The "gift of tears" was always considered by the masters of Christian spirituality as a grace from the Holy Spirit, for it is thanks to this gift that the soul surpasses itself and ascends to a degree of intensity of life which is certainly above that to which it is accustomed.

Now, the "gift of tears" is a comparatively recent spiritual phenomenon in the history of human spirituality. In the ancient world one wept only *ritually*, i.e. through verbal lamentations and through prescribed gestures of mourning or grief, and it was amongst the chosen people, Israel, that *real* weeping began. It was as a manifestation of the share that the chosen people had in the mission of preparing for the coming of Christ—who wept at the time of Lazarus' resuscitation and who sweated sweat and blood the night in the Garden of Olives—that real weeping came to have its rudimentary origin from the womb of this people. And to the present day the Jews preserve, cultivate and respect the "gift of tears". In fact, every revelation in the narrative of the *Zohar* is preceded or accompanied by the weeping of the one who had it and who comes to share it with the others. And, more recently, it was the same with the *tsaddikim* (righteous ones) of the Hassidim of eastern Europe. And the weeping wall in Jerusalem...

Therefore we owe to this people not only the Bible, not only Christ in the flesh, and not only the work of the apostles, but also the gift of tears—warm and sincere—which is the vivifying fluid that emanates from contact between the image and the likeness in us. Antisemitism...Good Lord! Ought not elementary gratitude suffice to grant the place of honour at the table of European culture to the Jews—or rather to humbly ask them to accept it—since this place is due to them by human and divine right? "Honour thy father and thy mother," says the divine commandment. And provided that we are not illegitimate children or foundlings, who are our spiritual parents — whom we are bound to honour — if not the Jews?. . . but I believe that in writing these things I am acting like a man who wants to force an open door. For I cannot imagine that your sentiments, dear Unknown Friend, are not identical to mine in this matter.

Above I said that the personages of the *Zohar* cry when they grasp a profound spiritual truth. The following is what there is to say on this subject from the point of view of Christian Hermeticism: There are three principal modes of authentic spiritual experience: *vision*, *inspiration* and *intuition* — or, perception of spiritual phenomena, spiritual communication and spiritual identification. Vision presents and shows us spiritual things, inspiration infuses us with understanding of them, and intuition reveals to us their essence by way of assimilation with our essence. Thus St. Paul had the *vision* of Christ on the way to Damascus, from whom he received *communications* that he obeyed and the carrying out of which constituted his apostolic work — including his journeys — and when he said, "I live, but it is no longer I who live, but Christ who lives in me" (Galatians ii, 20), this was knowledge through identification or *intuition*.

Now, vision augments experience; inspiration augments knowledge just as it does understanding; and intuition is the metamorphosis and growth no longer of what one experiences and understands, but rather of what one *is*. Through intuition one *becomes* another, through inspiration one apprehends new ways of thinking, feeling and acting, and through vision one's domain of experience is enlarged — one has a revelation of new facts inaccessible to the senses and to intellectual invention.

In practice it is not so that vision, inspiration and intuition are successive stages following the order — vision, inspiration, intuition. For there are those on the spiritual path who have only the experience of intuition, and still others who are only inspired, without ever having visions. But whatever the kind of mode of spiritual experience may be, at the final count it is always a matter of *becoming*, i.e. intuition. Thus one can say that *in principle* vision and inspiration are only means for arriving at intuition. Now, intuition takes place in the *blood*, inspiration in *tears*, and vision in *sweat*. For an authentic vision always entails an increase of effort in order to *bear* it, in order to remain upright in the face of it. Vision has a weight, sometimes overwhelming, which demands a great effort on the part of the soul in order not to give way under the weight of the vision.

Authentic inspiration always entails an inner upheaval. It *pierces* the soul like an arrow in wounding it and in making it experience that profound emotion which is a synthesis of sorrow and joy. The symbol of the Rose Cross — a cross from the centre of which a rose blossoms out — renders the essence of the experience of inspiration in the best way that I know. The Rose Cross expresses the mystery of tears, i.e. that of inspiration, with force and clarity. It portrays the joy of sorrow and the sorrow of joy, which together comprise inspiration.

With respect to intuition, it is no longer a matter either of the weight of riches or of the romance of the engagement of the Rose and the Cross, but rather of consummating the marriage of life and death. What lives, thereby dies; and what dies, thereby is re-born. Thereby blood is mingled with the Blood and is transformed alchemically from the "fluid of separation" into the "fluid of union".

There are three ways of "seeing" the Cross: the Crucifix, the Rose Cross, and the Gilded Cross bearing a rose of silver. The Crucifix is the greatest treasure of *vision*. It is the vision of divine and human love. The black Cross with a rose blossoming from it is the treasure of *inspiration*. This is divine and human love *speaking* in the soul. The Gilded Cross bearing a rose of silver is the treasure of *intuition*. This is love *transforming* the soul.

But the Mystery of the Cross is one and indivisible. Whoever does not worship the Crucifix cannot be inspired by it to the point of *accepting* it (which is inspiration) and still less can he *identify* himself with it (which is intuition). It is a matter of a single Cross—a single indivisible Christian Mystery. Therefore someone would certainly be in error if, instead of seeing in the Crucifix *the* way, *the* truth and *the* life, he were to think of founding, for example, a community or "fraternity of the Resurrection" with the Gilded Cross and rose of silver as its symbol, replacing the universal symbol of Christianity—the Crucifix. He would be in error, I say, because the Gilded Cross or the Rose Cross in no way replace the Crucifix, but are included and implied in it. It is the Cross of the Crucifix which becomes inspirative (the Rose Cross) and which is transformed into solar light (the Gilded Cross) bearing the receptive soul (the rose of silver). Resurrection is only crucifixion having reached the stage of fructification. It is *realised* crucifixion.

Therefore one should not—one cannot!—separate from one another the mortal *sweat* of the Crucifix, the inspirative *tears* of acceptance of the Cross (Rose Cross), and the *blood* transmuted through identification with the Cross (the Gilded Cross bearing the rose of silver). The mystery of sweat, tears and blood is *one* and indivisible.

It is the same with Christianity. It is *one* and indivisible. One should not—one cannot!—separate from so-called "exoteric" Christianity its gnosis and mysticism, or so-called "esoteric" Christianity. Esoteric Christianity is entirely *within* exoteric Christianity; it does not exist—and cannot exist—separately from it. Christian Hermeticism is only a special vocation within the universal Christian community—the vocation specific to the *dimension of depth*. Just as there are in the universal Church vocations to the priesthood, monastic life, religious knighthood, etc., so there is a vocation—as irresistible and irrevocable as the others—to Hermeticism. This is a vocation to a life lived in consciousness of the *unity* of cult (or Christian sacred magic), revelation (or Christian sacred gnosis) and salvation (or Christian sacred mysticism), just as the unity of the whole of mankind's authentic spiritual life throughout its entire history always was, is, and always will be *Christocentric*. Hermeticism is the vocation to live the universal and eternal truth of the prologue to St. John's Gospel:

> In the beginning was the Word, and the Word was with God,
> and the Word was God...*All* things were made through him
> and *nothing* that has been made was made without him. In him

was the life, and the life was the light of men...This was the
true light *that enlightens every man coming into the world*.
(John i, 1-4, 9)

Now: *unity* of the light in the whole past, in the present, and in the whole
future; *unity* of the light in the East, West, North and South; *unity* of the light
in magic, gnosis and mysticism; *unity* of the light, lastly, in cult, revelation and
salvation—this is the Hermetic vocation which is, I repeat, as irresistible and irrevocable as that of priest, monk or religious knight.

I may add that it is to you who are irresistibly and irrevocably called to Hermeticism that I address these Letters and that it is you whom I call "dear Unknown
Friends". I acknowledge that I have also "Known Friends". But with respect to these
latter, they are for the most part to be found in the spiritual world. All the more
do I address myself to them in these Letters...and how many times, in writing
these Letters, I have felt the fraternal embraces of these Friends, including here
Papus, Quaita, Péladan, Eliphas Lévi and Louis Claude de Saint-Martin!

Friends, Friends here and there, the Mystery is one and indivisible—sealed by
sweat, tears and blood! You, Friends who are *there*, now you know that there is
only *one* truth, *one* light, *one* Christ, *one* community—and that there is neither
separate exotericism and esotericism nor separate exoteric and esoteric communities. May the Friends who are *here* know this also!

Tears are the element proper to inspiration. And he who is moved to weep—
inwardly or outwardly is not important—before a Crucifix is already inspired by
it. He then contemplates the Rose Cross in the Crucifix. And he who fixes his
eyes on the Crucifix at the supreme moment of agony, where his blood begins
to chill, he—in drawing from it a new warmth to replace the warmth which is
leaving him—*lives* intuition. He already contemplates the Gilded Cross bearing
the rose of silver...

Inspiration is the principle acting in tears. Just like weeping, inspiration takes
place in the guise of "flowing between two vases". In inspiration, whatever its true
source of origin may be, a flow is active, which is produced between the higher
Self or image and the lower self or likeness. Here there is a flow which results from
the *simultaneous collaboration* of the "higher eye" (or "ear") and the "lower eye"
(or "lower ear"). This means to say that higher understanding and lower understanding, being in contact, vibrate in unison, each with its own voice and in terms
of its own language, and thus together produce a concrete inspiration.

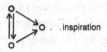

The "technique" of *vision* differs from that of inspiration in that in vision it
is not a matter of the simultaneous collaboration of two "eyes" (or "ears")—higher
and lower—but rather of the passive *imprint* that the lower self, alone, receives

from above. As it is not a matter of the collaboration of two "understandings", it can be that the lower self (the personality) experiences a vision without understanding it. It can, therefore, remain incomprehensible for a long time.

$$\overset{\circ}{\underset{\circ}{\downarrow}} \longrightarrow \text{vision}$$

Concerning intuition, this is due, likewise to a *single* active principle. Here the lower self identifies itself with the higher Self, i.e. it raises itself to the latter and effaces itself (in the higher Self) to the point of becoming a passive and mute presence. And then it is the higher Self alone which is active.

$$\overset{\circ}{\underset{\circ}{\uparrow}} \longrightarrow \text{intuition}$$

These three schematic representations represent at the same time the arcana of tears, sweat and blood. In intuition, where the lower self experiences a kind of death, which is transformed into life in the higher Self, the mystery of blood, symbolised by the Gilded Cross with the rose of silver, is accomplished. In vision, where the weight of revelation from above falls on the lower self and must be supported by it, it is a matter of the mystery of sweat, symbolised by the Cross of the Crucifix—the Cross that the Crucified One had to carry to Calvary, under the weight of which he fell three times. And in inspiration, where the unblemished image and the fallen likeness unite to give birth to a new word, it is a matter of the mystery of tears, symbolised by the Rose Cross.

It is the mystery of tears—and of inspiration—that the fourteenth Arcanum of the Tarot aims at in particular. It is the spiritual exercise dedicated to inspiration.

Inspiration, as follows from the whole of the preceding and as is evident from all authentic experience of it, is not something which simply *happens*, as in the case of vision. Nor is it something which results from the sum total of all efforts at self-sacrifice, mortification, and the reduction of oneself to nothing, as is the case with intuition. Rather, it is a *co-activity*, the concerted activity of the higher Self and the lower self. It is essentially the flow emanating from two vases at once.

The practical *arcanum* of inspiration is therefore the knowledge how to be active and passive at the same time: active—in what concerns the *question* or demand; passive—in what concerns the *answer* or solution. It would be false simply to formulate inwardly a question and subsequently assume a passive—though calm and silent—attitude of waiting for an answer through inspiration. One can thus certainly listen and wait for a long time—as a rule, nothing happens. It would be equally false to make a great effort at discursive thought and "divining" imagination so as to force inspiration as if it were a "salary for work done".

No, it is neither passivity in waiting nor, equally, activity of thought and imagination which realises the state of soul appropriate for inspiration; it is a matter of *simultaneous* activity and passivity. Let us try to explain.

Eighteenth century rationalism advanced the formula: what is clear is true. To which is added the corollary: what is not clear is not true. Now, we have inherited these two formulae, consciously or instinctively, from a century when thinking *modo geometrico* ("in a geometrical mode") was the ideal. Certainly we no longer believe that *everything* which is clear is true, but all the same we postulate that what is true should at the same time be clear. We demand that truth must entail clarity. Guided by this principle we endeavour to be *precise*, i.e. to delineate clear lines around the subject which occupies us. But in so doing we effect an intellectual *enclosure*. That which is enclosed is clear, yes, but it is separated by the enclosure from the great flood of truth (of which we have taken possession of only a drop). The drop is clear, but it is only a drop taken from the flood, i.e. from the great context of truth.

Having understood this, we can be prompted to think in another way. We can try *to think with the flood*, i.e. no longer to think *alone*, but rather *together* with the anonymous "choir" of thinkers above, below, yesterday and tomorrow. "*I think*" then gives way to "*it thinks*".

This "thinking together" is active and passive at the same time. It is active in so far as you are thinking, and it is passive in so far as "something" thinks with you. There are *two vases* from which thought flows—yours and also another. And this is precisely the state of soul that is necessary in order to have inspirations. The arcanum of inspiration, the fourteenth Arcanum of the Tarot, is that of *two* sources and *two* simultaneous currents of thought, which mingle, unite, and constitute authentic *inspiration*.

I have described above the process of "thinking together"—or that of inspiration—wholly as a kind of *special technique*. I had to do so for the sake of clarity. But clarity and truth are not identical. I must therefore correct what I had to sacrifice of the truth in favour of clarity. What follows is the correction.

There is, truth to tell, no technique in the intimate and spiritual domain of inspiration—just as no technique exists in the domains of vision and intuition. In these domains everything is essentially *moral*. For in order to "think together", one thing before everything else is required—and this is *humility*. In thinking, in order to "think together", I have to bow before an intelligence surpassing mine, and to do so not in general terms and in an abstract way but, rather, concretely—by yielding the "author's exclusive rights" to the anonymous co-thinker. "Thinking together" means to say *thinking on one's knees*, i.e. humbling oneself before the other—diminishing oneself so that he may increase. This is thought-prayer or prayer-thought.

Neither the concentration exercises of Raja-yoga nor the breathing (and other) exercises of Hatha-yoga will render us inspired. It is humility alone, due to poverty, obedience and chastity—the three universal and eternal vows—which renders us "inspirable".

It cannot be helped. . .the spiritual world is essentially moral. And inspiration is the fruit of humility in effort and of effort with humility. *Ora et labora* is therefore the key to the door of inspiration, as it is the key to many other doors besides.

What I have said concerning humility as the preliminary condition for inspiration calls for, in its turn, a further detail, if not a correction. For humility can sometimes prove not only sterile with respect to inspiration but can even be an obstacle put in its way. Thus, it is humility which paralyses the aspiration to knowledge of the truth and to perfection in the exercise of virtues and capabilities. Someone who humbly says the following will not receive inspiration: "I am not occupied with divine things and with the spiritual world, because for that one has to be a saint and a sage, and I am neither one nor the other." Preoccupation with the soul's salvation alone can certainly advance the soul quite far on the path of purity and innocence, but it can at the same time leave it in complete ignorance with respect to the world, history, and problems of mankind's spiritual life. Many an authentic saint did not know much concerning the world and its history, on account of the humility which protected him from going out from the circle of what is strictly necessary for salvation.

Hunger and thirst for the truth—which comprises God, the world and mankind —nevertheless underlie the inspiration which falls under the law of *ora et labora*. The Hermeticist, also, will not be inspired if he is not humble. But no more will he be inspired if he does not apprehend, in the aspiration to the truth, the art of forgetting himself. Whatever he may be—humble or presumptuous, innocent or sinful—he must be driven by hunger and thirst for the truth concerning God, the world and mankind.

One should know how to ask and one should dare to ask, whilst forgetting one's humility and one's presumption. Children know how to ask and dare to ask. Are they presumptuous? No, because each question that they pose is at the same time an avowal of their ignorance. Are they humble, therefore? They are in so far as they know and sense their ignorance, and they are not in so far as they are driven by hunger and thirst to know and understand to the point of forgetting them- selves—including all humility and all presumption in them. In this the Hermeticist imitates the child. He wants to know "who", "what", "how" and "why", concern- ing life and death, good and evil, creation and evolution, history and the human soul...People in the natural sciences whose hair is grey through study and research have abandoned these questions. "Childish questions", they say. They resign themselves to a single question: that of the technical "how". The "why" and the "what", not to speak of the "who", are pre-scientific questions which they leave to theology and the *belles-lettres*...

Still, we Hermeticists have conserved the whole repertoire of questions from our childhood—the "what" and the "how", the "why" and the "who". Are we backward? Have we progressed beyond others? Backward or progressive—it does not matter—we have kept living the hunger and thirst for knowledge and under- standing from our childhood and it is this which leads us to ask things that mature people of contemporary civilisation no longer ask.

What? Have we not learnt from the history of civilisation that these questions are unknowable, that the *ignoramus* ("we do not know") of today was preceded by the heroic effort of innumerable generations aspiring to answer these questions, and that it was after this unfruitful effort that one resigned oneself to the *ignoramus* ("we do not know")? What chance, therefore, what hope remains for us after all this?

Our chance, our hope...is *inspiration*. And it is precisely because we ask in the way that children do that we have the hope—no, the certainty—that our Father who is in heaven will give us the answer, that he will not give us a stone instead of bread, or a serpent in place of a fish. Inspiration—the two vases from whence flows the living water held by a winged Angel—is the hope and the chance for the survival of Hermeticism in the centuries to come!

Dear Unknown Friend, say to yourself that you know *nothing*, and at the same time say to yourself that you are able to know *everything*, and—armed with this healthy humility and this healthy presumption of children—immerse yourself in the pure and strengthening element of the "thinking together" of inspiration! May the winged Angel be present in this enterprise of yours, and may he hold the two vases from which inspiration will pour!

The arcanum of inspiration is of vital practical importance not only for Hermeticism but also for the spiritual history of mankind in general. For just as in the individual human biography there are decisive moments of inspiration, so there are in mankind's biography—which is history—decisive points where far-reaching inspirations enter into the spiritual life of humanity. The great religions are such inspirations. In ancient India the Rishis had inspiration, which became the source of the Vedas. In ancient Persia the great Zarathustra ("golden star") had inspiration, which became the source of the Zend-Avesta. Moses and the prophets had inspiration, which became the source of the Old Testament in the Bible. The Event of the life, death and resurrection of Christ was followed by the inspiration which was the source of the written Gospels—of which each author is twofold: man and inspiring Cherubim. Lastly, Islam refers to no other source than the inspiration that Mohammed received from the Archangel Gabriel, which became the source of the Koran.

With respect to Buddhism, which is the religion of humanism pure and simple, it also regards as the source of its origin the spiritual event in the soul of Gautama Buddha under the Bodhi tree, where the four sacred truths of Buddhism were revealed in a sudden way, excluding all doubt, i.e. by way of *inspiration*.

The great religions are therefore the inspirations of mankind. And the history of religion is that of inspiration. Misunderstandings with regard to inspiration and ignorance of its practical *arcanum* will also have distressing and tragic repercussions in mankind's history. There will be people who will believe that inspiration is obtained through effort, and others who will believe that it is produced only in complete passivity of the soul. Thus all forms of *Pelagianism* and *quietism* will arise in the history of religion. All those who do not know that the arcanum of inspiration is that of activity and passivity simultaneously will fall necessarily either into Pelagianism or into quietism.

Individual psychological experiences — including the experience of setbacks and disillusions — in the realm of aspiring to inspiration have played an enormous role in the catastrophic upheavals which have taken place in the history of Christianity. Thus, an Augustinian monk of the sixteenth century ardently desired inspiration. To this end he practised the rigourous asceticism of fasting, mortification of the flesh, and vigils of prayer. He believed that effort would procure inspiration for him; but . . . he had none. Then, disillusioned as he was, he advanced the doctrine of the vanity of work, of all effort. Faith alone suffices for salvation. Here lies the origin of Lutheran Protestantism.

In the same century a doctor of law underwent a sudden conversion, from which he concluded that inspiration is the work of God and God alone, without any participation of human effort and freedom. It is God, and God alone, who has chosen for all eternity those whom he has predestined to salvation amongst the mass predestined to perdition. Here lies the origin of Calvinist Protestantism.

If Martin Luther and John Calvin had known that inspiration is activity *and* passivity — or effort and grace simultaneously — the one would not have seen man as only a sinner and the other would not have conceived of God as a cosmic tyrant.

St. John of the Cross was needed to show that one can pass by the darkness and aridity of the senses and of the mind without drawing back and without despair, just as one can effect a profound reform — in the sense of the practice of the poverty and moral radicalism of the Gospels — without at the same time attacking the unity of the Church. In truth, St. John of the Cross *atoned* for Martin Luther.

Yet another saint, Ignatius of Loyola, was needed to demonstrate that man can choose God and his cause in the full freedom of love, instead of being chosen by God — and that just as Jacob wrestled until the break of day, saying "I will not let you go, unless you bless me" (Genesis xxxii, 26), so can each free human will, chosen or not, embrace the cause of God *voluntarily* and will be blessed by God. St. Ignatius of Loyola *atoned* for John Calvin by living in the voluntary obedience of love for the God of love, instead of the obedience of a poor wretch before the power of the Almighty.

With respect to Christian Hermeticism, it has knowledge of the arcanum of inspiration and it will never range itself on the side of those who believe that inspiration is *made*, nor on the side of those who believe that it is merited by pure and simple passivity of the soul. Hermeticism knows the law of the "marriage of opposites" and it knows that inspiration is the marriage of activity and passivity in the soul.

Read Louis Claude de Saint-Martin and you will nowhere find either Pelagianism or quietism, but rather throughout is the twofold faith — in God *and* man, in grace *and* human effort. *Ora et labora* is truly the practical view which is evident in the whole of the work of Saint-Martin. And the mature Eliphas Lévi? And Josephin

Péladan? And the mature Papus? They all professed to the twofold faith — in God and man, in grace and human effort. This amounts to saying that they knew the arcanum of inspiration — the arcanum which is found represented symbolically by the fourteenth Card of the Tarot.

I have mentioned some Hermeticists whom I suppose that you, dear Unknown Friend, know of. But there are many others who ought to be named as guardians of the ancient tradition of the arcanum of inspiration. But what will the name of Schmakov say to you, for example? Or the name Roudnikova? These are names which, like the yellow leaves of autumn, repose in forgetfulness beneath the immense white shroud of snow which covers pre-revolutionary Russia.

Be that as it may, there is a community of Hermeticists, known and unknown, but the majority of whose members are anonymous. And it is only a small part of this community which is composed of those who know one another and meet one another face to face in the full daylight of the world of the senses. Another part — still less numerous — is composed of those who know each other and meet each other face to face in *vision*. But it is *inspiration* which unites all members of the community of Hermeticists — without regard as to whether they are near to one another or far apart, whether they know each other or not, or whether they are living or deceased.

Inspiration, truth to tell, is what constitutes the Hermetic community. It is inspiration which is the link between its members and within which *all* its members meet one another. The community of inspiration — this is what in reality the community of Hermeticists is.

It is inspiration in common which underlies the mental and symbolic language common to Hermeticists — the language of analogy, the marriage of opposites, synthesis, moral logic, the dimension of depth added to those of clarity and breadth of knowledge, and above all the ardent belief that all is knowable and revealable, that the mystery *is* infinite knowability and revealability. . .

This common inspiration, this language that we have in common, is the inner *Word* which guides and impels us — inwardly and outwardly at the same time — in all our aspirations. The Papus of 1890 did not "know" what Papus would become in 1917, but he already directed his efforts towards what he would know, feel and realise — what he *would be*, in a word — in 1917. This was because he *knew* in 1890 what he did not "know". It was because the *inspiration* which underlies Christian Hermeticism was present and was working in him. And it was thanks to this inspiration that he broke with the neo-Buddhist stream of the Theosophical Society and that he preferred the intellectual Christianity of Saint-Yves d'Alveydre to the intellectual Buddhism of the Theosophical Society. And it was again thanks to this inspiration that he preferred the real Christianity of Maître Philip of Lyons to the Christian intellectualism of his youth. Yes, the Papus of 1917, praying and working, was the product of the *inspiration* which guided and impelled the young student of medicine, subsequent enthusiast for occult science, subsequent bold magician, and again, subsequently, the lover of great intellectual syntheses. Here we have a particular example of the gradual realisation of inspiration working from the days of youth.

"In the beginning was the Word" is the *law* not only of the world but also of the realisation of inspiration in each individual biography. And the entire community of Hermeticists lives under this law, under the *law of inspiration*.

Everyone lives under this law. The community of Hermeticists is distinguished from the rest of mankind only in that it is borne — in an irresistible way — *to be conscious of it* and *to know* what happens both to them and to the rest of humanity.

The *lot* of Hermeticists differs from that of every human being only in that the former hunger and thirst for comprehensive knowledge of that which the latter simply undergo. Their lot does not bring any privilege with it; on the contrary, rather, it is an added duty with which Hermeticists are charged, notably the inner duty to *understand* the totality of miracles and disasters which is life and the world. This duty makes them appear presumptuous or childish in the eyes of the world, but it is the arcanum of inspiration — the arcanum of the winged entity pouring living water from one vase into another — which renders them such as they are.

Meditation on the
Fifteenth Major Arcanum of the Tarot

THE DEVIL
LE DIABLE

LETTER XV

THE DEVIL

Dear Unknown Friend,

It is whilst still being impressed by the Arcanum of inspiration, with the winged entity pouring living water from one vase to another, that we find ourselves confronted by another winged entity holding a tapered torch above two beings bound to a pedestal, on which he is standing upright. This is the Arcanum of *counter-inspiration*, to which we now have to proceed.

And if the fourteenth Arcanum introduced us to the mystery of the *tears* and the *temperance* of inspiration, the fifteenth Arcanum of the Tarot will introduce us to the secrets of the *electrical fire* and the *intoxication* of counter-inspiration. This is a further chapter in the drama of the destiny of the divine image and likeness which we are now obliged to read.

But before we begin the meditation on the Arcanum of counter-inspiration, we must take account of the intrinsic difference between meditation on the other Arcana and meditation on the Arcanum "The Devil". It is as follows.

As it is a matter in the Tarot of a series of spiritual or Hermetic exercises, and as, on the other hand, every spiritual exercise tends to lead to the identification of the meditant with the subject of meditation, i.e. to an act of *intuition*, the fifteenth Arcanum of the Tarot, in so far as it is a spiritual exercise, cannot — and must not — lead to an experience of identification of the meditant with the subject of meditation. One should not arrive at an intuition of evil, since intuition is identification, and identification is *communion*.

Unfortunately many authors — occultist and non-occultist — have dealt without rhyme or reason with the profound things of both good and evil. They believed they should "do their best" with respect to depth and penetration in their treatment of the subject of the mysteries of good and, equally, that of the secrets of evil. It is thus that Dostoyevsky released into the world certain profound truths of Christianity, and, at the same time, certain secret practical methods of evil. This is above all the case in his novel *The Possessed*.

Another example of an excessive accentuation of the knowledge of evil — and therefore of an occupation of consciousness with evil — is the preoccupation with the problem of the twofold (even threefold) evil amongst German Anthroposophists. Lucifer and Ahriman (and even Adzura), the two principles of evil, subjective and objective, the seducing principle and the hypnotising principle, have so taken possession of the consciousness of Anthroposophists that there is hardly a single thing which would not fall under the category of being Ahrimanic or Luciferic. Science is Ahrimanic in so far as it is objective; Christian mysticism is Luciferic in so far as it is subjective. The East is under the domination of Lucifer, because it denies matter; the West is under the domination of Ahriman, because it has created a material civilisation and tends to materialism. All machines — including the apparatus of radio and television — incorporate Ahrimanic demons. Laboratories are the fortresses of Ahriman; theatres — and churches, some believe — are the fortresses of Lucifer. And so on. Anthroposophists are led to classify thousands of facts from the point of view of the category of evil which is revealed through them — which suffices to occupy them for the whole day. And to so occupy oneself amounts to contact with evil and a corresponding reduction of living and inspiring contact with good. The result is a lame wisdom without wings, deprived of creative élan, which only repeats and comments to satiety what the master, Dr. Rudolf Steiner, said. And yet Rudolf Steiner has certainly said things of a nature to awaken the greatest creative élan! His series of lectures on the four Gospels, his lectures at Helsingfors and Düsseldorf on the celestial hierarchies — without mentioning his book on the inner work leading to initiation (*Knowledge of the Higher Worlds. How is it achieved?*) — would alone suffice to inflame a deep and mature creative enthusiasm in every soul who aspires to authentic experience of the spiritual world. But it is the preoccupation with evil which has clipped the wings of the Anthroposophical Movement and which has rendered it such as it is since the death of its founder: a movement for cultural reform (art, education, medicine, agriculture) deprived of living esotericism, i.e. without mysticism, without gnosis and without magic, which have been replaced by lectures, study and intellectual work aiming at establishing a concordance between the writings and stenographed lectures of the master.

One ought not to occupy oneself with evil, other than in keeping a certain distance and a certain reserve, if one wishes to avoid the risk of paralysing the creative élan and a still greater risk—that of furnishing arms to the powers of evil. One can grasp profoundly, i.e. intuitively, only that which one loves. Love is the vital element of profound knowledge, intuitive knowledge. Now, one cannot love evil. Evil is therefore unknowable in its *essence*. One can understand it only at a distance, as an *observer* of its phenomenology.

This is why you will certainly find luminous descriptions—although schematic —of the celestial hierarchies by St. Dionysius the Areopagite, St. Bonaventura, St. Thomas Aquinas, and also in the Cabbala and in the work of Rudolf Steiner, but you will search in vain for an analogous tableau with regard to the hierarchies of evil. You will certainly find amongst sorcerers' grimoires and in the practical Cabbala (by Abramelin the Mage, for example) a host of names of particular beings belonging to the hierarchies of evil, but you will not find a description of their general classification in the manner of that by St. Dionysius the Areopagite of the celestial hierarchies. The world of the hierarchies of evil appears like a luxuriant jungle, where you can certainly, if necessary, distinguish hundreds and thousands of particular plants, but where you can never attain to a clear view of the totality. The world of evil is a *chaotic world*—at least, such as it presents itself to the observer.

One ought not to enter this jungle if one does not want to lose one's way there; one should be an observer from outside. This is why meditation on the Arcanum "The Devil" must obey the laws indicated above concerning the attitude towards evil. It will therefore be a matter of an effort to comprehend this Arcanum *at a distance* by means of the phenomenological method.

Let us proceed therefore to the phenomenology of the Card itself. Firstly, it represents three personages. The one in the middle is larger than the others, and he is standing upright on a pedestal to which the other two are attached. The personage in the middle is an androgynous entity equipped with bat's wings raised upwards. His right hand is raised. His left hand is directed downwards; it holds a lighted torch. His wings and legs are blue. On his head he wears a yellow skullcap with two yellow horns in the form of antlers. He is naked, save for his skullcap and a red girdle.

The two other personages before him and on either side of him represent a naked man and woman. They have tails and the ears of beasts. On their heads they are wearing red skull-caps and are bearing horns in the form of antlers. Their arms are tied behind their backs, and a cord passed around their necks fastens them to a central ring fixed on the lower red-coloured part of the central personage's pedestal. With respect to the latter, there is still a characteristic trait to mention: *he is cross-eyed*, his pupils focussing on the bridge of his nose.

What, therefore, is the set of ideas that is evoked, to begin with, by the Card? . . . ideas, I would like to say, of a nature having a *practical* spiritual significance, i.e. aiming at a practical *arcanum* of Hermeticism as a synthesis of mysticism, gnosis and magic.

Does it have to do with the cosmic metaphysics of evil, or the history of the rebellion of a part of the celestial hierarchies under the direction of the "ancient dragon" who "swept down a third of the stars" (Revelation xii, 3-4)? Is it related to the entity of whom Ezekiel spoke when he said:

> You were a guardian Cherubim, with outspread wings;
> I placed you on the holy mountain of God;
> You walked in the midst of the stones of fire.
> You were blameless in your ways,
> From the day you were created,
> Until iniquity was found in you . . .
> So I cast you as a profane thing
> From the mountain of God,
> And you, guardian Cherubim,
> Have been driven out
> From the midst of the stones of fire.
> Your heart was proud because of your beauty;
> You corrupted your wisdom
> For the sake of your splendour.
> I cast you to the ground . . .
>
> (Ezekiel xxviii, 14-17)

Evidently not. The Devil of the Card does not evoke ideas having to do with the cosmic drama of the fall of the "guardian Cherubim from the mountain of God", nor with the "ancient dragon" waging battle against the archistrategist Michael and his celestial army. The ideas that are evoked by the totality of the Card and its context are rather those of slavery, in which two personages are found who are attached to the pedestal of a monstrous demon. The Card does not suggest the metaphysics of evil, but rather an eminently practical lesson as to how it happens that beings can forfeit their freedom and become slaves of a monstrous entity which makes them degenerate by rendering them similar to it.

The theme of the fifteenth Arcanum of the Tarot is one of the *generation* of demons and of the power that they have over those who generate them. It is the Arcanum of the creation of artificial beings and of the slavery into which the creator can fall — becoming a slave of his own creation.

In order to be able to grasp this Arcanum, it is necessary firstly to take account of the fact that the world of evil consists not only of fallen entities of the celestial hierarchies (with the exception of Seraphim) but also of entities of *non-hierarchical origin*, i.e. entities who, in the manner of bacilli, microbes and viruses of infectious diseases in the domain of biology, owe their origin — to express it in the terms of Scholastic philosophy — neither to the primary cause, nor to secondary causes, but rather to tertiary causes, namely to arbitrary abuse on the part of autonomous creatures. Thus, there are hierarchies who are "of the left" and who act within the framework of the law, executing a strictly just function in their capacity as accusers and "putters to the trial" — whilst on the other hand there are "microbes of evil" or entities artificially created by incarnated human beings. These latter entities are demons whose soul is a special passion and whose body is the totality of "electro-magnetic" vibrations produced by this passion. These artificial demons can be engendered by human communities — such are many of the monstrous "gods" of the Phoenicians, Mexicans, and even Tibetans of the present day. The Canaan Moloch who demanded the bloody sacrifice of the first born, mentioned so often in the Bible, is not a hierarchical entity — either of good or of evil — but rather an evil *egregore*, i.e. a demon created artificially and collectively by human communities infatuated with the thrill of fear. The Mexican Quetzalcoatl is a similar instance of this. There, also, it was a matter of a demon created and worshipped collectively.

With respect to Tibet, we find there the singular phenomenon of the conscious — semi-"scientific" — practice of the creation and destruction of demons. It appears that in Tibet the Arcanum with which we are occupied is known, and it is practised as one of the methods of occult training of the will and imagination. The training consists of three parts: the creation of *tulpas* (magical creatures) through concentrated and directed imagination, then their evocation and, lastly, the freeing of consciousness from their hold on it by an act of knowledge which destroys them — through which it is realised that they are only a creation of the imagination, and therefore illusory. The aim of this training is therefore to arrive at disbelief in demons *after having created them* through the force of imagination and having confronted their terrifying apparitions with intrepidity. This is what Alexandra David-Neel, who wrote with a deep knowledge of the subject, said about it:

> I have questioned several lamas on this subject (of incredulity).
> "Incredulity comes sometimes," answered a *geshes* (graduate)
> from Derge (a town in Kham, Eastern Tibet). "Indeed, it is one
> of the ultimate objects of the mystic masters, but if the disciple
> reaches this state of mind before the proper time he misses
> something which these exercises are designed to develop, that
> is fearlessness. Moreover, the teachers do not approve of simple
> incredulity, they deem it contrary to truth. The disciple must
> understand that gods and demons do really exist for those who
> believe in their existence, and that they are possessed with the
> power of benefitting or harming those who worship or fear them.
> However, very few reach incredulity in the early part of their

training. Most novices actually *see* frightful apparitions. . ."
. . .I had the opportunity of talking with a *gomchen* of Ga
(Eastern Tibet) called Kushog Wanchen about sudden deaths
which occurred while calling up demons. This lama did not appear inclined towards superstition and I thought he would agree
with my opinion on this matter. "Those who died were killed
by fear. Their visions were the creations of their own imagination. He who does not believe in demons would never be killed
by them." I was much astonished when the anchorites replied
in a peculiar tone of voice: "According to that it must also follow
that a man who does not believe in the existence of tigers may
feel confident that none of them would ever hurt him even if
he were confronted by such a beast.". . .and he continued: "Visualising mental formations, either voluntarily or not, is a most
mysterious process. What becomes of these creations? May it not
be that like children born of our flesh, these children of our mind
separate their lives from ours, escape our control, and play parts
of their own? Must we not also consider that we are not the only ones capable of creating such formations? And if such entities
(*tulpas*, magical creatures) exist in the world, are we not liable
to come into touch with them, either by the will of their maker
or from some other cause? Could one of these causes not be that,
through our mind or through our material deeds, we bring
about the conditions in which these entities are capable of
manifesting some kind of activity?. . .One must know how to
protect oneself against the tigers to which one has given birth,
as well as against those that have been begotten by others."
(Alexandra David-Neel, *Magic and Mystery in Tibet*, London,
1967, pp. 146-148)

This is what the Tibetan masters thought of magic that creates demons. But the
French master of magic, Eliphas Lévi, hardly thought otherwise about it.

The devil-making magic which dictated the Grimoire of Pope
Honorius, the *Enchiridion* of Leo III, the exorcisms of the Ritual,
the verdicts of inquisitors, the suits of Laubardement, the articles of the Veuillot brothers, the books of MM. de Falloux, de
Montalembert, de Mirville, the magic of sorcerers and of pious
persons who are not sorcerers, is truly a thing to be condemned
in some and infinitely deplored in others. It is above all to combat these unhappy aberrations of the human mind by their ex-
posure that we have published this book. May it further the holy
cause! (*Ritual*, ch. xv).
Man is himself the creator of his heaven and hell, and there are
no demons except our own follies. Minds chastised by truth are
corrected by that chastisement, and dream no more of disturb-

ing the world (*Ritual*, ch. xxii). (Eliphas Lévi, *Transcendental Magic. Its Doctrine and Ritual*; trsl. A. E. Waite, London, 1968, pp. 322-323, 410)

For, in accordance with his experience of them, Eliphas Lévi saw in demons—such as incubi and succubi, the Leonard masters presiding over witches' sabbaths, and the demons of the possessed—only creations of human will and imagination, projecting, individually or collectively, their content into the malleable substance of the "astral light" and thus engendering demons, which are therefore engendered in Europe in exactly the same way as the Tibetan *tulpas*!

The art and method of "making idols", which is forbidden by the second of the ten commandments, is ancient and universal. It seems that at all times and everywhere demons have been engendered.

Both Eliphas Lévi and the Tibetan masters are in agreement not only with respect to the subjective and psychological origin of demons but also with respect to their *objective* existence. Engendered subjectively, they become forces independent of the subjective consciousness which engendered them. They are, in other words, *magical creations*, for magic is the *objectification* of that which takes its origin in subjective consciousness. Demons that have not arrived at the stage of objectification, i.e. at that of an existence separate from the psychic life of their parents, have a semi-autonomous existence which is designated in modern psychology by the term "psychological complex". C. G. Jung regarded these as parasitic entities, which are to the psychic organism what, for example, cancer is to the physical organism. A psychopathological "complex" is therefore a demon, when it has not come from outside but is engendered by the patient himself. In its state of gestation it is still not born, but it certainly has an almost autonomous life of its own, nourished by the psychic life of its parent. C. G. Jung said on this subject:

> It appears as an autonomous formation intruding upon consciousness...It is just as if the complex were an autonomous being capable of interfering with the intentions of the ego. Complexes do indeed behave like secondary or partial personalities possessing a mental life of their own. (C. G. Jung, *Psychology and Religion*; trsl. R. F. C. Hull, *The Collected Works of C. G. Jung*, vol. 11, London, 1958, pp. 13-14)

Now, "an autonomous being capable of interfering with the intentions of the ego" and which "possesses a mental life of its own" is nothing other than what we understand by a "demon".

It is true the "demon complex" still does not act from outside the psychic life of a single individual—it still does not have the "freedom of the city" of the motley and fantastic community of *tulpas* or objective demons, which can sometimes even bruise the victims of their assault with quite real blows, as was the case with St.

Anthony the Great and the holy priest of Ars, for example. The noise from such an assault that everyone hears and the bruise on the body of the victim which everyone sees is no longer purely and simply psychological — it is already objective.

How are demons engendered? As with all generation, that of demons is the result of the cooperation of the male principle and the female principle, i.e. the *will* and the *imagination*, in the case of generation through the psychic life of an individual. A desire that is perverse or contrary to nature, followed by the corresponding imagination, together constitute the act of generation of a demon.

The two personages, the one male and the other female, attached to the pedestal of the central personage of the Card of the fifteenth Arcanum — the Devil — are therefore not the creation or the children of the central personage, as one might be tempted to believe, seeing their small build in comparison with the size of the demon's stature. Rather, on the contrary, it is they who are the parents of the demon and who have become enslaved by their own creation. They represent perverse will and imagination contrary to nature, which have given birth to an androgynous demon, i.e. to a being endowed with desire and imagination, which dominates the forces that engendered it.

With respect to generation effected collectively, the demon — which in this case is known by the term *egregore* — is likewise the product of will and imagination, which in this case are collective. The birth of such an *egregore* in modern times is known to us:

"A spectre is haunting Europe — the spectre of communism" — such is the first phrase of the *Communist Manifesto* of Karl Marx and Friedrich Engels of 1848. The *Communist Manifesto* continues:

> "All the powers of old Europe have entered into a holy alliance to exorcise this spectre: Pope and Czar, Metternich and Guizot, French radicals and German police-spies." (Karl Marx and Friedrich Engels, *Manifesto of the Communist Party*; trsl. S. Moore, London, 1932, p. 8)

Meanwhile, we may add, the spectre has grown in stature and in power. Engendered by the will of the masses, born from the despair following the "industrial revolution" in Europe, nourished by the resentment accumulated amongst the masses through the generations, armed with a dummy intellectuality which is Hegel's dialectic misconstrued — this spectre has grown and continues to make the rounds in Europe, and in other continents. . .Today already one third of mankind is impelled to bow down before this god and to obey it in everything.

What I am saying here concerning the generation of the most imposing modern *egregore* is in perfect accord with Marxist teaching itself. Because for Marxism there is no God or gods — there are only "demons" in the sense of creations of the human will and imagination. This is the fundamental Marxist doctrine of the so-called "ideological superstructure". According to this doctrine it is the economic interest, i.e. the *will*, which creates, i.e. *imagines*, ideologies — religious, philosophical, social and political. For Marxism all religions are, therefore, only such "ideological superstructures", i.e. formations due to the human will and imagination. Marxism-Leninism itself is only an ideological superstructure, a product of intellectual imagination, on the basis of the will having arranged—or re-arranged—social, political and cultural things in a certain manner. And this method of production of ideological superstructures on the basis of the will is precisely what we understand by the collective generation of a demon or *egregore*.

Now, there is the Word, and there are *egregores* before whom humanity bows down; there is revelation of divine truth, and the manifestation of the will of human beings; there is the cult of God, and that of idols made by man. Is it not a diagnosis and prognosis of the whole history of the human race that at the same time that Moses received the revelation of the Word at the summit of the mountain, the people at the foot of the mountain made and worshipped a golden calf? The Word and idols, revealed truth and "ideological superstructures" of the human will, operate simultaneously in the history of the human race. Has there been a single century when the servants of the Word have not had to confront the worshippers of idols, *egregores*?

The fifteenth Card of the Tarot contains an important warning to all those who take magic seriously: it teaches them the magical Arcanum of the generation of demons, and of the power that the latter have over those who have engendered them.

We who have had experience of the demon or *egregore* in question above, and of the demon engendered by a collective will infatuated with national ambitions and making use of an imagination drawn from the province of biology—the national-socialist demon or *egregore*—know from first-hand experience what terrible power resides in our will and imagination, and what responsibility it entails for those who unleash it into the world! How true it is that he who "sows the wind, shall reap the whirlwind" (Hosea ix, 7)...and what a whirlwind!

We people of the twentieth century know that the "great pests" of our time are the *egregores* of "ideological superstructures", which have cost humanity more life and suffering than the great epidemics of the Middle Ages.

And having this knowledge, is it not time that we said to ourselves: let us be silent. Let us make our arbitrary will and imagination silent; let us impose on them the discipline of silence. Is this not one of the four traditional rules of Hermeticism: to dare, to will, to know, *to be silent*? To be silent is more than to keep things secret; it is more even than to guard oneself from profaning the holy things to which a respectful silence is owed. To be silent is, above all, *the great magical commandment of not engendering demons* through our arbitrary will and imagination; it is the task of silencing arbitrary will and imagination.

Let us resign ourselves, therefore, to the "great work" of contributing constructively to tradition—the spiritual, Christian, Hermetic, scientific tradition. Let us thoroughly immerse ourselves in it, let us study it, let us practise it, lastly, let us cultivate it, i.e. let us work not in order to overthrow but in order to build. Let us range ourselves amongst the builders of the "great cathedral" of mankind's spiritual tradition—and let us try to contribute to it. May the Holy Scriptures be holy for us; may the Sacraments be sacraments for us; may the hierarchy of spiritual authority be the hierarchy of authority for us; and may the "perennial philosophy" —and also *truly scientific* science—of the past and present have friends in us and, should it be the case, respectful collaborators! This is what the commandment *to be silent* entails—the commandment of not engendering demons.

Now, it is always excess owing to *intoxication* of the will and imagination which engenders demons. If—to return to the example cited above—Marx and Engels had simply defended the interests of the industrial workers without having let themselves be carried away by their intoxicated imagination to make statements of universal historical significance, and even cosmic significance, such as the statement that God does not exist, that all religion is only the "opium of the people", that all ideology is only a superstructure on the basis of material interests (and that this has always been so, everywhere), they would have been contributors to tradition. Because care for the rights and well-being of the poor is an integral part of the very essence of tradition—Christian, Jewish, Islamic, Buddhist, Hindu and humanist. Carried away by indignation—not devoid of a nobility of heart—and by the bitterness of disenchantment with the classes in power—not devoid of a foundation in experience—they cast in the same mould God, the bourgeoisie, the Gospels, capitalism, mendicant orders, industrial monopolies, idealistic philosophers, and bankers...and they declared all this, without a second thought, as riff-raff of the history of the human race. There is no doubt that with them it was a matter of an excess—a going beyond the limits of competence and sober and honest knowledge—which they did not in any way doubt, having been carried away by the intoxicating impulse of radicalism, i.e. by a fever of the will and imagination to change everything utterly at a single stroke. And it is this fever of desire to change everything utterly at a single stroke which gave birth to the demon of class hatred, atheism, disdain for the past, and material interest being placed above all else, which is now making the rounds in the world. This demon is being heroically combatted at present (1963) by the head of a large communist country, who is doing all that is humanly possible to replace it by a spirit of care for the people and for their well-being—the spirit which underlies the work of the *sober* Marx and Engels, i.e. taken into the framework of tradition, not exceeding either their competence or the limits of their cause itself.

To be silent is the Temperance of the fourteenth Arcanum of the Tarot, opposed to the intoxication whose essence and dangers are revealed by the fifteenth Arcanum of the Tarot. The inspiration of "Temperance" can be turned into the intoxication of "The Devil". The inspiration aiming at alleviating the lot of the poor and oppressed, and at re-establishing social justice, is able—as was the case with Marx and Engels—to change into the intoxication of radicalism, i.e. to become feverish will and imagination desiring to change everything utterly at a single stroke. This is the relationship between the inspiration of the Angel of the fourteenth Arcanum and the generation of the demon of the fifteenth Arcanum. The history of the human race supplies us with numerous examples of the transformation of the initial inspiration of Temperance into the subsequent intoxication generating demons.

It is the relationship between the fourteenth Arcanum and the fifteenth which explains how the religion of love was able to give way to the funeral-pyres of the Inquisition, how the idea of hierarchical collaboration within mankind became a caste system (or rather the struggle between the classes), how the scientific method was transformed into materialistic dogma, and how, lastly, the facts of biological evolution were used as a basis for the doctrine of intrinsic inequality between races and the corresponding superiority of certain nations. The list is in no way complete, but it suffices to show the practical significance of the relationship between the fourteenth and fifteenth Arcana of the Tarot. It is the relationship between inspiration and counter-inspiration.

One is in the habit — since the first centuries of the Christian era — of designating this counter-inspiration straight away as the "voice of the flesh", which subsequently promoted the flourishing of the principal dogma of the Manichaean and Cathar heresy, which declares Nature to be intrinsically bad. However, exact statements to the contrary were not lacking in Christian antiquity. For example, the following is what St. Anthony the Great said, who is, without doubt, an authority of the first order concerning the problem of "demon-flesh":

> I think that the body has a natural movement, adapted to it, but which is not produced if the soul does not want it; then only a movement without passion arises in the body. There is also another movement which comes from the nourishment and pleasure the body receives through food and drink. The warmth of blood that is thus provoked excites the body to action. . . And there is another movement, in those who are struggling, which comes from the snares and jealousy of demons. . . *It is known that the body has three kinds of carnal movements. The first is a natural movement, inherent in it. . . the second kind of movement in the body is produced by too abundant food and drink. . . the third movement comes from the evil spirits. . .* (St. Anthony the Great, *Apophthegmata*, xxii; trsl. of italicised text by E. Kadloubovsky and G. E. H. Palmer, *Early Fathers from the Philokalia*, London, 1954, p. 40)

These are, therefore, the principles — expounded with a clarity which leaves nothing to be desired — of traditional asceticism, based on experience and confirmed by the experience of thousands of spiritual seekers, including St. Teresa of Avila and St. Ignatius of Loyola in Spain. . . and Gautama Buddha in India. More than a century before Anthony, Origen said:

> We have often said that Christians have had to take up a struggle on two fronts. For the perfect, for those who are like Paul

of Ephesus, as the apostle himself said, ". . . are not contending against flesh and blood, but against Principalities and Powers, against the princes of the world of darkness, against the spiritual hosts of wickedness in heavenly places" (Ephesians vi, 12). Lesser ones—those who are not yet perfect—must struggle against flesh and blood; they are still struggling against the vices and weaknesses of the flesh. (Origen, *In libro Jesum Nave*, homily ix, 4; ed. W. A. Baehrens, *Die griechischen christlichen Schriftsteller der ersten drei Jahrhunderte*, vol. 7, Leipzig, 1921, pp. 349-350)

In other words, beginners have to struggle against the second movement of the body (following St. Anthony's schema) whilst the more advanced have to deal with demons and with hierarchies of the left. The scale of temptation therefore corresponds to that of spiritual advancement: temptation is progressively spiritualised as man becomes more spiritual. The temptations of "Principalities and Powers" (*archai kai exousiai*) which the spiritually advanced have to face are incomparably more subtle than those for a beginner. If one says, "merit necessitates" (*noblesse oblige*), one should add "simplicity protects". This is why Origen gave the following advice:

One should not . . . speak to disciples, at the beginning of their formative period, of profound and secret mysteries; but one should confide to them that which concerns the improvement of habits, the formation of discipline, and the first elements of religious life and simple faith. Such is the milk of the Church; such are the first elements for initial beginners. (Origen, *In libro Judicum*, homily v, 6; ed. Baehrens, pp. 496-497)

It is the law of temperance which is required. Now, the Arcanum of Temperance, the fourteenth Arcanum of the Tarot, represents a guardian Angel who is charged with his office. Origen is of the same opinion as we, and as the unknown author of the Tarot. He said, in fact:

When we begin to come to the cult of God, when we receive the principles of the word of God and of heavenly doctrine, it is the "princes of Israel" who must deliver these beginnings to us. By "princes of Israel" one should, in my opinion, understand the *Angels of Christian people* who, according to the word of the Lord, assist the smallest in the Church and look always upon the face of the Father in heaven. These are they who are "princes", and from whom we must receive the principles. . . (Origen, *In libro Judicum*, homily vi, 1; ed. Baehrens, p. 498)

Origen attributed not only the office of temperance to guardian Angels ("the Angels of Christian people") in conformity with the teaching of the fourteenth Arcanum of the Tarot, but he also taught the principle of the teaching concerning the "liberation of Angels" through man, as found in the preceding Letter. He said, in fact:

> But we must not always rely on the Angels to fight for us; they help us only at the beginning, when we ourselves are commencing. With the progress of time, we should arm ourselves for combat. Before we learn to do battle, so that we will consider giving ourselves up to the battles of the Lord, we are succoured by the "princes", by Angels. Initially, we receive the provision of celestial bread . . . as long as we are children, we are nourished by milk; when we begin to hold to the word of Christ, we live as children under the authority of tutors and procurators. But when we have tasted the sacraments of celestial militia, when we have nourished ourselves on the bread of life, listen how the apostolic trumpet invites us to combat! It is with a loud voice that Paul cried to us, saying: "Take the whole armour of God, that you may be able to withstand the wiles of the devil." He no longer permits us to hide ourselves under the wings of our nurse; he invites us to the fields of battle. "Gird yourself," he says, "with the breastplate of righteousness, and the helmet of salvation, and the sword of the Spirit, and above all the shield of faith, with which you can quench all the flaming darts of the evil one" (Ephesians vi, 13-17). (Origen, *In libro Judicum*, homily vi, 2; ed. Baehrens, pp. 498-500)

The same teaching is found twelve centuries later with St. John of the Cross. St. John of the Cross does not grow tired of repeating that the soul who seeks God is called to renounce every created being, above and below, every being — terrestrial and celestial. He summarised this teaching by saying:

> This knowledge is referred to by David when he says, "I have watched and am become as the lonely sparrow on the housetop" (*Vigilavi, et factus sum, sicut passer solitarius in tecto* — Psalm 101, 8), that is "I opened the eyes of my understanding, and was raised up above all natural comprehension, lonely, without them, on the housetop, lifted up above all earthly considerations." (St. John of the Cross, *A Spiritual Canticle* xv, 4; trsl. D. Lewis, London, 1909, p. 122)

This solitude and isolation is the consequence that one has ceased to live "like a child under the authority of tutors and procurators", as Origen expresses it, and that one has attained a mature spiritual age. The change which then takes place is characterised by St. John of the Cross in the following way:

> . . . it is at the time they (i.e. beginners) are going about their spiritual exercises with delight and satisfaction, when in their

opinion the sun of divine favour is shining most brightly on
them, that God darkens all this light and closes the door and
spring of the sweet spiritual water they were tasting as often and
as long as they desired. For since they were weak and tender,
no door was closed to them, as St. John says in the Apocalypse
(Rev. iii, 8). God now leaves them in such darkness that they
do not know which way to turn in their discursive imaginings;
they cannot advance a step in meditation, as they used to, now
that the interior sensory faculties are engulfed in this night. He
leaves them in such dryness that they not only fail to receive
satisfaction and pleasure from their spiritual exercises and works,
as they formerly did, but also find these exercises distasteful and
bitter. As I said, when God sees that they have grown a little,
he weans them from the sweet breast so that they might be
strengthened, lays aside their swaddling bands, and puts them
down from his arms that they may grow accustomed to walking
by themselves. (St. John of the Cross, *The Dark Night* I, viii,
3; trsl. K. Kavenaugh and O. Rodriguez in *The Collected Works
of St. John of the Cross*, London, 1966, p. 312)

Let us add: to walk by themselves in order to become, in the progress of time,
as Origen said, combatants in the ranks of the militia of God.

This progress is accompanied by more and more subtle temptations. The temptations of the "vices and weaknesses of the flesh" are therefore followed by the
assaults of artificial demons, engendered by others or engendered collectively,
which subsequently give way to more subtle temptations whose authors are entities of the fallen hierarchies. Lastly, on the threshold of the All—God himself—
there is the last temptation, by way of the void: the "dark night of the soul", of
which St. John of the Cross speaks, signifying simultaneously union with God
or, rather, the despair of nothing—complete and supreme nihilism.

For this is the truth of which St. Anthony the Great spoke:

No one, if he is not tempted, will be able to enter the kingdom
of heaven. For, take away the temptations and no one is saved.
(St. Anthony the Great, *Apophthegmata*, v)

This law is of such universality that Jesus Christ, also, had to face three temptations in the desert after the manifestation of the Holy Trinity at the time of the
Baptism in the Jordan. The ladder of perfection therefore entails that of temptation. And just as the former signifies progress from the gross to the subtle, so does
the latter signify an analogous progress. In other words, inspiration is followed
or accompanied by counter-inspiration.

How, therefore, does one distinguish one from the other? What are the criteria
by which one must abide in order to be able to distinguish inspiration from
counter-inspiration?

The following are answers given by the most experienced masters of spiritual practice:

St. Anthony the Great:

> ...it is quite possible to tell the difference between the good and the bad when God grants it. *A vision of the holy ones is not turbulent*...it comes so quietly and gently *that instantly joy and gladness and courage arise in the soul*...And the thoughts of the soul remain untroubled and unruffled, so that in its own bright transparency it is able to behold those who appear...Such, then, is the vision of the holy ones. *On the other hand, the attack and appearance of the evil ones is full of confusion*, accompanied by crashing, roaring, and shouting: it could well be the tumult produced by rude boys and robbers. *This at once begets terror in the soul, disturbance and confusion of thoughts*, dejection, hatred of ascetics, indifference, sadness, remembrance of kinsfolk, and fear of death; and then a desire for evil, a disdain for virtue, and a complete subversion of character. When, therefore, you have a vision (or experience some inspiration*) and are afraid, if then the fear is taken from you immediately and in its place comes ineffable joy and contentment; and courage and recovery of strength and calmness of thought and the other things I have mentioned, and stoutheartedness, too, and love of God, then be of good cheer and pray—*for your joy and your soul's tranquility* betoken the holiness of Him who is present...But when you have certain visions, and confusion overtakes you and there is tumult from without and earthly apparitions and threats of death and all the things I have mentioned, then know that the visit is from the wicked. (St. Athanasius, *The Life of Saint Anthony*; trsl. R. T. Meyer, Westminster, 1950, pp.49-51)

St. Teresa of Avila:

> Locutions (inspired*) that come from the devil not only lead to no good, but leave bad effects behind them. These I have experienced, though only on two or three occasions, and each time I have had an immediate warning from the Lord that they came from the devil. *Not only is the soul left in great dryness, but there is also a certain disquiet*, such as I have experienced on many other occasions when the Lord has allowed me to be subjected to great temptations and spiritual trials of various sorts. But although this disquiet torments me very often, as I shall say later, it is not easy to know where it comes from. *The soul seems to resist the experience and is upset and afflicted without*

---

*Author's note.

knowing why, for what is actually said is not evil but good...The pleasures and joys which the devil bestows differ greatly, I believe, from those which come from God...After visions of the kind that come from the devil, *the soul is not left in a calm state, but in a kind of bewilderment and most perturbed*... When the devil speaks to us, all good things seem to be hidden from the soul and to flee from it; it becomes restless and touchy, and suffers nothing but bad effects. It may seem to have good desires, but they are not strong; and the humility that remains behind is false, excitable, and lacking in tranquility. (*The Life of St. Teresa of Avila;* trsl. J. M. Cohen, London, 1957, pp. 177-179)

Now let us return to the first point. These communications may come either from the inferior or the superior part of the soul, or from without, which does not prevent their originating from God. The most certain signs of their being divine are in my opinion these: The *first* and truest is the *power and authority* they carry with them and their operation (i.e. they are communications and works at one and the same time)...I will explain myself at greater length. A soul is suffering all the sorrow and disquiet I have described: the mind is darkened and dry; but is set at peace, freed from all trouble and filled with light, merely by hearing the words: "*Be not troubled*." These deliver it from all its pains, although before, if the whole world and all its learned men had united to persuade it (that) there was no cause for grief, it could not, in spite of all their efforts, have got rid of its sadness...The *second sign* is a *great calm* and a devout and peaceful recollection which dwell in the soul, together with a desire to praise God...The *third proof* is that these words (interior communciations) *do not pass from the memory*, but remain there for a very long time; indeed, some are never forgotten... (St. Teresa of Avila, *The Interior Castle* vi, 6-7, 10-11; trsl. by the Benedictines of Stanbrook, revised by B. Zimmerman, London, 1906, pp. 157-159)

St. John of the Cross:

...there is a great difference between the visions of God and those of the evil one. For the effect of the latter is not like that of the former: those of Satan *result in dryness of spirit*, in a tendency to self-esteem, to accept and make much of visions; and in no degree whatever do they produce the gentleness of humility, and love of God. Again, the forms of the diabolic visions do not remain impressed on the soul with the sweet clearness of the others, *neither do they endure, yea, rather, are immediately effaced*, except when the soul attaches itself to them: in that case the importance attached to them causes them to be remembered naturally, but with great dryness of spirit, and without the fruit of humility and love, which issue out of the good visions, whenever they recur to the memory. . .The effects of these (latter) visions in the soul are quietness, enlightenment, joy like glory, sweetness, pureness, love, humility, inclination, or elevation of the mind to God, sometimes more of one, sometimes more of another. . . (St. John of the Cross, *The Ascent of Mount Carmel* II, xxiv, 6-7; trsl. D. Lewis, London, 1906, pp. 201-202)

This is the *traditional* doctrine, i.e. based on experience repeated and renewed through the centuries. People of the century of Descartes, Spinoza and Leibnitz were strongly impressed by *geometry*, because philosophical opinions change, whilst the arguments and conclusions of Euclid and Archimedes remain unalterably valid. Thus, people of the seventeenth century were led to prefer the geometrical mode (*modo geometrico*) of reasoning to all other kinds of reasoning. However, there exists still something else of as unalterable validity and universality as the geometrical method: this is authentic spiritual experience. As we see from the above quotations from spiritual masters of the fourth and sixteenth centuries, authentic spiritual experience remains the same across the ages just as geometrical reasoning remained the same across the ages—until Lobachevsky.

It is this immutable reality of spiritual experience which is the foundation and essence of *Hermeticism*, i.e. of knowledge founded on first-hand experience of spiritual reality across the ages. Hermeticism is therefore not limited to the spokesmen for so-called Hermetic orders, brotherhoods or societies, but it also includes all those who have had something to say with real knowledge of spiritual reality and of the path towards this reality—all those, in other words, who *bear witness* to the mysticism, gnosis and magic whose unity is Hermeticism. For this reason we have many more masters from whom we are able to learn—and, in fact, from whom we should learn—than are contained in the list of authors of so-called authorities: Cabbalists, Rosicrucians, esotericists, Theosophists, occultists, etc. In any case, this was really the point of view of Papus, Sédir, Marc Haven and others—all of whom belonged to orders, fraternities and societies for initiation—when they recognised in Maître Philip of Lyons their master, although not only did he not belong to any organisation for initiation but also he considered them more or less superfluous. And if this did not prevent them in any way from rallying around Maître Philip of Lyons, it was because they believed—not without reason, moreover—to have found a master in him, i.e. an authentic witness to spiritual reality, to Hermeticism understood in exactly the same sense as we understand it in these Letters: as the *tradition of authentic spiritual experience* across the ages, which has the aspects named "mysticism", "gnosis" and "magic".

Such was also the point of view of Louis Claude de Saint-Martin who, being a member of the initiation order of Martinez de Pasqually, did not hesitate to act in the same way with regard to the shoemaker of Goerlitz, Jacob Boehme, as Papus and his friends acted with regard to Maître Philip of Lyons.

Now, I know very well that neither St. Anthony the Great, nor St. Teresa of Avila, nor St. John of the Cross were members of any initiation organisation — that, therefore, they were not representatives of the so-called initiation tradition — but, as they are authentic witnesses to spiritual reality, I take the same attitude towards them as Papus and his friends took with regard to Maître Philip of Lyons or that Saint-Martin took with regard to Jacob Boehme. For Hermeticism is in no way exclusiveness, but *depth*. Therefore all that which is deep belongs to it. It is not "legitimate initiation" which constitutes the chain — or rather the flow — of the tradition — but rather the *niveau* and *authenticity* of spiritual experience and the *depth* of thought that it comprises. Therefore it is initiation *per se* which constitutes the Hermetic tradition across the ages, and not the transmission of initiation by way of rituals and formulae. If the tradition depended only on the latter, it would already long ago have been either extinguished or certainly lost in the jungle of quarrels over rights and legitimacy. Now, it is he who *knows from first-hand experience* who represents the tradition, and it is his authentic knowledge which is his legitimacy. If this were not so, the old argument "Can anything good come out of Nazareth?" would have rendered the tradition sterile by reducing it to the niveau of the scribes and Pharisees, i.e. to the niveau of erudition and rules. Let us add in parentheses that the one who advanced this argument historically, Nathanael, had the moral courage not to attribute to it the role of a decisive criterion, since he followed the invitation from Philip: "Come and see" (John i, 46). This had the consequence that he said, "Rabbi, you are the Son of God! You are the King of Israel!" and that he heard the words of the Master, "Truly, truly, I say to you, you will see heaven open and the Angels of God ascending and descending upon the Son of man" (John i, 49-51). This is the formula of the essence of the tradition: *to see heaven open and the Angels of God ascending and descending*.

Now, all those who have seen "heaven open and the Angels of God ascending and descending" belong to the tradition and represent the tradition, including St. Anthony the Great, St. Teresa of Avila and St. John of the Cross, to mention only those witnesses spoken of in this Letter.

Do you know, dear Unknown Friend, who is an initiate of the first order in the tradition of Christian Hermeticism? This is St. Francis of Assisi, the *poverello* without erudition and without rules — a star of the first order in the heaven of mysticism, gnosis and magic! For not only did he see heaven open and the Angels of God ascending and descending, but also he was rendered at one accord with the Initiator himself of all authentic initiations in the act of initiation accomplished by the Seraphim from above.

But let us return to the fifteenth Arcanum of the Tarot...Until now we have treated it from the point of view of the generation of "artificial demons"— individual generation and collective generation. Concerning the latter, i.e. the generation of *egregores*, the following is an important point that still needs to be specified:

Occult literature — above all in France — of the nineteenth and twentieth centuries advances the thesis (which has become almost classical, and seems to be generally accepted) that as well as bad *egregores* good ones can equally well be engendered through collective will and imagination, i.e. "good demons" are engendered in exactly the same way as evil ones. According to this thesis, all depends on the generating will and imagination: if they are good, they engender positive *egregores*; if they are bad, they engender negative *egregores*. There are, according to this thesis, good "artificial demons" as well as bad ones—just as there are good and bad thoughts.

From a practical point of view this thesis gives rise to a practice where one endeavours to collectively create an *egregore* for this special purpose: as a "group spirit" or spirit of the fraternity concerned. This *egregore* once created, it is believed that one is able to rely on it and that one has an efficacious magical ally in it. It is believed that every group has an active "group spirit" which renders it influential with regard to the outside world as well as with regard to its members. It is believed that real and effective traditions are, in the last analysis, only strong and well-nourished *egregores*, which live and act across the ages. Not only do all initiation orders and fraternities owe their life and influence to their *egregores*, but it is believed that churches do also. Therefore, Catholicism is believed to be an *egregore* generated by the collective will and imagination of believers . . . and similarly so with the eastern Orthodox Church, and with Lamaism, etc.

This is the thesis and its main consequence in practice. The exactness that I think I must give concerning this point amounts to the counter-thesis that *good "artificial demons" do not exist*, i.e. one cannot engender positive *egregores*. The reasons in support of this are as follows:

In order to engender a psychic or "astral" entity, it is necessary that the psychic and mental energy that you produce to this effect coagulates, i.e. *enfolds*. A form is not produced by *radiation*; it is produced only by coagulation or *enfoldment*. Now, good only radiates; it does not at all enfold. It is always evil which does this.

You cannot engender a "demon of pure love" or an "*egregore* of universal love" because the quality of will and imagination required to this end is not held together as a formation centred in itself, but forms an alliance—one of "radiating movement"—with the activity of the world of spiritual hierarchies. The psychic and mental energy of love would never give rise to the formation of an individualised psychic or "astral" entity; it would immediately put itself wholly at the disposal of the celestial hierarchies, saints, and God. Therefore, although one can certainly engender demons, one cannot engender artificial Angels.

If there are *egregores* of initiation orders and religious—and other—communities, they are always negative. The *egregore* of Catholicism, for example, is its parasitic double (the existence of which it would be futile to deny), which manifests itself as fanaticism, cruelty, "diplomatic wisdom" and excessive pretensions. But in so far as the *positive* spirits of communities are concerned, they are never *egregores*, but rather they are entities from the ten hierarchies (ten, because the tenth hierarchy—that of mankind—is included here). It is therefore a human soul, an Angel or an Archangel who assumes responsibility for the direction of a human community in a positive sense. Thus, it is not at all an *egregore* but rather St. Francis himself who is the spiritual director of the Franciscan order. It is similarly so for the Church. Its guiding spirit is Jesus Christ.

Nations are under the direction of Archangels, in so far as it is a matter of their true mission and spiritual progress. There are, at the same time, *egregores* or demons engendered by the collective will and imagination of nations. The "French cock" therefore disputes with the "Archangel of memory" over the direction of the French nation. And it is the same with other nations.

One could object: if the good — psychic and mental energy of good — does not accumulate, how can one explain miracles or the magical action of certain "holy places", statues, icons and relics, if not by the fact that they are "magnetised" by the faith, i.e. by the will and imagination, of believers?

Holy places, miraculous relics, statues and icons, are not depots for the psychic and mental energy of pilgrims and other believers, but rather places or objects where "heaven opens and Angels are able to ascend and descend". They are points of departure for spiritual radiation. This radiation certainly presupposes faith on the part of the believers in order to be effective, but it is not so that the "energy" which they radiate is drawn out from the believers. The faith of the latter is simply that which renders them *susceptible* to the healing and illuminating force which radiates from these places or objects, but it is not the source of this force.

Therefore, one can certainly say that relics, etc., are "magnetised" — long ago and by someone — in the sense that they have become doors, windows or window-frames, so to say, open to the heavens and allowing its activity to enter. But they are not "magnetised" by believers in the sense of being accumulators of fluid emanated by believers and constituting the active agent in subsequent healings, conversions and illuminations. The law of relics, etc., is that the more one takes from them, the more force they radiate, whilst the law of things magnetised fluidicly is that of an inverse ratio between the energy deposited and the energy consumed. The magnetiser knows very well that he cannot go beyond a certain level in the consumption of his vital fluid without risk to his health and his life — his vital fluid being regulated by the law of quantity: the more that is consumed, the less remains. The saint, however, does not heal by giving his vital fluid to the sick person; he heals him *by taking* the latter's sickness upon himself and by raising it within himself as an offering ("host") to heaven.

It is similarly so with talismens and relics. Talismens are depots of magical energy; they are under the law of quantity. In contrast, relics are windows open to heaven; they are under the law of quality, i.e. the more energy they give out, the more they become capable of giving out. They are inexhaustible as sources of energy. They are not depots for, or accumulators of, energy; rather, they are generators or sources of energy.

Consecrated water, for example, does not "lock up" the blessing — or the force of will and imagination of the priest who blessed it — but the blessing "hovers" above it. It re-establishes — through the sacred magic of analogy put into practice — the primordial relationship which existed between water and the spirit of God on the first day of creation, when "the spirit of God was moving over the face of the waters" (Genesis i, 2). Therefore, consecrated water is not water which has become a depot for the beneficial force of consecration, but rather it has been rendered susceptible to the presence of heaven. And a few drops of it are very effective for chasing demons away, as borne out by authentic witnesses across the centuries.

Now, here we arrive at an important question: Once artificial demons are generated, how does one combat them, and how does one protect oneself and rid oneself of them?

Firstly, how does one combat them? Good does not combat evil in the sense of destructive action. It "combats" it by the sole fact of its *presence*. Just as darkness gives way to the presence of light, so does evil give way before the presence of good.

Modern depth psychology has discovered and put into practice the therapeutic principle of bringing unconscious complexes to the light of consciousness. Because — so it affirms — the light of consciousness renders the obsessional complex not only visible but also impotent. This important discovery of modern psychology is in complete accord with the spiritual reality of the "struggle" of the celestial hierarchies against evil. Because this "struggle", also, amounts to their presence alone, i.e. to bringing evil to the light of day.

Light drives out darkness. This simple truth is the practical key to the problem of how to combat demons. A demon perceived, i.e. on whom the light of consciousness is thrown, is already a demon rendered impotent. This is why the desert fathers and other solitary saints had so much experience with demons. They cast their light on them. And they did so as representatives of human consciousness in general, for whoever withdraws from the world becomes representative of the world; he becomes a "son of man". And being a "son of man" the solitary saint attracted the demons haunting the subconscious of mankind, making them *appear*, i.e. bringing them to the light of consciousness and thus rendering them impotent. Whilst St. Athanasius the Great struggled against human errors and depravations in the daylight of his public life as bishop of Alexandria, his friend and brother, St. Anthony the Great, in the solitude of the Egyptian desert, struggled against the demons whose doings in the darkness of the subconscious were stirring up these very errors and depravations.

The famous "temptations" of St. Anthony were not, truth to tell, only temptations where it was a matter of the salvation and progress of his soul, but rather they were, in the first place, *acts of healing* the humanity of his time from demoniacal obsession. They were acts of sacred magic, bringing demons to the light of consciousness illumined from above, through which they were reduced to impotence. St. Anthony drew demons from darkness to the light of the consciousness of the "son of man". *He rendered them visible, and thus impotent.*

A demon rendered impotent is a deflated balloon. It is thus that certain demons engendered collectively in the Middle Ages became purely abstract and fell into forgetfulness—which was the lot, for example, of the famous demoniacal personage known by the name of "master Leonard" or the "goat of the sabbath". He disappeared from one day to the next thanks to a courageous and pure soul who deflated him.

Artificial demons, brought to the light of day and resisted, are dissipated. They disappear. With respect to "natural demons", i.e. entities of the hierarchies of the left, this is not so. The demon, for example, who loved Sarah, the daughter of Raguel, and who killed her suitors "fled through the air to Egypt. Raphael pursued him there, and bound and shackled him at once" (Tobit viii, 3), according to the Jerusalem Bible, and ". . .was overtaken by the Angel Raphael in the waste lands of Upper Egypt, and there held prisoner" (*tunc Raphael Angelus apprehendit daemonium, et religavit illud in deserto superioris Aegypti*, *Liber Tobiae* viii, 3), according to the Vulgate.

Here it is not a question of the annihilation of the demon, but rather of changing its field of activity and the place—or, rather, mode—of its existence. The vanquished demon in the story of Tobias (which is not generally found in the Protestant Bible) was forced by the Archangel Raphael to leave the country of his victim or protégée, and to take up "exile" in Egypt and to remain there. It was the *presence* of the Archangel Raphael—made possible by prayer and by the ritual carried out by Tobias during the three wedding nights—which forced the demon to withdraw and to go to Egypt.

Let us now proceed to the second part of our question: How does one protect oneself and rid oneself of demons? It follows from the foregoing that clarity of thought and rightness of moral attitude are both necessary—and also sufficient—in order to supply the light which renders demons impotent. Nevertheless, one needs rest—time during which one is left in peace by demons, i.e. time during which they are *absent*.

In order to assure this, one has to resort to sacred magic. Tradition, centuries of experience, teaches us what is necessary in order to protect oneself from the approach of demons—or, if one senses them approaching, what to do in order to drive them away—and gives the following practical advice: make the sign of the Cross towards the north, south, east and west, each time saying the first two verses of Psalm 68 (from David):

> Let God arise, let his enemies be scattered;
>   let those who hate him flee before him!
> As smoke is driven away, so drive them away;
>   as wax melts before fire,
>   let the wicked perish before God!

And here is further advice, as simple and as effective as the preceding: if one senses depression or any other sign of approach of a demon or demons, one spits three times to the left and crosses oneself.

These two procedures have been tried across the centuries and, I repeat, are very effective. They are so above all with regard to artificial demons. With respect to entities of the hierarchies of the left, it is not so simple to protect oneself against them. For the formula "Let God arise, let his enemies be scattered..." does not apply, truth to tell, to entities of the hierarchies of the left, because they are not enemies of God and also because they are not to be dissipated. In law one cannot win a cause simply by driving the attorney away. One must convince him of the innocence of the accused. Only then will he become silent and leave the latter in peace. It is the same with entities of the hierarchies of the left—hierarchies of "strict justice" as they are designated (with good reason) in the Cabbala. They have their joint functions as attorney or agents of the attorney, police, and witnesses for the prosecution. Imagine to yourself a law department whose agents are oc-cupied not only with establishing the facts of crimes committed but also—and above all—with putting potential criminals to the test by setting them in condi-tions favourable for crime, i.e. by submitting them to *temptations*. Such is, in fact, the activity of entities of hierarchies of the left towards mankind. The story of Job supplies us with a renowned example of this, where Satan, who is present amongst the sons of God, says to God concerning Job: "Does Job fear God for naught? Hast thou not put a hedge about him and his house and all that he has, on every side? Thou hast blessed the work of his hands, and his possessions have increased in the land. But put forth thy hand now, and touch all that he has, and he will curse thee to thy face" (Job i, 9-11). And with permission obtained, Satan puts Job to the test.

Thus, Satan does not accuse Job of sin committed but of a *potential sin*. And he sets to work so as to actualise it. They are "laboratory experiments", so to say, that he makes with Job in order to prove his prosecution thesis. Who needs them? God? No, because God is too noble and too generous a friend, and too tender a Father, to put his friends and children to the test. Moreover, God does not need an experimental verification of his statement made with certainty: "There is none like Job on the earth, a blameless and upright man, who fears God and turns away from evil" (Job i, 8). The one who needs to test is therefore Satan himself—and, perhaps, some of the "sons of God" present at the dialogue who could have been impressed by the accusation advanced by Satan.

Now, no magical means would have sufficed in Job's case to protect him against Satan, and to drive Satan away. Job had to endure to *convince* Satan of the futili-ty of his design to get him to curse God.

Entities of the hierarchies of the left must therefore be convinced during the course of real testing that they are wrong. There is no other means of making them go away. It was the same in the case of Tobias and the demon Asmodeus. Tobias had proved, having spent three nights in the wedding chamber with his fiancée in prayer, that he was not one of those "such as go about their marrying with all thought of God shut out of their hearts and minds, wholly intent on their lust, as if they were horse or mule, brutes without reason" (Tobias vi, 17—Vulgate).

Having done so, the Archangel Raphael made the demon leave and go to Egypt. The demon was therefore vanquished by the demonstration of the fact that Tobias was not like the seven preceding suitors for Sarah's hand. The demon who "loved" Sarah wanted to protect her against a marriage that he believed would be unworthy of her. Tobias proved that he was a husband worthy of her. Without this, the heart and liver of the fish alone would not have sufficed to make the demon give up his place as Sarah's protector to the Archangel Raphael and Tobias.

These examples—Job's "Satan" and Tobias' demon—are in themselves sufficient to understand the nature of the entities of hierarchies of the left and the way in which they operate, and likewise show how one struggles against them. They are critical spirits, i.e. prosecutors, and one can vanquish them only by convincing them—under "laboratory conditions", so to say—that the accusation lacks foundation, which is exceptional and difficult. For their accusation is usually the result of work done with indefatigable zeal, and with a very lucid and very well informed intelligence—save for the intimate human domain of moral conscience, which is not accessible to them. And it is precisely the intimate domain of moral conscience from whence the decisive factor can arise which can turn the accusation to the advantage of the accused. Because one is "righteous" and "holy" only if good *and* evil fall into agreement that it is so. This is why the procedure with an *advocatus diaboli* (devil's advocate) is not only allowed but also is required preceding the declaration of a new saint by the Church.

Concerning their function as prosecutor, entities of the hierarchies of the left fulfill it in a number of quite different ways. Some do it in the tragic sense of having to do what they no longer want to do and they no longer believe; others do it with fierce conviction and passionate indignation; there are also entities from the hierarchies of the left who accuse by making use of *ridicule*—farce—as a means of demonstrating their prosecuting thesis. An entity belonging to this latter category is known in the western world. This is Mephistopheles, whose portrait Goethe painted with astonishing exactness. As he is generally known—just as are Job's "Satan" and Tobias' demon—one can, without going beyond the limits of discretion in question (cf. the beginning of this Letter), add the example of Mephistopheles to those of the "Satan" of Job and the demon of Tobias.

The ridicule which Mephistopheles makes use of has a serious foundation. It is primarily human pretension and snobbery that he turns into ridicule. Here is an example of this:

A journalist, disenchanted with everything, and who was able to allow himself this luxury, retired with his wife from the vanity of the world and lived in a villa on a small island near Great Britain. As a good journalist with lots of experience, he took nothing for definite and he did not deny anything definitely.

He lived simply from breakfast to lunch, from lunch to five o'clock tea, and from tea to supper. But something extraordinary happened to him one day. He felt a sudden desire to take some paper and write. He did this. And he produced from inner dictation a series of manuscripts with drawings—he who had never drawn—whose author declared himself to be none other than Osiris himself, from ancient Egypt, and who now seized the opportunity to recount frankly and in detail what he knew of ancient wisdom and religion in the guise of a message to mankind of the twentieth century. One reads there, expounded with pompous simplicity, the history of the struggle between the good and the wicked, and how the wickedness of the latter had its punishment in the guise of the Atlantean catastrophe. One reads there details of the true cult celebrated in the temples of Osiris, and one sees there drawings of the candelabras, vases and other cult objects, and also portraits of Osiris and other important personages of pre-historic antiquity, who are all as alike as peas. The beneficiary of this prodigious revelation and his wife, enamoured by the grandeur of the revelation and the person of the revelator, looked at the work admiringly with a view to bearing the unheard of revelation to the knowledge of the whole of mankind. And this is how a special publishing house put before the world one volume after another of the revelation of Osiris...

This story that I have recounted is true; the publishing house is real; the volumes that it has put out are to be found, in fact, in public libraries in England; and there is, without doubt, a revelation and a revelator. Only the revelator is not Osiris but...Mephistopheles; and the whole revelation is only a farce made by him for the...credulous? no—for spiritual snobs. For, whoever the author of this "revelation" may be—you, dear Unknown Friend, not being obliged to believe me on my word alone—whoever the author may be, he actually said:

> You who hold for very little the scientific endeavour, the world of thought from Plato to Kant, the treasures of authentic witness of the great mystics, the riches of the Hermetic tradition and, lastly, the Holy Scripture, the sacraments, the blood and sweat of Gethsemane, the Cross of Calvary, the Resurrection... take, therefore, what you desire—these volumes of banalities presented in a pompous manner and communicated to you, as you would wish, in an extraordinary way.

This is an example of Mephistophelian accusation against those who do not seek the *truth* as such, but rather extraordinary circumstances of revelation...no matter what. I would still add to this example of Mephistophelian dupery that, with a little rightness of thought and moral judgement, it is an easy thing to avoid becoming a victim of it.

I believe, dear Unknown Friend, that the preceding has portrayed with sufficient clarity: firstly, the difference between on the one hand demons engendered artificially through human will and imagination and on the other hand entities of the hierarchies of the left; and secondly, that the fifteenth Arcanum of the Tarot is that of the generation and the enslaving role of so-called "artificial demons"— the Tibetan *tulpas*. It is a warning which says that we certainly have the force to generate demons but that the use of this force will render the generator a slave of the generated.

There still remains one last question for us: Were all of the pagan gods always demons—collectively engendered *egregóres*? Is paganism in general simply a cult of demons?

Before answering this question, one has to distinguish between the "paganism" of the philosophers and initiates into the mysteries, symbolic and mythological "paganism", naturalistic "paganism" and, lastly, demoniacal "paganism".

In other words, one has to distinguish firstly between the "paganism" of Hermes Trismegistus, Pythagoras, Plato, Aristotle, Plotinus, etc., and the "paganism" of Homer and Hesiod. Then one must distinguish between the latter and the totality of cults of the sun, moon, stars, fire, air, water and earth. And, lastly, one has to distinguish between the latter and the totality of cults of "divinities" engendered by perverse collective imagination and will—the cults of *egregores*, pure and simple.

It would be an error and a grave injustice to consider the four "paganisms" as the same thing, e.g. to see a priest of Moloch sacrificing human beings as a representative of the same cause as Plato. It would be a similar error to see the same "light" in the funeral-pyres of the Inquisition and the lighted lamps of the Resurrection festival—or even to see Mahatma Gandhi and a thug, a strangler for the glory of the goddess Kali, as representatives of the same cause, namely that of Hindu "paganism".

With this distinction made, one can say that the "pagan" initiates and philosophers knew of the unique God—the creator and supreme Good of the world. The Bhagavad-Gita, the books of Hermes Trismegistus, Plato, Plutarch, Plotinus and many other ancient sources prove this beyond any shadow of a doubt. The difference between the religion of the so-called "pagan" initiates and philosophers and that of Moses is simply the fact that the latter made monotheism a *popular religion*, whilst the former reserved it for the élite, for the spiritual aristocracy— although they were often fairly numerous.

With respect to the cult of the "gods" and the iconolatry that this cult entailed, the "pagan" initiates and philosophers saw in it the practice of *theurgy*, i.e. that of intercourse with entities of the celestial hierarchies either by raising themselves to them, or by rendering possible their descent and *presence* on earth—in the sanctuaries or temples or elsewhere. Hermes Trismegistus and Iamblichus treat this subject with sufficient clarity. Thus Iamblichus says:

> They (i.e. the Egyptians) also establish a pure intellect above the world, and one impartial intellect in the whole world, and another which is distributed into all the spheres. And these things they do not survey by mere reason alone, but through the sacerdotal theurgy, they announce that they are able to ascend to more elevated and universal essences, and to those that are established above Fate, viz. to God and the Demiurgus; neither employing matter, nor assuming any other thing besides, except the observation of a suitable time. This deific and anagogic path Hermes, indeed, narrated... (*De mysteriis* viii, 4-5). Again... such Gods as are truly divinities, are alone the givers of good; alone associate with good men, and with those that are purified by the sacerdotal art, and from these amputate all vice, and every passion. When these, also, impart their light, that which is evil, and at the same time demoniacal, vanishes from before more excellent natures, in the same manner as darkness when light is present; nor is it able to disturb theurgists in the smallest degree, who receive from this light every virtue, obtain worthy manners, become orderly and elegant in their actions, are liberated from passions, and purified from every disorderly motion, and from atheistical and unholy conduct (*De mysteriis* iii, 31). (Iamblichus, *De mysteriis*; trsl. T. Tayler, *Iamblichus on the Mysteries of the Egyptians, Chaldeans and Assyrians*, London, 1968, pp. 199, 306)

These are the principal traits of the theurgy of the "paganism" of the initiates and philosophers. You can also find important details in Plutarch's *De Iside et Osiride* 77, in Plotinus' *Enneads* iv, 3, 11, in Hermes Trismegistus' *Asclepius* 23-24, 37 and in Proclus' *De sacrificio et magia* (= *The Hieratic Art*). It goes without saying that the "paganism" of the initiates and sages, when not degenerated, had nothing to do with the cult of collectively engendered demons.

The "paganism" of the poets—symbolic and mythological paganism—was, in so far as it was not a symbolic version of the wisdom and magic (theurgy) of the mysteries, a universal *humanism*. Its "gods" were, truth to tell, human personages —heroes and heroines, divinised or poetised, who were prototypes of the development of the *human personality*, i.e. planetary and zodiacal types. Thus Jupiter, Juno, Mars, Venus, Mercury, Diana, Apollo, etc., were not at all demons, but leading prototypes of the development of the human personality who, in their turn, corresponded to cosmic—planetary and zodiacal—principles.

Concerning the third form of "paganism"—"naturalistic paganism"—it was "cosmolatry", i.e. it did not go beyond the limits of Nature—like natural science today. It was, therefore, "neutral" from the point of view both of the true spiritual world and of the demons. It accepted the latter as a *fact* with which it had to come to terms. But in bowing before Nature it did not engender demons, because this would be contrary to Nature—for the generation of demons presupposes a *perverse* will and imagination.

There remains, lastly, the fourth form of "paganism"—that of the worship of collectively engendered demons. This form of paganism, which is due to the degeneration of the other three forms—and above all of "naturalistic paganism"—is the only form of paganism where demons were engendered, worshipped and obeyed, and which led to the whole of paganism being renamed unjustly and calumniously as the "demoniacal religion". The Church fathers, who—with a few exceptions—treated it as such, had in truth to do above all with degenerate paganism and, consequently, were right in seeing in the popular pagan cult of their time either the cult of demons or the fables of poets. But those amongst them such as Clement of Alexandria, Origen, St. Augustine, and Synesius, who had knowledge of the paganism of the initiates and philosophers (which was the pure essence of paganism as such), spoke of what "all men possess as a healthy anticipation of the moral doctrine". As Origen expressed it:

> There is . . . nothing amazing about it if the same God has im-
> planted in the souls of all men the truths which He taught
> through the prophets and the Saviour. (Origen, *Contra Celsum*
> i, 4; trsl. H. Chadwick, Cambridge, 1953, pp. 8-9)

This is something quite different from paganism as the worship of demons.

With respect to Christian Hermeticism, it cannot see otherwise than that as the coming of Jesus Christ was an event of universal significance, it had its universal preparation, i.e. that just as the prophets of Israel until John the Baptist prepared the coming of Jesus Christ in the flesh, so did the initiates, sages and righteous men of the whole world prepare the world for his Word and his Spirit. The incarnated Logos was awaited everywhere wherever one suffered, died, believed, hoped, loved . . . The Jews prepared for the Incarnation; the pagans prepared themselves to recognise the Logos. Thus Christianity had its precursors everywhere—the "choir" of precursors included not only the prophets of Israel, but also the initiates and sages of paganism.

Meditation on the
Sixteenth Major Arcanum of the Tarot

THE TOWER OF DESTRUCTION
LA MAISON DIEU

My soul magnifies the Lord,
And my spirit rejoices in God my Saviour,
For he has regarded the low estate of his
  handmaiden.
For behold, henceforth all generations will call
  me blessed...
He has scattered those who have proud
  thoughts in their hearts,
He has put down the mighty from their
  thrones,
And he has exalted those of low degree.
He has filled the hungry with good things,
And the rich he has sent away empty-handed.
                          (Luke i, 46-48, 51-53)

He who exalts himself will be abased,
And he who humbles himself will be exalted.
                          (Luke xiv, 11)

The kingdom of God is as if a man should
scatter seed upon the ground, and should
sleep and rise night and day, and the seed
should sprout and grow, he knows not how.
                          (Mark iv, 26-27)

LETTER XVI

THE TOWER OF
DESTRUCTION

Dear Unknown Friend,

The generation of artificial demons and the nature of the entities of hierarchies
of the left constituted the principal theme of the preceding Letter. One could
ask oneself, after having let pass in review before the inner eye all that one knows
concerning the diverse beings of the world of evil, whether it is not so, given that the
flesh itself is innocent and the kernel of the human being is in the image of God,
that it is the demons and entities of the hierarchies of the left alone who are the
cause of evil, and that without them there would be no evil in human life and
in the history of mankind.

The question is not new. It was a preoccupation in antiquity, already in the third century of our era. This is what Origen says concerning it (born in Alexandria ca. A.D. 185):

> . . .the simpler sort of believers in Christ the Lord suppose that all the sins that men have committed come from the persistent influence of the contrary powers on the sinners' minds, because in this invisible contest the powers are found to be superior; that if, so to speak, there were no devil, no man would ever sin at all. We however, who look more carefully into the reason of things, do not think that this is so; especially when we consider the acts that arise clearly from the necessities of our body. Are we to suppose that the devil is the cause of our being hungry or thirsty? I suppose there is no one who would venture to maintain this. If then he is not the cause of our being hungry or thirsty, what of that condition when an individual has attained the age of puberty and this period has called forth the exciting movements of the natural heat? It follows without a doubt that, as the devil is not the cause of our being hungry or thirsty, so neither is he the cause even of that impulse which is naturally called forth at the time of maturity, that is, of the desire for sexual intercourse. It is certain that this impulse is by no means always aroused by the devil, so as to lead us to suppose that if there were no devil our bodies would not have the desire for such intercourse.
>
> Then again let us consider in regard to food,—if it be true, as we have shown above, that this is not sought for by men at the instance of the devil, but from a natural instinct—whether human experience, supposing there were no devil, could possibly employ such great self-control in partaking of food as absolutely never to exceed the limit, that is, never to take anything but what the occasion demanded or more than reason permitted, and that it should never happen that men went astray in the observance of due measure and moderation in their food. I for my part do not think that, even if there were no impulse from the devil to urge men on, this rule could be so observed by them that no one would exceed due measure and moderation in partaking of food, not at any rate before they had learned this lesson by long practice and experience. What then? In regard to foods and drink it would be possible for us to go wrong even apart from the instigation of the devil, if we happened to be caught at an intemperate or careless moment; and are we to suppose that in regard to the control of the sexual appetite and the natural desires we should not be affected in a similar way? My own opinion is that the same process of reasoning can also be applied to the rest of the natural emotions, such as covetousness, anger, sorrow or any others whatever, which by the fault of intemperance exceed the limits of their natural measure. The fact

is therefore clear that, just as in regard to things that are good the mere human will is by itself incapable of completing the good act,—for this is in all cases brought to perfection by divine help—so also in regard to things of the opposite kind we derive the beginnings and what we may call the seeds of sin from those desires which are given to us naturally for our use. But when we indulge these to excess and offer no resistence to the first movements towards intemperance, then the hostile power, seizing the opportunity of this first offence, incites and urges us on in every way, striving to extend the sins over a larger field; so that while we men supply the occasions and beginnings of our sins, the hostile powers spread them far and wide and if possible endlessly. (Origen, *De principiis* III, ii, 1-2; trsl. G. W. Butterworth, *On First Principles*, New York, 1966, pp. 213-214)

This is a clear answer: there is in man—notably in his soul, and not in his body—a seed of evil of his own, without which temptation coming from outside would not exert any action on him. Because temptation would be impotent if it did not find a terrain already prepared in the human soul.

Now, as the fifteenth Arcanum is related to demoniacal evil, so the sixteenth Arcanum is related to human evil, i.e. to evil which does not come from outside, but which certainly has its origin within the human soul.

The unfortunate misunderstanding locating innate human evil in the body instead of in the soul is due to a tendency towards a materialistic interpretation of the Biblical story of paradise and the Fall. Indeed, if paradise is understood as a place on the terrestrial or material plane, and if the Fall is similarly understood as having taken place on this plane, innate human evil cannot be understood otherwise than as biologically hereditary, i.e. that it is the flesh which bears it and transmits the seed of evil from generation to generation. Then it is the flesh which is the enemy of the soul and against which one has to struggle. Hence one "disciplines" it by flagellation, one weakens it by depriving it of food and sleep, and one scorns it and mistreats it in many ways—one is ashamed of one's body.

However, it is the body which, rightly, has more reason to be ashamed of the soul inhabiting it, than the latter of the body. For the body is a miracle of wisdom, harmony and stability, which does not merit scorn but rather the admiration of the soul. For example, can the soul boast of moral principles as stable as the body's skeleton? Is it as indefatigable and as faithful in its sentiments as, for example, the heart, which beats day and night? Does it possess a wisdom comparable to that of the body, which knows how to harmonise such opposing things as water and fire, air and solid matter? Whilst the soul is torn by opposing desires and feelings, this "contemptible" body knows how to unite opposing elements and make them collaborate: the air that it breathes, the solid matter of food, the water that it drinks, and the fire (warmth) that it produces unceasingly within it... And if this does not suffice to change scorn into respect, admiration and gratitude, then one can recall, if one is a Christian, that Jesus Christ, the Son of God, inhabited this flesh and that he honoured it to the point of uniting himself with it in the Incarnation. Similarly, if one is a Buddhist or Brahmanist, one should not forget that Buddha and Krishna, also, inhabited this flesh and that it served them well in the accomplishing of their respective missions.

Negative asceticism, directed *against* the body and not *for* celestial things, is the practical consequence of the materialistic interpretation of paradise and the Fall. However, the fact alone that a Cherubim "was placed at the east of the garden of Eden, with a flaming sword which turned every way, to guard the way to the tree of life" (Genesis iii, 24), suffices to drive away any shadow of a doubt: here it is a matter of a plane higher than the terrestrial plane, and it was therefore souls who committed the original sin — and the body had nothing to do with it.

The Fall occurred prior to the terrestrial life of mankind — this is the Hermetic doctrine (cf. *Kore Kosmu* 24-26), which was taken up by Pythagoras and Plato, and was represented in the first centuries of the Christian era by Origen. Origen taught that God had created all souls equal, but that amongst these souls some sinned in the spiritual world and had to leave it for the earth: these are human souls. Others on the contrary, in turning towards God, perfected themselves and became Angels. But let us give the words of Origen himself. This is what he says:

> . . .the following objection is raised by many, and particularly by those who come from the schools of Marcion, Valentinus and Basilides. . .they raise an objection on the score of the differences that exist among men on the earth. Some, they say, inherit at birth a happier lot, as for example the one who springs from Abraham and is born by promise, and the other, the child of Isaac and Rebecca who, while yet lying in the womb, supplants his brother and is said, before he is born, to be loved by God; and, speaking generally, one man is born among the Hebrews, with whom he finds instruction in the divine law, another among the Greeks who are themselves men of wisdom and no small learning, another among the Ethiopians, whose custom is to feed on human flesh, others among the Scythians, where parricide is practised as if sanctioned by law, or among the Taurians, where strangers are offered in sacrifice. If then they ask us, this great diversity and these various and different conditions of birth, in which certainly the power of free will has no place — for a man does not choose for himself either where or in what nation or what state of life he shall be born, — if, they say, all this is not caused by a diversity in the natures of souls, that is, a soul with an evil nature is destined for an evil nation and a good one for a good nation, what alternative is there but to suppose that it is the result of accident or chance?. . .We, however, speaking simply as men, will, in order not to nourish the insolence of the heretics (e.g. Marcion, Valentinus and

Basilides) by being silent, to the best of our ability reply to their objections with such arguments as may occur to us, as follows. We have frequently shown in the preceding chapters, by declarations which we were able to quote from the divine scriptures, that God the Creator of the universe is both good and just and omnipotent. Now when "in the beginning" he created what he wished to create, that is rational beings, he had no other reason for creating them except himself, that is, his goodness. As therefore he himself, in whom was neither variation nor change nor lack of power, was the cause of all that was to be created, he created all his creatures equal and alike, for the simple reason that there was in him no cause that could give rise to variety and diversity. But since these rational creatures, as we have frequently shown and will yet show again in its proper place, were endowed with the power of free will, it was this freedom which induced each one by his own voluntary choice either to make progress through the imitation of God or to deteriorate through negligence. This, as we have said before, was the cause of the diversity among rational creatures, a cause that takes its origin not from the will or judgement of the Creator, but from the decision of the creature's own freedom. . . For this reason the Creator will not appear to have been unjust when, according to the above principles, he placed everyone in a position proportionate to his merit; nor will the happiness or unhappiness of anyone's birth, or any condition whatever that may fall to his lot, be supposed to be due to chance; nor will it be believed that there are different creatures or souls that are diverse by nature. (Origen, *De principiis* II, ix, 5-6; trsl. G. W. Butterworth, *On First Principles*, New York, 1966, pp. 133-135)

The doctrine that the pre-existent soul, in having sinned, took into itself the seed of evil in the pre-terrestrial sphere, has as a practical consequence *positive* asceticism, i.e. that of the soul's atonement and reunion with God.

Positive asceticism does not struggle against the body but rather against the seed of evil in the soul, for the sake of its reunion with God. If, for example, the only food that Teresa Neumann had for decades was the host from the Sacrament of Holy Communion, this was not because she struggled against the body or despised it but rather because she really lived from the Holy Sacrament without prejudicing the health of the body. And if, for example, another passes the night in prayer, without sleep, he does not do so in order to deprive the body of rest, but rather in order to unite with God in prayer. St. Martin gave his coat to a poor man not because he wanted to make his body suffer from the cold but rather because he wanted to put an end to the suffering of his neighbour, whose body was deprived of protection against the cold. St. Anthony went into the desert not in order to make his body suffer but rather in order to be alone in the presence of God. A monk renounces marriage not because he hates love, women and children but rather because he is fired by the love of God and there is no room in him for another love.

Positive asceticism is universal. Everyone practises it. A scientist who shuts himself in his room with a view to pursuing his studies does so because he is taken up with the truth that he is seeking and not because he wants to deprive his body of sun, fresh air and other benefits or pleasures of the world outside his room. A ballerina fasts much so as to keep her body slender and supple. A doctor interrupts his sleep during the night if he is called out to a sick person. A missionary lives in a miserable hut in a village in Africa — as is his wish — not because he loves misery but because he wants to share the lot of his brothers.

The principle of positive asceticism is found enunciated in the Gospel in a way that could not be clearer:

> The kingdom of heaven is like treasure hidden in a field, which a man found and covered up; then in his joy he goes and sells all that he has and buys that field. Again, the kingdom of heaven is like a merchant in search of fine pearls, who, on finding one pearl of great value, went and sold all that he had and bought it. (Matthew xiii, 44-46)

Positive asceticism is therefore the exchange of good for better.

Let us now return to the problem of innate human evil. What is it?

It is *ahamkara*, the sense of self, due to *avidya*, primordial ignorance, caused by maya's power of projection (*viksepa-shakti*), associated with maya's power of obscuration (*avarana-shakti*), which consists in the illusory identification of the true Self (*atman*) with the empirical self — as is clearly attested by the revelation of Scripture (*shruti*), direct authentic experience (*pratyaksha*), tradition (*smirti*) and inference (*anumana*). This is the answer according to the ancient wisdom of India, from the mouth of Shankara (ninth century A.D.), the author of this summary and synthesis (cf. *Viveka-cuda-mani* 105-107, 111-113, 343-346; English trsl. by Swami Madhavananda, Mayavati, 1932).

It is desire (*tanha*), engendered by ignorance (*avidya*), which consists in attributing the central role to an illusory mental construction of the "self", whilst the centre is nowhere, or everywhere, answers Buddhism (cf. *The Prajnaparamita of Nagarjuna*).

The other current of tradition, the right wing of the entity of Wisdom, if you wish — the western (Egyptian-Jewish-Christian) current — gives another reply. According to it, innate human evil is not due to primordial ignorance (ἀγνωσία), but rather to the *sin of knowledge* at one's own instigation instead of that through God. Pre-Christian Hermetic treatises (e.g. *Kore Kosmu* and *The Divine Pymander*) and the Bible (Genesis) are in agreement that it is *original sin* which underlies innate human evil.

Both the Hermetic treatises and the Bible state that the original sin was committed in heaven (Hermeticism) or paradise (the Bible) before the original Fall (πρώτη κάθοδος). Both pre-Christian Hermeticism and the Bible describe this original sin as an act of disobedience towards God, i.e. a separation of the human will from that of God, and a discordance between these two wills, caused by the desire for another type of knowledge than that of revelation and for another subject of knowledge than God and his revelation through the world.

Among the Hermetic texts, it is *Kore Kosmu* which speaks in the most explicit way of the sin prior to the Fall (whose consequence and punishment was the Fall), where Isis says to Horus:

> "Having thus spoken, God mixed together the two remaining elements, water and earth, and breathed into them a certain life-giving substance, and spoke over them certain secret spells, potent indeed, but not so potent as those which he had uttered before. These things he stirred well together; and when the scum which floated on the surface of the mixture had become translucent, he took this scum, and out of it he fashioned the vital spirits of (from) the animal (circle, i.e. the zodiac)... (*Kore Kosmu* 18).
>
> "But the residue of the mixture he handed over to the souls that had by this time made progress, those souls that had ascended to 'the places near the stars', and had been given a new name, and were called ' holy daemons'; and he said to them, 'My children, offspring of my being, take the residue left over from my handiwork, and let each of you fashion something, relying on his own ability; and I will set before you as models these things which I have made'...and then he withdrew... (*Kore Kosmu* 19).
>
> "And God arranged the zodiac in accord with the movings of Nature; and having bestowed on it powers of all-various working, he bade it be productive of all the animals that were to be in all time to come (i.e. all that were to be born after the making of the first specimen, or pair, of each kind)*... (*Kore Kosmu* 20).
>
> "(And God promised) to join to the visible works of their hands the invisible vital-spirits, and to give to each of the creatures that should be made power to generate others like itself, in order that the souls might not thereafter be obliged to make anything else beside what they made at first..." (*Kore Kosmu* 21).
>
> *Horus*: "Tell me then, mother, what did the souls make?"—And Isis said: "When the souls, my son Horus, had received the min-

---

*Note added by Walter Scott.

gled mass, they first examined it, and sought to find out of what
ingredients it was compounded; but this it was not easy for them
to discover. Thereupon they feared they might incur the Father's
anger for having tried to find out; and they betook themselves
to doing the work they had been bidden to do. . .They fashioned
the race of birds. . .fishes. . .quadrupeds. . .reptiles. . . (*Kore
Kosmu* 22).

"But the souls, my son, thinking that they had now done something great, began to arrange themselves in presumptuous audacity, and transgress God's commands; for they sought to vie
with the gods in heaven, claiming nobility equal to theirs, in
that the souls themselves had been made by the same Maker.
And so they now began to overstep the bounds of their own divi-
sions of the atmosphere; for they would not any longer abide
in one place, but were ever on the move, and thought it death
to stay in one abode. . . (*Kore Kosmu* 24).

"But when the souls did thus, my son, the Lord of all (so Hermes
said . . .) failed not to mark it; and he sought a way to punish
them. And so the Ruler and Master of all, thought good to
fabricate the human organism, to the intent that in it the race
of souls might through all time suffer punishment. . ." (*Kore
Kosmu* 25).*

Now, let us look at the salient facts of this text: souls are entrusted with fashioning animals according to their celestial models in the zodiac; but instead of accomplishing this *synthetic* work, "they first examined it (the mixture), and sought
to find out of what ingredients it was compounded", i.e. they gave themselves
up to *analysis*, preferring *analytical knowledge* to *creative synthetic work*; this had
the consequence that they changed their fundamental attitude from the vertical
attitude (God-soul) to the horizontal attitude (soul-world) and "were ever on the
move" in the horizontal, "for they would not any longer abide in one place"—i.e.
the immobility of the vertical—since they "thought it death to stay in one abode".

Let us now compare these salient facts with those of the Biblical account. There,
man is placed by God in the garden of Eden—called to the creative *work* of "till-
ing it and keeping it" (Genesis ii, 15). He lives under the law of the vertical: there
are all the *trees* of the garden from which he eats, i.e. methods of ecstasy and
enstasy, whereby through prayer, meditation and contemplation the soul is elevated
to God. And there is only one prohibition—that of "eating" from a single "tree",
the Tree of Knowledge of Good and Evil, for on the day that he eats of it he will
die. Man in paradise "gave names to all the animals" that God placed under man's
dominion "so that whatever man called every living creature, that was its name"
(Genesis ii, 19-20). Lastly, moved by the desire "to have their eyes opened and
to be as gods, knowing good and evil" (Genesis ii, 5), Adam and Eve ate from

Kore Kosmu 18-22, 24-25; trsl. W. Scott, *Hermetica*, vol. i, Oxford, 1924, 469-473.

the forbidden tree and were driven out from the garden of Eden in order to cultivate the land.

The similarity, if not identity, of the two narratives leaps out at one. In both it is a matter of the sin of "presumptuous audacity" (or "impudent curiosity"); in both man follows the desire "to have his eyes opened and to be as a god"; in both man is entrusted with a creative magical task with regard to the animals; in both man changes his fundamental attitude from the vertical to the horizontal —which has the consequence that he incarnates, with the consequences of incarnation: suffering, toil and death.

Concerning the points of difference between the two accounts: souls fashioning animals, man only giving them their names; "the places near the stars", the garden of Eden; the multitude of souls, Adam and Eve; the composition of the mixture of the Father, the Tree of Knowledge of Good and Evil — they are easily understood if one takes account of the difference that there is in general between the Genesis of Moses and the treatise *Kore Kosmu*. The latter *teaches*, i.e. it gives an exposition of a teaching, whilst the former *recounts* the dawn of mankind and world history. The one is a *commentary* on the world, whilst the other is a *chronicle* of it. This is why even the facts and events in *Kore Kosmu* are presented in an intellectualised way, i.e. in so far as and in as much as they are stated with sufficient clarity as *ideas*. With regard to the narrative in Genesis, it only presents to the mind of the reader, with magical force, the facts relevant to the spiritual history of the world and mankind. *Kore Kosmu* wants to *convince*, whilst Genesis *awakens* profound memories of a remote past which slumber in the depths of the soul — memories from the "collective unconscious" as Jung would have said.

Being a magical text, Genesis does not say that man "fashioned" the animals, but rather that "he gave them *names*". Now, the "name" is the formative principle in the language of magic. To give a name means to say, in magic, to assign a mission, to charge with a function and at the same time to render capable of acquitting it. Man, according to Genesis, gave the animals created by God their specific missions and functions on the plane of realisation — which entailed a specific organism. He *fashioned* them by giving them names with respect to the plane of realisation.

With respect to "the places near the stars" and the garden of Eden, here again the Biblical account is magical: it does not aim so much at answering the question, "Where in the cosmos was mankind to be found before the primordial Fall?" as the question, "What was mankind doing and what was happening around it before the Fall?"

Now, the answer in Genesis is that mankind was set in a garden "in order to *till* it and *keep* it" (Genesis ii, 15). This means to say that the dawn of humanity did not take place either in a *desert* where nothing happens, or even in a *jungle* where everything sprouts forth and grows without the regulating and directing control of the Spirit or, lastly, in the conditions of a city or *town* where nothing sprouts forth and grows but where everything is caused and is done through the regulation and direction of the Spirit. A "garden" is thus a state of the world where there is cooperation and equilibrium between Spirit and Nature, whilst a "desert" is a state of immobile passivity both of Nature and Spirit, a "jungle" is the state of activity of Nature alone, and a "town", lastly, is that of activity of Spirit alone. One could say, making use of Hindu philosophical language, that a "garden" corresponds to the state of *sattva* of Nature (*prakriti*) towards the Spirit (*purusha*). And it was in such a "*sattvic*" milieu — or "garden"— that humanity was placed and was assigned its primordial and eternal mission: to cultivate and maintain this "garden".

Let us stop here for a moment, dear Unknown Friend, to breathe in again, after the magnitude and significance of this compressed and lapidary statement from Genesis (ii, 15) has so taken our breath from us. The primordial and eternal mission of mankind is thus to cultivate and maintain the "garden", i.e. the world in a state of equilibrium and cooperation between Spirit and Nature! What a world of content is found enclosed in seed form in this statement! May spiritual light — moral and practical, mystical, gnostic and magical — radiate forth when one opens one's heart and mind to the touch of this seed-statement!

One then understands in a split second. . .that it is not necessary either *to do*, or *to leave alone*; either to build systems of thought, or to let all thought pass through the head without control; either to devote onself to exercises of occult, ascetic and mystical training, or to do without constant and continuous endeavour . . .that it is necessary to work, and to allow growth; to think, and to await the growth and ripening of thought; and that it is necessary for the magical word to be accompanied and followed by the *magical silence*. In a word, it is necessary *to cultivate and maintain*!

To cultivate and to maintain. . .culture and tradition. . .To will and to dare. . .to know and to be silent.

Here is the essence of the mission of Hermeticism, which is the memory working in the depths of our souls of the primordial and eternal mission of mankind: that of cultivating and maintaining the unforgettable garden of the dawn of mankind. There are "trees" to cultivate and maintain in this garden: the methods or ways of uniting earth and heaven — the rainbow of peace between that which is below and that which is above. In India these methods or ways of union are called "yoga". There the following ways of union are taught: Hatha-yoga, Jnana-yoga, Bhakti-yoga, Karma-yoga, Tantra-yoga, Mantra-yoga and Raja-yoga, i.e. union through breathing and the circulatory movement of life (*prana*), union through thought, union through feeling, union through conduct, union through love, union through the magic of the word, and union through the will.

Black Elk, the guardian of the sacred pipe of the Sioux tribe, who went blind owing to his advanced age, revealed to Joseph Epes Brown (in *The Sacred Pipe*, Baltimore, 1953) the seven traditional Sioux rites or ways of man's union with the Father (the Great Spirit) and Mother (the earth), which constitute the soul of the spiritual life of the Red-Indian tribes from the coast of the Gulf of Mexico as far as Maine in the north and from Georgia as far as Idaho in the west.

But in so far as we—Christian Hermeticists—are concerned, the "trees" or "yogas" of the garden that we want to cultivate and maintain, are given to us in the "seven pillars of the house that Wisdom has built" (Proverbs ix, 1), i.e. the seven "days" of Creation (including the sabbath), the seven miracles of the Gospel of St. John, the seven "I am" sayings of Jesus Christ and, lastly, the seven Sacraments of the Church.

Such are the "trees" of the garden that we cultivate and maintain, i.e. the mysteries of union—mystical, gnostic, magical and Hermetic—of that which is below with that which is above. For mysticism, gnosis, magic and Hermetic science are the four branches of the "river" which flows out of our garden of Eden "to water"—the "river" which "divided and became four rivers" (Genesis ii, 10).

Let us therefore imitate with respect and gratitude both Swami Vivekananda of India and Black Elk of the North American Sioux, concerning their faithfulness to the task of cultivating and guarding that which providence wanted to entrust them with of the memory of the garden of Eden—by cultivating and guarding with the same faithfulness what providence certainly wants to entrust us with of the memory of this same garden. And let us not trouble ourselves about the lot of those whose culture and tradition differs from ours. God, who sees all, will certainly not forget to crown the head of every cultivator and faithful guardian of his garden.

Another point of difference between *Kore Kosmu* and Genesis is the multitude of souls, on the one hand, and Adam-Eve, on the other. Here again the difference is explained by the semi-philosophical nature of *Kore Kosmu*, in contrast to the magical nature of Genesis. *Kore Kosmu* has *substances* in mind, whilst Genesis speaks of the *act*. From the point of view of substance it was a multitude of souls who caused and underwent the Fall; from the point of view of the act they were only one, since their act was one—having been committed collectively—and it was Adam-Eve who committed it.

Thus, there are two answers to the question, "What is innate human evil?" The one—given by the left wing of traditional Wisdom—is *"ignorance"*; the other—given by the right wing of traditional Wisdom—is *the sin of illicit knowledge*.

A contradiction? Yes and no. The two answers are contradictory in so far as ignorance and knowledge are opposites. But they are in agreement in so far as innate ignorance is a consequence of the original sin of the will, which became infatuated with the desire to replace knowledge due to revelation by knowledge due to experimentation. There is certainly a difference, but there is in no way a contradiction. The difference consists in that the oriental tradition puts the accent on the *cognitive aspect* of the fact of discord between human consciousness and cosmic reality, whilst the occidental tradition puts it on the *moral aspect* of this same fact.

The oriental tradition sees in innate human evil a kind of misunderstanding, or undervaluing, where consciousness mistakes the empirical personality—relating to the body and the psychic life—for the true Self which is immutable and eternal. In contrast, the occidental tradition sees here the consequence of the sin of having wanted to be "like gods, knowing good and evil", i.e. the *disfiguration* of the "likeness of God", although the image—which corresponds to the "true Self" of the orientals—has remained intact. And it is the "empirical self" which bears the features of disfiguration due to original sin. Therefore it is not a question of the erroneous identification of the true Self (or "image of God") with the "empirical self", but rather of the disfiguration of this latter. The identification would be perfectly justifiable if the "empirical self" had remained in the "likeness of God", i.e. if it had not been disfigured as a consequence of the Fall.

In other words, the difference between the two traditions is that in the oriental tradition one aspires to divorce in the marriage of the "true Self" and the "empirical self", whilst the occidental tradition regards this marriage as indissoluble. The "true Self", according to the occidental tradition, cannot or should not rid itself of the "empirical self" by repudiating it. The two are bound by indissoluble links for all eternity and should together accomplish the work of re-establishing the "likeness of God". It is not the freedom of divorce but rather that of reunion which is the ideal of the occidental tradition.

It is thus in the *will* that the original sin took place and brought about the Fall. Genesis describes this sin of the will as the desire to arrogate to oneself knowledge of good and evil, to become "like gods".

But Genesis does not confine itself to the first stage of the Fall in paradise—although this is the decisive one—but adds three subsequent stages: notably *Cain's fratricide*, the *generation of giants*, and the *building of the tower of Babel* (Genesis iv, 1-16; vi, 1-4; xi, 1-9).

Although these three subsequent stages are simply a logical development from the original sin committed in paradise, they are nonetheless new stages in so far as the *realisation* of the original sin in the terrestrial domain of mankind's spiritual history is concerned. For Cain's fratricide is the primordial phenomenon (Goethe's *Urphaenomen*) containing the seed of all subsequent wars, revolutions and revolts in the history of the human race. The generation of giants is the primordial phenomenon which is the proto-historical seed of all subsequent pretensions in the history of the human race for individuals, groups and peoples to play a domineering role as divine sovereigns, and thus all pretensions of being "supermen". The Caesars who arrogated divine honour and authority to themselves, Nietzsche's "superman" (*Uebermensch*), and likewise the diverse fascist and communist *Führers* of our century, are only particular manifestations of the primordial "gigantism" of which Genesis speaks. And the building of the tower of Babel (Genesis xi, 1-9) is the primordial phenomenon containing in seed form all subsequent tendencies in the history of the human race towards the conquest of heaven by means of forces acquired and developed on the earth.

At the root of Cain's fratricide is the revolt of the "lower self" against the "true

Self"—of the fallen "likeness" against the intact "image". At the root of the generation of giants is the marriage of the "lower self" with entities of the fallen hierarchies—instead of with the "true Self". And at the root of the building of the tower of Babel is the collective will of "lower selves" to achieve the replacing of the "true Self" of the celestial hierarchies and God with a superstructure of universal significance fabricated through this will.

Revolt, possession, and substitution of the fabricated for the revealed—with these three sins there correspond three "falls" and effects entailed by them. Cain, who killed his brother Abel, became an *exile*—he became a wanderer. The generation of giants was followed by the *flood*. The building of the tower of Babel had as its effect the "thunderbolt" of the "descent of the Lord", who "confused their language"—that of the builders—and "scattered them abroad over the face of all the earth" (Genesis xi, 7-9), so that they would no longer understand one another's language.

Just as the building of the tower of Babel is the summary of the preceding stages of sin—those of revolt and "gigantism"—so the *effect* of the building of the tower of Babel—the thunderbolt dispersing its builders and confusing their language—is the summary of the effects of the two preceding sins. This is why, it seems, the sixteenth Card of the Major Arcana of the Tarot represents only the blasted tower and the thunderbolt—quite disregarding the flood and Cain's exile. For the tower blasted by lightning suffices to reveal to serious meditation the comprehensive *arcanum* of the relationship between the will and destiny—between what one wants and what happens.

For *to wander* is the inevitable lot of the revolt of the "lower self" against the "higher Self"; *to be drowned* is the lot entailed by the pretension to be a "superman"; and *to be blasted by a thunderbolt* is the fate—as inevitable as the two preceding—of building, collectively or individually, it does not matter, a tower of Babel.

The Arcanum "The Tower of Destruction" teaches a general and universal *law* that it presents in the comprehensive form of the tower of Babel. A general and universal law—this means to say a law which operates both on a small scale and on a grand scale, in individual biography as well as in that of mankind, and in the past, present and future equally. According to this law, he who rebels against his "higher Self" will no longer live under the law of the *vertical* but rather under that of the *horizontal*, i.e. he will be "a fugitive and a wanderer on the earth" (Genesis iv, 12).

He who unites himself with an entity of the fallen hierarchies, instead of with his "higher Self", to the point of being possessed, will be *drowned*, i.e. he will fall prey to madness. This happened to Nietzsche, the inspired author of works lauding the "superman" and the antichrist. Likewise, this happened to humanity at the time when "giants were on the earth"—"these were the mighty men of old, the men of renown" (Genesis vi, 4). For the flood inundated the earth not only with water but also with that other "water" which drowns consciousness and memory—that very "water" of forgetfulness and imbecility which inundated Nietzsche. It is thus that the very advanced civilisation of Atlantis was drowned in forgetfulness, just as the cradle continent of this civilisation was engulfed by waters. It is thus that the "primitive" tribes and nomadic peoples, disinherited from their past and obliged to begin everything again, began to live in caves or camp under trees. There were once powerful kingdoms and magnificent towns in Africa, but their descendants had lost all memory of them and gave themselves up entirely to the daily life of "primitive" tribes—the life of hunting, fishing, agriculture and war. The forgetting on the part of the indigenous Australians was even more complete.

Similarly, he who builds a "tower" to replace revelation from heaven by what he himself has fabricated, will be blasted by a thunderbolt, i.e. he will undergo the humiliation of being reduced to his own subjectivity and to terrestrial reality.

The "law of the tower of Babel" has already been stated in the thirteenth Letter on the Tarot with respect to certain occult practices aiming at achieving a kind of immortality by means of the crystallisation of energy emanated from the physical body to the point of resisting death. There it was a matter of building an individual "tower of Babel" consisting of superimposed "doubles" in ascending order from the physical body. It was the aspect of "building" alone which was in question there, without the other aspect of this law being dealt with—that of the "thunderbolt". Now, under the title of the sixteenth Major Arcanum of the Tarot there is occasion to deal with the entire law, i.e. that of the "thunderbolt" as well as the aspect of "building".

We pointed out above that the law of the tower of Babel is universal, i.e. that it works both in individual biography and in humanity—and even in other hierarchies. The point of this law is that all autonomous activity from below inevitably meets with divine reality above. What one has built through the autonomous effort of the "lower self" must, sooner or later, be confronted by divine reality, and undergo the effects of comparison with it. The law—or arcanum—of the tower of Babel is manifest, for example, in the fact of purgatory after death. For every man who is not a saint or fully righteous man builds a kind of "tower of Babel" which is his own. His actions, opinions and aspirations—autonomous or personal —constitute a "private world" that he has built and that he bears with himself into the spiritual world after his death. This subjective world must there pass through the trial of meeting with trans-subjective spiritual reality—the *thunderbolt*. And this meeting of subjectivity with spiritual reality is the essence of the post-mortem stage known by the name "purgatory".

Purgatory is therefore the state of the soul where the actions, opinions and aspirations of the past life are seen in the true light of day of trans-subjective consciousness. No one judges it; it is the soul itself who judges itself in the light of a completely awakened conscience.

One often speaks of the "darkness" into which the soul is plunged on entering purgatory, and also of the "solitary confinement" that it undergoes there. There is truth in these descriptions of the state of the soul in purgatory, but it is necessary firstly to understand them in order to be able to rightly appreciate their truth. Seen from *without*, a soul who enters the state of purgatory disappears from the sight of other souls and is thus plunged into the darkness of invisibility and inaccessibility. It is in this sense, i.e. in the sense of being inaccessible, that one can certainly say that the soul in purgatory undergoes "confinement". For the soul is then outside of contacts and relationships with the "free" beings of the spiritual world.

But seen from *within*, a soul who enters into purgatory is plunged into the absolute light of trans-subjective consciousness which, being so luminous, seems to envelop and make the soul so concentrated as to become inaccessible to everyone.

Concerning how the purification of the soul in purgatory takes place, the nature of the darkness and confinement of the state of purgatory and, lastly, the fruits of this state—no one has given a clearer idea and a more convincing description, being founded on authentic experience, than that given by St. John of the Cross in his *Dark Night of the Soul*. In the chapters where he deals with "the dark night of the spirit" we find an analogy that is as close as possible to the state of the soul in purgatory—the experience described being in every way analogous to the experience of purification that the soul undergoes in purgatory:

> The dark night is a certain inflowing of God into the soul which cleanses it of its ignorances and imperfections, habitual, natural and spiritual...But it may be asked: Why does the soul call the divine light, which enlightens the soul and purges it of its ignorances, the dark night? I reply that the divine wisdom is, for two reasons, not night and darkness only, but pain and torment also to the soul. The first is, the divine wisdom is so high that it transcends the capacity of the soul, and therefore is, in that respect, darkness. The second reason is based on the meanness and impurity of the soul, and in that respect the divine wisdom is painful to it, afflictive and dark also. To prove the truth of the first reason, we take for granted a principle of the philosopher, namely, the more clear and evident divine things are, the more dark and hidden they are to the soul naturally. Thus the more clear the light the more does it blind the eyes of the owl, and the stronger the sun's rays the more it blinds the visual organs; overcoming them, by reason of their weakness, and depriving them of the power of seeing. So the divine light of contemplation, when it beats on the soul, not yet perfectly enlightened, causes spiritual darkness, because it not only surpasses its strength, but because it blinds it and deprives it of its natural perceptions...This is the reason why the illuminating ray of hidden wisdom, when God sends it from Himself into the soul not yet transformed, produces thick darkness in the

understanding...The soul, by reason of its impurity, suffers exceedingly when the divine light really shines upon it. And when the rays of this pure light strike upon the soul, in order to expel its impurities, the soul perceives itself to be so unclean and miserable that it seems as if God had set Himself against it, and itself were set against God. So grievous and painful is this feeling—for it thinks now that God has abandoned it—that it was one of the heaviest afflictions of Job during his trial: "Why hast Thou set me contrary to Thee, and I become burdensome to myself?" (Job vii, 20). The soul seeing distinctly in this bright and pure light, though dimly, its own impurity, acknowledges its own unworthiness before God and all creatures. That which pains it still more is the fear it has that it never will be worthy, and that all its goodness is gone. In the second place, the pain of the soul comes from its natural, moral and spiritual weakness; for when this divine contemplation strikes it with a certain vehemence, in order to strengthen it and subdue it, it is then so pained in its weakness as almost to faint away...for sense and spirit, as if under a heavy and gloomy burden, suffer and groan in agony so great that death (annihilation) itself would be a desired relief...(this is a thing) wonderful and piteous...So great are the weakness and impurity of the soul that the hand of God, so soft and so gentle, is felt to be so heavy and oppressive, though neither pressing nor resting on it, but merely touching it, and that, too, most mercifully; for He touches the soul not to chastise it, but to load it with His graces... (*Dark Night* II, v, 1-4, 6, 8-9).

A sunbeam coming in by the window is perceived the less distinctly the more pure and free from atoms and motes the air is, but the more of these there are, the more distinct is the beam to the eye. The reason is that we do not see light itself, but by means of it we see the objects on which it falls, and these reflecting it, the light itself becomes a visible object; had it not struck them it would itself remain invisible...Thus this ray of divine contemplation, transcending as it does the natural powers, striking the soul with its divine light, makes it dark, and deprives it of all the natural affections and apprehensions which it previously entertained in its own natural light. Under these circumstances, the soul is left not only in darkness but in emptiness also, as to its powers and desires, both natural and spiritual, and in this emptiness and darkness is purified and enlightened by the divine spiritual light, but it does not imagine that it has it; yea, rather, it thinks itself to be in darkness, as we have said of the sunbeam which, though passing through the middle of the room, cannot be seen if the air is quite pure and there are no objects on which it may fall. However, the spiritual light falling on the soul if there is anything to reflect it, that is, upon any matter, however small, of perfection, which presents itself to the understanding or a decision to be made as to the truth or falsehood of anything, the soul sees it at once, *and understands the matter more clearly than it ever did before it entered into this darkness.* In the same way the soul discerns the spiritual light which is given it that it may easily recognise its own imperfection... (*Dark Night* II, viii, 5-6).

...the divine fire of contemplative love which, before it unites with, and transforms the soul into itself, purges away all its contrary qualities. It expels its impurities, blackens it and obscures it, and thus its condition is apparently worse than it was before, more impure and offensive. For while the divine purgation is removing all the evil and vicious humours, which, because so deeply rooted and settled in the soul, were neither seen nor felt, but now, in order to (effect) their expulsion and annihilation, are rendered clearly visible in the dim light of the divine contemplation, the soul—though not worse in itself, nor in the sight of God—seeing at last what it never saw before, looks upon itself not only as unworthy of His regard, but even as a loathsome object and that God does loathe it... (*Dark Night* II, x, 2).

...the light of God which illumines an Angel enlightens him, and sets him on fire with love, for he is a spirit already prepared for the infusion of that light; but man, being impure and weak, is ordinarily enlightened, as I said before, in darkness, in distress and pain—the sun's rays are painful in their light to weak eyes—till the fire of love, purifying him, shall have spiritualised and refined him, so that being made pure he may be able to receive with sweetness, like the Angels, the union of this inflowing love... (*Dark Night* II, xii, 4).

(St. John of the Cross, *The Dark Night of the Soul* II, v, viii, x, xii; trsl. D. Lewis, fourth ed., revised, London, 1916, pp. 83-88, 104-106, 118, 130)

The foregoing extracts from *The Dark Night of the Soul*, i.e. from chapters 5, 8, 10 and 12 of Book II (concerning "the dark night of the spirit"), are the most relevant here in the doctrine of St. John of the Cross. The purification portrayed in these extracts amounts to a school of humility, and the divine light present here, which puts the soul in darkness and bears down on it by making it experience the weight of the inevitable necessity of the confrontation of human nature with divine truth, can be summarised by the image of the tower blasted by a thunderbolt, and the fall of its constructors, i.e. by the Card of the sixteenth Arcanum of the Tarot. The *thunderbolt* which *blasts* is the divine light which *dazzles* and *bears down*; the blasted tower is what the human powers of understanding, imagination and will have erected, which find themselves confronted with divine reality; the constructors who fall represent the "school of humility" for the human powers of understanding, imagination and will. Purgatory, the way of purification which precedes illumination and mystical union, the great historical events which have had the effect that mankind had to begin again, lastly, the events in the biographies of individuals where the latter were overwhelmed by a thunderbolt-blast in order to rise again from it either illumined, like Saul of Tarsus, or alienated, like Nietzsche — all these things which appear so different are only diverse manifestations of the same law or arcanum: that of *the tower blasted by a thunderbolt*.

It is this law which is the theme of the *Magnificat* that I have put at the head of this Letter, where it is said:

> He has scattered those who have proud thoughts in their hearts,
> He has put down the mighty from their thrones. . .
> He has filled the hungry with good things,
> And the rich he has sent away empty-handed.
>
> (Luke i, 51-53)

It is the eternal law of the tower of Babel which is sung in the *Magnificat* — the law of the tower blasted by a thunderbolt, and of the humble heart raised by the same thunderbolt to divine illumination. For the *Magnificat* is the song of a heart struck by this very thunderbolt which "puts down the mighty from their thrones, and exalts those of low degree".

The essence of this law can hardly be expressed in a more precise and concise way than it is in the Gospel according to Luke: "Every one who exalts himself will be abased, and he who humbles himself will be exalted" (Luke xiv, 11). There are many ways of exalting oneself, and there is a single way of being abased.

In biology, for example, it has been established that in the process of evolution there are many ways which lead to a temporary advantage due to the specialisation of an organism in a determined direction, but which always ends in an impasse. Thus the great reptiles, the Saurians, attained uncontested dominion on the earth owing to their physical strength, their agility in movement, and their formidable natural weapons in the form of jaws and other members. But they lasted only to give way to small beings without the advantages of physical strength and natural weapons (i.e. tearing jaws and crushing limbs). These small warm-blooded beings, the first mammals, were not so specialised as the reptiles, and were insignificant beings alongside the latter.

> Their very insignificance enabled them to survive during the long period when the land was dominated by powerful and specialised types of reptile. (Julian Huxley, *Evolution in Action*, London, 1953, p. 123)

And it is also their lack of specialisation which allowed them to adapt to the radical change in climatic conditions, and other changes effected by the formation of mountains towards the end of the Mesozoic period, to which the dominant reptiles were unable to adapt; and thus they disappeared.

Therefore mammals replaced reptiles as masters of the earth. Much later, however, branches of mammals specialised, elevating themselves in their turn by developing organs and faculties which certainly gave them temporary advantages, but which brought them to an impasse, i.e. they were rendered incapable of further evolution. And it is the group of mammals who, instead of specialising themselves, were engaged in the *process of general growth*, or in a balanced evolution of the physical organism and the psychic faculties, who came to the crest of the wave of evolution and who eventually produced organisms capable of serving as instruments for human souls. Therefore, expressed in biological terms, "to exalt oneself" amounts to *specialisation*, which gives temporary advantages, and "to humble oneself in order to be exalted" means, in terms of biology, *general growth*, i.e. a balanced evolution, of the physical and psychic faculties of beings. And what is true in the domain of biology is also true in all other domains.

For this reason I thought it was the right place to add—at the head of this Letter—to the formula, "He who exalts himself will be abased, and he who humbles himself will be exalted" (Luke xiv, 11), the following text from the Gospel according to St. Mark:

> The kingdom of God is as if a man should scatter seed upon
> the ground, and should sleep and rise night and day, and the
> seed should sprout and grow, he knows not how. (Mark iv, 26-27)

For it is the way of *general growth* or that of "humbling oneself to the role of a seed", in opposition to the ways of *specialisation* or those of "exalting oneself by *building* towers", which sets this text in relief. To *grow* or to *build*—this is the choice which it comes down to in the last analysis: the "way of salvation" and the "way of perdition"; or the way of infinite perfection and that resulting in an impasse. The idea of hell is simply that of a definite spiritual impasse; that of purgatory refers to the process of the rejection of tendencies towards impasses of specialisation, with a view to safeguarding and keeping the way of perfection open—the "way of salvation".

To exalt oneself or to abase oneself, to specialise oneself in order to gain temporary advantages or to be moved only by the hunger and thirst for truth, beauty and goodness, to *build* a tower or to *grow* "sleeping and rising night and day... without knowing how"—here is the choice that every human being, every community, every tradition or spiritual school, *must* make.

Now, we occultists, magicians, esotericists and Hermeticists—all those who want to "do" instead of merely waiting, who want "to take their evolution in their own hands" and "to direct it towards an aim"—are confronted with this choice in a much more dramatic way, I should say, than is so for people who are not concerned with esotericism. Our principal danger (if not the *only* true danger) is that of preferring the role of "builders of the tower of Babel" (no matter whether personally or in a community) to watching over "as gardeners or vine-growers the garden or the vine of the Lord". Truth to tell, the only truly morally founded reason for keeping esotericism "esoteric", i.e. for not bringing it to the broad light of day and popularising it, is the danger of the great misunderstanding of confusing the *tower* with the *tree*, as a consequence of which "masons" will be recruited instead of "gardeners".

The Church was always conscious of this danger. This is why it always insisted — whilst appreciating and encouraging effort as such — on the principle of *grace* as the sole source for advancing on the way of perfection. This is also why it was always suspicious of so-called "initiation fraternities" or such-like groups who formed themselves at its periphery or beyond it. For, leaving rivalry and other human imperfections out of account, the *serious* reason for the Church to take a negative attitude towards initiation fraternities is the danger of the substitution of building for growth, of "doing" for grace, and of ways of specialisation for the way of salvation. I do not know if this explains the persecution of the Order of Templars, but it certainly explains the opposition of the Church with regard to Freemasonry.

Be that as it may for particular historical cases, what occupies us here is the arcanum of the tower blasted by a thunderbolt, i.e. the totality of relevant ideas and facts relating to the will "to exalt oneself", which produces specialisation, which in its turn leads inevitably to an impasse. It is therefore a matter of a choice between "building" and "growth" in the domain of esotericism.

You see a fakir who is insensible to the nails on which he stretches himself out, or who has himself buried alive for a week without being suffocated, or who makes a plant grow in your presence. This fakir has realised some advantages; he *can do* what you cannot do. But he has attained it at the expense of general development as a human being; he has specialised himself. He will never make a contribution of value to philosophy, religion or art. With respect to his general human progress he is at an impasse — awaiting a thunderbolt from above which can enable him to get out of it.

And then the problem that disquieted Agrippa of Nettesheim, author of the classic work on magic, *De Occulta Philosophia*: How could it be that the author of this book in which one finds a multitude of things based on authentic experience, how could it be that he, the enthusiastic adept, became the sceptic disenchanted with life who wrote *De Incertitudine et Vanitate Scientiarum* ("On the Uncertainty and the Vanity of the Sciences"), which was written during his last years of life?

The answer to this question is that Agrippa had built a "tower of Babel" which was later blasted by a "thunderbolt from above". It was higher reality which made all the "sciences of the supernatural" — to which he had devoted the best years of his life — appear vain to him. The tower was shaken, but the way of heaven was opened. He was free to begin again, i.e. in a condition to enter upon the way of *growth*.

The fakir and the magician both need equally the liberating thunderbolt from above in order to return to the way of purely *human* evolution, i.e. to that of general growth, without the impasses of specialisation. It is likewise with the specialised gnostic and mystic. This is why we have repeated so many times in these Letters that practical (i.e. *lived*) Hermeticism is neither occult science, nor magic, nor gnosis, nor mysticism, but rather their synthesis. For it is a *tree* and not a *tower*. And it is man himself, the *whole* man—who is at one and the same time philosopher and magician, gnostic and mystic—who is this tree.

Is this therefore the Sephiroth Tree of the Cabbala? Maybe. Or the Tree of Consciousness and Life in the middle of the garden of Eden? Yes. But above all I would most love to see here the Tree of Death and Resurrection—the Cross from which the Rose springs. This is the Cross that is mortifying and vivifying at the same time—the Cross where the agony of Calvary and the glory of the Resurrection are united. For the Cross is the law of *growth*: that of perpetual dying and becoming. It is the way which does not lead to impasses of specialisation, but rather to "throughways" of *purification*—which lead to *illumination* and end in *union*.

Practical Hermeticism is the mysticism, gnosis, magic and science of the Cross. The object of its pursuit, its basic impulse and reason for existence is the great work of *growth*—working through spiritual, psychic and corporeal transformation, sublimation, transubstantiation and transmutation. Yes, alchemy, the alchemical principle, is the soul of Hermeticism. One finds this principle expressed in the Gospel: "nothing should be lost. . .all should have eternal life" (John vi, 39-40). Can one imagine an ideal or aim where more faith, hope and love could be implied? Whilst those who lack perfect faith resort to the surgery of the separation of the true Self from the lower self, as is the case with Sankya and with yoga, those who lack hope make up for the absence of faculties and forces by resorting to artificial limbs, i.e. to the construction of mechanisms called to replace the functions of faculties which are absent—as is the case with the constructors of machines, the authors of philosophical systems, those who carry out rituals of ceremonial magic and, in general, *tower-builders*. Adepts of the "great work", however, confess to "the folly of the Cross" (I Corinthians i, 18), i.e. they believe, hope and desire that "nothing should be lost. . .all should have eternal life".

The "good news" that the world received more than nineteen centuries ago is in no way that of successful surgical operation of freedom from suffering; no more is it that of the successful construction of a tower attributed to man—small though the tower may be, or of unparalleled grandeur, i.e. "reaching up to heaven"; but rather it is that of *resurrection*—the great alchemical operation of the successful transmutation of the human being. Liberation through spiritual surgery, power owing to the construction of mental or other mechanisms, *or* resurrection thanks to the Cross, to the law of spiritual growth—here is the choice of ideal that every human soul must make.

Now, Hermeticism has made the choice. It has embraced for ever the law of "living life"—the Cross—as its way, and resurrection as its ideal. For this reason there is nothing mechanical about it, nor is there anything surgical about it. In Hermeticism one does not build any kind of tower and one does not seek to accomplish any divorce. It is a matter solely of the transmutation of the forces and faculties of human nature, i.e. the *great work* of human evolution, avoiding the impasses of specialisation.

I have said that in practical Hermeticism there is nothing mechanical or surgical. This means to say that one will not find any kind of device within it—mental, ceremonial or physiological—by means of which one would be able to know and accomplish things surpassing the capacity of the moral and intellectual faculties that one possesses by virtue of moral and intellectual growth due to experience, endeavour and the action of grace from above. You will not find, for example, a technical method of awakening the "lotus centres" by means of the pronunciation of mantric syllables accompanied by breathing specially adapted to this end. The "lotus centres" grow and mature in the light, warmth and life of the true, the beautiful and the good, without any special technical method being applied. The "lotuses", just like the whole human being, develop according to the general law:

> The kingdom of God is as if a man should scatter seed upon
> the ground, and should sleep and rise night and day, and the
> seed should sprout and grow, he knows not how. (Mark iv, 26-27)

It is *cordiality* which, in practical Hermeticism, renders the heart—the "twelve-petalled lotus"—warm, and not the awakening of the dormant Kundalini force through mantric syllables and respiration. It is *attention* due to the desire to understand which sets the lotus of intellectual initiative in motion—the "two-petalled lotus"—and not a mantric syllable and special mode of breathing; and so on. If it was otherwise, if one applied to each "lotus" a special method with a view to its development, one would achieve their development in the sense of *specialisation*, i.e. temporary advantages, but ultimately an impasse. It is the same with intellectual techniques. The calculating machine certainly has its place in the scientific work of today. But it—or anything analogous to it—has no place in Hermeticism, where personal and original effort of thought is irreplacable. Neither the *ars combinatoria* ("the art of combination") of Raymond Lull nor the "archeometry" of Saint-Yves d'Alveydre—ingenious and well-founded though they are—were accepted in Hermeticism as intellectual instruments for discoveries and classification. Similarly, the system of Aristotelian syllogisms such as was in use amongst Scholastic thinkers of the Middle Ages, gained hardly any access amongst Hermeticists.

It is because Hermeticism does not *want* to use *any instrument* that the above-mentioned excellent intellectual instruments were rejected by it. For Hermeticism has nothing to do with the desire to have "ready made answers" to all questions, obtained with minimum effort and maximum result. Its "questions" are *crises* and the "answers" that it seeks are *states of consciousness* resulting from these crises. This is why Hermeticism — being the *art of becoming*, the art of transformation, transubstantiation and transmutation of human consciousness — cannot make use of any intellectual instrument. The symbols which it uses — or rather that Hermeticists let themselves make use of — are not intellectual instruments. There is nothing mechanical about them. Quite on the contrary, the symbols are mystical-gnostic-magical "ferments" or "enzymes" of thought, whose troubling presence disquiets thinking, stimulates it, and calls it to immerse itself to ever new depths.

Therefore symbols are in no way instruments of thought, but rather they are its guides and active masters, just like the "symbol of faith", the Christian Creed, which is not an instrument of thought, but rather is a stellar constellation high above the head. And if this were not so, I repeat, if Hermeticism were a "system" or an intellectual instrument, it could only have led to an impasse and would have died long ago. For it would have become "specialised" in its development — and therefore non-viable. It would have become a tower of Babel awaiting a salutary thunderbolt from above.

About forty years ago, I knew an engineer who was twenty years older than me. He was an esotericist and I considered him to be a master. He had studied the three volumes of H. P. Blavatsky's *Secret Doctrine* in the solitude of the steppes of central Asia and had succeeded in reducing the mass of material of this work to a simple and elegant system — a circle with seven inner circles each in their turn subdivided into seven smaller circles. With time he had attained such an ability in manipulating this instrument that whatever question it was that he had to answer, he would find the answer to it almost immediately. The Russian revolution? This was 3 which aspired to 4. Science and religion? This was 5 and 4. European science and the esoteric wisdom of the Orient? This was 5 and 6.

And do not believe that all he said was these numbers. To the "non-initiated" he had many things to say each time — often very instructive and almost always quite to the point. The numbers were only for the "initiates", of whom I was one.

Now, the engineer, R., without doubt had an undeniable advantage in the instrument that he had constructed with the help of Blavatsky's *Secret Doctrine*. He was evidently superior to others who did not have the benefit of this instrument . . . temporarily, for some years. The great boredom of the impasse made his disciples disperse, of whom each sought a way of authentic experience of the living spirit. With respect to the author of this prodigious intellectual instrument, he finished by publishing a book . . . on the "white lady" who haunted an old house in the town where he lived. It was, I think, the same boredom which made him occupy himself with this phenomenon — a phantom, yes, but nevertheless a phenomenon of reality.

The arcanum of the tower blasted by a thunderbolt from above . . . how I would like to proclaim aloud the significance and meaning of it, so that it makes as deep an impression as possible on every seeker for profound truth! The English always

454   MEDITATIONS ON THE TAROT

say that it is sufficient to do one's best. But how can one know that it is *truly* one's best that one has done? Who can say with certainty that he has done his best? No, to say "I did my best" is quite convenient for someone who desires peace at any price, but this argument has no effect on anyone who desires the peace of certainty of conscience . . . But enough of personal torments—let us return to the arcanum with which we are occupied.

There never has been—nor *can* be—anything mechanical in practical Hermeticism, since it does not build "towers of Babel". I said also that there is nothing *surgical* in it. This means to say that, the alchemical principle being the soul of Hermeticism, it is the "*marriage* of opposites" and not their *divorce* which constitutes the basis of practical Hermeticism.

The marriage of opposites is a principle of universal significance. This is *not* a compromise that one contrives, but rather the *cross* and the magic of the cross. It is thus that the "true Self" is united to the "lower self" in the human being, where the "lower self" is the cross of the "true Self" and the "true Self" is the cross of the "lower self". The two poles of the human being then *live in the presence* of one another, the result of which is an alchemical process of gradual approach to one another.

It is similar with the hierarchies "of the right" and "of the left" in the world and in the history of the world. They can neither be united nor separated. They are engaged in a millennial-old discussion, where the arguments are facts and the conclusions are events. The hierarchies "of the left" are the cross of the hierarchies "of the right", and vice versa. There is no other hope in the world and in its history than the alchemical process of the transmutation of evil into good—the "sacrament of penance" on a cosmic scale. Divorce between the two sides would be an irreparable catastrophe.

Let us now take some historical examples nearer at hand. The wars of religion between Protestants and Catholics and also, before them, the wars between Christians and Mohammedans led—as in the recent Korean war—to the establishment of a line of demarcation, a "38th. parallel". The result was recognition of one another's existence and of the need to live in one another's presence, i.e. to suffer one another's presence. The decision was made to "carry the cross" instead of resorting to the surgery of war. Now the magic of the cross, the alchemical process of transmutation, could begin to work. And the result?

Both the Moslem and Christian world have at present not only no desire to convert one another by means of arms, but also not the least desire to populate hell with souls of the opposing religions. With respect to Protestants and Catholics, in Germany—the country which the Thirty Years' War ruined, no less than the Second World War of 1939-45—it is the united front of Catholics and Protestants, the CDU, which is in power.

It is similar in the conflict between the free world and the communist world. Whether we like it or not, we will have to mutually recognise one another and to tolerate the existence of one another, and to bear the suffering entailed thereby.

The 38th. parallel in Korea was the beginning of it. The result will be the operation of the magic of the cross, the alchemical process of transmutation. The free world, being in the presence of its judge and untiring competitor, will gradually eliminate what it recognises as social injustices; and the communist world, being in the presence of its judge and untiring competitor, will gradually liberalise itself and restore the freedoms that it recognises as postulates of human nature, which one cannot and must not violate.

It is the same again with the conflict between science and religion, both in the East and in the West. They will have to suffer one another. And the result will be that there will always be more Einsteins and more Teilhard de Chardins—believing scientists and scientific priests.

The magic of the cross, alchemy operating in the "marriage of opposites", is therefore the sole hope for the world, for mankind and for its history. And it is precisely this principle of the "marriage of opposites" which underlies Hermeticism. This is why it rejects the principle of divorce and war—the surgical principle—in practice as well as in theory, spiritually, morally and intellectually. The soul of Hermeticism is that "nothing should be lost...all should have eternal life" (John vi, 39-40).

Its fundamental thesis that all *can* be saved—this thesis which is Christian and alchemical at the same time—is without doubt that of faith, pure and simple, i.e. due to the experience of the divine breath. But it has the virtue of taking hold not only of the heart and the will but also of the understanding. The latter can find complete satisfaction here. The following is an example of how it can be found.

The parable of the lost sheep is well known. One generally understands it as portraying the care of the good pastor for the particular soul—and without doubt it does this. Nevertheless, one can, by analogy, apply it also to the inner life of the soul—its desires, aspirations, vices and virtues. If one does this, if one considers—by analogy—each particular force in the soul as a "sheep", one arrives at the understanding that the soul's faults and vices are not, fundamentally, monsters but rather, lost sheep. Thus, the eagerness to dominate, the desire to submit the will of other people to one's own is, fundamentally, a sheep which is lost. For at the root of the desire to dominate is found the dream of unity, union, the harmony of a choir. It is a "sheep". But instead of seeking the realisation of the dream of harmony by way of love, the will seeks to realise it by way of compulsion. This is a sheep that has lost its way. In order for it to return to the "flock", the fundamental will underlying the desire to dominate must be imprinted with the understanding that it is in the domain of love and not in that of commandment that it will find what it is seeking. Here is the return of the lost sheep—the alchemical process of transmutation of a "base metal" into "gold".

As it is the same with all the soul's faults and vices, we all have the mission of finding and bringing back to the flock (i.e. to the soul's choral harmony) the lost sheep in ourselves. We are missionaries in the subjective domain of our own soul, charged with the task of the conversion of our desires, ambitions, etc. We have to *persuade* them that they are seeking the realisation of their dreams in a false way, by showing them the true way. It is not a matter of commandment, but rather of the alchemy of the cross, i.e. making present an alternative way for our desires, ambitions, passions, etc. It is a matter, moreover, of the alchemical "marriage of opposites".

The practical way of doing this is *meditation*. It is deep meditation which makes present every "lost sheep" in us, with sufficient force to impress on it the alternative concerned. To meditate is to think in the presence of God—just as to pray is to speak in the presence of God.

Meditation is therefore the honest and courageous effort of the "lower self" to think together with the "higher Self" in divine light. And just as *concentration* necessarily precedes meditation, so does the latter lead soon or later to *contemplation*, i.e. a transition is made from consideration and discourse to the immobility and complete silence of supernatural communion, where one no longer thinks *something* from a distance, but where this Thing itself is present and reveals itself. Contemplation is the union of the thinker with reality. Here one does not arrive at a "conclusion", but one receives—or undergoes—the *imprint* of Reality.

This is therefore the "technique" (although there is, nevertheless, nothing technical in practical Hermeticism): the transition from concentration to meditation, and from meditation to contemplation.

In order to concentrate, it is necessary to have attained a certain degree of freedom and detachment. In order to meditate, one must place oneself within the light from above. And in order to experience contemplation, it is necessary to become one with this light. For this reason the states or stages of the soul corresponding to concentration, meditation and contemplation are those of *purification*, *illumination* and *union*. And it is the three sacred vows of obedience, chastity and poverty which render concentration, meditation and contemplation effective, with a view to the realisation of the soul's purification, illumination and union. These are the practical "secrets" of inner "gardening"—concerned with the laws of *growth* (and not those of *building*) of the human being, in the sense of his becoming ever more human, i.e. in the sense of *human evolution* without the impasses of specialisation.

The sixteenth Arcanum of the Tarot, that of the tower struck down by a thunderbolt, reveals the nature and danger of the impasses of specialisation. *One must not build; it is a matter of growth*—this is its essential teaching. For all the towers that are built will sooner or later be struck down by a thunderbolt—and let us add here that all freeing that owes its achievement to surgical operations entails the necessity of beginning again. The balloon that one makes fly higher, by cutting the strings of the ballast-bags and letting them fall, sooner or later will have to make a landing—the wind at some time will inevitably blow it down.

Towers will be *struck down by thunderbolts* and balloons will be *blown down by the wind*. In the last analysis, it is death and birth which constantly save human evolution, by acting as the thunderbolt which strikes down and as the wind which blows down. Is it not deeply significant that the spiritual head of the religion of liberation from the wheel of reincarnations is sought—and fourteen times was found—amongst children born immediately after his death?. . .that Dalai Lamas are found amongst children of the first generation after their decease, through the incontestable facts of concrete memories of their preceding incarnation?. . .that all fourteen Dalai Lamas are only successive reincarnations of a single soul or entity?

You will say: it is a mistake. Why? Can you prove that they are mistaken?. . .for those who are charged with the task of finding—or rather *refinding*—the Dalai Lama certainly have evidence to offer.

The Buddhists say that it is *mercy* which enables the soul of the Dalai Lama to return. But why could it not be a matter of the *wind*, i.e. the wind of compassion and mercy, just as the thunderbolt which strikes down towers is the divine love which saves us from impasses? For myself, on my part, I declare firmly that I have no doubt that death, which saves us from the impasse to which our bodily organisation leads, is the action of the thunderbolt of divine love, and that birth, which gives us the possibility of participating actively in the earthly history of the human race, is due fundamentally to the action of compassion for this earth and for mankind which inhabits it—at least, for a certain class of souls.

There is nothing mechanical or automatic at the foundation of world existence. Take away the mechanical appearances and you will find that the world is something moral—crucified love. Yes, mercenaries took His clothes and divided them into four parts, one for each mercenary, and they drew lots for His tunic; whereas the heart of the world—*naked*—is love crucified in the middle of two other crucified ones, on His right and on His left.

In fact, the mechanical sciences have divided the clothing of the Word and they dispute amongst themselves for priority in the application of the universal principle (the tunic) which manifests equally in each of their special domains—whether it can be reduced to the laws of physics, or the laws of chemistry, or the laws of energy, or lastly, biological laws.

But Hermeticism, decried and misunderstood as it is, does not in any way take part in dividing the clothing of the crucified Word, nor in drawing lots for its tunic. It strives to see the crucified Word clothed in appearance by the mechanical world. And this is why the alchemists, whose preoccupation was the chemistry of "puffers"—i.e. chemical, material processes directed by moral, psychic and spiritual breath—never took the clothing of the One to whom it belonged; their "chemistry" was not separated from the Word. This is why astrologers, also, whose preoccupation was the astronomy of "influences", or the "celestial breath", did not take the planetary and zodiacal world purely and simply as a mechanism; their "astronomy" was not separated from the Word. This is why also the magicians, whose preoccupation was the "physics of breath", i.e. movements and energies caused by the human word by analogy with the divine Word, did not take the clothing alone; their "physics" was not separated from the Word. Whatever the practical errors and abuses of alchemists, astrologers and magicians, at least they are not to be found amongst those who divide the clothing and draw lots for the tunic.

But Hermeticism is not alchemy, astrology and magic—although these "sciences" are derived from it by way of specialisation. For the fundamental principle of Hermeticism—as the synthesis of mysticism, gnosis, magic and philosophy—is *non-specialisation*. For this reason it *evolves* by avoiding the impasses of specialisation—the towers which sooner or later are struck down by thunderbolts.

Thus, Christian Hermeticism of today has not remained behind in the great spiritual events which have changed factors of the first order in the domain of astrology—which events now play the role of "the thunderbolt which blasts the tower of astrology". What I have in mind here is that the planetary influences and the days and hours of these influences have given way to a power of a higher order. It is true that the day Sunday is the day of the sun with respect to the human psycho-physical organism, but nowadays it is the day of resurrection, with respect to man's psycho-spiritual life. Saturday is still the day of Saturn, but it is so only with regard to the natural, lower part of the human being. For the soul which turns towards the spirit and for the human spirit itself, Saturday is the day of the Holy Virgin. And the influence of Venus has given way to Calvary, to Christ crucified—Friday. Tuesday is no longer the day of Mars—for the soul that aspires to the spirit, or for spiritual personages—it is the day of the Archistrategist Michael. Similarly, with respect to the soul turned towards the spirit and with respect to the lives of spiritual personages, Monday is the day of the Holy Trinity, instead of being that of the moon...Wednesday is the day of the human pastors of mankind, instead of Mercury...and Thursday is the day of the Holy Spirit, instead of Jupiter.

Consequently, sacred magic of the present day uses formulae and signs which correspond to the supernatural power of the day and not to the natural planetary influence of the day, although, I repeat, the latter remains valid in a restricted domain—more restricted than in the past—and remains of practical value in this domain. Therefore, one invokes and unites oneself with the Holy Spirit on Thursday, instead of invoking the "genius of Jupiter", etc. The priority of supernatural power with regard to the astral influences of days, hours and years—this is the "thunderbolt" which has "blasted" the tower of astrology and specialised astrological magic.

Here is an example of this "thunderbolt" in action: a horoscope indicates a baleful configuration, a conjuction of Saturn and Mars in the eighth house (that of death), predicting a violent death—however, it happens that it is not Saturn and Mars which act, but rather the Holy Virgin and the Archangel Michael, and instead of the predicted death a spiritual illumination takes place.

What is true here for astrology and magic is also true for alchemy, because everything which is specialised becomes a tower, i.e. it crystallises and therefore becomes deprived of the faculty of keeping step with spiritual evolution—it leads to an impasse. And it is then the "thunderbolt from above" which enters into play and removes the obstacle to further progress. The sixteenth Major Arcanum of the Tarot is therefore a warning addressed to all authors of "systems", where an important role is assigned to a mechanical ingredient—intellectual, practical, occult, political, social and other systems. It invites them to devote themselves to tasks of growth instead of those of construction—to tasks as "cultivators and guardians of the garden", instead of as builders of the tower of Babel.

Meditation on the
Seventeenth Major Arcanum of the Tarot

THE STAR

L'ÉTOILE

The righteous flourish like the palm tree,
And grow like a cedar in Lebanon...
They still bring forth fruit in old age,
They are ever full of sap and green...
(Psalm 92, 12-14)

Two things fill the mind with ever new
and increasing admiration and awe...
the starry heavens above me and the moral
law within me.
(Immanuel Kant)*

LETTER XVII

THE STAR

Dear Unknown Friend,

The sixteenth Major Arcanum of the Tarot presented us with the alternative of two ways—that of *construction* and that of *growth*; and it portrayed the dangers of the way of construction by presenting the law of the tower of Babel to our hearts and minds. Having understood this, one is led to decide upon the way of growth.

Now, the seventeenth Major Arcanum of the Tarot—"The Star"—is the Arcanum of growth, just as the sixteenth Arcanum is that of construction. Therefore, it is a matter now of a spiritual exercise devoted to growth, i.e. it is time for us to concentrate on the problem of growth and to meditate on its essential aspects with a view to arriving at a contemplation of its kernel or its mystical-gnostic-magical-

Critique of Practical Reason; trsl. L. W. Beck, Chicago, 1949, p. 258.

463

metaphysical essence—in a word: at its Hermetic essence. Let us therefore apply ourselves to this threefold task.

A tower is built; a tree grows. The two processes have this in common: that they present a gradual increase in volume with a pronounced tendency upwards. But there is at the same time the difference that the tower rises by leaps and bounds, whilst the tree shows a continuous elevation. This is because bricks or hewn stones are put one on top of the other in the process of building the tower, whilst the microscopic "bricks"—the cells—of a tree multiply through division and growth in volume. It is the *sap* in the tree, rising from the roots into the trunk and branches, which renders growth of the tree possible and which makes it shoot up through the multiplication and growth in volume of its cells. Whilst the tower is *dry*, the tree is filled with sap in movement, which underlies both the division of its cells and their growth—in a word, it underlies the process of growth.

Growth is flowing, whilst construction proceeds by leaps and bounds. And what is true of the artificial and the natural in the physical domain is also true in the psychic and spiritual domain. "The righteous flourish like the palm tree. . .they are ever full of sap and green. . ." (Psalm 92), but ". . .a down cast spirit dries up the bones. . ." (Proverbs xvii, 22).

Here we are in the presence of a theme of the same significance as that of the astral "magical agent", the link between consciousness and action, which so much is made of in occult literature—namely the theme of *the universal sap of life*, which is the theme of the seventeenth Arcanum, the Arcanum of growth. For just as there is a mysterious intermediary agent which effects the passage from imagination to reality, so there is also a no-less mysterious agent which effects the passage from the potential state of a seed to that of maturity, i.e. the passage from what is only potential to its realisation. This is *the agent of tranformation from the ideal to the real*.

Just as an intermediary force enters into play in the process which transforms imagination into action, i.e. into an objective event, so does the play of an unknown force take place in the process of *becoming*—where either an acorn becomes a branched oak, or a crying infant becomes a St. Augustine, or lastly a world in the state of "primordial mist" becomes a planetary system with forms of living beings, ensouled beings and intelligent beings. Whatever it is in question—it does not matter whether it is the growth of an organism, the development of an individual from birth to death, or cosmic evolution—it is necessary to postulate the existence of an active agent which effects the passage from the state of that which is only potential to one of reality. For *something has acted* during the time in which an acorn becomes an oak, or a fertilised egg becomes a mature man, or a primordial cosmic mist becomes a planetary system (including our globe inhabited by mankind). I know quite well that this reasoning is not in accordance with the rules of the game fixed by the natural sciences, but there are other rules—above all those of natural reasoning, with which this here is not only in agreement but which also is categorically demanded by them. Categorically. . .this means to say that one must either resign oneself to silence of thought with regard to problems of this order, or else reason in a way that conforms to the nature — to the *structural exigencies* — of the reasoning that is the rule of the game in Hermeticism. It is necessary, therefore, to postulate a structural "agent of growth", just as it is necessary to postulate a "magical agent" acting as intermediary between consciousness and events, if one decides to think about it.

What is the intrinsic difference between the "magical agent" and the "agent of growth"? It is as follows:

The magical agent is of an *electrical* nature — either terrestrial or celestial. It is of a nature to act through discharges, through the emission of sparks or flashes. It is *dry and warm* — of the nature of *fire*. The "blasted tower" of the sixteenth Arcanum is in fact only the meeting of two "drynesses"— that of the tower below and that of the thunderbolt from above; and the Arcanum "The Devil" (Arcanum XV) is essentially that of "warmth"— moreover two "warmths"; that of evil and that of good. The Arcana XV and XVI are therefore those of *fire*, whilst the Arcana XIV and XVII are those of *water*. For Angelic inspiration and the agent of growth have this in common that they *flow* — that they do not act through shocks and discharges, but in a continuous way. *Continuous transformation* is the essential manifestation of the agent of growth, just as *creative lightning* is that of the magical agent.

These two agents manifest themselves everywhere, including the domain of human intellectuality. There are minds who have sided with "water", and it is to them that we owe the ideas of "transformism": evolution, progress, education, natural therapy, living tradition, etc.; and there are others who have sided with "fire", to whom we owe the ideas of "creationism": creation *ex nihilo*, invention, election, surgery and prosthesis, revolution, etc. Thales (ca. 625-547 B.C.) believed that it is the agent of growth or water which plays the principal role in the world, whilst Heraclitus of Ephesus (flourished ca. 500 B.C.) attributed it to the magical agent or fire.

Goethe, in the "classical Walpurgis night" scene in part II of *Faust*, has Anaxagoras, a partisan of fire, discuss with Thales, a partisan of water, the theme of the priority of creative lightning or continuous transformation in Nature — a discussion which leads to the dramatic result of Anaxagoras' magical evocation of the threefold moon (Diana, Luna and Hecate), which he regrets. Thus he throws himself down, face to the ground, imploring the flashing forces, which threaten irreparable catastrophe, to calm down. With respect to Thales, he invites Homunculus to a joyous maritime festival (*zum heitern Meeresfeste*) — the festival of metamorphoses, the "ball" of transformism — where Thales cries out:

> All things are out of water created,
> All by water maintained. Thou Life-giving
> Ocean, vouchsafe us thine agency ever!

> (*Alles ist aus Wasser entsprungen*
> *Alles wird durch das Wasser erhalten*
> *Ozean, gönn' uns dein ewiges Walten!*)
> (Goethe, *Faust* II)*

It is not to be wondered at that Goethe, although he admits the reality of the magical agent or fire, ranges himself on the side of the agent of growth or water—for he was the author of four works on *metamorphosis*, the principal theme of his life, namely on the metamorphosis of light or colour (*Farbenlehre*), on the metamorphosis of plants (*Metamorphose der Pflanzen*), on the metamorphosis of animals (*Metamorphose der Tiere*), and on the metamorphosis of man (*Faust*), which is his principal work. His faith was that of transformism, evolution, the tradition of cultural progress without revolution—in a word, Goethe believed in and attached value to all that *flows*, all that grows without leaps and bounds. He ranged himself on the side of the principle of *continuity*.

The principle of continuity was portrayed in the intellectual domain in a particularly impressive and fruitful way by the German philosopher Leibnitz—who, moreover, wrote more in French and Latin than he did in German. Proceeding in his thought according to the principle of continuity, i.e. thinking without leaps and bounds, Leibnitz did not have to face the gulfs or abysses which separate one belief from another, or one thesis from another, or one human group from another. All theses are separated from their antitheses by abysses, but Leibnitz threw the bridge of the rainbow of continuity, i.e. gradual transition, across them. Just as red is transformed gradually into orange, and orange into yellow, which in its turn is transformed imperceptibly into green, in order later to become blue, indigo and violet, so is every thesis transformed into its antithesis. Thus the thesis "each centre of a particular existence (monad) is free" and the thesis "all is predetermined by the effective and final cause of the universe (pre-established harmony)" co-existed in peace in the rainbow of the totality of Leibnitz's ideas on the world, although they are clearly contradictory. But for Leibnitz they were no more nor less contradictory than red and violet in the rainbow.

Platonism, Aristotelianism, Scholasticism, Cartesianism, Spinozism and mysticism were for Leibnitz only "colours" of the rainbow of the "perennial philosophy" (*philosophia perennis*), and in his thoughts he moved according to the "zodiacal circle" of thought. His whole work was therefore that of *peace*, just as the work of Hermeticism is; for Leibnitz's method is nothing other than Hermeticism, pure and simple. And it was this "rainbow of peace" (the principle of continuity) which guided Leibnitz in his all-consuming activity, which aimed at two salient goals: the foundation of scientific academies, and the fusion of the Catholic and Reformed Churches.

The Berlin, St. Petersburg and Vienna scientific academies were the fruit of Leibnitz's efforts to introduce the "rainbow of peace" in its practical form of coop-

---

*Trsl. A. G. Latham, Everyman Library, London-New York, 1908, p. 175.

eration between scientists of all the different scientific disciplines in western civilisation. With respect to the work of uniting the Catholic and Reformed Churches undertaken together with Bossuet, the intellectual and moral bridge that he built then still exists and there has been a considerable to-and-fro across it since that time — the time immediately following the Thirty Years War.

It was again the principle of continuity, the "water" of Hermeticism, which led Leibnitz to the discovery of the basis of differential calculus in mathematics. For differential calculus is simply the application of the principle of continuity — the *fluidic* mode of thought instead of *crystallised* thought — in the domain of mathematics. Infinitesimal calculus, comprising differential and integral calculus — the alpha and omega of thought-become-fluidic in mathematics — is an application of the principle of continuity. It is the fruit of the admission of the agent of growth into the domain of mathematics, where previously the principle of construction reigned alone.

I take the occasion to rescue from oblivion the work of a man that is probably either already forgotten or has not been noticed, i.e. the engineer Schmakov's *Svyashtchennaya Kniga Tota — Velikiye Arkany Taro* ("The Sacred Book of Thoth — the Major Arcana of the Tarot"), published in Russia in 1916 or 1917, where on almost every page the author makes use of differential and integral calculus in dealing with such problems as individuality, God, freedom and cosmic order, planes of existence and consciousness, spirit and matter, etc. The author of the book (400 pages) impressed me all the more profoundly as, in addition to the numerous formulae of infinitesimal calculus strewn throughout the book, he did not deign to translate — or even to transcribe in Latin or Cyrillic characters — long passages from the *Zohar* and other books in Hebrew or Aramaic. And this magnificent disdain for popularity was at a time when the populace became all-powerful and when demagogy was the order of the day! I should add that the book was large, printed in Cyrillic, Latin, Greek and Hebrew characters on the best paper, and that it was the author himself who published it at his own expense.

Yes, there have been noble stars in the heaven of Hermeticism — and I hope that this will always be so. . .This tribute to a deceased Unknown Friend is not, however, without a contribution to the theme of this Letter, addressed to the living Unknown Friend. For the engineer Schmakov's contribution to the tradition of Hermeticism is a demonstration of the fruitfulness of the application of infinitesimal calculus in the domain where it belongs from right of birth — the domain of Hermeticism.

In enumerating the spirits who have grasped the Arcanum of the agent of growth, I cannot pass by a great spirit, a star in the heaven of the perennial philosophy, whom you, dear Unknown Friend, certainly know without doubt. This is Henri Bergson — again a Hermeticist by the grace of God alone, without any external affiliations with initiation orders or societies. Henri Bergson had the courage and the talent to re-affirm, with its scientific consequences, the principle of continuity and the mode of thought which grasps movement by moving with it and not by arresting it. The following is what he says himself concerning this:

If it is a question of movement, all the intelligence retains is a series of positions: first one point reached, then another, then still another. But should something happen between these points, immediately the understanding intercalates new positions, and so on indefinitely. It refuses to consider *transition* . . . Suppose we skip this intellectual representation of movement, which shows it as a series of positions. Let us go directly to movement and examine it without any interposed concept: we shall find it simple and all-of-a-piece. Let us go further; suppose we get it to coincide with one of those incontestably real and absolute movements which we ourselves produce. This time we have mobility in its essence, and we feel that it mingles with an effort whose duration is an indivisible continuity. . .We shall say as much for change; the understanding breaks it up into successive and distinct states, supposed to be invariable. If one looks a little more closely at each of these states, noticing that it varies, asking how it could endure if it did not change, the understanding hastens to replace it by a series of shorter states, which in their turn break up if necessary, and so forth ad infinitum. *But how can we help seeing that the essence of duration is to flow*, and that the fixed placed side by side with the fixed will never constitute anything which has duration. It is not the "states", simple snapshots we have taken once again along the course of change, that are real; on the contrary, *it is flux, the continuity of transition, it is change itself that is real* . . .What we have here is merely an uninterrupted thrust of change—of a change always adhering to itself in a duration which extends indefinitely. (Henri Bergson, *La pensée et le mouvement*; trsl. M. L. Andison in *The Creative Mind*, New Jersey, 1965, pp. 15-17)

Henri Bergson therefore invites us to grasp the agent of growth in action instead of occupying ourselves with its fossilised products—he invites us to experience what he calls *intuition*.

Amongst those who have given effect to the call and to the work of Henri Bergson, the most prominent is Father Teilhard de Chardin. Here is a summary of his life-work that we find on the last page of his diary, written 7th. April, 1955, three days before his death:

> *Last page of the journal of Pierre Teilhard de Chardin*
> *Maundy Thursday.*   *What I believe.*
>
> 1. St. Paul—the three verses: *En pasi panta Theos.*
>
> 2. Cosmos = Cosmogenesis-Biogenesis-Noogenesis-
>   Christogenesis.

3. The two articles of my creed:

$$\begin{cases} \text{The Universe is centrated} - \text{Evolutively} \begin{cases} \text{Upward} \\ \text{Forward} \end{cases} \\ \text{Christ is its Centre} \begin{cases} \text{The Christian Phenomenon} \\ \text{Noogenesis} = \text{Christogenesis} \\ (= \text{Paul}) \end{cases} \end{cases}$$

The three verses are from Paul's first letter to the Corinthians:
The last enemy to be destroyed is death. For he (the Christ) has
put all things in subjection under his feet. . .When all things
are subjected to him, then the Son himself will also be subjected
to him who put all things under him, that God may be everything to everyone (*en pasi panta Theos*) (I Corinthians xv,
26-28). (Pierre Teilhard de Chardin, *The Future of Man*; trsl.
N. Denny, London, 1964, p. 309)

Just as there is Fire and fire, i.e. the celestial Fire of divine love and the fire
of electricity due to friction, so there is also Water and water, i.e. the celestial Water
of the sap of growth, progress and evolution and the lower water of instinctivity —
the "collective unconscious", engulfing collectivity — which is the water of floods
and drowning. Thus, the woman represented on the Card of the seventeenth Arcanum pours water from *two* vases — held in her left and right hands — which blend
into the same stream.

. . .which blend into the same stream, alas! Here is the tragedy of human life
and mankind's history and cosmic evolution. The flow of continuity — in heredity, tradition and, lastly, evolution — bears not only all that which is healthy, noble, holy and divine of the past but also all that which was infectious, vile, blasphemous and diabolical. All is borne pell-mell, never ending, towards the future.
What Verlaine said of the river Seine in his *Poèmes Saturniens* could also be said —
with good reason — of the flow of human life, mankind's history, and cosmic
evolution:

Still, Seine, your crawling journey do you make,
Curving through Paris like some aged snake,
A muddy snake.* And all your ports are fed
With loads of wood, of coal and of the dead!

(*Et tu coules toujours, Seine, et, tout en rampant,*
Tu traînes dans Paris ton cours de vieux serpent,
De vieux serpent boueux, emportant vers tes havres
Tes cargaisons de bois, de houille et de cadavres!)
(Paul Verlaine, "Paris: A Nocturne")**

---

*The mud of the serpent of old.
**From *Poemes Saturniens*; trsl. B. Hill, *The Sky above the Roof*, London, 1957, p. 37.

The same again could be said — also with good reason — in the words of Victor Hugo:

As a river of the communal soul,	(*Comme un fleuve d'âme commune,*
From the white pylon to the rough rune,	*Du blanc pylône à l'âpre rune,*
From the Brahmin to the Roman flamen,	*Du brahme au flamine romain,*
From the hierophant to the Druid,	*De l'hierophante au druide,*
A kind of godly fluid	*Une sorte de Dieu fluide*
Runs through the veins of the human race.	*Coule aux veines du genre humain*.)

(Victor Hugo, "Les mages", 435-440)*

For both the "mud of the serpent of old" and "a kind of godly fluid" indeed flow in the veins of the human race.

Is this dualism, then? Do the serpent's venom and the tears of the Virgin therefore flow together eternally in the flow of Life?

Yes and no — the one as resolutely as the other. *Yes* for the present, which is action and will; *no* for the future, which is the star of the sea of understanding and hope. Because for action it is dualism which awakens the will and makes it pass from a passive state to an active state — all *effort* presupposes a practical and concrete dualism. The great masters of dualism in the history of humanity such as Zarathustra, Buddha and Mani did not want to *explain* the world through the dogma of cosmic duality (Zarathustra), or psychological duality (Buddha), or even psycho-cosmic duality (Mani), but rather they wanted to *awaken* dormant will for the effort which manifests itself by the power to say *yes* and *no*. Fatalism, resignation to routine, and quietism are the sleep of the will — sometimes harmless, at other times tinged with bitterness. The great masters of dualism made appeal to the will to awaken it and rid it of the weight of somnolence. They wanted to give courage and boldness to the point of exercising in practice the will's birth-right — that of choice, that of saying *yes* or *no*.

The great Zarathustra wanted *knights* to fight under the banner of light in the struggle against darkness — the Turanian idolaters, the demons of impurity and ignorance, and lastly the spirit of Ahriman or Satan. He wanted that there should be people able to say *yes* to the light — and who, consequently, learnt to say *no* to the darkness.

The great Buddha wanted to awaken the will to say *no* to the great routine of desires which make the wheel of births revolve. He wanted *ascetics* with regard

*From the collection *Les contemplations*.

to the automatic mechanism of the psyche, who would learn to say *yes* with regard to the free creativity of the spirit.

The great Mani, who taught a synthesis of the teachings of Zarathustra and Buddha within Christianity, wanted (leaving aside the question of whether the blend that he accomplished was good or not) to mobilise the good will of the whole of mankind — Pagan, Buddhist and Christian — for a single concerted and universal effort of *yes* towards the eternal spirit and *no* towards the transitory things of matter.

The aim which the great masters of dualism pursued was *practical*, i.e. relating to the domain of *yes* and *no*. And we, in so far as we pursue a practical earthly psychic or spiritual aim, cannot accept the flow of human life, mankind's history and cosmic evolution simply as it is and let ourselves be carried along by it. We are bound to distinguish here between the "mud of the serpent of old" and "a kind of godly fluid", and to say *yes* and *no* — with all the practical consequences that this *yes* and this *no* entail.

At the same time we must not forget that the seventeenth Arcanum is not only that of the water which flows from two vases and is mixed in a single flow but also that of the *star* — all the more so as the traditional name of the Card is "The Star".

The great central star of the Card — as, moreover, the whole constellation of eight stars — invites us to an effort of consciousness to unite contemplative justice (the yellow star with eight rays) with active justice (the red star with eight rays), i.e. to unite the guiding principle of understanding with the guiding principle of the will. In other words, it invites us to overcome dualism through the magical and alchemical operation of nailing opposites to one another — that which one calls the "marriage of opposites". The "marriage of opposites" makes that light-force radiate into the world which renders the future not only acceptable but also desirable, which transforms the future into *promise*, and which is the antithesis of the thesis of the author of Ecclesiastes, the son of David, king of Jerusalem, who said: "What has been is what will be, and what has been done is what will be done; and there is nothing new under the sun" (Ecclesiastes i, 9).

The light-force which emanates from the star — constituted through the marriage of contemplation with activity, and which is the antithesis of the thesis that "there is nothing new under the sun" — is *hope*. It proclaims to the world: "What has been is that which prepares what will be, and what has been done is that which prepares what will be done; there is only *that which is new* under the sun. Each day is a unique event and revelation which will never be repeated."

Hope is not something subjective due to an optimistic or sanguine temperament, or to a desire for compensation in the sense of modern Freudian and Adlerian psychology. It is a light-force which radiates objectively and which directs creative evolution towards the world's future. It is the celestial and spiritual counterpart of the terrestrial and natural instinct of biological reproduction — which, with mutation, produces natural selection, which latter, in its turn, produces with time biological progress. In other words, hope is what moves and directs *spiritual evolution* in the world. In so far as it moves, it is an objective force, and in so far as it orientates and directs, it is a subjective light. This is why we may speak of it as a "light-force".

Hope is for spiritual evolution what the instinct of reproduction is for biological evolution. It is the force and the light of the *final cause* of the world or, if you wish, the force and the light of the ideal of the world—the magical radiation of the "Omega point", according to Teilhard de Chardin. This "Omega point" towards which spiritual evolution is tending—or that of the "noosphere", which surges triumphantly above the "barysphere" and "biosphere"—is the central point of the hope of the "personalising world". It is the point of complete unity of the outer and inner, of matter and spirit, i.e. the God-Man, *the resurrected Jesus Christ*, just as the "Alpha point", the prime mover or the effective cause, is the Word which set in motion electrons, atoms, molecules, i.e. movement *directed* towards their association into planets, organisms, families, races, kingdoms...

"I am the Alpha and the Omega" (Revelation xxi, 6)—this is how the message of the central star of the Card of the seventeenth Arcanum of the Tarot reads—which means to say, "I am *activity*, the effective cause, who set all in motion; and I am *contemplation*, the final cause, who draws towards himself all that which is in movement. I am *primordial action*; and I am *eternal waiting*—for all to arrive where I am."

Here is why we say *no* to dualism seen in the light of the future, just as we say *yes* to it if we are looking at it in the light of the present. It is hope, the fruit of the marriage of opposites, which defends dualism for us and which not only invites us to believe in the final unity of opposites but also to work with a view to the realisation of this unity—which is the sense and the aim of the spiritual exercise which is the seventeenth Arcanum of the Tarot. For it has to be said yet again: the Major Arcana of the Tarot are spiritual exercises whose practice alone teaches the "arcanum" (that which one needs to know in order to make discoveries) of each Arcanum.

Now, the spiritual exercise of the seventeenth Arcanum is that of the endeavour to see together—"to contemplate"—the essence of biological growth (the agent of growth) and the essence of spiritual growth (hope), in order to find, or rather re-find, their analogy, their intrinsic kinship and, lastly, their fundamental identity. For it is a matter of grasping the essence of the *water* which flows both in the obscure process of growth, multiplication and continuity in biological reproduction and in the clarity of the serene heights of hope. It is a matter, therefore, of coming to an intuition of *water* such as it is understood in Moses' account of the second day of creation, where God "separated the waters which were under the firmament from the waters which were above the firmament" (Genesis i, 7), and of understanding ("under-standing") that the light which flows above consciousness and the instinctive drive which flows beneath consciousness are fundamentally the same thing—separated in order to act according to two different modes—namely *water*, which is the principle of growth and evolution, both biological and spiritual. Thus, it is necessary to attain to an intuitive perception, i.e. immediate and endowed with the certainty of obviousness, that the principle of fluid-sap and the principle of hope are one and the same, namely the principle of *water*. Fluid-sap is the bearer of the agent of growth; and so is hope, when it is a matter of growth in the sense of the "transformability" of things, i.e. their transformation in conformity with their divine prototypes. Thus, hope is the bearer of the agent of growth in spiritual evolution. It acts in the sphere situated above consciousness, whilst the agent of growth in biological evolution acts in the sphere beneath it (cf. Genesis i, 7 concerning the "waters above the firmament" and the "waters under the firmament").

This is why the Card of the seventeenth Arcanum of the Tarot represents the woman, the maternal principle, between the constellation of hope above her and the flow of continuity of biological life beneath her. Because every mother professes a double faith—the faith of celestial hope that the future will be more glorious than the present and the faith of terrestrial continuity that the flow of succeeding generations will go *forward*—in the direction indicated by hope from above. Every mother knows—in so far as she is a mother—that underlying the flow of generations there is at work the primordial magical impulse of the effective cause ("the Alpha") of the world and that the final cause ("the Omega") of the world will not fail to direct it and draw it towards itself. In other words, each mother professes—by the very fact that she is a mother—the divine origin of the world and the divine aim of the world. If this were not so, she would refuse to give birth, i.e. to give birth to children who otherwise would be destined to be the victims of absurdity. Therefore, we could also name the seventeenth Arcanum the "Arcanum of the Mother" or the "Arcanum of Eve". In her there are actively present, simultaneously, the intuition of celestial hope and the primordial magic of the benediction of the Creator ("be fruitful and multiply, and fill the earth and subdue it"—Genesis i, 28).

The ancients drew hope for life and for death in the mysteries of the Mother. I have in mind not only the mysteries of Eleusis but also a number of others, including those of Isis in Egypt. But one finds the essence of all these mysteries of the Mother expressed in the Epistle to the Romans of the apostle Paul:

> For the creation waits with eager longing for the revealing of the sons of God; for the creation was subjected to futility—not of its own will but by the will of him who subjected it—*in the hope that the creation itself will be set free from its bondage to decay and obtain the glorious liberty of the children of God. We know that the whole creation has been suffering the pangs of childbirth until now...* (Romans viii, 19-23)

Here is not only the soul of all the ancient mysteries of the Mother but also of all modern doctrines of "transformism" and biological and spiritual evolution! For modern evolutionism is, at root, only the renaissance in a scientific guise of the ancient mysteries of the Mother—the mysteries of hope and of the "pangs of childbirth". The mysteries of the Father contain the "what"—*salvation* through the Son; and the mysteries of the Mother contain the "how"—biological *and* spiritual evolution. Now, natural science is orientated towards the *how* of the world, and for this reason is on the way towards renewing the ancient mysteries of the Mother—knowledge of *evolution*; whilst the Christian religion is in the first place orientated towards the mysteries of the Father—*salvation* through the Son. It is to Teilhard de Chardin, a Hermeticist of our time, by the grace of God, that we owe the synthesis—or at least a way towards synthesis—of the *what* and the *how* of the world, i.e. of religion and science, which is the task and the mission of Hermeticism. Henceforth everyone can contemplate the serpent of evolution crucified on the cross of divine providence *and* the Son of God crucified on the cross of evolution of the serpent—and from thence draw hope for life and death. Here evolution and salvation—the two truths of science and religion—are no longer contradictory: they bear together the message of hope.

But let us not forget that this synthesis of today has had its history, and that this is due also to many "pangs of childbirth". It was born after a long series of continuous endeavours from century to century: the endeavour of Heraclitus, the philosopher of the perpetual change of matter; that of the Gnostics, who made the drama of the fall and return of Sophia Achamoth resound in human history; that of St. Augustine, the father of the philosophy of history, who brought to light the twofold current in mankind's history—that of the "terrestrial city" and that of the "city of God"; that of the Hermetic-alchemistic thinkers who affirmed and re-affirmed untiringly the principle of transformability of that which is base into that which is noble; that of Martinez de Pasqually, who wrote his *Traité de la réintégration des êtres* ("Treatise on the Reintegration of Beings"); that of Fabre d'Olivet, the author of *L'histoire philosophique du genre humain* ("Philosophical History of the Human Race"), showing the dynamic operation of the triangle fate-freedom-providence in mankind's history; that of H. P. Blavatsky, who added and opposed to Charles Darwin's materialistic evolution a breath-taking vision of the spiritual evolution of the universe; that of Rudolf Steiner, who emphasised that the centre of gravity of spiritual-cosmic evolution is Jesus Christ (it is then but a short step to Teilhard de Chardin's "Omega point"); all these endeavours have contributed—in a visible or invisible manner—to the synthesis of today. They *live*, all together, in the contemporary synthesis of evolution and salvation, which is the fruit of this collective endeavour from century to century. Truly, from the fusion of opinions truth shines forth. Because it is not the collision of opinions to which this synthesis is due, but rather to their fusion as constituent elements of the "rainbow of peace".

The synthesis of the truths of salvation and evolution is in fact a rainbow in which the immortal essences of the endeavours of the past are resplendent—purified of the temporary and accidental which has enveloped them. The modern "transformism" of biological *and* spiritual evolution is not due to a refutation of ancient and mediaeval alchemy, for example, but rather to the fact that the fundamental alchemical dogma of transmutability has been embraced by contemporary thinkers. Purified of temporary and accidental elements—like the orientation towards the aim of producing material gold, a material philosopher's stone and a material panacea—alchemy today celebrates its apotheosis in the splendour of the rainbow of the synthesis of salvation and evolution. Today alchemy has come out of the sombre alchemical kitchens where its adepts often lavished entire fortunes and the flower of their lives—in order to be installed in a laboratory more worthy of it: the vast extent of the universe. Now, it is the world which has become the alchemical laboratory, just as it has become the mystical oratory. Is this a loss or a gain for alchemy? Is it a loss or a gain for alchemy that it has ceased to be the secret—often maniacal—occupation of a sect, and that it has become the "prince of ideas" for mankind? What has become of the secret art of the transmutation of metals, the manufacture of the philosopher's stone and the preparation of the panacea—everyone's light of hope for a synthesis between salvation (the salvation of souls) and cosmic evolution? The answer is apparent: today we are witnesses of the triumph of alchemy—an unparalleled triumph, surpassing the most rash hopes of the past.

What is true of alchemy is also true of the Augustinian philosophy of history. The cross of the "terrestrial city" and the "city of God" that St. Augustine saw especially in the history of Israel and the Roman empire has today been transformed, whilst preserving its immortal essence, into the cross of salvation and evolution, that of religion and science—in the last analysis, the cross of *ora et labora* ("pray and work"), or grace and endeavour. The Augustinian vision therefore also lives in the rainbow of the modern synthesis of salvation and evolution.

And what is true of alchemy and of St. Augustine is also true of all other contributions—ancient, mediaeval and modern—to the synthesis of salvation and evolution. The work of all those who taught a *way*—the mystical and spiritual way of purification, illumination and union, or the historical and social way of the progress of civilisation through social and moral justice, or the biological way of evolution from the sphere of chemical elements to the sphere of living organisms and from the sphere of living organisms to that of beings endowed with thought and word—the work of all these, I say, which teaches us a *way* of individual and collective perfection, is now resplendent in the rainbow of the synthesis of salvation and evolution, the rainbow of mankind's hope. Because this rainbow is tradition in full flower—it is living tradition which has attained a certain degree of brilliancy. For this reason, let us also not forget the poet:

. . . it is he who, in spite of thorns,	(. . . *c'est lui qui, malgré les épines,*
Envy and derision,	*L'envie et la dérision,*
Walks, bent under your remains,	*Marche, courbé dans vos ruines,*
Gathering *tradition*.	*Ramassant la tradition.*
From fertile tradition	*De la tradition féconde*
Comes all that covers the world,	*Sort tout ce que couvre le monde,*
Everything that heaven can bless.	*Tout ce que le ciel peut bénir.*
Every idea, human or divine,	*Toute idée, humaine ou divine,*
Which is rooted in the past,	*Qui prend le passé pour racine*
Has its foliage in the future.	*A pour feuillage l'avenir.*)

(Victor Hugo, "Fonction du poète", 287-296)*

One cannot pass by poetry if one attaches value to tradition. The whole of the Bible breathes poetry—epic, lyric and dramatic—and likewise the *Zohar* is full of poetry.

The principal works of St. John of the Cross are simply commentaries on some pieces of poetry written by him. A poetic impetus vibrates in the whole work of Father Pierre Teilhard de Chardin, of a kind that his critics—as I understood from a conversation with one of them—see in it a weakness that is reprehensible from a scientific, philosophical and theological point of view. But they are mistaken, since poetry is élan and élan gives wings to imagination, and without winged imagination—directed and controlled by the strict laws of intrinsic coherence and conformity to facts—no progress is possible. One cannot pass by poetry, because one cannot do without the élan of imagination. One should only be on guard that one is not carried away by an imagination which seeks brilliance and not truth. With respect to an imagination that loves truth, i.e. which loves and seeks only what is coherent and in conformity with facts, it is what we name "genius" or fruitfulness in the domain of human endeavour.

Hermeticism, also, cannot pass by poetry. What is the *Emerald Table* of Hermes Trismegistus if not a piece of sublime poetry. Certainly, it is not "only poetry" in the pure and simple sense of verbal and musical aesthetics, since it advances a great mystical, gnostic, magical and alchemical dogma, but no more is it a discursive treatise in prose. It is a song of truth concerning three worlds.

And the Major Arcana of the Tarot? Are they not a call to the winged imagination, within a framework and in a direction proper to each of them? They are symbols. But what does one do with symbols if not apply the inspired imagination to them, directed towards their meaning via a will obedient to the laws of intrinsic coherence and in conformity with outward and inward—material and spiritual —facts of experience? Now, poetry is not simply a question of taste, but rather one of fertility (or sterility) of the spirit. Without a poetic vein there can be no access to the life of the Hermetic tradition.

Let us therefore love poetry and respect the poets. For it is not dukes, margraves and counts who constitute the true nobility of mankind, but rather the poets.

*From the collection *Les rayons et les ombres*, Paris, 1928, p. 19.

One is noble (in the sense of the "nobility of the heart") in so far as one is a poet at heart. And since every human soul is in principle a priest, a nobleman and a worker at one and the same time, let us not smother the nobility within us by an overestimation of practical aims or by a preoccupation with our salvation, but on the contrary let us ennoble our work and our religion by bringing in the breath of poetic inspiration. This will in no way adulterate the functions of priest and worker. The prophets of Israel were great poets, and the song of St. Paul concerning love (*caritas*) is a work of poetry which has yet to be surpassed. With respect to work, there is joy in it only in so far as it is elevated above the spirit of slavery by participating in the poetic élan of the "great human endeavour".

Be that as it may, we are bound to make a case concerning the problem of poetry under the title of the seventeenth Arcanum of the Tarot—the Arcanum of water above and beneath the firmament: the Arcanum of hope and continuity. For poetry is the union of the upper waters and the lower waters on the second day of creation. The poet is the point at which the separated waters meet and where the flow of hope and that of continuity converge.

It is when the circulation of the human blood, which bears continuity, and the radiation of hope, which is the blood of the spiritual world and of all the celestial hierarchies, meet, unite and begin to vibrate together that the poetic experience takes place. Poetic inspiration is the union of blood from above (hope) and blood below (continuity).

This is why it is necessary to be *incarnated*, i.e. to have the pulsation of warm earthly blood, in order to be able to create poetic works—and not only poetic works of subjective significance (*setrams*) but also those of objective significance (*mantrams*). It was necessary to be immersed in warm human blood, i.e. to be incarnated, and to rise above it by uniting with the luminous blood of heaven, i.e. with hope, in order that the Psalms of David, for example, could be born. It was not in heaven, but rather on earth, that the Psalms of David came to birth. And once born, they became an arsenal of magical mantrams not only on earth but also in heaven. Because the mantrams, i.e. magical formulae, of the Psalms are in use as such not only amongst beings with warm blood, i.e. human beings, but also amongst beings with luminous blood—entities from the celestial hierarchies.

Mantrams—formulae of magical significance in the three worlds—are born from the marriage of warmth and light: from earthly blood, the bearer of continuity, and from celestial blood, the bearer of hope.

On the other hand, every human word can become magical if it is sincere to the point of engaging the blood, and if at the same time it is filled by faith to the point of setting the luminous waters of hope from above in motion. The "great cry" uttered by Jesus Christ on the Cross when he gave up the spirit (cf. Matthew and Mark) was followed by trembling of the earth—". . .the curtain of the temple was torn in two, from top to bottom; and the earth shook, and the rocks were split; the tombs also were opened. . ." (Matthew xxvii, 51-52)—for this cry bore simultaneously the magic of the last drop of human blood shed and the whole ocean of the world's hope.

Therefore, it follows from the preceding that magical formulae are not invented — just as true poetry is not invented — but that they are *born* from blood and light. This is why one uses in sacred magic, as a rule, traditional formulae — and this not because they are ancient, but rather because they took birth in the above-indicated manner and they have proved themselves as such. This was well known to Martinez de Pasqually, for example. The rituals of his magical invocations consist only of traditional formulae, drawn above all from the Psalms — not because he was a practising Catholic but solely in view of their magical effectiveness (in the magic that he taught and practised).

Sacred magic differs from arbitary or personal magic — beyond the differences which we have stated in the third Letter — also in that it "makes use" of the agent of growth, whilst arbitrary magic works above all with the magical agent of electrical nature. Now, it is to these two agents that the following passage from the Sermon on the Mount relates:

> Again you have heard that it was said to the men of old: You shall not swear falsely, but shall perform to the Lord what you have sworn. But I say to you: Do not swear at all, either by heaven, for it is the throne of God, or by the earth, for it is his footstool, or by Jerusalem, for it is the city of the great King. And do not swear by your head, for you cannot make one hair white or black. Let what you say be simply "Yes" or "No"; anything more than this comes from evil. (Matthew v, 33-37)

For "to swear" includes all categories of magical acts designed to magically reinforce a simple promise or decision of the human will made within the limits of its competence, i.e. within the limits of "yes or no". The desire to go beyond these limits by evoking the aid of forces from beyond the precise circle of the will's competence, so as to render it more powerful by arranging to this end a dynamic mechanism that will serve it, necessarily makes appeal to the electrical forces of the serpent — or "evil". "To swear" is therefore a characteristic act representing the whole domain of arbitrary or personal magic, where it is a matter of rendering a personal will more powerful by reinforcing it through forces of an electric nature — flashing forth like lightning and acting through discharges — coming from beyond the will and submitting to its domination.

Now, the quoted passage says that reality is shielded from arbitrary human will — heaven and earth being assigned to God, Jerusalem being assigned to another individuality (that of "the great King"), and the head (one's own body) being reserved for the agent of growth, which is removed from human arbitrariness ("for you cannot make one hair white or black"). Heaven, earth, Jerusalem and the head are not only removed from human arbitrariness but also from that of the serpent—from the electrical force due to friction and conflict. It is not the magical agent which rules reality—heaven, earth, Jerusalem and the head—but rather another agent which serves only God and his servants ("the great King"). Now, this other agent—this agent removed from human arbitrariness and from the arbitrariness of the serpent—is what we have designated as the "agent of growth"; and it is this which is the agent of sacred or divine magic.

Here we have the whole problem of the difference between *magical phenomena* and *miracles*, between what personal or arbitrary magic realises and what sacred or divine magic accomplishes. Although this problem has been treated under the title of the third Major Arcanum of the Tarot, "The Empress", it is presented anew here, i.e. under the title of the seventeenth Arcanum, in a new and special aspect. For the problem of personal magic and divine magic was presented in the meditation on the third Arcanum above all from the aspect of the *author*, the source of the initiative of the magical operation—either personal or divine—whilst the same problem is presented now under the aspect of the *agent*, the active means of this operation.

Now, the agent of divine magic is essentially removed from the personal human will, whilst that of personal magic is not. It is the agent of growth which is used as "instrument" in divine magic; and it is therefore the dynamic means of *miracles*, if we understand by "miracle" the effect of the action of a force which is essentially and entirely removed from human personal will, but which is at the same time not indifferent towards the moral qualities of the aspirations of the human personal will—and can lend it a power of realisation higher than the forces of physical, biological, psychological and intellectual determinism, i.e. beyond natural, psychic and intellectual laws. Divine magic is therefore the moral consciousness which *invokes* the help of higher moral consciousness, which latter answers this invocation by setting in motion the agent of growth—the lower waters of the continuity of life and the higher waters of hope. And everywhere where hope and continuity act together in reply to the moral evocation of the human will, a miracle takes place. A miracle is the descent of hope, i.e. the "higher waters above the firmament", into the domain of continuity, i.e the "lower waters beneath the firmament", and it is the action of the two "waters" united.

Neither science nor personal or arbitrary magic can perform miracles. Only a series of "determinisms" (or "laws"), one against another, are set in play, e.g. wind moves the water, warmth moves the air, electricity produces warmth. Now, science supplies itself with mechanical movement by means of warmth and electricity. It effects the conversion of electricity into warmth and warmth into mechanical movement. In the "act of knowledge" science proceeds from the visible movement to its invisible causes, and in the "act of realisation" it proceeds from the invisible forces to their visible movement. The research thus pursued led to the discovery of nuclear energy. The electrons, protons, neutrons, etc., of nuclear atoms are invisible, but a nuclear explosion is certainly visible.

Here, therefore, is the circle of science: ascending from the visible to the in-

visible in theory, and descending from the invisible to the visible in practice. It
is the ancient symbol of the serpent which bites its tail:

Because this circle is closed—not in the sense of the circle's *dimension*, since it
can grow indefinitely, but rather in the sense that it is and always will be a *circle
without opening* (in contrast to the spiral, which is an "open circle"). The forces
of warmth, magnetism, electricity and nuclear forces are thus discovered—and
a series of other forces, more hidden and still more subtle, can be discovered—
but only *forces* are discovered, i.e. the causes of mechanical movement. It is in
that this circle is closed that it is why—without intervention from outside of it,
such as that of Teilhard de Chardin—it is a prison and captivity for the spirit.

What is true of natural science is also true of personal or arbitrary magic. The
latter proceeds exactly as the former—ascending in theory and descending in practice. Modern authors on magic are perfectly right in advancing the thesis that magic
is a science and that it has nothing to do with miracles as such:

> Magic is the study and practice of the control of Nature's secret
> forces. It is a science—pure, or dangerous—like all sciences...
> (Papus, *Traité méthodique de magie pratique*, Paris, 1970, p. v)

We have to add here only that this is true, and also that "Nature's secret forces"
are secret only for a limited time, notably until their discovery by natural science—
which simply discovers and renders controllable the "secret forces" of Nature one
after the other. It is therefore only a question of time until the pursuit of magic
and that of natural science coincide and become identical.

But, on the other hand, it is also true that the closed circle of science, which
is a prison and captivity for the spirit, applies also to personal magic. Magic, in
so far as it is a science—and it is one—has the same fate as science, i.e. captivity
in a closed circle. And when Papus says further on in the introduction to his *Traité
méthodique de magie pratique* that, "Magic, we could say, is the materialism of
the future knights of Christ..." (p. vi), he admits with this statement the fact
of the captivity of magic as such—in a closed circle of a single aspect of the world,
which he names "materialism". And he gives expression to his hope that in the
future there will be an intervention from beyond this closed circle by future magicians ("knights of Christ")...in other words, that future Teilhard de Chardins
will do for magic what he has done for science: that they will open the closed circle and transform it into a spiral.

When Louis Claude de Saint-Martin left the circle of disciples of Martinez de Pasqually, who were practising ceremonial magic, and abandoned the practice of this magic — without denying the effectiveness of its capacity for realisation — in order to embrace Jacob Boehme's kind of mysticism and gnosis, it was because he sensed that ceremonial magic is a closed circle, whilst he aspired to unlimited qualitative perfection, i.e. to God. For even if the supreme aim of the invocations of the ceremonial magic of Martinez de Pasqually had been realised, even if there had been success in the realisation of a "pass" at which the resurrected Jesus Christ would have appeared, it would have been a matter only of a "pass" with a phenomenal apparition rather than an immediate and certain revelation of the essence of Christ within the human soul. The circle of this type of magic, however sublime its aim may be, is *closed* in that it is always a matter of *apparitions* through "passes". But Saint-Martin had hunger and thirst for intuitive union — soul with soul, spirit with spirit — and nothing less than this could satisfy him. He says in his *Mon portrait historique et philosophique* ("My Philosophical and Historical Portrait"):

> There are people who are condemned to time. There are those who are condemned (or called) to eternity. I know someone of this latter kind; and when those who are condemned to time would wish to judge his eternity and govern him by the sceptre of their times, one may presume how they will treat him. (Louis Claude de Saint-Martin, *Mon portrait historique et philosophique, 1789-1803*, para. 1023, Paris, 1961, p. 411)

Being sentenced (or called) to eternity, Saint-Martin could not be content with that which is passing — including every "pass" realised by means of ceremonial magic. This is why he turned to the gnostic mysticism or mystical gnosis of Jacob Boehme.

> On the 9th day of the month of Brumaire (= November, 1800), I published my translation of Jacob Boehme's *L'Aurore naissante*. I felt in subsequently re-reading it at my leisure that this work is blessed by God and man, except for the whirlwind of the butterflies of this world, who will see nothing in it, or who will only make it the object of their criticism and sarcasm. (Louis Claude de Saint-Martin, *Mon portrait*, para. 1013, Paris, 1961, p. 408)

This is what he said concerning this book of Jacob Boehme, at the same time giving expression to his appreciation of Boehme's whole work: ". . .this work is blessed by God and man. . ." Elsewhere, concerning Boehme's work, he said:

> I would have been suffering and unhappy far too long if God had made known to me much sooner the things that he has acquainted me with now, thanks to the fruits born in me from

the fertile foundations of my friend B. (= Boehme). This is why
these maginificent gifts were deferred for so long. (Louis Claude
de Saint-Martin, *Mon portrait*, para. 902, Paris, 1961, p. 379)

Now, the "magnificent gifts" of which it is a matter here are not magical phenomena but rather revelations in the inner life of intuition and inspiration.

In returning to the problem of the difference between magical phenomena and
miracles, it should be said that the former fall under the heading of human scientific knowledge and power, whilst the latter fall under that of divine knowledge
and power—which means to say that conscious human participation in the miracles
of sacred magic begins with mysticism, proceeds to gnosis and results in miracles,
i.e. in practical sacred magic: *ex Deo, in Deo, per Deum* ("from God, in God,
through God"). It was the way *ex Deo, in Deo, per Deum* which was Saint-Martin's
inner vocation, and this is why he could not be content with the way *ex homine,
in homine, ad Deum* ("from man, in man, towards God")—the way of the most
noble kind of ceremonial magic of his time: that of the school of Martinez de
Pasqually. Saint-Martin, in leaving the closed circle of this school, nevertheless
remained grateful for the experience that he had had there and kept his veneration for the master of this school. He said of him:

If Martinez de Pasqually, who was the master for each one of
us, had wanted to know me, he would have led me in another
way than he did, and he would have made another person of
me, though, nevertheless, I have an inexpressible moral obligation to him, and I thank God every day for having allowed me
to participate—although only in a small measure—in the light
of this extraordinary man who, of all the people I know, has been
the only living person whom I could not have bypassed. (Louis
Claude de Saint-Martin, *Mon portrait*, para. 167, Paris, 1961,
p. 107)

It is thus that for Saint-Martin the circle of Martinez de Pasqually—a prison in
so far as being a closed circle—played the role of the first circle of a spiral. And
in having sought and found the way out, he could not see it otherwise than as
the first step of an "infinite spiral" in which he was engaged.

Having sought and found the way out, was the circle of ceremonial magic of
the school of Martinez de Pasqually therefore not closed, since Saint-Martin could
leave it?

The circle of ceremonial magic—just like that of science—*is* closed in principle, but every individual human soul can leave it by embracing a more elevated
ideal and by renouncing all the advantages that the circle offers him. This is an
important aspect of the meaning of the formula of Christ: "I am the door"—namely,
that there is an exit from every closed circle, from all captivity of the spirit. "I
am the door; if anyone enters by me, he will be saved, and will go in and out

and find pasture" (John x, 9), which means to say that if someone is moved by love of God and neighbour, he can enter each closed circle and he can leave it. Instead of prisons he will "find pasture", i.e. *he will move in a spiral*. It is thus, for example, that Teilhard de Chardin could enter the closed circle of science without being captured, and he could leave this circle by transforming it into a spiral. It is thus, also, that Saint-Martin could enter the closed circle of ceremonial magic without being captured by it, and he could also leave it by transforming it into a spiral.

The spiral: this is the "good news" (i.e. the "Gospel") to all those in captivity in closed circles. Jesus Christ said to Nathanael:

> Because I said to you, I saw you under the fig tree, do you believe? You shall see greater things than these. . .Truly, truly, I say to you, *you will see heaven opened, and the Angels of God ascending and descending upon the Son of man.* (John i, 50-51)

"Heaven opened"— it is the way of the spiral into the infinite which opens.

The spiral is the arcanum of growth — both spiritual and biological. A plant grows following the movement of a spiral; an idea, a problem, likewise grows following the movement of a spiral. Not only the branches of a tree are found arranged according to the spiral, but also the so-called "tree-ring" circles, which are formed each year between the bark and the centre of the trunk of the tree, constitute traces or effects of the operation of circular growth in two dimensions — vertical and horizontal — at the same time, i.e. proceeding in a spiral. With respect to ideas and problems, they grow in human consciousness through a series of expansions and contractions, i.e. through concentric circles, similar to tree-rings on the trunk of a tree, crossing in two directions — in breadth and height. Thus it was in 1919/20 that I was for the first time occupied with the Major Arcana of the Tarot under the four aspects comprising the divine name יהוה (YOD-HÉ-VAU-HÉ), which then were presented to me as a unity comprising Nature, man and heaven, or alchemy, ethical Hermeticism and astrology — united in theurgy. Now, after returning to this theme a number of times, the present meditations on the Tarot also deal with the four aspects which comprise the divine name יהוה, but they now already present themselves as the unity of mysticism, gnosis and sacred magic in Hermeticism. This is therefore an example of the growth of ideas and problems — taking place in a spiral in two dimensions.

Or, consider the history of the work of preparation for the coming of Christ. . . The Gospel according to Matthew summarises it in the guise of the genealogy of Jesus Christ which, in its turn, he summarises with a single phrase as follows:

> So all the generations from Abraham to David were fourteen generations, and from David to the deportation to Babylon fourteen generations, and from the deportation to Babylon to the Christ fourteen generations. (Matthew i, 17)

Here is the spiral of the history of the preparation for the coming of Christ—a spiral of three circles or "steps", each step being fourteen generations. The first circle or step of the spiral is that where the threefold imprint of the patriarchs Abraham, Isaac and Jacob—an imprint from above which corresponds to the sacrament of baptism in the name of the Father, Son and Holy Spirit—made possible the revelation on Mt. Sinai and the act of alliance that took place there, and resulted in the Law (Torah) becoming soul in a human personality: David. For it was in David that the commandments and ordinances of the Law—revealed with "thunders and lightnings, and a thick cloud upon the mountain . . . so that all the people trembled" (Exodus xix, 16)—became interiorised to the point of becoming love and conscience, the concern of a heart enamoured of their truth and beauty. The Law became soul in David; and this is why his transgressions, also, gave rise to the birth in the soul of a new force—that of inner penitence.

The first step of the spiral, the fourteen generations from Abraham to David, therefore corresponds to the process of interiorisation which takes place from the sacrament of *baptism* (the three patriarchs), through the sacrament of *confirmation* (the alliance of the Sinai desert), to the sacrament of *penance*. The second circle or step of the spiral, the fourteen generations from David to the deportation to Babylon, is the "school of David"—the school of inner penitence—which resulted in its outward aim, that of *expiation*, i.e. the deportation to Babylon. The third circle or step of the spiral, the fourteen generations from the deportation to Babylon to the Christ, corresponds to that which takes place spiritually between the last act of the sacrament of penance, i.e. *absolution*, and the sacrament of *holy communion* (the Eucharist)—that of the presence and reception of Christ.

John the Baptist "prepared the way of the Lord and made his paths straight" (Matthew iii, 3) by repeating—in abridged form—the entire history of the preparation of the coming of Christ, i.e. the way of penitence which was his "baptism by water". For the "son of David" was the "son of penitence" on his father's (Joseph's) side and the "son of innocence" on his mother's (Mary's) side. Jesus Christ could not come into another milieu than that of virginal innocence and innocence recovered through penitence. John the Baptist is therefore the one who—in the history of the world—accomplished the act of transition from penitence to communion; it is he who led by the hand the first penitent from the ancient world to the altar of grace of the new world. This moment of immense significance could not be more concisely described than in the Gospel according to John:

> The next day again John was standing with two of his disciples;
> and he looked at Jesus as he walked, and said: Behold, the Lamb
> of God! The two disciples heard him say this, and they followed
> Jesus. Jesus turned, and saw them following, and said to them:
> What do you seek? And they said to him: Master, where are you
> staying? He said to them: Come and see. They came and saw

where he was staying; and they stayed with him that day, for it was about the tenth hour. (John i, 35-39)

It was thus that John the Baptist transmitted the fruit of the world which had come to an end to the world which was beginning. If the three holy kings (magi) laid at the feet of the child Jesus the threefold quintessence of what the ancient world had achieved—gold, frankincense and myrrh—St. John the Baptist gave the Master a fourth gift: the pure heart which could see the Divine ("Behold, the Lamb of God"), of which the Master was to say: "Blessed are the pure in heart, for they shall see God" (Matthew v, 8).

Three times fourteen generations is therefore the spiral of the three steps of the way from Abraham to Christ, just as the ages of gold, frankincense and myrrh were the three steps of the spiral of mankind's spiritual way from the patriarchs of spirituality—the Rishis of ancient India—to the Christ. For the age of gold on this spiritual way, that of ancient India, was followed by the spiritual age of frankincense, that of ancient Iran, where the cosmic revelation of the Rishis became soul and an affair of the human heart; and the age of frankincense, in its turn, was followed by the age of myrrh—an age of mourning and penitence, of which ancient Egypt was the millennial-old torch . . . the ancient Egypt of which Hermes Trismegistus says in his treatise entitled *Asclepius*:

> Do you not know, Asclepius, that Egypt is an image of heaven, or, to speak more exactly, in Egypt all the operations of the powers which rule and work in heaven have been transferred to earth below? Nay, it should rather be said that the whole Cosmos dwells in this our land as in its sanctuary. And yet, since it is fitting that wise men should have knowledge of all events before they come to pass, you must not be left in ignorance of this: there will come a time when it will be seen that in vain have the Egyptians honoured the deity with heartfelt piety and assiduous service; and all our holy worship will be found bootless and ineffectual. For the gods will return from earth to heaven; Egypt will be forsaken, and the land which was once the home of religion will be left desolate, bereft of the presence of its deities. This land and region will be filled with foreigners . . . In that day will our most holy land, this land of shrines and temples, be filled with funerals and corpses . . . O Egypt, Egypt, of thy religion nothing will remain but an empty tale, which thine own children in time to come will not believe; nothing will be left but graven words, and only the stones will tell of thy piety. (*Asclepius* iii, 24b-25; trsl. W. Scott, *Hermetica*, vol. i, Oxford, 1924, pp. 341-343)

This is the voice of the embalmer, the sage of the wisdom of myrrh, who is familiar with death, with the laws of death—the voice of the Jeremiah of Egypt. And here is the voice of frankincense—that of the sage of the wisdom of frankincense—the voice of the psalmist of ancient Iran:

> We shall not, O Ahura Mazda! displease you and Asha (the Law) and Vahista Mananh (the Best Reason) who have been endeavouring in the gift of praises unto you...
> When I first conceived of Thee, O Mazda, in my mind—says Zarathustra—I sincerely regarded Thee as the First Actor in the universe, as the Father of Reason (Good Mind), as the true Originator of the Right Law (Righteousness), as the Governor over the actions of mankind...
> We praise the intelligence of Ahura Mazda, in order to grasp the holy word.
> We praise the wisdom of Ahura Mazda, in order to study the holy word.
> We praise the tongue of Ahura Mazda, in order to speak forth the holy word.
> We adore, every day and night, the mount Ushidarena, the Giver of Intelligence.
> (*Gathas* in R. P. Masani, *The Religion of the Good Life. Zoroastrianism*, London, 1938, pp. 52, 139)

And lastly the voice of a sage of the wisdom of gold, preaching cosmic humanism:

> The Purusha (Man) is this All,
>   that which was and which shall be.
> He is Lord of immortality,
>   which he grows beyond through (sacrificial) food...
> One fourth of him is all beings,
>   The three fourths of him is the immortal in heaven.
> Three fourths on high rose the Purusha,
>   One fourth of him arose again here (on the earth).
> Thence in all directions he spread abroad,
>   as that which eats and that which eats not.
> (*Rigveda* x, 90, 2-4)*

Here is the golden key to material and spiritual evolution, i.e. it is only the universal and transcendent human principle—the Adam Kadmon of the Cabbala, or the Purusha of the Vedas—who renders evolution intelligible.

The spiral of Israel's three steps, each of fourteen generations, and of the three steps of spirituality—those of gold, frankincense and myrrh—in the general history of mankind, thus constituted the preparation for the coming of Christ. Aren't

---

*Trsl. E. J. Thomas, *Vedic Hymns*, London, 1923, pp. 120-121.

the three weeks of Advent an abridgement of this preparation through millennia — the fourth week being their summary: the work of John the Baptist?

Be that as it may, it is the law of the spiral which occupies us here. For it is the spiral which characterises the action of the agent of growth which is the theme of the seventeenth Major Arcanum of the Tarot — whose Card shows us the relationship that there is between the stellar-, female-, fluidic- and growth-principles. There are stars in the sky, there is a naked woman who is pouring water from two vases, and there are two shrubs which are growing. It is the water which makes it possible for the shrubs to grow in the sandy desert; it is the woman who is pouring water; it is the stars, lastly, from whence the luminosity emanates which is transformed into fluidity through the woman as intermediary. The latter therefore transforms hope into the continuity of tradition and generations. It is thus that the shrubs are growing. The context of the Card therefore represents a spiral which descends from the stars (first step) to the woman (second step), then to the water (third step) and ends with the shrubs (the result, the fourth step).

The Card answers the question: What does a tree need to live? Stars, a woman, and water are needed — answers the Card. Indeed, what is required for mankind's evolution to continue? Hope, maternity and heredity are required.

What is essential in order that spiritual truth is not forgotten, and that it lives? Hope, true creativity and tradition are the essential factors. The corroborating testimony of *three* ever-present witnesses — spirit, blood and water — is necessary. True testimony through the spirit, through blood, and through water will never fall into forgetfulness. One can kill spiritual truth, but it will resurrect.

Now, the unity of hope, creativity and tradition is the agent of growth. It is the concerted action of spirit, blood and water. It is therefore *indestructible*; its action is *irreversible*; and its movement is *irresistible*. And it is the agent of growth which is, in the last analysis, the subject of the *Emerald Table* of Hermes Trismegistus.

"And as all things were by mediation of the One, so all things arose from this one thing by a single act of adaptation"— says the *Emerald Table* (*Tabula Smaragdina*, 3). Which amounts to saying: as the One is the creator of the *essence* of all things, thus there is a unique agent which adapts the *existence* of all things to their essence — the principle of the adaptation of that which is born to its created prototype. This is the agent of growth or the principle of *evolution*. It is engendered by the spontaneous light of hope (the sun) reflected in the movement of the lower waters (the moon), which produces the general impulse or "push" (the wind), which bears primordial hope towards its realisation in the material domain (the earth), which donates it with its constructive elements (i.e. nourishes or "nurses" it). Thus, the *Emerald Table* continues:

> The father thereof is the sun, the mother the moon; the wind carried it in its womb; the earth is the nurse thereof. (*Tabula Smaragdina*, 4)

The spontaneous light from above, the light reflected below, the impulse or push of evolution which results, and which uses material elements for its realisation — here is a complete analysis of the inner process of evolution and growth. It is a matter here of an agent which constantly *adapts* existence to essence — the agent of growth that the *Emerald Table* refers to with the term *thelema*:

> It is the father of all works of wonder (*thelema*) throughout the whole world. (*Tabula Smaragdina*, 5)

Now, the word *thelemos* (θέλημος) signifies in Greek, in poetic language, "voluntary, spontaneous", and the words *thelema* (τὸ θέλημα) and *thelesis* (ἡ θέλησις) signify in the language of the New Testament "desire" and "will". Therefore the author of the *Emerald Table* wants to explain the nature of the volitional and spontaneous impulse of the world in transformation and — as we say today — in evolution. He wants to reveal to us the origin and the constituent factors of the transforming agent of "transformism", the active agent underlying evolution. This agent is described in the sixteenth treatise of the *Corpus Hermeticum*, "An epistle of Asclepius to King Ammon":

> . . .with the light which is shed downward, and illuminates all the sphere of water, earth, and air, he puts life into the things in this region of the Cosmos (including the earth), and stirs them up to birth, and by successive changes (metamorphoses) remakes the living creatures and transforms them (one into the other in the manner of a spiral — ἕλικος τρόπον *helikos tropon* — the changing of the one into the other operating a continual change from type to type — γένη γενῶν, *gene genon* — and from species to species — εἴδη εἰδῶν, *eide eidon*). . . ("Asclepius to King Ammon", *Corpus Hermeticum* xvi, 8-9; trsl. W. Scott, *Hermetica*, vol. i, Oxford, 1924, pp. 267-269; the latter part of the translation, in brackets, is from the French translation of the *Corpus Hermeticum* by A. J. Festugière, vol. ii, Paris, 1945, p. 235)

Thus, this agent acts "in the manner of a spiral" between earth and heaven. For if one separates *thelema* (immanent desire in the depths of matter) from its material envelope, "it doth ascend from earth to heaven, and again it doth descend to earth, and uniteth in itself the force from things superior and things inferior" (*Tabula Smaragdina*, 8) — in the manner of a spiral which ascends and descends.

You see, therefore, dear Unknown Friend, that "transformism", the doctrine of evolution rediscovered by nineteenth-century science, was not only known as a fact in the Hermeticism of the Hellenistic epoch, but was also the subject of a profound philosophy which was occupied with the agent of "transformism" working "a continual change from type to type and from species to species" and transforming them "in the manner of a spiral" (*Corpus Hermeticum* xvi, 9).

Heliocentricity, also, was known in the Hermeticism of this epoch—at least thirteen or fourteen centuries before its rediscovery—as is evident from the above-cited Hermetic treatise:

> ...for he (the sun) is stationed in the midst (of the Cosmos), and wears the Cosmos as a wreath (crown) around him (μέσος γὰρ ἱδρύται στεφανωφορωητὸν κόσμον). And so he lets the Cosmos go on its course, not leaving it far separated from himself; for like a skilled driver, he has made fast and bound to himself the chariot of the Cosmos, lest it should rush away in disorder. ("Asclepius to King Ammon", *Corpus Hermeticum* xvi, 7; trsl. W. Scott, *Hermetica*, vol. i, Oxford, 1924, p. 267)

Could a more precise statement of the heliocentric solar system be given?

Now, the Hermeticists of antiquity knew the fact of evolution ("transformism") and they sought the active agent of "transformism", i.e. *thelema*—this volitional and spontaneous impulse working in the very depths of matter. And the *Emerald Table* of Hermes Trismegistus is the legacy given by them for posterity: it contains a summary of what they had found. It is a testament of the ancient world to the modern world, through which a gift is made to the latter of what the former had achieved—or, at least, what they believed they had achieved.

> ...it will separate the element of earth from that of fire, the subtle from the gross, gently and with great sagacity. It doth ascend from earth to heaven; again it doth descend to earth, and uniteth in itself the force from things superior and things inferior. Thus thou wilt possess the glory of the brightness of the whole world, and all obscurity will fly far from thee. This thing is the strongest of all powers, the force of all forces, for it overcometh every subtle thing and doth penetrate every solid substance. Thus was the world created. Hence there will be marvellous adaptations achieved, of which the manner is this. For this reason I am called Hermes Trismegistus, because I hold three parts of the wisdom of the world. That which I had to say about the operation of *sol* is (accomplished and) completed. (*Tabula Smaragdina*, 7-13; trsl. R. Steele and D. Singer, *Proceedings of the Royal Society of Medicine* xxi (1928), p. 42)

"Accomplished and completed" concludes this testament of antiquity. Is it foolish pretension, naive arrogance, pious illusion or an establishment of fact? It is a matter of conscience and experience to be answered by each individually.

Personally, I side with those who see here an establishment of fact—notably an establishment of fact concerning the agent of growth, which is "the strongest of all powers, the force of all forces" moving "every subtle thing" and penetrating "every solid substance".

The theme of the agent of growth has already been treated in these Letters, notably in the Letter on the third Arcanum and in that on the eleventh Arcanum of the Tarot. We cannot avoid the law of the spiral, which "rules" not only the totality of the series of Major Arcana of the Tarot but also the endeavours and the progress in consciousness of he who meditates on them. We have had to return to this theme for a third time in the present Letter, which thus represents the third step of the spiral—to continue to infinity—concerning the theme of growth and evolution.

The *Emerald Table* is a concise summary of what the ancient world had to say on the subject of the agent of growth and evolution. The Major Arcana of the Tarot are a summary, developed into a school or practical "system" of spiritual exercises, of what the mediaeval world had to say on the subject of this agent—as the fruit of its meditations on the *Emerald Table* and of its own efforts and spiritual experiences. In our time, therefore, it is a matter of the task of effecting the third step of the evolutionary spiral of the Hermetic tradition—the third "renaissance" on the subject of the *Emerald Table*. Our time makes appeal to the collective endeavour of Hermeticists of today to make a *third* summary, which will be for our time what the Tarot was for the Middle Ages and what the *Emerald Table* was for antiquity. Thus, just as the *Emerald Table* saved the essence of ancient wisdom, and just as the Tarot saved the essence of mediaeval wisdom, across the deluges which occurred in the time that separates us from them, may the essence of *modern wisdom* be saved in a spiritual "Noah's ark" from the deluge which is going to come, and may it thereby be transmitted to the future, just as the essence of ancient wisdom and that of mediaeval wisdom has been transmitted to us by means of the *Emerald Table* and the Major Arcana of the Tarot. The tradition of Hermeticism blossomed in the past and must live in the future. This is why a new, modern summary is required, which will be as viable as the *Emerald Table* and as the Major Arcana of the Tarot.

This is the message of the woman kneeling under the stars on the bank of a current which flows from the past into the future—a woman who never ceases to pour water from above into the flow of water below. It is she who is the mother of the future, and this is why her message confronts us with duty towards the future—the duty towards the flow of uninterrupted tradition. Let us therefore try to comply with this!

Meditation on the
Eighteenth Major Arcanum of the Tarot

THE MOON
LA LUNE

God forbade Lot and his family *to look back*:
but Lot's wife behind him looked back,
and she became a pillar of salt.

(Genesis xix, 26)

David's heart smote him
after he had numbered the people.
And David said to the Lord,
"I have sinned greatly in what I have done.". . .
So the Lord sent a pestilence upon Israel.

(II Samuel xxiv, 10, 15)

Our intelligence, as it leaves the hands of Nature,
has for its chief object the unorganised solid. . .
Of the discontinuous alone
does the intellect form a clear idea. . .
Of immobility alone
does the intellect form a clear idea. . .
The intellect lets what is *new*
in each moment of history escape.
It does not admit the unforeseeable.
It rejects all creation. . .
The intellect is characterised by
a natural inability to comprehend life. . .
But it is to the very inwardness of life
that *intuition* leads us—
by intuition I mean instinct
that has become disinterested,
self-conscious, capable of reflecting upon its object
and of enlarging it indefinitely.

(Henri Bergson)*

LETTER XVIII

THE MOON

Dear Unknown Friend,

The prohibition to Lot and his family against looking back, David's sin in having numbered the people of Israel, and the characteristic traits of human intelligence (as opposed to intuition) formulated by Henri Bergson, have this in common that they relate to the problem of the *inversion* of the forward movement of life, i.e. they relate to the problem of *retrograde movement*. Now, it is the problem of retrograde movement, contrary to that of life, which is suggested spontaneously by the Card of the eighteenth Major Arcanum of the Tarot—"The

Creative Evolution, ttsl. A. Mitchell, London, 1964, pp. 162-164, 174, 186.

494 MEDITATIONS ON THE TAROT

Moon". It is the antithesis of the seventeenth Arcanum "The Star". For if the latter evokes ideas, feelings and impulses of will relating to the evolution of life and
consciousness, concerning their infinite *development*, the former evokes ideas,
feelings and impulses of will relating to the *inversion* of the evolutionary movement of life and consciousness, i.e. to their *envelopment*, arrest of movement,
and retrograde movement. Instead of the current which flows and the verdant
shrubs of the Card of the seventeenth Arcanum, we find the stagnant water of
a swamp and two rigid stone towers in the Card of the eighteenth Arcanum. Instead of the naked woman who makes the current (which continues in its flow)
emanate from the two vases, we find an image of the most enveloped or shielded
creature — the crayfish — at the bottom of the swampy basin, and two dogs (or a
dog and a wolf) which are baying at the moon above. Lastly, instead of the radiant constellation of eight stars, we find the darkness of a total eclipse of the moon.

Through the totality of the context of its Card, the eighteenth Arcanum of the
Tarot invites us to a spiritual exercise — to a meditation on that which arrests evolutionary movement and tends to give it a direction in an inverse sense. And just
as the dominant and principal theme of the seventeenth Arcanum is the agent
of growth, so is it a matter in the eighteenth Arcanum of the special *agent of
diminution* — the principle of the eclipse. In the case of the eighteenth Arcanum
it is a matter neither of temptation from outside, which is the subject of the sixth
Arcanum, nor of the devil and demons — the intoxicating and enslaving forces —
which constitute the subject of the fifteenth Arcanum, nor even of the presumptuous tendency to build "towers of Babel", which is the subject of the sixteenth
Arcanum, but rather of something which is there, which is given and imposed
on every incarnated human soul by the very fact of being incarnated, i.e. which
the fate of being incarnated entails with necessity. The principle of the eclipse
or the "agent of diminution" would be present and active in us even if the devil
and all demons resigned, and even if all human beings learnt the lesson of humility
and abandoned the desire to build "towers of Babel".

The eighteenth Arcanum of the Tarot is the *arcanum* of the twofold current
that Henri Bergson designates as "intelligence — matter" or "materialistic intellectuality", contrary to the twofold current "duration — spirit" or "intuition —
conscience". For the current "intellectuality — materiality" that Bergson portrays
like no other thinker is precisely this "agent of diminution" or "eclipse principle"
that is suggested by the context of the Card of the eighteenth Arcanum. Because
the moon is the principle of *reflection*: just as it reflects the light of the sun, so
does human intelligence reflect the creative light of conscience — and the latter
is eclipsed when "materialistic intellectuality" prevails. Just as man's will to master
Nature sets "materialistic intellectuality" in motion and prescribes it the "rules
of the game" for its work, so is the moon of the eighteenth Arcanum in eclipse,
i.e. it is only fringed by rays of reflected sunlight, whilst the surface of the moon
itself reflects only the image of a human face in profile. Further, just as the crayfish
moves backwards in swimming, so does human intelligence move backwards, i.e.

in the direction "effect—cause", when it is engaged in the act of knowledge that is proper to it. The other details of this Card—the coloured drops which are *falling upwards*, the two towers, the two dogs which are baying, the stagnant water of the swamp—only make more specific, as we shall see through the following meditation on the central theme of this Arcanum, further aspects of the current "intellectuality—materiality" that is contrary to the current of creative evolution or "duration—spirit".

The sun, moon and stars are—according to Genesis—lights "in the firmament of the heavens to give light upon the earth" (Genesis i, 16-17), whose creation constituted the fourth day of the creation of the world.

Now, human consciousness is the field where *three* kinds of light are manifest: *creative* light, *reflected* light and *revealed* light. The first participates in the work of the creation of the world such as it has continued since the sixth day of creation, which we now call "creative evolution"; the second illumines the dark field of action of the human will, which we now call "matter"; the last orientates us towards transcendent values and truths which constitute, as it were, the supreme court of appeal, the ultimate criterion, of all that is of worth and of all that is true in space and time. It is thanks to these three types of light that man is at one and the same time a creator participating in creative evolution, a master of matter—author of the work of civilisation—and that he is a kneeling worshipper of God, capable of orientating his will towards the divine will. Creative consciousness, reflecting intelligence, and revelation from above are the three lights of the human microcosm—its "sun", "moon" and "stars".

The three Major Arcana of the Tarot—"The Star", "The Moon" and "The Sun" are those of light revealed from above, reflecting intelligence and creative consciousness. We were occupied with the stellar Arcanum in the last Letter. In the following Letter we shall be occupied with the solar Arcanum. In this Letter, it is a matter of the lunar Arcanum, i.e. the Arcanum of the inseparable couple—the earth and its satellite (the moon)—or, for the microcosm, materiality and intelligence. It should be formally pointed out that the eighteenth Arcanum of the Tarot reveals the *relationship* between the moon and the earth; it deals with the couple "moon—earth" as such—just as, for example, Henri Bergson deals with the couple "intelligence—matter" as such. For materiality (i.e. the material and mechanical aspect of the world) is to intelligence (i.e. to the faculty of consciousness which proceeds from effects to causes by induction and deduction) as the earth is to the moon. Intelligence is attuned to matter, and the latter is attuned to intelligence by lending itself easily to analysis and synthesis. Matter thus adapts itself to intelligence, and the latter "is characterised by the unlimited power of decomposing according to any law and of recomposing into any system" (Henri Bergson, *Creative Evolution*; trsl. A. Mitchell, London, 1964, p. 165). They constitute an inseparable couple.

Imagine what the state of intelligence would be if it were deprived of the environment of the material world, where there is the "unlimited power of decomposing according to any law and of recomposing into any system". Not only would it be incapable of separating out particular things from their enduring totality and grouping them into categories and classes, but also it would be powerless to manufacture the implements and machines which it makes use of to supplement the organs of action and perception with which Nature has endowed the human being.

The divisibility and malleability of inorganic matter (or matter *rendered* inorganic) are as indispensable to intelligence as water is to a fish which swims, or as the air is to a bird which flies. They constitute its vital element.

> The essential function of our intellect, as the evolution of life has fashioned it, is to be a light for our conduct, to make ready for our action on things, to foresee, for a given situation, the events, favourable or unfavourable, which may follow thereupon. Intellect therefore instinctively selects in a given situation whatever is like something already known; it seeks this out, in order that it may apply its principle that "like produces like". In just this does the prevision of the future by common sense consist. Science carries this faculty to the highest possible degree of exactitude and precision, but does not alter its essential character. Like ordinary knowledge, in dealing with things science is concerned only with the aspect of *repetition*. Though the whole be original, science will always manage to analyse it into elements or aspects which are approximately a reproduction of the past. Science can work only on what is supposed to repeat itself. . . Anything that is irreducible and irreversible in the successive moments of history eludes science. (Henri Bergson, *Creative Evolution*; trsl. A. Mitchell, London, 1964, p. 31)

At the same time there is reason to point out that the aspect of the *repetition* of things that intelligence seeks in the first place corresponds to the almost innate inclination of intelligence to reduce movement to immobility and to transform time into space. "Repetition" is only the immobile element in movement and the *spatial* element in time. When, for example, we speak of the yearly cycle of seasons, we turn the movement of time into space; we replace movement by the representation of a *circle* in space. And this circle signifies the stable *repetition* of the course of the seasons; springtime—summer—autumn—winter—springtime, etc.

No one has stated this postulate of intelligence—i.e. repetition, and the consequent transformation of time into space—with more force than Solomon, who says in Ecclesiastes:

> What has been is what will be, and what has been done is what will be done; and there is nothing new under the sun. Is there a thing of which it is said: See, this is new? It has been already,

LETTER XVIII THE MOON   497

in the ages before us. There is no remembrance of former things,
nor will there be any remembrance of later things yet to happen among those who come after. (Ecclesiastes i, 9-11)

Clearly, it is a matter here of a *postulate* — a dogma of faith for intelligence —
because the statement by Solomon surpasses the limits of experience by affirming that something which arises as new in the field of immediate experience *must*
be the repetition of something old, fallen into forgetfulness, and that it is only
ignorance due to the forgetfulness of the past which makes it appear as new, and
that it will be just the same in the future, i.e. everything that will be judged as
new will be thanks only to forgetfulness of what happens in the present. Time
creates nothing; it only combines and recombines that which is *given* for ever in
space. Time is like the wind, and space is like the sea; the wind produces waves
in infinite repetition on the surface of the sea, but the sea remains the same; it
does not change at all. Therefore there is nothing — and *there cannot be* anything
— new under the sun.

This is the postulate of intelligence, advanced some three thousand years ago,
which is still accepted and which underlies the way that intelligence works. And
here is its antithesis, formulated by Bergson:

> The universe endures. The more we study the nature of time,
> the more we shall comprehend that duration means invention,
> the creation of forms, the continual elaboration of the absolutely
> new. (Henri Bergson, *Creative Evolution*; trsl. A. Mitchell, Lon-
> don, 1964, p. 11)

We shall return later to the Bergsonian — and Hermetic — antithesis, when the
necessity for it will be blindingly apparent as the natural reply to this postulate
of intelligence, and when it will present itself to the mind as, so to say, the "com-
plementary colour" to the Arcanum "The Moon". For the Arcanum "The Moon",
in so far as it is a spiritual exercise, has no other aim than to evoke the conscious
desire to go further than intelligence, and to decide to make a "leap" in order
to leave its sphere.

But let us return to the pair "intelligence — matter" or "intellectuality —
materiality":

> ...the intellect aims, first of all, at constructing. This fabrica-
> tion is exercised exclusively on inert matter, in this sense, that
> even if it makes use of organised material, it treats it as inert,
> without troubling about the life which animated it. And of in-
> ert matter itself, fabrication deals only with the solid; the rest
> escapes by its very fluidity. If, therefore, the tendency of the in-
> tellect is to fabricate, we may expect to find that whatever is fluid
> in the real will escape it in part, and whatever is life in the liv-

ing will escape it altogether. Our intelligence, as it leaves the
hands of Nature, has for its chief object the unorganised solid.
(Henri Bergson, *Creative Evolution*; trsl. A. Mitchell, London,
1964, pp. 161-162)

Thus the axiom of intelligence that *the whole is greater than the part* is valid wholly
and without reserve when it is a matter of a solid body or a liquid measure (i.e.
when fluid is rendered similar to a solid body). Half a stone is evidently smaller
than the whole stone, and half a glass of water indicates less water than a whole
glass. But this axiom is not valid unreservedly when it is a matter of the functions
of a living organism. You can certainly have a leg cut off, which is many times
larger than the heart of the human body, without death ensuing, but you cannot
do without the heart, without dying. The *function* of the heart is more essential
to the life of the whole human organism than the leg, although the heart is very
much smaller than the leg. Thus, with respect to a living organism, the axiom
in question has to be modified—in the sense that, from the point of view of *functioning*, the functioning parts and the functioning whole can be *equal*. Therefore,
so far as the functioning of a living organism is concerned, one could bowl over
the bourgeois logician with the formula: *the whole can be equal to the part*.

The same axiom, applied to the *moral domain*, should undergo still further
an active modification. In the domain of pure values the axiom in question changes
its form and becomes transformed into its contrary. Indeed, Caiaphas' argument
in favour of a decision against Jesus, advanced to the assembly of the Sanhedrin,
"that it is expedient for you that one man should die for the people, and that
the whole nation should not perish" (John xi, 50), is evidently simply an appeal
to the logical axiom that the *whole* (the nation) *is greater* (is of higher value) *than
the part* (a single man). But the whole Jewish nation had no other reason for existence than part of it—the Messiah! Still more: Is the Word—through which all
things were made and outside of which nothing has come into existence, and which
became flesh (cf. John i, 3, 14)—a part or is it the whole of the Jewish nation
...mankind...lastly, the whole world?

Or again, take the parable of the lost sheep, where the Master says:

> If a man has a hundred sheep, and one of them has gone astray,
> does he not leave the ninety-nine on the hills and go in search
> of the one that went astray? And if he finds it, truly, I say to
> you, he rejoices over it more than over the ninety-nine that never
> went astray. (Matthew xviii, 12-13)

Is the axiom that the whole is greater than the part still valid in the domain of
moral *values*?

Or again, take the parables concerning the treasure hidden in a field, the pearl
of great price, and the lesson of the poor widow's two copper coins: Is it not evi-

dent from them that for the world of values the axiom in question should be *the part can be greater than the whole*?

These conclusions at which one arrives when one applies logic to the organic and moral spheres are shocking for intelligence, whose rules of logic are in accordance with inorganic solidity.

David's great sin — in ordering that the people of Israel be numbered (cf. II Samuel xxiv, 2) — consisted in the application of the method proper to human intelligence of reducing the living and moral to inorganic solidity, i.e. men to *things*: the living and moral (the community of Israel) to number. In giving the order to count the people of Israel, David committed the sin, in the spiritual domain, of having reduced living and feeling human beings to dead and inanimate things, i.e. to *corpses*. Thus he sinned against the commandment: Thou shalt not kill.

And it was not only during the darkest time of the year — when the nights are at their longest — but it was also under the sign of virgin intelligence eclipsed by human terrestrial intelligence that the nativity of Jesus Christ took place. For it took place at the time of an enrolment of the whole world: "In those days a decree went out from Caesar Augustus that all the world should be enrolled...when Quirinius was governor of Syria" (Luke ii, 1-2). It was a time when the sin of David was repeated, but on the scale of the Roman Empire — over "all the world". Then, Caesar Augustus decreed that all living and feeling human beings, including the incarnated Word, be treated as inanimate things. It was winter time as far as the sun is concerned...and the time of an eclipse of the moon as far as intelligence is concerned.

Our intelligence is only at ease, it is only entirely at home, when it is at work on raw matter, and in particular on solid objects:

> What is the most general property of the material world? It is extended: it presents to us objects external to other objects, and, in these objects, parts external to parts. No doubt, it is useful to us, in view of our ulterior manipulation, to regard each object as divisible into parts arbitrarily cut up, each part being again divisible as we like, and so on *ad infinitum*...To this possibility of decomposing matter as much as we please, and in any way we please, we allude when we speak of the continuity of material extension; but this continuity, as we see it, is nothing else but our ability, an ability that matter allows us to choose the mode of discontinuity we shall find in it. It is always, in fact, the mode of discontinuity once chosen that appears to us as the actually real one and that which fixes our attention, just because it rules our action. Thus discontinuity is thought for itself; it is thinkable in itself; we form an idea of it by a positive act of mind; while the intellectual representation of continuity is negative, being, at bottom, only the refusal of our mind, before any actually given

system of decomposition, to regard it as the only possible one. *Of the discontinuous alone does the intellect form a clear idea*. (Henri Bergson, *Creative Evolution*; trsl. A. Mitchell, London, 1964, pp. 162-163)

For this reason not only science decomposes, e.g. objects into chemical substances, the latter into molecules, molecules into atoms, and atoms into electrons, but also occult science (which would like to equal official science) decomposes. For example, the human being is decomposed into *three* principles — spirit, soul, and body — when it is a matter of the place that man occupies between God and Nature; or into *four* principles — physical body, vital body, astral body, and ego (self) — when it is a matter of the practical task of mastership by the operant of his "instruments", as is the case in Raja-yoga; or even into *seven* principles — physical body, etheric body, astral body, lower self, reason, intuition, and higher Self — when it is a matter of the evolution of the human being in time; or lastly into *nine* principles — three corporeal principles, three soul principles, and three spiritual principles — when it is a matter of the relationship between microcosm and macrocosm, with its nine spiritual hierarchies, which reflect, in their turn, the divine Holy Trinity. If we add here also that Christian theology divides man into only *two* principles — body and soul — that the Vedanta and the Cabbala divide him into *five* principles — for the Cabbala these are *basar*, *nephesh*, *neshamah*, *hayah*, and *yehidah* — that Cabbalists also divide man into *ten* principles, according to the ten Sephiroth, and that certain astrologers divide him into *twelve* principles, according to the twelve signs of the zodiac, it becomes evident that man easily allows himself diverse modes of decomposition, according to the aims of the intelligence which applies them. But he admits of this operation only in so far as he is given over to the manipulations of intelligence which treat him in the way proper to it, i.e. which decompose him according to a system corresponding in the best possible way to the ends that the will is aiming at. Because intelligence — *even when it is engaged in occult science* — clearly represents to itself only the discontinuous.

For this reason intelligence represents *motion* to itself as if it were discontinuous. It reconstructs motion by means of a motionless series that it places side by side, i.e. it makes the motion stop a desired number of times, obtaining in this way a cinematographic film, that it then makes roll:

Suffice it now to say that to the stable and immobile our intellect is attached by virtue of its natural disposition. *Of immobility alone does the intellect form a clear idea*. (Henri Bergson, *Creative Evolution*; trsl. A. Mitchell, London, 1964, p. 164)

The Greek philosopher Zeno of Elea (fifth century B.C.), author of the celebrated arguments concerning the "flying arrow" and "Achilles and the tortoise", who lived twenty-four centuries before cinematography, even denied the reality of motion for the reason that intelligence can represent only a succession of static positions in movement. Just as Solomon proclaimed, three thousand years ago, the postulate of intelligence "that there is nothing new under the sun", so did Zeno proclaim, twenty-four centuries ago, the other postulate of intelligence "that there is no continuous movement, there are only successive points of rest".

Intelligence is attached above all to *positions* of movement and not to the *progress* through which it passes from one position to another—progress which is movement itself:

> From mobility itself our intellect turns aside, because it has nothing to gain in dealing with it. If the intellect were meant for pure theorising, it would take its place within movement, for movement is reality itself, and immobility is always only apparent or relative. But the intellect is meant for something altogether different. Unless it does violence to itself, it takes the opposite course; it always starts from immobility, as if this were the ultimate reality... (Henri Bergson, *Creative Evolution*; trsl. A. Mitchell, London, 1964, p. 163)

Intelligence concentrates only on the *harvest*, i.e. on the *product*, and not on the *production*—which is, for it, only the means, a series of steps, for arriving at the product. It is always the *result* to which it aspires. It is always the "autumn" of things and events which it has in view. It is orientated towards facts—accomplished things—and not towards the process of creation, or that of becoming. The "springtime" and the "summer" of things and events either escape it or are taken into account only under the aspect of "autumn"—as its stages of preparation. Germination and growth are then considered only in relation to the harvest. Mobility coming into being—this is germination and growth; whilst the harvest is what is "become"—it is the product.

Quite other than the principle underlying intelligence—the principle of autumn—is that underlying the *intuition of faith*:

> In the beginning was the Word, and the Word was with God, and the Word was God. He was in the beginning with God; all things were made through him, and nothing that was made was made without him. In him was life, and the life was the light of men. (John i, 1-4)

The Gospel according to John advances here the principle of the intuition of faith, *the principle of springtime*. It is the *beginning*, the springtime of things of the world, to which the Gospel of St. John aspires, and it is the creative Word—the mobility itself at the heart of life and underlying the light of consciousness—

that it advances as the point of departure for all that follows. The Gospel of St. John invites us from the outset to an unparalleled act of violence to our intelligence—in transposing from autumn, where it is at home, to full springtime; from the harvest to the sowing; from things made to the creative Word; from vivified things to Life itself; from illumined things to Light itself.

We shall occupy ourselves in more detail with *creative intuition*—or the mystery of faith—in the Letter on the nineteenth Arcanum of the Tarot, "The Sun", which is the Arcanum of springtime. Here it is a matter simply of portraying more clearly the lunar (autumnal) principle of intelligence by means of contrasting the principle of creative intuition—such as it is stated in the first chapter of the Gospel of St. John—with the principle of intelligence, which is the theme of the eighteenth Arcanum of the Tarot.

Now, the Gospel of St. John appeals to the human soul to transpose its intelligence from autumn into full springtime—to rejuvenate it by placing it in the domain of creativity instead of that of the created, i.e. to accomplish a "conjunction" of the sun and moon, expressing it in astrological terms. This means to say that, if the postulate of intelligence is "that there is nothing new under the sun", it is invited to adapt itself to the pure and simple creativity expressed in the formula "in the beginning was the Word"; that if intelligence represents clearly to itself only immobility, it is bidden to plunge itself into the act of pure creation of the Word; that if intelligence represents clearly to itself only discontinuity, it finds itself confronted with the Word, in which is the life which is the light of men; that if intelligence has for its principal object inorganic solidity, it now has the task of understanding both the whole world as the organisatory act of the Word and Jesus Christ as the cosmic Word made flesh; that if, lastly, intelligence is characterised by a natural incomprehension of life, it has now to understand the Word at the heart of life, and the life underlying the light of consciousness. And all this it will do not in order to *understand*—i.e. in order to reap *that which is*—but rather in order to effect an act of becoming, in order to accomplish the birth of the new, i.e. of *that which is not*. Because "to all who received him, who believed in his name, he gave power to become children of God, who were born, not of blood nor of the will of the flesh nor of the will of man, but of God" (John i, 12-13).

Here is the difference between the nature of intelligence and that of intuition of faith, between the principle of autumn and that of spring. The former is *understanding of that which is*; the latter is *participation in the becoming of that which is to be*. When Abraham left Ur and went to a strange country by way of the desert in order to give birth to a people of the future—some centuries after him—he acted as a *man of the springtime*, or a man of faith. When Solomon, in the treatise known under the title "Ecclesiastes", summarised all that he had learnt during his life through experience and reflection, he acted as a *man of autumn*, a man of intelligence. Abraham was a "sower"; Solomon was a "reaper".

In so far as Hermeticism is concerned, it has a history of continuous and sustained effort aimed at an alliance of intelligence and the intuition of faith—the alchemical marriage of the moon and the sun. Is this marriage possible? St. Thomas

Aquinas, Henri Bergson and Pierre Teilhard de Chardin, amongst others, say *yes* — each in his own way. I have chosen these three names because they represent theology, philosophy and science. No doubt it is encouraging that these eminent representatives of religion, philosophy and science lend their assistance to our task, but if this were not so would we be able to aspire to anything else? Would we be able to abandon the millennial-old work and effort aimed at alliance — at the marriage and union of intelligence and faith? No, because whether we like it or not, we are engaged on this way for ever — even if it were a matter only of a mirage.

I say "even if it were a matter only of a mirage" because this alliance, this marriage, this union, has inspired (and still inspires) a continuous and sustained effort through the millennia, but this effort has never — as far as I know — been crowned with complete success. Intelligence and the intuition of faith sometimes approach quite near; they sometimes collaborate as allies; they sometimes complement one another in a way to give rise to the highest hope; but their true *fusion*, their complete and lasting alchemical marriage, is still not achieved. In the minds and hearts of certain workers at this great work, intelligence and the intuition of faith already act as an *engaged* couple, but not yet as a married couple. There has as yet been no complete success in obtaining the *alloy* of these two metals. It is always either silvered gold or gilded silver.

With Thomas Aquinas, for example, it is silvered gold; with most occultist-authors it is gilded silver. Origenes, Dionysius the Areopagite, Jacob Boehme, Louis Claude de Saint-Martin, Vladimir Soloviev and Nicolas Berdyaev, for example, show in their works a progress which is very advanced in *substantially* bringing together intelligence and the intuition of faith. The same could be said for Henri Bergson and Pierre Teilhard de Chardin.

Here is the endeavour that Henri Bergson proposes to us in the direction of a fusion of intelligence and intuition. After having ascertained that "the intellect is characterised by a natural inability to comprehend life", Bergson illumines the nature of *instinct*:

> Instinct, on the contrary, is moulded on the very form of life. While intelligence treats everything mechanically, instinct proceeds, so to speak, organically. If the consciousness that slumbers in it should awake, if it were wound up into knowledge instead of being wound off into action, if we could ask and it could reply, it would give to us the most intimate secrets of life... (trsl., p. 174).
>
> ...instinct and intelligence are two divergent developments of one and the same principle, which in the one case remains within itself, in the other steps out of itself and becomes absorbed in the utilisation of inert matter... (trsl., p. 177).
>
> A very significant fact is the swing to-and-fro of scientific theories of instinct, from regarding it as *intelligent* to regarding it as simply *intelligible*, or, shall I say, between likening it to an in-

telligence "lapsed" and reducing it to a pure mechanism. Each of these systems of explanation triumphs in its criticism of the other, the first when it shows us that instinct cannot be a mere reflex, the other when it declares that instinct is something different from intelligence, even fallen into unconsciousness... The concrete explanation, no longer scientific, but metaphysical (or Hermetic*), must be sought along quite another path, not in the direction of intelligence, but in that of "sympathy". Instinct is sympathy. If this sympathy could extend its object and also reflect upon itself, it would give us the key to vital operations—just as intelligence, developed and disciplined, guides us into matter. For—we cannot too often repeat it— intelligence and instinct are turned in opposite directions: the former towards inert matter, the latter towards life. Intelligence, by means of science, which is its work, will deliver up to us more and more completely the secret of physical operations; of life it brings us, and moreover only claims to bring us, a translation in terms of inertia. It goes all round life, taking from outside the greatest possible number of views of it, drawing it into itself instead of entering into it. But it is to the very inwardness of life that *intuition* leads us—by intuition I mean instinct that has become disinterested, self-conscious, capable of reflecting upon its object and of enlarging it indefinitely. (Henri Bergson, *Creative Evolution*, trsl. A. Mitchell, London, 1964, pp. 174, 177, 185-186)

Here, therefore, is the practical task of the endeavour. It envisages *rendering the instincts disinterested*, i.e. the true aim of all *asceticism*, or that part of the way towards mystical union that tradition calls *via purgativa*—the way of *purification* of the spiritual disciple—or also *purgatorium* ("purgatory"), when it is a matter of the way of human destiny; then it envisages *instinct becoming conscious of itself*, i.e. what tradition calls *via illuminativa*—the way of *illumination* of the spiritual disciple—or also *coelum* ("heaven"), when it is a matter of the way of human destiny; and then, lastly, it envisages *instinct becoming capable of reflecting upon its object and expanding indefinitely* whilst being completely united to it through sympathy, i.e. what tradition calls *via unitiva*—the way of *union*. The fruits of the way of union are *gnosis* (where "instinct is capable of reflecting upon its object") and the *mysticism* of contemplation (where "instinct is capable of expanding indefinitely")—or also the *visio beatifica* ("beatific vision"), which human souls enjoy in heaven after purgatory and after their celestial school in which they learn not to be dazzled by the divine light, but rather to see through it, when it is a matter of the way of human destiny.

Such is the task. But what is the endeavour? How is it to be realised?

It consists of the enterprise of the "going out" of intelligence from its milieu. Here is what Bergson has to say on this:

*Author's parentheses.

In vain, we shall be told, you claim to go beyond intelligence: how can you do that except by intelligence? All that is clear in your consciousness is intelligence. You are inside your own thought; you cannot get out of it. Say, if you like, that the intellect is capable of progress, that it will see more and more clearly into a greater and greater number of things; but do not speak of engendering it, for it is with your intellect itself that you would have to do the work.

The objection presents itself naturally to the mind. But the same reasoning would prove also the impossibility of acquiring any new habit. It is of the essence of reasoning to shut us up in the circle of the given. *But action breaks the circle.* If we had never seen a man swim, we might say that swimming is an impossible thing, inasmuch as, to learn to swim, we must begin by holding ourselves up in the water and, consequently, already know how to swim. Reasoning, in fact, always nails us down to the solid ground. But if, quite simply, I throw myself into the water without fear, I may keep myself up well enough at first by merely struggling, and gradually adapt myself to the new environment: I shall thus have learnt to swim. So, in theory, there is a kind of absurdity in trying to know otherwise than by intelligence; but if the risk be frankly accepted, action will perhaps cut the knot that reasoning has tied and will not unloose.

Besides, the risk will appear to grow less, the more our point of view is adopted. We have shown that intellect has detached itself from a vastly wider reality but that there has never been a clean cut between the two; all around conceptual thought there remains an indistinct fringe which recalls its origin. And further we compared the intellect to a solid nucleus formed by means of condensation. This nucleus does not differ radically from the fluid surrounding it. It can only be reabsorbed in it because it is made of the same substance. He who throws himself into the water, having known only the resistance of the solid earth, will immediately be drowned if he does not struggle against the fluidity of the new environment: he must perforce still cling to that solidity, so to speak, which even water presents. Only on this condition can he get used to the fluid's fluidity. *So of our thought, when it has decided to make the leap.*

But leap it must, that is, leave its own environment. Reason, reasoning on its powers, will never succeed in extending them, though the extension would not appear at all unreasonable once it were accomplished. Thousands and thousands of variations on the theme of walking will never yield a rule for swimming: come, enter the water, and when you know how to swim, you will understand how the mechanism of swimming is connected with that of walking. Swimming is an extension of walking, but walking would never have pushed you on to swimming. So you

may speculate as intelligently as you will on the mechanism of
intelligence; you will never, by this method, succeed in going
beyond it. You may get something more complex, but not
something higher nor even something different. *You must take
things by storm: you must thrust intelligence outside itself by
an act of will.* (Henri Bergson, *Creative Evolution*; trsl. A.
Mitchell, London, 1964, pp. 202-204)

This is the essence of "Bergsonian yoga", i.e. the practical method of making intelligence unite itself with instinct or the principle of sympathy, so that the latter
can extend its subject matter and reflect upon itself—or, in other words, so as to
develop *intuition*.

Now, the endeavour that Bergson has in mind is what the Cabbala calls KA-
VANA (כַּוָּנָה), and the result of this endeavor—that Bergson calls "intuition"—
is called DAATH (דַּעַת). KAVANA is profound meditation, i.e. the endeavour
of intelligence which aims at plunging into the depths of darkness surrounding it.
KAVANA differs essentially from Cartesian meditation, where it is a matter
notably of the concentration of the clarity of intelligence itself within itself,
and also from Kantian meditation, where intelligence strives to rise above itself
by making itself the object of observation, analysis and criticism. Profound meditation or KAVANA is neither only concentration of the light of intelligence
with a view to the intensification of its clarity, nor is it only the endeavour of intelligence to arrive at knowledge of itself. Profound meditation is the endeavour
of intelligence to probe the dark depths which surround it and to which it finds
access by means of *sympathy*, instead of through the exercise of its own logical,
analytical and critical faculties. Speaking in terms of the Cabbala, it is therefore
a matter of the marriage of the principle of intelligence—the Sephirah BINAH
(בִּינָה)—and the principle of wisdom—the Sephirah CHOKMAH (חָכְמָה)—in
the "middle pillar" of the Sephiroth Tree. DAATH is therefore the state of consciousness where intelligence and wisdom—acquired and acquirable knowledge,
on the one hand, and latent and actualisable knowledge, on the other hand—
become one. It is the same state of consciousness that the Church calls "intellect
illumined by grace" (*intellectus gratia illuminatus*)—grace being the principle
actualising within us latent knowledge of the "image and likeness of God", and
intellect being the "Bergsonian" intelligence which unites with and understands
things that it would never have understood from within itself. It is therefore
"illumined".

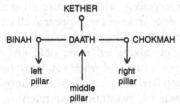

With respect to the Sephiroth Tree of the Cabbala, it must be pointed out that DAATH is nowhere to be found as a Sephirah or as a constituent element of the system (or "Tree") of Sephiroth. Whereas there are *four* Sephiroth to be found on the middle pillar—namely KETHER (בְּתֶר) or the Crown, TIPHERETH (תִּפְאֶרֶת) or Beauty, YESOD (יְסוֹד) or the Foundation, and MALKUTH (מַלְכוּת) or the Kingdom—DAATH is something to be created, to be added to the Sephiroth Tree. This means to say that a synthesis of the pillar of Wisdom—containing the Sephiroth GEDULAH (גְדוּלָה) or Majesty, and NETZACH (נֶצַח) or Victory—and the pillar of Intelligence—containing the Sephiroth GEBURAH (גְבוּרָה) or Power, and HOD (הוֹד) or Glory—is foreseen in the Sephiroth Tree only for the worlds of creation (*olam ha briah*) and formation (*olam ha yetzirah*), whilst in the world of emanation (*olam ha atziluth*) the synthesis constitutes the *point of departure* of emanation, creation and formation of the world; and the world of action (*olam ha assiah*) is itself the synthesis of the two columns (Wisdom and Intelligence).

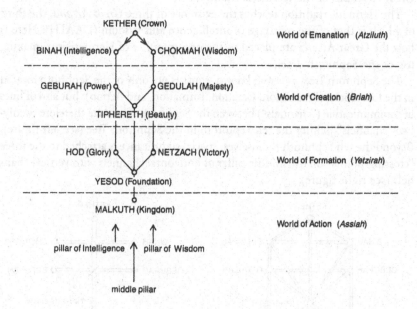

As is evident from this scheme of the Sephiroth Tree, there is a synthesis of the principles of Wisdom and Intelligence *preceding* the division of these two principles, which takes place in the Sephirah KETHER. There is also a synthesis which takes place in the world of action (MALKUTH); otherwise it is effected in artistic creativity (TIPHERETH), or in love between the sexes (YESOD), but it is not foreseen here for the *act of knowledge*, i.e. for the domain of gnosis.

Now, it is precisely the *act of knowledge* which is in question in the case of

DAATH, which is the aim of the spiritual school of the Cabbala — just as it is that of Hermeticism in general; it is nothing other than the task of the realisation of *intuition*, by uniting disinterested instinct and disinterested intelligence, as advanced by Henri Bergson. Cabbalists and Hermeticists (including Henri Bergson) therefore pursue the same aim, i.e. the union of intelligence and wisdom (or spontaneous knowledge) *other* than their union in artistic or aesthetic creativity and in love between the sexes. They have it in mind to achieve a *third* type of union of intelligence and wisdom: the "gnostic" union — DAATH or intuition.

We have spoken above of this millennial-old task of Hermeticism — this work and effort continued from century to century aiming at a complete fusion or marriage of the principles of intelligence and wisdom, i.e. of the power of knowledge acquired by logical discourse and the spontaneous knowledge of revelation. We have also pointed to some concrete facts, i.e. names of such personalities which are of a nature to inspire in us the hope that this work will one day be realised. Nevertheless, it is not yet so, because it is a matter of the realisation of the *third Great Arcanum* of the Hermetic tradition.

The Hermetic tradition teaches the existence of three *Great Arcana*, the third of which is that of the marriage of intelligence and wisdom (DAATH). Here is how the Great Arcana are placed in the *oral tradition* of Hermeticism, making use of the Sephiroth Tree:

The Sephiroth Tree, as is well known, consists not only of the Sephiroth located in the four worlds (Emanation, Creation, Formation, and Action), but also of lines of communication ("channels") between the Sephiroth. There are therefore twenty-two "channels" joining the ten Sephiroth in the Sephiroth Tree (see left figure). Beyond the ten Sephiroth themselves, special significance is attached to the three "crossing-points" on the middle pillar of horizontal channels with vertical channels (see right figure).

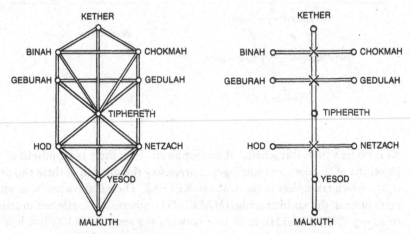

Figure: The Sephiroth Tree with twenty-two channels

Figure: The three crossing-points

These three crossing-points, each marked in the scheme by a St. Andrew's cross, indicate the "metaphysical or psychological points", where the three tasks—named "Great Arcana"—are to be realised.

The first Great Arcanum—called the "Great Magical Arcanum"—is situated at the crossing-point of the horizontal channel joining the Sephiroth NETZACH (Victory) and HOD (Glory), and the vertical channel joining TIPHERETH (Beauty) and YESOD (Foundation). It belongs to the world of formation.

The second Great Arcanum — the "Arcanum of moral geniality" — is situated at the crossing point of the horizontal channel joining the Sephiroth GEDULAH (Majesty) and GEBURAH (Power), and the vertical channel joining KETHER (Crown) and TIPHERETH (Beauty). It belongs to the world of creation.

The third Great Arcanum—that of geniality in the domain of knowledge, the "gnostic Arcanum"—is situated at the crossing-point of the horizontal channel joining the Sephiroth CHOKMAH (Wisdom) and BINAH (Intelligence), and the vertical channel joining KETHER (Crown) and TIPHERETH (Beauty). It is the state of consciousness that Cabbalists call DAATH, that the Hindu yogis call *samadhi*, and that we call here—with Henri Bergson—*intuition*. It belongs essentially to the world of emanation, i.e. the sphere of divine respiration, the sphere of the Holy Spirit.

The Great Magical Arcanum is therefore the centre of the cross formed by the current "Inspired Elevation—Certainty of Knowledge" and the current "Beauty—Love". It is a matter, therefore, of the task of realising the marriage of the creative fire of imagination with the limpid clarity of the waters of thought in the current which goes out from Beauty and ends in Love.

The Great Arcanum of the moral life is the centre of the cross formed by the binary "Magnanimity—Justice" in the current "Divine Radiation—Beauty". It is a matter of the realisation of the marriage of the charity which pardons all and everything with the judgement of strict justice in the current which emanates from divine Essence and arrives at the realisation of Beauty.

The Great Arcanum of knowledge is the centre of the cross formed by the binary "Wisdom—Intelligence" in the current "Divine Radiation—Beauty". It is a matter of the realisation of the marriage of revelation from above with argumentative intelligence based on experience.

The three Great Arcana of the tradition are therefore three crosses formed by the vertical middle pillar and three horizontal channels on the Sephiroth Tree. This is why the triple cross is the traditional symbol of complete initiation, and this is also why the title *Trismegistus* ("thrice greatest") is attributed to the founder of Hermeticism, the author of the *Emerald Table*.

Much has been written on the gnostic, moral and magical Great Arcana, and no doubt still more will be written in the future—their themes being central and inexhaustible at one and the same time. Here it is a matter simply of considering the Great Arcanum of the marriage of intelligence and wisdom in the context of the two other Great Arcana of the tradition. For the three Great Arcana are, truth to tell, only three aspects on three planes of one single Great Arcanum of the marriage of opposites in the head, in the heart and in the will. In other words, it is a matter of three aspects of the sole *Great Arcanum of the Cross*, since it is always the cross which realises the marriage of opposites—including that of the formal knowledge of intelligence and the material knowledge due to revelation from above.

The intuition of which Henri Bergson speaks is the fruit of the gradual transmutation of intelligence which has put its light at the disposal of the whispering—from black depths—of instinct-wisdom. It is the vow of obedience made by intelligence to the element which transcends it, which works its gradual transformation of the organ of formal knowledge (i.e. of the knowledge of the *relationships* of things and beings) into an organ of material knowledge (i.e. of the knowledge of *things and beings as such*). And it is the vow of poverty made by intelligence to the element which transcends it which renders it capable of perceiving this element and of receiving its intimate teaching, with regard to which it would be deaf and blind if it were not emptied of its own richness, i.e. if it did not know how to reduce itself to silence in order to listen. And it is, lastly, the vow of chastity made by intelligence to the element which transcends it, which transforms it gradually from an entity greedy for quantity of knowledge into an entity which seeks only the profound and essential, i.e. *quality*.

The gnostic aspect of the Great Arcanum of the conjunction of opposites (*conjunctio oppositorum*), or the marriage of opposites, is thus the transmutation of intelligence which is occupied with the "how" of things into an intuitive organ which is occupied with the "what" of things. It is, at the same time, the transformation of the revelation of wisdom from beyond the threshold of intelligence (which proceeds, from the point of view of intelligence, so spontaneously and in such a "dogmatic" manner that it appears to intelligence to be complete darkness from the unconscious) into intelligible language and communications that can be assimilated by the intelligence. In other words the unconscious, instead of shocking intelligence, allies itself with it, penetrates it, and becomes luminous within it. But this takes place only after the more-or-less long and painful experience of the crucifixion of consciousness on the cross formed by the pair of opposites: subjectivity—objectivity, and the pair of opposites: intelligence—unconscious wisdom (see figure). The four elements of this cross correspond to the first three Sephiroth (KETHER, CHOKMAH, BINAH) and the "middle pillar" between absolute subjectivity (KETHER) and absolute objectivity (MALKUTH).

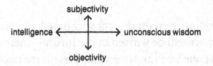

It is this cross where the gradual approach, alliance and, lastly, union of intelligence and unconscious wisdom is effected. At the beginning of this process intelligence and unconscious wisdom have so little in common that communication between them is reduced almost entirely to *dreams*, i.e. to the state of consciousness where intelligence, although present, is most passive. Then this communication is extended to the waking state also. The language of communication then becomes that of *symbols*, including those of the Tarot. Lastly, intelligence and wisdom—no longer unconscious—arrive at such a degree of mutual comprehension that they understand directly without the intermediary of dreams and symbols. It is only then that their union is achieved, i.e. that the state of consciousness that Bergson calls "intuition", and that Cabbalists identify with DAATH, is attained.

Direct communication between intelligence and wisdom is, truth to tell, only the development of *conscience*, which is extended from the domain of action to the domain of knowledge, and is awakened there to the point of becoming the light of intelligence. Conscience has two aspects, notably: a negative aspect (well-known and of which much is made in daily life), which manifests itself as warning disapproving an action before its execution or else as remorse disapproving of an action already committed; and a positive aspect (almost wholly ignored in daily life), which manifests itself as an impulse recommending an action before its execution and as serene joy after its execution. It is above all this positive aspect of conscience which becomes the illuminating and revelatory principle of intelligence, i.e. when the latter unites with unconscious wisdom (which is nothing other than the principle of conscience). Therefore intuition is, after all, only the marriage of intelligence (having renounced its absolute autonomy) with conscience awoken to the point of becoming a source of concrete and precise revelations for intelligence. One could also simply say that intuition is intelligence become entirely conscientious, and that it is conscience become entirely intelligible for intelligence.

Conscience thus offers intelligence as vast a world of inner experience as does the empirical world for outer experience. Intelligence can therefore develop itself and grow in two directions simultaneously—in the direction of the outer empirical world, thanks to the senses, and in that of the inner empirical world, thanks to conscience. Conscience is the door—the sole legitimate and healthy one—to a world at least as vast, and much more profound, than the world that we perceive with the senses. And it is the decision of intelligence to become "the servant of conscience" (*ancilla conscientiae*)—just as in the Middle Ages philosophy considered itself "the servant of theology" (*ancilla theologiae*)—which opens this door.

The leading role of conscience in the passage from the "surface world" to the "depth world" has long been known of in the tradition. It was dramatised and concretised by speaking of the "guardian of the threshold" and of the "meeting" with him. The decisive role was assigned to this meeting, concerning the passage across the "threshold" which separates the "surface world" from the "depth world". Because the admission or rejection of the aspirant depends on this meeting. He who could not bear the truth concerning himself, revealed to him by the "guardian of the threshold" at this meeting, fell back, i.e. decided to content himself with the "surface world"—the world of outer experience and constructions of argumentative intelligence. Whilst he who had the courage and humility necessary to bear the revelation of the truth concerning himself passed the threshold and was therefore admitted to the school of esoteric life, i.e. to the "depth world". The "guardian of the threshold" figures in the tradition (including more recent contributions to the tradition) either as a kind of double incorporating the whole past of the person in question, or also as a hierarchical entity of the rank of an Archangel who teaches the lesson of conscience by means (this is only one means) of projecting the double of the human personality aspiring to the "depth world". The latter conception of the "guardian of the threshold" and of the nature of the meeting with him is more complete and still more true. The guardian of the threshold is not a moral bogey for bowling over the "spiritual bourgeoisie", but rather our elder brother and servant of God, who helps us with infinite kindness and superhuman wisdom—although with perfect truthfulness—to advance from the surface to the depths. At least, such is the evidence of the experience of five people of this century known to me.

The guardian of the threshold spoken of in the Hermetic tradition is the great judge, charged with preserving the equilibrium of that which is above and that which is below. The traditional iconography of the Church represents him with a sword and balance. The sword is his vivifying and healing action, giving courage and humility to the soul which hungers and thirsts for the depths, and the balance is his action of presenting the precise account of what must be paid in order to have the right to go further.

It was Maître Philip of Lyons who, as much as any I know, had the most profound comprehension and the most complete knowledge of the practical manipulation of the balance referred to here. He did not tire of repeating:

> *Pay* your debts! *Pay* the debts of your neighbours! Because each will pay his debt, and it does not matter if it is paid in this world or in the other, provided that it is paid. (cf. Alfred Haehl, *Vie et paroles du Maître Philippe*, Lyon, 1959, and Philippe Encausse, *Le Maître Philippe de Lyon*, Paris, 1958)

This is why before healing a sickness he often asked the sick person and the people around him to pay "the price of healing", which he fixed as a certain time of abstention from slander with regard to others, which time he measured according to the case either by hours or by weeks.

Another way of paying debts—one's own or others'—is by giving money to the poor or to a good cause. Our ancestors had the right sentiment in leaving money to the poor, to the Church, to hospitals, or in accompanying their novenas of prayer for pardon and for healing by gifts of money paid to the poor or to good causes. They knew instinctively that debts must be paid and that it is better to pay them here than after death. They still had a feeling for the reality of the balance of the guardian of the threshold.

The guardian of the threshold spoken of in the tradition is therefore the administrator of the justice of conscience — and, at the same time, the master of the school of conscience. His balance signifies the negative aspect of conscience, and his sword signifies the positive aspect of conscience, i.e. the revelatory and healing aspect. One cannot dispense with the meeting with the guardian of the threshold when one wants to cross the threshold which separates the "surface world" from the "depth world". It is through the door of conscience that one must enter. And *intuition*, which reveals the "depth world", is nothing other than intelligence submitted to conscience — submitted from the point of view of being one with it.

There is therefore no esoteric or occult technique which is able to help us (without speaking of making us) pass from the "surface world" to the "depth world" other than the purely moral act of *sacrificium intellectus* — the sacrifice of intelligence to conscience. It is the recognition, once and for all, of the primacy of "moral logic"— its superiority to the "formal logic" of intelligence — which effects the passage from the state of reasoning to that of intuition. No exercise whatever for the concentration of attention or for the suppression of mental activity will, alone, help you to attain intuition. No breathing exercise or mental technique of itself will be of any use here. Because in order to attain an aim higher than intelligence and the body, one has to make use of means which are also higher than intelligence and the body. That which is spiritual is achieved only by spiritual means — and these comprise no technique beyond the purely moral act and endeavour.

A strange thing! The Christian Occident, which has developed technique and technology to such an extent on the material plane, possesses hardly any psycho-spiritual "technique and technology", whilst the Buddhist and pantheistic Orient — which has almost entirely neglected material technique — has developed a quite advanced body of pycho-spiritual "technique and technology". It seems that the "technological genius" of intelligence in the Orient is turned towards — and perhaps is exhausted in — the domain of the inner life, whilst the same "genius" of intelligence in the Occident has exhausted or continues to exhaust its creativity in the domain of external life. The consequence of this is that the spiritual life of the Occident — its mysticism, gnosis and magic — is developed above all under the sign of the *principle of grace*, and that the mysticism, gnosis and magic of the Orient are developed above all under the sign of the *principle of technology*, i.e. the scientific empirical principle of the observation and utilisation of the chain of cause and effects concerning efforts and that which results from them. Thus, for example, the classic work on yoga, *The Yogasutra of Patanjali*, recommends, *as useful to concentration*, devotion to a personal god — to be abandoned later when having lost its utility, i.e. when the yogi will have acquired the aptitude to concentrate himself on the formless and impersonal. "Yoga is the suppression of (involuntary) movements of the mental substance", says *The Yogasutra of Patanjali*, i.e. according to the law of causality—the chain of cause and effect—it is the suppression of mental movements which is the cause whose effect is yoga or union with the Absolute Being.

Now, St. John of the Cross, who was many times taken up in rapture through—or plunged in—union with the Absolute Being, also spoke in his writings of the state of the complete silence of personal intelligence, imagination and will—the state, therefore, where mental movements are suppressed; but he does not tire of repeating that it is the Divine Presence, of which the soul is enamoured, which effects this silence—this suppression of the mental movements—and not the human will. The state of complete silence of intelligence—and, moreover, of the imagination and will—is *present* in the soul set ablaze by the love of God. There is no psychospiritual "technology" here; it is the mutual love between the soul and God which does all.

Thus, here is the difference between the science of psycho-spiritual technique (Raja-yoga) and the "sheer grace" of love in the "night of the senses and the spirit" of St. John of the Cross. The term "sheer grace" which intends to specify this difference, is employed by St. John of the Cross himself. He says in his *Canciones del alma en la noche obscura* ("Songs of the Soul" in *The Dark Night of the Soul*):

One dark night, 　　　　　　　　　　　(*En una noche obscura,*
Fired with love's urgent longings 　　*Con ansias en amores inflamada,*
—*Ah, the sheer grace!*— 　　　　　　—*Oh dichosa ventura!*—
I went out unseen, 　　　　　　　　　*Salí sin ser notada,*
My house being now all stilled. 　　　*Estando ya mi casa sosegada.*)*

My house being now at rest...(the soul) goes forth into the
divine union of love...with the whole household of its powers
and desires sunk in sleep and silence...,

says St. John of the Cross in his commentary to the verse. He says elsewhere:

It was a sheer grace for the soul that God had brought it into
this dark night, from whence such great good came to it, and
into which it would never have been able to enter by itself.
Besides, no one would be capable through his own forces alone
of disengaging himself from all his tendencies ("the whole
household of powers and desires") in order to go forth to God.
(St. John of the Cross, *The Ascent of Mt. Carmel* I, i, 5)

Here he indicates the precise difference between the Christian way—the way of purification, illumination and the consummation of union—where there is

*Trsl. K. Kavanaugh and O. Rodriguez, *The Collected Works of St. John of the Cross*, London, 1966, p. 295.

nothing concerning technique, and that of yoga which comprises a scale ranging from techniques of physical preparation (Hatha-yoga) to psycho-mental techniques (Raja-yoga).

There is nothing of technique—here all is art and grace—in Christian mysticism, gnosis and magic. And how is it concerning the reciting of the rosary prayer amongst Catholics and the prayer of the heart (the "Jesus prayer") practised in the Orthodox Church? (The prayer of the heart is the uninterrupted repetition, day and night, with the beating of the heart, of the prayer: *Kyrie, Iesou Christe eleison*..."Lord Jesus Christ, Son of God, have mercy on me, a sinner.") Or, again, the Irish monks, who recited each day all the Psalms by heart? Is it not a matter here also of a technique?

The *principle of rhythm* and *that of technique* (or maximum effect with minimum effort) differ as biology differs from mechanics, or as a living organism from a machine. The repetition of ages and generations, festivals, the rituals of religious cult, breathing, the beating of the heart, prayer—with respect to the rosary prayer and the practice of the prayer of the heart, and also with respect to the daily recital of the Psalms—are manifestations and applications of the principle of rhythm, whilst, for example, the prayer wheel of the Tibetans, turning in the wind, is the application of a mechanical principle, i.e. the fundamental principle of the technique of minimum effort in order to obtain maximum effect.

Rhythm in prayer makes it pass from the psychological domain to that of *life*, from the domain of personal tendencies and moods to that of the fundamental and universal impulses of life itself. Speaking in occult terms, here it is a matter of carrying prayer over from the "astral body" (or "soul body") to the "etheric body" (or "vital body"), i.e. of making prayer employ the *language of life* instead of the language of personal feelings and desires. And just as life is like a river which flows unceasingly, so does the rosary prayer, for example, flow without stopping and *without fatigue*, because that which lives is at the same time *vivifying*. Calm and rhythmic prayer ("prayer-life") *does not take* forces—it does not tire—but *gives* forces to the person praying. This is why the anonymous author of the writing *The Way of a Pilgrim*—dealing with the experiences of a Russian pilgrim devoted to the practice of the prayer of the heart—speaks of the experience of plenitude and serene joy which filled him day and night, giving him a foretaste, already on the earth, of celestial beatitude. It is the same with the practice of the rosary prayer. The one hundred and fifty *Ave Marias* and the fifteen *Pater Nosters* of the rosary prayer introduce one to the universal river of spiritual life—which is the proof of a universal prayer—and thus lead one to joyous serenity. The pilgrim points out—in the third chapter of *The Way of a Pilgrim*—before his experience of the uninterrupted prayer of the heart, and even before he learnt of its existence, that in himself and his wife,

the wish for prayer was there, and the long prayers we said without quite understanding did not seem tiring, indeed we liked them. Clearly it is true, as a certain teacher once told me, that a secret prayer lies hidden within the human heart. The man himself does not know it, yet working mysteriously within his soul, it urges him to prayer according to each man's knowledge and power. (*The Way of a Pilgrim*; trsl. R. M. French, London, 1954, pp. 70-71)

It is perhaps this "secret prayer" in the unconscious of the soul which St. Paul has in mind in the Epistle to the Galatians where he says:

And because you are sons, God has sent the Spirit of his Son into our hearts crying: Abba! Father! (Galatians iv, 6)

Now, it is rhythm which unites conscious prayer and this unconscious "secret prayer", and it is as a consequence of their union that "prayer-effort" becomes "prayer-life", i.e. that prayer of the soul becomes spiritual prayer. The rosary prayer, the prayer of the heart, litanies and psalms that are repeated, etc., effect the transformation of "prayer-effort" into "prayer-life". Far from being means of the mechanisation of prayer, *they spiritualise it*.

Do not be scandalised, dear Unknown Friend, by the fact that you find yourself confronted with the rosary prayer in a *Hermetic* meditation on the eighteenth Arcanum of the Tarot—the Arcanum which teaches how to surmount "eclipsed lunar intelligence". Esotericism is not a collection of extraordinary and unknown things, but rather it is above all a less ordinary and less known way of *seeing* ordinary and known things—of seeing their profundity. And the rosary prayer, wholly "exoteric" and "known to satiety" as it is, reveals profound truths of spiritual life, including that of the union of prayer of the soul and spiritual prayer. It is, moreover, closely related to the theme of the eighteenth Arcanum of the Tarot: the Arcanum of knowing how to pass from intelligence eclipsed by terrestrial "technicality" to intelligence illumined by the spiritual sun—i.e. to *intuition*. In other words, the leap to which Henri Bergson invites our intelligence can be made by saying the rosary prayer. The opinion of a Capuchin friar? It could be, but why can't a Capuchin friar be right, sometimes at least?

Be that as it may, I declare openly that practical Hermeticism is above all the desire and capacity to learn from everyone and everything—and that "knowing better" is its coffin.

"Knowing better"—the state of consciousness which is present when one has made a review of the totality of efforts made in the past and the results obtained from them, by observing the fixed rules of the game—plunges intelligence into a pond of stagnant water with an exact geometrical border, which encloses it and makes it retreat, like a crayfish, in the face of all that is new and demands creative effort. Intelligence retreats into its element of stagnant water before the antinomy of mental psychism, i.e. the antinomy "credulous obedience—critical revolt". It does likewise in the face of the intellectual antinomy "thesis — antithesis", which rises up before it like two stone towers, rigid and immobile in their opposition. And above these antinomies, where the *third* term — the synthesis — should be found, it sees only a human face, only the projection of human will desirous of an intellectual arrangement so as to disencumber itself of disquieting contradictions. Whilst retreating, whilst refusing to decide to leap or fly either over the "dog" of submission to authority ("credulous obedience") and the "wolf" of criticism denying all authority ("critical revolt"), or over the intellectual "tower of Babel" of theses and that of their antitheses, intelligence nevertheless remains ill at ease — because of the imperceptible drops, emanating from the radiation of synthesis eclipsed by the projection of the shadow of arbitrary human will, which fall into its subconscious and constantly disturb it. For although the moon — intelligence illumined by the sun — is eclipsed, it nevertheless exercises a constant influence on intelligence through a kind of rain, whose drops fall into the subconsiousness of intelligence and produce there movement and confused, disquieting noise.

Yes, "knowing better", when it has once taken hold of intelligence, sets it fully in the scene of the Card of the eighteenth Arcanum of the Tarot — "The Moon". The context of the Card: the eclipsed moon above, the two towers and the two representatives of the canine species in the middle, and the pond with the crayfish below, says, "being confronted with two antinomies — one psychic and one intellectual — you have no other choice than to *advance* (which means to say, to raise yourself up) or to *retreat* (which means to say, to sink yourself into a stagnant element). Choose!

This choice being of utmost importance, its "environment" must be seen as clearly as possible. Therefore, here is the geometrical figure underlying the situation (see figure).

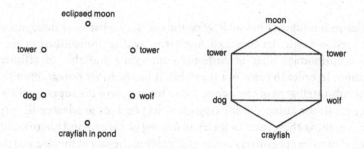

Now this figure — that of a square with two triangles opposed — is *magical*. Namely, it is the classical figure of sympathetic or voodoo magic, i.e. the magical operation or magical mechanism which immobilises the conscious will by means of two antinomies in the horizontal (the square) and an antinomy in the vertical (the two peaks of the opposed triangles). It goes without saying that it is not a matter of "poisonous magic" making use of "*aqua toffana*, poisoned nosegays, the shirt of Nessus, and other deadly instruments, still stranger and still less known" of which Eliphas Lévi speaks under the title of the eighteenth Arcanum of the Tarot in his *Dogme et rituel de la haute magie* (trsl. A. E. Waite, *Transcendental Magic. Its doctrine and ritual*, London, 1968, p. 155). No, it is a matter of something more serious and more profound, namely *the Arcanum of intelligence with conscience eclipsed*. It is the Arcanum of the magical mechanism, working behind the surface of the state of intelligence, which aims at explaining movement by the immobile, life by the non-living, consciousness by the unconscious, morality by the amoral. Indeed, how has it happened to mankind that many of its intelligent representatives—even its leaders and directors—have come to see in the brain not the instrument but the producer of consciousness, in chemistry not the instrument but the producer of life, in the economic sphere not the instrument but the producer of culture? How can it be that human intelligence has arrived—in so far as many of its representatives are concerned—at seeing man without a soul and the world without God? What secret and hidden force is at work pushing and forcing human intelligence to say first of all that the essential problems are insoluble—things transcending the senses and intelligence being unknowable—and then to deny their very existence? In other words, how has it happened that human intelligence finds itelf in a state of *metaphysical eclipse*?

It is sympathetic or voodoo magic—and it is the eighteenth Arcanum of the Tarot—which can give us the answer to these questions. "Answer" in this case—and in Hermeticism in general—signifies "enabling one to see" or "opening the eyes". For each Arcanum, in so far as it is an Arcanum, is not a doctrine but rather an event—that of opening the eyes, i.e. the opening up of an inner sense which permits things to be *seen* in a new way. And this is precisely the matter at hand in the case of the set of problems belonging to the eighteenth Arcanum of the Tarot.

Human intelligence has undergone the effects of what is no more, nor no less, than voodoo magic. Its conscious motivating will is immobilised in the square of two antinomies: that of authority—autonomy and that of affirmation—negation. In order to come out from this, it has to either *retreat* into the region of the sub-intelligent or else *advance* into the region of the super-intelligent, i.e. to retreat in the fashion of the crayfish in its pond, or to advance by surpassing itself—in rising above itself by means of *leaping* or *flying*—and not to build towers of Babel or to bay plaintively or howl furiously in the way of the dog and the wolf.

Now, it is retreat which has been chosen by many representatives of human intelligence. Others make only plaintive elegies to the romantic past, where intelligence was bathed in the light from above; still others make only "thunder and lightning" against the errors and sins of the tragic past with its dogmatism and authoritarianism. Others, lastly, unconcerned about what takes place around them in their intellectual environment, continue to build towers of intellectual systems of affirmation or negation, which are of the nature of towers of Babel. Thus, some retreat into the sub-intelligent, i.e. give themselves over to the way of seeing the cause of the advanced and the evolved in the primitive, the cause of consciousness in raw matter, the cause of the rational in the irrational, and the cause of the moral in the amoral; whilst others pour themselves out in elegies concerning the golden age of the past, or angrily make "thunder and lightning" concerning its imperfections; whilst, lastly, still others build intellectual towers of Babel founded on theses of affirmation or negation, chosen from the darkness of the inner ceiling of the skull, and eclipsing revelatory and directing consciousness.

One begins to see and to expect only the projection of the primary and elementary impulses of human nature: pleasure (Freud), the will to power (Nietzsche, Adler), material and economic concerns (Marx). The projection of the terrestrial element of human nature onto the nocturnal luminary—moral consciousness—causes its eclipse. One no longer sees anything worthwhile and one also no longer expects anything worthwhile.

The eclipsed moon with the human face instead of reflected solar light. . .the arid plain with two towers and with a dog and a wolf howling from below. . .the pond with stagnant water geometrically enclosed and shielding the crayfish—doesn't the totality of this imagery at first evoke troubling feelings, and then disquieting ideas relating to a far-reaching operation of voodoo magic whose victim is human intelligence?

Indeed, with Kant the limits of intelligence were brought to light, i.e. he demonstrated the fact of its imprisonment, and he addressed thinking humanity with the grave warning that one can formulate in the language of imagery of the eighteenth Arcanum of the Tarot as follows: "The nocturnal luminary is eclipsed! You find there the *face of a man* instead of the pure light of cosmic objective truth! One can escape the prison of this eclipse only by turning to the moral consciousness of the transcendent Self!" Since Kant, the fact of the spellbound state of intelligence has increased more and more in significance and certainty—up to the present day. In this Letter we have quoted Henri Bergson fully because he demonstrated this in an extremely lucid and well-founded manner, but Henri Bergson was not alone in ascertaining the subjective imprisonment of intelligence and making appeal to coming out of it. Whatever the divergence in their views and in other respects may be, Schopenhauer, Deussen, Vladimir Soloviev and Nicolas Berdyaev—to name only the well-known names—are in agreement in that which concerns the theme of the eighteenth Arcanum of the Tarot. Hegel even advanced a new metaphysical logic—the dialectic of thesis, antithesis and synthesis—which is, fundamentally, only the re-affirmation of the intellectual aspect of the Hermetic method of the "neutralisation of binaries" that one finds in alchemical treatises and with Jacob Boehme, Saint-Martin, Fabre d'Olivet, etc., which aims at intelligence coming out of its prison and raising itself to "objective knowledge" by means of intellectual intuition. In our time Pierre Teilhard de Chardin has advanced an objective "dialectic of evolution" which is no longer simply intellectual, but which is rather *a way of seeing* chemical, biological, psychic, intellectual, moral and spiritual processes *in evolution*, which proceeds according to an *objective* dialectic (i.e. everywhere ascertainable, through all means of experience) —namely, *divergence, convergence and emergence*. This is no longer an aspect of Hermeticism, but is Hermeticism pure and simple—including mysticism, gnosis and magic, as well as all experience of the physical world, as a unity.

The *fact* that human intelligence is spellbound is therefore not only recognised but also much effort is being made—and has already been made—towards freeing it. The question still remains with respect to the "technique" of the voodoo magic whose proven victim is intelligence.

The "technique" in question is summarised by a single word: doubt. Doubt—*dubium, Zweifel, somnenie*, etc.—is the state of consciousness faced with an antinomy, i.e. two theses which seem to it to be equally well-founded and which contradict one another. Kant, for example, formulated four fundamental antinomies:

1. The world has a beginning in time and a limit in space—the world has no beginning in time and is infinite in space;

2. substance consists of simple units—nothing in the world consists of simple units and there is nothing in the world which is simple;

3. there is no freedom, everything is determined by natural causality—determinism according to Nature's laws of causality is not the only kind that exists, for there also exists the determinism of causality having its source in freedom; and

4. the world presupposes an effective cause which is a necessary being—there does not need to be any being, either in the world or beyond the world, which is its effective cause.

In other words, the antinomies of the creation or the eternity of the world, of the simplicity or the infinite complexity of matter, of freedom or absolute determinism, of theism or atheism are those which confront intelligence and are able to reduce it to impotence, i.e. to paralyse it, according to Kant.

Leaving aside the question as to whether the Kantian antinomies are the only ones, or the most essential ones, they suffice to demonstrate *the discouraging and therefore paralysing effect* of antinomies on intelligence, no matter whether they are real or false. Now, the "technique" of voodoo magic acting on intelligence which has taken place in the history of the human race consists, in the first place, in having put it in the presence of antinomies—real or false—which discourage it and paralyse it, i.e. which make it stop and give up progressing forward in the direction towards the profound. Then this effort is intensified by the demonstration of the *subjective relativity* of the solutions to these antinomies and of the contradictory nature of these solutions: that it is, in the last analysis, only *taste* which determines for the authors of philosophical systems the foundation, structure and architecture of their intellectual edifices. Plato's idealism, Aristotle's realism, Descartes' rationalism, Leibnitz's monadism, Spinoza's monism, Schopenhauer's pessimistic voluntarism, Fichte's optimistic voluntarism, Hegel's dialectical absolutism, etc., are merely works of intellectual poetry whose differences depend only on the taste and talent of their authors—this is the second constituent element of the operation of voodoo magic with regard to human intelligence. Lastly, once ensnared in doubt, intelligence sees in illumination from above only manifestations of elements of human psychology—the "face of man on the moon"—and cannot see otherwise. Is the soul immortal? Or is it the desire for self-preservation which is manifested by this thesis? Is man a microcosm? Or is it the desire to be important which is at the root of this idea? Progress, evolution . . . an idea conceived of to render suffering, toil and death bearable. God? . . . an idea which guarantees that all will end well. Karma? . . . this idea appeases, if not consoles, the blind, the deaf and the dumb. The celestial hierarchies? . . . one is afraid of emptiness and therefore it is necessary to people a heaven with beings similar to us.

Thus, instead of asking if this or that thesis is *true*, intelligence comes to occupy itself with psychological motives hidden behind the so-called "game of rationalisation" fashioning intellectual superstructures. It projects the "face of man" on the moon and sees there only this face.

In this connection I must say that there are two categories of people with whom I have had the greatest difficulty in conversing, with any profit, during my life: these categories not being those of people who either passionately affirm or who passionately deny in the intellectual domain, but rather the two categories of people—that of the "psychologisers" and that of the "spiritualisers"—who *accept everything* with a tolerance which appears perfect. For you cannot speak with "psychologisers" about objective things and truths in the world and in life: they would understand these only as psychological manifestations that they accept as indisputable, although interpretable, "psychological facts". Therefore you cannot arrive at agreement, nor be in disagreement, with a "psychologiser" concerning things of the world and of life, since, if you speak of the moon, he will see only your face on the moon—if not his own. No more can you speak with a "spiritualiser", i.e. with someone who holds that his higher and true Self is identical with God—the higher and true Self of the world—and who consequently sees and understands only manifestations of this same absolute, universal and eternal truth which is revealed—it alone—relatively in all philosophical and religious opinions. Just as the "psychologiser" projects his lower human self onto the luminary illumining the darkness of the depths of the world and life, so does the "spiritualiser" project his higher human Self onto the same luminary. The one projects the human *psychic* face there and the other projects the human *spiritual* face—but it is, in both cases equally, the human face which is projected there.

Say to a "spiritualiser" that Jesus Christ was the son of God incarnated, and he will reply to you that it is true—since in Jesus Christ was realised the universal and eternal truth of the identity of the true higher Self with God. Then say to him that the Incarnation was an act of sacrifice of divine love, and he will say to you that it is true — since love is the identity of all individual "selves" in the universal Self of God, and that each individualisation comprises one incarnation and must necessarily be an act of sacrifice on the part of the higher, universal Self. If you then say to him that it was the victory over death, the resurrection of Jesus Christ, which signifies the uniqueness of the work accomplished by Jesus Christ, he will reply to you that there is no reason in the world to deny the fact of the resurrection of Jesus Christ, since the higher and universal Self can always project mental images — by *mayashakti* — to the point of making them appear visibly. Lastly, isn't the whole world a manifestation of mental force which renders the invisible visible? And if you say that Pentecost was the result of the work of Jesus Christ, he will reply to you — with evident benevolence — that to be sure it was Pentecost which necessarily had to result from the work of the avatar Jesus Christ, since it was Pentecost where his disciples, also, realised the universal and eternal truth of the identity of all individual "selves" in the higher universal Self — which is manifested by the fact that their speech became that of the higher Self of each person who listened to them. And if you say lastly — desperate as you are to come, at least, to a disagreement with your interlocutor — that there is evil in the world, that the Fall took place and that there is original sin, he will say to you that without any doubt there is the Fall and original sin, since the illusion of a plurality of individual consciousness has been arrrived at, whilst they are identical and one in the consciousness of the universal Self. A Fall was therefore certainly necessary in order to arrive at such an illusion . . .

Thus the "spiritualiser" as well as the "psychologiser" are not people to converse with about things concerning the world and life; they look at — and consequently see — only the *face*, either psychic or spiritual, *of man*. Here it is the effect of the Arcanum of the moon eclipsed by the face of man that is at work.

It is therefore hardly surprising that the intelligence of those who do not want to see the world as a display of human subjectivity and who, on the other hand, cannot or do not know how to make the *leap* of intelligence of which Henri Bergson speaks — that their intelligence is turned towards the "objective facts of the five senses". . . and hence the retreat into the framework of the pond with the crayfish of the Card of the eighteenth Arcanum of the Tarot. The operation of magical enchantment — the bringing into play of antinomies and the projection of the face of man onto the luminary called to illumine the enigmas and secrets of the depths beyond the threshold of consciousness (i.e. of the "night") — has attained its aim by making intelligence retreat in the face of heaven, and even from the surface of the earth, into a region situated *beneath* the surface of the earth, i.e. that which underlies the "facts of the senses", symbolised in the Card by the pond with the crayfish.

What is the state of intelligence which has abandoned all metaphysics and has decided to hold to and to limit itself solely to "objective facts of the senses"?

What is most characteristic of this state is that *intelligence no longer moves forwards but backwards*. It looks to the least developed and the most primitive for the cause and explanation of what is most developed and most advanced in the process of evolution. Thus, it looks for the effective cause of the world not in the heights of creative consciousness but rather in the depths of the unconscious — instead of going forward and elevating itself towards God, it retreats into matter. It does something with regard to the world which would be absurd with regard to a work of art, namely to explain it through the qualities — and quantities — of the materials of which it consists, instead of the style, the context, the meaning and the intention which the work of art reveals. Wouldn't it be absurd to want to understand one of Victor Hugo's poems, for example, by chemically analysing the ink with which it had been written and the paper on which it was written, or by counting the number of words and letters? Nevertheless, this is precisely what the intelligence under consideration does with regard to the world — the world in which Victor Hugo's poem makes up only a part and is only a single special case of the manifestation of the great process of the creation.

Now the moment has arrived to conclude our meditation on the eighteenth Arcanum of the Tarot. Here is the conclusion that it asserts:

Of the four *Hayoth* of the Cabbala, the four "sacred animals" of Hermeticism — the Eagle, the Man, the Lion and the Bull — we find *three* amongst the signs of the zodiac, i.e. the Bull, the Lion and the Man (or Waterbearer). But we do not find the *Eagle*. The Eagle's place in the zodiacal circle is occupied by the *Scorpion*. There, where the Eagle (the principle of elevation) ought to be, the Scorpion (the principle of retreat and suicide) is found. Now, the eighteenth Arcanum of the Tarot is that of the Eagle and the Scorpion — the Arcanum of the replacement of the one by the other. Because the crayfish of the Card of the Arcanum "The Moon" has the scorpion as its prototype — and as its aim. Intelligence which prefers retreating to flying must inevitably arrive at the impasse of absurdity — for example, the absurdity that we have pointed out above. And the absurd. . .this is *suicide* for intelligence. This is where "crayfish-intelligence" goes after having renounced becoming "eagle-intelligence".

The eighteenth Arcanum of the Tarot asks us: Do you want to choose the way of the eagle which rises above antinomies or the way of the crayfish which retreats before them until arriving at complete absurdity, i.e. at the scorpionic suicide of intelligence? This is the *point* — i.e. the message to the human *will* — of the eighteenth Major Arcanum of the Tarot.

Meditation on the
Nineteenth Major Arcanum of the Tarot

THE SUN
LE SOLEIL

When I began drawing the mandalas,
however, I saw that everything, all the paths
I had been following, all the steps I had
taken, were leading back to a single point
—namely, to the mid-point. It became
increasingly plain to me that the mandala is
the centre. It is the exponent of all paths. It
is the path to the centre, to individuation...
I knew that in finding the mandala as an
expression of the self I had attained what
was for me the ultimate. Perhaps someone
else knows more, but not I.

(C. G. Jung)*

Cor Jesu, Rex et centrum omnium cordium.
("Heart of Jesus, King and centre of all
hearts.")

(Litany of the Sacred Heart)

I am the Alpha and the Omega, the first and
the last, the beginning and the end.

(Revelation xxii, 13)

Under the combined influence of men's
thoughts and aspirations, the universe
around us is seen to be knit together
and convulsed by a vast movement of
convergence. Not only theoretically, but
experientially, our modern cosmogony is
taking the form of a cosmogenesis...at the
term of which we can distinguish a supreme
focus of personalising personality...
Just suppose that we *identify* (at least in his
"natural" aspect) the cosmic Christ of faith
with the Omega Point of science: then
everything in our outlook is clarified and
broadened, and falls into harmony.

(Pierre Teilhard de Chardin)**

LETTER XIX

THE SUN

Dear Unknown Friend,

The preceding Arcanum—"The Moon"—confronted us with the *task* of human intelligence to liberate itself from the magical enchantment which separates it from spontaneous wisdom, and to unite itself with the latter, i.e. to arrive at *intuition*. The nineteenth Arcanum—"The Sun"—is that of the accomplished union of intelligence and spontaneous wisdom: *the Arcanum of intuition*.

Intuition is what results from the intimate and profound alliance of intelligence

Memories, Dreams, Reflections; trsl. R. and C. Winston, London, 1967, p. 222.
**Christianity and Evolution*; trsl. R. Hague, London, 1971, p. 180.

and spontaneous wisdom. Now, the Card of the nineteenth Arcanum represents two children placed under the sun, where the one puts his right hand on the neck of the other as if he wanted to draw his head near to himself, whilst the other touches with his left hand the place on the body of the first where his heart is to be found. These two children thus represent intelligence endowed with childlike confidence with regard to the spontaneous wisdom of the heart, and spontaneous childlike wisdom which uses the language of the heart and which tends to draw the attention of the head, i.e. intelligence, to what it has to say. The image is therefore of two children united by bonds of a reciprocal confidence without reserve—where the one indicates and the other understands—placed under the sun. One could hardly better represent the relationship of intelligence and spontaneous wisdom brought into play in intuition than as it is in the Card of the Arcanum "The Sun". For this relationship presupposes such purity of intention as is found only with a child, and it postulates such reciprocal confidence, without a shadow of doubt or suspicion, which belongs naturally to children. Lastly, this relationship excludes tendencies to domination and authority—to pose as a pontiff and to pride oneself on the eminence of the guru or master whose favours one enjoys—which tendencies are also foreign to children.

"The children who are fraternising under the sun correspond all the better to *Gemini* because this zodiacal constellation brings in the longest days to us"—says Oswald Wirth (*Le Tarot des imagiers du moyen âge*, Paris, 1927, p. 208), thus locating the nineteenth Arcanum in the zodiacal circle of twelve cosmic mysteries or, speaking in the language of C. G. Jung, in the circle of twelve archetypal force-images of the collective unconscious which work in the depths of every human soul. For the zodiac is that which the human soul knows unconsciously; it is the book which the soul once "ate" and which is present and active only in his "bowels" —in the depths of his being—from whence it renders him strong or weak, fertile or arid, fervent or tepid, according to whether he is in harmony or not with its teaching-impulse.

Now, the teaching-impulse called "Gemini" can be expressed by paraphrasing a little the first statement of the *Emerald Table* of Hermes:

> May that which is below be as that which is above, and may that which is above be as that which is below to accomplish the miracles of one thing.

This is the principle of analogy put into practice, taking its point of departure from the *principle of cooperation*. It is the opposite of that of the *struggle for existence* advanced by Charles Darwin as the principle of evolution called "Sagittarius". Nature furnishes us at the same time with a great number of proofs of the principle of cooperation in the process of evolution—perhaps as many proofs as there are of the struggle for existence. The proofs are of a kind such that one could uphold the principle of cooperation to be worthy as the directing principle of natural evolution with the same justification as the principle of struggle may be upheld. Indeed, is it the struggle for existence within an organism — let us say the human body — which explains the effect of the activities of millions of biological units (cells) in the organism or, rather, is it their cooperation? Don't the cells of the muscles, the nervous system, the glands, the blood, etc., cooperate rather than struggle? And isn't the life and health of the whole organism due to this cooperation?

Bees and flowering plants cooperate. Air, light and plants cooperate in photosynthesis, where the miracle of the transformation of inorganic matter into organic matter takes place — where "stones" are transformed into "bread". And, lastly, if mankind had not cooperated more than it had struggled, it would not only not have achieved the international civilisation of our time but it would probably have been annihilated.

There is therefore no doubt that the principle of cooperation has at least the same rights to be considered as the directing principle of evolution as that of the struggle for existence advanced by Darwinism. In other words, the diurnal principle of Gemini plays a role at least equal to the nocturnal principle of Sagittarius in natural evolution.

One of the highest aspects of the principle of Gemini, the principle of cooperation, is that which is present in intuition: that of the cooperation between spontaneous wisdom and intelligence. Here it is a matter of a state of consciousness where intelligence advances from formal knowledge to material knowledge, i.e. from knowledge of the relationships of things to knowledge of the things themselves. Now, the "knowledge of things themselves" entails two functions: on the one hand what Henri Bergson happily designates as "sympathy", and on the other hand a sustained and profound deepening in that with which the sympathetic relationship is established. In other words, one has to enter into a contact of essential sympathy (i.e. from essence to essence) first of all, and then not to glide off to other contacts of the kind, but to dwell in this sympathy so as to result in sufficient intensity and clarity in order to be able to say, in all honesty, that in fact an act of material knowledge has taken place. Here is a concrete example:

You venerate (i.e. you love and respect) a non-incarnated being — a departed person, a saint, or a hierarchical being — in a disinterested manner. Your veneration — which includes love, respect, gratitude, the desire to conform, etc. — cannot fail to create an invisible link of sympathy with its object. It may be in a subtle and dramatic way, or rather in a slow, gradual and almost imperceptible way — this does not matter — the day will come when you will experience the *presence* . . . not a fluidic, semi-electrical presence close to you in space — as in the apparition of a phantom or a ghost — but a breath of radiant serenity, of which you know with certain knowledge that the source from which it emanates is not at all in you. It influences you and fills you but it does not take its origin in you; it comes from outside of you. Just as you know, in drawing near to a fireplace, that the warmth that you feel does not arise from you, but rather from the fireplace, so also do you feel that the breath of serenity in question is due to an objective presence. Here, therefore, a relationship of sympathy is established. After this it is up to you to remain silently concentrated so that the relationship established is subsequently developed, i.e. that it gains in intensity and clarity—that it becomes a *meeting* in full consciousness.

The meeting is thus the realisation of the relationship when it is borne to the limit of the intensity of clarity. According to the case, it can take either the character of a "conversation through forces" or that of a "conversation through words". In the former case it is not precise and articulated thoughts or images which are communicated to you, but rather "forces" or impulses—spiritual and psychic seeds impregnated germinally with moral ideas and judgements. In the case of the "conversation through words" a revelation of articulated thoughts and representations takes place. The revelation to the shepherds at Bethlehem can be considered as a prototype of the meeting whose character is "conversation through words" and the experience of the mages of the Orient—who saw the star of the "king of the Jews...in the East", but who had to ask at Jerusalem, "where is he who has been born king of the Jews?" (Matthew ii, 2)—is an example of the meeting whose character is "conversation through forces". The "star" of the king of the Jews gave them certainty concerning the coming of Christ and gave them the impulse to go and search where he was awaited, but it did not give them information with respect to the place and parents, whilst to the shepherds of Bethlehem it was revealed that "to you is born *this day* in the *city of David* a Saviour, who is Christ the Lord. And this will be a sign for you: you will find a babe wrapped in swaddling cloths and lying in a manger" (Luke ii, 11-12), i.e. precise and complete information was given to them with respect to time, place and external circumstances.

Now, the meeting whose character is "conversation through forces" always resembles the experience of the "star" of the mages from the East, and that whose character is "conversation through words" always resembles the experience of the shepherds of Bethlehem. The "star" does not speak, it *moves*; and it leaves to the subject of its revelation the work of research in the domain of intelligence and facts. The meeting whose character is "conversation through words", in contrast, moves *and* teaches—it bears also on the domain of intelligence and facts. It *guides*.

I am not in a position to say which of the two forms of revelatory meeting is more frequent or which is objectively preferable, although subjectively that of the shepherds of Bethlehem seems to me preferable to that of the mages of the Orient. Be that as it may, *intuition*—understood as the alliance of *active* wisdom and *active* intelligence, which is the theme of the nineteenth Arcanum of the Tarot and which not only underlies Hermeticism but is its very reason for existence—presupposes the *cooperation* of two principles and therefore falls in the category of the revelation whose character is "conversation through forces". Just as the mages from the Orient made a long journey and brought presents to the Child, in following the "star", so also Hermeticism is on the way from century to century to arrive at the manger—not to arrive there with empty hands, but to place there the presents which are the fruit of the millennial-old effort of human intelligence which follows the "star".

The manger: where the mages from the Orient and the shepherds of Bethlehem meet, of which the octogenerian C. G. Jung said—in calling it a "mandala"— that "all the paths I had been following. . .were leading back to a single point— namely, to the mid-point" and that "it became increasingly plain to me that the mandala is the centre. It is the exponent of all paths. It is the path to the centre, to individuation" (C. G. Jung, *Memories, Dreams, Reflections*; trsl. R. and C. Winston, London, 1967, p. 222). And of this Pierre Teilhard de Chardin said:

> Under the combined influence of men's thoughts and aspira-
> tions, the universe around us is seen to be knit together and con-
> vulsed *by a vast movement of convergence*. Not only theoretical-
> ly, but experientially, our modern cosmogony is taking the form
> of a cosmogenesis. . .at the term of which we can distinguish
> *a supreme focus of personalising personality*. (Teilhard de Char-
> din, *Christianity and Evolution*; trsl. R. Hague, London, 1971,
> p. 180)

The manger—the centre, the individuation of the psyche, the supreme focus of the personalising personality of the universe, or the mystery of the Incarnation of the Word in history, worshipped by the mages from the East and by the shep-herds of Bethlehem—is this not the centre of the movement of convergence, in time and space, of all efforts and all aspirations of those who have endeavoured throughout the centuries to transform the base into the precious, to listen and understand the message of the stars, to raise their problems to Angels, Archangels, Cherubim and Seraphim so as to consult them, and to guard and not forget the memory of all the altars and chalices of the past? In a word, is this not the centre also for Hermeticists?

The "star" which Hermeticists follow leads them to the manger—to the centre of history, to the centre of the psychic life (individuation), to the centre of universal evolution or the "supreme focus of the personalising personality", to the Alpha and Omega of revelations, to the Heart which is at the centre of all hearts. For there is a centre of gravitation of hearts, just as there is a centre of gravitation of the planets. Like the latter, it causes the "seasons" of the life of the soul. This is why it is not without reason that the manger is venerated by the Church each year and that a unique light is lit in the world each Christmas. What I want to say is that Christmas is not only the festival dedicated to the *memory* of the historical nativity of Christ but that it is in addition the *event* of the nativity which is repeated each year, where Christ becomes Child anew and where the history of mankind becomes the manger. Then all that which is in us of the nature of the shepherds of Bethlehem and all that which is in us of the nature of the mages from the East responds as in the past. That which is in us of the nature of the mages from the East is enamoured of the "star" and sets out *en route* with the little incense, myrrh and gold gathered during the year which is drawing to an end; and that which is in us of the shepherds of Bethlehem kneels down before the Child whose reality and presence is revealed from above.

The annual repetition of the nativity of Christ as a real event on the spiritual plane—like those of his miracles, his passion, his resurrection and ascension—means to say that just as the external sun eternally repeats springtime, summer, autumn and winter, so does the spiritual sun reveal his eternal springtime aspect—his infancy—at Christmas, his eternal summer aspect—his miracles, his eternal autumnal aspect—his passion and resurrection, and his eternal winter aspect—the ascension. This means to say, again, that the ages are eternal—that infancy, youth, middle age and old age are eternal. The Christ is eternally Child, Master, Crucified and Resurrected. Man bears in himself at one and the same time the child, the young man, the mature man and the old man. Nothing of the past is lost or destroyed; the past simply passes from the stage into the wings—from the framework of the conscious to the domain of the unconscious from where it operates in a no-less active way. It is the same with past epochs and civilisations of human history; they have not disappeared, but are present and active in the instinctivity of our epoch and civilisation. It is to the great merit of C. G. Jung that he discovered the presence of the remote past in contemporary psychic life and established the existence of "archaeological layers" in human psychic life—just as archaeology did for the material objects of past civilisations and as palaeontology did for material fossils of the biological past. Thanks to the work of Jung, "psychological excavations" can be added to archaeological and palaeontological excavations, and can come to their aid. The difference between the vestiges of the past with which archaeology and palaeontology work and the "psychic layers" of the past established by Jung is that the latter are *living*—although outside of the framework of consciousness dominated and determined by intelligence—whilst the materials of archaeology and palaeontology are *dead*; they are only skeletons of the past.

The sense of the *idea of resurrection* (the theme of the following Major Arcanum of the Tarot, the twentieth Arcanum) is the actualisation of the fullness of all spiritual, psychic and corporeal forces in latent being (latent is from the Latin *latere*: to be hidden), i.e. where they have withdrawn from the domain of action and intelligence to one of latent energy—the unconscious (in Jung's sense of the word). In other words, it is the domain that we call "the past" but which, according to Henri Bergson (who traced out a "footpath" for Jung), forms a part of indestructible *duration* and is therefore revivable or *recallable to the present through memory* (if it is a matter of the human psychic life) or *through resurrection* (if it is a matter of divine cosmic memory). Resurrection is thus the divine analogy of the act of human memory. Just as man, by remembering, evokes or actualises the part of duration that we name "the past", so does God actualise that which has become latent and evokes to consciousness that which lives in the domain of the unconscious by an anlogous magical act to that of human memory. The "resurrection of the dead" is therefore when God "remembers" the whole fullness of past duration. It is the act of divine magic whose human analogy is memory.

Now, it is resurrection which is the "good news" of Christianity. For this reason the history of Christianity is — and will be — that of the resurrection of all that which is worthy of resurrection from the past of the history of mankind and the world. It is — and will be — the history of a series of "renaissances"— in the manner of the renaissance of Graeco-Roman philosophy and arts which took place at the end of the Middle Ages. This "renaissance" will be followed by others, including that of ancient Egypt and Chaldaea. Modern evolutionism and "cosmism" are its dawn. The "renaissances" in question are only the first degree of resurrection: they bear on the spiritual life and realise — or restore — its continuity, i.e. its spiritual duration. Another series of "renaissances" will re-establish psychic continuity and will signify the second degree of resurrection: that of the *life of the soul*. This will be followed by the resurrection of the *body*—which will be its completion.

Complete resurrection, i.e. that of the body, is therefore preceded by spiritual and psychic "resurrection", where *duration* is re-established on earth—where memory triumphs over forgetfulness. And the history of Christianity is, in the last analysis, the history of these triumphs.

It is the same with the liturgical year of the Church. This is simply the yearly endeavour of human memory to unite itself with divine memory so as to realise resurrection, i.e. to make the past *live* in the present. The words of consecration, "This is my body, which is given for you; do this in memory of me," is the key to the liturgical year. One does these things in memory of him, his mother, the apostles, saints and martyrs — and he, his mother, the apostles, saints and martyrs are *present* and living and acting in the present. The whole liturgical year says to us: do not forget. Remember, for it is through memory that resurrection is accomplished.

All the festivals of the year aim at resurrection. And that of Christmas is the resurrection of the Child who was worshipped by the shepherds of Bethlehem and the mages of the Orient. But it is at the same time the festival of the resurrection of the shepherds and mages also, i.e. the time of the magical evocation of the spiritual and psychic forces made use of by revelation and gnosis. For just as the Child is present at Christmas, so also there is an awakening and activation at Christmas of forces (including individual souls) capable of receiving His revelation, be it from Angels or from the stars. It is thus that it happens that Hermeticism also undergoes each year the rejuvenating and inspiring effect of Christmas, and that Hermeticists — often without being aware of it — receive vivifying impulses and illuminating inspirations for their efforts. The mystery of the "star" is thus repeated.

But those who follow the "star" must learn a lesson once and for all: not to consult Herod and the "chief priests and scribes of the people" at Jerusalem, but to follow the "star" that they have seen "in the East" and which "goes before them", without seeking for indications and confirmation on the part of Herod and his people. The gleam of the "star" and the effort to understand its message ought to suffice. Because Herod, representing the anti-revelatory force and principle, is also eternal. The time of Christmas is not that of the nativity of the Child alone; it is also the time of the massacre of the children of Bethlehem—the time where autonomous intelligence is driven to kill, i.e. to strangle and push back into the unconscious, all the tender flowers of spirituality which threaten the absolute autonomy arrogated to itself by intelligence.

May those who follow the "star" do so completely and without reserve! May they not seek—once having the "star" before their eyes—scientific confirmation, approval or sanction...or, what would be still worse, direction on the part of science! May they follow the "star" above them and *nothing else*! *Noblesse oblige*.

There is a recent example from which everyone can learn: namely, how Carl Gustav Jung followed the "star" without ever seeking support from outside. Dear Unknown Friend, read his autobiography (*Memories, Dreams, Reflections*) and you will know what the crux of the matter is for those who follow the "star"; you will know that a whole world is at stake underlying the exhortation: follow the "star" above you and nothing else!

What I have in mind is Jung's spiritual biography, which gives a model example of a Hermeticist—a mage from the Orient—who followed the "star" all his life, and followed the "star" alone. I do not have the *results* of his work in mind, which are able to satisfy or not. They do not satisfy me, I confess, but what right have I to demand of Jung that he should have gone further than he did? What he has done he did in a way which can serve as a model for everyone—the model of a method carried to perfection. The essential is not the *presentation* to the world of the results of Jung's work, but rather his *method* of working. I mean to say that it is: the method of "free association", where the first Arcanum of the Tarot—that of "concentration without effort"—finds its application; the method of interpretation of dreams and of spontaneous phantasy, which is the application of the second Arcanum of the Tarot; the method of cooperation between the fertilising sphere (outside of and beyond normal consciousness) and fertilised consciousness, which corresponds to the third Arcanum of the Tarot; the method of the amplification of immediate data from the manifestation of the unconscious by means of alchemy, myths, and mysteries belonging to mankind's historical past, which is an application of the fourth Arcanum of the Tarot; the method of psychic healing which consists in making the patient understand the warnings of his unconscious and accept the latter as guide and master, where the fifth Arcanum of the Tarot is put into practice; the method of passing courageously through unparalleled temptations and conflicts of duties by making decisions according to the "arrow of inspiration" and not according to a code of rules of conduct, which is the sixth Arcanum of the Tarot; and, lastly, the method of not identifying oneself with the superhuman forces of archetypes—not allowing them to take possession of individual consciousness (so that the latter does not become a victim of *infla-tion*)—which is the application of the seventh Arcanum of the Tarot.

With respect to the nineteenth Arcanum of the Tarot, we find it again in the work of Jung in the guise of the active cooperation of intelligence and tran-scendental revelatory being, which cooperation is not only the mature fruit of the work of his long life, but also it is the principal thesis of his method of work in the domain of depth psychology, which he openly advanced and maintained. The *intuition* postulated by Henri Bergson as necessary in order to be able to under-stand life and the world was practised by Jung in order to understand and to heal the life of the human soul. He did not commit the error of the mages of the Orient. He did not consult Herod and his people.

Another example of faithfulness to the "star" is the life and work of Father Pierre Teilhard de Chardin. This mage from the Orient followed the "star" on a long voyage: through the paths of the universal evolution of the world throughout millions of years. What did he do, properly speaking? He showed the "star" above the universal evolution of the world, in a way that the latter "is seen to be knit together and convulsed by a vast movement of convergence . . . at the term of which we can distinguish a supreme focus of personalising personality" (Teilhard de Char-din, *Christianity and Evolution*; ttsl. R. Hague, London, 1971, p. 180). Darwin-ian evolution—this nightmare of a struggle for existence of species without number in life's feverishly multiplying endeavour, blind and groping, to produce that which is most viable—has therefore become henceforth the *way* leading to per-sonalisation, a movement which has direction and aim. Teilhard de Chardin, in having perceived the "star" above Darwinian evolution, has crowned the latter with this guiding "star" and has thus transformed it from the nightmare of ram-pant production attempting to produce the viable into *the way towards the manger*. In following this "star", he did not let himself be turned aside from the path indicated by it—neither by enemies of the new from the camp of religion nor by enemies of the transcendental in the camp of science: the "sanctioners" and the "scribes" of Herod. It was to his faithfulness to the "star" that he owed the singular force of his soul which allowed him to be a faithful son of the Church and at the same time a conscientious worker for science—and to remain so until his last breath. He never revolted against or broke with the Church and Academia. Having been loyal to them with his whole heart until the end, he therefore comes under the seventh beatitude of the Sermon on the Mount: "Blessed are the peace-makers, for they shall be called sons of God" (Matthew v, 9).

In writing of the force of soul resulting from faithfulness to the "star"—the force which manifests itself in the power to resist the weakness of revolt (for revolt is a weakness where one lets oneself be carried away by the current of emotional impatience—the fundamental weakness of all rebels, including religious reformers as well as political revolutionaries and the most celebrated social reformers) and in the power to procure peace between two aspirations which are, or are believed to be, opposed to one another—it is difficult for me not to pay homage to two

Hermeticists of our century, notably Francis Warrain and Dr. Paul Carton, both avowed Hermeticists. The former followed the "star" through the study of law, through creative work in the domain of sculpture, through the metaphysics of Hoéné Wronski, through mathematics, logic and Charles Henry's psychophysics, through the Cabbala and Jacob Boehme. "By combining as much as possible the resources of the intuitive mode proper to antiquity with the instruments put at our disposal by the discursive method," he defined the essential conditions for an intermediary gnosis allowing the antinomy between the absolute and the relative—between faith and reason—to be correctly resolved. Blessed are the peacemakers, for they shall be called sons of God!

Paul Carton followed the "star" as a naturopathic doctor and as a Christian super-naturalist, along the narrow way between the natural and the miraculous, which way is that of Hermeticism pure and simple. His book *La science occulte et les sciences occultes* (Brevannes, 1935), where the Major Arcana of the Tarot are also the object of study, bears witness to his life's endeavour to unite the divine super-natural and the human natural through the intermediary magic of the Hermetic tradition. Again: Blessed are the peacemakers, for they shall be called sons of God!

Intuition is therefore the cooperation of human intelligence with superhuman wisdom. It is what creates the link—or the "intermediary gnosis" and "intermediary magic"—between the absolute and the relative, between the supernatural and the natural, between faith and reason. Now, intuition can be developed only by peo-ple who have faith and who have reason. It is reserved for believing thinkers. Whosoever believes and does not think will never attain it. Whosoever thinks and does not believe will never have the certainty of transcendental things that intui-tion alone can give.

Intuition combines two certainties: essential certainty (that of essence), and con-sistent certainty (that of consistency). The former is of a *moral* order; its force of conviction resides in the good and the beautiful. The latter is of a cognitive order; its force of conviction resides in consistency in the vision of the relationships of things. Intuitive certainty is therefore "faith at first hand" combined with "in-telligence at first hand". Let us explain this. There is faith founded on extrinsic authority—a person, an institution, a book, etc.—and there is faith founded on intrinsic authority—the inner and intimate experience of the divine breath, and the direct impression of the divine realm. The latter is first hand. There is still a third kind of faith—the most heroic, perhaps—the "intermediary faith" between faith founded on extrinsic authority and that founded on the intrinsic authority of inner experience: this is *postulative faith*, where one believes without any sup-port, either from without or from within. It is the faith of "the voice of one cry-ing in the wilderness" (Matthew iii, 3)—the voice itself of the soul who cries, i.e. postulates in complete solitude ("in the wilderness") the things without which it could not live. Kant's three postulates: God, freedom of will, and the immortal-ity of the soul, are such a cry of the soul in the wilderness. For they are founded neither on extrinsic authority nor on mystical experience, but rather on semi-structural exigencies of the soul itself. It is the reality of hunger and thirst alone which bears witness to the existence of bread and water. "Freedom, immortality and God"—or the desperate night of nothingness—such is the cry from Kant's soul in the desert where he found himself.

Such was also the faith of John the Baptist before he had the experience of the descent of the Spirit from heaven upon Jesus, at the baptism in the Jordan. His faith, which is summed up by the conclusion of his sermon, "Repent, for the kingdom of heaven is at hand" (Matthew iii, 2), was a cry in the wilderness, i.e. the voice of supreme hunger and thirst for the kingdom of heaven. And it is precisely this faith which made John the Baptist the first "eyewitness", so to say, of the reality of the descent of the kingdom of heaven, and which made him the first human being to recognise the Christ. His faith was crowned with experience. John the Baptist became one who saw.

Now, it is postulative faith become faith at first hand (mysticism) which arrives at the perfect certainty of intuition as a consequence of the help of intelligence. John the Baptist still had need of this latter in order to have complete certainty. For this reason he—who had seen the Spirit descend upon Jesus—sent two disciples to Jesus to ask him, "Are you he who is to come, or shall we look for another?" (Matthew xi, 3). And Jesus had to reply in the framework of intelligence alone:

> Go and tell John what you hear and see: the blind receive their sight and the lame walk, lepers are cleansed and the deaf hear, and the dead are raised up, and the poor have the good news preached to them. (Matthew xi, 4-5)

In other words, Jesus said that these phenomenal effects indicate consistency between the revelation of the descent of the Spirit experienced by John the Baptist and the manifestation of this Spirit through Jesus Christ. It is the language of intelligence, pure and simple, which Jesus makes use of in order to fill the gap in John the Baptist's consciousness—which required the help of intelligence. And it was because of this gap that Jesus Christ said of John the Baptist that, although a prophet, he is "more than a prophet" and that "among those born of women there has risen no one greater than John the Baptist, yet he who is least in the kingdom of heaven is greater than he" (Matthew xi, 9, 11). For the kingdom of God brings with it the absolute certainty of the cooperation of faith at first hand and intelligence—it is the *kingdom of intuition*.

This is why the Master made appeal not only to faith but also to intelligence, not only to essential certainty but also to consistent certainty, by stating the fundamental principle of intelligence, i.e. judgement by effects, knowledge of things by their fruits:

> You will know them by their fruits. Are grapes gathered from thorns, or figs from thistles? So, every sound tree bears good fruit, but the bad tree bears evil fruit. A sound tree cannot bear evil fruit, nor can a bad tree bear good fruit. (Matthew vii, 16-18)

This is the briefest and most complete characteristic of intelligence and its role. Its role is immense, if one considers that intelligence is called to constitute an integral part of intuition which, in its turn, determines greatness and smallness in the kingdom of God.

This role was understood in the Middle Ages in the ecclesiastical milieu of the West. Believers set themselves to thinking. Scholasticism thus took its birth. It is not true that scholasticism is due to the desire to intellectualise faith and to replace it by philosophy—that it owes its birth to secret doubt in the hearts of believers of the Middle Ages. No, what is at the root of scholasticism is the *desire for the fullness of intuition*, i.e. that of "baptising" intelligence and winning its cooperation with faith. It was thus a matter, truth to tell, not of doubt, but of an act of ardent faith which did not at all doubt that human intelligence is also as "baptisable" and "Christianisable" as the heart and the will. St. Albertus Magnus and St. Thomas Aquinas were in no way impelled by doubt when they set out upon their grandiose work of thought; they were full of confidence that the Blood of Calvary would penetrate, warm and transfigure the domain of the cold clarity of thought that there was up until then. Their work was apostolic rather than apologetic. Just as missionaries went to non-Christian countries in order to bear the good news there, so did St. Albertus Magnus and St. Thomas Aquinas go to the non-Christianised land of human intelligence in order to Christianise it. Was this doubt? Indeed no! It was an act of apostolic faith and apostolic zeal!

Dear Unknown Friend, do not scorn mediaeval scholasticism. It is, in truth, as beautiful, as venerable and as inspiring as the great cathedrals that we have inherited from the Middle Ages. To it we owe a number of masterpieces of thought—thought in the light of faith. And, like all true masterpieces, those of mediaeval scholasticism are beneficial. They heal the disorientated, feverish and confused soul. Just as a doctor prescribes for certain physical illnesses a change of climate and air—a sojourn of several months in the mountains—so it would be right and beneficial for him to prescribe to many a person disturbed by "existential problems" and troubled by the "contradictions of life" that he should remove himself for some time into the climate of high scholasticism and breathe there pure air from mental mountains. It is not a matter of a conversion to scholastic philosophy, i.e. that the person in question embraces the scholastic doctrine, but rather of a more elevated intellectual *niveau* and, above all, of continuous work for some time with the clear and precise notions of scholasticism on this elevated niveau.

Perhaps the *quinque viae*, the five ways of reasoning, of St. Thomas Aquinas will not necessarily convince you, but you will emerge from meditative work on the five arguments (proposed to prove the existence of God) with a clear head and a calm heart, well-prepared and equipped to seek and find other ways to certainty. It is the *occupation* with these five ways of reasoning which will render you stronger and more calm, which will elevate you above all the entanglements due to the confused play of complexes which are a mixture of feelings in which personal preferences assert themselves and thoughts which are only a mouthpiece for these preferences. And it is this elevation above psychological complexes which is the salutary effect — even the healing action — of occupation with scholasticism, when one reads in the style of scholastic meditation.

One could object: Why not mathematics? Doesn't mathematics have the same effect of detachment and elevation above personal psychological limitations?

Without doubt mathematics also has a salutary effect. But it does not so engage the whole human being as does the totality of scholastic problems, and consequently its salutary effect does not have the same significance. What is at stake with scholasticism is God, the soul, freedom, immortality, salvation, good and evil. The triumph over psychological factors here is something quite different than triumph over the same psychological factors through occupying oneself with quantities and their functions alone. Scholasticism has more at stake than mathematics and in consequence its salutary effect is of greater significance. Therefore, do not despise mediaeval scholasticism, dear Unknown Friend; it is still of value.

No more is it true that the mystical impulse from the end of the thirteenth and into the seventeenth century was purely and simply a *reaction* against the "dry intellectualism" of scholasticism. No, the flowering of mysticism during this epoch was the *fruit* and the *result* of scholasticism, prefigured in the spiritual biography of St. Thomas Aquinas himself. Notably, St. Thomas towards the end of his life arrived at mystical contemplation of God and the spiritual world and said, on returning from this ecstasy, that his written works now appeared to him "like straw". Indeed, he wrote nothing after this.

The believing thinker thus became a seeing mystic. And this transformation did not take place in spite of his work of scholastic thought, but rather thanks to it — as its fruit and its crowning glory.

Now, what happened to St. Thomas Aquinas also happened to a group of individuals who formed the crest of the wave of scholasticism. Just as St. Thomas, through scholastic reasoning, arrived at contemplation, so did part of advanced scholasticism arrive at mysticism, i.e. at the *aim* of scholasticism, which is *intuition* or the state of union of faith and intelligence. Meister Eckhart, Ruysbroeck or, lastly, St. John of the Cross are spirits amongst whom you will search in vain for a spirit of opposition to scholasticism. For them also it was true that scholasticism was "like straw", but they knew at the same time from their own experience that this straw proved to be an excellent combustible. They certainly surpassed scholasticism, but they did so by attaining its aim. For the aim of scholastic endeavour is contemplation, and it is mysticism which is the fruit of the scholastic tree.

The mystics of the epoch under consideration were individuals who signified a successful outcome of the scholastic endeavour, i.e. in them intelligence was baptised and Christianised. The missionary work with regard to "pagan" intelligence undertaken by St. Albertus Magnus and St. Thomas Aquinas was crowned with success in the guise of the mystical impulse which followed high scholasticism. The marriage of faith and intelligence was consummated and believers and thinkers were reinforced by a third group: that of the *people of intuition*.

Thus, dear Unknown Friend, do not at all despise mediaeval scholasticism, but make use of it not only to re-establish the health of your soul, but also—by thinking in the light of faith—to arrive at intuition, without which Hermeticism is something merely literary. . .of doubtful literary value. It lives only from intuition, and without intuition it is something dead. And it is this dead thing alone that is seen by people of faith and people of science, who are genuinely astonished that there are people who take it seriously. They see only scientific and religious "tinsel" or, at most, a weak faith which borrows crutches from science or, perhaps, a childlike science which has not yet learnt to distinguish between what one believes and what one knows. And they are not at all mistaken: without the invisible cement of intuition, Hermeticism is indeed only an improvised assemblage of heterogeneous elements of science and religion.

It suffices to indicate the following analogy: it was neither the straw of the crib, nor the animals that were present, which guided and enabled the mages from the East to find the Child, but rather the "star" in heaven. Similarly, in Hermeticism one will find only straw and animals if one is not guided by its "star", which exists only for intuition. Now, it is the nineteenth Arcanum of the Tarot which invites us to occupy ourselves quite especially with the "star" of Hermeticism in the heaven of intuition. What is this "star"? The *Zohar* says:

> And God made the two great lights. . .originally, when the moon and sun were in intimate union, they shone with equal luminosity. The names JEHOVAH and ELOHIM were then associated as equals. . .and the two lights were dignified with the same name: MAZPAZ MAZPAZ. . .The two lights rose simultaneously and were of the same dignity. But. . .the moon humbled herself by diminishing her light, and renounced her place of higher rank. From that time she has had no light of her own, but derives her light from the sun. Nevertheless, her real light is greater than that which she radiates here below; for a woman enjoys no honour save in conjunction with her husband. The great light (the sun) has the name JEHOVAH and the lesser light (the moon) has the name ELOHIM, which is the last of the degrees and the close of thought. Originally she was inscribed above among the letters of the sacred name (YHVH), which are four in number; it was only after diminishing herself that she took the name ELOHIM. But her power is manifest in all directions. . . EL being "the dominion of the day", IM being "the dominion of the night" and HÉ in the middle being the remainder of the forces ("the stars"), participating in both dominions. (*Zohar*, *Bereshith* 20a; compare also with the English translation by H. Sperling and M. Simon in *The Zohar*, vol. i, London-Bournemouth, 1949, pp. 84-85)

It is left to us only to cite another passage from an ancient source—from the eleventh book of Apuleius' *Transformations*—in order to have all the elements necessary to grapple, sufficiently equipped, with the problem of the "star" of Hermeticism and "The Sun" of the nineteenth Arcanum of the Tarot. Apuleius summarised his great vigil at the temple of Isis—the "arcana of the sacred night" (*noctis sacratae arcana*)—in the following way:

> I approached the very gates of death and set one foot on Proserpine's threshold, yet was permitted to return, rapt through all the elements. *At midnight I saw the sun shining in its brilliant radiance*; I entered the presence of the gods of the under-world and the gods of the upper-world, stood near and worshipped them. (Apuleius, *Transformations: The Golden Ass*; trsl. R. Graves, Penguin, 1950, p. 286)

Let us now seek for the *reality*, having in view the above-cited passage from the *Zohar* and the statement made by Apuleius. The *Zohar* tells us that the moon "renounced her place of higher rank"—that of equality with the sun—and that "from that time she has had no light of her own, but derives her light from the sun; nevertheless, her real light is greater than that which she radiates here below". *Here below*, therefore, the moon reflects the light of the sun, whilst *above*— where her name is ELOHIM—"her power is manifest in all directions... EL being 'the dominion of the day', IM being 'the dominion of the night' and HÉ in the middle being the remainder of the forces ('the stars'), participating in both dominions."

Now, the moon, in so far as she is the nocturnal luminary here below, reflects the sun, but in so far as she is the nocturnal luminary above, she shines with her own light, and it is the sun which reflects her. In other words, the moon is "solar" above and "lunar" here below, whilst the sun is "solar" here below and "lunar" above. It is in this sense that EL, the radiant part of the moon's name above, has "the dominion of the day", i.e. it is the visible sun—reflecting the invisible moon during the day. Similarly, the visible moon reflects the sun (become invisible) during the night. *The spiritual moon is therefore the sun which shines at midnight*. And it is the spiritual moon—or Isis-Sophia—that Apuleius "saw shining at midnight in its brilliant radiance". For the long vigil in the Isis temple resulted in a vision of the cosmic principle of Isis, i.e. the spiritual moon or the "sun at midnight".

All these things, although presented to us in mythological clothing, relate to the profound reality of the relationship of intelligence and wisdom, and their union—intuition. For intelligence corresponds to the moon, wisdom to the sun, and intuition to the restoration of the "intimate union" of the two luminaries. *Here below* intelligence reflects wisdom—or, if it is eclipsed (see Letter XVIII), it reflects the terrestrial world of external experience. But there is another intelligence *above*, a transcendental intelligence, whose "light is greater than that which it radiates here below", and which—united intimately to wisdom—is "inscribed

above among the letters of the sacred name (YHVH), which are four in number",
and which shines in the middle of the night "in its brilliant radiance". This higher
intelligence, this "sun at midnight", which is the conjunction of the spiritual sun
and spiritual moon—or, in other words, the intimate union of intelligence and
wisdom—is the "star" of Hermeticism, and it is "The Sun" of the nineteenth Arcanum. "The Sun" of the nineteenth Arcanum is the "sun at midnight", i.e. the
"sun" that Apuleius "saw shining at midnight in its brilliant radiance", and it is
this "sun" which is the "star" of Hermeticism across the ages. It is the principle
of intuition, or the intimate union of transcendental intelligence and wisdom.

The Arcanum of intuition is therefore that of knowing how to raise to creative
intelligence the intelligence which reflects, and how to effect its union with
wisdom, i.e. that of the work of re-establishing, firstly, the union of intelligence
of diminished light here below with the intelligence of complete light above, and
then the union of intelligence-thus-reunited with divine wisdom (see figure). The
triangle of the figure shows in a most clear way what the relationships are: intelligence, attracted by wisdom, does not unite itself to the latter on the plane
of reflection, but raises itself to the creative plane, where it regains its higher "non-
fallen" status and unites with wisdom, the result of which union is intuition.

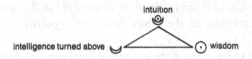

Therefore it is not thanks to the suppression of intelligence, or by becoming less
intelligent, that intuition is attained; but rather, on the contrary, it is thanks to
its intensification—until it becomes creative and is thus united to its higher,
transcendental aspect, *after which* it is united to wisdom. It is therefore by becoming more and more intelligent that one arrives at intuition—although there is
another way, that of "sunstroke", namely the annihilation of intelligence by the
brilliance of wisdom, which is the theme of the twenty-first (or zero) Arcanum
"The Fool". We shall therefore return to this in the twenty-first Letter on the Major Arcana of the Tarot, which is dedicated to "The Fool".

But those who hold to the tradition of Hermeticism—that of mysticism, gnosis,
magic and Hermetic philosophy—keep away from the way of "divine folly"
(*yurodivost* in Russian; *Narrheit in Gott* in German) and follow the way indicated
by the parable of the talents (Matthew xxv, 14-30), where the master entrusted
his servants with a number of talents, each according to his ability, so that they
should put them to good account. Thus, they *raise* intelligence to a level at which
it becomes capable of uniting with wisdom; they render it of maximum account—
which is intuition.

Just as the impulse of scholasticism, on the historical ladder of western civilisation, did not lead to a perfect system of scholastic philosophy, but rather to

mysticism, so does individual intelligence, on the ladder of individual development, lead to intuition and not to a state where it knows all and explains all. Intelligence is not the absolute aim; in developing, it is transformed into intuition. It is called to effect the passage from argumentative reasoning to comprehensive intuition.

In relation to the theme of the mission of intelligence being the way to intuition, it is relevant to indicate the fact that the philosophical work of Immanuel Kant—which scorched the pretensions to certainty of autonomous intelligence with respect to metaphysical things by demonstrating the set limits of knowledge possible to autonomous intelligence—has had an effect comparable to that of wind, which extinguishes the weak fire and which revives the strong fire: the one becoming sceptics and the others becoming mystics. Kant put an end to the speculative metaphysics of autonomous intelligence and opened up the way to a mysticism which non-autonomous intelligence or "practical reason" (*praktische Vernunft*) is capable of—Kant's "practical reason" being intelligence united to the wisdom of moral nature, i.e. intuition. Indeed, several times I have had occasion to observe the fact that with time Kantians become mystics—to name, for example, the German philosopher Paul Deussen, the author of a synthesis of Kantianism, Platonism and the Vedanta (cf. Paul Deussen, *The Elements of Metaphysics*; trsl. C. M. Duff, London-New York, 1894).

Deussen's fundamental thesis is that the incapability of autonomous intelligence attaining to the noumenon behind phenomenon (demonstrated by Kant) entails the task of resorting to intuitive perception of the essence of things, which is manifested in Platonism and in the Vedanta. It was probably with a view to showing the working of the intuitive method that Deussen translated and published sixty Upanishads from the Vedas (*Sechzig Upanishads des Veda*, Leipzig, 1897).

But let us return to the "star" of Hermeticism—to the midnight sun—which is the "sun" of the nineteenth Arcanum of the Tarot.

The *Zohar* and Apuleius have helped us to understand an important aspect of this sun, namely that of the "intimate union of the sun and moon"—or of wisdom and intelligence—in the guise of the midnight sun. A third ancient document can now help us to place ourselves in the presence of another important aspect of the problem occupying us, and presents it to us in its entirety. This is the Apocalypse of St. John, were we read:

> And a great portent appeared in heaven, a woman clothed with
> the sun, with the moon under her feet, and on her head a crown
> of twelve stars. (Revelation xii, 1)

The *Zohar* and Apuleius speak of the moon and the sun joined—the sign ☺ which is the sign of Isis. We find this sign again in the apocalyptic vision of the woman enveloped by the sun and with the moon under her feet. But the apocalyptic vision adds here a third element: the twelve stars.

In other words, intelligence united to wisdom in intuition still does not signify the achievement of the work of the reintegration of consciousness, if it is not crowned by a third element, which corresponds to the "stars" just as intelligence corresponds to the "moon" and wisdom to the "sun". What, therefore, is this third element?

In order to understand its role and nature it is still necessary for us to look at— and this time more closely—the experience of spirits who turned from intellectualism to intuitionism, as we indicated above in speaking of the effect of the work of Kant. We mentioned the German philosopher Paul Deussen, but perhaps it would be more to the point to mention his master, the German philosopher of worldwide renown—Arthur Schopenhauer. For it was he, author of the celebrated book *The World as Will and Representation*, who made the decisive step from Kant's thesis (that phenomena hide the essence of things, and that the essence remains inaccessible to intelligence as such) to the intuitive introspection of the essence of one thing—the Self—a thing that represents and contains the other things of the world.

This intuitive introspection allowed him to arrive at the conclusion that it is the will which is the essence of things, and that things are only representations of the will. Therefore the world is, according to Schopenhauer, a unique will which represents or "imagines" the multiplicity of things. And as Schopenhauer found that the same experience gave rise to almost the same conclusion in Indian mystical philosophy—above all in the Vedanta, based on the Upanishads of the Vedas— he said: "The Upanishads were my consolation in life, and they will also be so in death" (*Die Upanishads waren mein Trost im Leben; sie werden es auch im Tode sein*).

Thus, the mystical philosophy of India is the original and prototype of intuitionist philosophies of the West—such as that of Schopenhauer, Deussen and Eduard von Hartmann (cf. *Philosophy of the Unconscious*; trsl. W. C. Coupland, London, 1931). Let us therefore examine the fundamental experience and principal conclusion to be drawn from the mystical philosophy of India, as represented by the Vedanta of the Advaita ("non-dualist") school.

This philosophy is founded on intuitive introspection—as method. This is based on the one hand on experience of the will as the element underlying all intellectual, psychological, biological and mechanical movement, and on the other hand on the experience of the "inner eye" or detached transcendental Self, which observes the movements produced by the will. The will creates the multiplicity of mental, psychic, biological and mechanical phenomena, in contrast to the unity of "the Seer in seeing" (the transcendental Self). The transcendental Self does not move, therefore it does not change, therefore it is immortal, therefore it is not an entity separated from the real essence of the world, and thus it is one with it. The true Self of man and the essence of the real world—or God—are identical. *Aham Brahma asmi* ("I am Brahma")—this is the formula which gives a summary of the experience and conclusions drawn by the Vedanta.

Now, it suffices on the one hand not to identify with the will and its movements and on the other hand to identify with the transcendental Self—"the Seer in seeing"— in order to attain to the real being and essence of the world in the *intuitive experience* of Vedanta adherents and German intuitionist philosophers. But one could ask: Is the intuitive experience of the transcendental Self truly final and complete, so that nothing follows it or surpasses it? Is the experience of the transcendental Self truly the *nec plus ultra* ("the ultimate") of knowledge?

Indeed, it lacks something important: *the whole spiritual world*, i.e. the Holy Trinity and the nine spiritual hierarchies. The "great portent" of which the Apocalypse speaks indicates beyond the sun and moon *a crown of twelve stars on the head of the woman*.

The intuitive experience of the transcendental Self—sublime and stimulating as it may be—does not suffice, alone, to let us perceive, and to render us conscious of, the spiritual world. The union of the "moon" and the "sun" alone, in the human spiritual *microcosm*, still does not signify the experience of the spiritual *macrocosm*. It is not sufficient to elevate oneself to the transcendental Self; it is necessary, still further, that this transcendental Self perceives and becomes conscious of other "transcendental Selves"— many of which are higher than it. The transcendental Self of man, as eternal and immutable as it is, is not the ultimate summit in world evolution.

The transcendental Self is not God. It is in his image and after his likeness, according to the law of analogy or kinship, but it is not identical with God. There are still several degrees on the ladder of analogy which separate it from the summit of the ladder—from God. These degrees which are higher than it are its "stars"— or the ideals to which it aims. The Apocalypse specifies the number of them: there are *twelve* degrees higher than that of the consciousness of the human transcendental Self. It is necessary, therefore, in order to attain to the ONE God, to elevate oneself successively to degrees of consciousness of the nine spiritual hierarchies and the Holy Trinity. The conclusion of the Vedanta—*aham Brahma asmi*, declaring the identity of the transcendental Self and the One God—is therefore an error due to a confusion of values. Here the image and likeness of God is taken for God, and experience of the Divine, likewise, is taken to be God himself. All which glitters is not gold—and all which is transcendental and immortal is not God. For the devil, also, is transcendental and immortal.

This confusion can easily take place if one keeps exclusively to the empirical psychological method, whilst avoiding the principle of transcendental metaphysics. Thus even C. G. Jung only narrowly missed identifying his psychological experience of the seventh "archetype"— the (transcendental) Self (*das Selbst*)—with what religions call "God". It was only thanks to his prodigious prudence that he had, though, left a door open and did not go as far as to pretend to have had a psychological experience of God. Then again, consider disciples of the *Sankya* (or *Samkhya*) metaphysical school, concerning which Krishna said:

> Fools, not wise men, say that *Sankya* (renunciation of action to know God) and *Yoga* (pursuit of action living in God) are distinct. He who practises one, fully earns the fruits of both. The place which the follower of *Sankya* obtains is also gained by the followers of *Yoga*. He sees truly who sees the *Sankya* and the *Yoga* as one and the same. (*Bhagavad-Gita* v, 4-5; trsl. M. N. Dutt, *Bhishma Parva* xxix, 4-5 in *The Mahabharata* vi, Calcutta, 1896, p. 38)

They have, therefore, the same experience of the transcendental Self as yogis and Vedantins, yet without arriving at the conclusion that the transcendental Self is God. On the contrary, thanks to the principles of their metaphysics, they recognise the *plurality* of individual *purushas*, i.e. the plurality of "transcendental Selves". Thus, the same experience can give rise to different — even contrary — interpretations, if one applies different directing metaphysical principles. Yoga and Sankya are "one and the same" with respect to the *experience* of the transcendental Self, but they differ radically with respect to the interpretation of this experience: the "men of yoga" believe that with it they have attained God, whilst the "men of Sankya" do not pretend to have achieved anything other than the experience of the individual transcendental Self, the individual *purusha* (or *monad* — in the sense of Leibnitz's term).

One could also say, in the symbolical language of the Bible, that yoga attains to union (= yoga) of the two luminaries — the moon (or intelligence) and the sun (or spontaneous wisdom of the transcendental Self) — and halts there, whilst Sankya also attains this, but it takes account of still a further kind of "luminary": the "stars" (higher entities of the spiritual world). Sankya, whilst leaving the door open to that which transcends the "transcendental Self", does not occupy itself with it, it is true, in an explicit manner — which has given it the qualification "atheistic". However, its "atheism" does not amount to its denying the existence of a universal *Purusha* higher than all individual *purushas* (it professes to know nothing of this with certain knowledge), but rather to its denying the affirmation of yoga and Vedanta, i.e. that the "transcendental Self" *is* God.

In contrast, Judaeo-Christian Hermeticism, which ranges itself on the side of Sankya with respect to the negation of the identification of the "transcendental Self" with God, is intensely occupied with the third "luminary"— the "stars"— in the three aspects of astrology, angelology and trinitarian theology, which aspects correspond to the body, soul and spirit of the third "luminary". Judaeo-Christian Hermeticism is thus the sustained effort across the centuries to know and understand the *three* luminaries in their *unity*, i.e. to know and understand the "great portent which appeared in heaven — a woman clothed with the sun, with the moon under her feet, and on her head a crown of twelve stars" (Revelation xii, 1). It is the woman in this apocalyptic vision who unites the three "luminaries"— the moon, the sun and the stars, i.e. the luminaries of night, day and eternity.

It is she—the "Virgin of light" of the *Pistis Sophia*, the Wisdom sung of by Solomon, the *Shekinah* of the Cabbala, the Mother, the Virgin, the pure celestial Mary—who is the soul of the light of the three luminaries, and who is both the source and aim of Hermeticism. For Hermeticism is, as a whole, the aspiration to participation in knowledge of the Father, Son and Holy Spirit, and the Mother, Daughter and Holy Soul. It is not a matter of seeing the Holy Trinity with human eyes, but rather of seeing with the eyes—and in the light—of Mary-Sophia. For just as no one comes to the Father but by Jesus Christ (John xiv, 6), so does no one understand the Holy Trinity but by Mary-Sophia. And just as the Holy Trinity manifests itself through Jesus Christ, so *understanding* of this manifestation is possible only through intuitive apprehension of what the virgin mother of Jesus Christ understands of it, who not only bore him and brought him to the light of day, but who also was present—present as mother—at his death on the Cross. And just as Wisdom (Sophia)—as Solomon said—was present at the creation ("when he established the heavens, I was there, when he drew a circle on the face of the deep. . .then I was at work beside him"—Proverbs viii, 27-31) and "built her house. . .set up her seven pillars" (Proverbs ix, 1), so Mary-Sophia was present at the redemption and "was at work beside him", and "built her house. . .set up her seven pillars", i.e. she became Our Lady of the seven sorrows. For the seven sorrows of Mary correspond, for the work of the redemption, to the seven pillars of Sophia for the work of creation. Sophia is the queen of the "three luminaries"—the moon, the sun and the stars—as the "great portent" of the Apocalypse shows. And just as the *word* of the Holy Trinity became flesh in Jesus Christ, so did the *light* of the Holy Trinity become flesh in Mary-Sophia—the *light*, i.e. threefold receptivity, the threefold faculty of intelligent reaction, or *understanding*. Mary's words: *mihi fiat secundum verbum tuum* ("let it be to me according to your word"—Luke i, 38) are the key to the mystery of the relationship between the pure act and pure reaction, between the word and understanding—lastly, between Father, Son and Holy Spirit on the one hand and Mother, Daughter and Holy Soul on the other hand. They are the true key to the "seal of Solomon"—the hexagram: ✡

The hexagram is not at all the symbol of good and evil, but rather it is that of the threefold pure act or "fire" and the threefold pure reaction (the threefold *mihi fiat secundum verbum tuum*) or "light of fire", i.e. "water". "Fire" and "water" signify that which acts spontaneously and creatively on the one hand, and that which reacts reflectively on the other hand—the latter being the conscious "yes" or light of *mihi fiat secundum verbum tuum*. This is the elementary meaning of the "seal of Solomon"—elementary in the sense of the *elements* "fire" and "water", taken on their highest level.

But the still higher meaning that this symbol hides—or rather reveals—is that of the *luminous Holy Trinity*, i.e. that of *understanding* of the Holy Trinity.

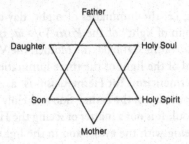

Then it is the hexagram comprising the two triangles: Father-Son-Holy Spirit; Mother-Daughter-Holy Soul (see figure). And these two triangles of the luminous Holy Trinity are revealed in the work of redemption accomplished through Jesus Christ and conceived through Mary-Sophia. Jesus Christ is its agent; Mary-Sophia is its luminous reaction. The two triangles reveal the *luminous Holy Trinity* in the work of creation accomplished by the creative Word and animated by the "yes" of Wisdom-Sophia. The luminous Holy Trinity is therefore the unity of the triune Creator and the triune *natura naturans*, i.e. the unity of the threefold *Fiat* and the threefold *mihi fiat secundum verbum tuum* which reveals itself in *natura naturata*, in the world created before the Fall; and it is the triune divine *spirit* and the triune *soul* of the world manifesting in the *body* of the world—in *natura naturata*.

The *Zohar* puts forward the idea of the luminous Holy Trinity. It teaches that the great name of GOD YHVH reveals the Father (Y = י), the supreme Mother (H = ה), the Son (V = ו), and the Daughter (the second HÉ of the divine name YHVH). Such is the eternal name YHVH. But in the history of the created world there are also revealed: the *Shekinah* (identified with the "community of Israel")—the true "Rachel weeping for her children" (Matthew ii, 18), who weeps in exile and who is the "beautiful virgin who has no eyes" (*Mishpatim* 95a; trsl. *The Zohar*, vol. iii, p. 285); the *Messiah-king* who "descends and reascends through all the heavens in order to exercise, with all the prophets who are to be found, the universal function of salvation" (L. Schaya, *L'homme et l'absolu selon la Kabbale*, Paris, 1958, p. 96); and the *Ruach hakodesch* (the "holy breath" or Holy Spirit), of which Saadya speaks, through the intermediary of which the thirty-two ways of wisdom are incorporated in the air that one breathes—the "holy breath" by means of which God is revealed, to the prophets, at the foundation of the secret of creation and which is called the "breath of the living God" (רוּחַ הָאֱלֹהִים חַיִּים") (cf. Henri Sérouya, *La Kabbale*, Paris, 1956, p. 136). The Messiah is the seventh term or principle of the hexagram Father, Son, Holy Spirit; Mother, Daughter, Holy Soul (= *Shekinah*, or the "community of Israel"). He is the *agent* of all, the active summary of the bi-polar Trinity or, as we have called it, the *luminous Holy Trinity*.

With respect to the concrete manifestation of the *Shekinah*, "it is as a woman that she now appears to the visionaries among the Cabbalists, like Abraham Halevi, a disciple of Luria, who in 1571 saw her at the wailing wall in Jerusalem as a woman dressed in black and weeping for the husband of her youth" (G. G. Scholem, *Major Trends in Jewish Mysticism*, London, 1955, p. 230). The weeping Lady of La Salette also wept at the foot of a wall no less real than the wailing wall in Jerusalem — the wall of universal sin which is placed between humanity and divine grace — but she differs from the *Shekinah* of the visions of the Cabbalists and Hassidim in that she is not the personification of a principle, i.e. she is not solely an *aspect* of the Divine, but rather is a human person who existed in the flesh at the bosom of the visible community of Israel twenty centuries ago. Similarly, the Messiah, whom many have seen and met during the last twenty centuries, is no more only a spirit who "descends and reascends through all the heavens in order to exercise, with all the prophets who are to be found, the universal function of salvation", but rather is a human person who existed at the bosom of the visible community of Israel twenty centuries ago. For just as the Word became flesh in Jesus Christ, so did the *Bath-Kol*, the "Daughter of the Voice", become flesh in Mary-Sophia. The Church worships her as the Virgin, as the Mother and as the celestial Queen, corresponding to the Mother, the Daughter and the "Virgin of Israel" of the Cabbala, and to the Sophianic Trinity—Mother, Daughter and Holy Soul—mentioned above.

The Athenians, also, had an analogous feminine triad, which played the principal role in the mysteries of Eleusis: Demeter—the Mother, Persephone—the Daughter, and "Athena the bringer of salvation" (cf. Olympiodorus, *In Platonis Phaedonem commentaria* = "Commentary on the Phaedo of Plato"; ed. W. Norvin, Leipzig, 1913, p. 111)—where Athena was at the same time the "community of Athens" or the "soul of Athens" as it were, analogous to the "Virgin of Israel".

Historical analogies and metaphysical parallels alone, however, do not suffice to attain the complete certainty of intuition: it is for the heart to say the last decisive word. Thus the following "argument of the heart" proved to be decisive, twenty-five years ago, to the one who writes these lines.

There is nothing which is more necessary and more precious in the experience of human childhood than parental love; nothing more necessary, because the human child, alone, is not viable if it is not taken from the first moments of its life into the circle of care of parental love or, lacking parental love, its substitute — charity; nothing more precious, because the parental love experienced in childhood is moral capital for the whole of life. In childhood we receive two dowries for life, two assets from which we can draw during the whole of life: the vital biological asset which is the treasure of our health and vital energy, and the moral asset which is the treasure of health of soul and its vital energy—its capacity to love, to hope and to believe. The moral asset is the experience of parental love that we have had in childhood. It is so precious, this experience, that it renders us capable of elevating ourselves to more sublime things—even to divine things. It is thanks to the experience of parental love that our soul is capable of raising itself to the love of God. Without it the soul could not truly enter into a living relationship with the living God, one of loving God — being unable to pass beyond the abstract conception of God as the "Architect" or the "First Cause" of the world. For it is the experience of parental love — and it is above all this — which renders us capable of *loving* the "Architect" or "First Cause" of the world as *our Father* who is in heaven. Parental love bears in itself true senses of the soul for the Divine — which are, by analogy, eyes and ears of the soul.

Now, the experience of parental love consists of two elements: the experience of maternal love and that of paternal love. The one and the other are equally necessary and equally precious. The one and the other render us capable of raising ourselves to the Divine. The one and the other signify to us the means of entering into a living relationship with God, which means to love God, who is the prototype of all paternity and all maternity.

Now, love teaches in its own way — with a certainty which excludes all doubt — that the divine commandment, "Honour thy father and thy mother", is truly *divine*, i.e. that it is significant in heaven as well as on earth. "Honour thy father and thy mother" is applicable therefore not only to transitory things but also to eternal things. Such is the commandment revealed to Moses on Mt. Sinai, and such is also the commandment emanating from the depths of the human heart. One should honour the Father who is in heaven *and* the celestial Mother. This is why practising believers of the traditional Church, i.e. the Roman Catholic Church and the Orthodox Church, caring little for the difference stated in dogmatic theology between the celestial Father and Mother, love and honour — in their practice of prayer — the celestial Mother no less than the Father who is in heaven.

Dogmatic theologians may well put believers on their guard against "exaggeration" in the domain of Mariology and Protestant critics may well advance criticism of the cult of the Virgin Mary as "idolatry", but practising believers of the traditional Church continue and will always continue to honour and love their celestial Mother as the eternal Mother of all that lives and breathes. If one says that "the heart has its own reasons, which the intellect does not know", one can also say that "the heart has its own dogmas, which theological reasoning does not know". Indeed this "dogma" of the heart, although as yet not formulated — being generally confined to the domain of the unconscious — nonetheless exercises a growing influence on the guardians of dogmatic orthodoxy of a kind such that the latter are constrained to give way, through the centuries, one position after another to this irresistible impulse: in liturgical forms and in the practice of prayer sanctioned by ecclesiastical authorities, the role accorded to the Virgin Mary does not stop growing. The Queen of the Angels, the Queen of the patriarchs, the Queen of the apostles, the Queen of martyrs, confessors, virgins, and saints, the Queen of peace, is, in the texts of liturgical prayers, also the Mother of God, the Mother of divine grace, and the Mother of the Church. In the churches of the Greek Orthodox Church one sings: "More honoured than the Cherubim, more glorious than the Seraphim — thou who art the true Mother of God, we honour thee". Now, the Cherubim and Seraphim are the first celestial hierarchy and the Holy Trinity alone is above them. This "dogma" of the heart is so powerful that the time will come when it will result in official recognition from the Church and will be formulated. For it is thus that all Church dogmas have arrived, in the past, at their promulgation: they live first of all in the hearts of the believers, then influence more and more the liturgical life of the Church, in order — lastly — to be promulgated as formulated dogmas. Dogmatic theology is only the last stage of the "way of dogma" which begins in the depths of the life of souls and results in ceremonious promulgation. This way is exactly what is understood by "the direction of the Church by the Holy Spirit". The Church knows it and has the patience to await — even for centuries — the time when the work of the Holy Spirit will have attained to maturity.

Be that as it may, whatever the duration of time for the mysterious process of the birth of the dogma raising maternal love to the level of the Holy Trinity may be, it is already well formulated and is at work across the centuries. All the same, it is a matter, whilst respecting the law of patience and abstaining from all attempts to force things, of cultivating feelings and ideas relating to divine maternal love and of meditating on the ancient Hermetic doctrines which reveal the mystical, gnostic and magical meaning of this aspect of divine love. In other words, it is a matter of meditating on the mystery of the luminous Holy Trinity, whose symbol is the "seal of Solomon":   ✡   — or again, on the symbol of the Trinity alongside that of the luminous Holy Trinity: △   ✡

This symbol of the development from the Holy Trinity to the luminous Trinity, i.e. from the triangle to the hexagram, is at the same time the divine meaning — or the highest that I know — of the number nine. Ten further spiritual exercises were necessary for us, after the meditation on the ninth Arcanum of the Tarot, in order to dare to touch on the theme of the development of the Holy Trinity into the luminous Holy Trinity, symbolised by the triangle alongside the hexagram.

We have indicated above that it is the practice of prayer and the liturgical life of the Church where the great truths anticipate their promulgation as dogmas. Now, the mystery of the number nine, that of the development of the Trinity into the luminous Trinity, also lives in the practice of prayer and ritual within the Church.

I have in mind the practice, universally diffused in the Catholic Church, of the novena — the most practised form of which is the act of prayer consisting of one *Pater Noster* and three *Ave Marias*, to which one devotes oneself for nine days. One makes a novena by appealing to the paternal love of the Father (*Pater Noster*) and to the maternal love of the Mother (the three *Ave Marias*) simultaneously for nine days, for the sake of a person or a cause. What depth there is underlying this practice that is so simple! In truth — in any case for the Hermeticist — the direction of the superhuman wisdom of the Holy Spirit is manifested here!

Similarly, it is so with the rosary prayer, where appeal to the two aspects of divine parental love in the prayer addressed to the Father and the Mother is made during meditation on the mysteries of the Joy, Suffering and Glory of the Blessed

Virgin. The rosary prayer is—in any case for the Hermeticist—again a masterpiece of simplicity, containing and revealing things of inexhaustible profundity...a masterpiece of the Holy Spirit!

Dear Unknown Friend, the Arcanum "The Sun" with which we are occupied is an Arcanum of children bathing in the light of the sun. Here it is not a matter of finding occult things, but rather of seeing ordinary and simple things in the light of day of the sun—and with the look of a child.

The nineteenth Arcanum of the Tarot, the Arcanum of intuition, is that of revelatory *naivety* in the act of knowledge, which renders the spirit capable of an intensity of look not troubled by doubt and by the scruples engendered by doubt, i.e. it is the vision of things such as they are under the eternally new day of the sun. It teaches the art of undergoing the pure and simple impression which reveals through itself—without intellectual hypotheses and superstructures—what things are. To render impressions *noumenous*—this is what it is a matter of in the Arcanum "The Sun", the Arcanum of intuition.

You will understand therefore, dear Unknown Friend, that in speaking of parental love and of its two aspects, in speaking of the practice of the novena and the rosary prayer, etc., we are in no way estranging ourselves from the theme of the nineteenth Arcanum of the Tarot; rather, on the contrary, we are penetrating to its very heart. For we are endeavouring to advance from an *understanding* of what intuition is to its *exercise*, i.e. from meditation on the Arcanum of intuition to the use of this Arcanum.

Meditation on the
Twentieth Major Arcanum of the Tarot

THE JUDGEMENT
LE JUGEMENT

The state of the brain
continues the remembrance;
it gives it a hold on the present
by the materiality which it confers upon it:
but pure memory is a spiritual manifestation.
With memory we are in very truth
in the domain of spirit.
                              (Henri Bergson*)

For as the Father raises the dead
And gives them life,
so also the Son gives life to whom he will.
The Father judges no one,
but has given all judgement to the Son...
                              (John v, 21-22)

LETTER XX

THE JUDGEMENT

Dear Unknown Friend,

The Card that we have before us bears the traditional name "The Judgement", and what it represents is the resurrection of the dead at the sound of the trumpet of the Angel of resurrection. It is a matter, therefore, of a spiritual exercise where the use of intuition—that of the nineteenth Arcanum "The Sun"—has to be carried to a maximum, the theme of resurrection being of the order of "last things", but all the same accessible to intuitive cognition.

Now, the "last things"—or the spiritual horizon of humanity—are not the same

Matter and Memory; trsl. N. M. Paul and W. S. Palmer, London, 1911, p. 320

for the whole of humanity. For some everything finishes with the death of the individual and with the complete dissipation—maximum entropy—of the warmth of the universe. For others there is a "beyond", an individual existence after death and an existence of a non-material universe after the end of the world. For still others there is not only spiritual life after death for the individual but also his return to terrestrial life—reincarnation—as well as cosmic reincarnation, i.e. an alternation of states of *manvantara* and *pralaya*. Others, again, see for the individual something beyond repeated incarnations, namely the state of supreme peace of union with the eternal and universal Being (the state of *nirvana*). Lastly, there is a part of mankind whose existential horizon goes beyond not only post mortem existence and reincarnation, but also even beyond the peace of union with God—it is *resurrection* which constitutes their spiritual horizon.

It is in the Iranian and Judaeo-Christian spiritual currents—i.e. in Zoroastrianism, Judaism and Christianity—that the idea and ideal of resurrection has taken root. The advent of the idea and ideal of resurrection was "as lightning coming from the east and shining as far as the west" (Matthew xxiv, 27). The inspired prophet of the East, namely the great Zarathustra in Iran, and the inspired prophets of the West—Isaiah, Ezekiel and Daniel in Israel—announced it almost simultaneously.

> Then he (*Saoshyant*) shall restore the world, which will (thenceforth) never grow old and never die, never decay and never perish, ever live and ever increase, and be master over its wish, when the dead will rise, when life and immortality will come, and the world will be restored at (God's) wish. (*Zamyad Yasht*; trsl. R. P. Masani, *The Religion of the Good Life. Zoroastrianism*, London, 1938, p. 113)

Here is expressed the Zoroastrian idea concerning the *ristakhez*, i.e. the resurrection from the dead. The prophet Isaiah says of it:

> Thy dead shall live, their bodies shall rise.
> O dwellers in the dust, awake and sing for joy!
> For thy dew is a dew of light,
> and on the land of the shades thou wilt let it fall.
> (Isaiah xxvi, 19)

What is the idea and ideal of resurrection? The following parable can be useful to us for understanding the meaning of the idea and ideal of resurrection:

Some people are near the bed of a sick person and give their opinions on his state and his prospects. One of them says: "He is not ill. It is his nature which is manifesting in this fashion. His state is only natural." Another says: "His illness is temporary. It will be followed naturally by the re-establishment of his health.

Cycles of sickness and health follow one after the other. This is the law of destiny."
A third says: "The illness is incurable. He is suffering in vain. It would be better
to put an end to his suffering and to give him, through pity, death." Then the
last one begins to speak: "His illness is fatal. He will not recover at all without
help from outside. It will be necessary to renew his blood, for his blood is infected.
I shall let his blood and then give him a transfusion of blood. I shall give my blood
for the transfusion." And the end of the story is that after treating him accordingly, the ill person—being healed—gets up.

These are the four principal attitudes towards the world. The pagan attitude
is that of accepting the world as it is. The "pagan", i.e. he who believes that the
world is perfect and for whom the world is the god "Cosmos", denies the fact that
the world is sick. There was no Fall of Nature. Nature is health and perfection itself.

The attitude of "spiritual naturism", i.e. that of minds whose horizon is enlarged
beyond the present state of the world to recognition of the semi-cyclical evolution
—the "seasons" of the great cosmic year—of the world, is that of believing that
degeneration and regeneration follow one another cyclically in the world, that
"falls" and "reintegrations" of the world alternate as do the seasons of the year.
For "spiritual naturism" the present world is certainly "sick", i.e. degenerate, but
it will re-establish itself, i.e. it will regenerate, necessarily and naturally, according to the law of cyclicity. One has only to wait for it.

The attitude of "spiritual humanism" is that of people who raise themselves
above the pure and simple cyclicity of "spiritual naturism" and who protest, in the
name of the individual being, against the interminable chain of cyclicity (be it
"seasons" of the world or individual reincarnations)—seeing here interminable
subjugation and suffering for the human being. This attitude is one of *negation*
both as a whole and in detail of past, present and future Nature—whether spiritual
or material, cyclical or unique. Life is suffering; therefore it would be cruel and
inhuman to affirm it. Human salvation, dictated by pity, is to cut for ever all links
of the human spirit with the world and its cyclicity.

The naive cosmolatry of paganism is the point of view of the first person in
our parable—the one who says: "He is not ill." The "spiritual naturism" of enlightened paganism is the point of view of the second person—the one who says
that illness is only a cyclic episode. The negation of the world of "spiritual humanism" is expressed by the third person who says: "The illness being incurable, it
is better to let the sufferer die."

Now, these three attitudes towards the world—historically manifested in pagan
Hellenism, in Hindu Brahminism, and in Buddhism—are distinguished from
the fourth, i.e. that of active intervention with a view to accomplishing the work
of the purification and regeneration of the world, in that they lack the *therapeutic
impulse* and *faith in therapy*, whilst the attitude which is manifested historically
in the prophetic religions (Iranian, Judaic and Islamic) and in the religion of salvation (Christianity), where *renewal* of the world is the motive force and final aim,
is essentially *therapeutic*. It is the fourth person of our parable—he who *acts*, heal-

ing the illness through a transfusion of his blood—who represents the *Christian attitude*, which includes and realises those of the prophetic religions. The Christian ideal is the renewal of the world—"a new heaven and a new earth" (Revelation xxi, 1), i.e. universal resurrection.

The idea and ideal of resurrection goes further than the negation of Nature, as is the case with the "spiritual humanism" of Buddhism; it signifies its complete transformation, the alchemical work on a cosmic scale of the transmutation of Nature—spiritual as well as material, "heaven" and "earth". There is no idea and ideal more bold, more contrary to all empirical experience, and more shocking to common sense than that of resurrection. Indeed the idea and ideal of resurrection presupposes a force of soul which renders it capable: not only of emancipation from the hypnotising influence of the totality of empirical facts, i.e. of breaking away from the world; not only of deciding to take part in the evolution of the world—that is to say, no longer in the capacity of an object of the world but also, and rather, as a subject, i.e. of becoming a motivating spirit instead of a "moved" spirit; not only of participating actively in the process of world evolution; but also of raising oneself to conscious participation in the work of divine magic—the magical operation on a cosmic scale whose aim is resurrection.

The idea, the ideal and the work of resurrection comprises the "fifth asceticism". For there is "natural asceticism"—that of moderation and putting the brakes on desires—with *health* in view; there is the "asceticism of detachment"—that of the spirit conscious of itself and of its immortality in the face of things that are transitory and of less value—with a view to *freedom*; there is the "asceticism of attachment"—that of the love of God, where loving him is divesting oneself of all that which intervenes between oneself and the Beloved—with a view to *union*; there is the "asceticism of activity"—that of active participation in evolution, i.e. of human work and endeavour aiming at *perfection*; and lastly there is the "asceticism of divine magic"—that of the great work of *resurrection*. This "fifth asceticism" includes and crowns all the other "asceticisms", since the work of divine magic *presupposes* union with the divine will, the realisation and surpassing of evolution, complete freedom of the spirit, and therapeutic action towards man and Nature.

The idea, ideal and work of resurrection therefore make appeal to that which is most creative, most generous and most courageous in the human soul. For the soul is invited to become a conscious and active instrument of accomplishment—neither more nor less—of a miracle on a cosmic scale. What faith, what hope and what love the idea, ideal and work of resurrection imply here! In the face of the idea and ideal of resurrection, does one not remember St. Paul's words:

> Where is the wise man? Where is the scribe? Where is the debator of this world?. . . For since the world through its wisdom did not know God in his wisdom, it pleased God to save those who believe through the folly of preaching. (I Corinthians i, 20-21)

The "folly of preaching". . .does the idea, ideal and work of resurrection necessarily fall under the heading of the "folly of preaching" today, i.e. nineteen centuries later. . .after nineteen centuries of effort and evolution of human religious, philosophical, scientific and—last but not least—Hermetic thought?. . .after St. Augustine, St. Albertus Magnus, St. Thomas Aquinas, St. Bonaventura, the great mystics, the masters of alchemy, and the pleiad of idealist philosophers?. . .after scientific "evolutionism", depth physics and depth psychology?. . .after Henri Bergson, Teilhard de Chardin, and Carl Gustav Jung? In other words, is not human thought, after the enormous work of nineteen centuries, better equipped and more evolved—given good will—to see in the idea, ideal and work of resurrection *more* than the "folly of preaching"?

An honest and profound meditation on the idea, ideal and work of resurrection —i.e. on the twentieth Arcanum of the Tarot—is the sole means of coming to an affirmative or negative answer to this question. Let us therefore apply ourselves to it!

Let us take account first of all of the context of the Card of this Arcanum. Both the Marseille Tarot (1761) and the Tarot of Fautriez (1753-1793), and also that of Court de Gébelin, represent a man and a woman who *contemplate* the resurrection from a tomb of a *third* person, an adolescent. The Card represents a kind of "parallelogram of resurrecting forces"—the Angel with the trumpet above, the parental love of the father (on the right) and the mother (on the left) and, below, the arising of the resuscitated one from an open tomb. The man and woman are outside of the tomb; it is only their child—an adolescent—who is resuscitated. Therefore we have before us a parallelogram (see figure).

This geometrical figure, derived from the image of the Card of the twentieth Arcanum, portrays the composition of the forces realising resurrection: the sound of the Angel's trumpet, the parental love of the father and mother, and the effort of arising of the resuscitated adolescent. It is the same composition of operative forces that we find in the raising of Lazarus at Bethany, where Jesus plays the role of the Angel, the father and the mother—all at once.

> Jesus wept. So the Jews said: See how he loved him. . .Jesus, deeply moved again, came to the tomb; it was a cave, and a stone lay before it. Jesus said: Take away the stone. . .So they took away the stone. . .He cried with a loud voice: Lazarus, come out. The dead man came out, his hands and feet bound with bandages, and his face wrapped with a cloth. Jesus said to them: Unbind him, and let him go. (John xi, 35-44)

Now, Jesus weeping manifests the tender love of the mother; Jesus, deeply moved again, coming to the tomb and saying, "Take away the stone", manifests the active love of the father; and Jesus crying with a loud voice, "Lazarus, come out", sounds the trumpet in serving as the Angel of resurrection. The loud voice crying, "Lazarus, come out" is the sound of the trumpet of resurrection, which changes the love of the mother and the love of the father into a magical call.

The magic of resurrection, aspired to by the twentieth Arcanum of the Tarot, is therefore that of the sound of the voice of love of the mother and that of love of the father united. Just as the earthly father and mother give life to the child at his incarnation, where the Angel of life sounds the trumpet in order to call his soul into incarnation—and the "trumpet" formed by his outspread wings is then turned above—so do the celestial Father and Mother restore the child to life at his resurrection, where the Angel of resurrection sounds the trumpet in order to call his soul and his body to resurrection—and the "trumpet" formed by his outspread wings is then turned below.

This is the general meaning of the Arcanum. It is now a matter of understanding the "details", i.e. of understanding concretely. There still remains a whole world, namely the *how* of resurrection.

Now, forgetting, sleep and death are opposed to remembering, wakefulness and birth in the earthly life of man. Forgetting, sleep and death are members of the same family. It is said that sleep is the younger brother of death; by the same token it would be right to say that forgetting is the younger brother of sleep. Forgetting, sleep and death are three degrees of a single thing, namely the process of elimination of a conscious and living being. It is noteworthy that the account of Lazarus' resurrection that we quoted above also brings the chain forgetting-sleep-death into consideration. It is said:

> Now Jesus loved Martha and her sister and Lazarus. So when he heard that Lazarus was ill, he stayed two days longer in the place where he was...then he said to them (the disciples): Our friend Lazarus has fallen asleep, but I go to awake him...Then Jesus told them plainly: Lazarus is dead...(Upon which) Thomas, called the Twin, said to his fellow disciples: let us also go, that we may die with him. (John xi, 5-16)

Thomas understood that the Master had allowed *forgetting* (by remaining a further two days in the place where he was after having learnt the news that Lazarus was ill), *sleep* (by saying, "Lazarus has fallen asleep") and *death* to accomplish their work. If such was the will of the Master, who so loved Lazarus, would it not be better, concluded Thomas, for the disciples, also, to die with Lazarus? Indeed, Thomas was not mistaken concerning the fact that the Master certainly gave full power to forgetting, sleep and death in this case. Hence the conclusion: let us go also, so as to die with Lazarus.

Let us now consider more closely the two analogous and opposed chains: that of forgetting, sleep and death, on the one hand, and that of remembering, wakefulness and birth, on the other hand, so as to acquire the conceptual equipment to be able to grapple with the mystery of resurrection.

We know that our ego consciousness, the consciousness that we have during the sixteen hours of the waking state each day, is only a weak part of the totality of our consciousness. It is only a cross-section of the whole, only a focal point of *action*, i.e. of judgement, word and deed.

Indeed, at each given moment the content of our consciousness in the waking state is limited to that which has reference to what we are engaged in judging, saying or doing, or else what we are going to judge, to say or to do. The rest, i.e. all that which is not concerned with inner or outer action, is not present in our consciousness and is "elsewhere". For action entails *concentration* of consciousness, i.e. selection from the totality of images and concepts belonging to our consciousness which interest us with a view to action. Thus all that you know of astronomy, chemistry, history and jurisprudence is absent and relegated to the darkness of temporary forgetfulnes when you discuss your garden with the gardener. In order to act, it is necessary to forget.

In return, action requires that one draws from the same darkness of temporary forgetfulness all the memory images and concepts of knowledge which could be useful. In order to act one has to recall.

To forget is therefore to dismiss the things which do not interest us to the darkness of latent memory; and to recall things is to call anew to active ego consciousness —because they interest us—from the same darkness of latent memory. It goes without saying that it is not the images and concepts which come to birth when we recall them, or perish when we forget them; rather, they are present in our mind or are removed from it. To be endowed with "good concentration" therefore amounts to the faculty of chasing away swiftly and completely all images and concepts which are not useful for action. It is mastery of the art of forgetting.

To be endowed with "good memory", in contrast, signifies mastery of the mechanism of recall—of that which *renders present* the images and concepts which one needs. It is mastery of the art of recalling.

There is therefore a continual coming and going between ordinary consciousness of the waking state (or cerebral consciousness) and the domain of memory. Each "going" corresponds to the action of falling asleep or dying. Each "coming" corresponds to awakening or *resurrection*. Every representation that goes from the field of cerebral consciousness experiences an analogous fate to that stated by the saying: "Our friend Lazarus has fallen asleep...Lazarus is dead." And every representation that one recalls has a fate analogous to that which took place when Jesus cried with a loud voice: "Lazarus, come out!"

Memory therefore supplies us with a key of analogy which allows intelligence not to remain simply taken aback in the face of the problem of resurrection. It renders it intelligible. Indeed, the analogy between the "loud voice" which called

Lazarus to life and the inner effort which evokes a memory reveals, *mutatis mutandis*, the essence of the magic of Jesus' "loud voice" and of the "sound of the trumpet" of the Angel of the resurrection — as the following shows.

Experience teaches us that we easily forget, and recall with difficulty, the things to which we attach no value — that we do not love. One forgets what one does not love and one never forgets what one loves. It is love which gives us the power to recall at any desired moment the things that our hearts preserve "warm". Indifference, in contrast, makes one forget everything.

It is the same with the "awaking and resurrection of the dead". Here it is not cosmic indifference (that we call "matter") which will effect anything, but rather it is cosmic love (that we call "spirit") which will accomplish the magical act of resurrection, i.e. the reintegration of an inseparable unity — the unity of spirit, soul and body — not by way of birth (reincarnation) but by way of the magical act of divine memory. . .What can one say about divine memory?

The clinical experience of modern neuro-pathology and the work of Henri Bergson together establish as certain fact that in reality nothing is forgotten from the totality of man's psychic life, and that so-called "forgotten" things are in the unconscious (i.e. extra-cerebral) part of the psychic life. There is complete memory in the depths of the unconscious, where nothing is forgotten.

Just as the microcosm, the human being, forgets nothing, so does the macrocosm, the world, not forget anything. What occult literature calls the "Akasha chronicle" is to history which is in the process of unfolding as the total memory of the psychic unconscious is to the conscious self's memory in action. The Akasha chronicle is the macrocosmic analogy to the total memory of the microcosmic unconscious (or, rather, the microcosmic "extra-conscious"). And just as total psychic memory is not inactive, often affecting psychic health, so does the Akasha chronicle often play a decisive role in the unfolding of universal history.

The two analogous terms — the "total psychic memory" of the individual and the "Akasha chronicle" (the memory of the cosmos) — are too general. It is still necessary to distinguish and specify — which both depth psychology and occult literature have hardly done. Indeed, the former as well as the latter treat total psychic memory and the Akasha chronicle *en bloc*, as if it were a matter of uniform and homogeneous unities without inner difference and contrast. However, both total psychic memory and the Akasha chronicle show, in fact, differences — and even contrasts — each with respect to its own domain. With respect to total psychic memory, one has to distinguish between three "memory tableaus": the pure and simple "tableau of the past", the "logical tableau", i.e. the *structure* of the past, and, lastly, the "moral tableau", i.e. the *travelled way* of the past. These three "tableaus" of psychic memory correspond to the three types of memory such as we know them in our conscious life — automatic memory, logical memory and moral memory. Automatic memory is the psycho-physical faculty of reproducing (semi-automatically thanks to the functioning of the mechanism of associations) in the imagination all the *facts* of the past that are relevant or not. It places the *tableau* of the past, purely and simply, as raw material at the disposal of the conscious self so that the latter makes use of it and extracts from it the elements that it needs. The tableau of the past presented by purely associative or automatic memory is indifferent in so far as logic and morality is concerned; it is only a complex of facts from the past unfolded before the inner eye like a cinematographic film in sound and colour. And it is up to the spectator, i.e. the conscious self, to extract salient and pertinent facts from it.

Automatic memory is the "trump card" of childhood and youth. It is thanks to it that children and young people are able to learn the enormous quantity of things—with the prodigious facility and rapidity that belongs to their age—that they need or could need in this world. However, it is no longer so with a person who has reached a mature age. Automatic memory is weakened in proportion to the extent with which age increases. A person between the two extremes of age will find that he can no longer reckon with his automatic memory to the same extent that he could ten or fifteen years previously—that a certain effort is necessary to make up for and fill in its ever more frequent lapses. It is then *logical* effort which comes to aid the semi-automatic functioning of the failing mechanism of associations. It is the logical sequence of cause and effect which then replaces little by little the automatic play of associations. One is led more and more to replace the semi-photographic tableau of memory of the past by the tableau of facts relating to the logical relationships between them.

Logical memory, where the evocating force of the past is intelligence instead of the irrational automatism of the play of associations, weaves a tableau of the past according to the lines of sequential reasoning that intelligence finds relevant. One does not recall things simply beause they took place, but rather because they *played a role* whose effects reach the present.

Just as automatic memory with time gives up its supremacy in the domain of evoking the past to logical memory, so does the latter yield its dominant role to moral memory.

Moral memory presents a tableau of the past where the context indicates facts and sequences of facts not in so far as they took place or in so far as they played a relevant logical role, but above all in so far as they reveal *moral value and meaning*. In old age moral memory more and more replaces logical memory, and the force of memory then depends on moral force—on the intensity of the moral and spiritual life of the person in question. And as there is nothing in the world which is so insignificant that it is beneath moral and spiritual values—and as there is nothing so lofty that it is above them—the moral memory in old age of a person with an awakened heart can, in principle, replace without fault all the functions of automatic memory and logical memory.

Now, a threefold macrocosmic memory—the threefold Akasha chronicle—corresponds to the threefold microcosmic memory: automatic memory, logical memory and moral memory. There are, in fact, *three* Akasha chronicles. Occult literature, however, makes a case for only one, which is customarily spoken of as a kind of cinematographic film of the world's past, unfolding—before the seer's eye—things and events of the past such as they were, with all their details and with semi-photographic exactness.

This chronicle—which, moreover, certainly exists—displays the remarkable characteristic that the more remote the past, the more two contrary tendencies are manifested: namely that of ascent towards higher spheres and, simultaneously, that of descent towards lower spheres. One could say that it is divided into two parts, where one rises above and the other descends below (see figure).

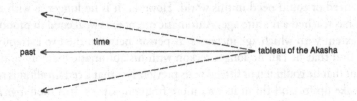

Thus, a twofold process takes place in the Akasha chronicle: it is spiritualised *and* at the same time concretised, in proportion to the extent that the distance from the present into the past increases. One could compare this process with what happens to the trees in autumn: the leaves are separated from the tree; they fall onto the ground and the tree itself—reduced to the essential of its form—stands out in more austere and precise lines against the background of the sky.

In fact, it is a matter of a process comparable to that of *abstraction*. Just as in the process of abstraction all that which is not essential is set apart and only that which is essential is retained, so a similar process takes place in the Akasha chronicle. A selection of the essential is retained, i.e. another, spiritualised Akasha chronicle is separated off, whilst the "waste" which remains—like dead leaves—constitutes another Akasha chronicle: the lower chronicle. This latter descends from sphere to sphere and ends in the subterranean sphere.

The Akasha chronicle which is present at first as one and undivided therefore divides into *two* distinct chronicles that must be sought for in different spheres. These two chronicles are distinguished above all by the difference in their general character. One is essentially *qualitative*, whilst the other has a *quantitative* character. This means to say that the higher chronicle consists solely of symbolic facts—typological facts representative of a whole series of facts—leaving their number out of account, and the lower chronicle consists precisely of the series of facts rejected as useless by the higher chonicle—rejected because they are already found to be qualitatively represented by a symbolic or typological fact.

Therefore, just as logical memory disengages itself from automatic memory and replaces it at a mature age in the life of the human individual, so does the Akasha chronicle disengage the higher chronicle—analogous to logical memory in the individual's life—to replace that which becomes the lower chronicle, which latter descends into the subterranean sphere.

The higher chronicle is the intelligent memory of the history of the world. It is the "book of truth" that one can not only read, i.e. see, but also "swallow", i.e. assimilate in such a way that it becomes always present in us—and which "will be bitter to your stomach, but sweet as honey in your mouth" (Revelation x, 9). The other book, the "book of archives" or the "book of facts", is no part of initiation, i.e. it cannot be "swallowed"; one can draw items of information from it only by procedures such as psychometry, mediumistic clairvoyance, or also by the intermediation of beings who have access to the subterranean region where it is to be found.

There is yet another "book"—the "book of life"—of which the Apocalypse speaks, where it is said:

> Books were opened . . . also another book was opened, which is the book of life. And the dead were judged by what was written in the books, by what they had done. (Revelation xx, 12)

The "book of life" is the *third* Akasha chronicle, which corresponds to moral memory in individual human life. It contains only what is of eternal value, i.e. that which is worthy of living eternally—*that which is worthy of resurrection*. The third Akasha chronicle—the "book of life"—contains the past only in so far as it is of significance for the future (and the future only in so far as it is of significance for eternity).

But do not think, dear Unknown Friend, that the third Akasha chronicle, or the "book of life", consists only of great things—that it does not have the things of ordinary or so-called "daily" life. It does so because, I repeat, there is nothing in the world which is so insignificant as to be beneath moral (i.e. eternal) value and there is nothing so lofty as to be above moral value. Indeed, this chronicle contains many a thing judged as "small"—but which is great in the moral context of life. One finds there, for example, complete texts of manuscripts written by authors—who, as editors, entrusted them to the four winds, addressing them to anyone into whose hands they would perhaps at some time fall. One also hears there the prayer borne by the last breath of a dying atheist or agnostic—the prayer which no one heard and no one expected. One sees there the radiation of the small coins put by "poor widows" in the "temple coffers"—and many things judged as small by the world.

The "book of life" is therefore the moral memory of the world. Therefore it does not contain forgiven and atoned-for sins. All forgiving and atonement entails change in the "book of life" or the third Akasha chronicle. For this reason it is constantly modified—written and re-written from day to day. For just as within the individual's moral memory the accounts to be adjusted are cancelled for those whom one has pardoned—consciously forgetting them—so forgiven and atoned-for sins are effaced from the "book of life". Divine memory *forgets* forgiven and atoned-for sins.

And it is the third Akasha chronicle, or the "book of life", which is the essence of *karma*. Since the Incarnation of Christ, karma has become the affair of the Lord of karma, who is Jesus Christ. For Jesus Christ not only *preached* the new law which must replace the old law of "an eye for an eye and a tooth for a tooth" (Exodus xxi, 24) but also *realised* it on the cosmic level by elevating the "book of life" above the "book of accounts" of strict justice. Karma is therefore no more the law of cause and effect solely, which works from incarnation to incarnation—it is now, above all, the means of salvation, i.e. the means of effecting new inscriptions in the "book of life" and of effacing other inscriptions from it. The cosmic sense of the sacrament of baptism is the act of the passage of the soul from ancient karma to new karma, i.e. from the law of the "regulation of accounts" to the law of pardon of the "book of life". And it is this truth that one confesses by saying the words of the Creed: *Confiteor unum baptisma in remissionem peccatorum* ("I acknowledge one baptism for the forgiveness of sins"). For the remission of sins signifies their effacement from the third Akasha chronicle, the "book of life".

The three Akasha chronicles are to be found in different spheres:

MORAL CHRONICLE
LOGICAL CHRONICLE
CHRONICLE OF FACTS

It is above all the first chronicle, that of facts, from which entities of the hierarchies of the left, i.e. those of strict justice, draw evidence for their accusations. It constitutes the archives of the cosmic prosecution.

With respect to the second chronicle, the logical chronicle, it is virtually the totality of accounts rendered in the millennial-old debate between the cosmic advocacy and the cosmic prosecution, i.e. between the hierarchies of the right and those of the left, or between good and evil. The second Akasha chronicle indicates for each given moment the *equilibrium* that there is in the world between good and evil.

The third Akasha chronicle is the source of strength for hierarchies of the right; it contains the supporting reasons for their faith in justice for the sake of world evolution and humanity, as well as for ultimate universal salvation. The third chronicle aspires to resurrection—to the reintegration of beings—whilst the second is the history of equilibrium, i.e. the karma of the world, the equilibrium between good and evil. The first chronicle—that of facts, pure and simple—supplies the points of support for the arguments of the hierarchies of the left, who do not believe in mankind and accuse mankind at all reproachable points.

Leibnitz, the German philosopher, is the author of the statement considered as the classical formula of the most radical philosophical optimism: "This world is the best of all conceivable worlds." This radical optimism from a man who, in that which concerned his personal life, was more unhappy than is usual, remains incomprehensible if his nocturnal experience of the third Akasha chronicle is not taken into consideration. Notably, the fact must be pointed out that certain individuals (their number is not important) are sometimes admitted to readership of the "book of life", i.e. by the grace of the guardian of this "book", the third Akasha chronicle is shown to them in the state of sleep. They must forget this experience in their day consciousness, since the latter could not support such an increase of knowledge, but what remains to them is its psychic summary in the guise of the force of optimistic faith — such as Leibnitz had, for example. His optimistic faith was the residue in day consciousness of the forgotten nocturnal knowledge.

Similarly, it can happen that someone can have the nocturnal experience of reading from the second Akasha chronicle, and as a result of this experience the unshakable conviction is formulated — as, for example, by Friedrich Schiller (*Die Weltgeschichte ist das Weltgericht*) — that the history of the world is the judgement of the world, i.e. that the history of the world is perpetual judgement or karma.

One should know that there are not only diverse Akasha chronicles but also *diverse ways* of experiencing or "reading" them. One can "see" the Akasha chronicle, one can "hear" it and one can be "seated" or "immersed" in it. This means to say that parts of the Akasha chronicle can be seen in vision, or can be heard as a dramatic or musical work, or also can become an integral or structural part of the spirit and soul of the one who experiences it. The latter identifies himself with it and it lives and works in him. It is this to which the Apocalypse of St. John aspires when there it is said that a book was *swallowed*: "It was sweet as honey in my mouth, but when I had eaten it my stomach was made bitter" (Revelation x, 10). For it is characteristic that the *intuitive* experience of the second Akasha chronicle comprises a state of psychic depression due to the gravity of its contents, but that this depression is transformed into joy as soon as the intuitive experience is grasped and understood by intelligence, i.e. when it becomes "articulated word". Then it becomes "sweet as honey in the mouth".

It should be added that whatever the way of "reading" the Akasha chronicle is, it is always a matter of parts or extracts from it, for no human spirit — even disincarnated — could bear the *whole*. One would have to be of the spiritual status of the Archangel Michael to be able to bear the whole of the second Akasha chronicle and of the status of the Cherubim guarding the entrance to paradise to be able to bear the whole of the third Akasha chronicle.

Therefore, the experiences of the Akasha chronicle undergone by occultists, esotericists, mystics and Hermeticists are always partial. As a general rule, the extent to which it is bearable is greater in the case of intuitive experience; it diminishes for inspirative experience; and it is more limited still for visionary experience. Thus, for example, Fabre d'Olivet founded his work *Histoire philosophique du genre humain* ("Philosophical History of the Human Race") on a number of visions or scenes from the second Akasha chronicle. It was a matter of extracts of some pages from a great book — and it was his intellectual speculation which established connecting links between the isolated scenes of his visions, and which filled the gaps between what he had seen and what he had not seen. This is why, quite rightly, he entitled his work *"Philosophical History of the Human Race"*—for the greater part of his work is due to his philosophy, i.e. to intellectual interpretation and speculation. It would therefore be a grave error to consider Fabre d'Olivet's book as *revelation* or purely and simply an account of what he read in the Akasha chronicle. There is to be found there not only things where the author's predilection plays a role but also quite marked prejudices (for example, that against Christianity). However, this does not bear any prejudice against his merit of having been an "angel of the tradition" at the beginning of the nineteenth century, and of having awoken—perhaps saved—some important aspects of the Hermetic tradition. For it was he who was the first to raise *history* to the niveau of Hermeticism—which, before Fabre d'Olivet, was strikingly lacking a vision of the history of the world.

Before Fabre d'Olivet the mystical aspect—the great alchemical work, the inner work of the new man and that of sacred magic—for a long time played the principal role in Hermeticism. It is thanks to him that a current of *esoteric history* was set in motion, which was represented by Saint-Yves d'Alveydre, H. P. Blavatsky and Rudolf Steiner—to name only the most well-known names. But since the time of Fabre d'Olivet esoteric historicism has undergone an unparalleled development: grandiose works have seen the light of day—for example, *From the Akasha Chronicle* (*Aus der Akasha-Chronik*) and chapters on cosmic history in *Occult Science* (*Geheimwissenschaft in Umriss*) by Rudolf Steiner.

What we said above concerning the work of Fabre d'Olivet is equally applicable to his successors in the domain of esoteric historicism based on the Akasha chronicle. For whatever the extent of their experience of the Akasha chronicle may be, however imposing the results of their efforts to do justice to this experience may be, it remains nonetheless fragmentary—and it is to the intellectual effort of the authors, more or less crowned with success, that we owe the logical or artistic sequence of their pretended *account* from the Akasha chronicle. Each of these authors of esoteric history has gaps in his experience of its source—the Akasha chronicle—and has filled them by taking recourse to his own means, to his intelligence and erudition.

Thus, the situation of esoteric historicism is at present such that one cannot swear by any particular work; here, also, collective work is necessary from generation to generation—i.e. a *living tradition*, where each continues the work of his predecessors, by confirming the truth, filling in the gaps, and correcting errors of interpretation or vision. Today no one should begin any more "wholly anew" from his own initiative in the domain of esoteric history, even if he is the most profound seer and greatest thinker. Henceforth it will be a matter not of isolated flashes of genius, but rather of a continuous collective endeavour of the *tradition*—which means to say of a slow but continuous growth of the light whose dawn was Fabre d'Olivet's work.

Dear Unknown Friend—you who are reading these lines written by a Hermeticist in 1965, after nearly fifty years of endeavour and experience in the domain of Hermeticism—I beg you not to regard what is written here as a vow made for the future of the current of Hermetic historicism, but rather as a testament making you who read these lines a trustee of the task in question—without reserve, but, however, with your consent. If you consent, do all that you judge to be proper, but one thing I implore you not to do: to found an organisation, an association, a society or an order which is charged with the task in question. For the tradition lives not thanks to organisations, but rather in spite of them. One should content oneself purely and simply with friendship in order to preserve the *life* of a tradition; it is not necessary to entrust it to the care of the embalmers and mummifiers *par excellence* that organisations are, save for that founded by Jesus Christ.

Let us return to the Akasha chronicle. It can reveal itself, as you see, in the human soul—either contracted to the point of an arrow as with the aforementioned statements by Leibnitz and Schiller ("This world is the best of all conceivable worlds" and "the history of the world is the judgement of the world"), or by way of a series of tableaus or dramatic pieces which give rise to volumes of works on the esoteric history of the world and humanity. Whatever its mode of revelation—extremely abridged or in almost unlimited deployment—its *effect* is always the same: cosmic optimism (the faith of Pierre Teilhard de Chardin!) and an increased sense of historical responsibility (the preoccupation of Carl Gustav Jung). In other words, in this respect your *soul* has the same gain, no matter whether you have the vision of long extracts from the Akasha chronicle in your day consciousness or whether you have only the psychic summary of it—the residue of the experience of the Akasha chronicle undergone in night consciousness, during sleep. The experience of the third chronicle (the "book of life") always has the effect that belief in God and in ultimate universal salvation—including the devil (the faith of Origen!)—becomes unshakable, and all experience of the second chronicle (that of the karma of the world) always has the effect that it awakens and intensifies the sense of the individual's responsibility for the universal lot (the meaning underlying the belief in "ten righteous men who justify the world").

With respect to the first chronicle ("the film which reproduces the past in all its details"), experience of it is comparable to that of organised espionage: it supplies a quantity of items of information—useful and useless, in a jumble—from which the meaning and logical sequence must be extracted through a work which is essentially the same as that done by a well-trained journalist or historian, as an eye-witness of recent events. This chronicle hardly teaches; it only informs. And it informs in such a way that it supplies a mass of facts simultaneously—without any selection and perhaps without relationship to the problem which interests you. The effect of experience of the first chronicle on the human soul is that the latter feels itself lost before an excessive number of unknown and even incomprehensible facts. It *tires* and fills to repletion even the most curious of minds.

The foregoing describes the essence of the Akasha chronicle. And the essential thing concerning this essence is its summarised *magic*, i.e. the vivifying and awakening effect that it produces when it becomes summarised. For the Akasha chronicle—vast and grand as it is—can be concentrated to a single word, to a single magical sound. And this magical concentration of the Akasha chronicle—the memory of the world—is precisely the *trumpet* of the Angel who figures in the "parallelogram of resurrecting forces" that the Card of the twentieth Arcanum of the Tarot represents.

The trumpet of the Angel is the entire Akasha chronicle concentrated in a single word or sound—awakening, vivifying and resuscitating. The symbol of the trumpet is related in general to the magical concentration of mystical and gnostic contents. It always signifies the transformation of a world of mystical experience and gnostic knowledge into magical action. The "trumpet"—in Hermetic symbolism—is *mysticism and gnosis which have become magic*.

The "parallelogram of forces" operating the resurrection represented by the twentieth Major Arcanum of the Tarot therefore consists of the following forces: the parental love of the father and mother, the sound of the trumpet from above, i.e. the magical summary of the Akasha chronicle, and the effort to arise of the one being resurrected. Until now we have been occupied with three of the forces of the parallelogram of the Arcanum—the love of the father, the love of the mother, and the "sound of the trumpet". It remains, therefore, to try to penetrate the fourth force meditatively—that of the active reaction to the action of the three forces which have been the object of our meditation until now.

Thus, it is a matter of considering such problems as the role of human endeavour (the theological problem of "work and grace"), the significance of resurrection (if it is complete, i.e. embraces spirit, soul and body, or if it is only spiritual) and, lastly, the nature of the resurrected body.

It stands to reason that man cannot resurrect himself. All the religious doctrines on resurrection (Zoroastrian, Judaic, Christian and Islamic), as well as the twentieth Arcanum of the Tarot, are in agreement on this point. Man does not resurrect himself; he will be resurrected . . . resurrection whether we like it or not? . . . come what may?

In other words, is resurrection something which purely and simply happens to man, without any participation on his part, or is it a comprehensive act which embraces the entire circle of that which is above and that which is below—including human will?

Let us return once again to Lazarus' resurrection at Bethany. There, Jesus, after being "deeply moved in spirit", after having wept, after having been "deeply moved again", and after having given thanks to the Father "that thou hast heard me", cried in a loud voice: "Lazarus, come out!" And "the dead man came out, his hands and feet wrapped with bandages, and his face wrapped with a cloth" (John xi, 33-44). Did Lazarus come out of the tomb like a somnambulant obeying the order of a hypnotist, i.e. under magical constraint? Or did he come out because the voice that he heard had awoken in him all the love, all the hope and all the faith which vibrated in it, and thus he experienced the ardent desire to be near the one who called him?

Eliphas Lévi in the third book of his work *The Key of the Mysteries* gives a positive answer to the last question. He says:

> The sacred books indicate to us the procedure which must be employed in such a case (to recall the soul of the deceased person to his body). The prophet Elijah and the apostle St. Paul employed it with success. The deceased must be magnetised by placing the feet on his feet, the hands on his hands, the mouth on his mouth. Then concentrate the whole will for a long time, call to itself the escaped soul, using all the loving thoughts and mental caresses of which one is capable. *If the operator inspires in that soul much affection or great respect, if in the thought which he communicates magnetically to it the thaumaturgist can persuade it that life is still necessary to it, and that happy days are still in store for it below, it will certainly return*, and for the man of everyday science the apparent death will have been only a lethargy. (Eliphas Lévi, *The Key of the Mysteries*; trsl. A. Crowley, London, 1969, p. 199)

Now, following Eliphas Lévi, it was the affection and respect that the Master inspired in the soul of Lazarus, just as it was the persuasion that life was still necessary for him and that precious experiences were still promised to him here below, which made Lazarus come out of the tomb. Indeed, no one who has had a little authentic experience of the spirituality of the world could doubt that there was not a shadow of constraint in the miracle of Lazarus' resurrection—and, consequently, that there will not be any shadow of constraint in the universal miracle of the resurrection of the dead.

The reaction of resuscitation at the "sound of the trumpet" and the parental love of the father and mother thus constitutes an essential factor in resurrection. The act of arising by the resuscitated adolescent—represented in the Card of the twentieth Arcanum of the Tarot—is therefore not a semi-mechanical result of the operation effected from above, but rather a free and conscious "yes" from the heart, intelligence and will of the resuscitated one. Just as Lazarus came out of the tomb moved by love, hope and faith, so does the adolescent of our Arcanum—i.e. the spiritual exercise having resurrection as its subject—raise himself, being moved not by the sound of the Angel's trumpet and by the force of appeal of his father and mother, but rather by his own *reaction* to this appeal and this sound—by his love, hope and faith in response to the appeal.

The Arcanum of resurrection is therefore one of morality, pure and simple, wholly contrary to a pure and simple act of power. It is not a matter of a feat of force—no matter whether divine, Angelic or human—but rather of the superiority of the moral order to the natural order, including death. Resurrection is not an all-powerful divine act, but rather the effect of the meeting and union of divine love, hope and faith with human love, hope and faith. The trumpet sounds from above the whole of divine love, hope and faith; and not only the human spirit and soul but also all the atoms of the human body respond "yes" in chorus, which is the free expression—a cry from the heart of the whole being and of each particular atom—of the love, hope and faith of man, and of Nature, which is represented by man. For man represents Nature towards God and he represents God towards Nature. For this reason, in addressing ourselves to the Father who is in heaven, we say: "Thy kingdom come; thy will be done, on earth as it is in heaven."

What would be the good of praying to the all-powerful Father for his kingdom to come and for his will to be done on earth as it is in heaven if we were not the connecting link between him and Nature?. . .if the Father still reigned in Nature, and if all that took place on earth were his will only?. . .if he had not yielded his rule over Nature to others, and if other wills than his were not developing on the earth?

The earth, i.e. Nature, has been given by the Father to the free human being as the field of deployment of his freedom. And it is this freedom alone which can—and is in the right to—address this prayer to the Father in the name of freedom and in the name of the whole of Nature: "Thy kingdom come; thy will be done, on earth as it is in heaven."

This prayer means to say: I desire your kingdom more than mine, for it is my ideal; and your will is the heart of hearts of my will—which languishes after your will, which is the *way* that my will seeks, the *truth* to which my will aspires, and the *life* from which my will lives. This prayer is therefore not only an act of submission of the human will to divine will, but it is above all the expression of hunger and thirst for union with the divine will; it does not adhere to fatalism, but rather to love.

It is to St. Augustine that we owe the remarkable statement: "God is more myself than I myself am"; he *knew* how to pray the Lord's prayer. For there is Prayer and prayer. One learns to pray the Lord's prayer, little by little, by becoming more and more conscious of what it is essentially concerned with. For this reason, the Lord's prayer that one prays in the Mass of the Catholic Church—after the preparation, the reading from the Epistles and the Gospels, the oblation of sacrifice and consecration, and at the beginning of the participation in the sacrifice (communion)—is preceded by the following words: *Praeceptis salutaribus moniti, et divina institutione formati, audemus dicere: Pater noster*. . .(Literally, "Illumined by the precepts of salvation and instructed by divine teaching, we dare to say: Our Father. . ." but in practice, "Let us pray with confidence to the Father in the words our Saviour gave us: Our Father. . ."). This means to say that the Lord's prayer requires preliminary elucidation and instruction. For to truly pronounce the petitions of the Lord's prayer, one has to have understood that our will is truly free only in union with that of God, and that God acts on the earth only through our free will freely united with his. Miracles are not proofs of divine omnipotence, but rather of the omnipotence of the *alliance* of divine will and human will. For this reason, anyone who preaches the pure and simple omnipotence of God sows atheism for the future. For he makes God responsible for the wars, concentration camps, and physical and psychic epidemics from which mankind has suffered and will suffer again. And sooner or later one arrives at the conclusion that God does not exist, because his omnipotence does not manifest where it should without doubt be manifested. The contemporary Marxist-communist movement has, truth to tell, no other argument for the non-existence of God than the lack of direct intervention by the all-powerful divinity. This argument amounts to that of the rulers and soldiers against the divinity of Christ, when they said to the face of the crucified One:

> He saved others; let him save himself, if he is the Christ, the Chosen One of God! The soldiers also mocked him, coming up and offering him vinegar, and saying: If you are the King of the Jews, save yourself!...One of the criminals who were hanged railed at him, saying: Are you not the Christ? Save yourself and us! (Luke xxiii, 35-37, 39)

But the other criminal crucified with him understood that it was not omnipotence which was at stake, but rather love — and he said:

> We (are) indeed justly (under the same sentence of condemnation); for we are receiving the due reward of our deeds; but this man has done nothing wrong. And he said: Jesus, remember me when you come in your kingly power. (Luke xxiii, 40-42)

He said, "Your kingly power"—meaning the reign of love and not that of omnipotence, pure and simple.

Thus, it is very dangerous to preach the omnipotence of God — and then to leave his sheep to extricate themselves from the inner conflicts that experience will sooner or later lead to. The petition of the Lord's prayer: "Thy will be done on earth as it is in heaven," when well understood, guards us from making divine omnipotence a stake of faith. It teaches us that divine will *is not done* on earth as it is in heaven, and that it is necessary for the human will to pray for it, i.e. to unite with it, in order that it may be done.

It is similarly so for the resurrection. It is not a unilateral act of divine omnipotence, but rather an act resulting from the union of *two wills* — namely, divine will and human will. Therefore it is not a semi-mechanical event according to the scheme "active will — instrument", but rather a *moral event*, i.e. the effect of the free union of two free wills.

The effect of the free union of two free wills...what effect?

Resurrection is the synthesis of life and death, or — using the accepted terminology of contemporary Hermeticism — the "neutralisation of the binary: life — death". This means to say that after the resurrection the resuscitated one can *act* as if he were living and, at the same time, he is free from terrestrial *links* as if he were dead. On the one hand, the risen Christ appeared in the midst of his disciples and disappeared again; on the other hand, he ate with them (cf. John xx, 19-23; 26-29; xxi, 9-13; Luke xxiv 28-31; 36-43). He materialised and dematerialised himself freely. He entered through closed doors, and he ate "broiled fish" (Luke xxiv, 42). He was therefore free as a disincarnated spirit and could act—show himself, speak and eat—as an incarnated person.

But there is one thing, a specific feature, which the Gospel account mentions several times: that the risen Christ was difficult to recognise—that he hardly resembled the Master that the disciples and women knew so well. Thus, Mary Magdalena took him to be the gardener; the two disciples on the way to Emmaus only recognised him at the moment that he broke the bread; the disciples did not recognise his appearance by the sea of Tiberias—and it was only after he had spoken that John, initially alone, recognised him and said to Peter, "It is the Lord!" (John xxi, 7). "When Simon Peter heard that it was the Lord, he put on his clothes, for he was stripped for work, and sprang into the sea" (John xxi, 7-8).

Why was the risen Jesus Christ difficult to recognise? Because he was without age. He did not have the appearance of Jesus on the eve of Calvary, nor that of the time of the baptism in the Jordan. Just as he was transfigured on Mt. Tabor, where he conversed with Moses and Elijah, so was he transfigured at his resurrection. The resurrected One was not only the synthesis of life and death, but also the synthesis of youth and old age. For this reason it was difficult for those who knew him between the ages of thirty and thirty-three to recognise him: at one time he appeared older to them, at another time younger than when they had known him.

And here we arrive at the full problem of the *resurrection body*. What is it?

Modern science has come to the understanding that matter is only condensed energy—which, moreover, was known by alchemists and Hermeticists thousands of years ago. Sooner or later science will also discover the fact that what it calls "energy" is only condensed psychic force—which discovery will lead in the end to the establishment of the fact that all psychic force is the "condensation", purely and simply, of consciousness, i.e. spirit. Thus, it will be known for certain that we walk not thanks to the existence of legs, but rather that legs exist thanks to the will for movement, i.e. that it is the will for movement which has fashioned the legs so as to serve as its instrument. Similarly, it will be known that the brain does not engender consciousness but that it is the latter's instrument of action.

Our physical body is therefore an instrument composed of the will for action and for perception. Its genesis is the vertical line:

| spirit |
| psychic force |
| energy |
| ↓ material organs |

Unfortunately, this vertical line is traversed by a horizontal one which runs counter to the freedom of the spirit in the fashioning — by the condensation of psychic forces and energy — of the material instrument in conformity with its task and mission. If our physical body were only the product of our own spirit alone, it would be the perfect instrument of our spiritual freedom. But, unfortunately, it is not so. Because the vertical line of condensation is traversed by the horizontal line of *heredity*. This constitutes the cross of human existence on earth (see figure).

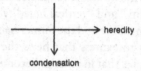

Heredity interposes a foreign element between the individual free spirit and its instrument of action (the body). This is a factor which can change considerably the vertical process: spirit-psychic force-energy-material organs. It is *another will* which mingles with the process of the fashioning of the instrument of action of the individual spirit — of a kind that the body becomes the instrument not only of the individual spirit but also of the collective will of ancestors.

Whatever the *physical mechanism* of heredity may be, the essence of the transmission to descendants of the physical and psychic characteristics of their ancestors is the *imitation*, voluntary or involuntary, of a ready-made model, instead of a purely creative act (from *nothing*, so to say) — that is, instead of pure and simple creation without any external model for it.

To imitate or to create — this is the choice and the trial of every soul in the process of incarnation. Now, there are strong — i.e. creative — souls, and there are weak — i.e. imitative — souls. The stronger a soul is, the greater the independence from the semi-hypnotic influence of the model presented by the preceding generations of the family chosen for the soul's incarnation. For this reason a strong incarnated soul shows in his or her psycho-physical personality fewer features traceable from the parents, and is in general less representative of family, people and race than of itself; he or she is more an individuality than a type. In contrast, a weak soul becomes an individual who seems to be only a pure and simple copy of the parents. In the former case — in the absence of sufficient information concerning the ancestry of the individual in question — it will certainly be said that, "the genes of a distant and unknown ancestor have prevailed". But whatever is said the fact remains incontestable that there are some cases where heredity is reduced to a minimum and that there are other cases where it manifests itself as almost all-powerful.

Heredity is the same imitation at work in the organic domain as that at work with children in the psychic domain — when they are learning to speak, to acquire useful habits and to form the first social qualities. If a child learns to speak by imitating its parents, this is only the consequence of the prior practice and more profound imitation of the nervous system, the circulatory system, and the structure of muscles and bones from the shaping of the organism in the uterus during the prenatal period.

Thus, every incarnated human being is the product of *two* shaping forces: the force of imitation, or heredity, and the creative force or self-realisation of the eternal individuality. The incarnated human being is at one and the same time representative of his ancestors and his individuality—the latter representing only itself.

One can also say that the incarnated human being is the product of two heredities—"horizontal heredity" and "vertical heredity", the latter being the imprint of the individuality from above and the former being the imprint of the ancestors here below. This seeks to express that he is the product of *two* imitations—horizontal and vertical, i.e. that in order to become what he is he owes it to imitation of his ancestors from the past and to that of himself above. In the last analysis, therefore, it is a matter on the one hand of horizontal heredity going back to the archetype (the "ancestor of ancestors") of terrestrial heredity, i.e. Adam, and on the other hand of vertical heredity rising up to the Father who is heaven, i.e. God. This is why it is so important to allow light from the dogma of the immaculate conception to convince us of its truth, for what is at stake is the line of vertical heredity—"God-man heredity".

"The Word became flesh and dwelt among us" (John i, 14)—this presupposes descent from above, instead of being the product of preceding generations. And it is this which holds out the promise that:

> . . .to all who received him, who believed in his name, he gave
> power to become children of God, who were born, not of blood
> nor of the will of the flesh nor of the will of man, but of God.
> (John i, 12-13)

Is it possible to state the re-establishment of "God-man heredity" (vertical heredity) more clearly and openly?

Now, the resurrection body is that of perfect freedom, i.e. the perfect manifestation of the individuality itself, without impediment on the part of heredity. Thus it is not an *instrument* which the soul makes use of, just as the soul itself is not an instrument which the spirit makes use of. For the very notion "instrument" presupposes a semi-mechanical relationship between master and implement; the master's will employs the implement without the latter consenting or making any contribution on its part, or taking any conscious and voluntary part of action. It is not so—it cannot be so—concerning the relationship between the soul and the resurrection body. The relationship between spirit, soul and resurrection body should be conceived of as a reflection of the Holy Trinity, i.e. as the re-establishment of the image and the likeness of God. This means to say that the relationship between spirit, soul and body will correspond, at the resurrection, to the relationship which exists between Father, Son and Holy Spirit. Man will be triune, as God is triune. Man's eternal individuality will be the unity underlying his spirit, his soul and his body. The resurrection body will therefore be one of three "persons" of the human trinity, analogous to the divine Trinity. It will be the "person of action" of the individuality, just as the soul will be the "person of heart" and the spirit will be the "person of contemplation". This means to say that the resurrection body will be the *magical realising agent* of the individuality, whilst contemplating eternity by way of his spirit and rendering it light and warmth in his soul.

Thus the resurrection body will have nothing mechanical, nothing automatic, about it. In no way will it be an assembly of implements pre-fabricated once and for all for the use of the will. In other words, it will not have ready-made and invariable "organs". No, the resurrection body will be absolutely mobile and will create for each action the "organ" which suits it. At one time it will be radiant light – such as Paul experienced on the way to Damascus – at another time it will be a current of warmth, or a breath of vivifying freshness, or a luminous human form, or a human form in the flesh. For the resurrection body will be *magical will*, contracting and expanding. It will be – we repeat – the synthesis of life and death, i.e. capable of acting here below as a living person and at the same time enjoying freedom from terrestrial links like a deceased person.

Will it be a new creation?. . .a sudden and gratuitous gift from God?

In order to answer this question, we have first of all to deepen the idea that we have of the "body" (i.e. the physical body). The general idea that we have of it is that it is a quantity of matter borrowed from Nature and organised in such a way as to serve as an instrument of action and as the scene of development of psychic life until its disintegration, i.e. death. "It has been made from dust and will return to dust" (Ecclesiastes iii, 20). If we replace the Biblical term "dust" by the modern term "multitude of atoms", this formula from Ecclesiastes expresses well, still today, our general idea of the body, no matter whether or not we believe in the soul's immortality. Here materialists and the spiritually-minded are in agreement, for both the former and the latter accept the empirical evidence of the complete disintegration of the individual body at death.

However, this is not the idea of the body according to Hermeticism. For, without denying the fact itself of the material disintegration of the body, Hermeticism denies the conclusion drawn from this fact that the individual body undergoes complete annihilation at death. Hermeticism advances the thesis that *the body is essentially as immortal as the soul and spirit* – that immortality is threefold and that the *whole* human being is essentially immortal. The immortality of the body, such as Hermeticism understands it, differs, of course, from the relative immortality that is accorded to it by biology (reproduction and heredity) and chemistry and physics (conservation of matter and energy), since it is a matter of *individual bodies* and not of the survival of the species or the conservation of amorphous matter.

According to Hermeticism, the essence of the body is not the matter of which it is composed nor the energy which is produced in it, but rather the fundamental *will* underlying matter and energy. And it is this will which is indestructible, because it exists prior to the birth of the body—and without it birth (here in the sense of incarnation) would not be possible. More particularly, there is an essential difference between incarnation-birth and propagation-birth (in the sense of the propagation of the species). The former is adapted to the *individuality* who is incarnating, whilst the latter aims at the pure and simple reproduction of the parents and ancestors without regard to the individuality who is going to incarnate —it is almost a *carte blanche*, inviting no matter what individuality to incarnate by accomodating him to the conditions and facilities that heredity offers him. Incarnation-birth is thus ruled by the law of the *vertical*, whilst propagation-birth falls under the law of the *horizontal*. The first is orientated towards the *individuality* above; the second is orientated towards the *species*, the race and the family, i.e. the past below. In the first case the individuality *incarnates himself*; in the second case he *falls* into incarnation.

This means to say that the individuality—in the case where his incarnation is ruled by the law of the vertical—descends consciously and of his own free will to birth, into an environment where he is wanted and awaited, whilst he is carried away by the general current of terrestrial attraction towards birth in the case where his incarnation comes under the law of the horizontal. Incarnation-birth presupposes conscious agreement between the will of the individuality above and the receiving will below. This is why all incarnation-births are *announced*, i.e. preceded by knowledge of the individuality who is going to incarnate himself due either to direct intuition or to intuition revealing itself in dream or, lastly, to revelation by means of a vision experienced by the future parents in full waking consciousness. Thus not only the Divine Incarnation was announced to Mary by the Archangel Gabriel, but also the incarnation of John the Baptist to his father Zacharias, the incarnation of Isaac to Abraham and Sarah (cf. Genesis xvii, 16-19), the incarnation of Siddhartha (Gautama Buddha) to his mother Maya and his father Suddhodana, king of Kapilavastu, the incarnation of Krishna to his mother Devaki, etc. Whatever the difference in the modes of preliminary annunciation for these incarnation-births and whatever the difference in their significance—as in the calibre of individual whose incarnation-birth had been announced or revealed—in each particular case it is a matter of one thing in common, namely the law ruling the incarnation of the individuality, or birth under the sign of the vertical, which law demands that the two ends of the vertical line—above and below—are in free agreement of will. This is why every incarnation-birth implies two events: revelation of the will above, or *annunciation*, and the *act of consent* of the will below. These two events—quite different as they are with respect to their mode, their significance, and the psychological and external circumstances in particular cases—are evident in the following formulae of Angelic salutation: "*Angelus Domini nuntiavit Mariae . . .*" ("The Angel of the Lord announced to Mary. . ."), and "*Ecce ancilla Domini, mihi fiat secundum verbum tuum*" ("Behold, I am the handmaid of the Lord; let it be to me according to your word"). For these two formulae serve as column headings, so to say, comprising all particular cases of incarnation-births, i.e. births ruled by the law of the vertical.

Therefore, it is thus that the body, in accordance above all with the individuality and not according to the line of hereditary descent, is the work of the will of the individuality who is descending to incarnation acting hand in hand with the will receiving him below. And it is this united will which constitutes *the indestructible and immortal kernel of the body*. It is the "philosopher's stone", which arranges the matter and energy given by Nature in such a way that it is adapted to the individuality—so that it becomes an imprint of it. Such an "individualised" body certainly returns to Nature (at the moment of death) the substances and energies that it had been given, but its active principle, its formative will-energy, survives death. It is the living memory, the formative will-memory, of the body that is born—in so far as it is thus born—under the law of the vertical. Thus the poet Baudelaire, in a moment of illumination through love, wrote:

> And yet you will be similar to that filth,
>   To that horrible infection,
> Star of my eyes, sun of my nature,
>   You, my angel and my passion!
>
> Yes! you will be like that, O queen of graces,
>   After the last sacraments,
> When you go, under the grass and rich blossomings,
>   To rot among the bones.
>
> Then, O my beauty, tell the vermin
>   Which will eat you with kisses,
> That I have kept the form and the divine essence
>   Of my decomposed loves!

> *Et pourtant vous serez semblable à cette ordure,*
>   *A cette horrible infection,*
> *Étoile de mes yeux, soleil de ma nature,*
>   *Vous, mon ange et ma passion!*
>
> *Oui! telle vous serez, ô la reine des grâces,*
>   *Après les derniers sacraments,*
> *Quand vous irez, sous l'herbe et les floraisons grasses,*
>   *Moisir parmi les ossements.*
>
> *Alors, ô ma beauté, dites à la vermine,*
>   *Qui vous mangera de baisers,*
> *Que j'ai gardé la forme et l'essence divine*
>   *De mes amours décomposés!*

(Charles Beaudelaire,
"Une Charogne/A Carrion")*

Les Fleurs du Mal; ttsl. W. Flowers, Bantam, 1964, pp. 46-47.

Baudelaire will not be alone in keeping "the form and the divine essence" of the body of the beloved. There is also One, One who is greater than he — and whose love is greater than his — who will guard them for all eternity. For if the love of the loving one preserves "the form and the divine essence" of the decomposed body of the person whom he loves, this is all the more reason for God — who is love — to preserve "the form and the divine essence" of this body. And it is this form and this essence which will resuscitate at the resurrection.

Thus, the resurrection body is prepared during the course of the ages. Each particular human incarnation is effected according to *the law of the cross*, i.e. it is vertical and horizontal at the same time. In reality it is only the proportion between the vertical of incarnation and the horizontal of heredity — i.e. the preponderance of the vertical over the horizontal or vice versa — which makes a particular incarnation emphasise either the law of the vertical or that of the horizontal. Hence the process of the growth of the resurrection body is gradual. The resurrection body matures from incarnation to incarnation, although in principle it should be possible for a single incarnation to suffice. In fact, however, it is so that many incarnations are necessary to bring the resurrection body to maturity.

What is the destiny of the kernel of the indestructible body — "the form and the divine essence" of the body — after death? Does it ascend with the soul and spirit to the spiritual world, leaving the mortal remains below?

Death — disincarnation — signifies the separation of the soul and spirit from the physical body, including its indestructible kernel or resurrection body. Whilst the soul and spirit ascend to the spiritual world — accompanied by the forces of vitality (the "etheric" or "vital body") and psychic forces (the "astral body", i.e. psychic habits, desires, character and psychic dispositions) — the resurrection body descends in the opposite sense, i.e. below, towards the centre of the earth. As it is active will during life, its descent is due to progressive relaxing of the will. The latter withdraws more and more within itself, instead of the effort concentrated previously on the task of rendering and maintaining the physical body in conformity with the soul and spirit of the incarnated individuality. This withdrawal of the resurrection body within itself after death amounts to what one understands by "peace" in speaking of the peace of the dead. *Memento etiam, Domine, famulorum famularumque tuarum, qui nos praecesserunt cum signo fidei, et dormiunt in somno pacis* ("Remember, Lord, those who have died and *sleep in peace*, who have gone before us marked with the sign of faith, especially those for whom we now pray...") — this is said in remembrance of the dead during the Eucharistic prayer of the Catholic Mass. The "rest" that is the case with cemetery inscriptions and the "sleep of peace" of the prayer for the dead does not apply to saints (who are active and work miracles of healing and help after their death) or to souls in purgatory (who, in their state of suffering, are not at all sleeping or at rest) but rather to the indestructible kernels of the bodies of the dead. Thus Saul's sin in having made the witch of Endor evoke the departed prophet Samuel did not consist in his having made the immortal soul of Samuel descend to the earth, but rather in that he made the indestructible body of the prophet *ascend* from its place of rest below. Here is the relevant text:

> The woman (the witch) said: Whom shall I bring up for you? He (Saul) replied: Bring up Samuel for me. When the woman saw Samuel, she cried out with a loud voice...The king (Saul) said to her: Have no fear; what do you see? And the woman said to Saul: *I see a god coming up out of the earth*...Then Samuel said to Saul: Why have you disturbed me by bringing me up? (I Samuel xxviii, 11-15)

Similarly, in St. Matthew's account of the death of Jesus it is not a matter either of souls descending from above or of phantoms — remains electrified by the passions and habits of the dead — but rather of the resurrection bodies of saints ascending or "coming out of the tombs". Here is the relevant text:

> Jesus cried out with a loud voice and yielded up his spirit. And behold, the curtain of the temple was torn in two, from top to bottom; and the earth shook, and the rocks were split; *the tombs also were opened, and many bodies of the saints who had fallen asleep were raised* (-καί πολλὰ σώματα τῶν κεκοιμημένων ἁγίων ἠγέρθησαν— *kai polla somata ton kekoimemenon hagion egerthesan*). And coming out of the tombs after his resurrection they went into the holy city and appeared to many. (Matthew xxvii, 50-53)

Thus, the evangelist is specific concerning the fact that it was the *bodies* (σώματα— *somata*) of the saints (τῶν ἁγίων— *ton hagion*) which came out of the opened tombs and which appeared to a large number of people in Jerusalem, and not the souls of the saints which descended from heaven and which were revealed to the inhabitants of the holy city. On the other hand the bodies of the saints were not at all material bodies; otherwise they would have gone in procession to Jerusalem instead of *appearing* there. The evangelist also takes note that it was the bodies of the *saints* (*ton hagion*) and not just any kind of dead. This means to say that the bodies were resurrection bodies which had already attained a certain advanced degree of maturity.

With respect to the resurrection of Lazarus (the seventh miracle in the Gospel according to St. John), this is the unique case of a *threefold* miracle — namely the recall of the soul of a departed one to terrestrial life, the healing of a body which had already been four days in the tomb and from which there was already an "odour" (John xi, 39) and, lastly, the evocation of Lazarus' resurrection body and its union with the healed material body.

The three statements concerning Lazarus —"Lazarus is ill", "Lazarus has fallen asleep" and "Lazarus is dead" that one finds in the gospel account (John xi) — are related to the threefold miracle of the healing, the awakening and the resurrection of Lazarus.

The Assumption of the Blessed Virgin is the unique event where separation from the body did not take place at all, i.e. where death, such as we know it, did not occur at all. Instead of separating from the material body and from the soul in order to descend below to the place of rest of the "sleep of peace", the resurrection body remained united with the soul and the material body, and ascended — united with the soul — to the spiritual world. With respect to the material body, it did not decompose but was wholly absorbed by the resurrection body. It dematerialised, spiritualising itself to the point of becoming one with the resurrection body — in its turn united inseparably with the soul of the Blessed Virgin. The tomb of the Blessed Virgin was in fact empty. The tradition which relates this is exact. One would search in vain for the terrestrial tomb of the Blessed Virgin; one would find nothing of it, since it does not exist. What exists is only the spot designated for laying to rest the body of the Virgin, but which never served this end.

The mystery of the Assumption of the Blessed Virgin is not identical to that of the resurrection. The latter is the last act of the drama of the Fall and the Redemption of mankind, whilst the Assumption brings out the history of the spirit and soul of non-fallen Nature. It is not a matter of the reintegration of a fallen being, but rather of the destiny of an entity who appeared in the fallen world without ever having been touched by original sin and the Fall that it brought with it, i.e. a *virgin* entity, in the most profound sense of this word.

The Blessed Virgin is therefore virgin Nature, virgin soul and virgin spirit since the dawn of the world, united and manifesting in a human person — Mary, daughter of Joachim and Anne. The Virgin Mary is therefore at one and the same time a human person and a cosmic entity: Wisdom (CHOKMAH חָכְמָה, *Sophia* Σοφία, *Sapientia*) according to Solomon, the "Virgin of light" of the gnostic *Pistis Sophia*, the "Virgin of the world" (*Kore Kosmu*, κόρη κόσμου) of the ancient Hermeticists, and the *Shekinah* of the Cabbalists. The dialogue between the Archangel Gabriel and Mary at the Annunciation has therefore, outside of human and Angelic significance, a cosmic significance. It was in the name of the divine Holy Trinity that the Archangel announced the Incarnation to come, and it was in the name of the threefold holy virgin Nature — Mother, Daughter and Holy Soul — that Mary gave the response which was the turning-point of the history of the world: *Ecce ancilla Domini, mihi fiat secundum verbum tuum* (ἰδού ἡ δούλη κυρίου γένοιτο μοι κατὰ τὸ ῥῆμα σου) — *idou he doule kyriou genoito moi kata to rema sou* — "Behold, I am the handmaid of the Lord; let it be to me according to your word" — Luke i, 38). It was *natura naturans* and non-fallen *natura naturata* which gave their reply at the same time that Mary pronounced these words. The eternal dialogue between creative will and executive will — where divine fire becomes light, where light becomes movement, and where movement becomes form—was projected in time and concentrated in the dialogue between the Archangel and Mary!

The Assumption of the Blessed Virgin was, consequently, neither disincarnation in the sense of separation of the soul and body, nor resurrection in the sense of union of the soul and the resurrection body, but rather the turning above—towards the spiritual world—of the current of life comprising spirit, soul and body: the ascent to heaven of the integral entity of the Blessed Virgin.

Thus, it follows from the preceding that the resurrection is the union of the spirits and the souls of the dead with their immortal bodies—their resurrection bodies—which will be awoken "by the sound of the trumpet" from above, and which will ascend to meet the descending souls. They will unite with the latter, never more to separate from them. Thus the "eternal incarnation" will begin, i.e. the epoch of cosmic history called in the Bible "the heavenly city of new Jerusalem" (Revelation xxi).

The universal resurrection has, however, another important aspect which has given the twentieth Major Arcanum of the Tarot its traditional name—"The Judgement". Though the Card represents only the resurrection, it nevertheless bears the name "The Judgement"—the last judgement being an essential part of the universal resurrection in the tradition. Tradition not only associates the resurrection and the last judgement, but also regards them as identical, as a single event seen from two sides. On what basis does the tradition draw an identification between the resurrection and the last judgement?

The resurrection is the final victory not only over *death* (as the separation of the soul from the body) but also over *sleep* (as the separation of the soul from the world of action) and over *forgetfulness* (as the separation of consciousness from the world of past memories). This means to say that resurrection signifies not only the re-establishment of the integral unity of the spirit, soul and body of the human being, but also the uninterrupted continuity of his activity and the uninterrupted continuity of his consciousness—the whole of his memory. Now, the emergence of complete memory of the entire past is equivalent, for consciousness, to the last *judgement*, where the whole past is reviewed in the light of conscience. It is conscience itself, the soul itself, which will judge itself. And it will then find that it is guilty under all the headings of accusation of divine law which live in the completely awakened conscience. And there will not be a single soul that will justify itself before its own awakened conscience. It is not authorised to justify itself. Justification lies in the realm of the Divine and it is only the Divine that is authorised to justify.

Thus, there will at first be the realisation of the complete equality of all members of the human community in the consciousness of their errors and their faults. This consciousness will be common to great initiates, high priests, heads of nations, and simple workers in the diverse domains of human effort in the past.

This great experience to come of human equality—in the light of completely awakened conscience—is prefigured in the penitential rite of the Mass, during the prayer at the foot of the altar, where priest and congregation say together: *Confiteor Deo omnipotenti et vobis, fratres, quia peccavi nimis cogitatione, verbo, opere et omissione: mea culpa, mea culpa, mea maxima culpa* ("I confess to almighty God, and to you, my brothers and sisters, that I have sinned through my own fault, in my thoughts and in my words, in what I have done, and in what I have failed to do. . ."—all strike their breast three times in saying the words *mea culpa, mea culpa, mea maxima culpa*). This rite, whose aim is to awaken the conscience of all and each is, at the same time, that of complete human *equality* before the divine law which operates in conscience. It prefigures the equality at the last judgement.

Thus, the last judgement will be essentially the experience by mankind of awakened conscience and completely restored memory. It will be mankind itself who will judge itself. It will be mankind alone who will play the role of the accuser. God will not accuse anyone. He will only acquit, justify and forgive. It is in response to the "act of accusation" (that the emergence of complete memory of the whole past of mankind will call forth) that he will open the "book of life", i.e. he will bring to light what we have called the third Akasha chronicle—the tableau of divine memory containing all that from the past of mankind which is worthy of eternity. This will be the divine "defence speech" at the last judgement—the act of indulgence, absolution and pardon. The last judgement will be the sacrament of penance on a cosmic scale, comprising universal confession and universal absolution. It will be only the impenitents who will exclude themselves from the grace of universal absolution, although it is difficult to imagine impenitence in this situation. The Church Father Origen could not do so, and believed that everyone, including the hierarchies of evil with Satan at their head, will be saved. Was he right or wrong? By way of answer, I will pose these two questions:

> 1. Is there in the world any person or group of people who know with certain knowledge who will be impenitent in the distant future?
> 2. Is there in the world any person or group of people who have the authority to specify the limits of God's love and mercy?
> . . . to state and decree that the love of God goes so far and no further?

These two questions are addressed to those who believe themselves to be in a position to affirm that Origen was wrong in believing in universal salvation. In cases where they cite the scriptures in their answer—the Prophetic Books, the Gospels and the Apocalypse, which speak of the fate of the damned—they should take into consideration the fact that neither the prophets, nor the Gospels, nor the Apocalypse treat the fate of the damned as inevitable for whoever this may be. They say that *if* human and hierarchical sinners are impenitent, *if* their conscience does not awaken by the end of time, *if* sinful souls refuse to the end to profit from the innumerable occasions which will be offered to them to turn towards the good, *then* their fate will be such as it is depicted in the scriptures as the lot of the damned. In other words, the lot of the damned is certainly real, but there is no one who is to be excluded from salvation. It is not the fear of hell, but rather the love of God and of good which ought to motivate the choice of souls.

The last judgement will be the last crisis. The Greek word for judgement is *krisis* (κρίσις), i.e. crisis. Friedrich Schiller said rightly that "the history of the world is the judgement of the world", i.e. it is a continual crisis, the stages of which are "historical epochs". The last judgement will therefore be the culminating point of history. It will be simultaneously the aim, the meaning and the summary of history — history condensed, i.e. *the* crisis that is in question in all the particular crises of history. For this reason Jesus Christ, who is the moral and spiritual centre of gravity of history, will be present there. The second coming will be the objective manifestation of the stake of history. In this sense Jesus Christ will be the "judge" at the last judgement. His presence alone will set in relief all that which is not like him, all that which is incompatible with him for the awakened conscience.

But he will not restrict himself to being present; he will participate in the last judgement and will take an active part, namely that of judge. But he will judge in his own way: he will not accuse, he will not condemn, and he will not impose punishments — rather, he will give forces to souls undergoing the trial that the awakening of conscience and complete memory entails. Christ's judgement is the comforting of those who judge themselves and his eternal commandment addressed to those who judge others is: "Let him who is without sin among you be the first to throw a stone. . ." (John viii, 7). It is thus that Jesus Christ judged during his life, thus that he judges now, and thus that he will judge at the last judgement.

Our meditation on the twentieth Arcanum of the Tarot — that of resurrection and the last judgement — is approaching an end. This is not to say that all that is essential has been said, but that the most essential of the essential is treated within the limits of the framework of an Arcanum of the Tarot — limits that we have to set in order to be able to carry through these meditations on the Major Arcana of the Tarot. Thus, it is now a matter of summarising:

Resurrection is the magical operation — divine and human at the same time — in which divine love and human love overcome forgetfulness, sleep and death. For love never forgets; it is always vigilant; and it is stronger than death.

At the resurrection the human spirit and soul descend from above and unite with their immortal body which ascends to meet them.

It is the love of the Father which makes souls and spirits descend to eternal incarnation; and it is love of the Mother which makes the resurrection bodies — which rest in the womb of the Mother — ascend.

Resurrected man will be the *image and likeness* of God; he will be triune as God is triune. The three principles of man — spirit, soul and body — will constitute the human trinity after the manner of the Holy Trinity, where there will be three persons and their fundamental unity will be the human individuality.

But the resurrection is at the same time the last judgement. As Paul said:

> . . . each man's work will become manifest; for the Day will disclose it, because it will be revealed with fire, and the fire will test what sort of work each one has done. If the work which any man has built on the foundation survives, he will receive a reward. If any man's work is burned up, he will suffer loss, though he himself will be saved, but only as through fire. (I Corinthians iii, 13-15)

*Meditation on the
Twenty-First Major Arcanum of the Tarot*

THE FOOL
LE MAT

Let no one deceive himself.
If any one among you thinks that he
is wise in this age,
let him become a fool
that he may become wise.
For the wisdom of this world
is folly before God.

                    (I Corinthians iii, 18-19)

Folly is a condition which prevents
that which is true from being grasped.
                    (Plato, *Définitions*)*

...consciousness succumbs all too easily
to unconscious influences, and these are
often truer and wiser than our conscious
thinking...Personality need not imply
consciousness. It can just as easily
be dormant or sleeping.
                    (C. G. Jung,
Conscious, Unconscious and Individuation)**

LETTER XXI

THE FOOL

Dear Unknown Friend,

I owe you, in the first place, an explanation of the fact of having changed—apparently arbitrarily—the order of the Cards of the Major Arcana of the Tarot, by making the Arcanum "The Fool" follow the twentieth Arcanum "The Judgement". The Arcanum "The Fool" does not bear any number and therefore cor-

*Cf. Plato, *Dialogues apocryphes* in *Oeuvres complètes*, vol. xiii, French trsl. by J. Souilhé, Paris, 1930, p. 173.
**Tran. R. F. C. Hull, *The Collected Works of C.G. Jung*, vol. 9, part vi, London, 1959, pp. 282-283.

responds to zero, whilst the Card of the Arcanum "The World" bears the number XXI in the Marseille Tarot pack. Thus, here is the reason—not for changing the number of the Card, but rather for why we have made the *meditation* on the Arcanum "The Fool" follow that on the twentieth Arcanum "The Judgement" and before the *meditation* on the twenty-first Arcanum "The World":

The principal reason is that the meditation on the Arcanum "The Fool" cannot conclude the series of meditations on the Major Arcana of the Tarot, which series is a "school" of spiritual training, i.e. an organic "system" of spiritual exercises. For the meditation on the Arcanum "The Fool", *as a spiritual exercise*, is not of a nature to summarise the whole preceding series of twenty-one meditations on the Tarot, i.e. to play the role of the last "point of view" of the experience that the symbolism of the Tarot renders possible.

There are still other reasons. One of them is indicated by Paul Marteau in his book *Le Tarot de Marseille*, where he says:

> This Card is not specified by any number, for it would be necessary to put '0' or '22'. It cannot be '0', otherwise the Fool would then represent the universal indefinite, when he is actually mobile and symbolises a passage of evolution. On the other hand, it cannot be characterised by '22', i.e. by two passivities, implying inaction, which is absolutely contrary to the bearing of the personage represented on the Card. (Paul Marteau, *Le Tarot de Marseille*, Paris, 1949, p. 93)

And here is a third reason: At St. Petersburg in Russia, around fifty years ago, there was a group of esotericists who composed the flower of the capital's "intelligentsia". This group was internally hierarchical, i.e. it comprised "grades"—Martinist, Templar and Rosicrucian. It was, properly said, a school of teaching and training comprising three "courses" or "classes"—first or Martinist, second or Templar, and highest or Rosicrucian.

At the head of the whole school was the professor of special mathematics from Pages College (*Pageskiy Korpus*) in St. Petersburg, Professor Gregory Ottonovitch Mebes.

Now, it was after the Bolshevik revolution (which, it goes without saying, put an end to this group and its work) that the one who is writing these lines met some members of this dispersed group and became friends with them. The friendship being true, i.e. based on unreserved mutual confidence, they (who belonged to the so-called "Rosicrucian" elite of the group) transmitted all that they knew and recounted everything concerning the work of their group, including the crises and painful experiences that they had undergone. This was in 1920. It was then that the one who is writing these lines—although he had already studied the masterly book by the engineer Schmakov, *Velikiye Arkany Taro* ("The Major Arcana of the Tarot"—a book almost twice as large as, for example, Oswald Wirth's

Le Tarot des imagiers du moyen âge or Paul Marteau's *Le Tarot de Marseille*) and the book on the Tarot by P. D. Ouspensky in 1917 — was struck to learn to what degree collective work on the Tarot can be fruitful for study, research, training and advancement in the esoteric domain. For the whole work of the Martinist-Templar-Rosicrucian group was founded on the Tarot. Study of the Cabbala, Magic, Astrology, Alchemy and Hermeticism was guided and inspired by the Tarot. This gave the whole work an exceptional coherence and organic unity. Every problem concerning the Cabbala, Magic, Astrology, Alchemy, etc., was treated as relating to a particular Arcanum of the Tarot. Thus, for example, one meditated on the twenty-two letters of the Hebrew alphabet, in order to derive their Cabbalistic meaning, in the light of the twenty-two Major Arcana of the Tarot. And one came to the conclusion that each letter of the Hebrew alphabet — understood Cabbalistically — corresponds to a particular Major Arcanum of the Tarot. Now, it is the letter *Shin* (ש), the twenty-first letter of the Hebrew alphabet, which was attributed to the Arcanum "The Fool". It was said that this is the letter of the Arcanum "The Fool". And confidentially it was added that the *esoteric name* of the Arcanum "The Fool" is AMOR (Love). Although the teaching and the experiences of this group of St. Petersburg esotericists lives now in the soul of the author of these Letters only as a general impulse received in his youth to penetrate the symbolism of the Tarot more deeply — indeed, until now he has not at all drawn upon this teaching for these Letters (the Tarot having been revealed to him during the forty-five years which followed in a new light and surpassing, with respect to its significance and its depth, all that he had learnt from the teaching and experience of the St. Petersburg group) — there is however one exception, namely the one that I have cited above, i.e. that the Arcanum "The Fool" corresponds to the letter *Shin* and that consequently its number is twenty-one, and its esoteric name is *Love*.

This is why, dear Unknown Friend, the meditation on the Arcanum "The Fool" follows that on the Arcanum "The Judgement" and precedes the meditation on the Arcanum "The World". It is a matter, therefore, beyond the two reasons concerning the scope of meditative work on the Tarot and the significance of the number twenty-one, of putting a "memorial wreath" on the non-existent tomb (i.e. non-existent here below) of the group of St. Petersburg esotericists from the beginning of this century.

First of all, let us examine the Card. It represents a man in baggy dress who is walking, leaning on a staff and carrying a hanging bag on another staff that he holds on his right shoulder. In walking, he is attacked from behind by a dog who is in the process of ripping his trousers. The man is wearing a yellow bonnet topped by a red ball; he has a blue collar with points terminating in small bells; he is wearing blue trousers and red slippers. His over-vest is red with blue arms coming out of yellow sleeves; he has a yellow belt or girdle to which little bells are attached. In a word, he has the clothing of a traditional mediaeval clown or fool.

The Fool is walking from left to right. He holds his staff with his right hand,

and with his left hand he balances on his right shoulder the staff from which the bag is hanging. His head is turned three-quarters to the right. So it is the Fool who has the tendency to the right. . .the Fool of good, not of evil, which is also evident from the fact that he does not defend himself against the dog—which he could easily chase away by means of the staff.

The Fool of good. . .it suffices to say these words in order to evoke the pale and thin figure of Don Quixote de la Manche—the knight-errant who made everyone laugh and who, from his life, merits the epithet *El Loco* ("The Fool") and who, after his death, merits that of *El Bueno* ("The Good"). O Don Quixote, you emerge from the pages of Miguel Cervantes' novel as a literary figure, but you have taken on a singular life, much more intense and real than that of a literary figure! You haunt the imagination from one generation to another, to the point of visionary experience. At evening time in an arid and rocky land, when the shadows are lengthening does one not see you silhouetted in distorted profile, of tall and stiff stature mounted on an emaciated nag?

Imagination, vision. . .what am I to say? One can meet you often in historically difficult situations—which resemble the arid and distorted landscape—where hearts have become hardened and heads have become obstinate. It is you. . .it is your voice which resounded more loudly than the beating of drums around the guillotine, one day in the month of Thermidor or Fructidor in the year II or III (of the French Republican calendar), with a cry from the top of the scaffolding, "Long live the King!"—before your chopped-off head rolled to the ground. It is you also who, in the presence of the jubilant revolutionary populace, tore down from the wall and ripped up a red placard announcing to the people of St. Petersburg the dawn of a New Era in Russia. . .and who was promptly run through by the bayonets of the red guards present. It is you again who declared openly to the German military authorities of the invaded and occupied Netherlands in 1941 that Germany, by occupying the land, was infringing the Hague Conventions that Germany herself had signed thirty years previously. . .

Don Quixote de la Manche *acts*. For Cervantes did not at all invent him, but only described him such as he appeared to him in Castille in the time of the twilight of the knighthood. Don Quixote existed and acted long before Cervantes, just as he continues to exist and act long after him. For he lives—from century to century—the life of an *archetype*, by revealing himself during the course of the ages through lots of people in lots of ways. Cervantes depicted him as a knight-errant, and the anonymous image-makers of the Middle Ages present him to us as the Fool of the Tarot. As an image, the Fool is mediaeval. This is obvious. But as an idea, as an archetype, and, lastly, as an Arcanum, what might his origin be? Greek? I should think so. Egyptian? I readily admit it. More ancient still? Why not?

Ideas, archetypes, arcana are ageless. It is only their representation, their imaged symbol, which can be attributed to a determined epoch. And this applies not only to "The Fool", but also to "The Magician", "The High Priestess", "The

Empress", "The Emperor", "The Pope", "The Lover", "The Chariot", "Justice", "The Hermit", "The Wheel of Fortune", "Force", "The Hanged Man"... For the Arcana of the Tarot are more than symbols and even more than spiritual exercises: they are magical entities, active initiating archetypes.

Not only Don Quixote, but also Orpheus, the wandering Jew, Don Juan, Tijl Uelenspiegel, Hamlet and Faust haunt the imagination of the western world.

Orpheus—such was the suffering of separation from the soul of his deceased love that it became magic, magic surpassing the river of sleep, forgetfulness and death which separates the dead from the living. Orpheus is present always and everywhere where the love of a soul torn away by death is not content with pious and resigned commemoration, but aspires to find and meet the departed one beyond the threshold of death. Such was Orpheus' love for Eurydice and such, also, was Gilgamesh's love for his friend and brother Eabani. And who can say how many human hearts have beaten, beat today, and will beat in the future, in union with that of Orpheus and that of Gilgamesh, the Babylonian hero?

The wandering Jew, or Ahasverus, is the archetype of the "other immortality"— that of crystallisation, which was in question in the letter on the thirteenth Arcanum of the Tarot "Death". He represents the principle and the soul of magic aspiring to the coagulation of the vital body (etheric body) to the point where it becomes "stone"—too hard for death's scythe. The formula underlying this magic is the reverse of that of life and grace; it is *Tu es non dignus ut intres sub tectum meum* ("You are not worthy to come under my roof"), i.e. the reverse of the formula *Domine, non sum dignus, ut intres sub tectum meum: sed tantum dic verbum, et sanabitur anima mea* ("Lord, I am not worthy that you should enter under my roof, but only speak the word and my soul will be healed"). This is the last secret and the "great arcanum" of those who sculpt themselves into stone and who want, with the resulting stones, to build the temple of humanity (cf. the meditation on the sixteenth Arcanum "The Tower of Destruction"). It goes without saying that it is only a handful amongst them who know this; the others, the majority, do not suspect it at all.

Don Juan is not purely and simply a blasphemous dissolute; he is rather a hierophant of this small god of great power known in antiquity under the name of Eros or Amor (Love). It is the magic of Eros that he represents, and it is the mysteries of Eros over which he presides in the capacity of a priest.

For if it were not thus so, if he were only a dissolute, pure and simple, how could he have exercised such power upon the imagination of poets such as Molière, Thomas Corneille, Lord Byron, Lorenzo da Ponte, Mozart (in music) and Alexis Tolstoy? It is above all the mystery poem of the latter which reveals the profound essence of Don Juan who, according to Alexis Tolstoy, was neither a blasphemous dissolute nor a false-hearted seducer, nor even a brutal adventurer, but rather an obedient and courageous servant of this childlike divinity who loves and commands élan, enthusiasm and ardour, and who detests and forbids the weighing, measuring and calculating of reason with its laws of utility and advantage, circumspection and respect for conventions and, lastly, its priority of a cold head over a warm heart. However, love has not only its right to exist, but also its transcendental metaphysics, philosophy and mysticism. For Alexis Tolstoy, Don Juan was more than a victim or dupe of love—this apparently capricious goddess. He embraced her philosophy and mysticism and was therefore her conscious collaborator, her hierophant initiated into her mysteries. And it is thus that he has become an archetype—*the archetype of love for its own sake*, the lover *par exellence*.

Don Juan lives through the energy of amorous influence for the energy of amorous influence—by nourishing it and maintaining it like a fire which should never be extinguished. This is because he is conscious of the value of this fire and of the mission that this fire has in the world. In the eternal conflict that there is between law—of right, of reason, and of the divine—and love, he takes the side of love, for which courage is necessary. And it is thus that Don Juan represents an idea, an archetype, an arcanum. He represents the young man on the Card of the sixth Arcanum of the Tarot "The Lover", who has chosen the fire of love as such and multiplicity instead of the unicity of the love of his eternal sister soul—since Babylon, the woman appointed to the mysteries of erotic magic, has convinced him.

Tijl Uelenspiegel, the Flemish tramp from Damme, near Bruges—the hero of numerous popular accounts of mystification and farce, and also the tragic hero of the epic by Coster—is the archetype of revolutionary anarchism who, as a consequence of complete disenchantment in human authority, has neither faith nor law. His is the spirit of rebellion against all authority in the name of the freedom of the individual—the freedom of a vagabond who has nothing, who obeys no one, who is afraid of nothing, who expects no recompense and who fears no chastisement, beyond as well as here below. . .the mocking spirit who, at the same time, turns the temples and altars of humanity upside down, making them collapse by means of his magic wand: ridicule. This wand, in touching things, transforms them: the solemn into the pompous, the moving into the sentimental, the courageous into the presumptuous, tears into snivelling, love into passing fancy . . .For this wand, also "has no other aim than to condense a great quantity of fluid emanated by the operator. . .and to direct the projection of this fluid onto a determined point" (Papus, *Traité méthodique de la magie pratique*, Paris, 1970 p. 204). And this "condensed fluid" of the operator is the operator's condensed faith that everything is only a great farce.

Tijl Uelenspiegel is an archetype because he is at work with his wand always and everywhere whenever a mocking spirit thinks of himself as being "enlightening" by turning the things, ideas and ideals to which others hold into ridicule. Thus not only the poetic verses of the Russian Bolshevik militant atheist Demyane Bedny, but also the works of such a respectable writer and thinker as Voltaire, show the presence and influence of Tijl Uelenspiegel. However, Tijl Uelenspiegel—in so far as he is an archetype—is not only purely and simply a mocker. This is only one side of his being. There is another side to him—it is that of militant anarchism:

the revolt of the humbler people against those who give the laws and prescribe what they should and should not do. The following act of a comparatively recent date is an example of this:

The sailors of a Russian Baltic fleet brought success to the Russian Bolshevik revolution in October 1917 by opening cannon fire from the cruiser "Aurora" upon the last nest of resistance of troops loyal to the democratic government (a battalion of women volunteers) at the Winter Palace in St. Petersburg, and taking it by assault. Thus they were the incontestable and celebrated heroes of the October revolution. However, it is a no less incontestable fact—although never celebrated—that the same sailors of this Baltic fleet rose up in February 1921 against the regime that they had decisively helped to establish in 1917. They took possession of the naval fortress at Kronstadt and a regular war of siege ensued. After a month of siege Kronstadt was taken by assault from the élite of the red guards—cadets or *coursants* (students of the Bolshevik naval school).

Now, to what was this radical change of attitude of the sailors of this Baltic fleet due? It was due to the fact that the sailors were fighting in October 1917 for anarchic freedom—for the soviets (councils) of workers, peasants, soldiers and sailors, without generals and admirals, without ministers, i.e. without those placed above the soviets. What they desired was the re-establishment of the community of comrades which existed in the sixteenth, seventeenth and eighteenth centuries known under the name *Sietch' Zaporozhskaya* (cossaks of the Ukraine)—the ideal of the communist anarchist community. However, in 1921 they realised that they had been mistaken. It was not a community of brothers and comrades which arose from the October revolution, but rather state control with a new, strong, dictatorial, police-regulated state, governed by a clique who had the say of everything in the face of a mass who had the say of nothing. The sailors of Kronstadt, having well understood the deception, took recourse to arms. And it was again Tijl Uelenspiegel who was invisibly at their head, just as he was at the head of the crowd who took the Bastille, and just as he was the author of the *carmagnole*, the revolutionary round danced in 1793, and of the song which accompanied it...

Soren Kierkegaard, the Danish religious thinker who initiated the philosophical and psychological current known under the name "existentialism", said:

> In modern philosophy there has been more than enough talk about speculation beginning with doubt, but on the other hand, as far as I have been able to concern myself occasionally with such reflections, I have sought in vain for illumination upon the point of difference between doubt and despair. I will here attempt to throw light upon this distinction... Doubt is a despair of thought, despair is a doubt of the personality; hence it is why I hold so stoutly to the category of choice, which is my solution, the very nerve of my views on life... (Soren Kierkegaard, *Either/Or*; trsl. W. Lowrie, vol. ii, London, 1944, pp. 177-178)

The existential philosophy of our time thus differs from traditional speculative philosophy in that it is founded on despair, i.e. upon the doubt of the whole personality, whilst speculative philosophy is founded on doubt, i.e. on the despair of thought alone. Now all despair, all doubt of the personality, amounts to—and is summarised by—Hamlet's famous question: "To be or not to be?" For just as Kierkegaard, the Danish thinker, is the author of modern existentialism, so is Hamlet, the prince of Denmark—hero of Shakespeare's drama and of the legend recounted by Saxo Grammaticus—the very archetype of existentialism, the despair of the personality. He is the archetype of the isolation of completely autonomous consciousness, cut off both from Nature and the spiritual world—man at the zero point between two fields of gravitation: terrestrial and celestial.

Doubt is more than a psychological state of indecision; it is the soul's sojourn in the intermediary sphere between the two fields of attraction—terrestrial and celestial—from which there is no other means of escape than a pure and simple act of faith, issuing from the soul itself without heaven and earth taking any part in it. It is therefore a matter of an act of the free personality in the face of complete silence from heaven and earth. Now, Hamlet is the archetype of this trial, where the following is at stake: either an act of faith, or despair and madness.

Doctor Faust is the synthesis of the forms of madness and wisdom of the *six* archetypes whom we have mentioned above: as Don Quixote he is in pursuit of unparalleled exploits; as Orpheus he is searching for a return to the light from the darkness of death from centuries past of Helen of Troy, whom he loves passionately in spite of the centuries and the threshold of death which separate him from her; as Don Juan he "sees Helen in every woman" and is searching for the "eternal feminine" (*das Ewig-Weibliche*) in and through particular loves; as Ahasverus he rejuvenates himself by means of dark magic so as to begin another life and a new terrestrial biography without interruption through death, i.e. a new incarnation without a preceding period of disincarnation; as Tijl Uelenspiegel he does away with every allegiance and all religious, scientific and political authority, and in Mephistopheles' company he mocks moral and other restraints impeding the freedom to dare and to will; as Hamlet, lastly, he has the trial of great existential doubt whether "to be or not to be" in the guise of the question "to live or not to live".

But beyond all that which he has in common with these six archetypes, Faust represents—at least, as Goethe conceived him—yet another archetype, an eternal archetype, namely that of the one who is tried and tempted: *eternal Job*, whom we find in the Bible. Faust is Job in the epoch of humanism, i.e. at the dawn of the modern age. Just as with the Biblical Job, he is the stake in a wager proposed to God by Mephistopheles, and accepted. But Faust's trial and temptation differs from that of the Biblical Job in that it does not consist in the reverse of fortune and in ill luck, but rather in favourable results and success. Mephistopheles has full power, accorded to him from above, to satisfy all Faust's desires. And the trial of which it is a matter here amounts to whether the relative and transitory world can for ever satisfy Faust — the man issuing from the modern age, the modern man. . .whether all pleasures here below, in detail and in general, can anaesthetise man's aspiration to the absolute and eternal by rendering him wholly satisfied and happy. Job demonstrated that the sorrow that the world can inflict is incapable of tearing the human soul away from God; Faust demonstrated that this is so also with the joy that the world can offer.

Oswald Spengler, the author of *The Decline of the West*, calls modern man "Faustian man" (*der faustische Mensch*) — and he was right to call him so. For Faust is indeed the dominant archetype of the epoch following the Middle Ages, which is characterised by the enormous growth of mankind's power over Nature and of the facilities for satisfying his desires — comprising those of the boldest of magicians of the past: flying through the air, seeing and hearing at a great distance, travelling without horses (e.g. by car), the evocation of living images and sounds of past events or events at a great distance, etc. It is just as if the prince of this world has obtained full power to satisfy, one after the other, all the desires of contemporary mankind, so as to demonstrate for himself that the power and enjoyment of the relative and transitory world here below can make man forget the absolute and eternal, can make him forget God. . .and with respect to God, it is so as to demonstrate to the hierarchies of evil that man is of another calibre than the relative and the transitory, that whatever the power and enjoyment is here below it can never satisfy him. The trial of our epoch is that of Faust. It is the trial of the satisfaction of desires.

A recent phenomenon of our epoch is communism — or, if you wish, social and collective state control. It openly pursues the aim of satisfying as completely as possible the needs and desires of as large a number of people living on the earth as possible. Well, let us suppose that it succeeds in Russia. Everyone will have well-furnished accommodation with a telephone, a radio, a television set, a refrigerator, a washing machine. . .And what then? Yes, cinema, theatre, concerts, ballet, sport. . .And what then? Yes, science will furnish new occasions and directions for activity, for the imagination and for. . .desire. One will visit the moon, the planets. . .And what then? There will be unparalleled adventures to experience and to know about, which as yet we cannot imagine — as, for example, the discovery of the existence of other intelligent beings, other "mankinds" on the planets. . .And what then? No answer.

No, there is certainly an answer: it is given by the parable of the prodigal son. What is the value of television sets, washing machines, supersonic aircraft, spaceships, flights to the planets and galactic exploration in comparison with the loving embrace of the Father upon the return of his son to the parental home?

The trial of our time is that of the satisfaction of desires. This applies not only to communists, capitalists and materialists, but also, and no less, to — I shall not say esotericists, but — occultists and magicians. For they also are under the sign of the same trial.

Louis Claude de Saint-Martin, for example, took part in the operations of ceremonial magic in the circle of Martinez de Pasqually's disciples. This magic proved itself to him to be effective and real. And it was after having been convinced of the reality and efficacy of ceremonial magic that—in full knowledge of what he was doing—he turned his back on these magical practices and embraced the mysticism of Jacob Boehme: the world of ineffable experiences, of relationships between the soul and God. Therefore he passed through the trial. Magical phenomena—the "passes"—did not succeed in arresting him on his path towards the absolute and the eternal, whilst his former companion and co-disciple, Jean Baptiste Willermoz, although spiritually orientated and sincerely believing, remained devoted to ceremonial magic and initiation ritualism until his death.

Eliphas Lévi, the author of *Dogme et rituel de la haute magie*, was without doubt the pioneer of the theory and practice of the ceremonial magic of the nineteenth century. It was he who had the courage—or the audacity, if you wish—to present magic to the light of day as something real and, at the same time, as something intelligible. . . and this after the vogue for the enlightenment and in the midst of the vogue for materialism! Can one reproach him for lack of courage? However, Madame H. P. Blavatsky reproached him. She said that he had subsequently disavowed his own magical teaching and turned to Christian mysticism —for fear of the ecclesiastical authorities taking him amiss. The truth is, however, that Eliphas Lévi—this intrepid magician who evoked Apollonius of Tyana in London—having surpassed the bounds of ceremonial magic, concentrated on the mysticism and gnosis of Christian Hermeticism. He passed through the Faustian trial, just as Saint-Martin did. For this reason, what Saint-Martin wrote to Kirchberger, Baron of Liebisdorf, on the reasons for his conversion from ceremonial magic to mysticism is applicable also in Eliphas Lévi's case:

> . . . the initiations I passed through in my first school, and which I have long since left behind me, to attend to the only initiation which is truly after my own heart . . . I can assure you I have received by the inward way, truths and joys a thousand times higher than those I have received from without. . . there is no initiation, but that of God only, and his Eternal Word within us . . . (L. Schauer and A. Chuquet, *La correspondance inédite de Louis Claude de Saint-Martin*; trsl. E. B. Penny, letters XIX and CX in *Saint-Martin's Correspondence*, Exeter, 1863, pp. 77-78, 375)

This applies also to Paul Sédir (Yvon de Loup), who was also devoted to practical magic and for two years utilised to this effect a room that he rented on the ground floor of 4, rue de Savoie in Paris (cf. Dr. Philippe Encausse, *Sciences occultes ou vingt-cinq années d'occultisme occidental. Papus, sa vie, son oeuvre*, Paris, 1949, p. 49). He was a member and dignitary of at least twenty fraternities, more or less secret—for example, the Cabbalistic Order of the Rose Cross, the Order of Martinists, the H. B. of L., the F. T. L., etc. But in January 1909 (his activity in this domain began in 1888) he retired from these fraternities, forsaking all the posts and titles that had been conferred on him. This surprised friends of his of long standing.

> But there was in his life an outward circumstance, a solemn and decisive event, which made him grasp the emptiness of secret sciences and societies, and which placed him for ever upon the sole way of the Gospel. (Dr. Philippe Encause, *Le Maître Philippe de Lyon*, Paris, 1958, p. 80)

This event was his meeting with Maître Philip of Lyons. Sédir himself wrote in a letter to "L'Echo du Merveilleux" in May 1910 (reprinted in *Bulletin des Amitiés Spirituelles*, April, 1933):

> ...For my reckoning I have, together with some companions, done the rounds of all esotericisms and explored all crypts with the most fervent sincerity, with the most vivid hope of success. But none of the certainties that I eventually grasped appeared to me to be the Certainty.
>   Rabbis have communicated unknown manuscripts to me; alchemists have admitted me to their laboratories; Sufis, Buddhists and Taoists have lead me, during long late-night sessions, to the abodes of their gods; a Brahmin let me copy his tables of mantrams; a yogi gave the secets of contemplation. But, one evening, after a certain meeting, all that these admirable men had taught me became for me like the soft haze which rises at dusk after an over-warm day. (Dr. Philippe Encausse, *Le Maître Philippe de Lyon*, Paris, 1958, pp. 80-81)

Papus also had the decisive meeting mentioned by Sédir. It was no less decisive for him than for Sédir, concerning the relationship between certainties and the Certainty, between values and the Value. But—being a doctor, and accustomed in the first place to consider the good of the patients who put their confidence in him—he did not forsake any of the responsibilities accepted in the past and did not retire from any group for which he had assumed responsibility, although his heart was already elsewhere. What changed for him was the priority of Christian spirituality, which he showed in a radical way—which won him the reproach of "having a soft spot for Catholicism" on the part of Robert Ambelain and merited his being treated as an inevitable "Jesuit" by certain Freemasons. But Papus' evolution—whatever one says, and whether it pleases one or not—was nothing other than the Faustian trial crowned with success.

These examples, although we could cite several more, suffice to illustrate the nature and experience of the Faustian trial in the domain of occultism. Every occultist must undergo this trial. For it is only after having passed through it, i.e.

after having known arbitrary magic, that an occultist finds the divine magic, gnosis and mysticism of Christian Hermeticism. Then he will transform himself from a scholar into a sage, from a magician into a mage, from a gnosticiser into a gnostic and from an amateur in the mysteries into a mystic. So be it.

The Faustian trial and the human prototype of Faust are prefigured in antiquity by the personality—whether legendary or real is not important—of Cyprian the Mage, who became a Christian and who, subsequently, was bishop of Nicodemia and, lastly, was martyred under the emperor Diocletian. The following are some extracts from the Coptic version of his "Confession" (the legend of Cyprian comprises three works: Conversion, Confession and Martyrdom):

> This is the repentance (μετάνοια) of Cyprian the Mage (μάγος) who became a Christian thanks to the virgin Justina; who was, subsequently, bishop in the town of Nicodemia; and who, lastly, with Justina, obtained the crown of a martyr under the king Diocletian, on 20th Phaopi, in peace, AMEN . . .
>
> I am Cyprian, he who was consecrated, from his adolescence, in the temple of Apollo, and who was instructed from childhood in the deceptions that the Dragon (δράγον) accomplishes. For, having not yet attained seven years of age, I was already devoted to the Mysteries of Mithra . . . And when I was fifteen years old I served Demeter and I walked before her, bearing torches in the procession. With respect to her daughter, who is called the "virgin" (παρθένος) I bore her mourning attire, clothed in brilliant clothing . . . I went to Olympus . . . that is called "the mountain of the gods". I was initiated into the secrets of the Image (εἰκών), into her way of speaking, which consists of a succession of noises, which are produced regularly at the time of a manifestation (φαντασία) of demons, when they reveal themselves . . . And I also saw the hearts of the demons—some singing, others, in contrast, setting traps, beguiling, and provoking trouble. And I saw arising before me the escort of each of the gods and goddesses. I passed 40 days and 40 nights in these places, nourishing myself solely from the sap of trees, after sunset . . . When I attained the age of fifteen, I was instructed by the priests, the seven prophets and the prophetess of the Devil (ἀντεκείμενος) with whom this latter they had mouth to mouth conversation. It is they, in fact, who procure work for each of the demons . . . The Devil (διάβολος) taught me how the earth is firmly established on its foundations. He taught me the law of the Air and the Ether. I visited the Sea as far as Tartar (τάρταρος). Lastly, I went to Argos; I celebrated the festival of Hera, and there I learnt how one separates women from their husbands and how one sows hate between brothers and friends. I learnt of the unity of the Air and the Ether, and of the way

in which the Earth enters into combination with Water and, on the other hand, how Water does so with the Ether.

And I left also for a town called Thalis (Elide?) which is in the country that is called Lacedemon. I learnt to know the mysteries of Helios and Artemis, the law of light and darkness, of the stars and their orbits. . .Subsequently, I went to the people that are called Phrygians. From them I learnt to know divination . . .And I knew also of the members of the body which make sudden convulsive movements, of the nerves which retract, provoking itching, and of others which get caught up in one another; I knew of the art of setting a trap with words, of the numbers that one obtains when one throws the fingers forward and also the numbers which fly away suddenly from the lips of men. I created things with my words, and I established that they were real. . .I also went to Memphis and Heliopolis. . .I visited their hidden underground chambers where the demons of the air enter into union with the demons who dwell on the earth; I learnt to know how they lead men into temptation. . .and how the spirits (πνεῦμος) struggle with demons. And I learnt to know how many Archontes of darkness there are, and the relationships that they have with souls and bodies deprived of reason, down to and including the fish; and I knew what work is accomplished by them (the Archontes); the one provokes the shunning of a man; another acts on his intelligence so that the man gives himself up to him; another acts on his memory; another inspires terror in him; another proceeds by way of guileful ruses; another by surprise; another provokes forgetfulness; another acts upon the crowd so that they revolt; and many other phenomena which are produced in the same way. . .I saw the souls of giants imprisoned in darkness — burdening the shadow of the earth — who appear like one who is bearing a heavy load. I saw dragons enter into contact with demons and I felt the bitter taste of venom coming out of their mouths. . .venom which the spirits (πνεῦμα) of the Air make use of to cause all these ills for human beings. . .I lived in these places: the spirit (πνεῦμα) of lying appearing in numerous aspects; the spirit of lewdness having a threefold face. . .; the spirit of anger which is like a hard stone. . .the spirit of trickery with a great number of sharpened tongues. . .the spirit of hate who is like a blind man, with eyes placed at the back of the head, all the time fleeing from the light. . .; the spirit of spitefulness who presents himself like a dried up bone. . .I saw also the appearance of the vainglory, virtue and sterile justice with which the demons deceived the Greek philosophers; they are, in fact, totally impotent and without force. Certain are like dust, whilst others are like shadows...The number of demons who acted as idols, leading the Greek philosophers into error, is 365. I could not tell you about all these things one by one without writing a number of books; but I shall tell you of some which will make the intensity of my blasphemy apparent.

When I attained thirty years of age, I left Egypt for the country of the Chaldeans, in order to learn how the Ether is. The people there say that it is established above the Fire; but the Sages among them claim that it dwells above the Light...the 365 parts of the Ether were enumerated to me, each part of which possesses its own nature and enters into contact with the force of material substances which are our body...Certain amongst them, however, do not obey the Word of Light, and maintain an attitude contrary to it. Likewise I was taught how one persuades them to participate in the designs of material beings, how one makes them know the Will of the Light and how they obey it. And I saw also the Mediators (μεσίτης) who are found amongst them. I was surprised by the number of spirits of darkness who are found in the air. . . I learnt to know the conventions (διαθήκη) that they elaborate amongst them and I was very astonished to learn that they are obedient to them. In this place there exists a constitution (διάθεσις), a good will (σπουδή), a commandment (ἐντολή) and a good sense allowing them to enjoy life in common...If you really want to believe me, I have seen him — the Devil — face to face. I made him appear before me through offerings. If you take my word to be the truth, I greeted him mouth to mouth. I spoke to him and he thought of me that I was one of the great ones before him. He called me "(a) gifted young man who is easy to instruct" and, also, "(a) little prince worthy of my society". . . He said, "I will help you through them (all the powers — ἐξουσίαι) in your life (βίος)", for I was highly thought of by him. . . As I was going to leave, he cried out my name, "O very zealous Cyprian, be a strong and persevering man in all that you do". . . And his appearance was similar to a flower of joy, adorned with precious stones; on his head he had a crown studded with these very stones, whose gleam was diffused throughout the whole place. And his clothing (στολή) radiated so strongly that the place where he sat moved... (R. P. Festugière, O. P., *La révélation d'Hermes Trismégiste*, vol. i, appendix 2, Paris, 1950, pp. 374-382)

Following this narrative of repentance, the account of Cyprian's conversion, properly said, begins. Well, here is one rich in experience and knowledge, for whom might be said (to use Paul Sédir's words):

> . . . after a certain meeting (with the Christian virgin Justina),
> all that the sages of Greece, Phrygia, Egypt and Chaldea had
> taught him became like the soft haze which rises at dusk after
> an over-warm day.

Furthermore, after having met face to face the master himself of the wisdom of this world, he renounced the wisdom of this world to give himself up to the wisdom of divine love—which is folly in the eyes of the sages of this world . . .

In other words Cyprian, the bishop and martyr—with the magical wand, cup, sword and pentacle of Cyprian the mage in a bag—took it on his shoulder and set off, without defence against the dogs who attacked him, and as a ridiculous clown in the eyes of the world, *en route* towards . . . the martyrdom which awaited him. His Greek, Phrygian, Egyptian and Chaldean co-initiates must have said: "There goes the Jester". Educated people and those of common sense of the society of his time would have said: "There goes the Fool". For in their eyes Cyprian had turned his back on the very principle of human culture and civilisation—the intellect . . . the intellect whose ruling genius himself he had met face to face and who had called him "(a) gifted young man who is easy to instruct". For the spirit of "knowledge for its own sake" spoke to him mouth to mouth and exhorted him to be "a strong and persevering man in all that he does".

Now, Cyprian proved to be stronger than the strength of arbitrary magic and more persevering than the perseverance required for "knowledge for its own sake". He surpassed arbitrary will itself and devoted himself to a higher science—to divine science, i.e. to the science of divine love. It is the Tarot Arcanum "The Fool" which is the decisive step that he made. Here lies its meaning and its actualising magic.

The Arcanum "The Fool" teaches the "know-how" of passing from intellectuality, moved by the desire for knowledge, to the higher knowledge due to love. It is thus a matter of transition from the consciousness that theosophical literature calls "lesser *manas*" to the consciousness that it calls "greater *manas*" (= "*manas-buddhi*")—which corresponds to the transition from ego consciousness to the consciousness of the spiritual self (= spirit-self) in anthroposophical literature. In other words, the Tarot Arcanum "The Fool" is related to the transformation of personal consciousness into cosmic consciousness, where the self (ego) is no longer the author of the act of consciousness but is its receiver—obedient to the law of poverty, obedience and chastity.

Now, the Arcanum "The Fool" has a double meaning. Indeed, it can be understood in two different ways: as a model and as a warning at the same time. For on the one hand it teaches the freedom of transcendental consciousness elevated above the things of this world, and on the other hand it clearly presents a very impressive warning of the peril that this elevation comprises—lack of concern, inadequacy, irresponsibility and ridicule . . . in a word, madness.

The Arcanum "The Fool" has in fact these two meanings. It teaches transcendental consciousness and it warns of its peril. It deals with two modes of sacrificing the intellect (*sacrificium intellectus*). For the intellect can be sacrificed in two different ways: it can be *placed in the service* of transcendental consciousness or it can be simply *abandoned*. Hermeticism chooses the first way of passing beyond intellectuality, whilst many a mystic — Christian or otherwise — has chosen the second way. However, let these two different attitudes not be confused with mystical ecstacism, pure and simple, on the one hand, and so-called "sober" mysticism, i.e. reasonable and prudent, on the other hand. St. John of the Cross was ravished in many bouts of ecstasy which went as far as levitation of the body; however, he was the author of books on mysticism whose clarity, profundity and sobriety of thought are hardly to be surpassed.

With St. John of the Cross, as he said himself, the intellect was silent in face of the divine Presence. It became absorbed by the divine Presence (for the length of time determined by the latter) in order to become active again — *more* active, in fact, than before — after which it comes out again from being immersed in the absolute light whose clarity dazzles the intellect and appears to plunge it into darkness. But this being plunged into the darkness of absolute light does not remain without a profound effect for the intellect: the latter comes out of it endowed with new tendencies, imprinted from the Arcana above. Each ecstasy of St. John of the Cross was therefore an initiation, i.e. the direct imprint of divine, absolute truth not in the domain of conscious thought but rather in the domain of the "will underlying thinking", i.e. that which *produces* conscious thoughts. Thus, it is not a matter of the antinomy: ecstasy — progressive growth of consciousness. No, in the passing beyond the intellect it is a matter of choosing between the decision to *replace* the intellect once and for all with the "breath from above" and the decision to *place* the intellect in the active service of this "breath", whether it produces ecstatic raptures or not. Thus, a whirling dervish who resorts to dance so as to exclude intelligence, or a Buddhist monk of the Zen sect who lives in a mindless state of "meditation" (where he meditates on nothing but simply stays awake with an empty consciousness without falling asleep — in the expectation of a sudden illumination), this dervish and this Zen monk, I say, have made their choice: they have decided not to pass beyond intellectual consciousness, but rather to dispense with it.

It is different in the case of a Christian contemplative monk who meditates, for example, on the stages of the Lord's Passion — and who wants to understand, feel and deepen himself in it to the point of identification with it — when he arrives at the state where his thought and imagination halt before the high pitch of the light. He passes beyond the intellect and the imagination, the activity of which halt after having attained their limit. But this halt is in reality only apparent; for just as a wheel turning with great speed appears to be immobile, so does the intellect and imagination of a soul in ecstasy appear to be immobile to ordinary consciousness — although they are (or, rather, because they are) overactive.

To pass beyond the intellect is therefore to render it overactive, whilst to bypass the intellect is to reduce it to complete passivity. These are the two quite different ways of sacrificing the intellect (*sacrificium intellectus*).

Now, I repeat, Hermeticism professes to the active surpassing of the intellect. This is why it comprises not only mystical experiences but also gnosis, magic and esoteric science. If it were not thus so, it would consist only of exercises or practical methods aspiring to illumination due to the suppression of intelletuality. The entire history of Hermeticism through the course of the ages is that of continuous inspiration from century to century, on the one hand, *and* the active response of human intelligence from century to century, on the other hand.

The twenty-first Arcanum of the Tarot is therefore that of the Hermeticist's method of sacrificing the intellect to spirituality in such a way that it grows and develops instead of becoming enfeebled and atrophied. It is the Arcanum of the marriage of opposites (*coniunctio oppositorum*, i.e. the conjunction of opposites) —namely discursive intellectuality and illuminative spirituality; or, in other words, it is the alchemical work of the union of human wisdom, which is folly in the eyes of God, with divine wisdom, which is folly in the eyes of man, in such a way that the result is not a double folly but rather a single wisdom which understands both that which is above and that which is below.

In order to understand better what the issue is here, let us first of all look at the byways of the relationship between intellectuality and spirituality, between knowledge and revelation, on the historical plane. Thus St. Paul wrote:

> . . . Jews demand signs (*semeia*) and Greeks seek wisdom (*sophian*), but we preach Christ crucified: a stumbling block to Jews and folly to Gentiles—but to those who are called, both Jews and Greeks: the power (*dynamin*) of God and the wisdom (*sophian*) of God. (I Corinthians i, 22-24)

Here he states precisely the state of things in the relationship between pagan intellectuality and the Jewish prophetic spirituality of his time. Because the aspirations of the best of the pagans—the "philosophers"—all converged on the "logos of the cosmos" (i.e. the "cosmic intelligence"), whilst Jewish spiritual leaders lived in expectation—and from expectation—of a miracle transforming the world: the manifestation of the power of the Celestial King through his Annointed One, a terrestrial king. The former wanted to understand the world, whilst the latter awaited its miraculous magical transformation. Now, the preaching of Christ crucified clashed with the philosophers' fundamental idea that the entire world is the incarnation of the Logos, as well as with the fundamental thesis of Jewish prophetism that the Celestial King is seated above the world and intervenes in wordly events only by emitting lightning-flashes of his power—through the prophets, through thaumaturgists, and through the Messiah—from his throne above the world.

The crucified Christ therefore satisfied neither those who were desiring to understand the world—being only a particular phenomenon amongst other phenomena of the world—nor those who were awaiting the magical transformative manifestation of the power of God—the death on the Cross being a failure and not a triumph of divine power. . ."a stumbling block to Jews and folly to Greeks". But St. Paul did not despair: Christ crucified, he said, revealed the power of God and the wisdom of God to those who are called, both Jews and Greeks, i.e. the Cross of Christ can be understood only through the cross of revelation (miracle) and wisdom (immanent Logos). Thus St. Paul set a problem to be solved—or rather a task to be accomplished—by mankind. And mankind's spiritual history since then consists only of stages crossed in the accomplishment of the task of the union of revelation and knowledge, of divine wisdom and human wisdom. The stages are as follows:

Initially there is pure and simple *opposition*, such as St. Paul stated it:

> If anyone among you thinks that he is wise in this age, let him become a fool that he may become wise. For the wisdom of this world is folly with God. (I Corinthians iii, 18-19)

Subsequently this opposition becomes *parallelism*, admitted and tolerated—a kind of "peaceful coexistence" of the spiritual and intellectual domains. The Gospel statement: "The sons of this age (*tou aionos toutou*) are wiser (*phronimoteroi*) in their own generation (*eis ten genean ten heauton*) than the sons of light (*huoi tou photos*)" (Luke xvi, 8) formulates admirably the fundamental idea underlying the parallelism of spirituality and intellectuality. This parallelism manifests itself historically in the admitted and tolerated duality of "philosophy" and "theology". Later, the parallelism was gradually replaced by *cooperation* between spirituality and intellectuality. The "wisdom of the Greeks"—above all the thoughts of Plato and those of Aristotle—which at the time of St. Paul saw only "folly in the preaching of Christ crucified" became an ally of revelation. First of all the Greek fathers (above all Clement of Alexandria and Origen), and also St. Augustine, did not hesitate to resort to the help of Platonic thought, and then it was St. Albertus Magnus and St. Thomas Aquinas who opened the way for the entrance of Aristotelian thought, also, in the domain of revealed truths.

It is above all the Dominicans to whom mankind's spiritual history owes the crossing of the stage in the gradual bringing together of spirituality and intellectuality which is the phenomenon called "scholasticism". Scholasticism signifies a great human endeavour, sustained through the course of centuries, aiming at an as complete as possible cooperation between spirituality and intellectuality.

Whilst endeavouring to render revelation intelligible, i.e. to understand it through intelligence, scholasticism made use of the latter only as an instrument for backing up revelation by means of argumentative or philosophical thought. The fundamental thesis of scholasticism was that philosophy is the servant of theology (*philosophia ancilla theologiae*). Intelligence certainly cooperated, but it played only a subordinate role. Thus, scholasticism did not succeed in achieving the alchemical work of the *fusion* of spirituality and intellectuality—the work of the "marriage of the sun and moon"—the result of which is a *third principle* called the "philosopher's stone" in alchemy.

The "philosopher's stone" of spiritual alchemy is described in the *Emerald Table* of Hermes Trismegistus as follows:

> The father thereof is the sun, the mother the moon.
> The wind carried it in its womb; the earth is the nurse thereof.
> It is the father of all works of wonder (*thelema*) throughout the
>   whole world.
> The power thereof is perfect, if it be cast on to earth.
> It will separate the element of earth from that of fire, the subtle
>   from the gross, gently and with great sagacity.
> It doth ascend from earth to heaven.
> Again it doth descend to earth, and uniteth in itself the force
>   from things superior and things inferior.
>   (*Tabula Smaragdina*, 4-8)*

This means to say that the process of induction (which "ascends from earth to heaven") and that of deduction (which "descends to earth"), the process of prayer (which "ascends from earth to heaven") and that of revelation (which "descends to earth")—i.e. human endeavour and the action of grace from above—unite and become a complete circle which contracts and concentrates to become a point where the ascent and descent are simultaneous and coincide. And this point is the "philosopher's stone"—the principle of the identity of the human and divine, of humanism and prophetism, of intelligence and revelation, of intellectuality and spirituality. It is the solution of the problem posed by St. Paul, or rather the accomplishment of the task given by him, when he wrote of the Cross being folly to the Greeks and a stumbling block to the Jews, but which "to those who are called, both Jews and Greeks, is the power of God and the wisdom of God" (I Corinthians i, 22-24).

Now, the historical and evolutionary mission of Hermeticism is to advance the progress of the alchemical work engaged in developing the "philosopher's stone" or the *union* of spirituality and intellectuality. It is called to be the crest of the wave of contemporary human effort aspiring to the fusion of spirituality and intellectuality. This effort and aspiration is larger than the group of Hermeticists, properly said, who are dispersed in the world. There are probably more people who are not avowed Hermeticists and who are engaged in the endeavour aiming at the fusion of spirituality and intellectuality than there are Hermeticists, prop-

*Trsl. R. Steele and D. W. Singer, *Proceedings of the Royal Society of Medicine* xxi, 1928, p. 42.

erly said. Neither Vladimir Soloviev, nor Nicolas Berdyaev nor Pierre Teilhard de Chardin, nor Carl Gustav Jung, for example, were declared Hermeticists, but how much they have contributed to the progress of the work in question! Christian existentialism (Berdyaev), Christian gnosis (Soloviev), Christian evolutionism (Teilhard de Chardin), and depth psychology of revelation (Jung) are, in fact, as many inestimable contributions to the cause of the union of spirituality and intellectuality. Although they did not make Hermeticism their calling, they served its cause and were inspired from the same sources from which Hermeticism is inspired. Hermeticism has, therefore, more than a few allies and collaborators beyond the ranks of its adherents. The Spirit blows where it will, but the task of the Hermetic tradition is to maintain—without pretension to a monopoly, God forbid! —the ancient ideal of "the *thelema* of the whole world. . .which ascends from earth to heaven. . .descends to earth, and uniteth in itself the force from things superior and things inferior". Its task is that of *guardian* of the great spiritual work.

To be a guardian signifies two things: firstly, the study of and practical application of the heritage of the past, and secondly continuous creative effort aiming at the advancement of the work. For the tradition lives only when it is deepened, elevated and increased in size. Conservation alone does not suffice at all. It is only a corpse which lends itself to conservation by means of mummification.

The great spiritual work—seen always on the historical plane—takes place under simultaneous action stemming from two contrasting sources: from above and from below, i.e. under the action of continuous revelation and that of the effort of human consciousness. In other words, it is the product of the collaboration of revelation and humanism, or of Avatars and Buddhas—to say it in terms of the Indo-Tibetan spiritual tradition. This latter awaits both a new wave of revelation, the culminating point of which will be the Kalki Avatar, and the manifestation of a new Buddha— the Maitreya Buddha. At the same time esoteric Islam (*batin*)—Shi'ism and Sufism—awaits the coming (*parousia*) of the twelfth Imam "who, at the end of our era, will bring the full revelation of the esotericism of all divine revelations" (Henri Corbin, *Histoire de la philosophie islamique*, Paris, 1964, p. 21), and believing Jews await the coming of the Messiah. We need hardly mention, also, the widespread expectation of the second coming of Christ.

Thus, there is a climate of expectation in the world—expectation sustained, contemplated and intensified through the course of the centuries. Without being nourished and directed from above, this energy of human expectation alone would have exhausted itself long ago. But it is not exhausted; rather, on the contrary, it is growing. This is because it aspires to a reality and not an illusion. And this reality is the historical accomplishment of the great work of uniting spirituality and intellectuality, revelation and humanism, on the vast scale of the whole of mankind.

Seen on the level of the history of the whole of mankind, this work presents itself as follows:

We mentioned above the oriental notions of Avatars and Imams, on the one hand, and that of Buddhas, on the other hand. Avatars and Imams represent personalities who are culminating points of the revelation from above, whilst Buddhas (Gautama Buddha being only one in a series of Buddhas) represent the culminating points of certain epochs of human history—not of revelation from above, but rather of the awakening of human consciousness. The word "Buddha" signifies "awakened", whilst that of "Avatar" signifies "descent"—"a descent, the birth of God in humanity, the Godhead manifesting itself in the human form and nature, (this is) the eternal Avatar" (Sri Aurobindo Ghose, *Essays on the Gita*, Madras, 1922, p. 190). Therefore, if Avatars are *descents* of the divine, Buddhas are *ascents* of the human—they are culminating points of stages of *humanism* in the process of evolution. The difference between the "revelatory ones" (Avatars and Imams) and the "awakened ones" (Buddhas) is analogous to that between "saints" and "righteous men" in the Judaeo-Christian world. Here "saints" correspond to Avatars in that they represent the revelation of divine grace through them and in them, and "righteous men" correspond to Buddhas in that they bring to evidence the fruits of human endeavour.

Thus Job was not a saint, but a righteous man—one of those righteous men who "maintain the world" through their merits. Righteous men show how great the value is of human nature when its very essence is awakened and revealed. Righteous men are the true humanists—the flowers of pure humanism. They bear witness to the fact that the essence of human nature is in the image and likeness of God. This was the witness borne by Job and it was also the witness borne by Socrates. The German philospher Immanuel Kant bore witness also, by declaring loudly that, however bereft the human soul might be of illuminating grace from above and revelation from above, it bears in itself the *categorical* imperative —immanent moral law (called *dharma* by the sages of India)—which makes it act and think as if it were eternal, immortal, and aspiring to infinite perfection. Thus Kant bore witness to the fundamental nobility of human nature—and this was his contribution to *faith in man*, whatever his limitations, and even errors, in the metaphysical domain may be. For just as there are two loves—love of God and love of neighbour—which are inseparable, so there are *two faiths* which are also inseparable—faith in God and faith in man. Saints and martyrs bear witness to God and righteous men bear witness to man, as being the image and likeness of God. The former restore and strengthen faith in God and the latter restore and strengthen faith in man. And it is faith in Jesus Christ, in the God-Man, which unites faith in God and that in man, just as love for Jesus Christ unites love of God and love of neighbour.

In Jesus Christ we have the perfect union of divine revelation and the most pure humanism. Which means to say that not only all Avatars but also all Buddhas of the past and of the future are summarised in Jesus Christ—being the Logos made flesh, and his Humanity having realised the most complete awakening of all that which is of divine essence in human nature. For Jesus Christ is the revelation that God is love, and he bears witness that the essence of human nature is love. And can one conceive of, can one imagine, anything more divine than love and anything more human than love? For this reason all Avatars (including all prophets and all Imams) and all Buddhas (including all sages, all initiates and all Boddhisattvas) were, are, and will be only degrees and aspects of the divine revelation and the human awakening realised in Jesus Christ.

This truth, evident for everyone whose head and heart are united in thought (i.e. for one who uses *moral logic*), is nevertheless very difficult for those making use of *formal logic*—in the domain of mankind's history or in the domain of philosophy—to understand and accept.

Now, the following words of Krishna in the *Bhagavad-Gita* relate to the doctrine of Avatars:

> Many births of yours and mine, O Arjuna, have taken place....
> Though I am unborn (having no birth), though I am imperishable, though I am master of the elements, yet out of my *maya*
> (power of illusion) I take birth, resting on (material) Nature.
> Whensoever, O Bharata, virtue (*adharmasya*, the law of righteousness) languishes and sin predominates, I create myself (I take birth). I take birth age after age, for the liberation of the good and the destruction of the wicked, and for the establishment of piety (true religion). (*Bhagavad-Gita* iv, 5-8; trsl. M. N.
> Dutt, *Bhishma Parva* xxviii, 5-8 in *The Mahabharata* vi, Calcutta, 1897, p. 37)

In commenting on this, Sri Aurobindo says:

> The Avatar comes as the manifestation of the divine nature in the human nature, the apocalypse of its Christhood, Krishnahood, Buddhahood, in order that the human nature may, by moulding its principle, thought, feeling, action, being on the lines of that Christhood, Krishnahood, Buddhahood, transfigure itself into the divine. The law, the Dharma which the Avatar establishes is given for that purpose chiefly; the Christ, Krishna, Buddha stands in its centre as the gate, he makes through himself the way men shall follow. That is why each Incarnation (Avatar) holds before men his own example and declares of himself that he is the way and the gate; he declares too the oneness of his humanity with the divine being, declares that the Son of Man and the Father above from whom he has descended are one, that Krishna in the human body...and the supreme Lord and Friend of all creatures are but two revelations of the same divine Purushottama, revealed there in his own being, revealed here in the type of humanity. (Sri Aurobindo Ghose, *Essays on the Gita*, Madras, 1922, pp. 190-191)

Nothing could be clearer and more convincing! Avatars are therefore periodic incarnations of the Divine; they incarnate periodically with a view to re-establishing the law, just like prophets, who arise to the same end, and they are, each time, doors and ways—Sons of God and Sons of Man who are one with their Father in heaven. And Sri Aurobindo concludes:

> Nor does it matter essentially in what form and name or put-
> ting forward what aspect of the Divine he (the Avatar) comes;
> for in all ways, varying with their nature, men are following the
> path set to them by the Divine which will in the end lead them
> to him and the aspect of him which suits their nature is that
> which they can best follow when he comes to lead them; in
> whatever way men accept, love and take joy in God, in that way
> God accepts, loves and takes joy in man. (Sri Aurobindo Ghose,
> *Essays on the Gita*, Madras, 1922, p. 226)

All this appears as the breath of pure reason—the most resolute ecumenism and universal tolerance. But is not this tolerance, this ecumenism and this reasonability of the doctrine of Avatars, such as it is professed by Sri Aurobindo, in principle identical with the reasonability, ecumenism and tolerance manifested by the leaders of the Roman empire who conceived of the idea of a temple for all the gods, i.e. the Pantheon?. . .the Pantheon with a place of honour given to Jesus Christ alongside Jupiter, Osiris, Mithras and Dionysius? For all these gods have this in common, that they are immortal and superior to man. And is not Christ immortal, since he resurrected from the dead?. . .and is he not superior to man, as his miracles prove? Therefore he belongs to the category of gods and has the right to be admitted to their ranks at the Pantheon.

Theoretically there are ten Avatars of Vishnu in Hinduism (e.g. Matsyavatara, Varahavatara, Narasimhavatara, Vamanavatara), but Rama and Krishna are the most popular and most celebrated amongst them. With respect to the Avatar to come, Kalkin or Kalki, he is spoken of in the *Kalki-Purana* as the Avatar who will mark the end of the age of iron; he will be clothed in the form of a giant, with the head of a horse—a symbol which appeals to our faculty of meditative deepening. Sri Aurobindo mentions—and this on many occasions—only Christ, Krishna and Buddha.

Nevertheless Buddha (whom, it is true, Hinduism has included in its pantheon, just as Islam sees in Jesus Christ one of the prophets, the last of whom was Mohammed) does not in any way correspond to the fundamental characteristic of Avatars given by Sri Aurobindo, namely:

> . . .each Incarnation (Avatar) holds before men his own exam
> ple and declares of himself that he is the way and the gate; he
> declares too the oneness of his humanity with the divine being

...that the Son of Man and the Father above from whom he
has descended are one... (Sri Aurobindo Ghose, *Essays on the
Gita*, Madras, 1922, p. 191)

It is an incontestable fact that Sakyamuni, the historical Buddha, never declared
the identity of his human being with divine being (not to mention that he never
declared himself to be one with the Father in heaven). The *Dishanikaya*, a long
collection of Buddha's discourses in Pali, contradicts it on each page and uses a
multitude of arguments and facts to the sole end of persuading the reader (or
listener to the Buddha's discourses) that Buddha was the *awakened man*, i.e. he
became completely conscious of the common and ordinary human experience on
earth—that of birth, sickness, old age and death—and drew from it practical and
moral conclusions which are summarised in his eightfold path. The point shown
by the *Dishanikaya* is that it is not the extraordinary experience of a mystic or
gnostic revelation which made the prince of Kapilavastu a Buddha, but rather
that he awoke to a new understanding of ordinary human experience—of the
human condition as such. It was a man—and not a messenger from heaven—
who awoke from the sleep of passive acceptance, habit, the stupefying influence
of transitory desires, and the hypnotic force of the totality of human conventions.

The Buddha's teaching is that of a human spirit who took account, in a state
of complete lucidity, of the human condition in general and of the practical and
moral consequences to be drawn from it. It is an analysis of the reality of human
life, and an establishment of the unique consequences which result necessarily
from this analysis, by a human spirit five centuries before Jesus Christ, who was
placed beyond the Jewish and Iranian prophetic tradition. The Buddha's teaching
is therefore humanism pure and simple, which has nothing to do with the revelation from above by prophets and Avatars.

It is necessary, therefore, to eliminate Buddha from the three Avatars mentioned
by Sri Aurobindo—"Christ, Krishna and Buddha".

Concerning Jesus Christ, he did not come solely "for the liberation of the good
and the destruction of the wicked, and for the establishment of the throne of
justice" (*Bhagavad-Gita* iv, 8), but above all to vanquish evil and death, for the
establishment of the throne of love. Jesus Christ was not only a divine *birth* but
also—and above all—the divine *death*, i.e. resurrection—which is not the mission of any Avatar, of the past or yet to come. The work of Jesus Christ differs from
that of Avatars in that it signifies the *expiatory sacrifice* for completely fallen
mankind. This means to say that mankind, who before Jesus Christ had only the
choice between renunciation and affirmation of the world of birth and death, is
put in the position, since the mystery of Calvary, of transforming it—the Christian
ideal being "a new heaven and a new earth" (Revelation xxi, 1). The mission of
an Avatar, however, is "the liberation of the good" in this fallen world, without
even attempting to transform it. It is a matter in the work of Jesus Christ of universal
salvation—the work of divine magic and divine alchemy, that of the transforma-

tion of the fallen world—and not only of the liberation of the good. The work of Jesus Christ is the divine magical operation of love aiming at universal salvation through the transformation of mankind and of Nature.

As well as Buddha, therefore, it is necessary to eliminate Jesus Christ, also, from the abridged list of Avatars given by Sri Aurobindo. Thus, only Krishna remains who is, in addition to Rama, the Avatar *par excellence* of Hinduism.

Although we refute Sri Aurobindo's classification of Buddha and Jesus Christ in the category of Avatars, we should do justice to this Indian sage: his idea of Jesus Christ is infinitely more elevated and nearer to the truth than that of self-styled Christian theologians of the so-called "liberal" Protestant school who regard Jesus Christ as a simple carpenter from Nazareth, who taught and lived the moral ideal of love of God and neighbour. Even every muezzin of Cairo or Baghdad has a notion of Jesus Christ that is more just than that of these theologians, since the former regard him as a prophet inspired by God. With respect to Sri Aurobindo, he regards Jesus Christ as a divine incarnation and makes it understood—by always placing Jesus Christ at the head of the other Avatars ("Christ, Krishna, Buddha")—that he, personally, considers him as a light of the first magnitude in the heaven of divine Avatars!

But let us now return to the Arcanum of the alchemical work of the fusion of spirituality and intellectuality, as seen on the historical plane.

After Jesus Christ—the God-Man, who was the complete unity not only of spirituality and intellectuality, but also of divine will and human will, and even of divine essence and human essence—the work of the fusion of spirituality and intellectuality can be nothing other than the germination of the Christic seed in human nature and consciousness. In other words, it is a matter of the progress of the *Christianisation* of mankind, not only in the sense of a growing number of baptised people, but above all in the sense of a qualitative transformation of human nature and consciousness. This latter will work in conformity with the law: general aspiration and longing; culminating point of success in an individuality; general diffusion spread out over a number of generations, i.e. the climate of general expectation will lead to the particular realisation which will subsequently become general. This is why Buddhists await the coming of the Maitreya Buddha and Hindus that of the Kalki Avatar. They await him having in view a step forward in mankind's spiritual evolution which will be crossed as a consequence of the manifestation of the new Buddha and the new Avatar. And this step forward will be nothing other than the fusion of spirituality and intellectuality.

This expectation is, moreover, not restricted to the Orient: theosophists made a considerable contribution to it by launching a movement of international scope aiming at preparing minds for the coming—supposedly at hand—of the new teacher. To this end they founded the Order of the Star of the East which numbered about 250,000 members, and which organised congresses, conferences and rallies all over the place, as well as publishing hundreds of books and brochures. Whilst spreading the idea of the imminent coming of a new teacher for mankind, the

Order of the Star of the East was, alas, too fixed on a particular personality—chosen not by heaven, but rather by the leaders of the Theosophical Society—who was extolled in advance so as to build up his prestige, which in the last analysis displeased this person, who disbanded the Order.

It was more discreetly, and without putting a particular person in the limelight as candidate, that Dr. Rudolf Steiner, founder of the Anthroposophical Society, predicted the manifestation—again in the first half of the twentieth century—not of the new Maitreya Buddha or Kalki Avatar, but rather of the Bodhisattva, i.e. the individuality in the process of becoming the next Buddha, whose field of activity he hoped the Anthroposophical Society would serve. A new disappointment! This time the disappointment was due not to an error with regard to the awaited individuality, nor even with regard to the time of the beginning of his activity, but rather to an overestimation of the Anthroposophical Society on the part of its founder—thus nothing became of it.

Be that as it may, the idea and the expectation of the coming of the new Buddha and new Avatar lives at present both in the western world and in the orient. There is much confusion concerning this idea, above all among theosophists, but there are also those who see clearly here. Rudolf Steiner, for example, saw very clearly: of all that has been written and said in public, the most correct is what was said by Rudolf Steiner. He was on the right track, at least.

Now, in following the same track—that leading to the culminating point of the fusion of spirituality and intellectuality—we arrive at the following synopsis:

Since it is a question of the work of the fusion of revelation and knowledge, of spirituality and intellectuality, it is a matter throughout of the fusion of the Avatar principle with the Buddha principle. In other words, the Kalki Avatar awaited by the Hindus and the Maitreya Buddha awaited by the Buddhists will manifest in a *single personality*. On the historical plane the Maitreya Buddha and the Kalki Avatar will be one.

This means to say that the awaited Avatar "with the body of a giant and the head of a horse" (Kalki) and the expected Buddha who will be the "bringer of good" (Maitreya) will be one and the same personality. And this personality will signify the complete union of the most elevated humanism (the principle of the Buddhas) and the highest revelation (the principle of the Avatars) of a kind that both the spiritual world and the human world will speak and act simultaneously and hand-in-hand through him. In other words, the Buddha-Avatar to come will *not only speak of the good, but he will speak the good*; he will not merely teach the way of salvation, but he will advance the course of this way; he will not be solely a witness of the divine and spiritual world, but he will make human beings into authentic witnesses of this world; he will not simply explain the profound meaning of revelation, but he will bring human beings themselves to attain to the illuminating experience of revelation, of a kind that it will not be he who will win authority, but rather He who is "the true light that enlightens every man coming into the world" (John i, 9)—Jesus Christ, the Word made flesh, who is the way, the truth and the life. The mission of the Buddha-Avatar to come will therefore not be the foundation of a new religion, but rather that of bringing human beings to first hand experience of the source itself of all revelation ever received from above by mankind, as also of all essential truth ever conceived of by mankind. It will not be novelty to which he will aspire, but rather the conscious certainty of eternal truth.

Maitreya-Kalki, the Buddha-Avatar, will represent the fusion of *prayer* and *meditation*, these two forms of spiritual activity being the motivating forces of spiritual religion and spiritual humanism. The apparent incompatibility of the state of consciousness represented by statues of the master of meditation, Gautama Buddha, plunged in meditation in the asana posture, and that of St. Francis of Assisi receiving the stigmata whilst kneeling in prayer—this apparent incompatibility, I say—will be surmounted by the Buddha-Avatar to come. The fire of prayer will unite with the limpid water of the peace of meditation; the alchemical marriage of the sun and moon, of fire and water, will take place in him.

The union of the principles of prayer and meditation which the future Buddha-Avatar will represent will be, in fact, the crowning of a long series of efforts aiming at this end through the course of the centuries—the result of a long preparation through the course of mankind's spiritual history. For not only was prayer introduced into the strictly meditative Indo-Tibetan Mahayana school of Buddhism —under the form of Lamaism—and into Hinduism under the form of Bhakti-yoga, but also meditation was introduced to the West in the guise of complementing and helping the life of prayer in the spiritual practice of the great religious orders. St. Bonaventura, for example, introduced it into the Franciscan Order, St. Teresa and St. John of the Cross introduced it into the Carmelite Order, and St. Ignatius of Loyola, the founder of the Jesuit Order, was a master not only of prayer but also of meditation. One could say that this latter to a large extent prefigured the fusion of spirituality and intellectuality, of prayer and meditation, which is the mission of the future Buddha-Avatar. The *calm warmth* of complete certainty, due to the cooperation of human effort and revelation from above, which St. Ignatius possessed and which his disciples (of his spiritual exercises) attained— where meditation and prayer are united—make an impressive prefiguring of the Buddha-Avatar to come.

I am well aware that St. Ignatius does not enjoy unreserved admiration either among Protestants or among Catholics themselves, and that neither among the former nor among the latter are there many who have much sympathy for him. At best he has gained the cold respect of the more perceptive intellectuals of the two confessions. But with regard to popularity or unpopularity there is good reason to say that it will not be popularity and general acclaim which will characterise the work of the Buddha-Avatar to come, but rather the fusion of spirituality and intellectuality, no matter whether this pleases or not. Without doubt there will be more opposition than appreciation, for neither the partisans of pure faith nor those of pure knowledge will hesitate to object that it is a matter of dangerously effacing the line of demarcation between faith and science. Look at the controversy of our time surrounding the work of Pierre Teilhard de Chardin!

With respect to St. Ignatius of Loyola, it is not only his heroic effort to unite spirituality and intellectuality which interests us — we who are engaged in meditating on the Tarot Arcanum "The Fool" — but also, and above all, the fact that St. Ignatius began as a "fool in Spirit" and that he succeeded in attaining to the wisdom of perfect equilibrium between the world of mystical revelations and the world of human tasks and actions. He learnt and openly lived the lesson of the twenty-first Arcanum of the Tarot.

Indeed, was it not as a "fool in Spirit" (acting in the spirit of the Fool of our Arcanum) when he "left on a bank (close to the place of embarkation at Barcelona) five or six pieces of silver obtained by begging in Barcelona, putting all his confidence, all his hope and all his assurance in God alone" — before embarking on board a ship destined for Italy? (cf. *Monumenta historica Societatis Jesu, Scripta de Sancto Ignatio*, vol. ii, Madrid, 1904). And compare the Ignatius of the time of his pilgrimage to the Holy Land with the Ignatius in Rome as the head of the Order, directing the very different activities at first of sixty, then of four hundred, and lastly of three thousand spiritual sons! And the step made by him — although contrary in direction to that made by Cyprian the mage — is again the putting into practice of the Tarot Arcanum "The Fool". For this Arcanum is that of the "hygienic experience", so to say, of man placed as an intermediary between two worlds — the divine world and the human world. It is the Arcanum of crossing the threshold of these two worlds in two directions — from below above (which was the case with Cyprian) and to return (which was, in fact, the case with St. Ignatius). It is therefore the Arcanum of the transformation of mental turmoil — the schizophrenia of two consciousnesses not in harmony with one another — into wisdom.

We have spoken here of the Buddha-Avatar to come, because he will be the guide in the transformation of potential schizophrenic madness into the wisdom of the harmony of the two worlds and of their experience. He will be the example and living model of realisation of the Arcanum which occupies us. For this reason he is represented as a Buddha in canonical Buddhist art not in a meditation posture with crossed legs, but rather seated as a European — this latter posture symbolising the synthesis of the principle of prayer and that of meditation. And for this reason, also, he is imagined in Indian "mythology" (as an Avatar) as a giant with the head of a horse, i.e. as a being with the human will of a giant and, at the same time, intellectuality placed completely in the service of revelation from above — the horse being the obedient servant of its rider. Thus, he represents in prodigious measure three activities of the human will: seeking, knocking and asking — conforming to the saying of the Master of all masters, "Ask, and it will be given you; seek, and you will find; knock, and it will be opened to you" (Matthew vii, 7). At the same time, he will not put forward personal opinions or reasonable hypotheses; for his intellectuality — his "horse's head" — will be moved solely by revelation from above. Like the horse, it will be directed by the rider. Nothing arbitrary will issue forth.

This is the Arcanum at work on the historical plane. Concerning its application in the domain of the individual's inner life, it is analogous to the work of spiritual alchemy which operates on the historical plane. This means to say that the individual soul begins initially with the experience of the separation and opposition of the spiritual and intellectual elements within it, then advances to—or resigns itself to—parallelism, i.e. a kind of "peaceful coexistence" of these two elements within it. Subsequently it arrives at cooperation between spirituality and intellectuality which, proving to be fruitful, eventually becomes the complete fusion of these two elements in a third element—the "philosopher's stone" of the spiritual alchemy of Hermeticism. The beginning of this final stage is announced by the fact that logic becomes transformed from formal logic (i.e. general and abstract logic)—passing through the intermediary stage of "organic logic"—into *moral logic* (i.e. material and essential logic).

In order to illustrate the transformation of formal logic into organic logic and this latter into moral logic, let us take the example of the axiom of formal logic: "the part is less than the whole." It is an axiom because the notion itself of "part" signifies nothing other than a quantity less than that of the whole. This is evident, when it is a matter of *quantities*. But this axiom is no longer absolutely valid with respect to the *functions* of a living organism. Here the part—and even a small part—can be as essential as the whole organism. The heart, for example, is only a small part of the body, but remove it from the body and the whole organism will cease to exist as a living organism. For the domain of organic functions it is therefore necessary to modify our axiom in the sense that "*the part can be equal to the whole*". But if we proceed from the organic world to the world of *values*, the moral world, we are obliged to modify the axiom still further. Here it should be said that "*the part can be greater than the whole*", because Caiaphas' reasoning that "it is expedient for you that one man should die for the people, that the whole nation should not perish" (John xi, 50) is right only with regard to the domain of quantities, but is false with regard to the domain of moral values. For this "one man" that he proposed to sacrifice in order to save the people was the very reason for the existence of this people: the Messiah. Moreover, history has shown that the measure taken on Caiaphas' counsel aiming at preventing military intervention by the Romans was in vain: the Romans came all the same in A.D. 70, destroying Jerusalem and the temple of Jerusalem after having massacred its inhabitants, which was exactly what Caiaphas wanted to avoid . . .

Moral logic, in contrast to formal logic and organic logic, operates with values instead of notions of grammar, mathematics, or biological functions. Thus, if formal logic can go only so far towards the idea of God as to postulate the necessity of admitting a beginning in the chain of cause and effect—postulating a First Cause (*primus motor*)—and if organic logic, that of functions, cannot come further than postulating in the order existing in the world the existence of God as the ordering principle — the "law of laws" of the world — moral logic comes to the postulate that God is the "value of values", that he is love.

And, since hate and indifference are not creative, it is love which is the source, cause and motivation of the creation of the world. One does not create what one detests and one does not proceed to the creative act being moved by indifference, i.e. by lack of interest. God is, therefore, creative love — the creative Father of the visible and invisible world..."Father", i.e. he who gives being to created beings. And since being is his gift to beings, and not a temporary loan, he does not take back his gift — once given; beings created by the Father are therefore *immortal*. Immortality is thus a necessary conclusion of moral logic concerning the idea that God is love...and so on, until all the essential articles of faith are established from the moral postulates necessary to moral logic. What are initially postulates of moral logic are confirmed, amplified and deepened through spriritual experience, which will not hesitate to come to the aid of thought, when head and heart are equally engaged. Because moral logic is the language of the spiritual world, and to make use of moral logic is to begin a *dialogue* with the spiritual world. For the latter does not remain mute and indifferent when addressed in its own language.

Moral logic, as we have stated, is the logic of the head and heart united. It is therefore that which unites *meditation* and *prayer*.

Prayer — which asks, thanks, worships and blesses — is the radiation, the breath and the warmth of the awakened heart: expressed in formulae of the articulated word, in the wordless inner sighing of the soul and, lastly, in the silence, both outward and inward, of the breathing of the soul immersed in the element of divine respiration and breathing in unison with it. Prayer has, therefore, different aspects: a "magical" aspect, i.e. prayer in formulae; a "gnostic" aspect, when it becomes inexpressible inner sighing; and, lastly, a "mystical" aspect, when it becomes the silence of union with the Divine. Thus, it is never in vain and without effect. Even a prayer-formula pronounced rapidly in a detached and impersonal manner has a magical effect, because the sum-total of ardour put into this formula in the past — by believers, saints and Angels — is evoked soley through the fact of pronouncing the prayer-formula. Every prayer-formula consecrated by use has a magical virtue, since it is *collective*. The voices of all those who have ever prayed it are evoked by it and join the voice of he who pronounces it with serious intention. This applies above all to all the formulae of liturgical prayer. Each phrase of the Roman Catholic Mass or Greek Orthodox Liturgy, for example, is a formula of divine sacred magic. There is nothing astonishing about this, since the Mass and the Liturgy consist only of the prayers of prophets, saints and Jesus Christ himself. But what is truly astonishing is that there are — and always have been — esotericists (such as Fabre d'Olivet, for example) who improvise cults, prayer-formulae, new "mantrams", etc., as if something is gained through novelty! Perhaps they believe that the formulae taken from Holy Scripture or given by the saints are used up through usage and have lost their virtue? This would be a radical misunderstanding. Because usage does not at all deplete a prayer-formula, but rather, on the contrary, it adds to its virtue. For this reason it is also deplorable that certain Protestant churches have the custom of the minister or preacher improvising prayers in their divine service—probably believing that it is the personal which is more effective and not the common and collective tradition.

One should know, dear Unknown Friend, that one never prays alone, i.e. that there are always others—above, or in the past on earth—who pray with you in the same sense, in the same spirit and even in the same words. In praying, you always represent a visible or invisible community together with you. If you pray for healing, you represent all the sick and all healers, and the community of sick people and healers then prays with you. For this reason the Lord's prayer is not addressed to "my Father in heaven", but rather to "*our* Father in heaven", and asks the Father to "give *us* this day *our* daily bread", that he "forgive *us our* trespasses", that he "leads *us* not into temptation" and that he "delivers *us* from evil". Thus, whatever the particular intention of the one who prays the Lord's prayer may be, it is in the name of the whole of mankind that he prays.

With respect to the prayer which is an inner, inexpressible sighing, that we have named "gnostic"—in contrast to the "magical" prayer in formulae—it is a transformation of the psycho-physical breathing into prayer. Thus it can be made permanent—day and night, awake and asleep, without interruption, as long as respiration lasts. This type of prayer (which is practised above all in the Christian Orient) has a virtue that is more than magical: it transforms man into a mirror of the spiritual and divine world. For this reason we have named it "gnostic"—gnostic experience being the reflection of mystical experience.

Concerning mystical prayer properly said, i.e. the state of the human soul united with the Divine, where it no longer has even its own breathing, but breathes in and through the breath of divine respiration alone, it is the profound silence of all soul faculties—intelligence, imagination, memory and will—which, for example, St. John of the Cross describes and explains in his works. It is the consummation of love between the soul and God.

Meditation, i.e. the gradual deepening of thought, also has its stages, which comprise pure and simple concentration on a subject, understanding the subject within the totality of relationships that it has with reality and, lastly, intuitive penetration into the very essence of the subject. Just as prayer leads to mystical union of the soul with the Divine, so does meditation lead to grasping a direct knowledge of eternal and immutable principles. René Guénon named this experience of the union of the particular intellect with the universal Intellect (the *nous* of Plotinus and the Stoics)—as well as the doctrines which result from it—"metaphysical". He summarised his leading ideas on this "metaphysics" in a conference on "oriental metaphysics" which he gave at the Sorbonne in 1925—which thesis one finds reproduced in Paul Sédir's book *Histoire et doctrine des rose-croix*:

> Metaphysics is knowledge *par excellence*. It is not natural knowledge, either with respect to its object or with respect to the faculties by which it is obtained. More particularly, it has nothing

to do with the scientific and rational domain. It is not a matter of operating with abstractions but of taking knowledge directly from eternal and immutable principles.

Metaphysics is not human knowledge. Thus, it is not in so far as he is man that man can attain it; it is the grasping in effective consciousness of supra-individual states. The very principle of metaphysical realisation is identification through knowledge — according to Aristotle's axiom: a being is all that he knows.

The most important means is concentration. Realisation consists initially in the unlimited development of all possibilities contained virtually in the individual, then in finally going beyond the world of forms to a degree of universality which is that of pure being.

The final aim of metaphysical realisation is the absolutely unconditioned state, free from all limitation. The liberated being is then truly in possession of the fullness of his possibilities. This is union with the supreme Principle.

True metaphysics cannot be determined in time; it is eternal. It is an order of knowledge reserved for an élite. . .[an élite, let us add with Sédir, which is composed of beings who are only intelligence]. . . and then, all existing manifestations of the Absolute are not there for the sake of being ignored; to abandon them because they encumber us, as the yogi (*sic*) or the arhat does, is not noble or Christian. . .(Paul Sédir, *Histoire et doctrine des rose-croix*, Paris, 1964, pp. 13-14)

Metaphysics as "direct knowledge of eternal and immutable principles" and as the realisation of "finally going beyond the world of forms to a degree of universality which is that of pure being" is only one of the applications of meditation, and is by no means the only one. There are still others.

Since Orientals aspire to deliverance by taking refuge in the abstract point of origin of all spatial forms, they therefore employ meditation to this end. However, Jewish esotericists — the Cabbalists — want to arrive at the worship and love of God that is most worthy of him. This is why their meditative efforts aim at a deepening of the divine mysteries which are revealed in scripture and in the creation. The *Zohar* is an inexhaustible source of teaching concerning this school of meditation and its fruits.

Christian meditation, also, pursues the aim of deepening the two divine revelations: holy scripture and the creation, but it does so above all with a view to awakening a more complete consciousness and appreciation of Jesus Christ's work of redemption. For this reason it culminates in the contemplation of the seven stages of the Passion: the washing of the feet, the scourging, the crowning with the crown of thorns, the way of the cross, the crucifixion, the laying in the tomb, and the resurrection.

The meditation of Christian Hermeticism—whose aim is to understand and advance the work of the alchemical transformation of the spirit, the soul, and matter, from the state of primordial purity before the Fall, to the state after the Fall, and from the latter to that of the Reintegration (the fulfillment of salvation)—proceeds, for example, from the seven "days" of the creation according to Genesis to the seven stages of the Fall, then to the seven miracles of St. John's Gospel, and then to the seven sayings of Jesus concerning himself (I am the resurrection and the life; I am the light of the world; I am the good shepherd; I am the bread of life; I am the door; I am the way, the truth and the life; I am the true vine), in order to conclude with the seven "words" of Jesus Christ crucified and the seven stages of the Passion indicated above.

Meditation can thus serve as a means to attain diverse ends, but whatever its aim it is always the means to realisation of a more and more intense awakening of the whole consciousness (and not only of intelligence) with respect to particular facts, ideas, ideals and, lastly, the reality of the human terrestrial and spiritual condition in general. It is also the means of awakening consciousness with respect to revelations from above. To meditate is to deepen; it is to go to the heart of things.

For this reason the practice of meditation entails the transformation of formal logic into organic logic and this latter into moral logic. The latter, in its turn, is developed by going beyond comprehension, by contemplation of things which surpass understanding: mysteries which—not being unknowable—allow of an infinite knowledge that one can understand and know ever more deeply, without end. Having attained this contemplation of things surpassing actual understanding, meditation becomes *prayer*—just as prayer which attains the state of contemplation without words becomes *meditation*.

And it is this "alchemical marriage" of prayer and meditation—of the sun and moon of the soul's inner heaven—which takes place in the soul of the human being who is in the process of realising the Arcanum "The Fool"...the Arcanum of the union of revelation from above and human wisdom, whilst avoiding madness...the Arcanum of the formation of the "philosopher's stone", where the twofold certainty of revelation from above and human knowledge is concentrated.

The foregoing are some glimpses that arise in the soul of one who meditates on the Card of the Arcanum "The Fool", representing a man walking, in the clothes of a buffoon, holding a bag and supporting himself with a staff, which he does not use to chase away the dog attacking him. Other—and more profound—glimpses are kept in reserve for those who will deepen their meditation on this Arcanum further than is indicated here. I greet them and hope that they may be able to make new light issue forth from their meditation on the Arcanum whose esoteric name is LOVE!

Meditation on the
Twenty-Second Major Arcanum of the Tarot

THE WORLD
—————
LE MONDE

When he drew a circle
on the face of the deep. . .
then I was at work beside him,
and I was daily his delight,
rejoicing before him always,
rejoicing in his inhabited world
and delighting in the sons of men.
                    (Proverbs viii, 27, 30-31)

Lust — tiefer noch als Herzeleid!
Weh spricht: Vergeh!
Doch alle Lust will Ewigkeit —
will tiefe, tiefe Ewigkeit!

(Joy — deeper yet than woe is she!
Saith woe: Hence, go!
Yet Joy would have Eternity —
Profound, profound Eternity!)
(Friedrich Nietzsche, *Thus Spake Zarathustra*)*

One truly lives only when one dances.
                    (Isadora Duncan)

LETTER XXII

THE WORLD

Dear Unknown Friend,

The above quotations are a musical prelude to the twenty-second Major Arcanum of the Tarot "The World". The Card represents a naked woman in a garland dancing and holding a wand in the left hand and a philtre in the right. She is wearing a scarf thrown lightly across her shoulder. In the four corners of the Card one sees the Angel and the Eagle above, and the Bull and the Lion below. The four sacred animals thus enclose the garland in which the naked dancer, with her floating scarf, is dancing.

*Trsl. A. Tille, revised M.M. Bozman, Everyman Library, 1958, p. 285.

Thus, the first ideas which come to mind in looking at the Card are those of dance, of flowering, and of the four elements—which in the first place turn the mind towards such problems as the essence of movement, of growth and of the spontaneous wisdom that we call "instinct". The first impression of the Card is therefore as if the last Major Arcanum of the Tarot would suggest a conception of the world as rhythmic movement or dance of the female psyche, sustained by means of the orchestral accompaniment of the four primordial instincts, which gives the appearance of a rainbow of colours and forms—or, in other words, that the world is a work of art. This idea is portrayed in a most impressive way by Edward Carpenter in his work *The World as a Work of Art*. This is tantamount to the thesis that the world is fundamentally neither a mechanism, nor an organism, nor even a social community—neither a school on a grand scale nor a pedagogical institution for living beings—but rather a work of divine art: at one and the same time a choreographic, musical, poetic, dramatic work of painting, sculpture and architecture.

Is this truly the last Arcanum of the twenty-two Major Arcana of the Tarot? Does the series of twenty-two spiritual exercises—each destined to teach how to find and employ a key to the mystery of the world—truly end with a meditation and an understanding of the world as a work of art?

The Card suggests it, but in order to arrive at certainty there is no other way than that of profound meditation. This is the only way that certainty can be attained. Let us therefore follow the general suggestion that the context of the Card conveys.

The idea of the world as a work of art is implicit in all cosmogonies which explain the origin of the world through a *creative act*, or through a series of creative acts, as is the case in Moses' Genesis. Creation—whatever its mode may be—entails the demiurgic rearranging of pre-existing matter from a chaotic state into a cosmic state, where the transformation from primordial chaos into cosmos is intelligible only by analogy with the magical art or the magic of art. "In the beginning God (Elohim) created (= magical act) the heavens and the earth (= work of art)" (Genesis i, 1)—so begins the account of the creation of the world in Moses' Genesis. Can one conceive of another idea here than that of the act transforming the ideal into the real, the intelligible (i.e. of the realm of intelligence) into the sense perceptible? And is this transformation into objective reality of that which exists only in divine thought and will analogous to the act of artistic creation as well as to the magical act? Is the divine magic implicit in Moses' account of the creation of the world one and the same as the divine art that is implicit therein?

Platonic philosophy, also, conceives of the visible world as the realisation of the invisible world of archetypes or ideas. Thus, the Neoplatonist Plotinus says that the idea "Man" is pre-existing and realises itself in each particular man:

> . . .when Man enters into human form there exists a particular
> man who, however, is still Man. From the one thing Man—man

in the Idea—material man has come to constitute many individual men: the one identical thing is present in multiplicity, in multi-impression, so to speak, from the one seal. (Plotinus,
Ennead VI, v, 6; trsl. S. MacKenna, *The Enneads*, London, 1969,
p. 536)

Here the metaphysics of magic and, at the same time, that of art are portrayed
with admirable clarity! By means of the biological knowledge available in the first
quarter of the twentieth century, Edgar Dacqué, in *Leben als Symbol* ("Life as
Symbol") reveals the nature of the "seal" spoken of by Plotinus ("the one identical thing is present in multiplicity, in multi-impression, from the one seal").
The following are two relevant quotations from *Leben als Symbol*:

> Schopenhauer once said that things appear to the child so
> bathed in splendour and of such a paradisical nature because
> they experience naively in each particular thing the idea of type
> (species). This splendour of inner reality is entirely lost for man
> who has attained to the maturity of rational thought, when he
> comes out of the "childlike state" of animated and living percep-
> tion and is given over to laws of pure abstraction. Thus, each
> time we are in the state of experiencing the idea in form, we
> are—like the child—within Nature. Goethe was such a child.
> (p. 114) If, therefore, as I have tried to show all along, man is
> the archetype of the evolutionary history of species and the centre
> of living Nature . . . if the animal kingdom, as the ancients al-
> ready knew, is man disintegrated—which we can now take in
> a realistic sense—then we have a solid basis for all totemism and
> animal cults that is well founded from the standpoint of natural
> science. (p. 191) (Edgar Dacqué, *Leben als Symbol*, Munich-
> Berlin, 1928, pp. 114, 191)

In other words, Edgar Dacqué—just like Pierre Teilhard de Chardin—sees the
world with its animal, plant and mineral kingdoms as variations of a single theme,
i.e. *man*, who is the archetype of Nature in evolution. Man is therefore the "seal"
spoken of by Plotinus, and the beings of Nature are partial imprints of him. Is
not the world in evolution, following Dacqué, a work of art in creation where the
idea—man—becomes reality?

With respect to Goethe, whom Dacqué cites as an example of one who perceived
the archetypal world in particular phenomena, he conceived of the creative, artistic act as an integral part of the creative activity which works in Nature, where
this activity becomes continued in man. For him, a flower which pushes forth from
the soil, and a poem which "pushes forth" from the "soil" of the soul of the poet,
are only two particular manifestations of the same creative magical-artistic force.
He called this force "metamorphosis". This is why Goethe, throughout his whole

life, occupied himself both with observing metamorphosis at work and with scientific and artistic works on metamorphosis. His writings on colour, *Zur Farbenlehre* ("Theory of Colours"), are nothing other than a description and analysis of the metamorphosis of light; his work *Metamorphose der Pflanzen* ("The Metamorphosis of Plants") is what its title says; his fragment *Metamorphose der Tiere* ("The Metamorphosis of Animals") is again what its title says, and his master work *Faust* is nothing other than the metamorphosis of the human soul since the epoch of the Renaissance. . .

To summarise, it must be admitted that everyone who believes that the invisible becomes visible in the creation and evolution of the world also believes that the creative act, where the idea is transformed into the objective reality of art (and magic), is analogous to what takes place in the formation and transformation of the world. He cannot think otherwise if he is not a materialist, i.e. if he does not bring his thinking to a halt already in the vestibule of the edifice of the intelligible. For the materialist proceeds like the reader of a manuscript who, instead of reading and understanding the thought of the author, occupies himself with the letters and syllables. He believes that the letters wrote themselves and combined themselves into syllables, being moved by mutual attraction, which, in its turn, is the effect of the chemical or molecular qualities of the ink as "matter" common to all the letters, and of which the letters and syllables are epiphenomena. It is not the materialistic *method*, but rather materialistic *faith* which I have in mind here.

Concerning the relationship between art and magic, Joséphin Péladan—himself an artist and magician—said:

> With respect to geniuses, they are intuitive people who bring to expression supernatural laws with images; they attract an influx from beyond and they are in direct relationship with the occult. Neither Dante, nor Shakespeare, nor Goethe carried out evocations, and all three understood the occult; they were wisely content to create eternal images; and in this they were incomparable mages. To create in the abstract, to create in the souls of men, vivifying reflections of the mystery—this is the great work. (Joséphin Péladan, *Introduction aux sciences occultes*, Paris, 1911; cf. E. Bertholet, *La pensée et les secrets du Sar Joséphin Péladan*, vol. ii, Paris, 1952, p. 377)

Thus, artistic creation differs from the operation of ceremonial magic in that the latter is more inward than the former. With respect to sacred magic, the relationship between sacred art and sacred magic amounts to that between the beautiful and the good, i.e. to the relationship between colours and warmth of the same light. The beautiful is the good which makes itself loved; the good is the beautiful which heals and vivifies.

But the good from which the beautiful is lost from sight hardens into principles and laws—it becomes pure duty; the beautiful which is detached from the good and loses it from sight becomes softened to pure enjoyment—stripped of obligation and responsiblity. The hardening of the good into a moral code and the softening of the beautiful to pure pleasure is the result of the separation of the good and the beautiful—be it morally, in religion, or in art. It is thus that a legalistic moralism and a pure aestheticism of little depth has come into existence. This has, at the same time, also engendered corresponding human types: on the one hand the "stiff-as-a-peg" human type, who was at his height during the reign of Puritanism in England—this form of life and religion without joy and without art—as also in the shape of *Huguenot ennui* in a large part of France and Switzerland, and on the other hand the human type of the bearded "artist", of shabby appearance with a mop of tufted hair, and with licentious morals, who is in full flower now (1966) all over the place.

The twenty-second Arcanum of the Tarot suggests the idea that the world is to be understood artistically rather than intellectually, since it is movement and rhythm (as the central figure is dancing). Does this Arcanum want to communicate this teaching only or does it, in the manner of the twenty-first Arcanum "The Fool", also give a warning? In other words, has it also two aspects—a teaching aspect and a warning aspect? For if the Arcanum whose Card represents an itinerant fool brought us to its more profound name, i.e. "Love", cannot the Arcanum whose Card represents a naked dancer in a garland bring us to its second, hidden name— "Folly"?

We shall see if this is so after having deepened our meditation on the Arcanum "The World" far enough to be able to be in a position to see clearly both the profound beauty of the world and the danger of the beauty of the world. May our meditation therefore be *sober*, and may it not let either the Arcanum's teaching or the warning that it entails escape us.

I say *sober* meditation, but since it is a matter of meditation on the world as a work of art, instead of conceiving of it as a system of laws, do we not—in advance—condemn ourselves to sterility by renouncing the élan of intoxication? Has not Baudelaire, an artist of genius, bequeathed us intoxication as the sole, indispensable key for creation and artistic creativity?

By posing this question we are here plunged fully into the Arcanum "The World" with its two aspects. For just as there is human Art and art, so also there is cosmic, divine, creative Art and the cosmic art of mirages. And just as there are ecstasies and illuminations from the Holy Spirit, so there are intoxications from the spirit of mirage—which is named the "false Holy Spirit" in Christian Hermeticism. Here is a criterion for distinguishing them: if you seek for the *joy* of artistic creation, spiritual illumination and mystical experience, you will inevitably more and more approach the sphere of the spirit of mirage and become more and more accessible to it; if you seek for *truth* through artistic creation, spiritual illumination and mystical experience, you will then approach the sphere of the

Holy Spirit, and you will open yourself more and more to the Holy Spirit. The revelations of truth issuing from the Holy Spirit *bring with them* joy and consolation (consolatory spirit = *Paraclete*), but are only *followed* by the joy which *results* from the revealed truth (spirit of truth— τὸ πνεῦμα τῆς ἀληθείας— *spiritus veritatis*; cf. John xvi, 13), whilst the revelations that we have called "mirages" follow the joy—they are born from the joy. (A mirage is not the same thing as a pure and simple illusion—a mirage being a "floating" reflection of a reality—but it is "floating", i.e. outside of the context of objective reality with its moral, causal, temporal and spatial dimensions).

The sobriety that we propose to maintain in this meditation on the Arcanum "The World" is therefore in no way a programme of dryness (although dryness is better than being swept away by the current of the pursuit of the enjoyment of "creative productivity" as such), but rather consciousness of the necessity of applying the above-mentioned criterion to meditation on the Arcanum in question: the necessity of keeping away from the spirit of mirage by means of faithfulness to the vows of chastity, poverty and obedience—these vows being the *sole means* of avoiding the dangers of the sphere of the spirit of mirage.

The joy which results from truth and the belief which results from joy—here is the key which opens the door to understanding the Arcanum of the world as a work of art. For it is this Arcanum which will reveal the world to us as a work of divine creative art, i.e. the world of Wisdom "who was at work beside him . . . rejoicing before him always" (Proverbs viii, 30), and it is this Arcanum again which will reveal the world to us as a work of art of deceptive mirage, i.e. the world of *maya*, the great illusion, who plays her game (*lila*) unceasingly—or, in other words, on the one hand the world which reveals God by manifesting him, and on the other hand the world which hides him by covering him.

But whether it is a matter of a revelatory world or of a deceptive world, whether it is a matter of the world seen in the light of the sphere of the spirit of truth or of the sphere of the spirit of mirage, it is *joy*—a twofold joy—which plays the key role here.

What is joy? What is it in its deeper sense?

Seen in the light of the Arcanum "The World"—the Arcanum of rhythmic movement or dance—joy is the harmony of rhythms, whilst suffering is their disharmony. The pleasure that one experiences in winter when one is seated close to a fire is only the restoration of an accord between the body's rhythm and the rhythm of the air—that which we call "temperature". The joy that friendship gives is the harmony between the psychic and mental rhythms of two or more people. The joy of good conscience is the accord between the moral rhythms of the lower self and the higher Self. The beatitude (Matthew v, 8) promising those who have a pure heart that they will "see God" signifies the accordance of their basic rhythm with the divine rhythm. Joy is therefore the state of harmony of inner rhythm with outer rhythm, of rhythm below with that from above, and, lastly, of the rhythm of created being with divine rhythm.

Now, the whole world is the accordance of innumerable rhythms. For its life is based on the preponderance of the accordance of particular rhythms, and not on their discordance. Thus life is basically joy.

It is therefore not without reason that the Septuagint—the Greek version of the Bible from the third century B.C.—renders the twenty-third verse of the third chapter of Genesis as follows: ". . .the Lord God sent him (Adam) forth out of the garden of delight to cultivate the ground out of which he was taken. . ." (καὶ ἀπέστειλεν αὐτὸν ὁ κύριος ὁ Θεὸς ἐκ τοῦ παραδίσου τῆς τρυφῆς ἐρ γάζεσθαι τὴν γὴν ἐξ ἧς ἐξεφύη). This version is taken over by the Vulgate —"*Et emisit eum Dominus Deus de paradiso voluptatis, ut operaretur terram de qua sumptus est*" (So the Lord God drove him out from that garden of delight, to cultivate the ground from which he came"— *Liber Genesis* iii, 23)—whilst the Hebrew Bible says only: "YHVH Elohim sent him forth from the garden of Eden, to till the ground (*adamah*) from which he was taken" (Genesis iii, 23). The translators of the Bible from the third century B.C., in translating the Hebraic term *gan-eden* (גַּן־עֵדֶן) by "garden of delight", were thereby advancing the thesis that the primordial state of man and Nature was joy—that the world, in so far as it is a divine creation, is the kingdom of joy. It was only after the Fall that suffering became added to joy.

This traditional conception is well supported both by logic and experience. Indeed, can one imagine a world in perpetual movement—living and ensouled— deprived of all vital élan, all satisfaction, and all *joie de vivre* ("joy of life")? Does not the very idea of movement—biological, psychic or intellectual, it does not matter—presuppose an affirmative impulse, a conscious or unconscious "yes", self-willed or instinctive, at the basis of all movement that is not purely mechanical? A lot is said in biology and psychology about the instinct of self-preservation, but what is this instinct if not the affirmation of existence—the manifestation of *joie de vivre*? If this were not so, universal weariness and disgust would have long ago put an end to all life.

Even the most austere asceticism bears witness in favour of this *joie de vivre*, for it wants to purify the mixture following the Fall: it aspires to the primordial and real joy of being. The idea of Buddhism and yoga—deliverance from terrestrial life—in the last analysis only affirms being, by commending the final surpassing of the world of forms to the degree of universality which is that of pure being. And the state of pure being—not of nothingness—is appraised in yoga as beatitude or blessedness (*ananda*) by postulating the equation:

$$sat \text{ (being)} = chit \text{ (consciousness)} = ananda \text{ (blessedness)}$$

With respect to the Buddhistic *nirvana*, this is the state of complete absence of the suffering entailed by earthly incarnation. If *nirvana* signified "void" pure and simple, and not the blessedness of pure being, no one—including the Buddha himself—would be able to find in himself the considerable energy demanded by the moral and intellectual effort on the way which leads to *nirvana*. In order to make this effort, one has to want—and one cannot want the void, i.e. that where there is nothing to want. Complete suicide? No, since suicide is an act of despair, whilst *nirvana* is the hope of the blissfulness of peace which one is able—or believes oneself to be able—to attain after having travelled a long path of discipline, renunciation and meditation. Do we not pray, we Christians, also, for the souls of the departed: *requiem aeternam dona eis, Domine* ("grant them eternal rest, O Lord")?...and *requiescant in pace* ("may they rest in peace")? Thus, Buddhists want nothing other than this *requies aeterna* ("eternal rest") that they call *nirvana*. There remains, lastly, the question of suicide. One says of some such person that he blew his brains out because he did not want to live any longer. Is it true that he did not want to live? Or rather, did he commit suicide because he wanted to live *otherwise*?...because he did not believe that he could change his life?

At the root of the depression and despair which lead to suicide, the element of *dissatisfaction* is to be found, i.e. the desire and assertion for another form of life or another way of living. One is not dissatisfied if one does not want anything. One does not despair, if one does not hope for anything. One does not kill oneself if one does not take life seriously. All dissatisfaction presupposes the affirmation of an imagined happiness. All despair presupposes a virtual hope. Thus, all suicide presupposes the passionate affirmation of some value in life: love, glory, honour, health, happiness...

Even in the fallen world, in the world which preserves only reflections of its primordial state, which was that of unblemished joy—the state of the "garden planted by God"—even in our fallen world, of which Schopenhauer said that the sum total of suffering far exceeds that of joy, even in this world, I say, it is the joy of life which moves it. Even if Schopenhauer was right that the *quantity* of suffering here exceeds that of joy, the quality of joy, although it is rarer and although it may be less long-lasting than suffering, is of a nature to make its memory be cherished, to keep it in memory, to make it awaken hope, in a word, to make it move the world. Nietzsche, in his *Thus Spake Zarathustra*, says:

> Joy—deeper yet than woe is she!   *Lust—tiefer noch als Herzeleid!*
> Saith woe: Hence, go!   *Weh spricht: Vergeh!*
> Yet Joy would have Eternity—   *Doch alle Lust will Ewigkeit—*
> Profound, profound Eternity!   *will tiefe, tiefe Ewigkeit!*

(Friedrich Nietzsche, *Thus Spake Zarathustra*)*

Nietzsche is right. The sources of joy are deeper than those of suffering. They still spring from the river which "flowed out of Eden to water the garden" (Genesis ii, 10). Joy is more ancient than suffering, and the world of joy preceded the world

---

* trsl. A. Tille, revised M. M. Bozman, Everyman Library, 1958, pp. 285

of suffering. Paradise was before the world of the struggle for existence and the survival of the fittest. Just as life precedes death, so does joy precede suffering.

This is why king Solomon in the book of Proverbs speaks of joyous Wisdom—a theme which was taken up twenty-eight centuries later by Nietzsche, who advanced the thesis of joyous science (*die fröhliche Wissenschaft*) contrasted to the spirit of heaviness (*Geist der Schwere*), i.e. the gravity of the science of his day and our day. Wisdom says of herself:

> Before his works of old I was set up from everlasting, from the beginning, or ever the earth was. When he established the heavens, I was there, when he drew a circle on the face of the deep, when he made firm the skies above, when he established the fountains of the deep, when he assigned to the sea its limits, so that the waters might not transgress his command, when he marked out the foundations of the earth, then I was at work beside him, and I was daily his delight, rejoicing before him always, rejoicing in his inhabited world and delighting in the sons of men. (Proverbs viii, 25-31)

This text portrays not only the artistic spirit which held sway at the dawn of the world, not only the joy of creation, but also the idea that joy is the accordance of rhythms. Indeed, Wisdom (*Sophia*, CHOKMAH) "was at work beside the Creator, and was daily his delight", which means to say that there was divine joy or accord between the rhythms of the Creator and of Wisdom "rejoicing before him always". And Wisdom "delighted in the sons of men", i.e. the human beings whose rhythm accorded with that of Wisdom "were her delight", just as she herself "was the delight" of the Creator by working in harmony with him.

There is still room to note that part of the above-quoted text—namely "rejoicing before him always, rejoicing in his inhabited world"—is found represented on the Card of the Arcanum "The World" of a Tarot printed at Paris in 1500, the existence of which was pointed out by Oswald Wirth in *Le Tarot des imagiers du moyen âge* (Paris, 1927). Here "The World" is represented by a globe, analogous to that held in the left hand of the Emperor (fourth Arcanum); above this globe of the world an entirely naked woman is dancing, who is holding up a huge curtain in her right hand, the extremity of which she gathers together in her left hand. Oswald Wirth says: "This is Truth manifesting itself unreservedly, by drawing aside the veil of appearances in order to communicate the secret of the essence of things" (ibid., p. 221). This variant of the Tarot evidently represents Wisdom "rejoicing before him always, rejoicing in his inhabited world".

Joy is the accordance of rhythms. Solomon speaks of the primordial joy which is the accordance of divine creative rhythms and the artistic creations of Wisdom. But he speaks also of another joy—that of accordance with the rhythm of "Folly" (the second name of the Arcanum "The World"):

Folly is a noisy woman,
    Wanton and without shame.
She sits at the door of her house,
    she takes a seat on the high places of the town,
calling to those who pass by,
    who are going straight on their way:
Whoever is simple, let him turn in here!
    And to him who is without sense she says:
Stolen water is sweet,
    and bread eaten in secret is pleasant!
But he does not know that those
    who go in there perish
—that her guests are in the depths of Sheol (the valley of the dead).
                              (Proverbs ix, 13-18)

The Septuagint adds to the last verse:

But hasten away, delay not in the place, neither fix thine eye
upon her: for thus shalt thou go through strange water; but thou
shouldst abstain from strange water (ἀπὸ δὲ ὕδατος ἀλλο-
τρίου ἀποσπάου), and drink not of a strange fountain, that
thou mayest live long, and years of life may be added to thee.
(Proverbs ix, 18)

There is, therefore, the joy of Wisdom and the joy of intoxication—called
"strange water" in the text of the Septuagint. The former springs from Wisdom,
whilst the latter produces a false wisdom which consists of mirages. For a sphere
of mirages exists in the invisible world, which constitutes the principal trap for
esotericists, gnostics and mystics—for all those who are seeking authentic spiritual
experience. Rudolf Steiner named it the "belt of lies" (*Lügengürtel*), and in traditional Christian Hermeticism it is called the "sphere of the false Holy Spirit". This
sphere (or belt) is closer to that of ordinary consciousness—so-called "ego-
consciousness"—than the "sphere of the Holy Spirit", where saints sojourn and
from whence they act on human terrestrial consciousness. Thus, in order to rise
to the sphere of the saints and the celestial hierarchies, one has first to "traverse",
i.e. to refuse to react to its attraction, the "sphere of the false Holy Spirit". It is
to the disciple "without sense" that the above-quoted text of the Septuagint is
addressed: "...delay not in the place, neither fix thine eye upon her: for thus shalt
thou go through strange water; but thou shouldst abstain from strange water"
(Proverbs ix, 18 in *The Septuagint Version of the Old Testament*; trsl. L. C. L. Bren-
ton, London, 1844, p. 653). Similarly, it is to the disciple "without sense" that
the false Holy Spirit, the spirit of "Folly", addresses herself by saying:

Stolen water is sweet,
    and bread eaten in secret is pleasant!

The lure of the sphere of mirages, following the book of Proverbs, is therefore "stolen water", i.e. the mobile element which flows and sweeps consciousness away in a delicious current of easily-won illuminations and inspirations without consciousness having to make the moral effort which is summarised in the three words: cross, prayer and penitence. Here consciousness finds itself in a state of flight and freedom which dispenses with all law, with no responsibility of rendering account to anyone at all about anything at all—as if the Cross did not exist—receiving illuminations gratis, that it has not prayed for. . . free from all memory of sin, free of all remorse and all responsibility for sins and errors of the past, as if sin and error were trifles hardly worth remembering. Filled with joy, savouring the creative élan, consciousness gives itself unreservedly to visionary and inspired speculation, where every image and every thought which are presented to it appear to be revelations from above, imprints of seals of superhuman wisdom. This "stolen water" is all the more dangerous because it *inundates* the soul with floods of psychic energy, which is an entirely new experience—the door to the belief that it is a matter of supernatural interference. On the other hand, the illuminations that these floods convey tally with the most intimate inclinations and desires of the soul, which redouble their convincing force and their hold on it.

It is thus that false prophets and messiahs arise. It is thus also that there were those illuminations in certain gnostic sects which resulted from immoral practices. For example, the following is the scene painted by Epiphanius—himself a witness of (and probably also a participant in) the gatherings of the Barbeliot sect—who recounts what he saw because he reckoned it impossible to keep silence:

> They have their wives in common, and when someone comes to them who knows nothing of their teaching, the men have towards the women, and the women towards the men, a sign of recognition whereby they determine whether the newcomer belongs to their sect. The sign is given as they are shaking hands: as they touch, they make a kind of tickling on the surface of the palm of the hand. After they have recognised one another, they set about supper right away. They put on the table a sumptuous repast—eating meat and drinking wine even if they are poor. When they have dined together thus and, as it were, are "brimming at the veins" with energy, they then get down to business. Each man separates himself from his wife, saying to her: Stand up and fulfil the love-feast (*agape*) with thy brother. . .
>
> . . . nevertheless, I shall not shy away from saying what they are not shy of doing, so that—with due consideration for the reader—I shall arouse a shudder with each obscene act perpetrated by them. After they have had intercourse, not satisfied with the depravity of their fornication, they elevate their disgrace towards heaven. Each man and woman takes the man's ejaculation in their hands. Then, stepping forward and directing themselves towards heaven with this filth in their hands, they pray,

as so-called "stratiotics" and "gnostics", offering to the Father
of All what they have in their hands, with the words: We bring
to thee this offering, the body of Christ...(Hans Leisegang, *Die
Gnosis*, Leipzig, 1924, pp. 190-191)

It was thus, also, that meetings of the Russian *Khlysty* sect ("flagellants") of the
nineteenth century sometimes finished, after the "descent of the Holy Spirit",
through orgies of free love resulting from the freedom communicated by the "Holy
Spirit".

It was also thanks to revelations from the sphere of mirages that, for example,
many families of Estonian peasants in the nineteenth century sold off their goods
in order to go to a place on the elevated side of the Baltic sea, to Lasnamägi
(Laksberg), so as to wait there for the arrival of a "white boat"—predicted by their
prophetically inspired leaders—which was to have taken them to a land of freedom,
where there would be neither barons nor taxes.

Lastly, it was thus that the medicine men of a number of tribes of Red Indians
in North America, exasperated by the disappearance of herds of bison in the last
quarter of the past century, had a revelation of a new magical cult—the "bison
dance"—the practice of which would make the herds of bison reappear in the
prairies, as it would also make the white man withdraw from the hereditary hunting terrain of the Red Indians. It was only after the bloody intervention of the
United States army that the practice of the magical cult came to an end.

Intellectual hallucinations of still greater significance have, in our century, had
their hold on entire peoples. It is not necessary to read Louis Pauwels and Jacques
Bergier's book *The Dawn of Magic* (trsl. R. Myers, London, 1963) to understand
that Hitler's Nazi adventure was due to a dynamism released through an intellectual hallucination of prodigious power—it suffices to know the facts of contemporary history to which we have been witness.

Another example of the semi-magical hold of an intellectual hallucination over
whole peoples in our times is given by Marxism-Leninism-Stalinism-Maoism. For
the intellectual system and principles underlying this movement are as at variance
with world reality as was the "myth of the twentieth century" of Nazi Germany.
The Marxist intellectual mirage paints a scene of the world and human history
where the spirit is only a kind of "exhalation"—in the guise of ideologies, religions
and moral codes—issuing forth from material things and interests. The spirit is
only an epiphenomenal superstructure upon biological and economic factors, produced and fashioned by them.

The success of Marxism-Leninism—apart from its appeal to feelings of resentment and indignation of the disinherited classes—is due to the putting to work
of a prodigious quantity of psychic energy instilled into the masses of militants
as a consequence of contact with the "sphere of the false Holy Spirit", inspired
by some leading inspired prophets. It is the sphere of mirages which explains not

only the semi-magical hold of Bolshevism on the masses but also its doctrines. This latter is the offspring of two different experiences: the experience of the sphere of mirages and that of economic material realities. The first experience engenders the fundamental dogma of Marxism-Leninism that the spirit—with ideologies, religions and moral codes as its functions—is only a projection of human interests and ambitions expressing the will to power; which is true if the experience of spiritual life goes no further than the sphere of mirages...if it stops at this sphere ...if it does not arrive at the sphere of the Holy Spirit, i.e. that of the saints and Angelic hierarchies. Thus it has happened that the authors of Marxist-Leninist doctrine have discovered the reality of the sphere of mirages as an almost inexhaustible source of psychic energy on the one hand, and as an immense fabric of superstructure, on the other hand, where all earthly interest receives its ideological, religious and moral clothing.

Now, purely earthly interests and aspirations amount to the will to power, which is the basis of the struggle for existence and the survival of the fittest in the general evolution of the species presented by Charles Darwin. On the other hand, power in the domain of human terrestrial life amounts to wealth, i.e. to control of production and enjoyment of the fruits of production; thus it amounts to control of the means of production. Now add to these conclusions drawn from experience of the sphere of mirages those drawn from experience of the earthly economic domain—with its inequality in the control of production and its inequality in the enjoyment of the fruits of production—and you arrive inevitably at the second fundamental dogma of Marxism-Leninism, namely that the means of production should belong to the whole community or society and not to individuals or groups of individuals. All other propositions of Marxist-Leninist doctrine— such as the social revolution, the dictatorship of the proletariat, the classless society, the decline of the state, etc.—follow from these two fundamental dogmas, founded on the interweaving of experience of the sphere of mirages and experience of the economic domain seen as the field of the struggle for existence and the survival of the fittest, the struggle between exploiters and the exploited.

With respect to the "myth of the twentieth century" of Nazi Germany, it also owed its hold on the masses as well as the dogmas of its doctrine to the influx of energy from, and to the illuminating effect of, the sphere of mirages. This time it was a matter not of the economic life, but rather of biological life—seen in the light emanated from the sphere of mirages. The factors of heredity and those of "blood" in Nazi doctrine took the place of the economic factors in Marxist-Leninist doctrine and differentiate it from the latter. The two doctrines have in common that it is the will to power—of classes in the one, and of races in the other—which move and must move human history.

Now, the Nazi mirage dissipated suddenly as a consequence of the hard experience of the reality of complete military defeat. With respect to the Marxist-Leninist mirage, it is dissipating little by little as a consequence of the hard and sobering experience of economic reality and the reality of human nature. "Revisionism", after having rejected Stalinism, is at work, and will not allow itself to be halted any more.

The mirages dissipate, but at what a price...

The sphere of mirages or the "sphere of the false Holy Spirit" is not only a thesis of the doctrine of Hermeticism, but is also the latter's trial and danger. Occultists, magicians, gnostics and mystics are its victims (or should I say "dupes"?) no less often than nations or than the authors and leaders of social and political movements. We have already cited the case of the moral aberration of the Barbeliot gnostics in Egypt, and we mentioned that of the *Khlysty* sect in Russia, nearer to our time. These cases could be banished from your thoughts, dear Unknown Friend, as of little relevance, since they relate to ancient and more recent *sects* and not to esotericists of an independent spirit, having as their slogan "neither Loyola, nor Voltaire" (Papus). It is nevertheless a fact that one can observe here and there that independent spirits—concerned about their freedom, and rejecting all submission to an authority external to their own conscience—that these spirits end up by becoming sectarian esotericists, with their own revelations and their own personal illuminations. As they are lacking the fruits of a disciplined training, and as there is no one of authority to whom they can turn at the times of danger which spiritual experience holds in store for them, they easily fall prey to the lures of the sphere of mirages, against which Solomon cautions us in the above-quoted passage from the book of Proverbs.

What can one say? Mankind is a unity and one person's experience is meant to help and serve others. One cannot dispense with the experience of others, i.e. with authority, if one wants to avoid the traps set along the way of spiritual experience. Truth to tell, the principal reason as to why occultism is "occult" and esotericism is "esoteric", i.e. demanding protection through secrecy, is the concern to protect "free spirits" above all against the dangers of enslavement through "inflation", as Carl Gustav Jung called it, which is an aspect of the sphere of mirages. On the other hand, the general reserve and refusal to accept occultism, esotericism, gnosis and mysticism—not to mention magic—that is manifested by the public opinion of all times, is due to the same reason. The sphere of mirages has in the past played too much of a role here, and has sown a profound mistrust in the conservative opinion of the public. The sober public does not want illusions —it has had enough of them.

Thus, it is the playing in of the sphere of mirages which is the historical cause of the veil of secrecy. By this means esotericism protects, on the one hand, audacious neophytes; just as, on the other hand, the exoteric public protects itself—through mistrust—against the danger of becoming engaged in the play of the sphere of mirages. For the way of esotericism—the way of personal and authentic spiritual experience—necessarily entails confronting the reality of the sphere of mirages or the "sphere of the false Holy Spirit".

This is why the mystics of eastern Christianity do not tire of warning beginners of the danger that they call "seductive illumination" (*prelestnoye prosveshtcheniye* in Russian) and insist upon the *nakedness* of spiritual experience, i.e. on experience of the spiritual world stripped of all form, all colour, all sound and all intellectuality. The intuition alone of divine love with its effect on moral consciousness is — they teach — the sole experience to which one should aspire. Ladyzhendsky — in his book *Vnoutrenny svet* ("The Inner Light"), published at St. Petersburg in 1915/16 — gave a well-documented exposition of the doctrine of orthodox mystics concerning true and false illumination. There he reproaches the mystics of western Christianity for their doctrine (namely that of admitting, under certain conditions, visions and illuminations of an intellectual nature), i.e. for not rejecting visions and illuminations from the outset.

Thus, the mystics of eastern Christianity are so impressed by the reality and the danger of the sphere of mirages that they prefer to renounce all spiritual experience of a visionary or intellectual nature, whatever it may be, rather than risk the danger of confrontation with the reality of this sphere. With respect to the mystics of western Christianity, they are also conscious of the reality of this sphere and its dangers, but they do not reject outright all vision and intellectual illumination. Their experience accumulated under the supervison of the religious orders (there are no religious orders in the East) and that of the hierarchical and centralised Church (in the East there is no directing centre which is in a position to accumulate and validate the experience of hundreds — or even thousands — of years of the spiritual life of Christian mankind) allows them to derive criteria needed to distinguish whether or not private revelations stem from the sphere of the Holy Spirit, i.e. from the sphere of the saints and the celestial hierarchies. These criteria amount to the strict observation of the vows of obedience, poverty and chastity, according to their letter and according to their spirit.

The *chaste mind* seeks the truth and not the joy of revelation of the truth, just as chaste love seeks union with the loved one and not the carnal pleasure of union. The chaste mind is therefore sober; it does not let itself be swept away by the "stolen water" which is sweet, i.e. by the intoxication arising from the ready afflux — gratis — of floods of illuminations, concerning which Solomon warns us in the Book of Proverbs. The *poor mind* refuses to drink the "stolen water", since it seeks only what is essential to the life of the body, the life of the soul, and the life of the spirit. It does not seek the superfluous — even if it is spiritual — and will not accept the invitation to take part in the orgy of spiritual illuminations that the sphere of mirages offers it. The *obedient mind* has an awake and cultivated sense of obedience, i.e. the *spiritual hearing of the will*, which renders it capable of recognising the *voice of truth* and distinguishing it from other voices. It is to this spiritual hearing, developed by obedience, that the Gospel of St. John refers in the following passage:

> He who does not enter the sheepfold by the door but climbs
> in by another way, that man is a thief and a robber; but he who

enters by the door is the shepherd of the sheep. To him the
gatekeeper opens; the sheep hear his voice, and he calls his own
sheep by name and leads them out. When he has brought out
all his own, he goes before them, and the sheep follow him, for
they know his voice. A stranger they will not follow, but they
will flee from him, for they do not know the voice of strangers.
(John x, 1-5)

True obedience is not at all the subjugation of the will to another will, but rather
the moral clairaudience of the will — the faculty of knowing and recognising the
voice of truth. And it is this which renders the soul inaccessible to the lures of
the sphere of mirages.

Although no practising esotericist is sheltered from the sphere of mirages, he
who has made the vows of obedience, poverty and chastity an affair of the heart
will come out victorious from the confrontation with this sphere. If St. Anthony
said radically, "No salvation without temptation," one could add: "No temptation vanquished without the three vows."

Unfortunately, it is a fact that esotericists, in contrast to monks and nuns, tend
as a general rule to make little of the vows of obedience, poverty and chastity. They
seem to have made their fundamental attitude scientific, where one relies on intelligence alone. The result of this is often — very often — a game of intellectual
fireworks which, in contrast to the light of the sun, does not illumine, does not
warm and does not vivify.

But, however, it is not sterility alone which is the principal danger of intellectual
flight at the expense of moral and spiritual progress; it is, above all, the reality
of the sphere of mirages. For the latter is always ready to supply not only visions
but also intellectual illuminations and intellectual mirages. Thus it happens that
the sphere of mirages enters into play and paints dazzling intellectual scenes for
the mind that is forgetful of the necessity of the vows of obedience, poverty and
chastity. Dazzled by the richness of the glimpses and the artistic breadth of the
intellectual edifice which is presented to his eyes, such a mind accepts it, believing himself to have been favoured by revelation from above.

What renders such an intellectual mirage all the more dangerous is that it is
not, as a general rule, purely and simply a delusion or illusion. It is a mixture
of truth and illusion, mixed in an inextricable way. The true serves to prop up
the false and the false seems to lend the true a new splendour. It is therefore a
mirage and not pure illusion, which would be easier to perceive. And as it is a
matter of an alloy of the true and the false, the true appears here in the light of
the false. Ideas which are true in themselves, as a consequence of their association
with false ideas, acquire here a falsified meaning. It is a net woven from the true
and the false which lays hold of the befuddled soul.

The sphere of mirages is also constantly at work to re-shuffle facts relating to
former lives and karmic relationships. For example, it can evoke a series of sub-

jective reminiscences or scenes from a distant past which, being a mixture of the true and the false, can completely disorientate the beneficiary—or rather the victim—of these revelations. For from this there result tasks and missions to accomplish in the present life which have only little—or even nothing—to do with the true tasks of this life. Mirages are above all frequent in the case of relationships between persons of the opposite sex who feel drawn to one another. It then often happens that the qualities, and even the identity, of one soul are projected upon another. Many a Tristan thinks he recognises his Isolde in a simple maid, just as many an Elsa of Brabant sees her Lohengrin in a gallant.

The conclusion which asserts itself from all that we have said above concerning the sphere of mirages is that practical esotericism demands at least the same prudence as exact science, but the prudence that it demands is of a nature that is not only intellectual but also, and above all, moral. In fact, it encompasses the whole human being with his faculties of reasoning, imagination and will. It is therefore a matter of *being* prudent.

For this reason the rule of every serious esotericist should be *to be silent*—often for a length of years—concerning every new illumination or inspiration that he has, so as to give it the necessary time to *mature*, i.e. to acquire that certainty which results from its accordance with moral consciousness, moral logic, the totality of spiritual and ordinary personal experience—and that of friends and spiritual guides of the past and present—as also with divine revelation, whose eternal dogmas are guiding constellations in the intellectual and moral heaven. And it will be only after having arrived at such an accordance that a personal illumination or inspiration can be considered communicable and presentable.

This applies not only to esotericists but also to artists. The latter—above all those who hold to the principle of "art for the sake of art"—are, as a general rule, playthings of the sphere of mirages. Whilst keeping to the dogma of autonomy and independence of truth and morality in the domain of art, they fall easy prey to the doings of the sphere of mirages to such a point that they even identify this sphere with the very source of their inspiration. For if one hardly concerns oneself with the "what" and seeks only the "how" of artistic creation, one will certainly end up by giving oneself up to illuminations and inspirations from the sphere of mirages—the sphere *par excellence* of so-called creative imagination, withdrawn from moral control.

This state of things was well understood by certain particularly artistic spirits. For example: Goethe, who wrote *Faust* over a period of sixty years, not only wanted to brush aside the sphere of mirages from his work but also to bring to the light of day in *Faust* the reality and mechanism of the action of this sphere. For him, art was not purely and simply a product of the play of the imagination, but rather a continuation in the subjective domain of the creative work which Nature carries out in the objective domain. He insisted on directed imagination—"exact imagination" (*exakte Phantasie*)—for artistic creation as well as for knowledge.

But the principles of Goethe's method are brushed aside by classing them in the category of "literary classicism", i.e. by making them a question of literary taste instead of seeing and recognising here an appeal to the conscience of the artist to stop drawing his inspirations from the sphere of mirages . . . at such a cost that the single work—*Faust*—could demand sixty years of work! Artists, like esotericists, are obliged to make their works pass the trial of time, so that the poisonous plants from the sphere of mirages can be uprooted, and there remains only the wheat—pure and ripe.

Thus there exists sacred art, which is distinguished from profane art, just as sacred magic is to be distinguished from profane magic and sorcery:

> Every sacred art is therefore founded on a science of forms, or in other words, on the symbolism inherent in forms. It must be borne in mind that a symbol is not merely a conventional sign. It manifests its archetype by virtue of a definite ontological law . . . a symbol *is* in a certain sense that to which it gives expression. For this very reason traditional symbolism is never without beauty: according to the spiritual view of the world, the beauty of an object is nothing but the transparency of its existential envelopes; an art worthy of the name is beautiful because it is true. (Titus Burckhardt, *Sacred Art in East and West*; trsl. Lord Northbourne, London, 1967, p. 8)

Sacred art is therefore founded upon a *science of forms* and not upon subjective artistic creative élan or upon the subject as such.

> When historians of art apply the term "sacred art" to any and every work that has a religious subject, they are forgetting that art is essentially form. An art cannot properly be called "sacred" solely on the grounds that its subjects originate in a spiritual truth; its formal language also must bear witness to a similar origin. Such is by no means the case with a religious art like that of the Renaissance or of the Baroque period, which is in no way distinct, so far as style is concerned, from the fundamentally profane art of that era; neither the subjects which it borrows, in a wholly exterior and as it were literary manner, from religion, nor the devotional feelings with which it is permeated in appropriate cases, nor even the nobility of soul which sometimes finds expression in it, suffice to confer on it a sacred character. No art merits that epithet unless its forms themselves reflect the spiritual vision characteristic of a particular religion . . . (p. 7)
>
> The doctrine common to traditional civilisations prescribes that sacred art must imitate the Divine Art, but it must be clearly understood that this in no way implies that the complete Divine creation, the world such as we see it, should be copied, for such would be pure pretension; a literal "naturalism" is foreign to

sacred art. What must be copied is the way in which the Divine Spirit works. Its laws must be transposed into the restricted domain in which man works as man, that is to say, into artisanship (p. 10). (Titus Burckhardt, *Sacred Art in East and West*; trsl. Lord Northbourne, London, 1967, pp. 7, 10)

It remains only to add to what Titus Burckhardt says that the transposition of the way in which the divine spirit works in the domain of human artisanship presupposes the three traditional vows of chastity, poverty and obedience. Purification must precede illumination and perfection. Sacred art, which imitates the way in which the divine spirit works, requires that the soul of the artist rids itself of its own inclinations and habits, i.e. that it becomes poor, so as to be able to receive the wealth of the divine spirit. . .that it reduces its own phantasy and its own predilections to silence, i.e. that it is chaste, so as not to disturb the limpid waters flowing from the divine source. . .and that it is obedient, so as to be able to imitate the divine spirit at work, i.e. to be able to work in concert with the divine spirit.

Now, the Card of the twenty-second Arcanum of the Tarot—"The World"— represents a dancer holding a magic wand in her hand, and a philtre in the other. The wand symbolises the creative power of realisation below of that which is above; she holds it vertically. This is the gesture of actualising below that which is above — the gesture of sacred art, i.e. the gesture imitating the way in which the divine creative spirit works. And the following is what Paul Marteau says concerning the philtre that the dancer is holding in her other hand:

It is the creative philtre of illusion on all the planes of Nature, for man can have both the illusion of love and that of spirituality. The philtre is opposed to the wand in the sense that the illusion created by man can give him an ephemeral kingly dignity. (Paul Marteau, *Le Tarot de Marseille*, Paris, 1949, p. 90)

In other words, the Arcanum "The World" has a twofold meaning: it *teaches* that joy, i.e. the accordance of rhythms, is at the root of creation; and it *warns*, at the same time, of the danger of seeking for creative joy instead of for creative truth. Thus he who seeks first and foremost for creative joy will drink from the philtre the intoxicating potion of illusion of the sphere of the "false Holy Spirit", i.e. the sphere of mirages, whilst he who seeks first and foremost for creative truth will not only find it through the sober effort of vertical elevation but will also participate actively in the accordance of rhythms, i.e. creative joy. He will learn the way of the wand, i.e. to put himself vertically in contact with the "sphere of the Holy Spirit"— the sphere of saints and the celestial hierarchies— by traversing the sphere of mirages unperturbed.

The Arcanum "The World" thus communicates to us a teaching of immense practical significance: "The world is a work of art. It is animated by creative joy. The wisdom that it reveals is joyous wisdom—that of creative-artistic élan, and not that of an engineer-technician or industrial designer. Happy is he who seeks wisdom in the first place, for he will find that wisdom is joyous! Unhappy is the one who seeks the joy of joyous wisdom in the first place, for he will fall prey to illusions! Seek first the creative wisdom of the world—and the joy of creativity will be given to you in addition."

From this teaching there results an important rule of "spiritual hygiene", namely: that he who aspires to authentic spiritual experiences never confounds the *intensity* of the experience undergone with the *truth* that is revealed—or is not revealed—through it, i.e. he does not regard the *force* of impact of an inner experience as a criterion of its authenticity and truth. For an illusion stemming from the sphere of mirages can bowl you over, whilst a true revelation from above can take place in the guise of a scarcely perceptible inner whispering. Far from imposing itself through force, authentic spiritual experience sometimes requires very awake and very concentrated attention so as not to let it pass by unnoticed. It is often difficult to even notice it, without speaking of being seized or bowled over by it. If this were not so, what good would exercises of concentration and profound meditation be? For all the exercises that all serious esotericism prescribes are necessary in order to render attention so awake and intense that it is in a position to perceive within the calm and silent domain of the depth of the soul where spiritual truth reveals itself. And this latter has the quite pronounced tendency to work gently and gradually, although—as in the case of St. Paul—there are exceptions. But as a general rule, the spiritual world does not at all resemble the surging of the sea—at work to break down the dams holding it back, so as to inundate the land. No, what characterises the spiritual world, i.e. the "sphere of the Holy Spirit", is the consideration that it has for the human condition. The amount and frequency of revelation from above, destined for a human being, is measured with a lot of care, so as to avoid every possible perturbation in the moral and physical equilibrium of this person. What the spiritual world prefers most of all is "reasonable inspiration", i.e. a gentle flow of inspiration which intensifies to the extent that the intellectual and moral forces of the recipient grow and mature. Here a succession of elements comprising a great truth are revealed little by little until the day when the great truth in its entirety shines within the human consciousness thus prepared. Then there will be joy, certainly, but not the perturbation of equilibrium which is intoxication—nor will there be nervous over-excitement or insomnia.

This is the law of the wand that the central personage of the Card of the twenty-second Arcanum is holding in one of her hands. But it is just the opposite which applies to the philtre that she is holding in the other hand. There, first and foremost, it is a matter of the joy and intoxication which result from mirage-revelations. The way of working of the "sphere of the false Holy Spirit" is to make human souls convinced of the truth of intellectual or visionary mirages through the intensity of the impression that they produce. "That which excites the most is true" seems to be the criterion advanced by the sphere of mirages.

It is true that the most advanced school of modern depth psychology—advanced in the sense of penetration into the domain of the psychic unconscious—that of Carl Gustav Jung, considers the *numinosum* in psychic experience as a manifestation of the *dynamic reality* of the unconscious (or subconscious, or even superconscious). (By *numinosum* is meant that which the soul experiences as something which is irresistibly imposed on it, or which is not mastered—or is even "unmasterable"—by it). The *numinosum* is thus a psychic experience (in dream, phantasy, phantasy-vision, or vision) which—through its irresistible fascination—subjugates he who experiences it. The *numinosum* does not present itself, it imposes itself. Consciousness submits to its action rather than calling it forth. The *numinosum* as such subjugates man independently of his will (cf. C. G. Jung, *Psychology and Religion*; trsl. R. F. C. Hull, *The Collected Works of C. G. Jung*, vol. 11, London, 1958, p. 7).

Now, according to Jung, the *reality* of the unconscious is manifested by action of a numinous character upon consciousness. This is what Jung says concerning the unconscious:

> . . . the unconscious. . . by definition and in fact, cannot be circumscribed. It must therefore be counted as something boundless: infinite or infinitesimal. Whether it may legitimately be called a microscosm depends simply and solely on whether certain portions of the world beyond individual experience can be shown to exist in the unconscious—certain constants which are not individually acquired but are *a priori* presences. The theory of instinct and the findings of biology in connection with the symbiotic relationship between plant and insect have long made us familiar with these things. . . A general proof of the rightness of this expectation lies in the ubiquitous occurrence of parallel mythologems, Bastian's "folk thoughts" or primordial ideas; and a special proof is the autochthonous reproduction of such ideas in the psyche of individuals where direct transmission is out of the question. . . Mythologems are the aforementioned "portions of the world" which belong to the structural elements of the psyche. They are constants whose expression is everywhere and at all times the same (C. G. Jung, "Medicine and Psychotherapy" in *The Practice of Psychotherapy*, trsl. R. F. C. Hull, *The Collected Works of C. G. Jung*, vol. 16, London, 1954, pp. 91-92)

The unconscious—with its numinous action—is therefore not confined to the individual soul; it surpasses it in every direction. Being "something boundless", the unconscious is the *world* seen under its psychic aspect. Which means to say that it consists not only of innate, i.e. prenatal, individual tendencies and inclinations, but that it also includes what we have designated as "spheres"—namely the "sphere of the Holy Spirit" and that of the "false Holy Spirit". Action of a numinous character from the unconscious, thus conceived, is certainly a criterion sufficient to distinguish the manifestation of the *reality* of the unconscious from the manifestation of the subjectivity of the individual soul through the latter's spontaneous fantasy, feeling and intellectuality, but *it does not at all suffice* to distinguish *the truth* within this reality, i.e. to distinguish the action of the sphere of the Holy Spirit from that of the sphere of mirages. For the sphere of mirages, also, is real— but *reality* is one thing and *truth* is another thing. A mirage is certainly real, but it is not true; it is deceiving.

Jung was, at the same time, quite conscious not only of the compensatory— i.e. guiding and correcting—role of the unconscious, but also of the gravity of the danger courted by human consciousness in submitting to the baleful, unrestrained influence of the unconscious. For him this influence could be auspicious or baleful—which corresponds to the teaching of Hermeticism concerning these two spheres, i.e. that of the Holy Spirit and that of mirages. Here is what he said concerning the danger which menaces mankind on account of the unconscious:

> Psychology constitutes nothing less than the most indispensable knowledge that we have. Indeed, it is apparent with an increasingly blinding clarity that that which constitutes the greatest danger threatening man is not famine or earthquakes or microbes or cancer but man's well being. The cause of this is quite straightforward: there still does not exist any effective protection against psychic epidemics—and these epidemics are infinitely more devastating than the worst catastrophes of Nature! The supreme danger which menaces both the individual and the populace as a whole is *psychic danger*. With regard to this, our understanding proves to be quite powerless, which is explained by the fact that rational arguments act on the conscious —but on the conscious alone—without having the least effect on the unconscious. Consequently, a major danger for man emanates from the mass, i.e. the crowd, at whose core the working of the unconscious accumulates—first muzzling, then stifling the pleas for reason on the part of the conscious. Every organisation of a crowd constitutes a latent danger, like that of piling up dynamite. Because it produces effects that no one wanted, and which no one is able to hold in check. For this reason one must ardently hope that psychology—knowledge of psychology and achievements in the domain of psychology — will spread on such a scale that human beings will finally understand the source of the supreme danger hanging over their heads. It is not by arming themselves to the teeth, every country of itself, that nations will be able, in the long run, to preserve themselves from the terrible catastrophes occasioned by modern

war. Accumulated arms demand war! On the contrary, would
it not be preferable in future to guard against and to avoid the
conditions delineated at present — in which the unconscious
breaks down the dams of the conscious and dispossesses the latter, making the world run the risk of inestimable devastation?
(C. G. Jung, *L'homme à la découverte de son âme*; French trsl.
by R. Cahen, Geneva, 1944, pp. 402-403 — epilogue written for
this French edition by Jung and dated Küsnacht-Zurich, January,
1944)

This is a warning from a man who speaks with real knowledge — with more knowledge, in fact, than many an authentic occultist — thanks to his prodigious experience accumulated during a long life directed by the will to heal. And it was this
will to heal which made him first of all an explorer and then an expert in the
world of depths, the door to which is the human soul.

But let us return to the Arcanum "The World" — the Arcanum of movement,
i.e. of the "how" of moving that which is moved by that which moves.

Until now we have been occupied with the central figure of the Card, i.e. with
joyous Wisdom with her wand and philtre, and with the way in which the wand
moves consciousness as well as with the way in which the philtre moves it. The
movement emanating from the "sphere of the Holy Spirit" and that emanating
from the "sphere of mirages" — the two movements corresponding to the wand and
the philtre — have this in common: that they move, as it were, from outside or
above the human soul and the world of action. In order to understand the whole
Arcanum of movement, i.e. the world, it is still necessary to consider the movement *immanent* in beings and things. This latter is represented in the Card by
the garland which surrounds the central figure, and by the four figures — the three
animals and the Angel — in the four corners of the Card, outside of the garland.

The garland represents the movement immanent in *growth* and the four figures
symbolise the movement immanent in *basic instinct*, or what the ancients called
the "four elements". For the four elements — "fire", "air", "water" and "earth" — are
not chemical substances, or even states of matter (namely warmth, gaseous, liquid
and solid), but rather modes of movement immanent in all substance . . . mental, psychic, organic, and also inorganic. They are therefore the four fundamental
instincts immanent in the world-in-movement; and this is why they are depicted
in the tradition of religious iconography in general — as also in the Card of the
Arcanum "The World" — as the cosmogonic quaternary of the Bull, the Eagle, the
Lion and the Angel.

The Angel and the three sacred animals are represented in the
firmament by stars of first magnitude located at the four cardinal points: *Aldebaran*, or the eye of the Bull; *Regulus*, or the
heart of the Lion; *Altair*, the light of the Eagle; and *Fomalhaut*
in the stellar Fish, which absorbs the water poured out by the

> Waterman. These stars mark the extremities of a cross whose cen-
> tre is the polar star which, because of its immobility in the mid-
> dle of the celestial rotation, corresponds in the Arcanum ("The
> World") to the young girl framed in an oval of greenery depicting
> the zone of the ecliptic. (Oswald Wirth, *Le Tarot des imagiers
> du moyen âge*, Paris, 1927, p. 220)

The idea underlying this correspondence between the four "sacred animals" of
the Evangelists and the stars of the signs of the zodiac is the *cosmic or zodiacal
significance* of the four "cosmic instincts" or "elements". It attributes a universal
and also a stable function to them in the planetary world of movement, just as
the fixed stars are attributed with this function in the zodiac.

But it is not the constellations of the zodiac which manifest the principle of
the quaternary of the "cosmic elements" or "basic instincts". This principle is found
manifested in the ineffable name of God—the *Tetragrammaton*, יהוה (YOD-
HE-VAU-HÉ)—the imprint of which on a cosmic scale constitutes the quaternary
in question. For what we know as the category (i.e. the structural disposition of
our intelligence) of *causality*—with its quaternary of effective causes, formal causes,
material causes and final causes—is only a special case of this imprint. Indeed,
we would not know how to perceive order in the universal movement that we call
"the world" if we did not apply causality, that is to say, if we did not distinguish
what moves from what is moved, what forms from what is formed, the source from
the aim, the beginning from the end. Without the application of causality to
universal movement, we would be able only to contemplate it "open-mouthed",
instead of being able to derive from it a "universal evolution", a "universal history",
and a "law of gravitation"—and also to find the causes of illnesses, disasters, and
all the dangers which lie in wait for us, so as to foresee them and avert them.

Now, that which manifests itself in the structure of our intelligence in the guise
of the category of causality—which is revered by Cabbalists in the guise of the
ineffable name of God, and which occupies the central place in Pythagorean
philosophy in the guise of the sacred tetrad—is what is manifested again in the
guise of the quaternary of "cosmic instincts" (or the "sacred animals" of the
Apocalypse and the prophet Ezekiel), i.e. the quaternary of spontaneous impulsion, reaction, transformability and "foldability" (or enfoldment), or the four
elements: fire, air, water and earth.

Impulsion, movement, formation and form—these four elements are at work
everywhere. They are to be found both in intellectual activity and in psychic and
biological activity, both in so-called "inorganic" matter and in organic matter,
both in the macrocosm and in the microcosm.

An eminent Christian Hermeticist, Dr. Paul Carton—now (regrettably) deceased
—made a precious contribution to the living tradition of Christian Hermeticism
with his masterly work on the four temperaments entitled *Diagnostic et conduite
des tempéraments* ("Diagnosis and Behaviour of the Temperaments"), where the
four temperaments (bilious, nervous, sanguine and lymphatic) are not only de-

scribed phenomenologically but also are explained as a manifestation of the universal law of the quaternary. We read there:

> Ancient Wisdom drew from the enigma of the Sphinx the four
> fundamental rules of human conduct: *to know* with the intel-
> ligence of the human brain; *to will* with the strength of the lion;
> *to dare* or to elevate oneself with the audacious power of the
> wings of the eagle; *to be silent* with the massive and concen-
> trated force of the bull. Applied to the behaviour of the tem-
> peraments, the allegory of the Sphinx teaches that man — in
> order to build himself wholly and to develop himself har-
> moniously — must normally cultivate, balance and hierarchise
> within himself the four essential functions of human life: the
> wilful energy of the bilious, the reflective understanding of the
> nervous, the vital power of the sanguine, the self-control of the
> lymphatic. (Paul Carton, *Diagnostic et conduite des tempéra-
> ments*, Paris, 1961, p. 20)

The four temperaments are, again, a special case of the universal quaternary of impulsion, movement, formation and form, of the four elements — fire, air, water and earth. And at the basis of these four elements the quaternary of the *motive instinct* immanent in the world is found. This instinct in turn reflects the four cosmic entities which bear the MERKABAH (the divine chariot) — the Angel, the Eagle, the Lion and the Bull from Ezekiel's vision of the chariot and from the vision of St. John. The latter describes them as follows:

> The first living creature was like a lion, the second living creature
> like an ox, the third living creature had the face of a man, and
> the fourth living creature was like a flying eagle. (Revelation iv, 7)

Ezekiel, however, stresses the fundamental unity of the four living creatures by saying:

> As for the likeness of the faces of the four living creatures, each
> had the face of a man in front; all four had the face of a lion
> on the right side; all four had the face of an ox on the left side;
> and all four had the face of an eagle at the back. (Ezekiel i, 10)

They are a unity because the divine name, the *Tetragrammaton*, is a unity (which, however, is made up of four elements) and because they represent this name, which is the divine chariot. Thus, the *Zohar* says concerning the four *Hayoth* (living creatures) of Ezekiel's vision:

> It is written concerning them, "And the likeness of their faces
> is as the *face of man*" (Ezekiel i, 10). They are all embraced in
> that likeness, and that likeness embraces them all . . . These like-

nesses are engraved on the throne — the supernal chariot which is comprised in the four letters of the *Tetragrammaton*, which is the name that comprises all. . . and the throne is decorated with these likenesses, one to the right, one to the left, one in front, and one behind, corresponding to the four corners of the world. . . (*Bereshith* 19a; trsl. H. Sperling and M. Simon, *The Zohar*, vol. i, London-Bournemouth, 1949, pp. 80-81)

The *Zohar* not only says that the four letters of the divine name (*Tetragrammaton*) correspond to the four corners of the world — the four cardinal points: East, West, North and South — but also speaks of Michael (whose likeness is as the *face of man*) directing himself towards the North with all the faces turned towards him (*Bereshith* 18b). In the further discourse, it is said:

The ox (i.e. the living creature with the face of an ox) ascends to seek guidance and gaze in the *face of man* . . . the eagle ascends to seek guidance and gaze in the *face of man* . . . the lion ascends to seek guidance and to gaze in the *face of man* . . . "man" contemplates all of them, and all ascend and contemplate him. (*Bereshith* 19b; trsl., p. 80)

The fourth living creature of Ezekiel's vision — the Angel (or the "man") — is thus the synthesis of all of them. Now, the *Zohar* describes how the Hebrew word SHINAN (Angel) embodies the mystery of the four living creatures:

"(On) the chariot of God are myriads of thousands of SHINAN (Angels)" (Psalm lxviii, 17): the word SHINAN expresses by means of its initials all the faces, the SHIN standing for SHOR (ox), the NUN for NESHER (eagle), and the ALEPH for ARYEH (lion), and the final NUN representing by its shape man, who walks erect, and who mystically combines male and female. (*Bereshith* 18b; trsl., pp. 79-80)

All these myriads of thousands of Angels — continues the *Zohar* — issue from the archetypes symbolised by the name SHINAN, and from these types they diverge into groups (characterised by their respective faces). All the Angels with faces other than the *face of man* have two faces — firstly, that which is their particular one, and secondly, that which they have borrowed from the "man" by contemplation of the *face of man* (i.e. in beholding Michael): by reflecting the characteristic of strength (EL), for Angels with the face of the bull; by reflecting the characteristic of greatness (GADDOL), for those with the face of the eagle; by reflecting the characteristic of power (GHIBOR), for those with the face of the lion. The "man" contemplates all the other faces, and they "all ascend and contemplate him". It is thus that they all receive the particular imprint of the "man", who is characterised by the name "tremendous" (NORAH). For this reason, the names by which the Holy One is called in the scripture are: "the strong, the great, the mighty and the tremendous" (Nehemiah ix, 32).

> These names are engraved above on the supernal chariot which is comprised in the four letters of the *Tetragrammaton*, which is the name that comprises all. . .These four supernal names bear along the throne, and the throne is comprised in them. . .It descends with its burden like a tree laden with branches on all sides and full of fruit. As soon as it descends, these four likenesses come forth in their several shapes emitting bright flashes which scatter seed over the world. (*Bereshith* 19a; trsl., pp. 80-81)

This is the moving account from the *Zohar*—which emanates such fascinating and rejuvenating freshness—concerning the chariot of God and the four spirits of the four elements whose symbols are found represented in the four corners of the Card of the Arcanum "The World".

The three-coloured garland surrounding the central figure portrays the idea of the immanence of all passivity (blue colour), all activity (red colour) and all neutrality (yellow colour) in the world-in-movement—the world of impulses emanating from the four spirits of the four elements. These three colours signify the three essential modes of energy—passivity (latency), activity (deployment), and neutrality (harmony of equilibrium)—described in the *Bhagavad-Gita* and designated as the three qualities *tamas*, *rajas* and *sattva*, which are the modes of manifestation of the four elements.

> *Sattva* action is that. . .which is performed in the Shastras, which is performed without attachment, desire or aversion, and without the desire for any fruit by the performer.
> *Raja* action is that which is attended with great trouble and which is performed by one who desires for the fruit of action, and who is filled with egoism.
> *Tama* action is that which is performed from delusion, without regard to consequences, and with one's own loss and injury as well as of others.
> *Sattva* agent is he who is free from attachment and egoism, who is full of constancy and energy, and who is unmoved both in success and failure.
> *Raja* agent is he who is full of affections, who desires for the fruit of actions, who is covetous, cruel and impure, and feels both joy and sorrow.

Tama agent is he who is void of application, who is without discernment, who is obstinate, deceitful, malicious, idle, despond-
ing and procrastinating.
(*Bhagavad-Gita* xviii, 23-28; trsl. M. N. Dutt, *Bhishma Parva*
xlii, 23-28 in volume vi, 1897, of *The Mahabharata*, 18 vols.,
Calcutta, 1895-1905)

One can amplify indefinitely the manifestations of the three qualities (*gunas*)
in all domains of existence. Thus the mineral kingdom is in the *tamasic* state,
the animal kingdom is in the *rajasic* state, and the plant kingdom is in the *sattvic*
state. The sage (*brahmin*) is in the *sattvic* state, the warrior (*kshattriya*) is in the
rajasic state, and the servant (*shudra*) is in the *tamasic* state. The sun is *sattvic*,
lightning is *rajasic*, and the moon is *tamasic*, etc. It is always a matter of equilibrium
(*sattva*), activity (*rajas*) and passivity (*tamas*), which are the modes of manifestation of the four elements.

Now, the three-coloured garland is the *field of manifestation* of the four elements acting at the heart of life's phenomena in the guise of *vital élan*, inherent
in the current of life. It is "the river flowing out of Eden to water the garden, which
divided and became four rivers" (Genesis ii, 10). The ancient Greeks named the
river which divides itself into four branches the "ether", which is divided into four
elements, i.e. fire, air, water and earth. Hindu doctrine names the fifth element,
which is the root of the four elements, *akasha*—generally translated by "ether".
And mediaeval alchemy sets great store on the quintessence (*quinta essentia*, or
"fifth essence") at the root and basis of the four elements. Thus, we read in
*Hermetis Trismegisti Tractatus vere Aureus. De Lapidis philosophici secreto, cum
Scholiis Dominici Gnosti* (Leipzig, 1610):

> *Divide lapidem tuum in quatuor elementa. . .et conjunge in
> unum et totum habebis magisterium* ("Divide your stone into
> four elements. . .and rejoin them as one, and you will have the
> whole *magisterium*").

That is, the *magisterium* or "know-how" of the "great work" is the separation of
the four elements from the *prima materia* ("primal substance") and then the
realisation of their unity in the *quinta essentia* (or "ether" of the ancients—cf.
Aristotle, *De coelo* i, 3).

This corresponds to the context of the Card of the Arcanum "The World", where
there are four figures in the corners of the Card, with the dancer at the centre.
The three-coloured garland which surrounds her represents the intermediary stage
of the analysis 1-3-4 or of the synthesis 4-3-1 (i.e. the progress of the four elements
to the three qualities or *gunas*, and of the three qualities to the unity of the
quintessence). The three qualities correspond to the three *regimina* of alchemy,

through which the four elements are transformed and then synthesised in the quintessence. Thus, the first *regimen* transforms earth into water; the second *regimen* transforms water into air; and the third *regimen* transforms air into fire (▽ into ▽ , ▽ into △ , and △ into △). The Arcanum "The World" is therefore that of analysis and synthesis. It teaches the art of *distinguishing*, within the totality of the experience of movement, the illusory from the real (the two hands of the dancer with the philtre and the wand), then the three "colours" (*gunas* or *regimina*) of movement, and lastly the four elements or impulses inherent within all that is in motion. And it also teaches the art of "perceiving" (alchemically realising) the *basic unity* of the four elements, the three colours, and the two effects, i.e. the *quintessence*. Or, speaking Cabbalistically, the Arcanum in question is that of the "unfolding" of the sacred name of God and of its subsequent "refolding"—the two operations being analogous to the work of *creation* and that of *salvation*. (Whoever wishes to penetrate this thesis to the relevant details should consult Professor Friedrich Weinreb's masterly work *De Bijbel als schepping*; The Hague, 1963, concerning the divine plan of creation in the Bible).

It goes without saying that one could extend the analysis (followed by subsequent synthesis) of the Arcanum "The World" further—much further indeed. One could, for example, establish the role of the four elements in the four worlds (or planes)— namely, the world of emanation, the world of creation, the world of formation, and the world of action (*Atziluth*, *Briah*, *Yetzirah*, and *Assiah*)—according to the Sephiroth Tree, by taking the ten Sephiroth for each plane and by summarising for each plane (by means of synthesis) the result obtained.

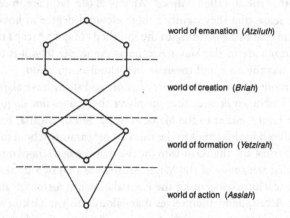

world of emanation (*Atziluth*)

world of creation (*Briah*)

world of formation (*Yetzirah*)

world of action (*Assiah*)

If we were to do this, what would we obtain?

We would obtain the system of the *Minor Arcana* of the Tarot, i.e. the four times ten Cards numbered 1 to 10 and the four times four figures synthesising the teaching of the four elements in relation to the four worlds. We would thus obtain the forty numerical Cards, and the sixteen Cards of figures, of the system of Minor Arcana of the Tarot, i.e. ten numerical Cards of pentacles, ten numerical Cards of swords, ten numerical Cards of cups, and ten numerical Cards of wands, as well as the four Cards of figures of pentacles, four Cards of figures of swords, four Cards of figures of cups, and four Cards of figures of wands. With regard to the sixteen Cards of figures, the correspondence between the four worlds and figures is: knave—world of action; knight—world of formation; queen—world of creation; king—world of emanation. Concerning the four "suits"—pentacles, swords, cups and wands—they correspond exactly to the structure of the sacred name YHVH and, consequently, to the four elements. Wands represent the emanating principle, the YOD of the divine name; cups represent the conceiving principle, the first HÉ of the divine name; swords represent the formative principle, the VAU of the divine name; and pentacles symbolise the principle of form, the second HÉ of the divine name.

The fifty-six Minor Arcana of the Tarot are, therefore, simply a development from the last Major Arcanum of the Tarot, "The World", developed Cabbalistically —rigorously and mathematically—where systematisation is pushed so far that one asks oneself involuntarily if it is not a matter of a rationalistic performance, pure and simple. Indeed, it is difficult to accept, in the first instance, the Minor Arcana of the Tarot as *arcana* in the sense of the Major Arcana that we have been meditating upon. For the rational arrangement so jumps out at one that one is tempted to reject it as "playing around" and therefore as something far inferior to the Major Arcana of the Tarot. Nevertheless, there was a school (that of St. Petersburg in the first quarter of this century, mentioned in Letter XXI) where it was taught that the so-called "Minor" Arcana of the Tarot are in reality *Major* Arcana in the sense that they signify a more elevated degree of knowledge and experience than that corresponding to the so-called "Major" Arcana of the Tarot. The Minor Arcana are to the Major Arcana as the upper school is to the lower school—such was the accepted thesis at the school in question.

Now, after more than forty-five years of effort and study have elapsed, I must tell you, dear Unknown Friend, that the above thesis does not do justice to the Arcana of the Tarot—either to the Major or to the Minor Arcana. For the Major Arcana are reduced in this thesis to the role of a preparatory school for the Minor Arcana—which they are, thanks only to the use that the said school made of them. And the use that was made of the Major Arcana was that of a framework for an encyclopaedic teaching concerning the Cabbala, magic, astrology and alchemy. As the Major Arcana lend themselves marvellously to the task of serving as a framework for such an encyclopaedic teaching, they were therefore made use of for this purpose. Thus, the Major Arcana played the role of a *general teaching programme* for the traditional occult sciences, aiming at giving general knowledge concerning their nature and methods, whilst the role of *psychurgical practice* was reserved for the Minor Arcana, i.e. the transformation of consciousness rising from plane to plane, which followed, as it were, as the upper school follows on from the lower school (the "lower school" being that of the Major Arcana). However the Major Arcana *are not*, in their totality, a teaching programme for the occult sciences, but rather a school of meditation aiming at awakening consciousness to the laws and forces—to the *arcana*—which are at work beneath the intellectual, moral and phenomenological surface. And the Minor Arcana constitute a systematised summary of experiences gained during meditation on the Major Arcana, in the guise of amplification—analysis and synthesis pushed to the extreme—on the Major Arcanum "The World". They are, if you like, a detailed elaboration of the Major Arcanum "The World"—or, again, its *application* in the domain of the various planes of consciousness, rising from the plane of action to the plane of emanation.

As it would ask too much of your forces, dear Unknown Friend, if I were to present you—in addition to the present twenty-two meditations on the Major Arcana of the Tarot—another fifty-six meditations on the Minor Arcana, and as, also, the time necessary for this task is lacking, I invite you, dear Unknown Friend, to do this work yourself, to write—in the manner of these Letter-Meditations—Letter-Meditations on the Minor Arcana of the Tarot. It is so as to facilitate this task that I propose the following considerations, which can serve as a key to the Minor Arcana of the Tarot—these are:

The Minor Arcana of the Tarot represent the way of ascent from consciousness belonging to the world of action (the phenomenal world) through the world of formation and the world of creation to the world of emanation. Thus, it is a matter of four degrees (including the summit) of ascent from the world of sensual and intellectual imagery, which corresponds to *pentacles*, to the world (or degree) of destruction of this imagery—or the "wilderness"—which corresponds to *swords*, so as to attain to that degree of spiritual poverty which is necessary to become a receptacle for revelation from above—which degree corresponds to *cups*. The summit is attained when the cup of consciousness which receives the revelation from above is transformed—by cooperating with revelatory action—into this latter. It then becomes revelatory activity itself, being actively united with the world of emanation. Then the degree of *wands* or *sceptres* is attained, i.e. that of pure creative activity.

Therefore the way begins in the world of coins or pentacles. This is the world of the imagery of facts, intellectual constructions and imagined ideals. Here consciousness surrounds itself with a world of images—on the one hand the memories of experiences, and on the other hand the formulae and schemes of the intellect, as well as those of moral imagination, which latter we call "ideals". This world of images is neither reality nor illusion. It consists of values/images *corresponding* to reality and which are therefore "convertible" into reality; for this reason *coins* are its symbol. For just as pieces of money are not themselves board, heating and lodging but can be converted into board, heating and lodging, so do memory images and the formulae and schemes of the intellect and moral imagination *represent* realities—being "worths" that may be converted into reality.

Now, the world of coins—the world of images—has a twofold significance. It signifies, on the one hand, the *wealth* acquired by consciousness, and on the other hand it signifies the totality of that which must be renounced if consciousness wants to come to spiritual reality. Because in order to convert money into real things, i.e. in order to buy them, one has to pay. One has to become "poor in spirit" in order to have the kingdom of heaven.

This payment, where one divests oneself of one's wealth of spirit, is that of swords. Here, the values/images (or coins) that one has struck through intellectual, moral and artistic effort are destroyed, one after the other, in the same (*Sephirothic*) order in which they were formed. This can last an instant, an hour, or decades. With St. Thomas Aquinas it took the time of a single ecstasy, whilst with Plato it seems that it was a slow process extending over several years. With respect to St. Thomas, it was probably at the end of 1273 that he underwent the decisive ecstasy. It lasted so long that his sister, with whom he was staying at the time, became concerned and thus questioned Brother Reginald (Raynald).

> *Qui dixit ei: "Frequenter Magister in spiritu rapitur cum aliqua contemplatur: sed nunquan tanto tempore, sicut nunc, vidi ipsum sic a sensibus alienum." Unde port aliquam horam ivit socius ad Magistram, et trahens ipsum per cappam fortiter, quasi a somno contemplationis ipsum ultimo excitavit. Qui suspirans dixit: "Raynalde fili, tibi in secreto revelo prohibens, ne in vita mea alicui audeas revelare. Venit finis scripturae meae, quia talia sunt mihi revelata, quod ea quae scripsi et docui modica mihi videntur, et ex hoc spero in Deo, quod sicut doctrinae meae sic cito finis erit et vitae."*
> (Who said to her: "The master is often caught up in spiritual rapture when he contemplates anything: but I have never before seen him taken out of his senses for so long." And so, after about an hour or so, the *socius*, i.e. Brother Reginald, went to the master, and tugging hard at his cloak, finally woke him out of his sleeping contemplation. He said with a sigh: "Reginald, my son, I reveal to you something in secret, forbidding you to reveal it to anyone as long as I live. *I have come to the end of all my writing, because such things have been shown to me, such that all that I have written and taught now seems to me very insignificant*, and this leads me to hope in God, that as I have come to the end of my teaching, so very soon will I come to the end of my life.") (William of Tocco, *Vita Sancti Thomae Aquinatis*, ch. 47; cf. P. Mandonnet, "La Canonisation de S. Thomas d'Aquin", *Mélanges Thomistes* (1923), pp. 1-48, esp. p. 8)

The ecstasy that St. Thomas underwent persuaded him that all that he had written and taught was of little significance (*ea quae scripsi et docui modica mihi videntur*). This is a case of passing through the sphere of swords.

Concerning the other "rich man"—Plato, whose works, in eight volumes, are

before me as I write these lines—he made the astonishing statement in his letter
to the parents and friends of Dion (Plato's *Seventh Letter*, which the ancients
designated with the name of the "great letter"—(ἡ μεγάλη ἐπιστολή)—written
by Plato at about the age of seventy-five):

> I have written no treatise on these matters (*reality*— τὸ ὄν),
> nor shall I ever write one. These matters cannot be expressed
> in words as other subjects can, but after persistent occupation
> in the study of these matters, after living for some time with
> them, suddenly a flash of understanding, as it were, is kindled
> by a spark that leaps across, and once it has come into being
> within the soul it proceeds to nourish itself. (Plato, *Seventh Let-
> ter* 341, c-d; cf. trsl. by R. S. Bluck in *Plato's Life and Thought*,
> London, 1949, p. 174)

Thus Plato, at about the age of seventy-five, bears judgement on his philosophical
work: "I have written no treatise on these matters . . ." (which he describes in this
letter as "the matters with which I concern myself"). Either Plato is mocking (but
irony of this kind is as far as possible from the general tone of the *Seventh Letter*), or he is serious and declaring himself to be a contemplative, i.e. that the
enormous work that he did in the domain of argumentation with its four elements
—words (or names, ὄνομα), definitions (λόγος), images (εἴδωλον), and
science (ἐπιστήμη)—is not suited to the knowledge of Being (οὐσία, τὸ ὄν)
that he calls simply "the matters with which I concern myself (περί ὦν ἐγώ σπογ-
δά ζω) and that his endeavour aspires towards mystical intuition of Being itself.
And this endeavour occupied him so completely in his last years that it seemed
to him that he could affirm that he had never written anything on "the matters
with which I concern myself" (*Seventh Letter* 341 c).

This is another case of the passage through the sphere of swords. Plato, as did
St. Thomas Aquinas, arrived at the "spiritual poverty" which is necessary to become
a "cup" and "sceptre" (or "wand"), i.e. to become a receptacle for the revelation
of Being, and then to become an active cooperator—which means to say "initiated".

The "worlds" or "spheres" of pentacles (coins), swords, cups and wands correspond to the degrees of the traditional way of preparation, purification (*purgatio*,
κάθαρσις), illumination (*illuminatio*, ψωτισμός) and perfection (*perfectio*,
unio mystica, τὰ τέλη)·

What one acquires through observation, study, reasoning and discipline constitutes the *degree of preparation*, or the world of coins.

This "world" exposed to the action of the breath of the Real, constitutes the
degree of purification, or the world of swords.

That which remains after this trial becomes the virtue or faculty of the soul
to receive illumination from above. This is the *degree of illumination*, or the world
of cups.

And, lastly, to the extent that the soul raises itself from receptivity to active cooperation with the Divine, it is admitted to the *degree of perfection*, or to the world of sceptres or wands.

These are the things which can serve as a key to the Minor Arcana of the Tarot, for your work, dear Unknown Friend, on these Arcana.

Adieu, dear Unknown Friend,

Festival of the Holy Trinity
21 May 1967.

Afterword

Cardinal Hans Urs von Balthasar

A thinking, praying Christian of unmistakable purity reveals to us the symbols of Christian Hermeticism in its various levels of mysticism, gnosis and magic, taking in also the Cabbala and certain elements of astrology and alchemy. These symbols are summarised in the twenty-two so-called "Major Arcana" of the Tarot cards. By way of the Major Arcana the author seeks to lead meditatively into the deeper, all-embracing wisdom of the Catholic Mystery.

Firstly, it may be recalled that such an attempt is to be found nowhere in the history of philosophical, theological and Catholic thought. The Church Fathers understood the myths born from pagan thought and imagination in a quite general way as veiled presentiments of the Logos, who became fully revealed in Jesus Christ (which once again Schelling undertook to show at length in his later philosophical work). Origen in particular, completing this line of thought, undertook as a Christian to elucidate not only the pagan philosophical wisdom in the light of Biblical revelation, but also the "wisdom of the rulers of this world" (I Cor.ii,6), by which he meant the so-called "secret wisdom of the Egyptians" (especially the Hermetic writings supposedly written by "Hermes Trismegistus", the Egyptian god Thoth). He also had in mind the "astrology of the Chaldeans and Indians ... which purports to impart knowledge concerning supersensible matters" and nothing less than the "manifold teachings of the Greeks concerning the Divine". He believed it possible that the cosmic powers ("rulers of this world") do not bring their wisdom to human beings "in order to harm them, but because they themselves hold these things to be true".[1] Similar ideas are to be found in the work of Eusebius (cf. *Praeparation evangelica*).

It is known how Christian philosophy was widely influenced during the Middle Ages, from Arabic sources and elsewhere, by the beliefs concerning cosmic powers or "intelligences" (conceived of partly as thoughts of God, partly as Angels). Above all during the Renaissance, through the continuing influence of these conceptions, the best minds were occupied with accommodating the Jewish magical-mystical Cabbala into the Christian faith. As has now been observed,[2] many of the Church Fathers had already attributed a place of honour among the heathen prophets and wisemen to the mysterious Hermes Trismegistus. Hermetic books had already circulated in the early and high Middle Ages.[3] Later, during the Renaissance, Hermes Trismegistus was celebrated as the great contemporary of Moses, and as the father of the wisdom of the Greeks (one may call to mind the portrayal honouring him at Siena Cathedral, inset in the cathedral floor). Poets, painters and theologians drew enthusiastically and reverently from the teachings of Hermes, and from other sources of pagan wisdom, the scattered rays of divine illumination, bringing it to a focus in the Christian faith. Yet the other source from which enlightenment was gathered, the Cabbala, was, if anything, still more important (the secret, oral tradition of the Cabbala is likewise dated back to the time of Moses.)

The first discussions for or against the secret teachings of the Cabbala go back to the converted or non-converted Spanish Jews of the twelfth century. Among those who later endeavored to understand these teachings were Reuchlin in Germany, Ficino and especially Pico della Mirandola in Italy,[4] whilst the extraordinary Cardinal Giles of Viterbo (1469–1552) wanted to explain the Holy Scripture with the help of the Cabbala "with a method that is not foreign, but which is intrinsic (to it)" (*non peregrina sed domestica methodo*).[5] Enjoined by Pope Clement VII, this zealous, reform-hungry Cardinal wrote his ebullient dissertation on the "Shekinah", dedicated to Emperor Charles V.[6] Alongside these few names resounding from the past, a multitude of lesser predecessors and imitators could be mentioned.

Here the important point is that although this penetration into the secret teachings of pagan and Jewish origin was pursued in the spirit of humanism, in the hope

1. Origen, *Peri Archon* III,3,1–3. So-called "magi and magicians" are also spoken of in this text, as well as "*daimons*", from whom human beings "purified through much abstinence" are able to receive inspired communications.
2. S. Gasparra, "L'ermetismo nelle testimonianze dei Padri", *Studia Patristica*, vol.II (Berlin, 1972), pp. 58–64.
3. L. Thorndike, *A History of Magic and Experimental Science*, vol.2 (New York, 1947), pp. 214–228.
4. F. Secret, *Les Kabbalistes chrétiens de la Renaissance* (Paris, 1964).
5. J.W. O'Malley, "Giles of Viterbo on Church and Reform", *Studies in Medieval and Reformation Thought*, vol. 5 (Leiden, 1968); G. Signorelli, *Il Cardinale Egidio da Viterbo, Agostiniano, umanista e riformatore* (Florence, 1929); J. Blau, *The Christian Interpretation of the Cabala in the Renaissance* (New York, 1944).
6. Published in 1559; critical edition by F. Secret, *Edizione nazionale dei Classici del Pensiero Italiano*, Series II (Rome, 1959), pp. 10ff.

of bringing new life into rigidified Christian theology through collecting such scattered revelation and illumination, no one for a moment doubted that despite the disparities everything could be accommodated into the true Christian faith. That Pico, in particular, did not aim at syncretism, he himself made quite clear: "I bear on my brow the name Jesus Christ and would die gladly for the faith in him. I am neither a magician nor a Jew, nor an Ishmaelite nor a heretic. It is Jesus whom I worship, and his cross I bear upon my body."[7] The author of these *Meditations* could also have affirmed this oath of allegiance.

There are other historical examples analogous to that of the gathering and accommodation of Hermetic and Cabbalistic wisdom into Biblical and Christian thought: above all, the transposition of Chassidism to a modern horizon of thought by Martin Buber (Chassidism is deeply influenced by the Cabbala). However, just as strong in its creative power of transformation is the incorporation of Jacob Boehme's Christosophy into the Catholic world-conception by the philosopher Franz von Baader. A third, less clear-cut transposition will be referred to briefly: that of the ancient magic/alchemy into the realm of depth psychology by C. G. Jung. The author's *Meditations on the Tarot* are in the tradition of the great accomplishments of Pico della Mirandola and Franz von Baader, but are independent of them. The mystical, magical, occult tributaries which flow into the stream of his meditations are much more encompassing; yet the confluence of their waters within him, full of movement, becomes inwardly a unity of Christian contemplation.

II.

It is remarkable that the *Meditations* take the ancient symbolic pictures of the Tarot cards as their point of departure. Naturally the author knows about the magical-divinatory application of these cards. However, although he does not feel inhibited about using the multi-meaning word "magic", in the *Meditations* he is not at all interested in the practice of "laying the cards" (cartomancy). For him it is only the symbols or their essential meaning which are important — individually or in their mutual reference to one another. Since he often refers to C. G. Jung, we may tentatively designate them as "archetypes". However, we must guard against interpreting them simply as inner psychological facts of the collective unconscious — which Jung, also, does not do categorically. They can just as well be understood as principles of the objective cosmos; and here we touch upon the sphere of the "powers and mights", as they are called in the Bible.

7. H. de Lubac, *Pic de la Mirandole* (Paris, 1974), pp. 90–113. Quote (p. 100) from *Apologia* (Opp. 1572, p. 116). There is of course another stream, deriving strongly from Joachim of Fiore, active from the Middle Ages through the Renaissance into modern times, which aspires to elevate the dogmatic faith of the Church in the direction of a "third kingdom of the Spirit". Henri de Lubac follows this step-by-step in his work *La postérité spirituelle de Joachim de Flore* (Paris, 1979), but as this is irrelevant to the work of our author, we do not need to discuss it further.

The origin of the Tarot is obscure, as is the historical background of its symbols — representations of which, moreover, have varied markedly in the course of the centuries. The attempt to trace them back to Egyptian or Chaldean wisdom remains fantastic, whilst to explain the use and spread of the cards by way of wandering gypsies is plausible. The oldest surviving cards date from the end of the fourteenth century.[8] Correspondences between the Tarot symbols and the Cabbala, astrology and the Hebrew alphabet were established relatively late, towards the end of the eighteenth century — supposedly first of all by the French archeologist Court de Gébelin (1728–1784).[9]

Repeated attempts have been made to accommodate the Cabbala and the Tarot to Catholic teaching. The most extensive undertaking of this kind was that of Eliphas Lévi (the pseudonym of Abbé Alphonse-Louis Constant), whose first work (*Dogme et rituel de la haute magie*) appeared in 1854. The author knows the work of Eliphas Lévi well and in the *Meditations* deepens the often naive expositions of the latter. There have also been other spiritual streams — such as the "Hermetic Order of the Golden Dawn" — which have worked partly to hinder the realisation of the Christian aspect of the Tarot symbols. (Arthur Edward Waite, who published in 1910 *The Pictorial Key of the Tarot*, was a member of the "Hermetic Order of the Golden Dawn".) Among numerous other attempts to interpret the Tarot cards, that of the Russian author P. D. Ouspensky could be mentioned. Like the anonymous author, who refers to him critically in the *Meditations*, Ouspensky was a Russian emigrant, and was also an influential teacher.[10] In his work *A New Model of the Universe*, he expounds the game of Tarot according to the general outline of his world-view, partly in the framework of Eastern religion and partly in that of depth psychology imbued with erotic elements.

It is not necessary to enumerate here the many authors — occultists, theosophists and anthroposophists — with whom the author of the *Meditations* enters into dialogue. There are those whom he rejects as lacking competence, and others, in contrast, from whom he borrows a thought that appears valuable to him, which he then incorporates into his meditations — whether an interpretation of the Sephiroth (from the Cabbala), or a thought from Jacob Boehme or Rudolf Steiner, from Jung or Péladan, from Papus or Maître Philippe, or whoever it may be. Often he refers also to the great philosophers and theologians, such as Thomas Aquinas, Bonaventura, Leibniz, Kant, Kierkegaard, Nietzsche, Bergson, Solovieff, Teilhard de

8. Before the year 1377 no authentic reference to playing cards is known from any European source, and the earliest definite reference to the Tarot cards is from the year 1442 in the *Registro dei Mandati* for the court of Ferrara, northern Italy (cf. M. Dummett, *The Game of Tarot*, London, 1980, p. 10 and p. 67).
9. Cf. S. R. Kaplan, *The Encyclopedia of the Tarot* (New York, 1978), p. 12: "In 1781, writing in *Monde Primitif*, Court de Gébelin advanced the theory that the Major Arcana cards constituted the Egyptian hieroglyphic Book of Thoth, saved from the ruins of burning Egyptian temples thousands of years ago."
10. Ouspensky was born on March 5, 1878, in Moscow and died on October 2, 1947, in Lyne, Mendham, New Jersey. J. D. Beresford, Algernon Blackwood, Christopher Isherwood and Aldous Huxley are among those who studied under him.

Chardin; or to dramatists and poets, such as Shakespeare, Goethe, De Coster, Cervantes, Baudelaire, and many others.

The basic spiritual direction of an author is recognisable by the fact of who — in the spiritual tradition — stands close to him: Whom does he frequently refer to, often with loving reverence? Again and again the names of St. Anthony the Great, St. Albertus Magnus and St. Francis of Assisi appear; and he quotes extensively above all from the works of St. John of the Cross and St. Teresa of Avila.

He immerses himself lovingly and with deep earnestness in the symbols of the Major Arcana of the Tarot. They inspire him; he allows himself to be borne aloft on the wings of his imagination, to behold the depths of the world and of the soul. Thereby a memory of something known or read in the past may spontaneously occur to him; and occasionally the various lines of thought intertwine and cross threads. The formidable power of his spiritual vision lies less in the detail than in the ineluctable certainty that at the depths of existence there is an interrelationship between all things by way of analogy. This lends his vision a unifying power of surveyance, which holds the remotely scattered individual insights magnetically in place and enables them to be appropriately ordered. For him this "magical" capacity has nothing to do with the human being's despotic nature — the commonplace, magical will-to-power, which seeks by way of world forces to gain dominion in the realm of knowledge and in the sphere of destiny. Rather, it is something very different. One can only call it the "magic of grace", the magic of which issues forth from the very heart of the mysteries of the Catholic faith. Since this faith itself neither is nor aspires to be magical, the magic amounts to the content of faith: that all cosmic "mights and powers" are subject to the sole rulership of Christ. The New Testament depicts this subjugation of the cosmic powers to Christ as a process which — although achieved in principle — will continue until the end of the world.[11] Thereby a dangerous possibility emerges: the temptation — through curiosity or the desire for power — to prematurely give oneself up to the cosmic powers instead of approaching them by way of the triumphant victory of Christ. The right approach is only possible through faith and, ultimately, through truly Christian wisdom.

Insight into this is of decisive importance for a proper assessment of the *Meditations* (a work that many a reader will certainly find confusing). The author is able to enter into all the varieties of occult science with such sovereignty, because for him they are secondary realities, which are only able to be truly known when they can be referred to the absolute mystery of divine love manifest in Christ. He does

11. One can refer also to the Apocalypse of John. Here it is evident that certain cosmic world-powers play a role — always a subordinate one — in the drama between God and mankind: Angels of wind, fire, water . . . Such an extremely mythological interpretation as that of Boll (*Aus der Offenbarung Johannis. Hellenistische Studien zum Weltbild der Apokalypse*, Leipzig, 1914) must be treated with caution, yet one can nevertheless concede the validity of such a background (cf. Burch, *Anthropology and the Apocalypse. An Interpretation of the Book of Revelation in Relation to the Archeology, Folklore and Religious Literature and Ritual of the Near East*, 1939).

not in any way conceive of the Christian revelation as some kind of imprint —potential or real —of archetypes, be they subjective or objective. Rather, the latter merely form the cosmic material into which the unique Christian revelation finally incarnates; and since the incarnation of divine love, becoming human, is the ultimate aim of cosmic evolution, they comprise a round of allegories and schematic patterns announcing this event by way of "mirrors and enigmas".

In order to grasp this, a parallel work — *The Greater Trumps* (i.e. the Major Arcana of the Tarot) — may be referred to, even if it stems from a somewhat different kind of spirituality. The Christian author, Charles Williams (1886–1945) — the mysterious and learned friend of T. S. Eliot, C. S. Lewis, Tolkien, Dorothy Sayers — was a profound thinker, who likewise pondered deeply upon the magic of the Tarot and its deeper significance for the religious life. In an earlier novel — *The Place of the Lion* (1933)[12] — he allows Platonic ideas to suddenly enter in as forces into the phenomenal world. Here everything depends on how the characters react towards them: one becomes terribly afraid, another ecstatically worships them, yet another is gripped with the desire to possess them, in order to rule the world by means of ideas, and the last one finds the only truly appropriate attitude: facing up to the superior strength of the cosmic powers, he devotes himself in freedom towards the grace intrinsic to their inner being. *The Greater Trumps* (1950)[13] depicts the cosmic principles of the Tarot which, once released, possess a frightful, destructive power if put solely at the disposal of magic; but ultimately — when confronted by totally selfless love — the negative is banished, and they submit to their supreme Lord.

As with the author of the *Meditations*, we encounter in Charles Williams a new form of the ancient Christian wisdom, which in the early centuries of Christianity fought with might and main against all forms of fatalism — notably astrology — in the name of the sovereignty and freedom of God in the face of all cosmic powers. The existence of these secondary cosmic principles was not denied, nor that providence could make use of them in order to guide the course of destiny.[14] Here again the teaching of St. Paul may be recalled (Col. ii, 15): the "elemental spirits of the universe" (worshipped by many as Angelic powers), the "principalities and powers", the "princes of this world" are recognised as real beings with effective powers, but Christ having disarmed them triumphs over them — they go before his triumphal chariot.

For Christians who want to investigate, as an aspect of the reality of the world, the realm in which these secondary cosmic principles act,[15] Williams shows dramatically that it is not easy to develop this kind of science strictly within the framework of theology. The task is very much more difficult than that of the purely

---

12. New edition of *The Place of the Lion* published by W. B. Eerdmans (Grand Rapids, Michigan, 1978).

13. New edition of *The Greater Trumps* with a foreword by W. L. Gresham (Avon, New York, 1969).

14. For the classical theological teaching concerning destiny (*fatum*), cf. Thomas Aquinas, *S. theol.* I, q 116; *C. gent.* III. 93; *Comp. theol.* 138; *Opusc.* 28 *de fato*.

15. Cf. H. Schlier, "Mächte und Gewalten im Neuen Testament", *Quaest. Disp.*, vol. 3 (Freiburg, 1958).

conceptual transposition from the realm of non-Christian philosophy to the domain of theology. The history of astrology in the Byzantine Empire and throughout centuries of Western culture shows this most clearly. Here many who play the sorcerer's apprentice become, through their dilettantish arts, caught up in an existential web that robs them of their Christian freedom (freedom before God), which was the main concern of the Church Fathers. The flourishing trade of some of the daily press and of much second-rate literature in the interpretation of horoscopes totally unrelated to the individual does something else by substituting illusory superstition for true faith. Much more than a professional training and a serious moral responsibility are called for here. Other qualities beyond these are really necessary: a certain sixth sense and also a feeling for the boundaries of that which can be communicated, together with a respectful and reserved attitude towards the mystery of the individual's religious path.

Meditations on the Tarot ranks in a category far beyond that of the numerous examples of second-rate occult literature. As a whole it comprises solely meditations. Also, it refrains from giving any concrete indications as to how the "occult" sciences could be practised under the aegis of Christian wisdom. Presumably any kind of general, exoteric indication did not come into question at all for the author. For him it was a matter solely of accomplishing something similar to that which Bonaventura achieved for all levels of worldly theoretical and practical knowledge in his dissertation *De reductione artium ad theologiam.* (Bonaventura showed that they all converge upon the incarnation of the divine Logos, the divine Archetype, from which they remain suspended as on a chain, one interlocking the other.) Another possible comparison could be drawn with the grandiose world-conception of St. Hildegard of Bingen (1098–1179). Here, as perhaps nowhere else, the cosmic powers (according to how they were viewed at that time) are incorporated in the great Christocentric drama between creation and redemption, between heaven and earth. Truly, in Hildegard's world-picture there are "more things than you with all your education could ever dream of, Horatio".

To analyse in detail as to how far a Christian synthesis for these in-between realms is possible or communicable would exceed the scope and competence of this Afterword.

Certainly, the author always seeks with great religious conscientiousness to keep to the middle way of Christian wisdom. The superabundance—almost too much—of genuine, fruitful insights which he conveys, certainly justifies bringing these *Meditations* to a wider circle of readers.

The author wanted to remain anonymous in order to allow the work to speak for itself, to avoid the interposition of any kind of personal element between the work and the reader—reasons that we respect.

Translated from the German Edition, Herder, Basel, 1983, by Robert A. Powell

Index

About the Authors

Written anonymously and published posthumously at the wishes of the author, *Meditations on the Tarot* has been translated from the original French by author and esotericist **Robert Powell,** who lives in Germany. More of Powell's work is online at *www.sophiafoundation.org.*

Widely considered one of the greatest Catholic theologians of the twentieth century, the Swissborn **Hans Urs von Balthasar** was nominated by Pope John Paul II as a Cardinal in 1988, and died in June of that year, two days before his consecration. Upon his death, the Pope called him "One of the most extraordinary theologians and social scientists, who deserves a special place of honor in the cultural life of today."

About the Author

A Note to Readers

Readers wishing to learn more about *Meditations on the Tarot* can visit *www. medtarot.freeserve.co.uk.*

A Note to Readers